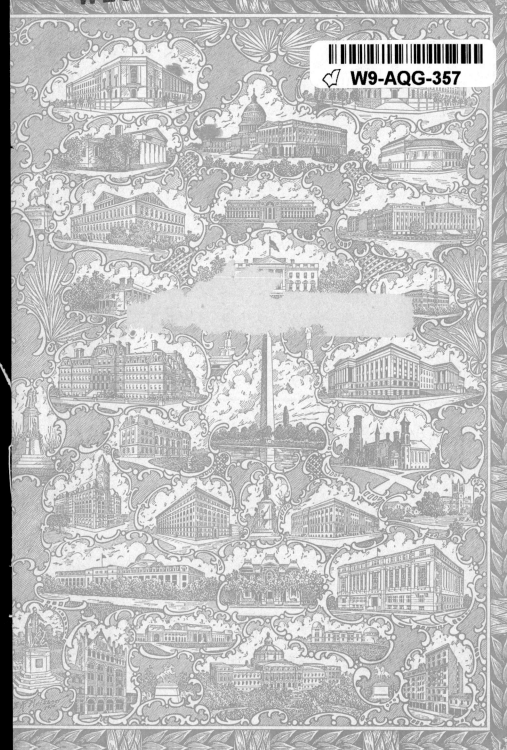

Washington Monument

THE WASHINGTON MONUMENT

AN APPRECIATION BY MR. GLENN BROWN

Architect; Author, "History of United States Capitol"

GRAY in the dawn, brilliant in the sunlight, black in the thunder-storm, pink in the afterglow, mysterious in the moonlight, vanishing in the mist, lost in the clouds, always majestic, stands the memorial to the Father of his Country.

Its phases forcibly remind us of the shifting and changing fortunes of our great chief. Standing alone, simple and dignified, it is as self-contained and practical as was his character in life. Enshrouded in the mists, shadowy, weird, vanishing from sight, a mere suggestion of an outline visible, it recalls the clouded reputation of Washington when surrounded by foes, false comrades, and encompassed by the fierce elements. Black in the thunderstorm, it brings to mind dark days and bridled passions. Apparently floating in the air when the base is obscured by the fog, it suggests his struggles without reasonable foundation or hope. Brilliantly illuminated at its base and the pinnacle lost in the clouds, it typifies great victories with the ultimate results in doubt. Piercing the shifting clouds as they float past, with the base and crown illuminated by the sunlight, it vividly recalls the force which enabled him to penetrate the darkest shadows. Reflecting the pink blush of the evening glow, it points to the brightness dawning as his life advanced. A column of light in the moon's rays, it is a beacon leading us, as did his life, to forget self in our country's service. Glorious in the sunshine, scintillating, brilliant against the clear blue sky, it forcibly reminds us of the great results springing from an unselfish life of duty.

The aluminum crest sparkles as a beautiful star; its rays are beams of light guiding us to patriotic efforts.

A factor in the artistic composition of the city, it is a charming end to many vistas. Viewed from the Capitol, the White House and the Mall, it stands imposing in its grandeur; from the river it rises pure and simple, with the green hills of Maryland as a noble exhedra, and from the heights, visible through the valley, it always produces a thrill of pleasure. In the sunlight and shadow, thunderstorm and mist, in the clouds and in the clear sky, against the golden sunrise and the red sunset, against the midday sky of blue, and the midnight sky scintillating with stars, against the bright white clouds and the dark gray clouds, moving with the wind, bowing to the warmth of the sun, receiving the lightning's stroke, ever changing, it is always stately, always beautiful.

The corner-stone of the Washington Monument was laid July 4, 1848, but soon the work languished and then stopped entirely. Work was resumed in 1876, and the monument was finally completed December 6, 1884. It is 555 feet high and 50 feet square at the base. The entire cost of the monument was $1,187,710.

THE WASHINGTON MONUMENT

A factor in the artistic composition of the city, it is a charming end to many vistas. Viewed from the Capitol, the White House and the Mall, it stands important in its grandeur, from the river it rises pure and simple, with the green hills of Maryland as a noble cathedral, and from the heights, visible through the valley, it always produces a thrill of pleasure. In the sunlight and shadow, thunder storm and mist, in the clouds, and in the clear sky, against the golden sunrise and the red sunset, against the midday sky of blue, and the midnight sky scintillating with stars, against the bright white clouds and the dark gray clouds, moving with the wind, bowing to the warmth of the sun, receiving the lightning's stroke, ever changing, it is always grand, it is always beautiful.

The corner stone of the Washington Monument was laid July 4, 1848, but soon the work ragged and then stopped entirely. Work was resumed in 1876, and the monument was finally completed December 6, 1884. It is 555 feet high and 50 feet square at the base. The entire cost of the monument was $1,187,710.

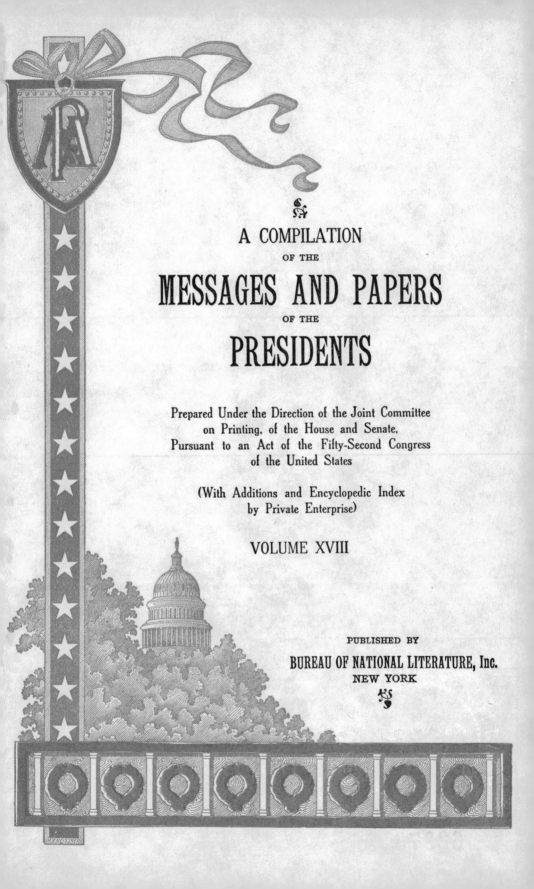

A COMPILATION

OF THE

MESSAGES AND PAPERS

OF THE

PRESIDENTS

Prepared Under the Direction of the Joint Committee
on Printing, of the House and Senate,
Pursuant to an Act of the Fifty-Second Congress
of the United States

(With Additions and Encyclopedic Index
by Private Enterprise)

VOLUME XVIII

PUBLISHED BY

BUREAU OF NATIONAL LITERATURE, Inc.

NEW YORK

ILLUSTRATIONS IN VOLUME EIGHTEEN

tribution, and to facilitate the movement, of foods, feeds, fuel, including fuel oil and natural gas, fertilizer and fertilizer ingredients, tools, utensils, implements, machinery, and equipment required for the actual production of foods, feeds, and fuel, hereafter in this Act called necessaries; to prevent, locally or generally, scarcity, monopolization, hoarding, injurious speculation, manipulations, and private controls, affecting such supply, distribution, and movement; and to establish and maintain governmental control of such necessaries during the war. For such purposes the instrumentalities, means, methods, powers, authorities, duties, obligations, and prohibitions hereinafter set forth are created, established, conferred, and prescribed. The President is authorized to make such regulations and to issue such orders as are essential effectively to carry out the provisions of this Act."

And, Whereas, it is further provided in said Act as follows:

"That, from time to time, whenever the President shall find it essential to license the importation, manufacture, storage, mining, or distribution, of any necessaries, in order to carry into effect any of the purposes of this Act, and shall publicly so announce, no person shall, after date fixed in the announcement, engage in or carry on any such business specified in the announcement of importation, manufacture, storage, mining, or distribution of any necessaries as set forth in such announcement, unless he shall secure and hold a license issued pursuant to this section. The President is authorized to issue such licenses and to prescribe regulations for the issuance of licenses and requirements for systems of accounts and auditing of accounts to be kept by licensees, submission of reports by them, with or without oath or affirmation and the entry and inspection by the President's duly authorized agents of the places of business of licensees."

And, Whereas, it is essential in order to carry into effect the provisions of the said Act, and in order to secure an adequate supply and equitable distribution, and to facilitate the movement of certain necessaries hereafter in this proclamation specified that the license powers conferred upon the President by said Act be at this time exercised, to the extent hereinafter set forth.

Now, Therefore, I, Woodrow Wilson, President of the United States of America, by virtue of the powers conferred upon me by said Act of Congress, hereby find and determine and by this proclamation do announce that it is essential in order to carry into effect the purposes of said Act, to license the importation, manufacture and refining of sugar, sugar syrups and molasses, to the extent hereinafter specified.

All persons, firms, corporations and associations engaged in the business either of importing sugar, of manufacturing sugar from sugar cane or beets, or of refining sugar or of manufacturing sugar syrups or molasses, (except those specifically exempted by said Act of Congress), are hereby required to secure on or before October 1, 1917, a license, which license will be issued under such rules and regulations governing the conduct of the business as may be prescribed.

Applications for licenses must be made to the United States Food Administrator, Washington, D. C., upon forms prepared by him for that purpose.

Any person, firm, corporation or association, other than those hereinbefore excepted, who shall engage in or carry on the business either of importing sugar, manufacturing sugar, or refining sugar, or of manufacturing sugar syrups or molasses after October 1, 1917, without first securing such license, will be liable to the penalties prescribed by said Act of Congress.

In Witness Whereof, I have hereunto set my hand and caused the seal of the United States to be affixed.

Done in the District of Columbia, this seventh day of September in the year of our Lord one thousand nine hundred and [SEAL.] seventeen, and of the Independence of the United States of America, the one hundred and forty-second.

WOODROW WILSON.

By the President:
ROBERT LANSING, *Secretary of State.*

EXECUTIVE ORDER

[Suspending law admitting foreign-built ships to American entry.]

THE WHITE HOUSE, *7 September, 1917.*

In pursuance of the authority conferred upon the President of the United States by Section 2 of the Act approved August 18, 1914, entitled "An Act to provide for the admission of foreign built ships to American registry for the foreign trade, and for other purposes," it is hereby ordered:

That the provisions of law requiring survey, inspection and measurement, by officers of the United States, of foreign built ships admitted to United States registry under said Act are hereby suspended so far and for such length of time as is herein provided, namely: The said provisions shall not apply to any such foreign built ship during the period of two years from September 1, 1917, provided the Secretary of Commerce is satisfied in the case of any such ship that the ship is safe and sea-worthy and that proper effort is being made to comply with the said provision.

WOODROW WILSON.

By the President of the United States of America

A PROCLAMATION

[Exports of Coin, Bullion and Currency Unlawful.]

Whereas Congress has enacted, and the President has on the fifteenth day of June, 1917, approved a law which contains the following provisions:

"Whenever during the present war the President shall find that the public safety shall so require, and shall make proclamation thereof, it shall be unlawful to export from or ship from or take out of the United States to any country named in such proclamation any article or articles mentioned in such proclamation, except at such time or times, and under such regulations and orders, and subject to such limitations and exceptions as the President shall prescribe, until otherwise ordered by the President or by Congress: Provided, however, that no preference shall be given to the ports of one State over those of another.

"Any person who shall export, ship, or take out, or deliver or attempt to deliver for export, shipment, or taking out, any article in violation of this title, or of any regulation or order made hereunder, shall be fined not more than $10,000, or, if a natural person, imprisoned for not more than two years, or both; and any article so delivered or exported, shipped, or taken out, or so attempted to be delivered or exported, shipped, or taken out, shall be seized and forfeited to the United States; and any officer, director, or agent of a corporation who participates in any such violation shall be liable to like fine or imprisonment, or both.

"Whenever there is reasonable cause to believe that any vessel, domestic or foreign, is about to carry out of the United States any article or articles in violation of the provisions of this title, the collector of customs for the district in which such vessel is located is hereby authorized and empowered, subject to review by the Secretary of Commerce, to refuse clearance to any such vessel, domestic or foreign, for which clearance is required by law, and by formal notice served upon the owners, master, or person or persons in command or charge of any domestic vessel for which clearance is not required by law, to forbid the departure of such vessel from the port, and it shall thereupon be unlawful for such vessel to depart. Whoever, in violation of any of the provisions of this section shall take, or attempt to take, or authorize the taking of any such vessel out of port or from the jurisdiction of the United States, shall be fined not more than $10,000 or imprisoned not more than two years, or both; and, in addition, such vessel, her tackle, apparel, furniture, equipment, and her forbidden cargo shall be forfeited to the United States."

And whereas the President has heretofore by proclamation, under date of the twenty-seventh day of August in the year one thousand nine hundred and seventeen, declared certain exports in time of war unlawful, and the President finds that the public safety requires that such proclamation be amended and supplemented in respect to the articles hereinafter mentioned:

Now, Therefore, I, Woodrow Wilson, President of the United States of America, do hereby proclaim to all whom it may concern that the public safety requires that, except at such time or times, and under such regulations and orders, and subject to such limitations and exceptions as the President shall prescribe, until otherwise ordered by the President or by Congress, the following articles, namely: coin, bullion and currency: shall not, on and after the 10th day of September in the year one thousand nine hundred and seventeen, be exported from or shipped from or taken out of the United States or its territorial possessions to Albania, Austria-Hungary, Belgium, Bulgaria, Denmark, her colonies, possessions or protectorates, Germany, her colonies, possessions or protectorates, Greece, Liechtenstein, Luxembourg, The Kingdom of the Netherlands, Norway, Spain, her colonies, possessions or protectorates, Sweden, Switzerland or Turkey, Abyssinia, Afghanistan, Argentina, Bolivia, Brazil, China, Chile, Colombia, Costa Rica, Cuba, Dominican Republic, Ecuador, Egypt, France, her colonies, possessions or protectorates, Guatemala, Haiti, Honduras, Italy, her colonies, possessions or protectorates, Great Britain, her colonies, possessions or protectorates, Japan, Liberia, Mexico, Monaco, Montenegro, Morocco, Nepal, Nicaragua, the colonies, possessions or protectorates of The Netherlands, Oman, Panama, Paraguay, Persia, Peru, Portugal, her colonies, possessions or protectorates, Roumania, Russia, Salvador, San Marino, Serbia, Siam, Uruguay, or Venezuela.

The regulations, orders, limitations and exceptions prescribed will be administered by and under the authority of the Secretary of the Treasury, from whom licenses in conformity with said regulations, orders, limitations and exceptions will issue.

Except as hereby amended and supplemented, the above mentioned proclamation under date of August 27, 1917, shall continue in full force and effect.

In Witness Whereof, I have hereunto set my hand and caused the seal of the United States of America to be affixed.

Done in the District of Columbia, this 7th day of September in the year of our Lord one thousand nine hundred and seven-
[SEAL.] teen and of the Independence of the United States of America the one hundred and forty-second.

WOODROW WILSON.

By the President:

ROBERT LANSING, *Secretary of State.*

EXECUTIVE ORDER

[Regulations relating to the exportation of coin, bullion and currency.]

THE WHITE HOUSE, *September 7, 1917.*

By virtue of the authority vested in me, I direct that the regulations, orders, limitations, and exceptions prescribed in relation to the exportation of coin, bullion, and currency shall be administered by and under the authority of the Secretary of the Treasury; and upon the recommendation of the Secretary of the Treasury I hereby prescribe the following regulations in relation thereto:

1. Any individual, firm or corporation desiring to export from the United States or any of its territorial possessions to any foreign country named in the proclamation dated September 7th, 1917, any coin, bullion, or currency, shall first file an application in triplicate with the Federal Reserve Bank of the district in which such individual, firm or corporation is located, such application to state under oath and in detail the nature of the transaction, the amount involved, the parties directly and indirectly interested and such other information as may be of assistance to the proper authorities in determining whether the exportation for which a license is desired will be compatible with the public interest.

2. Each Federal Reserve Bank shall keep a record copy of each application filed with it under the provisions of this regulation and shall forward the original application and a duplicate to the Federal Reserve Board at Washington together with such information or suggestions as it may believe proper in the circumstances and shall in addition make a formal recommendation as to whether or not in its opinion the exportation should be permitted.

3. The Federal Reserve Board, subject to the approval of the Secretary of the Treasury, is hereby authorized and empowered upon receipt of such application and the recommendation of the Federal Reserve Bank to make such ruling as it may deem proper in the circumstances and if in its opinion the exportation in question be compatible with the public interest, to permit said exportation to be made; otherwise to refuse it. WOODROW WILSON.

A PROCLAMATION

[Urging school children to enroll in Red Cross Service.]

September 15, 1917.

To the School Children of the United States:

The President of the United States is also President of the American Red Cross. It is from these offices joined in one that I write you a word of greeting at this time when so many of you are beginning the school year.

The American Red Cross has just prepared a Junior Membership with School Activities in which every pupil in the United States can find a chance to serve our country. The school is the natural center of your life. Through it you can best work in the great cause of freedom to which we have all pledged ourselves.

Our Junior Red Cross will bring to you opportunities of service to your community and to other communities all over the world and guide your service with high and religious ideals. It will teach you how to save in order that suffering children elsewhere may have the chance to live. It will teach you how to prepare some of the supplies which wounded soldiers and homeless families lack. It will send to you through the Red Cross Bulletins the thrilling stories of relief and rescue. And best of all, more perfectly than through any of your other school lessons, you will learn by doing those kind things under your teacher's direction to be the future good citizens of this great country which we all love.

And I commend to all school teachers in the country the simple plan which the American Red Cross has worked out to provide for your cooperation, knowing as I do that school children will give their best service under the direct guidance and instruction of their teachers. Is not this perhaps the chance for which you have been looking to give your time and efforts in some measure to meet our national needs?

(Signed)   WOODROW WILSON,
President.

LETTER

[To Mr. Max Eastman, concerning suppression of certain periodicals during the War with Germany.]

THE WHITE HOUSE, *September 18, 1917.*

MY DEAR MR. EASTMAN:

I thank you very warmly for your generous appreciation of my reply to the Pope, and I wish that I could agree with those parts of your letter which concern the other matters we were discussing when you were down here. I think that a time of war must be regarded as wholly exceptional and that it is legitimate to regard things which would in ordinary circumstances be innocent as very dangerous to the public welfare. But the line is manifestly exceedingly hard to draw, and I cannot say that I have any confidence that I know how to draw it. I can only say that a line must be drawn and that we are trying—it may be clumsily, but genuinely—to draw it without favor or prejudice. Cordially and sincerely yours,

WOODROW WILSON.

MEMORANDUM

[To Secretary of Labor, concerning Labor Disputes.]

THE WHITE HOUSE, *September 19, 1917.*

I am very much interested in the labor situation in the mountain region and on the Pacific coast. I have listened with attention and concern to the numerous charges of misconduct and injustice that representatives both of employers and of employees have made against each other. I am not so much concerned, however, with the manner in which they have treated each other in the past as I am desirous of seeing some kind of a working arrangement arrived at for the future, particularly during the period of the war, on a basis that will be fair to all parties concerned. To assist in the accomplishment of that purpose, I have decided to appoint a commission to visit the localities where disagreements have been most frequent as my personal representatives. The commission will consist of William B. Wilson, Secretary of Labor; Col. J. L. Spangler, of Pennsylvania; Verner C. Reed, of Colorado; John H. Walker, of Illinois; and E. P. Marsh, of Washington. Felix Frankfurter, of New York, will act as secretary of the commission.

It will be the duty of the commission to visit, in each instance, the governor of the state, advising him that they are there as the personal representatives of the President with a view to lending sympathetic counsel and aid to the state government in the development of a better understanding between laborers and employers, and also themselves to deal with employers and employees in a conciliatory spirit, seek to compose differences and allay misunderstanding, and in any way that may be open to them to show the active interest of the National Government in furthering arrangements just to both sides. Wherever it is deemed advisable conferences of employers and employees should be called with the purpose of working out a mutual understanding between them which will insure the continued operation of the industry on conditions acceptable to both sides. The commission should also endeavor to learn the real causes for any discontent which may exist on either side, not by the formal process of public hearings but by getting into touch with workmen and employers by the more informal process of personal conversation. I would be pleased to have the commission report to me from time to time such information as may require immediate attention.

WOODROW WILSON.

EXECUTIVE ORDERS

[Suspending eight-hour day in Bureau of Standards.]

THE WHITE HOUSE, *September 20, 1917.*

Under authority contained in the Naval Appropriation Act approved March 4, 1917 (Public No. 391, 64th Congress) whereby it is provided—

> "That in case of national emergency the President is authorized to suspend provisions of law prohibiting more than eight hours labor in any one day of persons engaged upon work covered by contracts with the United States: *Provided further,* That the wages of persons employed upon such contracts shall be computed on a basic day rate of eight hours work with overtime rates to be paid for at not less than time and one-half for all hours work in excess of eight hours;"

it is hereby ordered that during the present national emergency the provisions of law limiting the hours of daily service of mechanics and laborers to eight hours in any one day on work under contracts to which the United States is a party are suspended with respect to all contracts of the Bureau of Standards, Department of Commerce, for the construction of an emergency laboratory building to be used for the purpose of standardizing equipment, instruments, and apparatus for the Army and Navy, and other buildings that may be erected and used for research, testing and experimental work in connection with the present national emergency. This order shall take effect from and after this date.

WOODROW WILSON.

[Creating Divisions of Pictures, Films and Publications under Committee on Public Information.]

THE WHITE HOUSE, *25 September, 1917*

I hereby create, under the jurisdiction of the Committee on Public Information, heretofore established by Executive Order of April 14, 1917, (1) a Division of Pictures; (2) a Division of Films; (3) a Division of Publications; for the purpose of stimulating recruiting and patriotic interest in the war; to the end that the utmost cooperation of all citizens in the successful prosecution of the war be secured.

The Secretary of State, the Secretary of War, and the Secretary of the Navy are authorized each to detail an officer or officers to the work of the committee.

WOODROW WILSON.

[Suspending the eight-hour day in construction of Immigrant Station at Baltimore, Md.]

THE WHITE HOUSE, *September 27, 1917.*

In order to effect the more expeditious construction of the buildings for the new Immigration Station, Baltimore, Maryland, the early completion of the buildings for military purposes creating a national emergency, the same to be turned over to the War Department by the Department of Labor for hospital purposes, etc., and by virtue of the provisions of the Act of Congress approved March 4, 1917, entitled "An Act Making Provisions for the Naval Service for the Fiscal Year Ending June 30, 1918, and for other Purposes," whereby it is provided that in case of national emergency the President is authorized to suspend provisions of law prohibiting more than eight hours labor in any one day by persons engaged upon work covered by contracts with the United States; provided further, that the wages of persons employed upon such contracts shall be computed on a basic day rate of eight hours work with overtime rate to be paid for at not less than time and one-half for all hours work in excess of eight hours, I do hereby suspend the provisions of law prohibiting more than eight hours of labor in any one day by persons engaged in the construction of the new Immigration Station at Baltimore, Maryland. This order shall take effect from and after this date.

WOODROW WILSON.

[Assigning quarantine duties in Virgin Islands to Treasury Department.]

THE WHITE HOUSE, *27 September, 1917.*

Whereas, an Act of Congress approved June 19, 1906, provides "that the Secretary of the Treasury shall have the control, direction, and management of all quarantine stations, grounds, and anchorages, established by authority of the United States * * *."

Now, therefore, I, Woodrow Wilson, President of the United States, by virtue of the authority in me vested, and pursuant to Section 1 of the Act approved March 3, 1917, entitled "An Act to provide a temporary government for the West Indies Islands, acquired by the United States from Denmark, etc.," do hereby order that the provisions of the Act of Congress approved February 15, 1893, entitled "An Act granting additional quarantine powers and imposing additional duties upon the Marine-Hospital Service," and all rules and regulations heretofore prescribed by the Secretary of the Treasury under this Act are to be given full force and effect in the islands of St. Thomas, St. Croix, and St. John, West Indies, and all public property of the former government of the Virgin Islands, ceded heretofore to the United States, consisting of quarantine reservations, buildings, wharves, docks connected therewith, and equipment, be, and hereby are, taken for uses and purposes of the United States, and the Secretary of the Treasury, through the Surgeon General of the Public Health Service, is hereby charged with all administrative duties relating to said quarantine service, and the Secretary of the Treasury shall have estimates prepared by the Surgeon General of the Public Health Service, and submitted to Congress for an appropriation for the maintenance of said quarantine service, and securement of reservations where necessary, and additional facilities for the proper enforcement of quarantine preventive measures.

WOODROW WILSON.

[Giving chief of staff control over War Department in absence of Secretary of War and Assistant Secretary of War.]

THE WHITE HOUSE, *29 September, 1917.*

In accordance with the provisions of Section 179 of the Revised Statutes, as amended by an Act making appropriations for the legislative, executive, and judicial expenses of the Government, approved August 5, 1882 (22 Stats., 238), the Chief of Staff, United States Army, is authorized and directed to perform the duties of Secretary of War during the illness or temporary absence from the seat of Government of the Secretary of War, whenever during such illness or absence the Assistant Secretary of War is also absent.

WOODROW WILSON.

BY THE PRESIDENT OF THE UNITED STATES OF AMERICA

PROCLAMATIONS

[License of Commodities.]

Whereas, under and by virtue of an Act of Congress entitled "An Act to provide further for the national security and defense by encouraging the production, conserving the supply, and controlling the distribution of food products and fuel," approved by the President on the 10th day of August, 1917, it is provided among other things as follows:

"That, by reason of the existence of a state of war, it is essential to the national security and defense, for the successful prosecution of the war, and for the support and maintenance of the

Army and Navy, to assure an adequate supply and equitable distribution, and to facilitate the movement, of foods, feeds, fuel including fuel oil and natural gas, and fertilizer and fertilizer ingredients, tools, utensils, implements, machinery, and equipment required for the actual production of foods, feeds, and fuel, hereafter in this Act called necessaries; to prevent, locally or generally, scarcity, monopolization, hoarding, injurious speculation, manipulations, and private controls, affecting such supply, distribution, and movement; and to establish and maintain governmental control of such necessaries during the war. For such purposes the instrumentalities, means, methods, powers, authorities, duties, obligations, and prohibitions hereinafter set forth are created, established, conferred and prescribed. The President is authorized to make such regulations and to issue such orders as are essential effectively to carry out the provisions of this Act."

And, whereas, it is further provided in said Act as follows:

"That, from time to time, whenever the President shall find it essential to license the importation, manufacture, storage, mining or distribution, of any necessaries, in order to carry into effect any of the purposes of this Act, and shall publicly so announce, no person shall, after a date fixed in the announcement, engage in or carry on any such business specified in the announcement of importation, manufacture, storage, mining, or distribution of any necessaries as set forth in such announcement, unless he shall secure and hold a license issued pursuant to this section. The President is authorized to issue such licenses and to prescribe regulations for the issuance of licenses and requirements for systems of accounts and auditing of accounts to be kept by licensees, submission of reports by them, with or without oath or affirmation, and the entry and inspection by the President's duly authorized agents of the places of business of licensees."

And, Whereas, It is essential, in order to carry into effect the provisions of the said Act, that the powers conferred upon the President by said Act be at this time exercised, to the extent hereinafter set forth,

Now, Therefore, I, Woodrow Wilson, President of the United States of America, by virtue of the powers conferred upon me by said Act of Congress, hereby find and determine and by this proclamation do announce that it is essential, in order to carry into effect the purposes of said Act, to license the importation, manufacture, storage and distribution of necessaries, to the extent hereinafter specified.

All persons, firms, corporations and associations engaged in the business either of, (1) operating cold storage warehouses (a cold storage warehouse, for the purposes of this proclamation, being defined as any place artificially or mechanically cooled to or below a temperature of 45 degrees above zero Fahrenheit, in which food products are placed and held for thirty days or more), (2) operating elevators, warehouses or other places for the storage of corn, oats, barley, beans, rice, cotton seed, cottonseed cake, cottonseed meal or peanut meal, or (3) importing, manufacturing (including milling, mixing or packing), or distributing (including buying and selling) any of the following commodities:

Wheat, wheat flour, rye or rye flour; barley or barley flour; oats, oatmeal or rolled oats; corn, corn grits, cornmeal, hominy, corn flour, starch from corn, corn oil, corn syrup or glucose; rice, rice flour; dried beans; pea seed or dried peas; cotton seed, cottonseed oil, cottonseed cake or cottonseed meal; peanut oil or peanut meal; soya bean oil, soya bean meal, palm oil or copra oil; oleomargarine, lard, lard substitutes, oleo oil or cooking fats; milk, butter or cheese; condensed, evaporated or powdered milk; fresh, canned or cured beef, pork or mutton; poultry or eggs; fresh or frozen fish; fresh fruits or vegetables; canned: peas, dried beans, tomatoes, corn, salmon or sardines; dried: prunes, apples, peaches or raisins; sugar, syrups or molasses,—

Excepting, however,

(1) Operators of elevators or warehouses handling wheat or rye, and manufacturers of the derivative products of wheat or rye, who have already been licensed,

(2) Importers, manufacturers and refiners of sugar, and manufacturers of sugar syrups and molasses, who have already been licensed,

(3) Retailers whose gross sales of food commodities do not exceed $100,000.00 per annum,

(4) Common carriers,

(5) Farmers, gardeners, cooperative associations of farmers or gardeners, including live stock farmers, and other persons with respect to the products of any farm, garden or other land owned, leased or cultivated by them,

(6) Fishermen whose business does not extend beyond primary consignment,

(7) Those dealing in any of the above commodities on any exchange, board of trade or similar institution as defined by Section 13 of the Act of August 10th, 1917, to the extent of their dealings on such exchange or board of trade,

(8) Millers of corn, oats, barley, wheat, rye or rice operating only plants of a daily capacity of less than seventy-five barrels,

(9) Canners of peas, dried beans, corn, tomatoes, salmon or sardines whose gross production does not exceed 5,000 cases per annum,

(10) Persons slaughtering, packing and distributing fresh, canned

or cured beef, pork or mutton, whose gross sales of such commodities do not exceed $100,000.00 per annum,

(11) Operators of poultry or egg packing plants, whose gross sales do not exceed $50,000.00 per annum,

(12) Manufacturers of maple syrup, maple sugar and maple compounds,

(13) Ginners, buyers, agents, dealers or other handlers of cotton seed who handle yearly, between September 1st and August 31st, less than one hundred and fifty tons of cotton seed,
are hereby required to secure on or before November 1, 1917, a license, which license will be issued under such rules and regulations governing the conduct of the business as may be prescribed.

Application for license must be made to the United States Food Administration, Washington, D. C., Law Department—License Division, on forms prepared by it for that purpose, which may be secured on request.

Any person, firm, corporation or association other than those hereinbefore excepted, who shall engage in or carry on any business hereinbefore specified after November 1, 1917, without first securing such license will be liable to the penalty prescribed by said Act of Congress.

In Witness Whereof, I have hereunto set my hand and caused the seal of the United States to be affixed.

Done in the District of Columbia, this eighth day of October, in the year of our Lord one thousand nine hundred and
[SEAL] seventeen, and of the Independence of the United States of America, the one hundred and forty-second.

WOODROW WILSON.

By the President:
Robert Lansing, *Secretary of State.*

[Liberty Day.]

The Second Liberty Loan gives the people of the United States another opportunity to lend their funds to their Government to sustain their country at war. The might of the United States is being mobilized and organized to strike a mortal blow at autocracy in defense of outraged American rights and of the cause of Liberty. Billions of dollars are required to arm, feed and clothe the brave men who are going forth to fight our country's battles and to assist the nations with whom we are making common cause against a common foe. To subscribe to the Liberty Loan is to perform a service of patriotism.

Now, therefore, I, Woodrow Wilson, President of the United States of America, do appoint Wednesday, the twenty-fourth of October, as Liberty Day, and urge and advise the people to assemble in their respective communities and pledge to one another and to the Government that represents them the fullest measure of financial support. On the afternoon of that day I request that patriotic meetings be held in every city, town and hamlet throughout the land, under the general direction of the Secretary of the Treasury and the immediate direction of the Liberty Loan Committees which have been organized by the Federal Reserve Banks. The people responded nobly to the call of the First Liberty Loan with an oversubscription of more than fifty per cent. Let the response to the Second Loan be even greater and let the amount be so large that it will serve as an assurance of unequaled support to hearten the men who are to face the fire of battle for us. Let the result be so impressive and emphatic that it will echo throughout the Empire of our enemy as an index of what America intends to do to bring this war to a victorious conclusion.

For the purpose of participating in Liberty Day celebrations, all employees of the Federal Government throughout the country whose services can be spared, may be excused at twelve o'clock noon, Wednesday, the twenty-fourth of October.

In Witness Whereof, I have hereunto set my hand and caused the seal of the United States to be affixed.

Done in the District of Columbia, this twelfth day of October, in the year of our Lord, one thousand nine hundred and [SEAL] seventeen, and of the Independence of the United States of America the one hundred and forty-second.

WOODROW WILSON.

By the President:

ROBERT LANSING, *Secretary of State.*

EXECUTIVE ORDER

[Vesting power and authority in designated officers and making rules and regulations under Trading with the Enemy Act and Title VII of the act approved June 15, 1917.]

THE WHITE HOUSE, *October 12, 1917.*

By virtue of the authority vested in me by "An Act to Define, Regulate and Punish Trading with the Enemy and for Other Purposes," approved October 6, 1917, and by Title VII of the Act approved June 15, 1917, entitled "An Act to Punish Acts of Interference with the Foreign Relations, the Neutrality and the Foreign Commerce of the United States, to Punish Espionage and Better to Enforce the Criminal Laws of the United States and for Other Purposes," (hereinafter designated as the Espionage Act), I hereby make the following orders and rules and regulations:

WAR TRADE BOARD

I. I hereby establish a War Trade Board to be composed of representatives, respectively, of the Secretary of State, of the Secretary of the Treasury, of the Secretary of Agriculture, of the Secretary of Commerce, of the Food Administrator, and of the United States Shipping Board.

II. I hereby vest in said Board the power and authority to issue licenses under such terms and conditions as are not inconsistent with law, or to withhold or refuse licenses, for the exportation of all articles, except coin, bullion or currency, the exportation or taking of which out of the United States may be restricted by proclamations heretofore or hereafter issued by me under said Title VII of the Espionage Act.

III. I further hereby vest in said War Trade Board the power and authority to issue, upon such terms and conditions as are not inconsistent with law, or to withhold or refuse, licenses for the importation of all articles the importation of which may be restricted by any proclamation hereafter issued by me under Section 11 of the Trading with the Enemy Act.

IV. I further hereby vest in said War Trade Board the power and authority not vested in other officers by subsequent provisions of this order, to issue, under such terms and conditions as are not inconsistent with law, or to withhold or refuse, licenses to trade either directly or indirectly with, to, or from, or for, or on account of, or on behalf of, or for the benefit of, any other person, with knowledge or reasonable cause to believe that such other person is an enemy or ally of enemy, or is conducting or taking part in such trade directly or indirectly for, or on account of, or on behalf of, or for the benefit of, an enemy or ally of enemy.

V. I further hereby vest in said War Trade Board the power and authority, under such terms and conditions as are not inconsistent with law, to issue to every enemy or ally of enemy, other than enemy or ally of enemy insurance or reinsurance companies, doing business within the United States through an agency or branch office, or otherwise, applying therefor within thirty days of October 6, 1917, licenses temporary or otherwise to continue to do business, or said Board may withhold or refuse the same.

VI. And I further hereby vest in said War Trade Board the executive administration of the provisions of Section 4 (b) of the Trading with the Enemy Act relative to granting licenses to enemies and enemy allies to assume or use other names than those by which they were known at the beginning of the war. And I hereby authorize said Board to issue licenses not inconsistent with the provisions of law or to withhold or refuse licenses to any enemy, or ally of enemy, or partnership of which an enemy or ally of enemy is a member or was a member at the beginning of the war, to assume or use any name other than that by which such enemy or ally of enemy or partnership was ordinarily known at the beginning of the war.

VII. I hereby revoke the executive order* of August 21, 1917, creating the Exports Administrative Board. All proclamations, rules, regulations and instructions made or given by me under Title VII of the Espionage Act and now being administered by the Exports Administrative Board are hereby continued, confirmed and made applicable to the War Trade Board, and all employees of the Exports Administrative Board are hereby transferred to and constituted employees of the War Trade Board in the same capacities, and said War Trade Board is hereby authorized to exercise without interruption, the powers heretofore exercised by said Exports Administrative Board.

VIII. The said War Trade Board is hereby authorized and empowered to take all such measures as may be necessary or expedient to administer the powers hereby conferred. And I hereby vest in the War Trade Board the power conferred upon the President by Section 5 (a) to make such rules and regulations, not inconsistent with law, as may be necessary and proper for the exercise of the powers conferred upon said Board.

*Not published.

WAR TRADE COUNCIL

IX. I hereby establish a War Trade Council to be composed of the Secretary of State, Secretary of the Treasury, Secretary of Agriculture, Secretary of Commerce, the Food Administrator and the Chairman of the Shipping Board, and I hereby authorize and direct the said War Trade Council thus constituted to act in an advisory capacity in such matters under said Acts as may be referred to them by the President or the War Trade Board.

SECRETARY OF THE TREASURY

X. I hereby vest in the Secretary of the Treasury the executive administration of any investigation, regulation or prohibition of any transaction in foreign exchange, export or earmarking of gold or silver coin, or bullion or currency, transfers of credit in any form (other than credits relating solely to transactions to be executed wholly within the United States) and transfers of evidence of indebtedness or of the ownership of property between the United States and any foreign country, or between residents of one or more foreign countries, by any person within the United States; and I hereby vest in the Secretary of the Treasury the authority and power to require any person engaged in any such transaction to furnish under oath complete information relative thereto, including the production of any books of account, contracts, letters or other papers in connection therewith in the custody or control of such person, either before or after such transaction is completed.

XI. I further hereby vest in the Secretary of the Treasury the executive administration of the provisions of subsection (c) of Section 3 of the Trading with the Enemy Act relative to sending, or taking out of, or bringing into, or attempting to send, take out of, or bring into, the United States, any letter, writing or tangible form of communication, except in the regular course of the mail; and of the sending, taking, or transmitting, or attempting to send, take, or transmit, out of the United States, any letter, or other writing, book, map, plan or other paper, picture, or any telegram, cablegram, or wireless message, or other form of communication intended for or to be delivered, directly or indirectly, to an enemy or ally of enemy. And said Secretary of the Treasury is hereby authorized and empowered to issue licenses to send, take or transmit out of the United States anything otherwise forbidden by said subsection (c) and give such consent or grant such exemption in respect thereto, as is not inconsistent with law, or to withhold or refuse the same.

XII. I further authorize the Secretary of the Treasury to grant a license under such terms and conditions as are not inconsistent with law or to withhold or refuse the same to any "enemy" or "ally of enemy" insurance or reinsurance company doing business within the United States through an agency or branch office or otherwise, which shall make application within thirty days of October 6, 1917.

XIII. I hereby authorize and direct the Secretary of the Treasury, for the purpose of such executive administration, to take such measures, adopt such administrative procedure, and use such agency or agencies as he may from time to time deem necessary and proper for that purpose. The proclamation of the President, dated September 7, 1917, made under authority vested in him by Title VII of said Act of Congress, approved June 15, 1917, shall remain in full force and effect. The executive order, dated September 7, 1917, made under the authority of said title shall remain in full force and effect until new regulations shall have been established by the President, or by the Secretary of the Treasury, with the approval of the President, and thereupon shall be superseded.

CENSORSHIP BOARD

XIV. I hereby establish a Censorship Board to be composed of representatives, respectively, of the Secretary of War, the Secretary of the Navy, the Postmaster General, the War Trade Board, and the Chairman of the Committee on Public Information.

XV. And I hereby vest in said Censorship Board the executive administration of the rules, regulations and proclamations from time to time established by the President under subsection (d) of section 3, of the Trading with the Enemy Act, for the censorship of communications by mail, cable, radio or other means of transmission passing between the United States and any foreign country from time to time specified by the President, or carried by any vessel, or other means of transportation touching at any port, place or territory of the United States and bound to or from any foreign country.

XVI. The said Censorship Board is hereby authorized to take all such measures as may be necessary or expedient to administer the powers hereby conferred.

FEDERAL TRADE COMMISSION

XVII. I further hereby vest in the Federal Trade Commission the power and authority to issue licenses under such terms and conditions as are not inconsistent with law or to withhold or refuse the same, to any citizen of the United States or any corporation organized within the United States to file and prosecute applications in the country of an enemy or ally of enemy for letters patent or for registration of trade-mark, print, label, or copyright, and to pay the fees required by law and the customary agents' fees, the maximum amount of which in each case shall be subject to the control of such Commission; or to pay to any enemy or ally of enemy any tax, annuity or fee which may be required by the laws of such enemy or ally of enemy nation in relation to patents, trade-marks, prints, labels and copyrights.

XVIII. I hereby vest in the Federal Trade Commission the power and authority to issue, pursuant to the provisions of Section 10 (c) of the Trading with the Enemy Act, upon such terms and conditions as are not inconsistent with law, or to withhold or refuse, a license to any citizen of the United States, or any corporation organized within the United States, to manufacture or cause to be manufactured a machine, manufacture, composition of matter, or design, or to carry on or cause to be carried on a process under any patent, or to use any trade-mark, print, label, or copyrighted matter owned or controlled by an enemy or ally of enemy, at any time during the present war; and also to fix the prices of articles and products manufactured under such licenses necessary to the health of the military and the naval forces of the United States, or the successful prosecution of the war; and to prescribe the fee which may be charged for such license, not exceeding $100.00 and not exceeding 1 per centum of the fund deposited by the licensee with the Alien Property Custodian as provided by law.

XIX. I hereby further vest in the said Federal Trade Commission the executive administration of the provisions of section 10 (d) of the

Trading with the Enemy Act, the power and authority to prescribe the form of, and time and manner of filing statements of the extent of the use and enjoyment of the license and of the prices received and the times at which the licensee shall make payments to the Alien Property Custodian, and the amounts of said payments, in accordance with the Trading with the Enemy Act.

XX. I further hereby vest in the Federal Trade Commission the power and authority, whenever in its opinion the publication of an invention or the granting of a patent may be detrimental to the public safety or defense, or may assist the enemy, or endanger the successful prosecution of the war, to order that the invention be kept secret and the grant of letters patent withheld until the end of the war.

XXI. The said Federal Trade Commission is hereby authorized to take all such measures as may be necessary or expedient to administer the powers hereby conferred.

THE POSTMASTER GENERAL

XXII. I hereby vest in the Postmaster General the executive administration of all the provisions (except the penal provisions) of Section 19, of the Trading with the Enemy Act, relating to the printing, publishing or circulation in any foreign language of any news item, editorial, or other printed matter respecting the Government of the United States or of any nation engaged in the present war, its policies, international relations, the state or conduct of the war or any matter relating thereto, and the filing with the Postmaster at the place of publication, in the form of an affidavit of a true and complete translation of the entire article containing such matter proposed to be published in such print, newspaper or publication, and the issuance of permits for the printing, publication and distribution thereof free from said restriction. And the Postmaster General is authorized and empowered to issue such permits upon such terms and conditions as are not inconsistent with law and to refuse, withhold or revoke the same.

XXIII. The sum of $35,000.00 or so much thereof as may be necessary is hereby allotted out of the funds appropriated by the Trading with the Enemy Act, to be expended by the Postmaster General in the administration of said section 19 thereof.

XXIV. The Postmaster General is hereby authorized to take all such measures as may be necessary or expedient to administer the powers hereby conferred.

SECRETARY OF STATE

XXV. I hereby vest in the Secretary of State the executive administration of the provisions of subsection (b) of Section 3 of the Trading with the Enemy Act relative to any person transporting or attempting to transport any subject or citizen of an enemy or ally of enemy nation, and relative to transporting or attempting to transport by any owner, master or other person in charge of a vessel of American registry, from any place to any other place, such subject or citizen of an enemy or enemy ally.

XXVI. And I hereby authorize and empower the Secretary of State to issue licenses for such transportation of enemies and enemy allies or to withhold or refuse the same.

XXVII. And said Secretary of State is hereby authorized and empowered to take all such measures as may be necessary or expedient to administer the powers hereby conferred and to grant, refuse, withhold or revoke licenses thereunder.

SECRETARY OF COMMERCE

XXVIII. I hereby vest in the Secretary of Commerce the power to review the refusal of any Collector of Customs under the provisions of Sections 13 and 14 of the Trading with the Enemy Act, to clear any vessel, domestic or foreign, for which clearance is required by law.

ALIEN PROPERTY CUSTODIAN

XXIX. I hereby vest in an Alien Property Custodian, to be hereafter appointed, the executive administration of all the provisions of Section 7 (a), Section 7 (c), and Section 7 (d) of the Trading with the Enemy Act, including all power and authority to require lists and reports, and to extend the time for filing the same, conferred upon the President by the provisions of said Section 7 (a), and including the power and authority conferred upon the President by the provisions of said Section 7 (c), to require the conveyance, transfer, assignment, delivery or payment to himself, at such time and in such manner as he shall prescribe, of any money or other properties owing to or belonging to or held for, by or on account of, or on behalf of, or for the benefit of any enemy or ally of an enemy, not holding a license granted under the provisions of the Trading with the Enemy Act, which, after investigation, said Alien Property Custodian shall determine is so owing, or so belongs, or is so held.

XXX. Any person who desires to make conveyance, transfer, payment, assignment or delivery, under the provisions of Section 7 (d) of the Trading with the Enemy Act, to the Alien Property Custodian of any money or other property owing to or held for, by or an account of, or on behalf of, or for the benefit of an enemy or ally of enemy, not holding a license granted as provided in the Trading with the Enemy Act, or to whom any obligation or form of liability to such enemy or ally of enemy is presented for payment, shall file application with the Alien Property Custodian for consent and permit to so convey, transfer, assign, deliver or pay such money or other property to him and said Alien Property Custodian is hereby authorized to exercise the power and authority conferred upon the President by the provisions of said Section 7 (d) to consent and to issue permit upon such terms and conditions as are not inconsistent with law, or to withhold or refuse *the same.*

XXXI. I further vest in the Alien Property Custodian the executive administration of all the provisions of Section 8 (a), Section 8 (b), and Section 9 of the Trading with the Enemy Act, so far as said Sections relate to the powers and duties of said Alien Property Custodian.

XXXII. I vest in the Attorney General all powers and authority conferred upon the President by the provisions of Section 9 of the Trading with the Enemy Act.

XXXIII. The Alien Property Custodian to be hereafter appointed is hereby authorized to take all such measures as may be necessary or expedient, and not inconsistent with law, to administer the powers hereby conferred; and he shall further have the power and authority to make such rules and regulations not inconsistent with law as may be necessary and proper to carry out the provisions of said Section 7 (a), Section 7 (c), Section 7 (d), Section 8 (a), and Section 8 (b), conferred upon the President by the provisions thereof and by the provisions of Section 5 (a), said rules and regulations to be duly approved by the Attorney General.

XXXIV. The Alien Property Custodian to be hereafter appointed shall, "under the supervision and direction of the President, and under such rules and regulations as the President shall prescribe," have administration of all moneys (including checks and drafts payable on demand) and of all property, other than money which shall come into his possession in pursuance of the provisions of the Trading with the Enemy Act, in accordance with the provisions of Section 6, Section 10, and Section 12 thereof.

WOODROW WILSON.

EXECUTIVE ORDER

[Free consular services.]

THE WHITE HOUSE, *October 13, 1917.*

During the continuance of the war and until further orders, any services which American consular officers shall be called upon to perform under items 8, 12, 31, 32, 33, 38, 39, 40, 41, 42, and 43 of the Tariff of United States Consular Fees for any person in the military or naval service of the United States, shall be rendered free of charge.

WOODROW WILSON.

STATEMENT

[Urging State Banks to join Federal Reserve System.]

THE WHITE HOUSE, *Oct. 13, 1917.*

It is manifestly imperative that there should be a complete mobilization of the banking resources of the United States. All who are familiar with financial operations must appreciate the importance of developing to the maximum our banking power and of providing financial machinery adequate for meeting the very great financial requirements imposed upon our country by reason of the war.

A vigorous prosecution and satisfactory termination of the war will depend in no small degree upon the ability of the Government not only to finance itself, but also to aid the governments associated with it in the war, which must be kept supplied with munitions, fuel, food, and supplies of all kinds.

The banking problem involved is one which concerns all banks alike. Its solution does not depend upon the national banks alone, nor upon the State banks. The burden and the privilege must be shared by every banking institution in the country. The important functions of the Federal Reserve Banks in the sale of the Government's securities, in receiving and transferring the billions of dollars involved, in supplying credit facilities, and in protecting the reserves of the country have become so familiar to all that I am sure it is unnecessary to dwell upon or expound them.

The extent to which our country can withstand the financial strains for which we must be prepared will depend very largely upon the strength and staying power of the Federal Reserve Banks. The Federal Reserve act is the only constructive financial legislation which we have ever had which was broad enough to accommodate at the same time banks operating under powers granted by the general Government and banks whose charters are granted by the respective States. The unification of our banking system and the complete mobilization of reserves are among the fundamental principles of the act.

The State banking institutions for some reason have until recently seemed inclined to hold aloof. Congress a few months ago prescribed very generous terms for the admission of the State banks into the Federal Reserve system, which have removed the objections heretofore raised by State banks when considering membership. As the law now stands, it leaves member State banks and trust companies practically undisturbed in the exercise of all the banking powers conferred upon them by the States. The law provides also in definite terms the conditions upon which any State bank or trust company may withdraw from the system.

Many of the largest State banks and trust companies are now becoming members, realizing that to win the war we must conserve all of the physical, financial, and moral resources of our country; that our finances must rest on the firmest possible foundation, and that they must be adequately and completely conserved so as to respond instantly to every legitimate demand. How can this necessary condition be brought about and be made permanently effective better than by the concentration of the banking strength of our country in the Federal Reserve system?

May I not, therefore, urge upon the officers and directors of all non-member State banks and trust companies which have the required amount of capital and surplus to make them eligible for membership to unite with the Federal Reserve system now, and thereby contribute their share to the consolidated gold reserves of the country? I feel sure that as member banks they will aid to a greater degree than is possible otherwise in promoting the national welfare, and that at the same time, by securing for themselves the advantages offered by the Federal Reserve system, they will best serve their own interest and the interest of their customers. I believe that co-operation on the part of the banks is a patriotic duty at this time and that membership in the Federal Reserve system is a distinct and significant evidence of patriotism.

There are probably eight or nine thousand State banks and trust companies eligible for membership which have not yet united with the system. These institutions have it in their power to add enormously to the resources of the Federal Reserve Banks, thereby broadening and strengthening the foundation upon which our whole financial structure must rest. Permit me to urge that every bank officer and bank director owes a solemn obligation to the country, which I am sure they wish to discharge. I therefore wish again to impress upon them my solemn conviction that they can best measure up to their duties and responsibilities through membership in the Federal Reserve system.

WOODROW WILSON.

LETTER

[To Mrs. Carrie Chapman Catt, concerning the Woman Suffrage Campaign in New York State.]

THE WHITE HOUSE, *October 13, 1917.*

My Dear Mrs. Catt:

May I not express to you my very deep interest in the campaign in New York for the adoption of Woman Suffrage, and may I not say that I hope that no voter will be influenced in his decision with regard to this matter by anything which the so-called pickets may have done here in Washington? However justly they may have laid themselves open to serious criticism, their action represents, I am sure, so small a fraction of the women of the country who are urging the adoption of Woman Suffrage that it would be most unfair and argue a narrow view to allow their actions to prejudice the cause itself. I am very anxious to see the great State of New York set a great example in this matter.

Cordially and sincerely,

WOODROW WILSON.

EXECUTIVE ORDERS

[Suspending civil service rules in training camp activities.]

THE WHITE HOUSE, *October 15, 1917.*

Civilian employees of the Commissions on Training Camp Activities may be appointed without regard to the requirements of the Civil Service rules.

The staffs of employees of the Commissions on Training Camp Activities, heretofore paid from private funds, are to be taken into the service of the War and Navy Departments and paid from Government appropriations, and it is desired that the established organizations be continued. In the opinion of the Secretary of War and the Secretary of the Navy, it is impracticable to secure qualified employees for this work by competitive examination.

WOODROW WILSON.

[Providing for Requisitioning of Foods and Feeds.]

Under and by virtue of an Act of Congress, entitled "An Act to provide further for the national security and defense by encouraging the production, conserving the supply, and controlling the distribution of food products and fuel," approved August 10, 1917, I, Woodrow Wilson, President of the United States, hereby authorize and direct Herbert Hoover, United States Food Administrator, from time to time, to requisition any and all foods and feeds, and storage facilities for the same, that said Herbert Hoover, United States Food Administrator, may deem are necessary for any public use connected with the common defense, other than the support of the Army or the maintenance of the Navy, and to ascertain and pay a just compensation therefor.

Done in the District of Columbia, this twenty-third day of October, in the year of our Lord one thousand nine hundred and seventeen, and of the Independence of the United States of America, the one hundred and forty-second.

WOODROW WILSON.

[Waiving civil service regulations for confidential positions under Trading with the Enemy Act.]

THE WHITE HOUSE, *October 25, 1917.*

Newspaper readers and translators selected by the Postmaster General for filling certain confidential positions under the Trading with the Enemy Act may be appointed during the period of the war with Germany without examination under the civil service law. The Postmaster Gene. al states that there are available to the Post Office Department for appointment in these lines men whose loyalty has been proven and who in some cases will accept employment at a nominal salary through patriotic desire to give service at this time.

The Civil Service Commission concurs in the issuance of this order in view of the highly confidential character of the employments and the particular qualifications required.

WOODROW WILSON.

BY THE PRESIDENT OF THE UNITED STATES OF AMERICA

PROCLAMATIONS

[Supplication and prayer.]

Whereas, the Congress of the United States, by a concurrent resolution adopted on the fourth day of the present month of October, in view of the entrance of our nation into the vast and awful war which now afflicts the greater part of the world, has requested me to set apart by official proclamation a day upon which our people should be called upon to offer concerted prayer to Almighty God for His divine aid in the success of our arms;

And, Whereas, it behooves a great free people, nurtured as we have been in the eternal principles of justice and of right, a nation which has sought from the earliest days of its existence to be obedient to the divine teachings which have inspired it in the exercise of its liberties, to turn always to the supreme Master and cast themselves in faith at His feet, praying for His aid and succor in every hour of trial, to the end that the great aims to which our fathers dedicated our power as a people may not perish among men, but be always asserted and defended with fresh ardor and devotion and, through the Divine blessing, set at last upon enduring foundations for the benefit of all the free peoples of the earth:

Now, therefore, I, Woodrow Wilson, President of the United States, gladly responding to the wish expressed by the Congress, do appoint October twenty-eighth, being the last Sunday of the present month, as a day of supplication and prayer for all the people of the nation, earnestly exhorting all my countrymen to observe the appointed day, according to their several faiths, in solemn prayer that God's blessing may rest upon the high task which is laid upon us, to the end that the cause for which we give our lives and treasure may triumph and our efforts be blessed with high achievement.

In Witness Whereof, I have hereunto set my hand and caused the seal of the United States to be affixed.

Done in the District of Columbia this nineteenth day of October, in the year of our Lord one thousand nine hundred and seven- [SEAL] teen, and of the Independence of the United States of America the one hundred and forty-second.

WOODROW WILSON.

By the President:

ROBERT LANSING, *Secretary of State.*

[Manufacture, etc., of explosives in time of war unlawful.]

Whereas, under and by virtue of an Act of Congress entitled "An Act to prohibit the manufacture, distribution, storage, use and possession in time of war of explosives, providing regulations for the safe manufacture, distribution, storage, use and possession of the same, and for other purposes," approved by the President on the 6th day of October, 1917, it is provided among other things that from and after forty days after the passage and approval of said Act no person shall manufacture, distribute, store, use or possess explosives or ingredients thereof, not including explosives for the military or naval service of the United States of America under the authority of the Government or ingredients in small quantities not used or intended to be used in the manufacture of explosives, and not including small arms or shotgun cartridges, unless such person shall obtain a license issued in the name of the Director of the Bureau of Mines, except that any workman may purchase or accept explosives or ingredients thereof under prescribed conditions from a licensed superintendent or foreman.

And, Whereas, it is further provided in said Act as follows:

"That the Director of the Bureau of Mines, with the approval of the President, is hereby authorized to utilize such agents, agencies, and all officers of the United States and of the several States, Territories, dependencies, and municipalities thereof, and the District of Columbia, in the execution of this Act, and all agents, agencies, and all officers of the United States and of the several States and Territories, dependencies, and municipalities thereof, and the District of Columbia, shall hereby have full authority for all acts done by them in the execution of this Act when acting by the direction of the Bureau of Mines."

Now, therefore, I, Woodrow Wilson, President of the United States of America, by this proclamation do announce the following:

That from and after the 15th day of November, 1917, and during the present war with Germany, it will be unlawful to manufacture, distribute, store, use, or possess explosives or ingredients thereof, except as provided in said Act.

That the Director of the Bureau of Mines is hereby authorized to utilize, where necessary for the proper administration of said Act, the services of all officers of the United States and of the several States, Territories, dependencies, and municipalities thereof, and of the District of Columbia, and such other agents and agencies as he may designate, who shall have full authority for all acts done by them in the execution of the said Act when acting under his direction.

In Witness Whereof, I have hereunto set my hand and caused the seal of the United States to be affixed.

Done in the District of Columbia, this twenty-sixth day of October, in the year of our Lord one thousand nine hundred and [SEAL] seventeen, and of the Independence of the United States of America, the one hundred and forty-second.

WOODROW WILSON.

By the President:
ROBERT LANSING, *Secretary of State.*

APPEAL FOR FOOD CONSERVATION

THE WHITE HOUSE, *October 28, 1917.*

The chief part of the burden of finding food supplies for the peoples associated with us in war falls for the present upon the American people, and the drain upon supplies on such a scale necessarily affects the prices of our necessaries of life. Our country, however, is blessed with an abundance of foodstuffs, and if our people will economize in their use of food, providently confining themselves to the quantities required for the maintenance of health and strength; if they will eliminate waste; and if they will make use of those commodities of which we have a surplus, and thus free for export a large proportion of those required by the world now dependent upon us, we shall not only be able to accomplish our obligations to them, but we shall obtain and establish reasonable prices at home.

To provide an adequate supply of food both for our own soldiers on the other side of the seas and for the civil populations and the armies of the Allies, is one of our first and foremost obligations; for, if we are to maintain their constancy in this struggle for the independence of all nations, we must first maintain their health and strength. The solution of our food problems, therefore, is dependent upon the individual service of every man, woman, and child in the United States.

The great voluntary effort in this direction which has been initiated and organized by the Food Administration under my direction offers an opportunity of service in the war which is open to every individual and by which every individual may serve both his own people and the peoples of the world. We cannot accomplish our objects in this great war without sacrifice and devotion, and in no direction can that sacrifice and devotion be shown more than by each home and public eating place in the country pledging its support to the Food Administration and complying with its requests.

WOODROW WILSON.

EXECUTIVE ORDER

[Fixing salary of and vesting certain power and authority in the alien property custodian appointed under Trading-with-the-Enemy Act.]

THE WHITE HOUSE, *October 29, 1917.*

By virtue of the authority vested in me by "An act to define, regulate, and punish trading with the enemy," approved October 6, 1917, I hereby make and establish the following order:

1. I hereby fix the salary of the Alien Property Custodian heretofore appointed at the sum of $5,000 per annum. I direct that said Alien Property Custodian shall give a bond in the amount of $100,000 with security to be approved by the Attorney General, and which bond shall be conditioned to well and faithfully hold, administer, and account for all money and property in the United States due or belonging to an enemy or ally of enemy or otherwise, which may be paid, conveyed, transferred, assigned, or delivered to said custodian under the provisions of the trading-with-the-enemy act.

2. I hereby authorize and empower the Alien Property Custodian to employ and appoint in the manner provided in the trading-with-the-enemy act in the District of Columbia and elsewhere, and to fix the compensation of, such clerks, attorneys, investigators, accountants, and other employees as he may find necessary for the due administration of the powers conferred on such Alien Property Custodian by law or by any order of the President heretofore or hereafter made.

3. I hereby vest in the Alien Property Custodian the executive administration of the provisions of Section 12 of the trading-with-the-enemy act pertaining to the designation of a depositary, or depositaries, and requiring all such designated depositaries to execute and file bonds and prescribing the form, amount, and security thereof. And I authorize and empower the Alien Property Custodian to designate any bank, or banks, or trust company, or trust companies, or other suitable depositary or depositaries located and doing business in the United

States, as the depositary or depositaries with which said Alien Property Custodian may deposit any stocks, bonds, notes, time drafts, time bills of exchange, or other securities or property (except money, or checks, or drafts payable on demand) of an enemy or ally of enemy, and to prescribe the bond or bonds and the form, amount, and security thereof which shall be given by said depositary or depositaries.

4. The following sums, or so much thereof as may be necessary, are hereby allotted out of the funds appropriated by the trading-with-the-enemy act to the following named officers:

To the Alien Property Custodian............$100,000

To the Federal Trade Commission........... 25,000

To the Secretary of the Treasury............ 15,000

To the War Trade Board................... 25,000

to be expended in the administration of the powers vested respectively in them by law or by any order heretofore or hereafter made by me.

5. The powers and authority herein vested in said Alien Property Custodian are in addition to the powers and authority vested in said Alien Property Custodian by the Executive Order of October 12, 1917.

WOODROW WILSON.

STATEMENT

[An appeal to the American people for Armenian and Syrian Relief.]

THE WHITE HOUSE, *October 29, 1917.*

One year ago, in compliance with resolutions passed by the Senate and by the House of Representatives, I appointed days upon which the people of the United States might make such contributions as they felt disposed for the aid of the stricken Armenian and Syrian peoples.

American diplomatic and consular representatives and other American residents recently returned from Western Asia assure me that many thousands of lives were saved from starvation by the gifts of the American people last winter. They also bring full assurance of the continued effective distribution of relief and report that the suffering and death from exposure and starvation will inevitably be very much greater this winter than last unless the survivors can be helped by further contributions from America.

Reports indicate that of orphans alone there are more than 400,000, besides women and other dependent children, reaching a total of more than 2,000,000 destitute survivors. The situation is so distressing as to make a special appeal to the sympathies of all.

In view of the urgent need, I call again upon the people of the United States to make such further contributions as they feel disposed in their sympathy and generosity for the aid of these suffering peoples.

Contributions may be made through the American Red Cross, Washington, D. C., or direct to the American Committee for Armenian and Syrian Relief, Cleveland H. Dodge, Treasurer, 1 Madison Avenue, New York City.

WOODROW WILSON.

By the President of the United States of America.

PROCLAMATIONS

[Thanksgiving—1917.]

It has long been the honored custom of our people to turn in the fruitful autumn of the year in praise and thanksgiving to Almighty God for His many blessings and mercies to us as a nation. That custom we can follow now even in the midst of the tragedy of a world shaken by war and immeasurable disaster, in the midst of sorrow and great peril, because even amidst the darkness that has gathered about us we can see the great blessings God has bestowed upon us, blessings that are better than mere peace of mind and prosperity of enterprise.

We have been given the opportunity to serve mankind as we once served ourselves in the great day of our Declaration of Independence, by taking up arms against a tyranny that threatened to master and debase men everywhere and joining with other free peoples in demanding for all the nations of the world what we then demanded and obtained for ourselves. In this day of the revelation of our duty not only to defend our own rights as a nation but to defend also the rights of free men throughout the world, there has been vouchsafed us in full and inspiring measure the resolution and spirit of united action. We have been brought to one mind and purpose. A new vigor of common counsel and common action has been revealed in us. We should especially thank God that in such circumstances, in the midst of the greatest enterprise the spirits of men have ever entered upon, we have, if we but observe a reasonable and practicable economy, abundance with which to supply the needs of those associated with us as well as our own. A new light shines about us. The great duties of a new day awaken a new and greater national spirit in us. We shall never again be divided or wonder what stuff we are made of.

And while we render thanks for these things let us pray Almighty God that in all humbleness of spirit we may look always to Him for guidance; that we may be kept constant in the spirit and purpose of service; that by His grace our minds may be directed and our hands strengthened; and that in His good time liberty and security and peace and the comradeship of a common justice may be vouchsafed all the nations of the earth.

Wherefore, I, Woodrow Wilson, President of the United States of America, do hereby designate Thursday, the twenty-ninth day of November next as a day of thanksgiving and prayer, and invite the people throughout the land to cease upon that day from their ordinary occupations and in their several homes and places of worship to render thanks to God, the great ruler of nations.

In witness whereof, I have hereunto set my hand and caused the seal of the United States to be affixed.

Done in the District of Columbia this 7th day of November, in the year of our Lord one thousand nine hundred and seventeen, [SEAL] and of the independence of the United States of America the one hundred and forty-second.

WOODROW WILSON.

By the President:

ROBERT LANSING, *Secretary of State.*

[Licensing Bakers.]

Whereas, Under and by virtue of an Act of Congress entitled "An Act to provide further for the national security and defense by encouraging the production, conserving the supply, and controlling the distribution of food products and fuel," approved by the President on the 10th day of August, 1917, it is provided among other things as follows:

"That by reason of the existence of a state of war, it is essential to the national security and defense, for the successful prosecution of the war, and for the support and maintenance of the Army and Navy, to assure an adequate and equitable distribution, and to facilitate the movement, of foods, feeds, fuel, including fuel oil and natural gas, and fertilizer and fertilizer ingredients, tools, utensils, implements, machinery, and equipment required for the actual production of foods, feeds, and fuel, hereafter in this Act called necessaries; to prevent, locally or generally, scarcity, monopolization, hoarding, injurious speculation, manipulations, and private controls, affecting such supply, distribution, and movement; and to establish and maintain governmental control of such necessaries during the war. For such purposes the instrumentalities, means, methods, powers, authorities, duties, obligations, and prohibitions hereinafter set forth are created, established, conferred, and prescribed. The President is authorized to make such regulations and to issue such orders as are essential effectively to carry out the provisions of this Act."

And, whereas, it is further provided in said Act as follows:

"That, from time to time, whenever the President shall find it essential to license the importation, manufacture, storage, mining, or distribution of any necessaries, in order to carry into effect any of the purposes of this Act, and shall publicly so announce, no person

PRESIDENT WILSON ADDRESSING CONGRESS.

One of the features of the administration of Woodrow Wilson was his resumption of the habit, discarded since the days of Jefferson, of reading his messages to the Senate in person. The messages of his predecessors had been read by a clerk, and little attention was usually paid to the reading by the members of Congress, who later read the message for themselves at leisure. President Wilson's utterances delivered by him to joint sessions of Congress were always brief documents which went straight to the point, couched in the magnificent English which flows so readily from his pen. The President is described as reading his messages quietly, but with a feeling emphasis which drove their meanings home to the hearts of all who heard them.

STATEMENT

[Urging Assistance in Making a Complete Inventory of Draft Registrants.]

THE WHITE HOUSE, *November 9, 1917.*

The task of selecting and mobilizing the first contingent of the National Army is nearing completion. The expedition and accuracy of its accomplishment were a most gratifying demonstration of the efficiency of our democratic institutions. The swiftness with which the machinery for its execution had to be assembled, however, left room for adjustment and improvement. New regulations putting these improvements into effect are therefore being published today. There is no change in the essential obligations of men subject to selection. The first draft must stand unaffected by the provisions of the new regulations. They can be given no retroactive effect.

The time has come for a more perfect organization of our man power. The selective principle must be carried to its logical conclusion. We must make a complete inventory of the qualifications of all registrants in order to determine, as to each man not already selected for duty with the colors, the place in the military, industrial or agricultural ranks of the nation in which his experience and training can best be made to serve the common good. This project involves an inquiry by the selective boards into the domestic, industrial and educational qualifications of nearly ten million men.

Members of these boards have rendered a conspicuous service. The work was done without regard to personal convenience and under a pressure of immediate necessity which imposed great sacrifices. Yet the services of men trained by the experience of the first draft must of necessity be retained and the selection boards must provide the directing mechanism for the new classification. The thing they have done is of scarcely one-tenth the magnitude of the thing that remains to be done. It is of great importance both to our military and to our economic interests that the classification be carried swiftly and accurately to a conclusion. An estimate of the time necessary for the work leads to the conclusion that it can be accomplished in sixty days; but only if this great marshaling of our resources of men is regarded by all as a national war undertaking of such significance as to challenge the attention and compel the assistance of every American.

I call upon all citizens, therefore, to assist local and district boards by proffering such service and such material conveniences as they can offer and by appearing before the boards, either upon summons or upon their own initiative, to give such information as will be useful in classifying registrants. I urge men of the legal profession to offer themselves as associate members of the legal advisory boards to be provided in each community for the purpose of advising registrants of their rights and obligations and of assisting them in the preparation of their answers to the questions which all men subject to draft are required to submit. I ask the doctors of the country to identify themselves with the medical advisory boards which are to be constituted in the various districts throughout the United States for the purpose of making a systematic physical examination of the registrants. It is important also that police officials of every grade and class should be informed of their duty under the selective service law and regulations, to search for persons who do not respond promptly and to serve the summons of local and district boards. Newspapers can be of very great assistance in giving wide publicity to the requirements of the law and regulations and to the numbers and names of those who are called to present themselves to their local boards from day to day. Finally, I ask that during the time hereafter to be specified as marking the sixty-day period of the classification all citizens give attention to the task in hand in order that the process may proceed to a conclusion with swiftness and yet with even and considerate justice to all.

(Signed)   WOODROW WILSON.

ADDRESS

[Before Annual Convention of American Federation of Labor at Buffalo, New York, November 12, 1917.]

Mr. President, Delegates of the American Federation of Labor, Ladies and Gentlemen: I esteem it a great privilege and a real honor to be thus admitted to your public councils. When your Executive Committee paid me the compliment of inviting me here, I gladly accepted the invitation, because it seems to me that this, above all other times in our history, is the time for common counsel, for the drawing not only of the energies but of the minds of the nation together. I thought that it was a welcome opportunity for disclosing to you some of the thoughts that have been gathering in my mind during the last momentous months.

I am introduced to you as the President of the United States, and yet I would be pleased if you would put the thought of the office into the background and regard me as one of your fellow-citizens who had come here to speak, not the words of authority, but the words of counsel, the words which men should speak to one another who wish to be frank in a moment more critical perhaps than the history of the world has ever yet known, a moment when it is every man's duty to forget himself, to forget his own interests, to fill himself with the nobility of a great national and world conception, and act upon a new platform elevated above the ordinary affairs of life, elevated to where men have views of the long destiny of mankind.

I think that in order to realize just what this moment of counsel is it is very desirable that we should remind ourselves just how this war came about and just what it is for. You can explain most wars very simply, but the explanation of this is not so simple. Its roots run deep into all the obscure soils of history, and in my view this is the last decisive issue between the old principles of power and the new principles of freedom.

The war was started by Germany. Her authorities deny that they started it. But I am willing to let the statement I have just made await the verdict of history. And the thing that needs to be explained is why Germany started the war. Remember what the position of Germany in the world was—as enviable a position as any nation has ever occupied. The whole world stood at admiration of her wonderful intellectual and material achievements, and all the intellectual men of the world went to school to her. As a university man, I have been surrounded by men trained in Germany, men who had resorted to Germany because nowhere else could they get such thorough and searching training, particularly in the principles of science and the principles that underlie modern material achievements.

Her men of science had made her industries perhaps the most competent industries in the world, and the label "Made in Germany" was a guarantee of good workmanship and of sound material. She had access to all the markets of the world, and every other man who traded in those markets feared Germany because of her effective and almost irresistible competition.

She had a place in the sun. Why was she not satisfied? What more did she want? There was nothing in the world of peace that she did not already have and have in abundance.

We boast of the extraordinary pace of American advancement. We show with pride the statistics of the increase of our industries and of the population of our cities. Well, these statistics did not match the recent statistics of Germany. Her old cities took on youth, grew faster than any American cities ever grew; her old industries opened their eyes and saw a new world and went out for its conquest; and yet the authorities of Germany were not satisfied.

You have one part of the answer to the question why she was not satisfied in her methods of competition. There is no important industry in Germany upon which the Government has not laid its hands to direct it and, when necessity arise, control it.

You have only to ask any man whom you meet who is familiar with the conditions that prevailed before the war in the matter of international competition to find out the methods of competition which the German manufacturers and exporters used under the patronage and support of the Government of Germany. You will find that they were the same sorts of competition that we have tried to prevent by law within our own borders. If they could not sell their goods cheaper than we could sell ours, at a profit to themselves, they could get a subsidy from the Government which made it possible to sell them cheaper anyhow; and the conditions of competition were thus controlled in large measure by the German Government itself.

But that did not satisfy the German Government. All the while there was lying behind its thought, in its dreams of the future, a political control which would enable it in the long run to dominate the labor and the industry of the world. They were not content with success by superior achievement; they wanted success by authority.

I suppose very few of you have thought much about the Berlin-to-Bagdad Railway. The Berlin-to-Bagdad Railway was constructed in order to run the threat of force down the flank of the industrial undertakings of half a dozen other countries, so that when German competition came in it would not be resisted too far—because there was always the possibility of getting German armies into the heart of that country quicker than any other armies could be got there.

Look at the map of Europe now. Germany, in thrusting upon us again and again the discussion of peace, talks about what? Talks about Belgium, talks about Northern France, talks about Alsace-Lorraine. Well, those are deeply interesting subjects to us and to them, but they are not talking about the heart of the matter.

Take the map and look at it. Germany has absolute control of Austria-Hungary, practical control of the Balkan States, control of Turkey, control of Asia Minor. I saw a map in which the whole thing was printed in appropriate black the other day, and the black stretched all the way from Hamburg to Bagdad—the bulk of the German power inserted into the heart of the world. If it can keep that, she has kept all that her dreams contemplated when the war began. If she can keep that, her power can disturb the world as long as she keeps it, always provided—for I feel bound to put this proviso in—always provided the present influences that control the German Government continue to control it.

I believe that the spirit of freedom can get into the hearts of Germans and find as fine a welcome there as it can find in any other hearts. But the spirit of freedom does not suit the plans of the Pan-Germans. Power cannot be used with concentrated force against free peoples if it is used by a free people.

You know how many intimations come to us from one of the Central Powers that it is more anxious for peace than the chief Central Power; and you know that it means that the people in that Central Power know that if the war ends as it stands they will, in effect, themselves be vassals of Germany, notwithstanding that their populations are compounded with all the people of that part of the world, and notwithstanding the fact that they do not wish, in their pride and proper spirit of nationality, to be so absorbed and dominated.

Germany is determined that the political power of the world shall belong to her. There have been such ambitions before. They have been in part realized. But never before have those ambitions been based upon so exact and precise and scientific a plan of domination.

May I not say that it is amazing to me that any group of people should be so ill-informed as to suppose, as some groups in Russia apparently suppose, that any reforms planned in the interest of the people can live in the presence of a Germany powerful enough to undermine or overthrow them in intrigue or force? Any body of free men that compounds with the present German Government is compounding for its own destruction. But that is not the whole of the story. Any man in America, or anywhere else, who supposes that the free industry and enterprise of the world can continue if the Pan-German plan is achieved and German power fastened upon the world is as fatuous as the dreamers of Russia.

What I am opposed to is not the feeling of the pacifists, but their stupidity. My heart is with them, but my mind has a contempt for them. I want peace, but I know how to get it, and they do not.

You will notice that I sent a friend of mine, Colonel House, to Europe, who is as great a lover of peace as any man in the world; but I did not send him on a peace mission. I sent him to take part in a conference as to how the war was to be won, and he knows, as I know, that that is the way to get peace if you want it for more than a few minutes.

All of this is a preface to the conference that I referred to with regard to what we are going to do. If we are true friends of freedom—our own or anybody else's—we will see that the power of this country, the productivity of this country, is raised to its absolute maximum and that absolutely nobody is allowed to stand in the way of it.

When I say that nobody is allowed to stand in the way, I don't mean that they shall be prevented by the power of the Government, but by the power of the American spirit. Our duty, if we are to do this great thing and show America to be what we believe her to be, the greatest hope and energy of the world—then we must stand together night and day until the job is finished.

While we are fighting for freedom, we must see, among other things, that labor is free; and that means a number of interesting things. It means not only that we must do what we have declared our purpose to do, see that the conditions of labor are not rendered more onerous by the war—but also that we shall see to it that the instrumentalities by which the conditions of labor are improved are not blocked or checked. That we must do. That has been the matter about which I have taken pleasure in conferring from time to time with your President, Mr. Gompers. And, if I may be permitted to do so, I want to express my admiration of his patriotic courage, his large vision, and his statesmanlike sense of what is to be done. I like to lay my mind alongside of a mind that knows how to pull in harness. The horses that kick over the traces will have to be put in a corral.

Now to "stand together" means that nobody must interrupt the processes of our energy, if the interruption can possibly be avoided without the absolute invasion of freedom. To put it concretely, that means this: Nobody has a right to stop the processes of labor until all the methods of conciliation and settlement have been exhausted; and I might as well say right here that I am not talking to you alone. You sometimes stop the courses of labor, but there are others who do the same. And I believe that I am speaking of my own experience not only, but of the experience of others, when I say that you are reasonable in a larger number of cases than the capitalists.

I am not saying these things to them personally yet, because I haven't had a chance. But they have to be said, not in any spirit of criticism, but in order to clear the atmosphere and come down to business. Everybody on both sides has got to transact business, and the settlement is never impossible when both sides want to do the square and right thing. Moreover, a settlement is always hard to avoid when the parties can be brought face to face.

I can differ with a man much more radically when he isn't in the room than I can when he is in the room, because then the awkward thing is that he can come back at me and answer what I say. It is always dangerous for a man to have the floor entirely to himself. And therefore we must insist in every instance that the parties come into each other's presence and there discuss the issues between them, and not separately in places which have no communication with each other.

I always like to remind myself of a delightful saying of an Englishman of a past generation, Charles Lamb. He was with a group of friends, and he spoke very harshly of some man who was not present. I ought to say that Lamb stuttered a little bit. And one of his friends said: "Why, Charles, I didn't know that you knew so-and-so?"

"Oh," he said, "I don't. I can't hate a man I know."

There is a great deal of human nature, of very pleasant human nature, in that saying. It is hard to hate a man you know. I may admit parenthetically that there are some politicians whose methods I do not at all believe in, but they are jolly good fellows, and if they only would not talk the wrong kind of politics with me, I would love to be with them.

And so it is all along the line in serious matters and things less serious. We are all of the same clay and spirit, and we can get together if we desire to get together. Therefore, my counsel to you is this: Let us show ourselves Americans by showing that we do not want to go off in separate camps or groups by ourselves, but that we want to co-operate with all other classes and all other groups in a common enterprise, which is to release the spirit of the world from bondage.

I would be willing to set that up as the final test of an American. That is the meaning of democracy. I have been very much distressed, my fellow-citizens, by some of the things that have happened recently. The mob spirit is displaying itself here and there in this country. I have no sympathy with what some men are saying, but I have no sympathy with the men that take their punishment into their own hands, and I want to say to every man who does join such a mob that I do not recognize him as worthy of the free institutions of the United States.

There are some organizations in this country whose object is anarchy and the destruction of law, but I would not meet their efforts by making myself a partner in destroying the law. I despise and hate their purposes as much as any man, but I respect the ancient processes of justice, and I would be too proud not to see them done justice, however wrong they are. And so I want to utter my earnest protest against any manifestation of the spirit of lawlessness anywhere or in any cause.

Why, gentlemen, look what it means: We claim to be the greatest democratic people in the world, and democracy means, first of all, that we can govern ourselves. If our men have not self-control, then they are not capable of that great thing which we call democratic government. A man who takes the law into his hands is not the right man to co-operate in any form of or development of law and institutions. And some of the processes by which the struggle between capital and labor is carried on are processes that come very near to taking the law into your own hands. I do not mean for a moment to compare them with what I have just been speaking of, but I want you to see that they are mere gradations of the manifestations of the unwillingness to co-operate.

And the fundamental lesson of the whole situation is that we must not only take common counsel, but that we must yield to and obey common counsel. Not all of the instrumentalities for this are at hand. I am hopeful that in the very near future new instrumentalities may be organized by which we can see to it that various things that are now going on shall not go on. There are various processes of the dilution of labor, and the unnecessary substitution of labor, and bidding in distant markets, and unfairly upsetting the whole competition of labor, which ought not to go on—I mean now on the part of employers—and we must interject into this some instrumentality of co-operation by which the fair thing will be done all around. I am hopeful that some such instrumentalities may be devised, but, whether they are or not, we must use those that we have, and upon every occasion where it is necessary to have such an instrumentality, originated upon that occasion, if necessary.

And so, my fellow-citizens, the reason that I came away from Washington is that I sometimes get lonely down there. There are so many people in Washington who know things that are not so; and there are so few people in Washington who know anything about what the people of the United States are thinking about, I have to come away to get reminded of the rest of the country; I have to come away and talk to men who are up against the real thing, and say to them, "I am with you if you are with me." And the only test of being with me is not to think about me personally at all, but merely to think of me as the expression for the time being of the power and dignity and hope of the United States.

BY THE PRESIDENT OF THE UNITED STATES OF AMERICA

PROCLAMATIONS

[Additional Regulations Prescribing the Conduct of Alien Enemies.]

WHEREAS the Congress of the United States in the exercise of the constitutional authority vested in them have resolved, by joint resolution of the Senate and House of Representatives bearing date of April 6th, 1917, "That the state of war between the United States and the Imperial German Government which has been thrust upon the United States is hereby formally declared";

WHEREAS it is provided by Section four thousand and sixty-seven of the Revised Statutes, as follows;

> Whenever there is declared a war between the United States and any foreign nation or government, or any invasion or predatory incursion is perpetrated, attempted or threatened against the territory of the United States, by any foreign nation or government, and the President makes public proclamation of the event, all natives, citizens, denizens, or subjects of the hostile nation or government, being males of the age of fourteen years and upwards, who shall be within the United States, and not actually naturalized, shall be liable to be apprehended, restrained, secured, and removed, as alien enemies. The President is authorized, in any such event, by his proclamation thereof, or other public act, to direct the conduct to be observed, on the part of the United States, toward the aliens who become so liable; the manner and degree of the restraint to which they shall be subject, and in what cases, and upon what security their residence shall be permitted, and to provide for the removal of those who, not being permitted to reside within the United States, refuse or neglect to depart therefrom; and to establish any other regulations which are found necessary in the premises and for the public safety;

WHEREAS, by Section four thousand and sixty-eight, four thousand and sixty-nine, and four thousand and seventy, of the Revised Statutes, further provision is made relative to alien enemies;

AND WHEREAS, by a proclamation dated April 6th, 1917, I declared and established certain regulations prescribing the conduct of alien enemies;

Now, THEREFORE, I, WOODROW WILSON, President of the United States of America, pursuant to the authority vested in me, hereby declare and establish the following regulations, additional and supplemental to those declared and established by said proclamation of April 6th, 1917, which additional and supplemental regulations I find necessary in the premises and for the public safety:

13. An alien enemy shall not approach or be found within one hundred yards of any canal; nor within one hundred yards of any wharf, pier or dock used directly by or by means of lighters by any vessel or vessels of over five hundred (500) tons gross engaged in foreign or domestic trade other than fishing; nor within one hundred yards of any warehouse, shed, elevator, railroad terminal or other terminal, storage or transfer facility adjacent to or operated in connection with any such wharf, pier or dock; and wherever the distance between any two of such wharves, piers or docks, measured along the shore line connecting them, is less than eight hundred and eighty yards, an alien enemy shall not approach or be found within one hundred yards of such shore line.

14. Whenever the Attorney General of the United States deems it to be necessary, for the public safety and the protection of transportation, to exclude alien enemies from the vicinity of any warehouse, elevator or railroad depot, yard or terminal which is not located within any prohibited area designated by this proclamation or the proclamation of April 6th, 1917, then an alien enemy shall not approach or be found within such distance of any such warehouse elevator, depot, yard or terminal as may be specified by the Attorney General by regulation duly made and declared by him; and the Attorney General is hereby authorized to fix, by regulations to be made and declared from time to time, the area surrounding any such warehouse, elevator, depot, yard or terminal from which he deems it necessary, for the public safety and the protection of transportation, to exclude alien enemies.

15. An alien enemy shall not, except on public ferries, be found on any ocean, bay, river or other waters within three miles of the shore line of the United States or its territorial possessions; said shore line for the purpose of this proclamation being hereby defined as the line of sea coast and the shores of all waters of the United States and its territorial possessions connected with the high seas and navigable by ocean going vessels; nor on any of the Great Lakes, their connecting waters or harbors, within the boundaries of the United States.

16. No alien enemy shall ascend into the air in any airplane, balloon, airship, or flying machine.

17. An alien enemy shall not enter or be found within the District of Columbia.

18. An alien enemy shall not enter or be found within the Panama Canal Zone.

19. All alien enemies are hereby required to register at such times and places and in such manner as may be fixed by the Attorney General of the United States and the Attorney General is hereby authorized and directed to provide, as speedily as may be practicable, for registration of all alien enemies and for the issuance of registration cards to alien enemies and to make and declare such rules and regulations as he may deem necessary for effecting such registration; and all alien enemies and all other persons are hereby required to comply with such rules and regulations; and the Attorney General in carrying out such registration is hereby authorized to utilize such agents, agencies, officers and departments of the United States and of the several states, territories, dependencies and municipalities thereof and of the District of Columbia as he may select for the purpose, and all such agents, agencies, officers and departments are hereby granted full authority for all acts done by them in the execution of this regulation when acting by the direction of the Attorney General. After the date fixed by the Attorney General for such registration, an alien enemy shall not be found within the limits of the United States, its territories or possessions, without having his registration card on his person.

20. An alien enemy shall not change his place of abode or occupation or otherwise travel or move from place to place without full compliance with any such regulations as the Attorney General of the United States may, from time to time, make and declare; and the Attorney General is hereby authorized to make and declare, from time to time, such regulations concerning the movements of alien enemies as he may deem necessary in the premises and for the public safety, and to provide in such regulations for monthly, weekly or other periodical report by alien enemies to federal, state or local authorities; and all alien enemies shall report at the times and places and to the authorities specified in such regulations.

This proclamation and the regulations herein contained shall extend and apply to all land and water, continental or insular, in any way within the jurisdiction of the United States.

IN WITNESS WHEREOF, I have hereunto set my hand and caused the seal of the United States to be affixed.

DONE in the District of Columbia, this sixteenth day of November, in the year of our Lord one thousand nine hundred and [SEAL] seventeen, and of the independence of the United States the one hundred and forty-second.

WOODROW WILSON.

By the President:

FRANK L. POLK, *Acting Secretary of State.*

[Regulation and Prohibition of Imports.]

Whereas, Congress has enacted, and the President has on the 6th day of October, 1917, approved a law which contains the following provisions:

> Whenever during the present war the President shall find that the public safety so requires and shall make proclamation thereof, it shall be unlawful to import into the United States from any country named in such proclamation any article or articles mentioned in such proclamation, except at such time or times, and under such regulations or orders, and subject to such limitations and exceptions as the President shall prescribe, until otherwise ordered by the President or by Congress. Provided, however, that no preference shall be given to the ports of one State over those of another.

Now, therefore, I, Woodrow Wilson, President of the United States of America, do hereby proclaim to all whom it may concern that the public safety requires that the following articles, namely:

Antimony, antimony ore, or any chemical extracted therefrom; asbestos, beans of all kinds, balata, burlap, castor seed, castor oil, cotton, chrome, chrome ore, or any ferro-alloy or chemical extracted therefrom; cocoanut oil, cobalt, cobalt ore, or any ferro-alloy or chemical extracted therefrom; copra, industrial diamonds, all ferro-alloys, flax, gutta joolatong, gutta percha, gutta siak, hemp, hides and skins, jute, iridium, leather, manganese, manganese ore, or any ferro-alloy or chemical extracted therefrom; mica, molybdenum, molybdenum ore, or any ferro-alloy or chemical extracted therefrom; naxos emery and naxos emery ore, nickel, nickel ore, matte, or any ferro-alloy or chemical extracted therefrom; sodium, potassium, or calcium nitrates, optical glass, palm oil, platinum, plumbago, pyrites, rice, rubber, raw, reclaimed, waste or scrap; scheelite, shellac, sisal, soya bean oil, spiegeleisen, sugars, tanning materials, tin in bars, blocks, pigs, or grain, or granulated; ton ore and tin concentrates, or any chemical extracted therefrom; titanium, titanium ore, or any ferro-alloy or chemical extracted therefrom; tobacco, tungsten, tungsten ore, or any ferro-alloy or chemical extracted therefrom; vanadium, vanadium ore, or any ferro-alloy or chemical extracted therefrom; wheat and wheat flour, wolframite, or wool.

Shall not, from and after the date of this proclamation, be imported into the United States or its territorial possessions from Abyssinia, Afghanistan, Albania, Argentina, Austria-Hungary, Belgium, her colonies, possessions and protectorates; Bolivia, Brazil, Bulgaria, China, Chile, Colombia, Costa Rica, Cuba, Denmark, her colonies, possessions and protectorates; Dominican Republic, Ecuador, Egypt, France, her colonies, possessions and protectorates; Germany, her colonies, possessions and protectorates; Great Britain, her colonies, possessions and protectorates; Greece, Guatemala, Haiti, Honduras, Italy, her colonies, possessions, and protectorates; Japan, Liechtenstein, Liberia, Luxembourg,

Mexico, Monaco, Montenegro, Morocco, Nepal, the Netherlands, her colonies, possessions, and protectorates; Nicaragua, Norway, Oman, Panama, Paraguay, Persia, Peru, Portugal, her colonies, possessions, and protectorates; Rumania, Russia, Salvador, San Marino, Serbia, Siam, Spain, her colonies, possessions, and protectorates; Sweden, Switzerland, Turkey, Uruguay, or Venezuela.

Except under license granted by the War Trade Board in accordance with regulations or orders and subject to such limitations and exceptions as have heretofore been made or shall hereafter be prescribed in pursuance of the powers conferred by said act of October 6, 1917, and the Executive Order of October 12, 1917.

In witness whereof, I have hereunto set my hand and caused the seal of the United States of America to be affixed.

Done in the District of Columbia, this 28th day of November, in the year of our Lord, one thousand nine hundred and seventeen, [SEAL] and of the independence of the United States of America, the one hundred and forty-second.

WOODROW WILSON.

By the President:

ROBERT LANSING, *Secretary of State.*

[Additional Regulation and Prohibition of Exports.]

Whereas, Congress has enacted, and the President has on the fifteenth day of June, 1917, approved a law which contains the following provisions:

> Whenever during the present war the President shall find that the public safety shall so require and shall make proclamation thereof, it shall be unlawful to export from or ship from or take out of the United States to any country named in such proclamation any article or articles mentioned in such proclamation, except at such times or times, and under such regulations and orders, and subject to such limitations and exceptions as the President shall prescribe, until otherwise ordered by the President or by Congress; provided, however, that no preference shall be given to the ports of one State over those of another.

Now, therefore, I, Woodrow Wilson, President of the United States of America, do hereby proclaim to all whom it may concern that the public safety requires that the following articles (in addition to the articles controlled by the second division of the proclamation of August 27, 1917), namely:

Iron and steel wire rope, cable and strands consisting of six or more wires, stud link chain cable, micrometers and calipers, lathe chucks, antimony, antimony ore, asbestos, balata, mica, mica splittings, strontium ores, titanium, wolframite and iridium, arsenic and its compounds, opium, caustic soda, soda ash, methylethyl katone and wood alcohol, acetic acid, glacial acetic acid, acetate of cellulose and all acetates, animal oils and vegetable oils, beans, eggs, peanut meal, flaxseed, soya bean meal, soya bean oil, starch, canned peas, canned tomatoes, canned corn, dried prunes, dried apricots, dried apples, dried raisins and dried peaches, quebracho and chestnut extracts; vegetable fibre bags and bagging, except cotton bags and bagging; rubber, sponges, gutta joolatong, gutta percha, gutta siak, shellac seedlac and chinchona bark; hospital gauze and surgical instruments; yellow pine wood measuring 1' by 1' by 25' and larger, and poster paper.

Shall not, after the first day of December, in the year one thousand nine hundred and seventeen, be exported from or shipped from or taken out of the United States or its territorial possessions to

Abyssinia, Afghanistan, Argentina, Belgium, her colonies, possessions or protectorates, Bolivia, Brazil, China, Chile, Colombia, Costa Rica, Cuba, Dominican Republic, Ecuador, Egypt, France, her colonies, possessions or protectorates; Great Britain, her colonies, possessions or protectorates; Guatemala, Haiti, Honduras, Italy, her colonies, possessions or protectorates; Japan, Liberia, Mexico, Monaco, Montenegro, Morocco, Nepal, Nicaragua, the colonies, possessions or protectorates of The Netherlands; Oman, Panama, Paraguay, Persia, Peru, Portugal, her colonies, possessions or protectorates; Rumania, Russia, Salvador, San Marino, Serbia, Siam, Uruguay or Venezuela, or to any territory occupied by the military forces of the United States or the nations associated with the United States in the war.

Except at such time or times, and under such regulations and orders, and subject to such limitations and exceptions as the President shall prescribe, until otherwise ordered by the President or by Congress.

The regulations, orders, limitations and exceptions prescribed will be administered by and under the authority of the War Trade Board, from whom licenses, in conformity with said regulations, orders, limitations and exceptions, will issue. Said proclamation of August 27, 1917, is hereby confirmed and continued, and all rules and regulations heretofore made in connection therewith or in pursuance thereof, including the executive order of October 12, 1917, are likewise confirmed and continued and made applicable to this proclamation.

In witness whereof, I have hereunto set my hand and caused the seal of the United States of America to be affixed.

Done in the District of Columbia this twenty-ninth of November in the year of Our Lord One thousand nine hundred and seventeen and of the Independence of the United States of America the one hundred and forty-second.

[SEAL]

WOODROW WILSON.

By the President:
ROBERT LANSING, *Secretary of State.*

EXECUTIVE ORDERS

[Directing the Determination and Enforcement of Reasonable Profits in the Sale of Food.]

THE WHITE HOUSE, *November 27, 1917.*

I hereby authorize and direct the United States Food Administrator, in prescribing regulations for licenses under Section 5 of the Act of Congress approved August 10, 1917, entitled An Act to Provide Further for the National Security and Defense by Encouraging the Production, Conserving the Supply, and Controlling the Distribution of Food Products and Fuel, and in enforcing and carrying into effect, so far as it relates to foods, feeds, and their derivative products, that part of Section 5, which reads as follows:

"Whenever the President shall find that any storage charge, commission, profit, or practice of any licensee is unjust or unreasonable, or discriminatory or unfair, or wasteful, and shall order such license, within a reasonable time fixed in the order, to discontinue the same, unless such order which shall recite the facts found, is revoked or suspended, such licensee shall, within the time prescribed in the order, discontinue such unjust, unreasonable, discriminatory, and unfair storage charge, commission, profit, or practice. The President may, in lieu of any such unjust, unreasonable, discriminatory, and unfair storage charge, commission, profit, or practice, find what is a just, reasonable, non-discriminatory, and fair storage charge, commission, profit, or practice, and in any proceeding brought in any court such order of the President shall be prima facie evidence."

To find that a just, reasonable, and fair profit is the normal average profit which persons engaged in the same business and place obtained prior to July 1, 1914, under free competitive conditions; to indicate, if he shall see fit to do so, what margin over cost will return such a just, reasonable, and fair profit; and to take such legal steps as are authorized by said act to prohibit the taking of any greater profit.

WOODROW WILSON.

[Changing Coal Prices.]

THE WHITE HOUSE, *November 28, 1917.*

The scale of prices prescribed August 23, 1917, by the President of the United States for anthracite coal at the mines, adjusted as to pea coal October 1, 1917, by order of the United States Fuel Administrator, is hereby amended by adding the sum of thirty-five (35) cents to each of the prices so prescribed or adjusted, provided, however, that this increase in prices shall not apply to any coal sold at the mines under an existing contract containing a provision for an increase in the price of coal thereunder, in case of an increase of wages paid to miners.

This order shall become effective at 7 A. M. on December 1, 1917.

WOODROW WILSON.

ADDRESS TO CONGRESS

[Delivered to Joint Session of Congress, December 4, 1917.]

GENTLEMEN OF THE CONGRESS: Eight months have elapsed since I last had the honor of addressing you. They have been months crowded with events of immense and grave significance for us. I shall not undertake to detail or even to summarize those events. The practical particulars of the part we have played in them will be laid before you in the reports of the executive departments. I shall discuss only our present outlook upon these vast affairs, our present duties, and the immediate means of accomplishing the objects we shall hold always in view.

I shall not go back to debate the causes of the war. The intolerable wrongs done and planned against us by the sinister masters of Germany have long since become too grossly obvious and odious to every true American to need to be rehearsed. But I shall ask you to consider again and with a very grave scrutiny our objectives and the measures by which we mean to attain them; for the purpose of discussion here in this place is action, and our action must move straight toward definite ends. Our object is, of course, to win the war; and we shall not slacken or suffer ourselves to be diverted until it is won. But it is worth while asking and answering the question, When shall we consider the war won?

From one point of view it is not necessary to broach this fundamental matter. I do not doubt that the American people know what the war is about and what sort of an outcome they will regard as a realization of their purpose in it.

As a nation we are united in spirit and intention. I pay little heed to those who tell me otherwise. I hear the voices of dissent—who does not? I hear the criticism and the clamor of the noisily thoughtless and troublesome. I also see men here and there fling themselves in impotent disloyalty against the calm, indomitable power of the Nation. I hear men debate peace who understand neither its nature nor the way in which we may attain it with uplifted eyes and unbroken spirits. But I know that none of these speaks for the Nation. They do not touch the heart of anything. They may safely be left to strut their uneasy hour and be forgotten.

But from another point of view I believe that it is necessary to say plainly what we here at the seat of action consider the war to be for and what part we mean to play in the settlement of its searching issues. We are the spokesmen of the American people, and they have a right to know whether their purpose is ours. They desire peace by the overcoming of evil, by the defeat once for all of the sinister forces that interrupt peace and render it impossible, and they wish to know how closely our thought runs with theirs and what action we propose. They are impatient with those who desire peace by any sort of compromise—deeply and indignantly impatient—but they will be equally impatient with us if we do not make it plain to them what our objectives are and what we are planning for in seeking to make conquest of peace by arms.

I believe that I speak for them when I say two things: First, that this intolerable thing of which the masters of Germany have shown us the ugly face, this menace of combined intrigue and force which we now see so clearly as the German power, a thing without conscience or honor or capacity for covenanted peace, must be crushed and, if it be not utterly brought to an end, at least shut out from the friendly intercourse of the nations; and second, that when this thing and its power are indeed defeated and the time comes that we can discuss peace—when the German people have spokesmen whose word we can believe and when those spokesmen are ready in the name of their people to accept the common judgment of the nations as to what shall henceforth be the bases of law and of covenant for the life of the world—we shall be willing and glad to pay the full price for peace, and pay it ungrudgingly.

We know what that price will be. It will be full, impartial justice—justice done at every point and to every nation that the final settlement must affect, our enemies as well as our friends.

You catch, with me, the voices of humanity that are in the air. They grow daily more audible, more articulate, more persuasive, and they come from the hearts of men everywhere. They insist that the war shall not end in vindictive action of any kind; that no nation or people shall be robbed or punished because the irresponsible rulers of a single country have themselves done deep and abominable wrong. It is this thought that has been expressed in the formula, "No annexations, no contributions, no punitive indemnities."

Just because this crude formula expresses the instinctive judgment as to right of plain men everywhere, it has been made diligent use of by the masters of German intrigue to lead the people of Russia astray—and the people of every other country their agents could reach—in order that a premature peace might be brought about before autocracy has been taught its final and convincing lesson and the people of the world put in control of their own destinies.

But the fact that a wrong use has been made of a just idea is no reason why a right use should not be made of it. It ought to be brought under the patronage of its real friends. Let it be said again that autocracy must first be shown the utter futility of its claim to power or leadership in the modern world. It is impossible to apply any standard of justice so long as such forces are unchecked and undefeated as the present masters of Germany command. Not until that has been done can right be set up as arbiter and peacemaker among the nations. But when that has been done—as, God willing, it assuredly will be—we shall at last be free to do an unprecedented thing, and this is the time to avow our purpose to do it. We shall be free to base peace on generosity and justice, to the exclusions of all selfish claims to advantage even on the part of the victors.

Let there be no misunderstanding. Our present and immediate task is to win the war and nothing shall turn us aside from it until it is accomplished. Every power and resource we possess, whether of men, of money, or of materials, is being devoted and will continue to be devoted to that purpose until it is achieved. Those who desire to bring peace about before that purpose is achieved I counsel to carry their advice elsewhere. We will not entertain it. We shall regard the war as won only when the German people say to us, through properly accredited representatives, that they are ready to agree to a settlement based upon justice and reparation of the wrongs their rulers have done. They have done a wrong to Belgium which must be repaired. They have established a power over other lands and peoples than their own—over the great empire of Austria-Hungary, over hitherto free Balkan states, over Turkey and within Asia—which must be relinquished.

Germany's success by skill, by industry, by knowledge, by enterprise we did not grudge or oppose, but admired, rather. She had built up for herself a real empire of trade and influence, secured by the peace of the world. We were content to abide by the rivalries of manufacture, science and commerce that were involved for us in her success, and stand or fall as we had or did not have the brains and the initiative to surpass her. But at the moment when she had conspicuously won her triumphs of peace she threw them away, to establish in their stead what the world will no longer permit to be established, military and political domination by arms, by which to oust where she could not excel the rivals she most feared and hated. The peace we make must remedy that wrong. It must deliver the once fair lands and happy peoples of Belgium and Northern France from the Prussian conquest and the Prussian menace, but it must deliver also the peoples of Austria-Hungary, the peoples of the Balkans and the peoples of Turkey, alike in Europe and Asia, from the impudent and alien dominion of the Prussian military and commercial autocracy.

We owe it, however, to ourselves, to say that we do not wish in any way to impair or to rearrange the Austro-Hungarian Empire. It is no affair of ours what they do with their own life, either industrially or politically. We do not purpose or desire to dictate to them in any way. We only desire to see that their affairs are left in their own hands, in all matters, great or small. We shall hope to secure for the peoples of the Balkan peninsula and for the people of the Turkish Empire the right and opportunity to make their own lives safe, their own fortunes secure against oppression or injustice and from the dictation of foreign courts or parties.

And our attitude and purpose with regard to Germany herself are of a like kind. We intend no wrong against the German Empire, no interference with her internal affairs. We should deem either the one or the other absolutely unjustifiable, absolutely contrary to the principles we have professed to live by and to hold most sacred throughout our life as a nation.

The people of Germany are being told by the men whom they now permit to deceive them and to act as their masters that they are fighting for the very life and existence of their empire, a war of desperate self-defense against deliberate aggression. Nothing could be more grossly or wantonly false, and we must seek by the utmost openness and candor as to our real aims to convince them of its falseness. We are in fact fighting for their emancipation from the fear, along with our own—from the fear as well as from the fact of unjust attack by neighbors or rivals or schemers after world empire. No one is threatening the existence or the independence of the peaceful enterprise of the German Empire.

The worst that can happen to the detriment of the German people is this, that if they should still, after the war is over, continue to be obliged to live under ambitious and intriguing masters interested to disturb the peace of the world, men or classes of men whom the other peoples of the world could not trust, it might be impossible to admit them to the partnership of nations which must henceforth guarantee the world's peace. That partnership must be a partnership of peoples, not a mere partnership of governments. It might be impossible, also, in such untoward circumstances, to admit Germany to the free economic intercourse which must inevitably spring out of the other partnerships of a real peace. But there would be no aggression in that; and such a situation, inevitable, because of distrust, would in the very nature of things sooner or later cure itself, by processes which would assuredly set in.

The wrongs, the very deep wrongs, committed in this war will have to be righted. That, of course. But they cannot and must not be righted by the commission of similar wrongs against Germany and her allies. The world will not permit the commission of similar wrongs as a means of reparation and settlement. Statesmen must by this time have learned that the opinion of the world is everywhere wide awake and fully comprehends the issues involved. No representative of any self-governed nation will dare disregard it by attempting any such covenants of selfishness and compromise as were entered into at the Congress of Vienna. The thought of the plain people here and everywhere throughout the world, the people who enjoy no privilege and have very simple and unsophisticated standards of right and wrong, is the air all governments must henceforth breathe if they would live.

It is in the full disclosing light of that thought that all policies must be received and executed in this midday hour of the world's life. German rulers have been able to upset the peace of the world only because the German people were not suffered under their tutelage to share the comradeship of the other peoples of the world either in thought or in purpose. They were allowed to have no opinion of their own which might be set up as a rule of conduct for those who exercised authority over them. But the Congress that concludes this war will feel the full strength of the tides that run now in the hearts and consciences of free men everywhere. Its conclusions will run with those tides.

All those things have been true from the very beginning of this stupendous war; and I cannot help thinking that if they had been made plain at the very outset the sympathy and enthusiasm of the Russian people might have been once for all enlisted on the side of the Allies, suspicion and distrust swept away, and a real and lasting union of purpose effected. Had they believed these things at the very moment of their revolution, and had they been confirmed in that belief since, the sad reverses which have recently marked the progress of their affairs towards an ordered and stable government of free men might have been avoided. The Russian people have been poisoned by the very same falsehoods that have kept the German people in the dark, and the poison has been administered by the very same hand. The only possible antidote is the truth. It cannot be uttered too plainly or too often.

From every point of view, therefore, it has seemed to be my duty to speak these declarations of purpose, to add these specific interpretations to what I took the liberty of saying to the Senate in January. Our entrance into the war has not altered out attitude towards the settlement that must come when it is over.

When I said in January that the nations of the world were entitled not only to free pathways upon the sea, but also to assured and unmolested access to those pathways, I was thinking, and I am thinking now, not of the smaller and weaker nations alone which need our countenance and support, but also of the great and powerful nations and of our present enemies as well as our present associates in the war. I was thinking, and am thinking now, of Austria herself, among the rest, as well as of Serbia and of Poland.

Justice and equality of rights can be had only at a great price. We are seeking permanent, not temporary, foundations for the peace of the world, and must seek them candidly and fearlessly. As always, the right will prove to be the expedient.

What shall we do, then, to push this great war of freedom and justice to its righteous conclusion? We must clear away with a thorough hand all impediments to success, and we must make every adjustment of law that will facilitate the full and free use of our whole capacity and force as a fighting unit.

One very embarrassing obstacle that stands in our way is that we are at war with Germany but not with her allies. I, therefore, very earnestly recommend that the Congress immediately declare the United States in a state of war with Austria-Hungary. Does it seem strange to you that this should be the conclusion of the argument I have just addressed to you? It is not. It is in fact the inevitable logic of what I have said. Austria-Hungary is for the time being not her own mistress but simply the vassal of the German Government.

We must face the facts as they are and act upon them without sentiment in this stern business. The Government of Austria and Hungary is not acting upon its own initiative or in response to the wishes and feelings of its own peoples, but as the instrument of another nation. We must meet its force with our own and regard the Central Powers as but one. The war can be successfully conducted in no other way.

The same logic would lead also to a declaration of war against Turkey and Bulgaria. They also are the tools of Germany, but they are mere tools and do not yet stand in the direct path of our necessary action. We shall go wherever the necessities of this war carry us, but it seems to me that we should go only where immediate and practical considerations lead us, and not heed any others.

The financial and military measures which must be adopted will suggest themselves as the war and its undertakings develop, but I will take the liberty of proposing to you certain other acts of legislation which seem to me to be needed for the support of the war and for the release of our whole force and energy.

It will be necessary to extend in certain particulars the legislation of the last session with regard to alien enemies, and also necessary, I believe, to create a very definite and particular control over the entrance and departure of all persons into and from the United States.

Legislation should be enacted defining as a criminal offense every wilful violation of the presidential proclamation relating to alien enemies promulgated under section 4067 of the revised statutes and providing appropriate punishments; and women, as well as men, should be included under the terms of the acts placing restraints upon alien enemies.

It is likely that as time goes on many alien enemies will be willing to be fed and housed at the expense of the Government in the detention camps, and it would be the purpose of the legislation I have suggested to confine offenders among them in the penitentiaries and other similar institutions where they could be made to work as other criminals do.

Recent experience has convinced me that the Congress must go further in authorizing the Government to set limits to prices. The law of supply and demand, I am sorry to say, has been replaced by the law of unrestrained selfishness. While we have eliminated profiteering in several branches of industry, it still runs impudently rampant in others. The farmers, for example, complain with a great deal of justice that, while the regulation of food prices restricts their incomes, no restraints are placed upon the prices of most of the things they must themselves purchase; and similar inequities obtain on all sides.

It is imperatively necessary that the consideration of the full use of the water power of the country, and also of the consideration of the systematic and yet economical development of such of the natural resources of the country as are still under the control of the Federal Government should be immediately resumed and affirmatively and constructively dealt with at the earliest possible moment. The pressing need of such legislation is daily becoming more obvious.

The legislation proposed at the last session with regard to regulated combinations among our exporters in order to provide for our foreign trade a more effective organization and method of co-operation ought by all means to be completed at this session.

And I beg that the members of the House of Representatives will permit me to express the opinion that it will be impossible to deal in any but a very wasteful and extravagant fashion with the enormous appropriations of the public moneys which must continue to be made if the war is to be properly sustained, unless the House will consent to return to its former practice of initiating and preparing all appropriation bills through a single committee, in order that responsibility may be centered, expenditures standardized and made uniform, and waste and duplication as much as possible avoided.

Additional legislation may also become necessary before the present Congress again adjourns in order to effect the most efficient co-ordination and operation of the railways and other transportation systems of the country; but to that I shall, if circumstances should demand, call the attention of Congress upon another occasion.

If I have overlooked anything that ought to be done for the more effective conduct of the war, your own counsels will supply the omission. What I am perfectly clear about is that in the present session of the Congress our whole attention and energy should be concentrated on the vigorous, rapid and successful prosecution of the great task of winning the war.

We can do this with all the greater zeal and enthusiasm because we know that for us this is a war of high principle, debased by no selfish ambition of conquest or spoiliation; because we know, and all the world knows, that we have been forced into it to save the very institutions we live under from corruption and destruction. The purpose of the Central Powers strikes straight at the very heart of everything we believe in; their methods of warfare outrage every principle of humanity and of knightly honor; their intrigue has corrupted the very thought and spirit of many of our people; their sinister and secret diplomacy has sought to take our very territory away from us and disrupt the union of the states. Our safety would be at an end, our honor forever sullied and brought into contempt, were we to permit their triumph. They are striking at the very existence of democracy and liberty.

It is because it is for us a war of high, disinterested purpose, in which all the free peoples of the world are banded together for the vindication of right, a war for the preservation of our nation, of all that it has held dear, of principle and of purpose, that we feel ourselves doubly constrained to propose for its outcome only that which is righteous and of irreproachable intention, for our foes as well as for our friends. The cause being just and holy, the settlement must be of like motive and equality. For this we can fight, but for nothing less noble or less worthy of our traditions. For this cause we entered the war and for this cause will we battle until the last gun is fired.

I have spoken plainly because this seems to me the time when it is most necessary to speak plainly, in order that all the world may know that, even in the heat and ardor of the struggle and when our whole thought is of carrying the war through to its end, we have not forgotten any ideal or principle for which the name of America has been held in honor among the nations and for which it has been our glory to contend in the great generations that went before us. A supreme moment of history has come. The eyes of the people have been opened and they see. The hand of God is laid upon the nations. He will show them favor, I devoutly believe, only if they rise to the clear heights of His own justice and mercy.

BY THE PRESIDENT OF THE UNITED STATES OF AMERICA.

A PROCLAMATION.

[Announcing state of war with Austria-Hungary.]

Whereas, the Congress of the United States, in the exercise of the constitutional authority vested in them, have resolved, by joint resolution of the Senate and House of Representatives, bearing date of Dec. 7, 1917, as follows:

"Whereas, the Imperial and Royal Austro-Hungarian Government has committed repeated acts of war against the Government and the people of the United States of America; therefore, be it

"Resolved, by the Senate and House of Representatives of the United States of America in Congress assembled, that a state of war is hereby declared to exist between the United States of America and the Imperial and Royal Austro-Hungarian Government; and that the President be, and he is hereby, authorized and directed to employ the entire naval and military forces of the United States and the resources of the Government to carry on war against the Imperial and Royal Austro-Hungarian Government; and to bring the conflict to a successful termination all the resources of the country are hereby pledged by the Congress of the United States."

Whereas, by Sections Four Thousand and Sixty-seven, Four Thousand and Sixty-eight, Four Thousand and Sixty-nine, and Four Thousand and Seventy of the Revised Statutes, provision is made relative to natives, citizens, denizens, or subjects of a hostile nation or Government, being males of the age of 14 years and upward who shall be in the United States and not actually naturalized;

Now, Therefore, I, Woodrow Wilson, President of the United States of America, do hereby proclaim to all whom it may concern that a state of war exists between the United States and the Imperial and Royal Austro-Hungarian Government; and I do specially direct all officers, civil or military, of the United States that they exercise vigilance and zeal in the discharge of the duties incident to such a state of war, and I do, moreover, earnestly appeal to all American citizens, that they, in loyal devotion to their country, dedicated from its foundation to the principles of liberty and justice, uphold the laws of the land, and give undivided and willing support to those measures which may be adopted by the constitutional authorities in prosecution of the war to a successful issue and in obtaining a secure and just peace;

And, acting under and by virtue of the authority vested in me by the Constitution of the United States and the aforesaid sections of the Revised Statutes, I do hereby further proclaim and direct that the conduct to be observed on the part of the United States toward all natives, citizens, denizens, or subjects of Austria-Hungary, being males of the age of 14 years and upward, who shall be within the United States and not actually naturalized, shall be as follows:

All natives, citizens, denizens, or subjects of Austria-Hungary, being males of 14 years and upward, who shall be within the United States and not naturalized, are enjoined to preserve the peace toward the United States and to refrain from crime against the public safety, and from violating the laws of United States and of the States and Territories thereof, and to refrain from actual hostility or giving information, aid, or comfort to the enemies of the United States, and to comply strictly with the regulations which are hereby or which may be from time to time promulgated by the President; and so long as they shall conduct themselves in accordance with law they shall be undisturbed in the peaceful pursuit of their lives and occupations and be accorded the consideration due to all peaceful and law-abiding persons, except so far as restrictions may be necessary for their own protection and for the safety of the United States; and toward such of said persons as conduct themselves in accordance with law all citizens of the United States are enjoined to preserve the peace and to treat them with all such friendliness as may be compatible with loyalty and allegiance to the United States.

And all natives, citizens, denizens, or subjects of Austria-Hungary, being males of the ages of 14 years and upward, who shall be within the United States and not actually naturalized, who fail to conduct themselves as so enjoined, in addition to all other penalties prescribed by law, shall be liable to restraint, or to give security, or to remove and depart from the United States in the manner prescribed by Sections 4,069 and 4,070 of the Revised Statutes, and as prescribed in regulations duly promulgated by the President;

And pursuant to the authority vested in me I hereby declare and establish the following regulations, which I find necessary in the premises and for the public safety:

(1) No native, citizen, denizen, or subject of Austria-Hungary, being a male of the age of 14 years and upward, and not actually naturalized, shall depart from the United States until he shall have received such permit as the President shall prescribe, or except under order of a court, Judge, or Justice, under Sections 4,069 and 4,070 of the Revised Statutes;

(2) No such person shall land in or enter the United States, except under such restrictions and at such places as the President may prescribe;

(3) Every such person of whom there may be reasonable cause to believe that he is aiding or about to aid the enemy, or who may be at large to the danger of the public peace or safety, or who violates or attempts to violate or of whom there is reasonable ground to believe that he is about to violate any regulation duly promulgated by the President, or any criminal law of the United States, or of the States or Territories thereof, will be subject to summary arrest by the United States Marshal, or his deputy, or such other officers as the President shall designate, and to confinement in such penitentiary, prison, jail, military camp, or other place of detention as may be directed by the President.

This proclamation and the regulations herein contained shall extend and apply to all land and water, continental or insular, in any way within the jurisdiction of the United States.

In witness whereof, I have hereunto set my hand and caused the seal of the United States to be affixed.

Done in the District of Columbia, this eleventh day of December, in the year of our Lord one thousand nine hundred and seventeen, [SEAL]   and of the independence of the United States the one hundred and forty-second.

WOODROW WILSON.

By the President:
    ROBERT LANSING,
        Secretary of State.

By the President of the United States of America

A PROCLAMATION

[Taking Over the Transportation Systems of the Country.]

Whereas, the Congress of the United States, in the exercise of the constitutional authority vested in them, by joint resolution of the Senate and House of Representatives, bearing date April 6, 1917, resolved:

That the state of war between the United States and the Imperial German Government which has thus been thrust upon the United States is hereby formally declared, and that the President be, and he is hereby, authorized and directed to employ the entire naval and military forces of the United States and the resources of the Government to carry on war against the Imperial German Government, and to bring the conflict to a successful termination all of the resources of the country are hereby pledged by the Congress of the United States.

And by joint resolution, bearing date December 7, 1917, resolved:

That a state of war is hereby declared to exist between the United States of America and the Imperial and Royal Austro-Hungarian Government, and that the President be, and he is hereby, authorized and directed to employ the entire naval and military forces of the United States and the resources of the Government to carry on war against the Imperial and Royal Austro-Hungarian Government, and to bring the conflict to a successful termination all the resources of the country are hereby pledged by the Congress of the United States.

And, whereas, it is provided by Section 1 of the act approved August 29, 1916, entitled "An Act Making Appropriations for the Support of the Army for the Fiscal Year Ending June 30, 1917, and for Other Purposes," as follows:

The President, in time of war, is empowered, through the Secretary of War, to take possession and assume control of any system or systems of transportation, or any part thereof, and to utilize the same, to the exclusion as far as may be necessary of all other traffic thereon, for the transfer or transportation of troops, war material and equipment, or for such other purposes connected with the emergency as may be needful or desirable.

And, whereas, it has now become necessary in the national defense to take possession and assume control of certain systems of transportation and to utilize the same, to the exclusion as far as may be necessary of other than war traffic thereon, for the transportation of troops, war material and equipment therefor, and for other needful and desirable purposes connected with the prosecution of the war;

Now, therefore, I, Woodrow Wilson, President of the United States, under and by virtue of the powers vested in me by the foregoing resolutions and statute, and by virtue of all other powers thereto enabling, do hereby, through Newton D. Baker, Secretary of War, take possession and assume control at twelve o'clock noon on the twenty-eighth day of December, 1917, of each and every system of transportation and the appurtenances thereof located wholly or in part within the boundaries of the continental United States and consisting of railroads, and owned or controlled systems of coastwise and inland transportation, engaged in general transportation, whether operated by steam or by electric power, including also terminals, terminal companies and terminal associations, sleeping and parlor cars, private cars and private car lines, elevators, warehouses, telegraph and telephone lines, and all other equipment and appurtenances commonly used upon or operated as a part of such rail or combined rail and water systems of transportation—to the end that such systems of transportation be utilized for the transfer and transportation of troops, war material and equipment to the exclusion so far as may be necessary of all other traffic thereon, and that so far as such exclusive use be not necessary or desirable, such systems of transportation be operated and utilized in the performance of such other services as the national interest may require and of the usual and ordinary business and duties of common carriers.

It is hereby directed that the possession, control, operation, and utilization of such transportation systems hereby by me undertaken shall be exercised by and through William G. McAdoo, who is hereby appointed and designated Director General of Railroads. Said Director may perform the duties imposed upon him so long, and to such extent, as he shall determine, through the boards of directors, receivers, officers, and employes of said systems of transportation. Until and except so far as said Director shall from time to time by general or special orders otherwise provide, the boards of directors, receivers, officers, and employes of the various transportation systems shall continue the operation thereof in the usual and ordinary course of the business of common carriers in the names of their respective companies.

Until and except so far as said Director shall from time to time otherwise by general or special orders determine, such systems of transportation shall remain subject to all existing statutes and orders of the Interstate Commerce Commission, and to all statutes and orders of regulating commissions of the various States in which said systems or any part thereof may be situated. But any orders, general or special, hereafter made by said Director shall have paramount authority and be obeyed as such.

Nothing herein shall be construed as now affecting the possession, operation, and control of street electric passenger railways, including railways commonly called interurbans, whether such railways be or be not owned or controlled by such railroad companies or systems. By subsequent order and proclamation, if and when it shall be found necessary or desirable, possession, control, or operation may be taken of all or any part of such street railway systems, including subways and tunnels, and by subsequent order and proclamation possession, control, and operation in whole or in part may also be relinquished to the owners thereof of any part of the railroad systems or rail and water systems, possession and control of which are hereby assumed.

The Director shall, as soon as may be after having assumed such possession and control, enter upon negotiations with the several companies looking to agreements for just and reasonable compensation for the possession, use, and control of the respective properties on the basis of an annual guaranteed compensation above accruing depreciation and the maintenance of their properties, equivalent, as nearly as may be, to the average of the net operating income thereof for the three-year period ending June 30, 1917, the results of such negotiations to be reported to me for such action as may be appropriate and lawful.

But nothing herein contained, expressed or implied, or hereafter done or suffered hereunder shall be deemed in any way to impair the rights of the stockholders, bondholders, creditors, and other persons having interests in said systems of transportation or in the profits thereof, to receive just and adequate compensation for the use and control and operation of their property hereby assumed.

Regular dividends hitherto declared, and maturing interest upon bonds, debentures, and other obligations, may be paid in due course; and such regular dividends and interest may continue to be paid until and unless the said Director shall from time to time otherwise by general or special orders determine. And, subject to the approval of the Director, the various carriers may agree upon and arrange for the renewal and extension of maturing obligations.

Except with the prior written assent of said Director, no attachment by mesne process or on execution shall be levied on or against any of the property used by any of said transportation systems in the conduct of their business as common carriers; but suits may be brought by and against said carriers and judgments rendered as hitherto until and except so far as said Director may, by general or special orders, otherwise determine.

From and after twelve o'clock on said twenty-eighth day of December, 1917, all transportation systems included in this order and proclamation shall conclusively be deemed within the possession of said Director, without further act or notice. But for the purposes of accounting said possession and control shall date from twelve o'clock midnight on Dec. 31, 1917.

In witness whereof, I have hereunto set my hand and caused the seal of the United States to be affixed.

Done by the President, through Newton D. Baker, Secretary of War, in the District of Columbia, this twenty-sixth day of December, in the year of Our Lord one thousand nine hundred and seventeen and of the independence of the United States the one hundred and forty-second.

By the President: WOODROW WILSON.

    ROBERT LANSING, *Secretary of State.*

    NEWTON D. BAKER, *Secretary of War.*

STATEMENT

[Explaining the Proclamation Taking Over the Transportation Systems of the Country.]

WASHINGTON, D. C., *December 26, 1917.*

I have exercised the powers over the transportation systems of the country which were granted me by the act of congress of August, 1916, because it has become imperatively necessary for me to do so. This is a war of resources no less than of men, perhaps even more than of men, and it is necessary for the complete mobilization of our resources that the transportation systems of the country should be organized and employed under a single authority and a simplified method of coördination, which has not proved possible under private management and control.

The committee of railroad executives who have been coöperating with the government in this all-important matter have done the utmost that it was possible for them to do; have done it with patriotic zeal and with great ability; but there were differences that they could neither escape nor neutralize. Complete unity of administration in the present circumstances involves upon occasion and at many points a serious dislocation of earnings, and the committee was, of course, without power or authority to rearrange charges or effect proper compensations and adjustments of earnings.

Several roads which were willingly and with admirable public spirit accepting the orders of the committee have already suffered from these circumstances and should not be required to suffer further. In mere fairness to them the full authority of the government must be substituted. The government itself will thereby gain an immense increase of efficiency in the conduct of the war and of the innumerable activities upon which its successful conduct depends.

The public interest must be first served and, in addition, the financial interests of the government and the financial interests of the railways must be brought under a common direction. The financial operations of the railways need not then interfere with the borrowings of the government, and they themselves can be conducted at a great advantage.

Investors in railway securities may rest assured that their rights and interests will be as scrupulously looked after by the government as they could be by the directors of the several railway systems. Immediately upon the reassembling of Congress I shall recommend that these definite guarantees be given: First, of course, that the railway properties will be maintained during the period of Federal control in as good repair and as complete equipment as when taken over by the government, and, second, that the roads shall receive a net operating income equal in each case to the average net income of the three years preceding June 30, 1917; and I am entirely confident that the Congress will be disposed in this case, as in others, to see that justice is done and full security assured to the owners and creditors of the great systems which the government must now use under its own direction or else suffer serious embarrassment.

The Secretary of War and I are agreed that, all the circumstances being taken into consideration, the best results can be obtained under the immediate executive direction of the Honorable William G. McAdoo, whose practical experience peculiarly fits him for the service and whose authority as Secretary of the Treasury will enable him to coördinate as no other man could the many financial interests which will be involved and which might, unless systematically directed, suffer very embarrassing entanglements.

The government of the United States is the only great government now engaged in the war which has not already assumed control of this sort. It was thought to be in the spirit of American institutions to attempt to do everything that was necessary through private management, and if zeal and ability and patriotic motive could have accomplished the necessary unification of administration it would certainly have been accomplished; but no zeal or ability could overcome insuperable obstacles, and I have deemed it my duty to recognize that fact in all candor now that it is demonstrated and to use without reserve the great authority reposed in me. A great national necessity dictated the action and I was therefore not at liberty to abstain from it.

WOODROW WILSON.

By the President of the United States of America

A PROCLAMATION

[Vessels in Ports of the United States.]

Whereas, under and by virtue of an Act of Congress entitled "An Act to punish acts of interference with the foreign relations, the neutrality, and the foreign commerce of the United States, to punish espionage, and better to enforce the criminal laws of the United States, and for other purposes," approved by the President on the 15th day of June, 1917, it is provided among other things as follows:

"Section I. Whenever the President by proclamation or Executive order declares a national emergency to exist by reason of actual or threatened war, insurrection, or invasion, or disturbance or threatened disturbance of the international relations of the United States, the Secretary of the Treasury may make, subject to the approval of the President, rules and regulations governing the anchorage and movement of any vessel, foreign or domestic, in the territorial waters of the United States, may inspect such vessel at any time, place guards thereon, and, if necessary in his opinion in order to secure such vessels from damage or injury, or to prevent damage or injury to any harbor or waters of the United States, or to secure the observance of the rights and obligations of the United States, may take, by and with the consent of the President, for such purposes, full possession and control of such vessel and remove therefrom the officers and crew thereof and all other persons not specially authorized by him to go or remain on board thereof. * * *"

And, whereas, in a proclamation made by me on the 6th day of April, 1917, it was proclaimed that a state of war exists between the United States and the Imperial German Government,

And, whereas, it is essential, in order to carry into effect the provisions of the said Act, which are quoted herein, that the powers conferred upon the President therein be at this time exercised,

Now, therefore, I, Woodrow Wilson, President of the United States of America, by virtue of the powers conferred upon me by the provisions of the said Act of Congress quoted herein, do hereby proclaim that a national emergency exists by reason of the existence of a state of war between the United States and the Imperial German Government,

And the Secretary of the Treasury is therefore hereby authorized to make rules and regulations governing the anchorage and movement of any vessel, foreign or domestic, in the territorial waters of the United States, and to inspect such vessel at any time, place guards thereon, and, if necessary in his opinion in order to secure such vessels from damage or injury, or to prevent damage or injury to any harbor or waters of the United States, or to secure the observance of the rights and obligations of the United States, to take, for such purposes, full possession and control of such vessel and remove therefrom the officers and crew thereof and all other persons not specially authorized by him to go or remain on board thereof.

In witness whereof, I have hereunto set my hand and caused the seal of the United States to be affixed.

Done in the District of Columbia, this third day of December, in
    the year of Our Lord One Thousand Nine Hundred and Sev-
[SEAL]   enteen, and of the Independence of the United States of Amer-
    ica, the One Hundred and Forty-Second.

WOODROW WILSON.

By the President:

    ROBERT LANSING, *Secretary of State.*

EXECUTIVE ORDER

[Supplemental to Executive Order of October 12, 1917, Vesting Power and
Authority in Designated Officers and Making Rules and Regulations Under
Trading with the Enemy Act and Title VII of the Act Approved June
15, 1917.]

THE WHITE HOUSE, 7 December, 1917.

By virtue of the authority vested in me by "An Act to Define, Regulate
and Punish Trading with the Enemy and for Other Purposes," approved
October 6, 1917, I hereby make the following orders, rules and regulations:

I. I hereby prohibit any and all foreign insurance companies from
doing business within the United States after February 1, 1918, unless
such companies shall first obtain from the Secretary of the Treasury
licenses to do business.

II. I further hereby vest in the Secretary of the Treasury the power
and authority to issue at any time, upon such terms and conditions as
the Secretary of the Treasury may deem proper and as are not inconsistent with law, or to refuse, a license to any foreign insurance company
to do business within the United States through agencies, branch offices
or otherwise.   WOODROW WILSON.

BY THE PRESIDENT OF THE UNITED STATES OF AMERICA

A PROCLAMATION

[Limiting Alcoholic Content of Malt Liquor.]

Whereas, under and by virtue of an act of Congress entitled "An Act
to provide further for the national security and defense by encouraging
the production, conserving the supply, and controlling the distribution
of food products and fuel," approved by the President on August 10,
1917, it is provided in Section 15, among other things, as follows:

    "Whenever the President shall find that limitation, regulation, or
prohibition of the use of foods, fruits, food materials, or feeds in
the production of malt or vinous liquors for beverage purposes, or
that reduction of the alcoholic content of any such malt or vinous
liquor, is essential, in order to assure an adequate and continuous

supply of food, or that the national security and defense will be subserved thereby, he is authorized, from time to time, to prescribe and give public notice of the extent of the limitation, regulation, prohibition, or reduction so necessitated. Whenever such notice shall have been given and shall remain unrevoked, no person shall, after a reasonable time prescribed in such notice, use any foods, fruits, food materials, or feeds in the production of malt or vinous liquors, or import any such liquors except under license issued by the President and in compliance with rules and regulations determined by him governing the production and importation of such liquors and the alcoholic content thereof ;"

Now, therefore, I, Woodrow Wilson, President of the United States of America, by virtue of the powers conferred on me by said Act of Congress, do hereby find and determine that the national security and defense will be subserved by the limitation of the amount of foods, fruits, food materials and feeds used in the production of malt liquor, and by reduction of the alcoholic content of malt liquor produced in the United States. And by this proclamation I prescribe and give public notice that on and after January 1, 1918, the total amount of foods, fruits, food materials and feeds used by any person in the production of malt liquor shall not exceed seventy per cent (70%) of the average consumption of any such foods, fruits, food materials or feeds in the production of such malt liquor by such person during the period from January 1, 1917 to January 1, 1918, the unit of time to be fixed by regulation ; and that on and after January 1, 1918, no malt liquor except ale and porter shall be produced in the United States containing more than two and three-quarters per cent (2.75%) of alcohol by weight.

No person shall, after January 1, 1918, use any foods, fruits, food materials or feeds in the production of malt liquor, unless he secures a license so to do, to be issued by the Commissioner of Internal Revenue, and complies with rules and regulations to be hereafter promulgated governing the production of such liquor and the alcoholic content thereof ; and no person shall import any such liquor except under license to be issued by the Division of Customs, Treasury Department, and in compliance with any rules and regulations governing the importation of such liquors which may be promulgated.

In witness whereof, I have hereunto set my hand and caused the seal of the United States to be affixed.

Done in the District of Columbia, this eighth day of December in the year of our Lord One Thousand, Nine Hundred and Sev-

[SEAL] enteen, and of the Independence of the United States of America, the One Hundred and Forty-Second.

WOODROW WILSON.

By the President:

ROBERT LANSING, *Secretary of State.*

VILLA—CARRANZA—HUERTA

LEADING FIGURES IN THE MEXICAN REBELLION OF 1913-14

The portrait to the right is that of Victoriano Huerta, who became Provisional President of Mexico after the overthrow and assassination of Madero. His authority was opposed by Venustiano Carranza, whose portrait is in the middle, who was Governor of Coahuila and leader of the Constitutionalist Party; and by Pancho Villa, portrait on the left, who was field general of the armies opposing Huerta.

The United States refused to recognize Huerta, because of his unlawful assumption of authority and his assassination of Madero. Carranza and Villa finally defeated and exiled Huerta; but they soon found themselves unable to co-operate in the government, and Villa took up arms against Carranza. President Wilson lent his support to Carranza, and Villa became a bandit. The story of Villa's raids upon United States territory, the results thereof, and the whole recent history of the relations between Mexico and the United States are fully described in the article Mexico in the Encyclopedic Index.

PROCLAMATION

[To the People, Asking Ten Million Members for the American Red Cross.]

To the People of the United States:

Ten million Americans are invited to join the American Red Cross during the week ending with Christmas Eve. The times require that every branch of our great national effort shall be loyally upheld and it is peculiarly fitting that at Christmas season the Red Cross should be the branch through which your willingness to help is expressed.

You should join the American Red Cross because it alone can carry the pledges of Christmas good will to those who are bearing for us the real burdens of the world war both in our Army and Navy and in the nations upon whose territory the issues of the world war are being fought out. Your evidence of faith in this work is necessary for their heartening and cheer.

You should join the Red Cross because this arm of the national service is steadfastly and efficiently maintaining the overseas relief in every suffering land, administering our millions wisely and well and awakening the gratitude of every people.

Our conscience will not let us enjoy the Christmas season if this pledge of support to our cause and the world's weal is left unfulfilled. Red Cross membership is the Christmas spirit in terms of action.

(Signed)

WOODROW WILSON.
President of American Red Cross.

LETTER

[To William J. Bryan, Denying That Mr. Bryan's Resignation from the Cabinet Had Been Asked or Desired.]

THE WHITE HOUSE, *December 17, 1917.*

MY DEAR MR. BRYAN: My attention has been called to a book in which the author states, by very clear implication, that I demanded your resignation as Secretary of State because of language used by you in an interview with Ambassador Dumba soon after the first Lusitania note. You may quote me as saying that I did not ask for your resignation or desire it, as anyone can learn from my note accepting your resignation. And this statement ought also to be a sufficient answer to the criticism of you based upon the Dumba interview, for I could not make it if I thought you responsible for the misinterpretation placed upon that interview in Berlin. But knowing at the time all the facts I did not give the matter serious thought and, I may add, in justice to you, that as you promptly corrected the misinterpretation when, within a few days, it was brought to your attention, it could not have affected the diplomatic situation.

Cordially and sincerely yours,
WOODROW WILSON.

Hon. W. J. Bryan,
  Hotel Lafayette,
  Washington, D. C.

ADDRESS TO CONGRESS

[January 4, 1918, Announcing Federal Control of Railroads.]

Gentlemen of the Congress: I have asked the privilege of addressing you in order to report that on the twenty-eighth of December last, during the recess of Congress, acting through the Secretary of War, and under the authority conferred upon me by the act of Congress approved August 29, 1916, I took possession and assumed control of the railway lines of the country and the systems of water transportation under their control. This step seemed to be imperatively necessary in the interest of the public welfare, in the presence of the great tasks of war with which we are now dealing. As our experience develops difficulties and makes it clear what they are, I have deemed it my duty to remove those difficulties wherever I have the legal power to do so. To assume control of the vast railway systems of the country is, I realize, a very great responsibility, but to fail to do so in the existing circumstances would have been much greater. I assumed the less responsibility rather than the weightier.

I am sure that I am speaking the mind of all thoughtful Americans when I say that it is our duty as the representatives of the nation to do everything that it is necessary to do to secure the complete mobilization of the whole resources of America by as rapid and effective means as can be found. Transportation supplies all the arteries of mobilization. Unless it be under a single and unified direction, the whole process of the nation's action is embarrassed.

It was in the true spirit of America, and it was right, that we should first try to effect the necessary unification under the voluntary action of those who were in charge of the great railway properties, and we did try it. The directors of the railways responded to the need promptly and generously. The group of railway executives who were charged with the task of actual coordination and general direction performed their difficult duties with patriotic zeal and marked ability, as was to have been expected, and did, I believe, everything that it was possible for them to do in the circumstances. If I have taken the task out of their hands, it has not been because of any dereliction or failure on their part, but only because there were some things which the Government can do and private management cannot. We shall continue to value most highly the advice and assistance of these gentlemen, and I am sure we shall not find them withholding it.

It had become unmistakably plain that only under Government administration can the entire equipment of the several systems of transportation be fully and unreservedly thrown into a common service without injurious discrimination against particular properties. Only under Government administration can absolutely unrestricted and unembarrassed common use be made of all tracks, terminal facilities and equipment of every kind. Only under that authority can new terminals be constructed and developed without regard to the requirements or limitations of particular roads. But under Government administration all these things will be possible—not instantly, but as fast as practical difficulties, which cannot be merely conjured away, give way before the new management.

The common administration will be carried out with as little disturbance of the present operating organizations and personnel of the railways as possible. Nothing will be altered or disturbed which it is not necessary to disturb. We are serving the public interest and safeguarding the public safety, but we are also regardful of the interest of those by whom these great properties are owned and glad to avail ourselves of the experience and trained ability of those who have been managing them. It is necessary that the transportation of troops and of war materials, of food and of fuel, and of everything that is necessary for the full mobilization of the energies and resources of the country should be first considered, but it is clearly in the public interest also that the ordinary activities and the normal industrial and commercial life of the country should be interfered with and dislocated as little as possible, and the public may rest assured that the interest and convenience of the private shipper will be as carefully served and safeguarded as it is possible to serve and safeguard it in the present extraordinary circumstances.

While the present authority of the Executive suffices for all purposes of administration, and while, of course, all private interests must for the present give way to the public necessity, it is, I am sure you will agree with me, right and necessary that the owners and creditors of the railways, the holders of their stocks and bonds, should receive from the Government an unqualified guarantee that their properties will be maintained throughout the period of Federal control in as good repair and as complete equipment as at present, and that the several roads will receive under Federal management such compensation as is equitable and just alike to their owners and to the general public. I would suggest the average net railway operating income of the three years ending June 30, 1917. I earnestly recommend that these guarantees be given by appropriate legislation, and given as promptly as circumstances permit.

I need not point out the essential justice of such guarantees and their great influence and significance as elements in the present financial and industrial situation of the country. Indeed, one of the strong arguments for assuming control of the railroads at this time is the financial argument. It is necessary that the values of railway securities should be justly and fairly protected, and that the largest financial operations every year necessary in connection with the maintenance, operation, and development of the roads should, during the period of the war, be wisely related to the financial operations of the Government.

Our first duty is, of course, to conserve the common interest and the common safety, and to make certain that nothing stands in the way of the successful prosecution of the great war for liberty and justice; but it is an obligation of public conscience and of public honor that the private interests we disturb should be kept safe from unjust injury, and it is of the utmost consequence to the Government itself that all great financial operations should be stabilized and coordinated with the financial operations of the Government. No borrowing should run athwart the borrowings of the Federal Treasury, and no fundamental industrial values should anywhere be unnecessarily impaired. In the hands of many thousands of small investors in the country, as well as in national banks, in insurance companies, in savings banks, in trust companies, in financial agencies of every kind, railway securities, the sum total of which runs up to some ten or eleven thousand millions, constitute a vital part of the structure of credit, and the unquestioned solidity of that structure must be maintained.

The Secretary of War and I easily agreed that, in view of the many complex interests which must be safeguarded and harmonized, as well as because of his exceptional experience and ability in this new field of governmental action, the Honorable William G. McAdoo was the right man to assume direct administrative control of this new executive task. At our request, he consented to assume the authority and duties of organizer and director-general of the new railway administration. He has assumed those duties, and his work is in active progress.

It is probably too much to expect that even under the unified railway administration which will now be possible sufficient economies can be effected in the operation of the railways to make it possible to add to their equipment and extend their operative facilities as much as the present extraordinary demands upon their use will render desirable, without resorting to the national Treasury for the funds. If it is not possible, it will, of course, be necessary to resort to the Congress for grants of money for that purpose. The Secretary of the Treasury will advise with your committees with regard to this very practical aspect of the matter. For the present, I suggest only the guarantees I have indicated and such appropriations as are necessary at the outset of this task.

I take the liberty of expressing the hope that the Congress may grant these promptly and ungrudgingly. We are dealing with great matters, and will, I am sure, deal with them greatly.

ADDRESS TO CONGRESS, JANUARY 8, 1918

[On War Aims and Peace Terms.]

Gentlemen of the Congress:

Once more, as repeatedly before, the spokesmen of the Central Empires have indicated their desire to discuss the objects of the war and the possible basis of a general peace. Parleys have been in progress at Brest-Litovsk between Russian representatives and representatives of the Central Powers, to which the attention of all the belligerents has been invited for the purpose of ascertaining whether it may be possible to extend these parleys into a general conference with regard to terms of peace and settlement. The Russian representatives presented not only a perfectly definite statement of the principles upon which they would be willing to conclude peace, but also an equally definite program for the concrete application of those principles. The representatives of the Central Powers, on their part, presented an outline of settlement which, if much less definite, seemed susceptible of liberal interpretation until their specific program of practical terms was added. That program proposed no concessions at all, either to the sovereignty of Russia or to the preferences of the population with whose fortunes it dealt, but meant, in a word, that the Central Empires were to keep every foot of territory their armed forces had occupied—every province, every city, every point of vantage—as a permanent addition to their territories and their power. It is a reasonable conjecture that the general principles of settlement which they at first suggested originated with the more liberal statesmen of Germany and Austria, the men who have begun to feel the force of their own peoples' thought and purpose, while the concrete terms of actual settlement came from the military leaders who have no thought but to keep what they have got. The negotiations have been broken off. The Russian representatives were sincere and in earnest. They cannot entertain such proposals of conquest and domination.

The whole incident is full of significance. It is also full of perplexity. With whom are the Russian representatives dealing? For whom are the representatives of the Central Empires speaking? Are they speaking for the majorities of their respective Parliaments or for the minority parties, that military and imperialistic minority which has so far dominated their whole policy and controlled the affairs of Turkey and of the Balkan States which have felt obliged to become their associates in this war? The Russian representatives have insisted, very justly, very wisely, and in the true spirit of modern democracy, that the conferences they have been holding with the Teutonic and Turkish statesmen should be held with open, not closed, doors, and all the world has been audience, as was desired. To whom have we been listening, then? To those who speak the spirit and intention of the resolutions of the German Reichstag of the ninth of July last, the spirit and intention of the liberal leaders and parties of Germany, or to those who resist and defy that spirit and intention and insist upon conquest and subjugation? Or are we listening, in fact, to both, unreconciled and in open and hopeless contradiction? These are very serious and pregnant questions. Upon the answer to them depends the peace of the world.

But whatever the results of the parleys at Brest-Litovsk, whatever the confusions of counsel and of purpose in the utterances of the spokesmen of the Central Empires, they have again attempted to acquaint the world with their objects in the war and have again challenged their adversaries to say what their objects are and what sort of settlement they would deem just and satisfactory. There is no good reason why that challenge should not be responded to, and responded to with the utmost candor. We did not wait for it. Not once, but again and again, we have laid our whole thought and purpose before the world, not in general terms only, but each time with sufficient definition to make it clear what sort of definite terms of settlement must necessarily spring out of them. Within the last week Mr. Lloyd George has spoken with admirable candor and in admirable spirit for the people and Government of Great Britain. There is no confusion of counsel among the adversaries of the Central Powers, no uncertainty of principle, no vagueness of detail. The only secrecy of counsel, the only lack of fearless frankness, the only failure to make definite statement of the objects of the war, lie with Germany and her allies. The issues of life and death hang upon these definitions. No statesman who has the least conception of his responsibility ought for a moment to permit himself to continue this tragical and appalling outpouring of blood and treasure unless he is sure beyond a peradventure that the objects of the vital sacrifice are part and parcel of the very life of society and that the people for whom he speaks think them right and imperative as he does.

There is, moreover, a voice calling for these definitions of principle and of purpose which is, it seems to me, more thrilling and more compelling than any of the many moving voices with which the troubled air of the world is filled. It is the voice of the Russian people. They are prostrate and all but helpless, it would seem, before the grim power of Germany, which has hitherto known no relenting and no pity. Their power apparently is shattered. And yet their soul is not subservient. They will not yield either in principle or in action. Their conception of what is right, of what is humane and honorable for them to accept, has been stated with a frankness, a largeness of view, a generosity of spirit, and a universal human sympathy which must challenge the admiration of every friend of mankind; and they have refused to compound their ideals or desert others that they themselves may be safe. They call to us to say what it is that we desire, in what, if in anything, our purpose and our spirit differ from theirs; and I believe that the people of the United States would wish me to respond with utter simplicity and frankness. Whether their present leaders believe it or not, it is our heartfelt desire and hope that some way may be opened whereby we may be privileged to assist the people of Russia to attain their utmost hope of liberty and ordered peace.

It will be our wish and purpose that the processes of peace, when they are begun, shall be absolutely open, and that they shall involve and permit henceforth no secret understandings of any kind. The day of conquest and aggrandizement is gone by; so is also the day of secret covenants entered into in the interest of particular governments and likely at some unlooked-for moment to upset the peace of the world. It is this happy fact, now clear to the view of every public man whose thoughts do not still linger in an age that is dead and gone, which makes it possible for every nation whose purposes are consistent with justice and the peace of the world to avow now or at any other time the objects it has in view.

We entered this war because violations of right had occurred which touched us to the quick and made the life of our own people impossible unless they were corrected and the world secured once for all against their recurrence. What we demand in this war, therefore, is nothing peculiar to ourselves. It is that the world be made fit and safe to live in; and particularly that it be made safe for every peace-loving nation which, like our own, wishes to live its own life, determine its own institutions, be assured of justice and fair dealings by the other peoples of the world, as against force and selfish aggression. All the peoples of the world are in effect partners in this interest, and for our own part we see very clearly that unless justice be done to others it will not be done to us.

The program of the world's peace, therefore, is our program, and that program, the only possible program, as we see it, is this:

I.—Open covenants of peace, openly arrived at, after which there shall be no private international understandings of any kind, but diplomacy shall proceed always frankly and in the public view.

II.—Absolute freedom of navigation upon the seas, outside territorial waters, alike in peace and in war, except as the seas may be closed in whole or in part by international action for the enforcement of international covenants.

III.—The removal, so far as possible, of all economic barriers and the establishment of an equality of trade conditions among all the nations consenting to the peace and associating themselves for its maintenance.

IV.—Adequate guarantees given and taken that national armaments will be reduced to the lowest point consistent with domestic safety.

V.—Free, open-minded, and absolutely impartial adjustment of all colonial claims, based upon a strict observance of the principle that in determining all such questions of sovereignty the interests of the population concerned must have equal weight with the equitable claims of the Government whose title is to be determined.

VI.—The evacuation of all Russian territory and such a settlement of all questions affecting Russia as will secure the best and freest cooperation of the other nations of the world in obtaining for her an unhampered and unembarrassed opportunity for the independent determination of her own political development and national policy, and assure her of a sincere welcome into the society of free nations under institutions of her own choosing; and, more than a welcome, assistance also of every kind that she may need and may herself desire. The treatment accorded Russia by her sister nations in the months to come will be the acid test of their good-will, of their comprehension of her needs as distinguished from their own interests, and of their intelligent and unselfish sympathy.

VII.—Belgium, the whole world will agree, must be evacuated and restored, without any attempt to limit the sovereignty which she enjoys in common with all other free nations. No other single act will serve as this will serve to restore confidence among the nations in the laws which they have themselves set and determined for the government of their relations with one another. Without this healing act the whole structure and validity of international law is forever impaired.

VIII.—All French territory should be freed and the invaded portions restored, and the wrong done to France by Prussia in 1871 in the matter of Alsace-Lorraine, which has unsettled the peace of the world for nearly fifty years, should be righted, in order that peace may once more be made secure in the interest of all.

IX.—A readjustment of the frontiers of Italy should be effected along clearly recognizable lines of nationality.

X.—The peoples of Austria-Hungary, whose place among the nations we wish to see safeguarded and assured, should be accorded the freest opportunity of autonomous development.

XI.—Rumania, Serbia, and Montenegro should be evacuated; occupied territories restored; Serbia accorded free and secure access to the sea; and the relations of the several Balkan States to one another determined by friendly counsel along historically established lines of allegiance and nationality; and international guarantees of the political and economic independence and territorial integrity of the several Balkan States should be entered into.

XII.—The Turkish portions of the present Ottoman Empire should be assured a secure sovereignty, but the other nationalities which are now under Turkish rule should be assured an undoubted security of life and an absolutely unmolested opportunity of autonomous development, and the Dardanelles should be permanently opened as a free passage to the ships and commerce of all nations under international guarantees.

XIII.—An independent Polish State should be erected which should include the territories inhabited by indisputably Polish populations, which should be assured a free and secure access to the sea, and whose political and economic independence and territorial integrity should be guaranteed by international covenant.

XIV.—A general association of nations must be formed under specific covenants for the purpose of affording mutual guarantees of political independence and territorial integrity to great and small states alike.

In regard to these essential rectifications of wrong and assertions of right, we feel ourselves to be intimate partners of all the governments and peoples associated together against the imperialists. We cannot be separated in interest or divided in purpose. We stand together until the end.

For such arrangements and covenants we are willing to fight and to continue to fight until they are achieved; but only because we wish the right to prevail and desire a just and stable peace, such as can be secured only by removing the chief provocations to war, which this program does remove. We have no jealousy of German greatness, and there is nothing in this program that impairs it. We grudge her no achievement or distinction of learning or of pacific enterprise such as have made her record very bright and very enviable. We do not wish to injure her or to block in any way her legitimate influence or power. We do not wish to fight her either with arms or with hostile arrangements of trade, if she is willing to associate herself with us and the other peace-loving nations of the world in covenants of justice and law and fair dealing. We wish her only to accept a place of equality among the peoples of the world—the new world in which we now live—instead of a place of mastery.

Neither do we presume to suggest to her any alteration or modification of her institutions. But it is necessary, we must frankly say, and necessary as a preliminary to any intelligent dealings with her on our part, that we should know whom her spokesmen speak for when they speak to us, whether for the Reichstag majority or for the military party and the men whose creed is imperial domination.

We have spoken, now, surely, in terms too concrete to admit of any further doubt or question. An evident principle runs through the whole program I have outlined. It is the principle of justice to all peoples and nationalities, and their right to live on equal terms of liberty and safety with one another, whether they be strong or weak. Unless this principle be made its foundation, no part of the structure of international justice can stand. The people of the United States could act upon no other principle, and to the vindication of this principle they are ready to devote their lives, their honor, and everything that they possess. The moral climax of this, the culminating and final war for human liberty, has come, and they are ready to put their own strength, their own highest purpose, their own integrity and devotion to the test.

EXECUTIVE ORDER

[Division created under Public Information Committee.]

THE WHITE HOUSE, *December 17, 1917.*

I hereby create, under the jurisdiction of the Committee on Public Information, heretofore established by Executive Order of April 14th, 1917, a Division of Foreign Picture Service for the purpose of stimulating interest in the war and furnishing entertainment and instruction by means of motion pictures to American Soldiers at home and abroad, also to lend similar aid to the armies and citizens of our allies through the medium of the Young Men's Christian Association and other agencies of like character.

WOODROW WILSON.

EXECUTIVE ORDER

[Rules for government of Virgin Islands.]

THE WHITE HOUSE, *December 26, 1917.*

Whereas, Section Two of the Act of Congress approved March 3, 1917, entitled "An Act to Provide for a Temporary Government of the Virgin Islands of the United States," provides as follows:

[Here follow the two paragraphs quoted on page 8332.]

Now, therefore, in virtue of the authority vested in me by the said Sections Two and Five of the said Act of Congress, I do hereby prescribe the following rules:

"Repeals, Alterations and Amendments of local laws of Virgin Islands of United States by Colonial Council having jurisdiction, shall be effective and enforced when, and to the extent, said Repeals, Alterations and Amendments are approved by the Governor of said islands, the Governor to state specifically in each case whether his approval is in whole or in part, and if in part only, what part is approved and what part not approved. The President reserves the right to disapprove and set aside any enactments of the Colonial Council"; "The duties, less the cost of collection, and the taxes collected in the Virgin Islands of the United States, shall be expended for the government and benefit of said islands in accordance with the annual budget prepared and modified by the local laws; provided, that during this current fiscal year of said islands, in order to provide for the payments of those expenses of said islands formerly paid by Denmark and not provided for in said budgets, and to provide further for other necessary and unforseen expenses of government, the Governor may authorize such additional expenditures from said funds as, in his discretion, may be necessary for the government and benefit of said islands during this current local fiscal year."

WOODROW WILSON.

BY THE PRESIDENT OF THE UNITED STATES OF AMERICA

PROCLAMATIONS

[Prohibiting Aircraft Expositions.]

Whereas, a state of war exists, and the military and naval forces of the United States are endangered by enemy aircraft, and

Whereas, this danger will be increased by communicating to the enemy the present state of aircraft invention in the United States, and

Whereas, the holding of so-called expositions of aircraft is a method of collecting and distributing information important to the enemy,

Now, Therefore, I, Woodrow Wilson, President of the United States, by virtue of the authority vested in me by the Constitution and the laws of the United States, do hereby, for the protection of such forces, proclaim to all whom it may concern that, under the pains and penalties prescribed by the laws of war and the statutes of the United States, throughout the present war no exposition of aircraft shall be held in the United States or its possessions.

In Witness Whereof, I have hereunto set my hand and caused the seal of the United States to be affixed.

Done in the District of Columbia, this first day of January, in the
year of our Lord one thousand nine hundred and eighteen,
[SEAL.] and of the independence of the United States the one hundred
and forty-second.

WOODROW WILSON.

By the President:

ROBERT LANSING,
Secretary of State.

[License of Ammonia Industry.]

Whereas, Under and by virtue of an Act of Congress entitled "An
Act to provide further for the national security and defense by
encouraging the production, conserving the supply, and controlling the
distribution of food products and fuel," approved by the President on
the 10th day of August, 1917, it is provided among other things as
follows:

[Here follow the two paragraphs quoted on pages 8322 and 8323.]

And, Whereas, it is essential in order to carry into effect the provisions of the said Act, and in order to secure an adequate supply and
equitable distribution, and to facilitate the movement of certain
necessaries hereafter in this proclamation specified that the license
powers conferred upon the President by said Act be at this time exercised to the extent hereinafter set forth.

Now, Therefore, I, Woodrow Wilson, President of the United
States of America, by virtue of the powers conferred on me by said
Act of Congress, hereby find and determine and by this proclamation
do announce that it is essential in order to carry into effect the purposes
of said Act, to license the importation, manufacture, storage and
distribution of the following necessaries: ammonia, ammoniacal liquors,
and ammonium sulphate from whatever source produced.

All persons, firms, corporations and associations (except those
specifically exempted by said Act of Congress) engaged in the business
of importing, manufacturing, storing or distributing ammonia, ammoniacal liquors or ammonium sulphate from whatever source produced
are hereby required to secure a license on or before January 21, 1918,
which will be issued under such rules and regulations governing the
conduct of the business as may be prescribed.

The Secretary of Agriculture shall supervise, direct and carry into
effect the provisions of said Act, and the powers and authority thereby
given to the President as far as the same apply to ammonia, ammoniacal
liquors and ammonium sulphate from whatever source produced, and
to any and all practices, procedure and regulations applicable thereto,

authorized or required under the provisions of said Act, and in this behalf he shall do and perform such acts and things as may be authorized or required of him from time to time by direction of the President and under such rules and regulations as may be prescribed by the President from time to time. All departments and agencies of the Government are hereby directed to cooperate with the Secretary of Agriculture in the performance of the duties hereinbefore set forth.

Applications for licenses must be made to the Law Department—License Division, United States Food Administration, Washington, D. C., upon forms prepared for that purpose.

Any person, firm, corporation or association, other than those hereinbefore excepted, who shall engage in the business of importing, manufacturing, storing or distributing ammonia, ammoniacal liquors or ammonium sulphate from whatever source produced after the date aforesaid, without first securing such license, will be liable to the penalties prescribed by said Act of Congress.

In Witness Whereof, I have hereunto set my hand and caused the seal of the United States to be affixed.

Done in the District of Columbia, this third day of January in the year of Our Lord One Thousand Nine Hundred and Eighteen, and of the Independence of the United States of America, the One Hundred and Forty-second.

[SEAL.]

WOODROW WILSON.

By the President:
ROBERT LANSING, *Secretary of State.*

[Licensing the importation, manufacture, storage and distribution of feeds, and certain other food commodities.]

Whereas, Under and by virtue of an Act of Congress entitled "An Act to provide further for the national security and defense by encouraging the production, conserving the supply, and controlling the distribution of food products and fuel," approved by the President on the 10th day of August, 1917, it is provided among other things as follows:

[Here follow the two paragraphs quoted on pages 8322 and 8323.]

And, whereas, It is essential in order to carry into effect the provisions of the said Act, that the powers conferred upon the President by said Act be at this time exercised, to the extent hereinafter set forth.

Now, therefore, I, Woodrow Wilson, President of the United States of America, by virtue of the powers conferred upon me by said Act of Congress, hereby find and determine and by this proclamation do announce that it is essential, in order to carry into effect the purposes of said Act, to license the importation, manufacture, storage, and distribution of feeds, and certain other food commodities, to the extent hereinafter specified.

(1) All persons, firms, corporations and associations engaged in the business of

(a) Importing, manufacturing (including mixing and processing of all kinds), storing or distributing any commercial mixed feeds (including dairy feeds, horse and mule feeds, stock feeds, hog feeds, and poultry feeds);

(b) Manufacturing feeds from any of the following commodities or importing, storing or distributing any of the following commodities as feeds or feed ingredients:

Buckwheat, kaffir, milo, feterita, broom corn, cane seed, spelt, emmer, millet, sunflower seed, grain and seed screenings, lentils, linseed oil cake, linseed oil meal, beans, peas, dried brewers grains, dried distillers grains, dried yeast grains, malt sprouts, baled hay, baled alfalfa, baled straw, animal or fish products or by-products, tankage;

(c) Importing, manufacturing, storing or distributing as feed any products or by-products of any of the following commodities except products or by-products whose importation, manufacture, storage or distribution is already covered by a license held by any such person, firm, corporation or association:

Shelled corn, ear corn, oats, barley, wheat, rye, buckwheat, sorghum grains, rice, grain and seed screenings, soya beans, velvet beans, peas, peanuts, copra, palm nut, palm kernel, sugar beets, sugar cane, hay, alfalfa, straw;

(2) All persons, firms, corporations, and associations engaged in the business of malting barley, or other grains, or in the business of storing or distributing malt, except brewers of malt liquor who do not malt their own grain;

(3) All persons, firms, corporations and associations engaged in the business of importing, manufacturing or distributing copra, palm kernels, palm kernel oil, and peanuts;

(4) All salt water fishermen not already licensed by the United States Food Administration, whether fishing independently or on shares, engaged at any period of the year, in the commercial distribution, including catching and selling, of any or all varieties of salt water fish including menhaden and of shellfish and crustaceans;

(5) All persons, firms, corporations, and associations engaged in the business of canning peas, dried beans, corn, tomatoes, salmon or sardines not already licensed whose gross production is more than five hundred (500) cases per annum, except home canners and bona fide boys' and girls' canning clubs recognized by the Departments of Agriculture of the several States in the United States;

(6) All persons, firms, corporations, and associations not already licensed, engaged in the business of manufacturing tomato soup, tomato catsup, or other tomato products;

(7) All persons, firms, corporations and associations engaged in the business of manufacturing alimentary paste;

(8) All persons, firms, corporations and associations, not already licensed, engaged in the business of manufacturing any products derived from wheat or rye, Excepting, however,

> (1) Retailers whose gross sales of food commodities do not exceed One Hundred Thousand Dollars ($100,000) per annum;

> (2) Common carriers as to operations necessary to the business of common carriage;

> (3) Farmers, gardeners, cooperative associations of farmers or gardeners, including live stock farmers, and other persons with respect to the products of any farm, garden or other land owned, leased or cultivated by them;

Are hereby required to secure on or before February 15, 1918, a license, which license will be issued under such rules and regulations governing the conduct of the business as may be prescribed.

All persons hereby made subject to license must apply, specifying the kind of license desired, to the United States Food Administration, License Division, Washington, D. C., on forms prepared by it for that purpose which may be secured on request.

Any person, firm, corporation or association other than those hereinbefore excepted, who shall engage in or carry on any business hereinbefore specified after February 15, 1918, without first securing such license, will be liable to the penalty prescribed by said Act of Congress.

In witness whereof, I have hereunto set my hand and caused the seal of the United States to be affixed.

Done in the District of Columbia, this tenth day of January, in the year of our Lord one thousand nine hundred and eighteen, [SEAL] and of the independence of the United States of America, the one hundred and forty-second.

WOODROW WILSON.

By the President:

ROBERT LANSING, *Secretary of State.*

[Calling on citizens for further conservation of food.]

THE WHITE HOUSE, *January 18, 1917.*

Many causes have contributed to create the necessity for a more intensive effort on the part of our people to save food in order that we may supply our associates in the war with the sustenance vitally necessary to them in these days of privation and stress. The reduced productivity of Europe because of the large diversion of man power to the war, the partial failure of the harvests, and the elimination of the more distant markets for foodstuffs through the destruction of shipping places the burden of their subsistence very largely on our shoulders.

The Food Administration has formulated suggestions which, if followed, will enable us to meet this great responsibility, without any real inconvenience on our part.

In order that we may reduce our consumption of wheat and wheat products by 30 per cent—a reduction imperatively necessary to provide the supply for overseas—wholesalers, jobbers and retailers should purchase and resell to their customers only 70 per cent of the amounts used in 1917. All manufacturers of alimentary pastes, biscuits, crackers, pastry, and breakfast cereals should reduce their purchases and consumption of wheat and wheat flour to 70 per cent of their 1917 requirements, and all bakers of bread and rolls to 80 per cent of their current requirements. Consumers should reduce their purchases of wheat products for home preparation to at most 70 per cent of those of last year, or when buying bread should purchase mixed cereal breads from the bakers.

To provide sufficient cereal food, homes, public eating places, dealers, and manufacturers should substitute potatoes, vegetables, corn, barley, oats, and rice products, and the mixed cereal bread and other products of the bakers which contain an admixture of other cereals.

In order that consumption may be restricted to this extent, Mondays and Wednesdays should be observed as wheatless days each week, and one meal each day should be observed as a wheatless meal.

In both homes and public eating places, in order to reduce the consumption of beef, pork, and sheep products, Tuesdays should be observed as meatless days in each week, one meatless meal should be observed in each day, while, in addition, Saturday in each week should further be observed as a day upon which there should be no consumption of pork products.

A continued economy in the use of sugar will be necessary until later in the year.

It is imperative that all waste and unnecessary consumption of all sorts of foodstuffs should be rigidly eliminated.

The maintenance of the health and strength of our own people is vitally necessary at this time, and there should be no dangerous restriction of the food supply; but the elimination of every sort of waste and the substitution of other commodities of which we have more abundant supplies for those which we need to save will in no way impair the strength of our people and will enable us to meet one of the most pressing obligations of the war.

I, therefore, in the national interest, take the liberty of calling upon every loyal American to take fully to heart the suggestions which are being circulated by the Food Administration and of begging that they be followed. I am confident that the great body of our women, who have labored so loyally in co-operation with the Food Administration for the success of food conservation, will strengthen their efforts and will take it as a part of their burden in this period of national service to see that the above suggestions are observed throughout the land.

WOODROW WILSON.

ORDER TO ARMY AND NAVY

[Enjoining Sabbath observance.]

THE WHITE HOUSE, *January 20, 1918.*

The President, commander in chief of the Army and Navy, following the reverent example of his predecessors, desires and enjoins the orderly observance of the Sabbath by the officers and men in the military and naval service of the United States. The importance for man and beast of the prescribed weekly rest, the sacred rights of Christian soldiers and sailors, a becoming deference to the best sentiment of a Christian people, and a due regard for the Divine Will demand that Sunday labor in the Army and Navy be reduced to the measure of strict necessity. Such an observance of Sunday is dictated by the best traditions of our people and by the convictions of all who look to Divine Providence for guidance and protection, and, in repeating in this order the language of President Lincoln, the President is confident that he is speaking alike to the hearts and to the consciences of those under his authority. WOODROW WILSON.

EXECUTIVE ORDER

[Prescribing rules and regulations under section 5 of the Trading with the Enemy Act and supplementing rules and regulations heretofore prescribed under Title 7 of the Espionage Act.]

THE WHITE HOUSE, *January 26, 1918.*

Whereas, by virtue of the authority vested in me by the act approved June 15, 1917, known as the Espionage Act, I directed by Executive order, dated September 7, 1917, that the regulations, orders, limitations, and exceptions prescribed by me in relation to the export of coin, bullion, and currency should be administered by the Secretary of the Treasury, and upon his recommendation prescribed certain regulations in relation thereto; and

Whereas, by Executive order, dated October 12, 1917, made under authority of the act aforesaid and of the act approved October 6, 1917, known as the Trading with the Enemy Act, I vested in the Secretary of the Treasury the executive administration of any investigation, regulation, or prohibition of any transactions in foreign exchange, export, or earmarking of gold or silver coin or bullion or currency, transfers of credit in any form (other than credits relating solely to transactions to be executed wholly within the United States) and transfers of evidences of indebtedness or of the ownership of property between the United States and any foreign country or between residents of one or more foreign countries by any person within the United States, and I further vested in the Secretary of the Treasury the authority and power to require any person engaged in any such transaction to furnish, under oath, complete information relative thereto, including the production of any books of account, contracts, letters, or other papers in connection therewith in the custody or control of such person, either before or after such transaction is completed; and

Whereas, by said Executive order, dated October 12, 1917, I authorized and directed the Secretary of the Treasury for the purpose of such executive administration to take such measures, adopt such administrative procedure, and use such agency or agencies as he may from time to time deem necessary and proper for that purpose; and

Whereas, the Secretary of the Treasury, with the approval of the President, by order dated November 23, 1917, adopted certain administrative procedure for the executive administration, authority and power vested in the Secretary of the Treasury by said Executive order, dated October 12, 1917, and designated the Federal Reserve Board to act as the agency of the Secretary of the Treasury, subject to the approval of the Secretary of the Treasury, to carry out such executive administration, authority and power vested in the Secretary of the Treasury as hereinbefore recited:

Now, therefore, upon the recommendation of the Secretary of the Treasury, and in order to vest all necessary authority in the Federal Reserve Board to act as the agency of the Secretary of the Treasury, in the performance of the duties hereby imposed upon it, I hereby prescribe the following orders, rules, and regulations in respect of such executive administration, authority and power, and I hereby amend the regulations heretofore prescribed by said Executive order dated September 7, 1917, as herein provided.

DEFINITIONS.

The term *person* as used herein shall be deemed to mean an individual partnership, association, company or other unincorporated body of individuals, or corporation or body politic.

The term *dealer* as used herein shall be deemed to mean any person engaged primarily or incidentally in the business (1) of buying, selling, or dealing in foreign exchange, or (2) of buying, selling, or dealing in securities *for* or *through* foreign correspondents, or (3) any person who carries accounts or securities *with* or *for* foreign correspondents.

Dealers who engage in the business of buying, selling, or dealing in foreign exchange, or of buying, selling, or dealing in securities *for* or *through* foreign correspondents, and who may or may not carry accounts or securities *with* or *for* foreign correspondents shall be known as dealers of *Class A*.

Dealers who carry accounts or securities *with* foreign correspondents or who buy, sell or deal in securities *through* such correspondents but who do not carry accounts or securities *for* foreign correspondents and who do not engage in the business of buying, selling, or dealing in foreign exchange or of buying, selling, or dealing in securities *for* foreign correspondents shall be known as dealers of *Class B*.

Dealers who carry accounts or securities *for* foreign correspondents or who buy, sell, or deal in securities *for* such correspondents but who do not carry accounts or securities *with* foreign correspondents and who do not engage in the business of buying, selling, or dealing in foreign exchange or of buying, selling, or dealing in securities *through* foreign correspondents shall be known as dealers of *Class C*.

The term *foreign exchange* as used herein shall be deemed to mean checks, drafts, bills of exchange, cable transfers, or any form of negotiable or assignable instrument, or order used (a) to transfer credit or to order the payment of funds in any foreign country, or (b) to transfer credit or to order the payment of funds within the United States for foreign account.

The term *securities* as used herein shall be deemed to mean all evidences of ownership of property not included in the foregoing definition of foreign exchange.

The term *correspondent* as used herein shall be deemed to mean any person who acts as the agent of, or for, or on behalf of, or as the depositary of, another person, or any person who is the principal for, or on behalf of, whom another person acts as agent.

The term *customer* as used herein shall be deemed to mean any person other than a dealer who buys foreign exchange from a dealer or sells foreign exchange to a dealer.

TRANSACTIONS IN FOREIGN EXCHANGE AND CERTAIN OTHER TRANSACTIONS PROHIBITED EXCEPT AS HEREIN AUTHORIZED.

All transactions in foreign exchange, export or earmarking of gold or silver coin or bullion or currency, transfers of credit in any form (other than credits relating solely to transactions to be executed wholly within the United States) and transfers of evidences of indebtedness or of the ownership of property between the United States and any foreign country, whether enemy, ally of enemy, or otherwise, or between residents of one or more foreign countries, by any person within the United States, except any such transactions or transfers conducted in conformity herewith, are hereby prohibited.

TRANSACTIONS IN FOREIGN EXCHANGE OR IN SECURITIES FOR OR THROUGH FOREIGN ACCOUNT.

Certain persons required to obtain registration certificates.

No person, other than a customer, shall, after February 10, 1918, engage in any transaction or make any transfer described in the next preceding subdivision hereof who shall not have obtained, on or before that date, a registration certificate, as hereinafter provided.

Every person who is a dealer upon the date hereof, as promptly as possible and in any event on or before January 31, 1918, shall file, with the Federal Reserve Board, through the Federal Reserve Bank of his district, an application for a registration certificate. Such application shall be in form approved by the Federal Reserve Board and shall show the character of business engaged in and whether or not an enemy or ally of enemy of the United States or any subject or citizen of an enemy or ally of enemy, wherever resident or domiciled, has any interest directly or indirectly in such business. Such application shall embody an agreement on the part of the applicant to comply with the regulations of the Federal Reserve Board, and to permit the inspection at any time of his books and accounts and to make reports as and when required on forms to be approved by the Federal Reserve Board.

The Federal Reserve Board may issue to such applicant the appropriate registration certificate in form approved by it, entitling the holder to engage in the class or classes of foreign exchange or other transactions specified in such certificate, subject to all applicable provisions of law and to such Executive orders of the President and administrative regulations as shall have been issued or may from time to time be issued by the Federal Reserve Board.

Any person who is not a dealer at the date hereof but who hereafter desires to become a dealer must first obtain a registration certificate.

Any person, other than a customer, who does not desire to become a dealer but who nevertheless desires to engage in one or several transactions or to make one or several transfers described in the next preceding subdivision hereof, may be permitted by the Federal Reserve Board, in its discretion, to engage in any such transaction or to make any such transfer without first obtaining a registration certificate, and the Federal Reserve Board may likewise waive any requirement hereof, other than any which relates to trading with an enemy or ally of enemy, whenever it is satisfied that such waiver is not incompatible with the best interests of the United States.

Nothing herein shall be construed to abrogate or modify any existing requirement that licenses shall be obtained from the War Trade Board in respect of any transaction with, or for account of, an enemy or ally of enemy, or any person acting for, or on behalf of, or for the benefit of, an enemy or ally of enemy.

Revocation of registration certificates.

Any or all such registration certificates may be revoked at any time by direction of the Secretary of the Treasury or of the Federal Reserve Board.

Books and accounts.

Each Federal Reserve Bank through which any such registration certificate shall be issued shall furnish, to the applicant, copies of all forms of reports required and the books and records of such applicant shall thereafter be kept in a manner which will make it possible to furnish information called for in such reports without delay.

General reports.

After obtaining a registration certificate, each holder thereof shall file with the Federal Reserve Bank through which such certificate shall be issued a report, on forms to be furnished by the Federal Reserve Board, showing all accounts or securities carried *with* or *for* foreign correspondents as of the close of business on January 30, 1918, or on such other date as the Federal Reserve Board may require, and such other information as may be called for on such forms and shall thereafter file with the Federal Reserve Board, through such Federal Reserve Bank, on dates specified by the Federal Reserve Board, reports showing all changes in such accounts and all purchases, sales, and other transactions in foreign exchange or securities *for* or *through* foreign correspondents.

Customers' statements.

A dealer shall require every customer purchasing foreign exchange from him or selling foreign exchange to him, to file a statement showing the purpose of such purchase or sale with such details as the Federal Reserve Board may require, including a declaration to the effect that no enemy or ally of enemy of the United States has any interest directly or indirectly in such purchase or sale. The Federal Reserve Board shall prescribe the form of such declaration. Copies of such statements shall be furnished by such dealer upon request to the Federal Reserve Board, through the several Federal Reserve Banks.

Reports made through domestic correspondents.

Dealers to whom registration certificates have been issued, and who buy, sell, or deal in foreign exchange through domestic correspondents, (for example, banking or other institutions located in the United States) unless otherwise directed by the Federal Reserve Board, shall arrange with such correspondents to include such transactions in the reports of such correspondents.

Such dealers will be required to report to the Federal Reserve Board only those foreign exchange transactions which are not included in the reports of such correspondents but may be called upon for any information in regard thereto desired by the Federal Reserve Board, and shall keep all books and records in a manner which will make it possible to furnish such information.

Special reports.

Whenever any holder of a registration certificate shall have reason to believe that any transaction within his knowledge involves or may involve directly or indirectly the payment of funds or delivery of securities to or the transfer of credit or securities for the benefit of an enemy or ally of enemy, or which may involve any other transaction with an enemy or ally of enemy, he shall immediately report the facts and circumstances to the Federal Reserve Board through a Federal Reserve Bank.

Filing and verification of reports.

All reports, statements, and declarations herein required, unless otherwise specified, shall be filed with the Federal Reserve Board through the Federal Reserve Banks.

Any or all such reports, statements, or declarations shall, in the discretion of the Federal Reserve Board, be verified by oath of the person making same.

Examinations.

The books and records of all dealers must at all times be open to inspection by examiners designated by the Federal Reserve Board.

DECLARATION OF FOREIGN CORRESPONDENT TO BE OBTAINED BY HOLDERS
OF REGISTRATION CERTIFICATES.

After dates to be fixed by the Federal Reserve Board in respect of each foreign country, respectively, no holder of a registration certificate shall engage in transactions *with, through,* or *for* any foreign correspondent in such foreign country unless he shall have obtained from such correspondent a declaration to the following effect:

"Having arranged with............................to act as

[Holder of registration certificate.]

the agent or correspondent in the United States for, or on behalf of, the undersigned, under regulations issued by the appropriate authorities of the United States Government and/or the undersigned having agreed to act as the foreign correspondent of the said.............. ....I/we do hereby declare that I/we will not deal or attempt to deal, directly or indirectly, with said agent or correspondent in any transaction for or on account of, or for the benefit of, an enemy or ally of enemy of the United States, and will not make available for the use of an enemy or ally of enemy of the United States any funds or property received or credits established as a result of any transaction engaged in with or through said agent or correspondent, and will not transmit to said agent or correspondent for collection or credit any negotiable instrument bearing the signature or indorsement of an enemy or ally of enemy of the United States.

"The words 'enemy' and 'ally of enemy' are used herein as now or hereafter defined by laws of the United States or by Proclamation of the President of the United States."

NOTE.—If foreign correspondent is incorporated this certificate must be executed by a duly authorized officer of such corporation.

SUSPENSION OF RELATIONS WITH FOREIGN CORRESPONDENTS.

If any foreign correspondent of a dealer in the United States or any person proposing to become the foreign correspondent of a dealer in the United States, shall refuse or fail to make the foregoing declaration as herein required, or if the Federal Reserve Board shall have reason to believe that any such foreign correspondent or any such person is dealing or trading with an enemy or ally of enemy of the United States, contrary to the provisions of the declaration of noninterest of enemies, herein required, or if in the judgment of the Federal Reserve Board the best interest of the United States requires such action, it may prohibit any dealer or dealers in the United States from engaging in any transaction *with, through, for,* or *on behalf of* such correspondent or such person.

SUSPENSION OF TRANSACTIONS.

Whenever the Federal Reserve Board shall have reason to believe that any transaction in foreign exchange or any transfer of securities carried *with* or *for* a foreign correspondent involves or may involve trading with an enemy, or ally of enemy, or in its judgment is incompatible with the best interest of the United States, it may cause notice to be served on the parties in interest to postpone the consummation of such transaction for a period of ninety days pending investigation of the facts, and upon investigation if the Federal Reserve Board is of the opinion that the best interests of the United States require such action it may prohibit the consummation of such transaction.

The Secretary of the Treasury may likewise prohibit the consummation of any such transaction by notice served on the parties in interest (either directly or through the Federal Reserve Board) in any case in which in his judgment the best interests of the United States require such action.

SPECIAL PROVISIONS AS TO COLLECTION OF DIVIDENDS, INTEREST OR MATURING OBLIGATIONS FOR FOREIGN ACCOUNT.

Every person presenting for collection maturing obligations, or coupons, checks or drafts issued for dividends or interest, for account of any foreign Government or person resident in any foreign country, shall make a declaration in form approved by the Federal Reserve Board, to the effect that such collections are not made for, or on behalf of, or for the benefit of, any enemy or ally of enemy; that the proceeds of such collections will not be made available for any enemy or ally of enemy; and that the maturing obligations, or the obligations and stocks upon which dividends or interest are to be paid, are not the property of any enemy or ally of enemy; have not been owned by, or held for the account of, any enemy or ally of enemy, since January 26, 1918, and were not purchased by the present owner from any enemy or ally of enemy or from any person acting for or on behalf of or for the benefit of an enemy or ally of enemy since February 3, 1917.

Provided, however, that any holder of a Class A or Class C registration certificate may collect maturing obligations and coupons, checks, or drafts issued for dividends or interest for account of a person resident in a foreign country, without making such declaration, if such holder has filed with the Federal Reserve Board a similar declaration executed by the person for whom collection is made.

Interest or dividend checks payable for foreign account.

Every person issuing checks or drafts for interest or dividends after January 26, 1918, payable to any foreign Government or to any person resident in a foreign country shall attach to or shall print on the back of such check or draft the following statement:

"This check or draft will not be paid unless the following declaration is executed by the person to whom it is sent for collection by the payee, or his agent, or by the person who acts as the agent in the United States for the payee.

"From actual personal knowledge, or in reliance upon declarations or affidavits furnished the undersigned by the parties in interest, I/we do hereby expressly declare that no enemy or ally of enemy of the United States is directly or indirectly interested in the proceeds of this check or draft and that such proceeds will not be made available for the use of an enemy or ally of enemy of the United States; that the stock upon which this dividend is paid (or the obligation upon which this interest is paid) is not and has not been owned by or held for account of an enemy or ally of enemy of the United States since January 26, 1918, and has not been purchased by the present owner from an enemy or ally of enemy or from a person acting for or on behalf of or for the benefit of an enemy or ally of enemy since February 3, 1917."

DEALINGS IN SECURITIES FOR OR THROUGH FOREIGN ACCOUNT.

No person shall purchase, sell, or deliver any securities for account of any foreign Government, or for account of any person resident in a foreign country, unless such Government or such person, as the case may be, shall have made a declaration, in form approved by the Federal Reserve Board, similar in effect to that required in the case of the collection of maturing obligations, for account of a foreign Government or person resident in a foreign country.

PROCEDURE WHERE DECLARATION OF NONINTEREST OF ENEMY OR ALLY OF ENEMY CANNOT BE MADE.

Any person who is unable to make a declaration of noninterest of enemy or ally of enemy required hereunder may apply to the Federal Reserve Board for a waiver of such declaration, submitting to such board all facts and circumstances relating to the transaction involved which are in the possession of the applicant. If upon investigation the Federal Reserve Board shall determine that there is no reason to believe that any enemy or ally of enemy is directly or indirectly interested in the transaction involved, and that its consummation will not be incompatible with the best interests of the United States, it may permit the transaction to be consummated without the declaration herein required. If the Federal Reserve Board shall have reason to believe that an enemy or ally of enemy is or may be directly or indirectly interested in the transaction, it shall transmit to the War Trade Board all records in the case for such action as that board may determine to be necessary.

EXPORT AND EARMARKING OF COIN, BULLION, OR CURRENCY.

The following regulations prescribed by Executive order, dated September 7, 1917, shall continue in force as herein amended.

Any person desiring to export from the United States or any of its territorial possessions to any foreign country named in the proclamation dated September 7, 1917, any coin, bullion, or currency, shall first file an application in triplicate with the Federal Reserve Bank of the district in which such person is located for a special or general license. Applications filed must contain statements under oath and showing in detail the nature of the transaction, the amount involved, the parties directly and indirectly interested, and such other information as may be of assistance to the proper authorities in determining whether the exportation for which a license is desired will be compatible with the public interest. All such applications should be made on the standard form prescribed by the Federal Reserve Board.

Each Federal Reserve Bank shall keep a record copy of each application filed with it under the provisions of this regulation and shall forward the original application and a duplicate to the Federal Reserve Board at Washington, together with such information or suggestions as it may believe proper in the circumstances, and shall in addition make a formal recommendation as to whether or not, in its opinion, the exportation should be permitted.

The Federal Reserve Board, subject to the approval of the Secretary of the Treasury, is hereby authorized and empowered, upon receipt of such application and the recommendation of the Federal Reserve Bank, to make such ruling as it may deem proper in the circumstances; and if, in its opinion, the exportation in question be compatible with the public interest, to permit said exportation to be made; otherwise to refuse it.

No gold or silver coin, or bullion, or currency shall be set aside and earmarked for safekeeping for any person without the written approval of the Federal Reserve Board.

LICENSES FROM WAR TRADE BOARD IN TRANSACTIONS INVOLVING TRADING
WITH AN ENEMY OR ALLY OF ENEMY.

Applications to the Federal Reserve Board for permission to export or earmark gold or silver coin or bullion or currency shall be accompanied by a certified copy of a license issued by the War Trade Board, whenever any such transactions involve trading directly or indirectly with an enemy or ally of enemy or with any person acting for, or on behalf of, or for the benefit of, an enemy or ally of enemy.

APPLICATIONS FOR REGISTRATION CERTIFICATES AND EXPORT LICENSES,
PROVIDED FOR HEREUNDER, BY PERSONS RESIDING IN ANY DEPEND-
ENCY OF THE UNITED STATES.

Applications to the Federal Reserve Board either for registration certificates or for licenses to export coin, bullion or currency may be made by persons residing in any dependency of the United States (including the Philippine Islands, Alaska, Guam, Hawaii, Porto Rico, Virgin Islands, and Canal Zone) through such agency located in any such dependency as may be hereafter designated by the Federal Reserve Board, instead of through a Federal Reserve Bank; but until an agency has been so designated in any such dependency, persons residing therein may make such applications through any Federal Reserve Bank. The Federal Reserve Board may from time to time postpone, in respect of any one or more of such dependencies, the date on and after which persons residing therein shall be prohibited from engaging in any of the transactions or making any transfer hereinbefore prohibited without having obtained registration certificates, in case such registration certificates can not be obtained on or before the date hereinbefore specified. WOODROW WILSON.

BY THE PRESIDENT OF THE UNITED STATES OF AMERICA

PROCLAMATIONS

[Licensing bakers and importers or distributors of green coffee.]

Whereas, Under and by virtue of an Act of Congress entitled "An Act to provide further for the national security and defense by encouraging the production, conserving the supply, and controlling the distribution of food products and fuel," approved by the President on the 10th day of August, 1917, it is provided among other things as follows:

[Here follow the two paragraphs quoted on pages 8322 and 8323.]

And, whereas, It is essential, in order to carry into effect the provisions of the said Act, that the powers conferred upon the President by said Act be at this time exercised, to the extent hereinafter set forth,

Now, therefore, I, Woodrow Wilson, President of the United States of America, by virtue of the powers conferred upon me by said Act of Congress, hereby find and determine and by this proclamation do announce that it is essential, in order to carry into effect the purpose of said Act, to license the importation, manufacture, and distribution of necessaries, to the extent hereinafter specified.

All persons, firms, corporations, and associations, who manufacture for sale bread in any form, cake, crackers, biscuits, pastry, or other bakery products (excepting, however, those already licensed and those whose consumption of any flour and meal in the manufacture of such products is, in the aggregate, less than three barrels a month), are hereby required to procure a license on or before February 4, 1918.

This includes hotels, restaurants, other public eating places, and clubs, which serve bread or other bakery products of their own baking.

All persons, firms, corporations, and associations engaged in the business of importing or distributing green coffee are hereby required to procure a license on or before February 4, 1918.

Application for license must be made to the United States Food Administration, Washington, D. C., License Division, on forms prepared by it for that purpose, which may be obtained on request.

Any person, firm, corporation, or association, other than those hereinbefore excepted, who shall engage in or carry on any business hereinbefore specified after February 4, 1918, without first procuring such license, will be liable to the penalty prescribed by said Act of Congress.

In witness whereof, I have hereunto set my hand and caused the seal of the United States to be affixed.

Done in the District of Columbia, this 30th day of January, in the year of our Lord one thousand nine hundred and eighteen, [SEAL.] and of the independence of the United States of America, the one hundred and forty-second.

WOODROW WILSON.

By the President:

ROBERT LANSING, *Secretary of State.*

[License of fuel oil industry.]

Whereas, Under and by virtue of an Act of Congress entitled "An Act to provide further for the national security and defense by encouraging the production, conserving the supply, and controlling the distribution of food products and fuel," approved by the President on the 10th day of August, 1917, it is provided among other things as follows:

[Here follow the two paragraphs quoted on pages 8322 and 8323.]

And, whereas, It is not possible to move promptly our abundant supplies of fuel oil by reason of the traffic congestion on our railways and the transfer to trans-Atlantic service of a large number of tank steamers ordinarily engaged in coastwise trade, and it therefore seems desirable that a plan of control be made effective in case the distributing companies are unable to transport as required fuel oil to all consumers now being served,

And, whereas, It is essential, in order to carry into effect the provisions of the said Act, that the powers conferred upon the President by said Act be at this time exercised, to the extent hereinafter set forth.

Now, therefore, I, Woodrow Wilson, President of the United States of America, by virtue of the powers conferred upon me by said Act of

Congress, hereby find and determine and by this proclamation do announce that it is essential, in order to carry into effect the purposes of said Act, to license the importation, manufacture, storage and distribution of fuel oil to the extent hereinafter specified.

All persons, firms, corporations, and associations engaged in the business of both manufacturing and distributing fuel oil (including gas oil), whose gross sales of fuel oil (including gas oil) amount to more than one hundred thousand (100,000) barrels per annum, are hereby required to secure on or before February 11, 1918, a license, which license will be issued under such rules and regulations governing the conduct of the business as may be prescribed. Application for license must be made to the United States Fuel Administration, Washington, D. C., License Division.

Any person, firm, corporation or association other than those hereinbefore excepted who shall engage in or carry on any business hereinbefore specified on and after February 11, 1918, without first securing such license, will be liable to the penalty prescribed by said Act of Congress.

In witness whereof, I have hereunto set my hand and caused the seal of the United States to be affixed.

Done in the District of Columbia, this thirty-first day of January, in the year of our Lord, one thousand nine hundred and [SEAL] eighteen, and of the Independence of the United States of America, the one hundred and forty-second.

WOODROW WILSON.

By the President:

FRANK L. POLK, *Acting Secretary of State.*

[Germans and Austro-Hungarians in the custody of the War Department included within the term "enemy" for the purposes of the Trading with the Enemy Act.]

Whereas paragraph (c) of Section Two of the Act entitled "An Act to define, regulate, and punish trading with the enemy, and for other purposes," approved October 6, 1917, known as the Trading with the Enemy Act, provides that the word "enemy" as used therein shall be deemed to mean, for the purposes of such trading and of said Act, in addition to the individuals, partnerships or other bodies of individuals or corporations specified in paragraph (a), and in addition to the Government and political or municipal subdivisions, officers, officials, agents or agencies thereof specified in paragraph (b), of said Section Two, the following:

"Such other individuals, or body or class of individuals, as may be natives, citizens, or subjects of any nation with which the

United States is at war, other than citizens of the United States, wherever resident or wherever doing business, as the President, if he shall find the safety of the United States or the successful prosecution of the war shall so require, may, by proclamation, include within the term 'enemy';"

And, whereas, under the provisions of and by virtue of the power and authority granted in Sections four thousand and sixty-seven, four thousand and sixty-eight, four thousand and sixty-nine and four thousand and seventy, of the Revised Statutes, and in accordance with proclamations and regulations which have been or which may hereafter be made and established thereunder by the President of the United States, certain alien enemies have been, or may from time to time be, transferred after arrest into the custody of the War Department for detention during the war;

Now, therefore, I, Woodrow Wilson, President of the United States of America, pursuant to the authority vested in me, and in accordance with the provisions of the said Act of October 6, 1917, known as the Trading with the Enemy Act, do hereby find that the safety of the United States and the successful prosecution of the present war require that all natives, citizens or subjects of the German Empire or of the Austro-Hungarian Empire who, by virtue of the provisions of Sections four thousand and sixty-seven, four thousand and sixty-eight, four thousand and sixty-nine, and four thousand and seventy, of the Revised Statutes, and of the proclamations and regulations thereunder, have been heretofore or may be hereafter transferred after arrest into the custody of the War Department for detention during the war, shall be included within the meaning of the word "enemy" for the purposes of the Trading with the Enemy Act and of such trading; and I do hereby proclaim to all whom it may concern that every such alien enemy who is so transferred, after arrest, into the custody of the War Department for detention during the war, shall be and hereby is included within the meaning of the word "enemy" and shall be deemed to constitute an "enemy" for said purposes.

In witness whereof, I have hereunto set my hand and caused the seal of the United States to be affixed.

Done in the District of Columbia, this 5th day of February, in the year of our Lord one thousand nine hundred and eighteen, [SEAL] and of the independence of the United States the one hundred and forty-second.

WOODROW WILSON.

By the President:

FRANK L. POLK, *Acting Secretary of State.*

EXECUTIVE ORDER

[Changes in Trading with the Enemy Act.]

THE WHITE HOUSE, *February 5, 1918.*

By virtue of the authority vested in me by an Act to define, regulate, and punish trading with the enemy, approved October 6, 1917, known as the Trading with the Enemy Act, I hereby make the following orders, rules and regulations:

1. Paragraph XXX of the Executive Order dated October 12, 1917, and made by me pursuant to said Act of Congress, is hereby revoked; and in place thereof it is hereby ordered:

XXX. Any person not an enemy, or ally of enemy, who owes to, or holds for or on account of, or on behalf of, or for the benefit of, an enemy or an ally of enemy, not holding a license granted by or in the exercise of the power and authority of the President under the provisions of said Trading with the Enemy Act any money or other property, or to whom any obligation or form of liability to such enemy, or ally of enemy, is presented for payment, may, having first obtained the consent of the Alien Property Custodian, pay, convey, transfer, assign, or deliver, to or upon the order of the Alien Property Custodian, said money or other property, with like effect as if such payment, conveyance, transfer, assignment or delivery were made in obedience to requirement pursuant to the provisions of Section 7, subsection (*c*), of said Trading with the Enemy Act.

2. Paragraph XXXI of said Executive Order dated October 12, 1917, is hereby revoked; and in place thereof it is hereby ordered:

XXXI. I hereby vest in the Alien Property Custodian the executive administration of all provisions of Section 8 (*a*) and Section 8 (*b*) of the Trading with the Enemy Act, including the power, authority and duty conferred or imposed upon the President by the provisions of said Section 8 (*a*), and the notice therein required to be given to the President shall be given to the Alien Property Custodian.

WOODROW WILSON.

ADDRESS TO CONGRESS

[Discussion of peace probabilities and outlook.]

February 11, 1918.

Gentlemen of the Congress: On the eighth of January I had the honor of addressing you on the objects of the war as our people conceive them. The Prime Minister of Great Britain had spoken in similar terms on the fifth of January. To these addresses the German Chancellor replied on the twenty-fourth and Count Czernin, for

Austria, on the same day. It is gratifying to have our desire so promptly realized that all exchanges of view on this great matter should be made in the hearing of all the world.

Count Czernin's reply, which is directed chiefly to my own address on the eighth of January, is uttered in a very friendly tone. He finds in my statement a sufficiently encouraging approach to the views of his own Government to justify him in believing that it furnishes a basis for a more detailed discussion of purposes by the two Governments. He is represented to have intimated that the views he was expressing had been communicated to me beforehand and that I was aware of them at the time he was uttering them; but in this I am sure he was misunderstood. I had received no intimation of what he intended to say. There was, of course, no reason why he should communicate privately with me. I am quite content to be one of his public audience.

Count von Hertling's reply is, I must say, very vague and very confusing. It is full of equivocal phrases and leads it is not clear where. But it is certainly in a very different tone from that of Count Czernin, and apparently of an opposite purpose. It confirms, I am sorry to say, rather than removes, the unfortunate impression made by what we had learned of the conferences at Brest-Litovsk. His discussion and acceptance of our general principles lead him to no practical conclusions. He refuses to apply to them the substantive items which must constitute the body of any final settlement. He is jealous of international action and of international counsel. He accepts, he says, the principle of public diplomacy, but he appears to insist that it be confined, at any rate in this case, to generalities and that the several particular questions of territory and sovereignty, the several questions upon whose settlement must depend the acceptance of peace by the twenty-three states now engaged in the war, must be discussed and settled, not in general council, but severally by the nations most immediately concerned by interest or neighborhood. He agrees that the seas should be free, but looks askance at any limitation to that freedom by international action in the interest of the common order. He would without reserve be glad to see economic barriers removed between nation and nation, for that could in no way impede the ambitions of the military party with whom he seems constrained to keep on terms. Neither does he raise objection to a limitation of armaments. That matter will be settled of itself, he thinks, by the economic conditions which must follow the war. But the German colonies, he demands, must be returned without debate. He will discuss with no one but the representatives of Russia what disposition shall be made of the peoples and the lands of the Baltic provinces; with no one but the Government of

PHOTO FROM AEROPLANE OF TRENCHES

VIEW OF TRENCHES FROM AEROPLANE.

Volumes have been written in description of the method of fighting in trenches, but no words could reveal the nature of the trenches so vividly as does the preceding illustration. In the view taken from an aeroplane, it is clearly shown how the trenches zig-zag in all directions across the face of a country, not only to take advantage of every favorable contour of the ground, but also to present a jagged line to the guns of the enemy, so that a shot finding the trenches will not mow down a whole column of men. Only the depressions in the preceding picture which are filled with men are trenches; the other holes in the ground show the spots where shells from the large guns have exploded, and give an idea both of the accuracy of the marksmanship and of the ever-constant danger of sudden death at the front.

France the "conditions" under which French territory shall be evacuated; and only with Austria what shall be done with Poland. In the determination of all questions affecting the Balkan states he defers, as I understand him, to Austria and Turkey; and with regard to the agreements to be entered into concerning the non-Turkish peoples of the present Ottoman Empire, to the Turkish authorities themselves. After a settlement all around, effected in this fashion, by individual barter and concession, he would have no objection, if I correctly interpret his statement, to a league of nations which would undertake to hold the new balance of power steady against external disturbance.

It must be evident to everyone who understands what this war has wrought in the opinion and temper of the world that no general peace, no peace worth the infinite sacrifice of these years of tragical suffering, can possibly be arrived at in any such fashion. The method the German Chancellor proposes is the method of the Congress of Vienna. We cannot and will not return to that. What is at stake now is the peace of the world. What we are striving for is a new international order based upon broad and universal principles of right and justice,—no mere peace of shreds and patches. Is it possible that Count von Hertling does not see that, does not grasp it, is in fact living in his thought in a world dead and gone? Has he utterly forgotten the Reichstag Resolutions of the nineteenth of July, or does he deliberately ignore them? They spoke of the conditions of a general peace, not of national aggrandizement or of arrangements between state and state. The peace of the world depends upon the just settlement of each of the several problems to which I adverted in my recent address to the Congress. I, of course, do not mean that the peace of the world depends upon the acceptance of any particular set of suggestions as to the way in which those problems are to be dealt with. I mean only that those problems each and all affect the whole world; that unless they are dealt with in a spirit of unselfish and unbiased justice, with a view to the wishes, the natural connections, the racial aspirations, the security, and the peace of mind of the peoples involved, no permanent peace will have been attained. They cannot be discussed separately or in corners. None of them constitutes a private or separate interest from which the opinion of the world may be shut out. Whatever affects the peace affects mankind, and nothing settled by military force, if settled wrong, is settled at all. It will presently have to be reopened.

Is Count von Hertling not aware that he is speaking in the court of mankind, that all the awakened nations of the world now sit in judgment on what every public man, of whatever nation, may say on the issues of a conflict which has spread to every region of the world? The Reichstag Resolutions of July themselves frankly accepted the decisions of that court. There shall be no annexations, no contributions, no punitive damages. Peoples are not to be handed about from one sovereignty to another by an international conference or an understanding between rivals and antagonists. National aspirations must be respected; peoples may now be dominated and governed only by their own consent. "Self-determination" is not a mere phase. It is an imperative principle of action, which statesmen will henceforth ignore at their peril. We cannot have general peace for the asking, or by the mere arrangements of a peace conference. It cannot be pieced together out of individual understandings between powerful states. All the parties to this war must join in the settlement of every issue anywhere involved in it; because what we are seeking is a peace that we can all unite to guarantee and maintain and every item of it must be submitted to the common judgment whether it be right and fair, an act of justice, rather than a bargain between sovereigns.

The United States has no desire to interfere in European affairs or to act as arbiter in European territorial disputes. She would disdain to take advantage of any internal weakness or disorder to impose her own will upon another people. She is quite ready to be shown that the settlements she has suggested are not the best or the most enduring. They are only her own provisional sketch of principles and of the way in which they should be applied. But she entered this war because she was made a partner, whether she would or not, in the sufferings and indignities inflicted by the military masters of Germany, against the peace and security of mankind; and the conditions of peace will touch her as nearly as they will touch any other nation to which is entrusted a leading part in the maintenance of civilization. She cannot see her way to peace until the causes of this war are removed, its renewal rendered as nearly as may be impossible.

This war had its roots in the disregard of the rights of small nations and of nationalities which lacked the union and the force to make good their claim to determine their own allegiances and their own forms of political life. Covenants must now be entered into which will render such things impossible for the future; and those covenants must be backed by the united force of all the nations that love justice and are willing to maintain it at any cost. If territorial settlements and the political relations of great populations which have not the organized power to resist are to be determined by the contracts of the powerful governments which consider themselves most directly affected, as Count von Hertling proposes, why may not economic questions also? It has come about in the altered world in which we now find ourselves that justice and the rights of peoples affect the whole field of international dealing as much as access to raw materials and fair and equal conditions of trade. Count von Hertling wants the essential bases of commercial and industrial life to be safeguarded by common agreement and guarantee, but he cannot expect that to be conceded him if the other matters to be determined by the articles of peace are not handled in the same way as items in the final accounting. He cannot ask the benefit of common agreement in the one field without according it in the other. I take it for granted that he sees that separate and selfish compacts with regard to trade and the essential materials of manufacture would afford no foundation for peace. Neither, he may rest assured, will separate and selfish compacts with regard to provinces and peoples.

Count Czernin seems to see the fundamental elements of peace with clear eyes and does not seek to obscure them. He sees that an independent Poland, made up of all the indisputably Polish peoples who lie contiguous to one another, is a matter of European concern and must of course be conceded; that Belgium must be evacuated and restored, no matter what sacrifices and concessions that may involve; and that national aspirations must be satisfied, even within his own Empire, in the common interest of Europe and mankind. If he is silent about questions which touch the interest and purpose of his allies more nearly than they touch those of Austria only, it must of course be because he feels constrained, I suppose, to defer to Germany and Turkey in the circumstances. Seeing and conceding, as he does, the essential principles involved and the necessity of candidly applying them, he naturally feels that Austria can respond to the purpose of peace as expressed by the United States with less embarrassment than could Germany. He would probably have gone much farther had it not been for the embarrassments of Austria's alliances and of her dependence upon Germany.

After all, the test of whether it is possible for either government to go any further in this comparison of views is simple and obvious. The principles to be applied are these:

First, that each part of the final settlement must be based upon the essential justice of that particular case and upon such adjustments as are most likely to bring a peace that will be permanent;

Second, that peoples and provinces are not to be bartered about from sovereignty to sovereignty as if they were mere chattels and pawns in a game, even the great game, now forever discredited, of the balance of power; but that

Third, every territorial settlement involved in this war must be made in the interest and for the benefit of the populations concerned, and not as a part of any mere adjustment or compromise of claims amongst rival states; and

Fourth, that all well defined national aspirations shall be accorded the utmost satisfaction that can be accorded them without introducing new or perpetuating old elements of discord and antagonism that would be likely in time to break the peace of Europe and consequently of the world.

A general peace erected upon such foundations can be discussed. Until such a peace can be secured we have no choice but to go on. So far as we can judge, these principles that we regard as fundamental are already everywhere accepted as imperative except among the spokesmen of the military and annexationist party in Germany. If they have anywhere else been rejected, the objectors have not been sufficiently numerous or influential to make their voices audible. The tragical circumstance is that this one party in Germany is apparently willing and able to send millions of men to their death to prevent what all the world now sees to be just.

I would not be a true spokesman of the people of the United States if I did not say once more that we entered this war upon no small occasion, and that we can never turn back from a course chosen upon principle. Our resources are in part mobilized now, and we shall not pause until they are mobilized in their entirety. Our armies are rapidly going to the fighting front, and will go more and more rapidly. Our whole strength will be put into this war of emancipation,—emancipation from the threat and attempted mastery of selfish groups of autocratic rulers,—whatever the difficulties and present partial delays. We are indomitable in our power of independent action and can in no circumstances consent to live in a world governed by intrigue and force. We believe that our own desire for a new international order under which reason and justice and the common interests of mankind shall prevail is the desire of enlightened men everywhere. Without that new order the world will be without peace and human life will lack tolerable conditions of existence and development. Having set our hand to the task of achieving it, we shall not turn back.

I hope that it is not necessary for me to add that no word of what I have said is intended as a threat. That is not the temper of our people. I have spoken thus only that the whole world may know the true spirit of America,—that men everywhere may know that our passion for justice and for self-government is no mere passion of words but a passion which, once set in action, must be satisfied. The power of the United States is a menace to no nation or people It will never be used in aggression or for the aggrandizement of any selfish interest of our own. It springs out of freedom and is for the service of freedom.

PROCLAMATIONS

[Imports in time of war.]

Whereas, Congress has enacted, and the President has on the Sixth day of October, 1917, approved, a law which contains the following provisions:

"Whenever during the present war the President shall find that the public safety so requires and shall make proclamation thereof it shall be unlawful to import into the United States from any country named in such proclamation any article or articles mentioned in such proclamation except at such time or times, and under such regulations or orders, and subject to such limitations and exceptions as the President shall prescribe, until otherwise ordered by the President or by Congress: Provided, however, that no preference shall be given to the ports of one State over those of another."

And, whereas, the President has heretofore by proclamation dated November 28, 1917, declared certain imports in time of war unlawful, and the President now finds that the public safety requires that such proclamation be amended and supplemented in respect to the articles and countries hereinafter mentioned;

Now, therefore, I, Woodrow Wilson, President of the United States of America, do hereby proclaim to all whom it may concern that the public safety requires that the following articles, namely:

All kinds of arms, guns, ammunition and explosives, machines for their manufacture or repair, component parts thereof, materials or ingredients used in their manufacture, and all articles necessary or convenient for their use; all contrivances for or means of transportation on land or in the water or air, machines used in their manufacture or repair, component parts thereof, materials or ingredients used in their manufacture, and all instruments, articles and animals necessary or convenient for their use; all means of communication, tools, implements, instruments, equipment, maps, pictures, papers and other articles, machines and documents necessary or convenient for carrying on hostile operations; all kinds of fuel, food, foodstuffs, feed, forage and clothing, and all articles and materials used in their manufacture; all chemicals, drugs, dyestuffs and tanning materials; cotton, wool, silk, flax, hemp, jute, sisal and other fibers and manufactures thereof; all earths, clay, glass, sand, stone, and their products; animals of every kind, their products and derivatives; hides, skins and manufactures thereof; all non-edible animal and vegetable products; all machinery, tools, dies, plates, and apparatus, and materials necessary or convenient for their manufacture; medical, surgical, laboratory and sanitary supplies and equipment; all metals, minerals, mineral oils, ores, and all derivatives and manufactures thereof; paper pulp, books and all printed matter, and materials necessary and convenient for their manufacture; rubber, gums, rosins, tars and waxes, their products, derivatives and substitutes, and all articles containing them; wood and wood manufactures; coffee, cocoa, tea and spices; wines, spirits, mineral waters and beverages; and all other articles of any kind whatsoever,

Shall not, on or after the sixteenth day of February, in the year one thousand nine hundred and eighteen, be imported into the United States or its territorial possession from

Abyssinia, Afghanistan, Albania, Argentina, Austria-Hungary, Belgium, her colonies, possessions and protectorates, Bolivia, Brazil, Bulgaria, China, Chile, Colombia, Costa Rica, Cuba, Denmark, her colonies, possessions and protectorates, Dominican Republic, Ecuador, Egypt, France, her colonies, possessions and protectorates, Germany, her colonies, possessions and protectorates, Great Britain, her colonies, possessions and protectorates, Greece, Guatemala, Haiti, Honduras, Italy, her colonies, possessions and protectorates, Japan, Liechtenstein, Liberia, Luxembourg, Mexico, Monaco, Montenegro, Morocco, Nepal, The Netherlands, her colonies, possessions and protectorates, Nicaragua, Norway, Oman, Panama, Paraguay, Persia, Peru, Portugal, her colonies, possessions and protectorates, Roumania, Russia, Salvador, San Marino, Serbia, Siam, Spain, her colonies, possessions and protectorates, Sweden, Switzerland, Turkey, Uruguay, or Venezuela,

Except under license granted in accordance with regulations or orders and subject to such limitations and exceptions as have heretofore been, or shall hereafter be prescribed in pursuance of the powers conferred by said Act of October 6, 1917. The said proclamation of November 28, 1917, and paragraph III of the executive order of October 12, 1917, are hereby confirmed and continued and all rules and regulations heretofore made in connection therewith or in pursuance thereof are likewise hereby confirmed and continued and made applicable to this proclamation.

In witness whereof, I have hereunto set my hand and caused the seal of the United States of America to be affixed.

Done in the District of Columbia, this 14th day of February in the year of our Lord one thousand nine hundred and eighteen, [SEAL]   and of the independence of the United States of America the one hundred and forty-second.

WOODROW WILSON.

By the President:

ROBERT LANSING, *Secretary of State.*

[Exports in time of war.]

Whereas, Congress has enacted, and the President has, on the fifteenth day of June, 1917, approved a law which contains the following provisions:

"Whenever during the present war the President shall find that the public safety shall so require, and shall make proclamation thereof, it shall be unlawful to export from or ship from or take out of the United States to any country named in such proclamation any article or articles mentioned in such proclamation, except at such time or times, and under such regulations and orders, and subject to such limitations and exceptions as the President shall prescribe, until otherwise ordered by the President or by Congress: Provided, however, that no preference shall be given to the ports of one State over those of another."

And, whereas, the President has heretofore by proclamations dated July 9, 1917, August 27, 1917, September 7, 1917, and November 28, 1917, declared certain exports in time of war unlawful, and the President now finds that the public safety requires that such proclamations be amended and supplemented in respect to the articles and countries hereinafter mentioned;

Now, therefore, I, Woodrow Wilson, President of the United States of America, do hereby proclaim to all whom it may concern, that the public safety requires that the following articles, namely:

[The list is identical with that of the preceding proclamation.]

Shall not, on and after the sixteenth day of February in the year one thousand nine hundred and eighteen, be exported from, or shipped from, or taken out of the United States or its territorial possessions to

[The list of countries is identical with that of the preceding proclamation]

Except under license granted in accordance with regulations or orders and subject to such limitations and exceptions as have heretofore been, or shall hereafter be prescribed in pursuance of the powers conferred by said Act of June 15, 1917. The said proclamations of July 9, 1917, August 27, 1917, September 7, 1917, and November 28, 1917; and paragraph II of the executive order of October 12, 1917, are hereby confirmed and continued and all rules and regulations heretofore made in connection therewith or in pursuance thereof are likewise hereby confirmed and continued and made applicable to this proclamation.

In witness whereof, I have hereunto set my hand and caused the seal of the United States of America to be affixed.

Done in the District of Columbia, this 14th day of February in the year of our Lord one thousand nine hundred and eighteen, [SEAL] and of the independence of the United States of America the one hundred and forty-second.

WOODROW WILSON.

By the President:

ROBERT LANSING, *Secretary of State.*

MESSAGE

[Condemning strike of carpenters in Eastern shipyards before awaiting arbitration.]

February 17, 1918.

WILLIAM L. HUTCHESON,
  General President, United Brotherhood of Carpenters and Joiners of America, New York.

I have received your telegram of yesterday and am very glad to note the expression of your desire as a patriotic citizen to assist in carrying on the work by which we are trying to save America and men everywhere who work and are free. Taking advantage of that assurance, I feel it to be my duty to call your attention to the fact that the strike of the carpenters in the shipyards is in marked and painful contrast to the action of labor in other trades and places. Ships are absolutely necessary for the winning of this war. No one can strike a deadlier blow at the safety of the Nation and of its forces on the other side than by interfering with or obstructing the shipbuilding program. All the other unions engaged in this indispensable work have agreed to abide by the decisions of the Shipbuilding Wage Adjustment Board. That board has dealt fairly and liberally with all who have resorted to it.

I must say to you very frankly that it is your duty to leave to it the solution of your present difficulties with your employers and to advise the men whom you represent to return at once to work pending the decision. No body of men have the moral right in the present circumstances of the Nation to strike until every method of adjustment has been tried to the limit. If you do not act upon this principle you are undoubtedly giving aid and comfort to the enemy, whatever may be your own conscious purpose. I do not see that anything will be gained by my seeing you personally until you have accepted and acted upon that principle. It is the duty of the Government to see that the best possible conditions of labor are maintained, as it is also its duty to see to it that there is no lawless and conscienceless profiteering, and that duty the Government has accepted and will perform. Will you cooperate or will you obstruct?

WOODROW WILSON.

By the President of the United States of America:

PROCLAMATIONS

[Fixing guaranteed prices for wheat.]

Whereas, under and by virtue of an Act of Congress entitled "An Act to provide further for the national security and defense by encouraging the production, conserving the supply, and controlling the distribution of food products and fuel," approved by the President on the 10th day of August, one thousand nine hundred and seventeen, it is provided, among other things, as follows:

"Sec. 14. That whenever the President shall find that an emergency exists requiring stimulation of the production of wheat and that it is essential that the producers of wheat, produced within the United States, shall have the benefits of the guaranty provided for in this section, he is authorized, from time to time, seasonably and as far in advance of seeding time as practicable, to determine and fix and to give public notice of what, under specified conditions, is a reasonable guaranteed price for wheat, in order to assure such producers a reasonable profit. The President shall thereupon fix such guaranteed price for each of the official grain standards for wheat as established under the United States Grain Standards Act approved August eleventh, nineteen hundred and sixteen. The President shall from time to time establish and promulgate such regulations as he shall deem wise in connection with such guaranteed prices, and in particular governing conditions of delivery and payment, and differences in price for the several standard grades in the principal primary markets of the United States, adopting number one northern spring or its equivalent at the principal interior primary markets as the basis. Thereupon, the Government of the United States hereby guarantees every producer of wheat produced within the United States that, upon compliance by him with the regulations prescribed, he shall receive for any wheat produced in reliance upon this guarantee within the period, not exceeding eighteen months, prescribed in the notice, a price not less than the guaranteed price therefor as fixed pursuant to this section. In such regulations the President shall prescribe the terms and conditions upon which any such producer shall be entitled to the benefits of such guaranty. The guaranteed prices for the several standard grades of wheat for the crop of nineteen hundred and eighteen shall be based upon number one northern spring or its equivalent at not less that $2 per bushel at the principal interior primary markets. This guaranty shall not be dependent upon the action of the President under the first part of this section, but is hereby made absolute and shall be binding until May first, nineteen hundred and nineteen."

Now, therefore, I, Woodrow Wilson, President of the United States, by virtue of the powers conferred upon me by said Act of Congress, and especially by section 14 thereof, do hereby find that an emergency exists requiring stimulation of the production of wheat, and that it is essential that the producers of wheat produced within the United States shall have the benefits of the guarantee provided for in said section; and, in order to make effective the guarantee by Congress for the crop of nineteen hundred and eighteen and to assure such producers a reasonable profit, I do hereby determine and fix, and give public notice of reasonable guaranteed prices for No. 1 Northern Spring wheat and its equivalents at the respective principal primary markets as follows, to wit:

Chicago, Illinois, Two Dollars and Twenty Cents ($2.20) per bushel;

Omaha, Nebraska, Two Dollars and Fifteen Cents ($2.15) per bushel;

Kansas City, Missouri, Two Dollars and Fifteen Cents ($2.15) per bushel;

St. Louis, Missouri, Two Dollars and Eighteen Cents ($2.18) per bushel;

Minneapolis, Minnesota, Two Dollars and Seventeen Cents ($2.17) per bushel;

Duluth, Minnesota, Two Dollars and Seventeen Cents ($2.17) per bushel;

New York, New York, Two Dollars and Twenty-eight Cents ($2.28) per bushel;

Philadelphia, Pennsylvania, Two Dollars and Twenty-seven Cents ($2.27) per bushel;

Baltimore, Maryland, Two Dollars and Twenty-seven Cents ($2.27) per bushel;

Newport News, Virginia, Two Dollars and Twenty-seven Cents ($2.27) per bushel;

Charleston, South Carolina, Two Dollars and Twenty-seven Cents ($2.27) per bushel;

Savannah, Georgia, Two Dollars and Twenty-seven Cents ($2.27) per bushel;

Portland, Oregon, Two Dollars and Five Cents ($2.05) per bushel;

Seattle, Washington, Two Dollars and Five Cents ($2.05) per bushel;

San Francisco, California, Two Dollars and Ten Cents ($2.10)
per bushel;

Los Angeles, California, Two Dollar and Ten Cents ($2.10) per
bushel;

Galveston, Texas, Two Dollars and Twenty Cents ($2.20) per
bushel;

New Orleans, Louisiana, Two Dollars and Twenty Cents ($2.20)
per bushel;

Salt Lake City, Utah, Two Dollars ($2.00) per bushel;

Great Falls, Montana, Two Dollars ($2.00) per bushel;

Spokane, Washington, Two Dollars ($2.00) per bushel;

Pocatello, Idaho, Two Dollars ($2.00) per bushel;

Fort Worth, Texas, Two Dollars and Nine Cents ($2.09) per
bushel;

Oklahoma City, Oklahoma, Two Dollars and Five Cents ($2.05)
per bushel;

Wichita, Kansas, Two Dollars and Eight Cents ($2.08) per
bushel,

and that the guaranteed price for the other grades established under
the United States Grain Standards Act approved August 11, 1916,
based on said price for No. 1 Northern Spring wheat at the respective
principal primary markets of the United States above mentioned, will
assure the producers of wheat produced within the United States a
reasonable profit; the guaranteed prices in the principal primary markets above mentioned being fixed by adopting No. 1 Northern Spring
wheat or its equivalents at the principal interior markets, as the basis.

For the purposes of such guaranty only, I hereby fix the guaranteed
prices at the respective principal primary markets above mentioned for
the following grades of wheat to wit: No. 1 Northern Spring, No. 1
Hard Winter, No. 1 Red Winter, No. 1 Durum, No. 1 Hard White.
The guaranteed prices at the respective principal primary markets
aforesaid of all other grades of wheat established under the United
States Grain Standards Act approved August 11, 1916, shall be based
on the above guaranteed prices and bear just relation thereto.

The sums thus determined and fixed are guaranteed by the Government of the United States at the respective primary markets of
the United States above mentioned, to every producer of wheat of
any grade so established under the United States Grain Standards
Act, upon the condition that said wheat is harvested in the United
States during the year 1918, and offered for sale before the first day
of June, 1919, to such agent or employee of the United States, or
other person as may be hereafter designated, at any one of the above-
mentioned cities, which are, for the purposes of this Act, hereby
declared to be the principal primary markets of the United States,

and provided that such producer complies with all regulations which may be hereafter promulgated in regard to said guaranty by the President of the United States.

In witness whereof, I have hereunto set my hand and caused the seal of the United States to be affixed.

Done in the District of Columbia, this twenty-first day of February in the year of our Lord one thousand nine hundred and
[SEAL]   eighteen, and of the independence of the United States of America the one hundred and forty-second.

WOODROW WILSON.

By the President:
ROBERT LANSING, *Secretary of State.*

[License of fertilizer industry.]

Whereas, under and by virtue of an Act of Congress entitled "An Act to provide further for the national security and defense by encouraging the production, conserving the supply, and controlling the distribution of food products and fuel," approved by the President on the 10th day of August, 1917, it is provided, among other things, as follows:

[Here follow the two paragraphs quoted on pages 8322 and 8323.]

And, whereas, it is essential in order to carry into effect the purposes of said Act, and in order to secure an adequate supply and equitable distribution, and to facilitate the movement, of certain necessaries hereafter in this proclamation specified, that the license powers conferred upon the President by said Act be at this time exercised to the extent hereinafter set forth;

Now, therefore, I, Woodrow Wilson, President of the United States of America, by virtue of the powers conferred on me by said Act of Congress, hereby find and determine and by this proclamation do announce, that it is essential, in order to carry into effect the purposes of said Act, to license the importation, manufacture, storage and distribution of the following necessaries: fertilizers and fertilizer ingredients, including sulphuric acid, phosphate rock, acid phosphate, bones (raw, ground or steamed), bone black, basic slag, sodium nitrate, ammonia sulphate, cottonseed meal, slaughter house tankage, garbage tankage, castor pomace, fish scrap, base goods, cyanamid, calcium nitrate, dried blood, acidulated leather, hair, hoof meal, horn dust, ground leather, other unacidulated ammoniates, potash salts, cement dust, blast furnace dust, kelp ash, kelp char, dried kelp, wood ashes, cottonseed hull ashes, potassium nitrate, tobacco waste, mixed fertilizers, sulphur, and all other fertilizers and fertilizer ingredients.

All individuals, partnerships, associations, and corporations engaged in the business of importing, manufacturing, storing or distributing fertilizers or fertilizer ingredients (except those specifically exempted by said Act of Congress, and except to the extent to which licenses have been issued under the Proclamation of the President of January 3, 1918, relating to ammonia, ammoniacal liquors and ammonium sulphate) are hereby required to secure licenses on or before March 20, 1918, which will be issued under such rules and regulations governing the conduct of the business as may be prescribed.

The Secretary of Agriculture shall carry into effect the provisions of said Act, and shall supervise and direct the exercise of the powers and authority thereby given to the President, as far as the same apply to fertilizers and fertilizer ingredients, and to any and all practices, procedure and regulations applicable thereto, authorized or required under the provisions of said Act, and in this behalf he shall do and perform such acts and things as may be authorized or required of him from time to time by direction of the President and under such rules and regulations as may be prescribed by the President from time to time. All departments and agencies of the Government are hereby directed to cooperate with the Secretary of Agriculture in the performance of the duties hereinbefore set forth.

Applications for licenses must be made to the Law Department— License Division, United States Food Administration, Washington, D. C., upon forms prepared for that purpose.

Any individual, partnership, association or corporation, other than as hereinbefore excepted, who shall engage in or carry on the business of importing, manufacturing, storing or distributing fertilizers or fertilizer ingredients after the date aforesaid, without first securing such license, will be liable to the penalties prescribed by said Act of Congress.

In witness whereof, I have hereunto set my hand and caused the seal of the United States to be affixed.

Done in the District of Columbia, this 25th day of February in the year of our Lord one thousand nine hundred and eighteen, [SEAL] and of the independence of the United States of America the one hundred and forty-second.

WOODROW WILSON.

By the President:

ROBERT LANSING, *Secretary of State.*

EXECUTIVE ORDER

[Prescribing rules and regulations respecting the exercise of the powers and authority and the performance of the duties of the Alien Property Custodian under the "Trading with the Enemy Act" and prior Executive orders pursuant thereto, and respecting the deposit and investment of moneys received by or for the account of the Alien Property Custodian.]

THE WHITE HOUSE, *February 26, 1918.*

By virtue of the authority vested in me by "An Act to define, regulate, and punish trading with the enemy, and for other purposes," approved October 6, 1917, known as the "Trading with the Enemy Act," I hereby make the following orders, rules and regulations:

(1) *Definitions.*

(a) The word "person," as used herein, shall be deemed to mean an individual, partnership, association, company, or other unincorporated body of individuals, or corporation or body politic.

(b) The word "enemy," as used herein (including subsequent definitions) shall be deemed to mean either an "enemy" or "ally of enemy," as the case may be.

(c) The words "right," "title," "interest," "estate," "power," and "authority" of the enemy, as used herein, shall be deemed to mean, respectively, such right, title, interest, estate, power, and authority of the enemy as may actually exist and also such as might or would exist if the existing state of war had not occurred, and shall be deemed to include, respectively, the right, title, interest, estate, power and authority in law or equity or otherwise of any representative of or trustee for the enemy or other person claiming under or in the right of, or for the benefit of, the enemy.

(d) Any requirement made by the Alien Property Custodian pursuant to Section 7, subsection "c" of the "Trading with the Enemy Act" may be known as and called a demand and will be hereinafter referred to as a demand.

(2) *Demands Pursuant to Section 7, Subsection "c."*

(a) The Alien Property Custodian may make demand for the conveyance, transfer, assignment, delivery, and payment of any money or other property owing or belonging to or held for, by, on account of, or on behalf of or for the benefit of an enemy not holding a license granted by me or in the exercise of my power and authority, which the Alien Property Custodian after investigation, shall determine is so owing or so belongs or is so held, together with every right, title, interest, and estate of the enemy in and to such money or other property and every power and authority of the enemy thereover, including (but without limiting the generality of the foregoing) the power and authority to affirm, ratify, approve, revoke, repudiate or disapprove, in whole or in part, and at any time or times, any power, agency, trust or other relation at the time existing, and also any act or omission theretofore done in the exercise of or pursuant to any power, agency, trust or other relation which the enemy could or might lawfully revoke, repudiate, disaffirm, affirm, ratify or approve, and also including (but without limiting the generality of the foregoing) the power and authority to direct, supervise, and control the future exercise of any power, agency, trust or other relation over such money or other property to the extent that the enemy could or might lawfully direct, supervise, and control the same. Or the Alien Property Custodian may qualify or limit any such demand in such manner and to such extent as he may in any case see fit and (without limiting the generality of the power to qualify and limit demands) he may in any case demand all or only such power and authority over the money or other property as he may see fit without demanding any conveyance, transfer, assignment, delivery or payment of such money or other property or any other right, title, interest, or estate therein or thereto except such as may be included within the power and authority demanded in the particular case over such money or other property.

A demand for the conveyance, transfer, assignment, delivery and payment of money or other property unless expressly qualified or limited shall be deemed to include every right, title, interest, and estate of the enemy in and to the money or other property demanded as well as every power and authority of the enemy thereover.

(b) Notice of any demand made by the Alien Property Custodian may be given to any person who, alone or jointly with others, may hold or have the custody or control of or may be exercising any right, power, or authority in or over or may be performing any duty concerning the money or other property mentioned in the demand; and, in any notice given, the Alien Property Custodian may require of the person notified the performance of any act or thing within the power of the person notified which may be necessary or proper to make the demand fully effective, or to establish proper acknowledgment, recognition, or evidence of the right, title, interest, and estate of the Alien Property Custodian in and to such money or other property and of the power and authority of the Alien Property Custodian thereover, and it shall be the duty of any person so notified to perform any act or thing so required. Such notice may be given in person or by mail.

(c) When demand shall be made and notice thereof given, as hereinbefore provided, such demand and notice shall forthwith vest in the Alien Property Custodian such right, title, interest, and estate in and to and possession of the money or other property demanded and such power or authority thereover as may be included within the demand,

and the Alien Property Custodian may thereupon proceed to administer such money or other property in accordance with the provisions of the "Trading with the Enemy Act" and with any orders, rules, or regulations heretofore, hereby, or hereafter made by me or heretofore or hereafter made by the Alien Property Custodian.

(3) *Powers of Administration*

(a) The Alien Property Custodian may appoint and clothe with necessary power and authority such agents, bailees, and attorneys in fact as he may find to be necessary or proper to carry out the provisions of the "Trading with the Enemy Act" and the Executive orders, rules, and regulations heretofore, hereby, or hereafter made, and prescribe the duties and fix the compensation of such agents, bailees, and attorneys in fact; and any depositary designated by the Alien Property Custodian may be appointed as such agent, bailee or attorney in fact. And the Alien Property Custodian may require bonds of such agents, bailees and attorneys in fact and fix the penalty and conditions thereof.

(b) The Alien Property Custodian may pay all reasonable and proper expenses which may be incurred in or about securing possession or control of money or other property and in or about collecting dividends, interest and other income therefrom, and in otherwise practicing and administering the same. So far as may be, all such expenses shall be paid out of, and in any event recorded as a charge against, the estate to which such money or other property belongs.

(c) The Alien Property Custodian may authorize depositaries designated by him and agents, bailees, and attorneys in fact appointed by him to deduct all expenses authorized or approved by the Alien Property Custodian, including the compensation of such depositaries, agents, bailees, and attorneys in fact, from any moneys collected by them and the payment by them to the Alien Property Custodian or into the Treasury of the United States of the net amount remaining in their hands.

(d) The Alien Property Custodian may exercise any right, power, or authority of the enemy in, to and over corporate stock, shares or certificates representing beneficial interests owing or belonging to or held for, by, on account of, or on behalf of or for the benefit of an enemy, including (1) the right to receive all notices issued by the corporation, unincorporated association, company or trustee which issued such stock, shares or certificates, to the holders or owners of similar stock, shares or certificates, (2) the right to exercise all voting power appertaining to such stock, shares or certificates, and (3) the right to receive all subscription rights, dividends and other distributions and payments, whether of capital or income, declared or made on account of such stock shares or certificates, regardless of whether or not such stock, shares or certificates be in the possession of the Alien Property Custodian and regardless of whether or not such stock, shares or certificates have been transferred to the Alien Property Custodian upon the books of the corporation, association, company or trustee issuing the same.

The Alien Property Custodian may nominate persons who may, when duly elected or appointed, serve as directors, officers or employees of any corporation whose corporate stock or shares, in whole or in part, are owing or belonging to, or are held for, by, on account of, or on behalf of or for the benefit of any enemy.

The Alien Property Custodian may demand the transfer of corporate stock, shares or certificates representing beneficial interests to be made upon the books of any corporation, unincorporated association, company or trustee, issuing the same, into the name of the Alien Property Custodian or into the name of any depositary designated by the Alien Property Custodian for the account of the Alien Property Custodian, or, in the case of corporate stock or shares, into the name of any other person for the purpose of qualifying such person to serve as a director of the corporation issuing such corporate stock or shares; and it shall be the duty of any corporation, unincorporated association, company, or trustee to comply with such demand when accompanied by the presentation of the certificates which represent such corporate stock, shares or beneficial interests. Provided that corporate stock or shares transferred into the name of any other person than the Alien Property Custodian or a designated depositary shall be indorsed by such person in blank and delivered to and held by the Alien Property Custodian or by a duly designated depositary.

(e) In respect of moneys, accounts payable, credits, notes or other obligations owing or belonging to or held for, by, on account, or on behalf of or for the benefit of an enemy, whether the payment or delivery or the mere transfer and assignment thereof be demanded, the Alien Property Custodian may exercise discretion in enforcing payment, granting indulgence, making extension or accepting security, and in exercising any other right, power or authority of the enemy.

(f) The Alien Property Custodian may sell and deliver any commodity or other tangible property which may be perishable or which may in the preservation thereof involve expense. And the Alien Property Custodian may sell and deliver any rights appurtenant to the ownership of corporate stock, shares or certificates of beneficial interests in cases where such rights would lapse unless exercised within a limited time. The Alien Property Custodian may manage, conduct, and operate any business belonging to or held for, by, on account of, or on behalf of or for the benefit of an enemy in cases where the continuation of such business may seem to be necessary to prevent waste or to protect such business. And the Alien Property Custodian may sell or otherwise dispose of such business or any part thereof, or the assets or any part thereof, whenever such sale shall seem to be necessary to prevent waste or to protect such business. And in the management, operation, conduct, sale or other disposition of such business the Alien Property Custodian may exercise every right, power and authority of the enemy.

(g) In cases of liquidation of an estate belonging to a partnership, association or unincorporated company in which an enemy may have an interest, the Alien Property Custodian may exercise every right, power, and authority of the enemy, including the right, power, and authority to sell the interest of the enemy in the event such sale seems necessary to prevent waste or to protect such interest.

(h) All sales made by the Alien Property Custodian may be conducted privately or publicly, with or without advertisement, and on such terms and conditions as to the Alien Property Custodian may seem proper.

In all cases of sales made by the Alien Property Custodian, all reasonable expenses incurred in and about such sales shall be deducted from the proceeds and the net amount remaining paid into the Treasury of the United States.

(i) The Alien Property Custodian is authorized to exercise any power conferred upon him by any license issued by me or in the exercise of the power and authority conferred upon me under the "Trading with the Enemy Act" wherever such license involves any act or thing concerning any money or other property owing or belonging to or held for, by, on account of, or on behalf of or for the benefit of any enemy.

(4) *Statutory Powers of the Alien Property Custodian.*

Nothing herein contained is intended, nor shall anything herein contained be construed, to limit the powers conferred upon the Alien Property Custodian by the "Trading with the Enemy Act."

(5) *Deposit and Investment of Moneys Received by the Alien Property Custodian*

There shall be deposited in the Treasury of the United States, through the office of the Secretary of the Treasury—

(a) Any and all moneys (including checks and drafts payable on demand) paid to or received by the Alien Property Custodian pursuant to the "Trading with the enemy Act";

(b) Any and all moneys (including checks and drafts payable on demand) collected or received by the Alien Property Custodian, as dividends or interest or income that may become due upon any stocks, bonds, notes, time drafts, time bills of exchange, or other securities or property held by the Alien Property Custodian or by any depositary or depositaries designated as provided in said Act for the account of the Alien Property Custodian.

(c) Any and all moneys collected as the proceeds of any and all maturing obligations held by the Alien Property Custodian or by any such depositary or depositaries for the account of the Alien Property Custodian; and

(d) Any and all moneys paid to or received by the Alien Property Custodian as the proceeds of any sale or sales, made at any time pursuant to such rules and regulations as the President shall prescribe, or any and all property or rights which shall come into the possession of the Alien Property Custodian in pursuance of the provisions of said Act;

Provided, however, that the Alien Property Custodian may fix stated periods, not longer than quarter-yearly, for accounting by depositaries, agents, bailees, and attorneys in fact of all moneys received by them, and for the payment thereof by such depositories, agents, bailees, and attorneys in fact to the Alien Property Custodian, who shall forthwith pay the same into the Treasury of the United States, as provided above, and that checks and drafts payable on demand received by designated depositaries in payment of dividends, interest and income from property held by or for the account of the Alien Property Custodian may be collected by such depositaries for the account of the Alien Property Custodian, but that all other checks and drafts payable on demand shall be forthwith deposited by the Alien Property Custodian in the Treasury of the United States, as provided above.

Any and all moneys so deposited in the Treasury of the United States, as herein provided, as well as all moneys, if any, which may be paid to the Treasurer of the United States, as provided in Section 12 of said Act, and all interest, dividends or other income, if any, in respect of any property conveyed, transferred, assigned or delivered to the Treasurer of the United States, as provided in said Section 12, shall be credited by the Treasurer of the United States to the Secretary of the Treasury "for account of the Alien Property Custodian."

Any and all moneys so deposited in the Treasury of the United States, as herein provided, together with any interest or income received from the investment thereof, shall be subject to withdrawal by the Secretary of the Treasury for the purpose of making any payment or payments pursuant to the provisions of said Act, and, until so withdrawn, may be invested and reinvested, from time to time, by the Secretary of the Treasury in United States bonds or United States certificates of indebtedness. The bonds and certificates of indebtedness, in which such moneys shall be so invested, shall be held by the Secretary of the Treasury for account of the Alien Property Custodian, subject to the provisions hereof and of said Act and to such further orders, rules or regulations as may, from time to time, be prescribed by me.

(6) *Amendments and Modifications of Prior Executive Orders.*

All other Executive orders heretofore made are hereby amended and modified to such extent as may be necessary to conform with the provisions hereof. WOODROW WILSON.

By the President of the United States of America.

A PROCLAMATION

[Regulating the flying of civilian aircraft.]

Whereas, The United States of America is now at war, and the Army and Navy thereof are endangered in their operations and preparations by aircraft, I, Woodrow Wilson, President of the United States, by virtue of the authority vested in me by the Constitution as Commander-in-Chief of the Army and Navy of the United States and of the Militia of the several States when called into the actual service of the United States, do hereby for the protection of such forces issue the following proclamation.

I. A license must be obtained from the Joint Army and Navy Board on Aeronautic Cognizance by or in behalf of any person who contemplates flying in a balloon, aeroplane, hydroplane, or other machine or device over or near any military or naval forces, camp, fort, battery, torpedo station, arsenal, munition factory, navy yard, naval station, coaling station, telephone or wireless or signal station, or any building or office connected with the National Defense, or any place or region within the jurisdiction or occupation of the United States which may be designated by the President as a zone of war-like operations or of war-like preparation.

II. The license will specify the person to whom it is issued, the machine to be used, the persons to operate the machine and all other persons to be carried therein, the mode of marking or otherwise identifying the machine, and other details intended to assure the military and naval forces of the peacefulness of the errand.

III. The license will also specify the territory and the time wherein it shall be available.

IV. In case any aircraft shall disregard this proclamation or the terms of the license, it shall be the right and duty of the military or naval forces to treat the aircraft as hostile and to fire upon it or otherwise destroy it, notwithstanding the resultant danger to human life.

V. For the present, the President designates as a zone of military operations and of military preparation the whole of the United States and its territorial waters and of the insular possessions and of the Panama Canal Zone.

VI. The provisions of this proclamation do not apply to aircraft operated by the Army or Navy of the United States.

VII. No private flying without a license will be permitted after the expiration of thirty days from the date of this proclamation.

In witness whereof, I have hereunto set my hand and caused the seal of the United States to be affixed.

Done in the District of Columbia, this 28th day of February, in the
   , year of our Lord one thousand nine hundred and eighteen,
[SEAL.] and of the independence of the United States the one hundred and forty-second.

WOODROW WILSON.

By the President:
ROBERT LANSING, *Secretary of State.*

MESSAGE

[To the All-Russian Congress of Soviets, meeting at Moscow, Russia, March 12, 1918.]

WASHINGTON, D. C., U. S. A., March 11, 1918.

May I not take advantage of the meeting of the Congress of the Soviets to express the sincere sympathy which the people of the United States feel for the Russian people at this moment when the German power has been thrust in to interrupt and turn back the whole struggle for freedom and substitute the wishes of Germany for the purpose of the people of Russia?

Although the Government of the United States is, unhappily, not now in a position to render the direct and effective aid it would wish to render, I beg to assure the people of Russia through the Congress that it will avail itself of every opportunity to secure for Russia once more complete sovereignty and independence in her own affairs and full restoration to her great role in the life of Europe and the modern world.

The whole heart of the people of the United States is with the people of Russia in the attempt to free themselves forever from autocratic government and become the masters of their own life.

(Signed) WOODROW WILSON.

APPEAL

[To boys of working age, to do farm work.]

THE WHITE HOUSE, *March 13, 1918.*

The Department of Labor has set aside the week beginning March 18 as National Enrollment Week for the United States Boys' Working Reserve. The purpose of this national enrollment work is to call the attention of the young men of the nation to the importance of increasing the food supply by working on the farms, and to urge them to enroll in the reserve.

I sincerely hope that the young men of the country of 16 years of age and over not now permanently employed, and especially the boys in our high schools, will enter heartily into this work and join the Boys' Working Reserve in order that they may have the privilege, for such I believe it to be, of spending their spare time in a productive enterprise which will certainly aid the nation to win the war by increasing the means of providing for the forces at the front, and for the maintenance of those whose services are so much needed at home.

(Signed)   WOODROW WILSON.

BY THE PRESIDENT OF THE UNITED STATES OF AMERICA

A PROCLAMATION

[Relative to the fuel administration and licenses for certain classes of distributors of coal and coke.]

Whereas, Under and by virtue of an Act of Congress entitled "An Act to provide further for the national security and defense by encouraging the production, conserving the supply, and controlling the distribution of food products and fuel," approved by the President on the 10th day of August, 1917, it is provided among other things as follows:

[Here follow the two paragraphs quoted on pages 8322 and 8323.]

And whereas, It is further provided in said Act as follows:

"That the President of the United States shall be, and he is hereby, authorized and empowered, whenever and wherever in his judgment necessary for the efficient prosecution of the war, to fix the price of coal and coke, wherever and whenever sold, either by producer or dealer, to establish rules for the regulation of and to regulate the method of production, sale, shipment, distribution, apportionment, or storage thereof among dealers and consumers, domestic or foreign."

And whereas, It is further provided in said Act as follows:

"That in carrying out the purposes of this Act the President is

authorized to enter into any voluntary arrangements or agreements, to create and use any agency or agencies,"

And whereas, The President has heretofore designated and appointed
Harry A. Garfield United States Fuel Administrator for the purpose
of carrying into effect the provisions of said Act, relating to fuel, and
has directed that:

"Said Fuel Administrator shall supervise, direct and carry into
effect the provisions of said Act and the powers and authority
therein given to the President so far as the same apply to fuel as
set forth in said Act, and to any and all practices, procedure and
regulations authorized under the provisions of said Act applicable
to fuel, including the issuance, regulation and revocation under
the name of said United States Fuel Administrator of licenses
under said Act" and has authorized said Fuel Administrator to
employ such assistants and subordinates as may from time to time
be deemed by him necessary, said Fuel Administrator and such
assistants and subordinates together constituting the governmental
organization called the United States Fuel Administration.

And whereas, It is essential in order to carry into effect the provisions of said Act, and in order to secure an adequate supply and
equitable distribution, and to facilitate the movement of certain necessaries hereafter in this proclamation specified, that the license powers
conferred upon the President by said Act be at this time exercised to
the extent hereinafter set forth,

Now, therefore, I, Woodrow Wilson, President of the United States
of America, by virtue of the powers conferred on me by said Act of
Congress, hereby find and determine and by this proclamation do
announce that it is essential in order to carry into effect the purposes
of said Act, to license certain classes of distributors of coal and coke to
the extent hereinafter provided:

All persons, firms, corporations and associations (except those specifically exempted by said Act of Congress, producers and miners of coal
and manufacturers of coke, distributing exclusively their own product,
and retail dealers, as defined in the United States Fuel Administrator's
Order of October 1, 1917, Publication No. 7) engaged in the business
of distributing coal or coke as jobber, broker, selling agent, purchasing
agent, wholesaler, or in any capacity whatsoever, are hereby required
to secure a license on or before April 1, 1918, which license will be
issued under such rules and regulations governing the conduct of the
business, as may from time to time be prescribed by the President of
the United States or by the United States Fuel Administrator acting by
virtue of the authority heretofore as aforesaid, or hereby, delegated to
him by the President.

The United States Fuel Administrator shall supervise, direct and carry into effect the provisions of said Act, and the powers and authority thereby given to the President, as the same applies to coal, coke, and other fuel, and to any and all practices, procedure and regulations authorized or required under the provisions of said Act, including issuance, regulation, and revocation, in the name of said Fuel Administrator, of licenses under said Act, and in this behalf he shall also do and perform such other acts and things as may be authorized or required of him from time to time by direction of the President, and under such rules and regulations as may be prescribed by the President from time to time.

For all the purposes aforesaid the United States Fuel Administrator may make use of the said governmental organization called the United States Fuel Administration.

Application for licenses may be made to the United States Fuel Administrator, Washington, D. C., upon forms prepared by him for that purpose.

Any person, firm, corporation or association, other than those hereinbefore excepted, who, without a license, issued pursuant to this proclamation, or whose license shall have been revoked, knowingly engages in or carries on, after the date aforesaid, any business for which a license is required under this proclamation, will be liable to the penalties prescribed by said Act of Congress.

In witness whereof I have hereunto set my hand and caused the seal of the United States to be affixed.

Done in the District of Columbia, this 15th day of March, in the year of our Lord 1918, and of the independence of the United
[SEAL.]   States of America the one hundred and forty-second.
By the President: WOODROW WILSON.
    ROBERT LANSING, *Secretary of State.*

EXECUTIVE ORDER

[Creating Service Bureau under Public Information Committee.]

THE WHITE HOUSE, *March 19, 1918.*

I hereby create under the direction of the Committee on Public Information, created by Executive order of April 14th, 1917, a Service Bureau, for the purpose of establishing a central office in the city of Washington, where complete information records may be available as to the function, location and personnel of all government agencies.

I hereby ask the several departments of Government, when so requested by the Chairman of the Committee on Public Information, to detail such person or persons as may be necessary in gathering the information needed and carrying on the work of the Bureau so far as it relates to such departments; to give opportunity to the director of the Bureau, or such person as he may designate, to secure information from time to time for the purpose of keeping the records up to date; to supply the director of the Bureau on form cards, furnished by him, with information as to personnel, function and location.

WOODROW WILSON.

LETTER

[To Democrats of New Jersey, meeting at a dinner on March 20, 1918.]

THE WHITE HOUSE, *March 20, 1918.*

My Dear Mr. Toastmaster:

I sincerely regret that matters of pressing importance will prevent my taking part in the reorganization banquet to which you have generously invited me. It is my feeling, as I am sure it will be the feeling of those present, that my clear duty is to stay here on the job. My work can be properly done only if I devote my whole thought and attention to it and think of nothing but the immediate task in hand.

At the same time it is clear that in the present posture of affairs in New Jersey I cannot overlook my responsibility as leader of a great party, and that it is my privilege to point out what I believe to be the duty of the Democrats in New Jersey, now and in the months to come, in order that the exigency of a great hour of crisis may properly be met.

During the months that I had the privilege of serving the people of New Jersey in the office of Governor we sought to accomplish this definite purpose, namely, to open the processes of government to the access and inspection of every citizen, in order that the people might feel that the Government of New Jersey represented their hopes, their impulses, and their sympathies. It was with this great purpose in mind that we succeeded in establishing electoral machinery which took away from selfish political leaders the power to hold the mass of the party voters of the State in subjection to themselves. In the matter of employers' liability we substituted for the cold letter of the old law the warm and wholesome tonic of humane statute.

In every act of legislation we cut a clear pathway of public service and achieved a record remarkable for its variety and humanity, in every way comprehensive in character and touching no vital interest in the State with a spirit of injustice or demagogy. We gave the people, after many tedious and discouraging years of waiting, a government which they could feel was their own, free and unhampered by special privilege.

A time of grave crisis has come in the life of the Democratic party in New Jersey—a time when its friends and supporters must face the facts of the situation if they would serve the cause of free government in New Jersey. Every sign of these terrible days of war and revolutionary change, when economic and social forces are being released upon the world whose effect no political seer dare venture to conjecture, bids us search our hearts through and through and make them ready for the birth of a new day—a day, we hope and believe, of greater opportunity and greater prosperity for the average mass of struggling men and women, and of greater safety and opportunity for children.

The old party slogans have lost their significance and will mean nothing to the voter of the future, for the war is certain to change the mind of Europe as well as the mind of America. Men everywhere are searching democratic principles to their hearts in order to determine their soundness, their sincerity, their adaptability to the real needs of their life, and every man with any vision must see that the real test of justice and right action is presently to come as it never came before.

The men in the trenches, who have been freed from the economic serfdom to which some of them had been accustomed, will, it is likely, return to their homes with a new view and a new impatience of all mere political phrases, and will demand real thinking and sincere action.

Let the Democratic party in New Jersey, therefore, forget everything but the new service which they are to be called upon to render. The days of political and economic reconstruction which are ahead of us no man can now definitely assess, but we know this, that every program must be shot through and through with utter disinterestedness; that no party must try to serve itself, but every party must try to serve humanity; and that the task is a very practical one, meaning that every program, every measure in every program, must be tested by this question, and this question only: Is it just; is it for the benefit of the average man, without influence or privilege; does it embody in real fact the highest conception of social justice and of right dealing without respect of person or class or particular interest?

This is a high test. It can be met only by those who have genuine sympathy with the mass of men and real insight into their needs and opportunities, and a purpose which is purged alike of selfish and of partisan intention. The party which rises to this test will receive the support of the people because it serves it.

Very sincerely yours,
WOODROW WILSON.

EXECUTIVE ORDER

[Defining non-combatant service and prescribing treatment of conscientious objectors.]

THE WHITE HOUSE, *March 20, 1918.*

1. By virtue of authority contained in Section 4 of the Act approved May 18, 1917, entitled, "An Act to authorize the President to increase temporarily the military establishment of the United States," whereby it is provided—

"And nothing in this Act contained shall be construed to require or compel any person to serve in any of the forces herein provided for who is found to be a member of any well recognized religious sect or organization at present organized and existing and whose existing creed or principles forbid its members to participate in war in any form and whose religious convictions are against war or participation therein in accordance with the creed or principles of said religious organizations; but no person so exempted shall be exempted from service in any capacity that the President shall declare to be noncombatant."

I hereby declare that the following military service is noncombatant service:

a. Service in the Medical Corps wherever performed. This includes service in the sanitary detachments attached to combatant units at the front; service in the divisional sanitary trains composed of ambulance companies and field hospital companies, on the line of communications, at the base in France, and with the troops and at hospitals in the United States; also the service of supply and repair in the Medical Department.

b. Any service in the Quartermaster Corps, in the United States may be treated as noncombatant. Also, in rear of zone of operations, service in the following: Stevedore companies, labor companies, remount depots, veterinary hospitals, supply depots, bakery companies, the subsistence service, the bathing service, the laundry service, the salvage service, the clothing renovation service, the shoe repair service, the transportation repair service, and motor-truck companies.

c. Any engineer service in the United States may be treated as noncombatant service. Also, in rear of zone of operations, service as follows: Railroad building, operation and repair; road building and repair; construction of rear line fortifications, auxiliary defenses, etc.; construction of docks, wharves, storehouses and of such cantonments as may be built by the Corps of Engineers; topographical work; camouflage; map reproduction; supply depot service; repair service; hydraulic service; and forestry service.

2. Persons ordered to report for military service under the above Act who have (*a*) been certified by their Local Boards to be members of a religious sect or organization as defined in Section 4 of said Act; or (*b*) who object to participating in war because of conscientious scruples but have failed to receive certificates as members of a religious sect or organization from their Local Board, will be assigned to noncombatant military service as defined in paragraph 1 to the extent that such persons are able to accept service as aforesaid without violation of the religious or other conscientious scruples by them in good faith entertained. Upon the promulgation of this order it shall be the duty of each Division, Camp, or Post Commander, through a tactful and considerate officer, to present to all such persons the provisions hereof with adequate explanation of the character of noncombatant service herein defined, and upon such explanations to secure acceptances of assignment to the several kinds of noncombatant service above enumerated; and whenever any person is assigned to noncombatant service by reason of his religious or conscientious scruples, he shall be given a certificate stating the assignment and reason therefor, and such certificate shall thereafter be respected as preventing the transfer of such persons from such noncombatant to combatant service by any Division, Camp, Post, or other Commander under whom said person may thereafter be called to serve, but such certificate shall not prevent the assignment of such person to some other form of noncombatant service with his own consent. So far as may be found feasible by each Division, Camp, or Post Commander, future assignments of such persons to noncombatant military service will be restricted to the several detachments and units of the Medical Department in the absence of a request for assignment to some other branch of noncombatant service as defined in paragraph 1 hereof.

3. On the first day of April, and thereafter monthly, each Division, Camp, or Post Commander shall report to The Adjutant General of the Army, for the information of the Chief of Staff and the Secretary of War, the names of all persons under their respective commands who profess religious or other conscientious scruples as above described and who have been unwilling to accept, by reason of such scruples, assignment to noncombatant military service as above defined, and as to each such person so reported a brief, comprehensive statement as to the nature of the objection to the acceptance of such noncombatant military service entertained. The Secretary of War will from time to time classify the persons so reported and give further directions as to the disposition of them. Pending such directions from the Secretary of War, all such persons not accepting assignment to noncombatant service shall be segregated as far as practicable and placed under the command of a specially qualified officer of tact and judgment, who will

be instructed to impose no punitive hardship of any kind upon them, but not to allow their objections to be made the basis of any favor or consideration beyond exemption from actual military service which is not extended to any other soldier in the service of the United States.

4. With a view to maintaining discipline, it is pointed out that the discretion of courts-martial, so far as any shall be ordered to deal with the cases of persons who fail or refuse to comply with lawful orders by reason of alleged religious or other conscientious scruples, should be exercised, if feasible, so as to secure uniformity of penalties in the imposition of sentences under Articles of War 64 and 65, for the wilful disobedience of a lawful order or command. It will be recognized that sentences imposed by such courts-martial, when not otherwise described by law, shall prescribe confinement in the United States Disciplinary Barracks or elsewhere as the Secretary of War or the reviewing authority may direct, but not in a penitentiary; but this shall not apply to the cases of men who desert either before reporting for duty to the military authorities or subsequently thereto.

5. The Secretary of War will review the sentences and findings of courts-martial heretofore held of persons who come within any of the classes herein described, and bring to the attention of the President for remedy, if any be needed, sentences and judgments found at variance with the provisions hereof.   WOODROW WILSON.

By the President of the United States of America.

A PROCLAMATION

[Possession and utilization of Netherlands vessels.]

Whereas, The law and practice of nations accords to a belligerent power the right in time of military exigency and for purposes essential to the prosecution of war, to take over and utilize neutral vessels lying within its jurisdiction:

And whereas, The Act of Congress of June 15, 1917, entitled, "An Act making appropriations to supply urgent deficiencies in appropriations for the Military and Naval Establishments on account of war expenses for the fiscal year ending June 30th, 1917, and for other purposes," confers upon the President power to take over the possession of any vessel within the jurisdiction of the United States for use or operation by the United States:

Now, therefore, I, Woodrow Wilson, President of the United States of America, in accordance with international law and practice, and by virtue of the Act of Congress aforesaid, and as Commander-in-Chief of the Army and Navy of the United States, do hereby find and proclaim that the imperative military needs of the United States require the immediate utilization of vessels of Netherlands registry, now lying within the territorial waters of the United States; and I do therefore authorize and empower the Secretary of the Navy to take over on behalf of the United States the possession of and to employ all such vessels of Netherlands registry as may be necessary for essential purposes connected with the prosecution of the war against the Imperial German Government. The vessels shall be manned, equipped and operated by the Navy Department and the United States Shipping Board, as may be deemed expedient; and the United States Shipping Board shall make to the owners thereof full compensation, in accordance with the principles of international law.

In testimony whereof, I have hereunto set my hand and caused the seal of the United States to be affixed.

Done in the District of Columbia, this twentieth day of March, in the year of our Lord one thousand nine hundred and [SEAL.] eighteen, and of the independence of the United States of America the one hundred and forty-second.

WOODROW WILSON.

By the President:

ROBERT LANSING, *Secretary of State.*

EXECUTIVE ORDERS

[Possession of vessels of the Netherlands.]

THE WHITE HOUSE, *March 28, 1918.*

In Pursuance of the authority conferred upon the President of the United States by the Act approved June 15, 1917, entitled, "An Act making appropriations to supply urgent deficiencies for the fiscal year ending June 30, 1917, and for other purposes," the Secretary of the Navy is hereby authorized and directed to take over, on behalf of the United States, possession of all tackle, apparel, furniture and equipment and all stores, including bunker fuel, aboard each of the vessels of Netherlands registry now lying within the territorial jurisdiction of the United States, possession of which was taken in accordance with the proclamation of the President of the United States promulgated March 20, 1918; and in every instance in which such possession has heretofore been taken of such tackle, apparel, furniture, equipment and stores, such taking is hereby adopted and made of the same force and effect as if it has been made subsequent to the signing of this Executive Order.

The United States Shipping Board shall make to the owners of any tackle, apparel, furniture, equipment and stores taken under the authority of this order full compensation in accordance with the principles of international law.   WOODROW WILSON.

[Certain sales to be conducted by the Alien Property Custodian pursuant to the "Trading with the Enemy" Act, and amendments thereof.]

THE WHITE HOUSE, *April 2, 1918.*

By virtue of the authority vested in me by "An Act to define, regulate and punish trading with the enemy, and for other purposes," approved October 6, 1917, known as the "Trading with the enemy Act", and the amendment to such Act embodied in "An Act making appropriations to supply urgent deficiencies in appropriations for the fiscal year ending June 30, 1918, and prior fiscal years, on account of war expenses, and for other purposes", approved March 28, 1918, I hereby, in the public interest, make the following determination, order, rule and regulation:

The Alien Property Custodian may sell at private sale, without public or other advertisement, any live stock, feed or food stuffs, hides and other animal products, agricultural products, fertilizers, chemicals, drugs, essential oils, lumber, cotton, tobacco, furniture, books, glass and china ware, wearing apparel, jewelry, precious stones, pictures, ornaments, bric-a-brac, objects of art, raw or finished textile materials, trunks, boxes, casks and containers of all kinds, partially or completely manufactured metals, fabrics or other articles, rubber and rubber products, and all kinds of merchandise, in lots having a market value at the time and place of sale not exceeding Ten Thousand Dollars ($10,000) per lot. Any such sale may be conducted at the place where such property, or the greater portion thereof, is situated, or elsewhere, and upon such terms and conditions as to the Alien Property Custodian, or his authorized agent, may seem proper.

My reasons for the foregoing determination, order, rule and regulation are:

(*a*) The properties described in the lots mentioned are not customarily sold and cannot usually be sold to advantage either at public sale after public or other advertisement, or at the place where such properties, or the greater portion thereof, are situated.

(*b*) The sales hereby authorized may be made at the time and place of favorable demand, and upon such terms and conditions as may be necessary to secure the market price.

(*c*) Unnecessary expense, delay and inconvenience may be avoided.

WOODROW WILSON.

BY THE PRESIDENT OF THE UNITED STATES OF AMERICA.

A PROCLAMATION

[Copyright—Australia and Territories of Papua and Norfolk Island.]

Whereas it is provided by the Act of Congress of March 4, 1909, entitled "An Act to Amend and Consolidate the Acts Respecting Copyright," that the provisions of said Act, "so far as they secure copyright controlling the parts of instruments serving to reproduce mechanically the musical work, shall include only compositions published and copyrighted after this Act goes into effect, and shall not include the works of a foreign author or composer unless the foreign state or nation of which such author or composer is a citizen or subject grants, either by treaty, convention, agreement, or law, to citizens of the United States similar rights:"

And Whereas it is further provided that the copyright secured by the Act shall extend to the work of an author or proprietor who is a citizen or subject of a foreign state or nation, only upon certain conditions set forth in section 8 of said Act, to wit:

(*a*) When an alien author or proprietor shall be domiciled within the United States at the time of the first publication of his work; or

(*b*) When the foreign state or nation of which such author or proprietor is a citizen or subject grants, either by treaty, convention, agreement, or law, to citizens of the United States the benefit of copyright on substantially the same basis as to its own citizens, or copyright protection substantially equal to the protection secured to such foreign author under this Act or by treaty; or when such foreign state or nation is a party to an international agreement which provides for reciprocity in the granting of copyright, by the terms of which agreement the United States may, at its pleasure, become a party thereto:

And Whereas it is also provided by said section that "The existence of the reciprocal conditions aforesaid shall be determined by the President of the United States, by proclamation made from time to time as the purposes of this Act may require":

And Whereas there has been received from the Government of Great Britain satisfactory official assurance that the Government of Australia has issued an Order in Council, effective March 15, 1918, providing that the existing copyright law of that country and the territories of Papua and Norfolk Island, including the provisions as to existing works, shall, subject to the provisions of the said law and of the said Order, apply:

(*a*) to literary, dramatic, musical and artistic works the authors whereof were at the time of the making of the works citizens of the United States of America in like manner as if the authors were British subjects:

(*b*) in respect of residence in the United States of America in like manner as if such residence had been residence in the Commonwealth of Australia and the territories of Papua and Norfolk Island:

Provided That—

(I) the term of copyright within the Commonwealth of **Australia**

VIEWS OF THE ENGLISH AND GERMAN FLEETS

GERMAN AND ENGLISH FLEETS.

The historian of the great European War will record, and contemporary historians are recording, that the deciding factors in the conflict were wrapped up in the control of the seas. Despite several severe naval engagements (which are described in the article European War in the Encyclopedic Index), the main fleets of the nations involved did not exchange broadsides. The main German fleet did not challenge England's control of the seas, nor her absolute blockade of the ports of the Central Powers; and the Imperial German Government retaliated only by the ruthless use of her large fleet of submarines. The accompanying picture is especially interesting in that it shows aeroplanes hovering over the English men-of-war; for there can be little doubt that aircraft were of inestimable value in preventing the destruction of the English ships by bombs from German Zeppelins.

and the territories of Papua and Norfolk Island shall not exceed that conferred by the law of the United States of America;

(II) the enjoyment of the rights conferred by this Order shall be subject to the accomplishment of the conditions and formalities prescribed by the law of the United States of America;

(III) in the application to existing works of the provisions of Section 24 of the Imperial Copyright Act, 1911, the commencement of this Order shall be substituted for the 26th July, 1910, in sub-section 1 (b).

Now, therefore, I, Woodrow Wilson, President of the United States of America, do declare and proclaim that one of the alternative conditions specified in section 8 (b) of the Act of March 4, 1909, now exists and is fulfilled in respect to the citizens of Australia and the territories of Papua and Norfolk Island, and that such citizens shall be entitled to all the benefits of section 1(e) of the said Act, including "copyright controlling the parts of instruments serving to reproduce mechanically the musical work" in the case of all musical compositions by composers of Australia and the territories of Papua and Norfolk Island published and duly registered in the United States on and after March 15, 1918, for copyright in the United States.

In Testimony Whereof, I have hereunto set my hand and caused the seal of the United States to be affixed.

Done in the District of Columbia this third day of April, in the year of our Lord one thousand nine hundred and eighteen and of [SEAL.] the Independence of the United States of America the one hundred and forty-second.

WOODROW WILSON.

By the President:

ROBERT LANSING,
     Secretary of State.

ADDRESS

[Delivered in Baltimore, Md., on April 6, 1918, on the occasion of the first anniversary of America's participation in the European War and the inauguration of the Third Liberty Loan.]

Fellow-citizens: This is the anniversary of our acceptance of Germany's challenge to fight for our right to live and be free, and for the sacred rights of freemen everywhere. The nation is awake. There is no need to call to it. We know what the war must cost, our utmost sacrifice, the lives of our fittest men, and, if need be, all that we possess. The loan we are met to discuss is one of the least parts of what we are called upon to give and to do, though in itself imperative. The people of the whole country are alive to the necessity of it, and are ready to lend to the utmost, even where it involves a sharp skimping and daily sacrifice to lend out of meagre earnings. They will look with reprobation and contempt upon those who can and will not, upon those who demand a higher rate of interest, upon those who think of it as a mere commercial transaction. I have not come, therefore, to urge the loan. I have come only to give you, if I can, a more vivid conception of what it is for.

The reasons for this great war, the reason why it had to come, the need to fight it through, and the issues that hang upon its outcome, are more clearly disclosed now than ever before. It is easy to see just what this particular loan means, because the cause we are fighting for stands more sharply revealed than at any previous crisis of the momentous struggle. The man who knows least can now see plainly how the cause of justice stands, and what the imperishable thing he is asked to invest in. Men in America may be more sure than they ever were before that the cause is their own, and that, if it should be lost, their own great nation's place and mission in the world would be lost with it.

I call you to witness, my fellow-countrymen, that at no stage of this terrible business have I judged the purposes of Germany intemperately. I should be ashamed in the presence of affairs so grave, so fraught with the destinies of mankind throughout all the world, to speak with truculence, to use the weak language of hatred or vindictive purpose. We must judge as we would be judged. I have sought to learn the objects Germany has in this war from the mouths of her own spokesmen, and to deal as frankly with them as I wished them to deal with me. I have laid bare our own ideals, our own purposes, without reserve or doubtful phrase, and have asked them to say as plainly what it is that they seek.

We have ourselves proposed no injustice, no aggression. We are ready, whenever the final reckoning is made, to be just to the German people, deal fairly with the German power, as with all others. There can be no difference between peoples in the final judgment, if it is indeed to be a righteous judgment. To propose anything but justice, even-handed and dispassionate justice, to Germany at any time, whatever the outcome of the war, would be to renounce and dishonor our own cause, for we ask nothing that we are not willing to accord.

It has been with this thought that I have sought to learn from those who spoke for Germany whether it was justice or dominion and the execution of their own will upon the other nations of the world that the German leaders were seeking. They have answered—answered in unmistakable terms. They have avowed that it was not justice, but dominion and the unhindered execution of their own will.

The avowal has not come from Germany's statesmen. It has come from her military leaders, who are her real rulers. Her statesmen have said that they wished peace, and were ready to discuss its terms whenever their opponents were willing to sit down at the conference table with them. Her present Chancellor has said—in indefinite and uncertain terms, indeed, and in phrases that often seem to deny their own meaning, but with as much plainness as he thought prudent—that he believed that peace should be based upon the principles which we had declared would be our own in the final settlement. At Brest-Litovsk her civilian delegates spoke in similar terms; professed their desire to conclude a fair peace and accord to the peoples with whose fortunes they were dealing the right to choose their own allegiances. But action accompanied and followed the profession. Their military masters, the men who act for Germany and exhibit her purpose in execution, proclaimed a very different conclusion. We can not mistake what they have done—in Russia, in Finland, in the Ukraine, in Rumania. The real test of their justice and fair play has come. From this we may judge the rest. They are enjoying in Russia a cheap triumph in which no brave or gallant nation can long take pride. A great people, helpless by their own act, lies for the time at their mercy. Their fair professions are forgotten. They nowhere set up justice, but everywhere impose their power and exploit everything for their own use and aggrandizement, and the peoples of conquered provinces are invited to be free under their dominion!

Are we not justified in believing that they would do the same things at their western front if they were not there face to face with armies whom even their countless divisions cannot overcome? If, when they have felt their check to be final, they should propose favorable and equitable terms with regard to Belgium and France and Italy, could they blame us if we concluded that they did so only to assure themselves of a free hand in Russia and the East?

Their purpose is, undoubtedly, to make all the Slavic peoples, all the free and ambitious nations of the Balkan Peninsula, all the lands that Turkey has dominated and misruled, subject to their will and ambition, and build upon that dominion an empire of force upon which they fancy that they can then erect an empire of gain and commercial supremacy—an empire as hostile to the Americas as to the Europe which it will overawe—an empire which will ultimately master Persia, India, and the peoples of the Far East. In such a program our ideals, the ideals of justice and humanity and liberty, the principle of the free self-determination of nations, upon which all the modern world insists, can play no part. They are rejected for the ideals of power, for the principle that the strong must rule the weak, that trade must follow the flag, whether those to whom it is taken welcome it or not, that the peoples of the world are to be made subject to the patronage and over-lordship of those who have the power to enforce it.

That program once carried out, America and all who care or dare to stand with her must arm and prepare themselves to contest the mastery of the world—a mastery in which the rights of common men, the rights of women and of all who are weak, must for the time being be trodden underfoot and disregarded and the old, age-long struggle for freedom and right begin again at its beginning. Everything that America has lived for and loved and grown great to vindicate and bring to a glorious realization will have fallen in utter ruin and the gates of mercy once more pitilessly shut upon mankind!

The thing is preposterous and impossible; and yet is not that what the whole course and action of the German armies has meant wherever they have moved? I do not wish, even in this moment of utter dis-illusionment, to judge harshly or unrighteously. I judge only what the German arms have accomplished with unpitying thoroughness through-out every fair region they have touched.

What, then, are we to do? For myself, I am ready, ready still, ready even now, to discuss a fair and just and honest peace at any time that it is sincerely proposed—a peace in which the strong and the weak shall fare alike. But the answer, when I proposed such a peace, came from the German commanders in Russia and I cannot mistake the meaning of the answer.

I accept the challenge. I know that you accept it. All the world shall know that you accept it. It shall appear in the utter sacrifice and self-forgetfulness with which we shall give all that we love and all that we have to redeem the world and make it fit for free men like ourselves to live in. This now is the meaning of all that we do. Let everything that we say, my fellow-countrymen, everything that we henceforth plan and accomplish, ring true to this response till the majesty and might of our concerted power shall fill the thought and utterly defeat the force of those who flout and misprize what we honor and hold dear. Germany has once more said that force, and force alone, shall decide whether justice and peace shall reign in the affairs of men, whether right as America conceives it or dominion as she conceives it shall determine the destinies of mankind. There is, therefore, but one response possible from us: Force, force to the utmost, force without stint or limit, the righteous and triumphant force which shall make right the law of the world and cast every selfish dominion down in the dust.

By the President of the United States of America.

A PROCLAMATION

[Establishment of a National War Labor Board.]

Whereas, In January, nineteen hundred and eighteen, the Secretary of Labor, upon the nomination of the President of the American Federation of Labor and the President of the National Industrial Conference Board, appointed a War Labor Conference Board for the purpose of devising for the period of the war a method of labor adjustment which would be acceptable to employers and employees; and

Whereas, Said Board has made a report recommending the creation for the period of the war of a National War Labor Board with the same number of members as, and to be selected by the same agencies that created, the War Labor Conference Board, whose duty it shall be to adjust labor disputes in the manner specified, and in accordance with certain conditions set forth in the said report; and

Whereas, The Secretary of Labor has, in accordance with the recommendation contained in the report of said War Labor Conference Board dated March 29, 1918, appointed as members of the National War Labor Board Hon. William Howard Taft and Hon. Frank P. Walsh, representatives of the General Public of the United States; Messrs. Loyall A. Osborne, L. F. Loree, W. H. Van Dervoort, C. E. Michael and B. L. Worden, representatives of the employers of the United States; and Messrs. Frank J. Hayes, William L. Hutcheson, William H. Johnston, Victor A. Clander and T. A. Rickert, representatives of the employees of the United States:

Now, therefore, I, Woodrow Wilson, President of the United States of America, do hereby approve and affirm the said appointments and make due proclamation thereof and of the following for the information and guidance of all concerned:

The powers, functions, and duties of the National War Labor Board shall be: To settle by mediation and conciliation controversies arising between employers and workers in fields of production necessary for the effective conduct of the war, or in other fields of national activity, delays and obstructions in which might, in the opinion of the National Board, affect detrimentally such production; to provide, by direct appointment, or otherwise, for committees or boards to sit in various parts of the country where controversies arise and secure settlement by local mediation and conciliation; and to summon the parties to controversies for hearing and action by the National Board in event of failure to secure settlement by mediation and conciliation.

The principles to be observed and the methods to be followed by the National Board in exercising such powers and functions and performing such duties shall be those specified in the said report of the War Labor Conference Board dated March 29, 1918, a complete copy of which is hereunto appended.

The National Board shall refuse to take cognizance of a controversy between employer and workers in any field of industrial or other activity where there is by agreement or Federal law a means of settlement which has not been invoked.

And I do hereby urge upon all employers and employees within the United States the necessity of utilizing the means and methods thus provided for the adjustment of all industrial disputes, and request that during the pendency of mediation or arbitration through the said means and methods, there shall be no discontinuance of industrial operations which would result in curtailment of the production of war necessities.

In witness whereof, I have hereunto set my hand and caused the seal of the United States to be affixed.

Done in the District of Columbia, this eighth day of April, in the year of our Lord one thousand nine hundred and eighteen, [SEAL]   and of the independence of the United States the one hundred and forty-second.   WOODROW WILSON.

By the President:

ROBERT LANSING, *Secretary of State.*

EXECUTIVE ORDER

[Revoking power and authority in designated officers under the Trading with the Enemy Act.]

THE WHITE HOUSE, *April 11, 1918.*

By virtue of the power and authority vested in me by "An Act to define, regulate, and punish trading with the enemy and for other purposes," approved October 6, 1917, I hereby make the following orders and rules and regulations:

SECRETARY OF THE TREASURY.

I. I hereby revoke the authority and power vested in the Secretary of the Treasury by Section XI of the Executive Order of October 12, 1917, to issue licenses to send, take or transmit out of the United States any letter or other writing, book, map, plan or other paper, picture, or any telegram, cablegram, or wireless message, or other form of communication intended for or to be delivered, directly or indirectly, to an enemy or ally of enemy, in any way relating to letters patent, or registration of trade-mark, print, label, or copyright, or to any applications therefor; and no such license shall be granted until further order.

FEDERAL TRADE COMMISSION.

II. I hereby revoke the power and authority vested in the Federal Trade Commission by Section XVII of the Executive Order of October 12, 1917, to issue licenses to any citizen of the United States or any corporation organized within the United States, to file or prosecute applications in the country of an enemy or ally of enemy for letters patent or for registration of trade-mark, print, label or copyright, and to pay any fees or agents' fees in connection therewith; or to pay to any enemy or ally of enemy any tax, annuity or fee in relation to patents, trade-marks, prints, labels and copyrights; and no such license shall be granted until further order.

WOODROW WILSON.

By the President of the United States of America.

PROCLAMATIONS

[Possession and control of certain transportation systems.]

Whereas, the Congress of the United States, in the exercise of the constitutional authority vested in them, by joint resolution of the Senate and House of Representatives bearing date April 6, 1917, resolved:

"That the state of war between the United States and the Imperial German Government which has thus been thrust upon the United States is hereby formally declared; and that the President be, and he is hereby, authorized and directed to employ the entire naval and military forces of the United States and the resources of the Government to carry on war against the Imperial German Government; and to bring the conflict to a successful termination all of the resources of the country are hereby pledged by the Congress of the United States."

And by joint resolution bearing date of December 7, 1917, resolved:

"That a state of war is hereby declared to exist between the United States of America and the Imperial and Royal Austro-Hungarian Government; and that the President be, and he is hereby, authorized and directed to employ the entire naval and military forces of the United States and the resources of the Government to carry on war against the Imperial and Royal Austro-Hungarian Government; and to bring the conflict to a successful termination all the resources of the country are hereby pledged by the Congress of the United States."

And, whereas, it is provided by section 1 of the act approved August 29, 1916, entitled "An act making appropriations for the support of the Army for the fiscal year ending June 30, 1917, and for other purposes," as follows:

"The President in time of war is empowered, through the Secretary of War, to take possession and assume control of any system or systems of transportation, or any part thereof, and to utilize the same, to the exclusion, as far as may be necessary, of all other traffic thereon, for the transfer or transportation of troops, war material, and equipment, or for such other purposes connected with the emergency as may be needful or desirable."

And, whereas, it has now become necessary in the national defense to take possession and assume control of certain systems of transportation and to utilize the same, to the exclusion, as far as may be necessary, of other than war traffic thereon, for the transportation of troops, war material, and equipment therefor, and for other needful and desirable purposes connected with the prosecution of the war;

Now, therefore, I, Woodrow Wilson, President of the United States, under and by virtue of the powers vested in me by the foregoing resolutions and statute, and by virtue of all other powers thereto me enabling, do hereby, through Benedict Crowell, Acting Secretary of War, take possession and assume control at 12:01 A. M. on the 13th day of April, 1918, of each and every system of transportation and the appurtenances thereof as follows, to wit: Clyde Steamship Company, a corporation of the State of Maine; Mallory Steamship Company, a corporation of the State of Maine; Merchants & Miners Transportation Company, a corporation of the State of Maryland, and Southern Steamship Company, a corporation of the State of Delaware, consisting of steamships, tugs, lighters, barges, ships, boats, and marine craft of any and every kind or description and all the tackle appurtenances to and appliances thereof, together with all wharves, docks, warehouses and other property of every kind or nature, real or chattel, owned, leased, chartered, controlled or used by said companies or either of them in conducting, or in connection with said transportation systems, to the end that such systems of transportation be utilized for the transfer and transportation of troops, war material, and equipment, to the exclusion so far as may be necessary of all other traffic thereon; and that so far as such exclusive use be not necessary or desirable such systems of transportation be operated and utilized in the performance of such other services as the national interest may require and of the usual and ordinary business and duties of common carriers.

It is hereby directed that the possession, control, operation, and utilization of such transportation systems, hereby by me undertaken, shall be exercised by and through William G. McAdoo, who has been duly appointed and designated Director General of Railroads. Said

Director General may perform the duties imposed upon him, so long and to such extent as he shall determine, through the boards of directors, officers and employees of said systems of transportation. Until and except so far as said Director General shall from time to time by general or special orders otherwise provide, the boards of directors, officers, and employees of said transportation systems shall continue the operation thereof in the usual and ordinary course of the business of common carriers, in the names of their respective companies.

Until and except so far as said Director General shall from time to time otherwise by general or special orders determine, such systems of transportation shall remain subject to all existing statutes of the United States and orders of the Interstate Commerce Commission and to all statutes and orders of regulating commissions of the various States in which said systems or any part thereof may be situated. But any orders, general or special, hereafter made by said Director General shall have paramount authority and be obeyed as such.

The Director General shall, as soon as may be after having assumed such possession and control, enter upon negotiations with the several companies looking to agreements for just and reasonable compensation for the possession, use, and control of their respective properties and fix such just compensation as provided by law.

But nothing herein contained, expressed or implied, or hereafter done or suffered hereunder, shall be deemed in any way to impair the rights of the stockholders, bondholders, creditors, and other persons having interests in said systems of transportation or in the profits thereof to receive just and adequate compensation for the use and control and operation of their property hereby assumed.

That none of said carriers while under Federal control shall, without the prior approval of the President, declare or pay any dividends in excess of its regular rate of dividends during the three years ended June thirtieth, nineteen hundred and seventeen; Provided, however, that such carriers as have paid no regular dividends or no dividends during said period may, with the prior approval of the President, pay dividends at such rate as the President may determine.

Except with the prior assent of said Director General, no attachment by mesne process or on execution shall be levied on or against any of the property used by any of said transportation systems in the conduct of their business as common carriers; but suits may be brought by and against said carriers and judgments rendered as hitherto until and except so far as said Director General may, by general or special orders, otherwise determine.

From and after 12:01 A. M. on said 13th day of April, 1918, all transportation systems included in this order and proclamation shall conclusively be deemed within the possession and control of said Director General without further act or notice.

In witness whereof, I have hereunto set my hand and caused the seal of the United States to be affixed.

Done by the President, through Benedict Crowell, Acting Secretary of War, in the District of Columbia, this 11th day of April, in the year of our Lord one thousand nine hundred and [SEAL] eighteen, and of the independence of the United States the one hundred and forty-second.

WOODROW WILSON.

By the President:

ROBERT LANSING, *Secretary of State.*

BENEDICT CROWELL, *Acting Secretary of War.*

[Liberty Day.]

An enemy who has grossly abused the power of organized government and who seeks to dominate the world by the might of the sword, challenges the rights of America and the liberty and life of all the free nations of the earth. Our brave sons are facing the fire of battle in defense of the honor and rights of America and the liberty of nations. To sustain them and to assist our gallant associates in the war, a generous and patriotic people have been called upon to subscribe to the Third Liberty Loan.

Now, therefore, I, Woodrow Wilson, President of the United States of America, do appoint Friday, the twenty-sixth day of April, one thousand nine hundred and eighteen, as Liberty Day. On the afternoon of that day I request the people of the United States to assemble in their respective communities and liberally pledge anew their financial support to sustain the Nation's cause. Patriotic demonstrations should be held in every city, town and hamlet throughout the land under the general direction of the Secretary of the Treasury and the immediate direction of the Liberty Loan Committees organized by the Federal Reserve Banks. Let the Nation's response to the Third Liberty Loan express in unmistakable terms the determination of America to fight for peace, the permanent peace of justice.

For the purpose of participating in Liberty Day celebrations, all employees of the Federal Government throughout the country whose services can be spared, may be excused at twelve o'clock noon, Friday, the twenty-sixth of April.

In witness whereof, I have hereunto set my hand and caused the seal of the United States to be affixed.

Done in the District of Columbia, this eighteenth day of April, in the year of our Lord one thousand nine hundred and eighteen, [SEAL] and of the independence of the United States of America the one hundred and forty-second.

WOODROW WILSON.

By the President:

ROBERT LANSING, *Secretary of State.*

[Extending regulations prescribing the conduct of alien enemies to women.]

Whereas, by Act of Congress, approved the sixteenth day of April, one thousand nine hundred and eighteen, entitled "An Act to amend section four thousand and sixty-seven of the Revised Statutes by extending its scope to include women," the said section four thousand and sixty-seven of the Revised Statutes is amended to read as follows:

Whenever there is a declared war between the United States and any foreign nation or government, or any invasion or predatory incursion is perpetrated, attempted, or threatened against the territory of the United States by any foreign nation or government, and the President makes public proclamation of the event, all natives, citizens, denizens, or subjects of the hostile nation or government, being of the age of fourteen years and upwards, who shall be within the United States, and not actually naturalized, shall be liable to be apprehended, restrained, secured, and removed, as alien enemies. The President is authorized, in any such event, by his proclamation thereof, or other public act, to direct the conduct to be observed, on the part of the United States, toward the aliens who become so liable; the manner and degree of the restraint to which they shall be subject, and in what cases, and upon what security their residence shall be permitted, and to provide for the removal of those who, not being permitted to reside within the United States, refuse or neglect to depart therefrom; and to establish any other regulations which are found necessary in the premises and for the public safety;

Whereas, by sections four thousand and sixty-eight, four thousand and sixty-nine, and four thousand and seventy, of the Revised Statutes, further provision is made relative to alien enemies;

And, whereas, a state of war has heretofore been declared and proclaimed to exist between the United States and the Imperial German Government and between the United States and the Imperial and Royal Austro-Hungarian Government;

Now, therefore, I, Woodrow Wilson, President of the United States of America, acting under and by virtue of the authority vested in me by the Constitution of the United States and the said sections of the Revised Statutes, do hereby further proclaim and direct that the conduct to be observed on the part of the United States towards all natives, citizens, denizens, or subjects of Germany or Austria-Hungary of the age of fourteen years and upwards, who shall be within the United States and not actually naturalized, shall be as follows:

All such natives, citizens, denizens or subjects of Germany or Austria-Hungary are enjoined to preserve the peace towards the United States and to refrain from crime against the public safety, and from violating the laws of the United States and of the States and Territories thereof, and to refrain from actual hostility or giving information, aid or comfort to the enemies of the United States, and to comply strictly with the regulations which are hereby or which have been or may be from time to time promulgated by the President; and so long as they shall conduct themselves in accordance with law, they shall be undisturbed in the peaceful pursuit of their lives and occupations and be accorded the consideration due to all peaceful and law-abiding persons, except so far as restrictions may be necessary for their own protection and for the safety of the United States; and towards such of said persons as conduct themselves in accordance with law, all citizens of the United States are enjoined to preserve the peace and to treat them with all such friendliness as may be compatible with loyalty and allegiance to the United States.

And all of such natives, citizens, denizens or subjects of Germany or Austria-Hungary who fail to conduct themselves as so enjoined, in addition to all other penalties prescribed by law, shall be liable to restraint, or to give security, or to remove and depart from the United States in the manner prescribed by sections four thousand and sixty-nine and four thousand and seventy of the Revised Statutes, and as prescribed in the regulations duly promulgated by the President;

And pursuant to the authority vested in me, I hereby declare and proclaim, as necessary in the premises and for the public safety, that Regulations 1 to 12, inclusive, in the Proclamation issued by me under date of April 6th, 1917, and Regulations 13 to 20, inclusive, in the Proclamation issued by me under date of November 16th, 1917, shall be and they hereby are, extended to and declared applicable to all natives, citizens, denizens or subjects of Germany, being females of the age of fourteen years and upwards, who shall be within the United States and not actually naturalized; provided, that this extension of Regulation 4 of the Proclamation issued by me under date of April 6th, 1917, shall not become effective until such time as may be fixed and declared by the Attorney General of the United States.

And pursuant to the authority vested in me, I hereby declare and proclaim, as necessary in the premises and for the public safety, that

Regulations 1 to 3, inclusive, in the Proclamation issued by me under date of December 11th, 1917, shall be, and they are hereby, extended to and declared applicable to all natives, citizens, denizens or subjects of Austria-Hungary, being females of the age of fourteen years and upwards, who shall be within the United States and not actually naturalized.

This Proclamation and the Regulations herein contained shall extend and apply to all land and water, continental or insular, in any way within the jurisdiction of the United States.

In witness whereof, I have hereunto set my hand and caused the seal of the United States to be affixed.

Done in the District of Columbia, this nineteenth day of April, in the year of our Lord one thousand nine hundred and eighteen, [SEAL] and of the independence of the United States the one hundred and forty-second.

WOODROW WILSON.

By the President:

FRANK L. POLK, *Acting Secretary of State.*

LETTER

[To Senator Overman, concerning the bill to remove sedition and espionage cases to military courts.]

THE WHITE HOUSE, *April 20, 1918.*

My dear Senator:

Thank you for your letter of yesterday. I am heartily obliged to you for consulting me about the Court-martial bill, as perhaps I may call it for short. I am wholly and unalterably opposed to such legislation, and very much value the opportunity you give me to say so. I think it is not only unconstitutional, but that in character it would put us upon the level of the very people we are fighting and affecting to despise. It would be altogether inconsistent with the spirit and practice of America, and, in view of the recent legislation, the Espionage bill, the Sabotage bill, and the Woman Spy bill, I think it is unnecessary and uncalled for.

I take the liberty, my dear Senator, of expressing myself in this emphatic way, because my feeling is very deep about the matter, as I gather your own is.

It is admirable the way you have been handling these important bills, and I thank you with all my heart for standing by the bill which bears your own name, without any compromise of any kind.

It gives me the greatest satisfaction to tell you how much I have appreciated what you have been doing.

Cordially and sincerely yours,
WOODROW WILSON.

Hon. Lee S. Overman,
United States Senate.

PROCLAMATION

[Red Cross Week.]

Inasmuch as the War Fund of 1917, so generously contributed by the American people to the American Red Cross for the administration of relief at home and abroad, has been practically exhausted by appropriations for the welfare of the men in our military and naval forces, and for those dependent upon them, and for the yet more urgent necessities of our Allies, military and civilian, who have long borne the brunt of war;

And, inasmuch as the American Red Cross has been recognized by law and international convention as the public instrumentality for war relief;

And, inasmuch as the year of our own participation in the war has brought unprecedented demands upon the patriotism and liberality of our people, and made evident the necessity of concentrating the work of relief in one main organization which can respond effectively and universally to the needs of humanity under stress of war;

And, inasmuch as the duration of the war and the closer and closer cooperation of the American Red Cross with our own Army and Navy, with the governments of our Allies, and with foreign relief organizations, have resulted in the discovery of new opportunities of helpfulness under conditions which translate opportunity into duty;

And, inasmuch as the American Red Cross War Council and its Commissioners in Europe have faithfully and economically administered the people's trust;

Now, Therefore, by virtue of my authority as President of the United States and President of the American Red Cross, I, Woodrow Wilson, do hereby proclaim the week beginning May 20, 1918, as "Red Cross Week," during which the people of the United States will be called upon again to give generously to the continuation of the important work of relieving distress, restoring the waste of war, and assisting in maintaining the morale of our own troops and the troops and people of our Allies by this manifestation of effort and sacrifice on the part of those, who, though not privileged to bear arms, are of one spirit, purpose, and determination with our warriors.

In Witness Whereof, I have hereunto set my hand and caused the seal of the United States to be affixed.

Done in the District of Columbia, this 4th day of May, in the year of our Lord One Thousand Nine Hundred and Eighteen, and [SEAL.] of the Independence of the United States of America, the One Hundred and Forty-second.

WOODROW WILSON.

By the President:

WILLIAM PHILLIPS,
Acting Secretary of State.

BY THE PRESIDENT OF THE UNITED STATES.

A PROCLAMATION

[Humiliation, Prayer and Fasting.]

Whereas the Congress of the United States, on the second day of April last, passed the following resolution:

"Resolved by the Senate (the House of Representatives concurring), That, it being a duty peculiarly incumbent in a time of war humbly and devoutly to acknowledge our dependence on Almighty God and to implore His aid and protection, the President of the United States be, and he is hereby, respectfully requested to recommend a day of public humiliation, prayer, and fasting, to be observed by the people of the United States with religious solemnity and the offering of fervent supplications to Almighty God for the safety and welfare of our cause, His blessings on our arms, and a speedy restoration of an honorable and lasting peace to the nations of the earth;

And Whereas it has always been the reverent habit of the people of the United States to turn in humble appeal to Almighty God for His guidance in the affairs of their common life.

Now, therefore, I, Woodrow Wilson, President of the United States of America, do hereby proclaim Thursday, the thirtieth day of May, a day already freighted with sacred and stimulating memories, a day of public humiliation, prayer, and fasting, and do exhort my fellow-citizens of all faiths and creeds to assemble on that day in their several places of worship and there, as well as in their homes, to pray Almighty God that He may forgive our sins and shortcomings as a people and purify our hearts to see and love the truth, to accept and defend all things that are just and right, and to purpose only those righteous acts and judgments which are in conformity with His will; beseeching Him that He will give victory to our armies as they fight for freedom, wisdom to those who take counsel on our behalf in these days of dark struggle and perplexity, and steadfastness to our people to make sacrifice to the utmost in support of what is just and true, bringing us at last the peace in which men's hearts can be at rest because it is founded upon mercy, justice and good will.

In Witness Whereof, I have hereunto set my hand and caused the seal of the United States to be affixed.

Done in the District of Columbia this eleventh day of May, in the year of our Lord Nineteen hundred and eighteen and of the [SEAL.]   independence of the United States the one hundred and forty-second.

WOODROW WILSON.

By the President:

ROBERT LANSING, *Secretary of State.*

EXECUTIVE ORDER

[National Research Council.]

THE WHITE HOUSE, *May 11, 1918.*

The National Research Council was organized in 1916 at the request of the President by the National Academy of Sciences, under its congressional charter, as a measure of national preparedness. The work accomplished by the Council in organizing research and in securing cooperation of military and civilian agencies in the solution of military problems demonstrates its capacity for larger service. The National Academy of Sciences is therefore requested to perpetuate the National Research Council, the duties of which shall be as follows:

1. In general, to stimulate research in the mathematical, physical and biological sciences, and in the application of these sciences to engineering, agriculture, medicine and other useful arts, with the object of increasing knowledge, of strengthening the national defense, and of contributing in other ways to the public welfare.

2. To survey the larger possibilities of science, to formulate comprehensive projects of research, and to develop effective means of utilizing the scientific and technical resources of the country for dealing with these projects.

3. To promote cooperation in research, at home and abroad, in order to secure concentration of effort, minimize duplication, and stimulate progress; but in all cooperative undertakings to give encouragement to individual initiative, as fundamentally important to the advancement of science.

4. To serve as a means of bringing American and foreign investi-

gators into active cooperation with the scientific and technical services of the War and Navy Departments and with those of the civil branches of the Government.

5. To direct the attention of scientific and technical investigators to the present importance of military and industrial problems in connection with the war, and to aid in the solution of these problems by organizing specific researches.

6. To gather and collate scientific and technical information, at home and abroad, in cooperation with governmental and other agencies, and to render such information available to duly accredited persons.

Effective prosecution of the Council's work requires the cordial collaboration of the scientific and technical branches of the Government, both military and civil. To this end representatives of the Government, upon the nomination of the National Academy of Sciences, will be designated by the President as members of the Council, as heretofore, and the heads of the departments immediately concerned will continue to cooperate in every way that may be required.

WOODROW WILSON.

By the President of the United States of America.

PROCLAMATIONS

[Licensing Packers of Canned Tuna and Others.]

Whereas, Under and by virtue of an Act of Congress entitled "An Act to provide further for the national security and defense by encouraging the production, conserving the supply, and controlling the distribution of food products and fuel," approved by the President on the 10th day of August, 1917, it is provided among other things as follows:

[Here follow the two paragraphs quoted on pages 8322 and 8323.]

And, Whereas, It is essential, in order to carry into effect the provisions of the said Act, that the powers conferred upon the President by said Act be at this time exercised, to the extent hereinafter set forth.

Now, Therefore, I, Woodrow Wilson, President of the United States of America, by virtue of the powers conferred upon me by said Act of Congress, hereby find and determine and by this proclamation do announce that it is essential, in order to carry into effect the purposes of said Act, to license the importation, manufacture, storage and distribution of necessaries, to the extent hereinafter specified.

All persons, firms, corporations and associations engaged in business as:

(1) Packers of canned tuna.

(2) Packers of mild cured, hard cured, salted, dried, smoked, pickled or otherwise preserved salmon.

(3) Operators of poultry and egg packing plants not already licensed by the United States Food Administration.

(4) Ginners, buyers, agents, dealers or other handlers of cotton seed not already licensed by the United States Food Administration who handle yearly between September 1 and August 31 more than twenty (20) tons of cotton seed.

(5) Importers, manufacturers or distributors of cottonseed hulls, and owners of elevators, warehouses or other places for the storage of cottonseed hulls.

(6) Manufacturers of fermented beverages containing less than one-half of one per cent of alcohol.

Excepting, however,

(1) Retailers whose gross sales of food commodities do not exceed One Hundred Thousand Dollars ($100,000) per annum;

(2) Common carriers as to operations necessary to the business of common carriage;

(3) Farmers, gardeners, co-operative associations of farmers or gardeners, including live stock farmers, and other persons with respect to the products of any farm, garden or other land owned, leased or cultivated by them;

Are hereby required to secure on or before June 1, 1918, license, which license will be issued under such rules and regulations governing the conduct of the business as may be prescribed.

Application for license must be made to the United States Food Administration, Washington, D. C., License Division, on forms prepared by it for that purpose, which may be secured on request.

Any person, firm, corporation or association who shall carry on any business hereinbefore specified after June 1, 1918 without first securing such license, will be liable to the penalty prescribed by said Act of Congress.

In Witness Whereof, I have hereunto set my hand and caused the seal of the United States to be affixed.

Done in the District of Columbia, this 14th day of May in the year of Our Lord One Thousand Nine Hundred and Eighteen, [SEAL.]   and of the Independence of the United States of America, the One Hundred and Forty-second.

WOODROW WILSON.

By the President:

ROBERT LANSING,
    Secretary of State.

[License of Farm Equipment Industry.]

Whereas under and by virtue of an Act of Congress entitled "An Act to Provide further for the national security and defense by encouraging the production, conserving the supply, and controlling the distribution of food products and fuel," approved by the President on the 10th day of August, 1917, it is provided among other things as follows:

[Here follow the two paragraphs quoted on pages 8322 and 8323.]

And whereas it is essential, in order to carry into effect the purposes of said Act and in order to secure an adequate supply and equitable distribution and to facilitate the movement of certain necessaries hereafter in this proclamation specified, that the license powers conferred upon the President by said Act be at this time exercised to the extent hereinafter set forth;

Now, therefore, I, Woodrow Wilson, President of the United States of America, by virtue of the powers conferred on me by said Act of Congress, hereby find and determine, and by this proclamation do announce, that it is essential, in order to carry into effect the purposes of said Act, to license the importation, manufacture, storage, and distribution of certain necessaries, hereinafter called farm equipment, including attachments and repair parts thereof, required for farm use in the actual production of foods and feeds, as follows: binders, boilers, brooders, bunchers, carriers, carts, cleaners, covers, crushers, cultivators, diggers, distributors, drills, elevators, evaporators, fencing, forges, forks, fountains, gates, graders, grinders, grind-stones, harrows, harvesters, headers, hillers, hitches, hullers, huskers, incubators, jacks, listers, loaders, markers, milkers, mills, mowers, pens, pickers, planters, plows, powers, presses, pullers, pulleys, pulverizers, pumps, racks, rakes, rollers, scales, seeders, separators, shellers, shredders, silos, sleds, slings, sorters, sowers, sprayers, spreaders, stalls, stanchions, tanks, tedders, testers, threshers, towers, tractors, trailers, troughs, trucks, wagons, weeders, weighers, windmills and all other tools, utensils, implements, and machinery, required for farm use in the actual production of foods and feeds.

All individuals, partnerships, associations, and corporations engaged in the business of importing, manufacturing, storing, or distributing the said farm equipment (except those specifically exempted by said Act of Congress), are hereby required to secure licenses on or before June 20, 1918, which will be issued under such rules and regulations governing the conduct of the business as may be prescribed under said Act.

The Secretary of Agriculture shall carry into effect the provisions of said Act, and shall supervise and direct the exercise of the powers and authority thereby given to the President, as far as the same apply to the said farm equipment, and to any and all practices, procedure, and regulations applicable thereto, authorized or required under the provisions of said Act, and in this behalf he shall do and perform such acts and things as may be authorized or required of him from time to time by direction of the President under such rules and regulations as may be prescribed by the President from time to time. All departments and agencies of the Government are hereby directed to cooperate with the Secretary of Agriculture in the performance of the duties hereinbefore set forth.

Applications for licenses must be made to the Law Department, License Division, United States Food Administration, Washington, D. C., upon forms prepared for that purpose.

Any individual, partnership, association, or corporation, other than as hereinbefore excepted, who shall engage in or carry on the business of importing, manufacturing, storing, or distributing such farm equipment, after the date aforesaid, without first securing such license, will be liable to the penalty prescribed by said Act of Congress.

In Testimony Whereof, I have hereunto set my hand and caused the seal of the United States to be affixed.

Done in the District of Columbia this 14th day of May, in the year of our Lord one thousand nine hundred and eighteen, and of [SEAL.] the independence of the United States of America the one hundred and forty-second.

WOODROW WILSON.

By the President:
  ROBERT LANSING,
    Secretary of State.

ADDRESS

[Delivered in New York City on the Opening of the Second Red Cross Drive for $100,000,000, May 18, 1918.]

Mr. Chairman and Fellow-Countrymen:

I should be very sorry to think that Mr. Davidson in any degree curtailed his exceedingly interesting speech for fear that he was postponing mine, because I am sure you listened with the same intent and intimate interest with which I listened to the extraordinarily vivid account he gave of things which he had realized because he had come in contact with them on the other side of the waters. We compass them with our imagination; he compassed them in his personal experience, and I am not come here tonight to review for you the work of the Red Cross. I am not competent to do so, because I have not had the time nor the opportunity to follow it in detail. I have come simply to say a few words to you as to what it all seems to me to mean, and it means a good deal.

There are two duties with which we are face to face. The first duty is to win the war. And the second duty, that goes hand in hand with it, is to win it greatly and worthily, showing the real quality of our power not only, but the real quality of our purpose and of ourselves. Of course, the first duty, the duty that we must keep in the foreground of our thought, until it is accomplished, is to win the war.

I have heard men recently say that we must get five million men ready. Why limit it to five million? I have asked the Congress of the United States to name no limit because the Congress intends, I am sure, as we all intend, that every ship which can carry men or supplies shall go laden upon every voyage with every man and every supply she can carry.

And we are not to be diverted from the grim purpose of winning the war by any insincere approaches on the subject of peace. I can say with a clear conscience that I have tested those intimations, and have found them insincere. I now recognize them for what they are— an opportunity to have a free hand, particularly in the East, to carry out purposes of conquest and exploitation. Every proposal with regard to accommodation in the West involves a reservation with regard to the East. Now, so far as I am concerned, I intend to stand by Russia as well as by France. The helpless and the friendless are the very ones that need friends and succor, and if any man in Germany thinks we are going to sacrifice anybody for our own sake, I tell him now he is mistaken. For the glory of this war, my fellow-citizens, so far as we are concerned, is that it is, perhaps for the first time in history, an unselfish war. I could not be proud to fight for a selfish purpose, but I can be proud to fight for mankind.

If they wish peace, let them come forward through accredited representatives and lay their terms on the table. We have laid ours, and they know what they are.

But behind all this grim purpose, my friends, lies the opportunity to demonstrate not only force, which will be demonstrated to the utmost, but the opportunity to demonstrate character, and it is that opportunity which we have most conspicuously in the work of the Red Cross. Not that our men in arms do not represent our character, for they do, and it is a character which those who see and realize appreciate and admire; but their duty is the duty of force. The duty of the Red Cross is the duty of mercy and succor and friendship.

Have you formed a picture in your imaginations of what this war is doing for us and for the world? In my own mind, I am convinced that not a hundred years of peace could have knitted this nation together as this single year of war has knitted it together; and better even than that, if possible, it is knitting the world together. Look at the picture. In the centre of the scene, four nations engaged against the world, and at every point of vantage, showing that they are seeking selfish aggrandisement; and against them twenty-three Governments representing the greater part of the population of the world, drawn together in a new sense of community of interest, a new sense of community of purpose, a new sense of community of life.

The Secretary of War told me an interesting incident the other day. He said that when he was in Italy a member of the Italian Government was explaining to him the many reasons why Italy felt near to the United States. He said, "If you want to try an interesting experiment, go up to any one of these troop trains and ask in English how many of them have been in America and see what happens."

He tried the experiment. He went up to a troop train and he said, "How many of you boys have been in America?" and he said it seemed to him as if half of them sprang up: "Me from San Francisco. Me from New York;" all over. There was part of the heart of America in the Italian Army. People that had been knitted to us by association, who knew us, who had lived among us, who had worked shoulder to shoulder with us, and now friends of America, were fighting for their native Italy.

Friendship is the only cement that will ever hold the world together. And this intimate contact of the Red Cross with the peoples who are suffering the terrors and the deprivations of this war is going to be one of the greatest instrumentalities of friendship that the world ever knew. And the centre of the heart of it all, if we sustain it properly, will be this land that we so dearly love.

My friends, a great day of duty has come, and duty finds a man's soul as no kind of work can ever find it. May I say this? The duty that faces us all now is to serve one another, and no man can afford to make a fortune out of this war. There are men among us who have forgotten that, if they ever saw it. Some of you are old enough—I am old enough—to remember men who made fortunes out of the Civil War, and you know how they were regarded by their fellow-citizens. That was a war to save one country—this is a war to save the world. And your relation to the Red Cross is one of the relations which will relieve you of the stigma.

You can't give anything to the Government of the United States; it won't accept it. There is a law of Congress against accepting even services without pay. The only thing that the Government will accept is a loan, and duties performed; but it is a great deal better to give than to lend or to pay, and your great channel for giving is the American Red Cross.

Down in your hearts you can't take very much satisfaction in the last analysis in lending money to the Government of the United States, because the interest which you draw will burn your pockets. It is a commercial transaction, and some men have even dared to cavil at the rate of interest, not knowing the incidental commentary that constitutes upon their attitude. But when you give, something of your heart, something of your soul, something of yourself goes with the gift, particularly when it is given in such form that it can never come back by way of direct benefit to yourself. You know there is the old cynical definition of gratitude as "the lively expectation of favors to come." Well, there is no expectation of favors to come in this kind of giving. These things are bestowed in order that the world may be a fitter place to live in, that men may be succored, that homes may be restored, that suffering may be relieved, that the face of the earth may have the blight of destruction taken away from it, and that wherever force goes there shall go mercy and helpfulness. And when you give, give absolutely all that you can spare, and don't constitute yourself liberal in the giving. If you give with self-adulation, you are not giving at all— you are giving to your own vanity; but if you give until it hurts, then your heart-blood goes with it.

And think what we have here! We call it the American Red Cross, but it is merely a branch of a great international organization, which is recognized not only by the statutes of each of the civilized governments of the world, but is recognized by international agreement and treaty, as the recognized and accepted instrumentality of mercy and succor. And one of the deepest stains upon the reputation of the German Army is that it has not respected the Red Cross. That goes to the root of the matter. They have not respected the instrumentality they themselves participated in setting up as the thing which no man was to touch because it was the expression of common humanity.

We are members, by being members of the American Red Cross, of a great fraternity and fellowship which extends all over the world, and this cross which these ladies bore here today is an emblem of Christianity itself. It fills my imagination, ladies and gentlemen, to think of the women all over this country who are busy tonight and are busy every night and every day doing the work of the Red Cross, busy with a great eagerness to find out the most serviceable thing to do, busy with a forgetfulness of the old frivolities of their social relationships, ready to curtail the duties of the household in order that they may contribute to this common work that all their hearts are engaged in, and in doing which their hearts become acquainted with each other. When you think of this, you realize how the people of the United States are being drawn together into a great intimate family whose heart is being used for the service of the soldiers not only, but for the service of civilians, where they suffer and are lost in a maze of distresses and distractions. And you have then this noble picture of justice and mercy as the two servants of liberty. For only where men are free do they think the thoughts of sympathy; only where they are free are they mutually helpful; only where they are free do they realize their dependence upon one another and their comradeship in a common interest and common necessity.

I heard a story told the other day that was ridiculous, but it is worth repeating because it contains the germ of truth. An Indian was enlisted in the Army. He returned to the reservation on a furlough. He was asked what he thought of it. He said, "Not much good; too much salute, not much shoot." Then he was asked, "Are you going back?" "Yes." "Well, do you know what you are fighting for?" "Yes, me know; fight to make whole damn world Democratic Party." He had evidently misunderstood some innocent sentence of my own.

But, after all, although there is no party purpose in it, he got it right as far as the word "Party"—to make the whole world democratic in the sense of community of interest and of purpose; and if you ladies and gentlemen could read some of the touching dispatches which come through official channels (for even through those channels there come voices of humanity which are infinitely pathetic), if you could catch some of the voices that speak the utter longing of oppressed and helpless peoples all over the world, to hear something like the Battle Hymn of the Republic, to hear the feet of the great hosts of liberty going to set them free, to set their minds free, set their lives free, set their children free, you would know what comes into the heart of those who are trying to contribute all the brains and power they have to this great enterprise of liberty.

I summon you to the comradeship. I summon you in this next week to say how much and how sincerely and how unanimously you sustain the heart of the world.

ADDRESS TO CONGRESS

[May 27, 1918, on the need for increased taxation for war purposes.]

Gentlemen of the Congress:

It is with unaffected reluctance that I come to ask you to prolong your session long enough to provide more adequate resources for the Treasury for the conduct of the war. I have reason to appreciate as fully as you do how arduous the session has been. Your labors have been severe and protracted. You have passed a long series of measures which required the debate of many doubtful questions of judgment and many exceedingly difficult questions of principle as well as of practice. The summer is upon us, in which labor and counsel are twice arduous, and are constantly apt to be impaired by lassitude and fatigue. The elections are at hand, and we ought, as soon as possible, to go and render an intimate account of our trusteeship to the people who delegated us to act for them in the weighty and anxious matters that crowd upon us in these days of critical choice and action. But we dare not go to the elections until we have done our duty to the full. These are days when duty stands stark and naked, and even with closed eyes we know it is there. Excuses are unavailing. We have either done our duty or we have not. The fact will be as gross and plain as the duty itself. In such a case lassitude and fatigue seem negligible enough. The facts are tonic and suffice to freshen the labor.

And the facts are these. Additional revenues must manifestly be provided for. It would be a most unsound policy to raise too large a proportion of them by loan, and it is evident that the four billions now provided for by taxation will not of themselves sustain the greatly enlarged budget to which we must immediately look forward. We cannot in fairness wait until the end of the fiscal year is at hand to apprise our people of the taxes they must pay on their earnings of the present calendar year, whose accountings and expenditures will then be closed. We cannot get increased taxes unless the country knows what they are to be and practises the necessary economy to make them available. Definiteness, early definiteness, as to what its tasks are to be is absolutely necessary for the successful administration of the Treasury. It cannot frame fair and workable regulations in haste, and it must frame its regulations in haste if it is not to know its exact task until the very eve of its performance. The present tax laws are marred, moreover, by inequities which ought to be remedied. Indisputable facts, every one; and we cannot alter or blink them. To state them is argument enough.

And yet, perhaps, you will permit me to dwell for a moment upon the situation they disclose. Enormous loans freely spent in the stimulation of industry of almost every sort produce inflations and extravagances which presently make the whole economic structure questionable and insecure, and the very basis of credit is cut away. Only fair, equitably distributed taxation of the widest incidence and drawn chiefly from the sources which would be likely to demoralize credit by their very abundance can prevent inflation and keep our industrial system free of speculation and waste. We shall naturally turn, therefore, I suppose, to war profits and incomes and luxuries for the additional taxes. But the war profits and incomes upon which the increased taxes will be levied will be the profits and incomes of the calendar year 1918. It would be manifestly unfair to wait until the early months of 1919 to say what they are to be. It might be difficult, I should imagine, to run the mill with water that had already gone over the wheel.

Moreover, taxes of that sort will not be paid until the June of next year, and the Treasury must anticipate them. It must use the money they are to produce before it is due. It must sell short-time certificates of indebtedness. In the autumn a much larger sale of long-time bonds must be effected than has yet been attempted. What are the bankers to think of the certificates if they do not certainly know where the money is to come from which is to take them up? And how are investors to approach the purchase of bonds with any sort of confidence or knowledge of their own affairs if they do not know what taxes they are to pay and what economies and adjustments of their business they must effect? I cannot assure the country of a successful Administration of the Treasury in 1918 if the question of further taxation is to be left undecided until 1919.

The consideration that dominates every other now, and makes every other seem trivial and negligible, is the winning of the war. We are not only in the midst of the war, we are at the very peak and crisis of it. Hundreds and thousands of our men, carrying our hearts with them and our fortunes, are in the field, and ships are crowding faster and faster to the ports of France and England with regiment after regiment, thousand after thousand, to join them until the enemy shall be beaten and brought to reckoning with mankind. There can be no pause or intermission. The great enterprise must, on the contrary, be pushed with greater and greater energy. The volume of our might must steadily and rapidly be augmented until there can be no question of resisting it. If that is to be accomplished, gentlemen, money must sustain it to the utmost. Our financial program must no more be left in doubt or suffered to lag than our ordnance program or our ship program or our munitions program, or our program for making millions of men ready. These others are not programs, indeed, but mere plans upon paper, unless there is to be an unquestionable supply of money.

That is the situation, and it is the situation which creates the duty; no choice or preference of ours. There is only one way to meet that duty. We must meet it without selfishness or fear of consequences. Politics is adjourned. The elections will go to those who think least of it; to those who go to the constituencies without explanations or excuses, with a plain record of duty faithfully and disinterestedly performed. I, for one, am always confident that the people of this country will give a just verdict upon the service of the men who act for them when the facts are such that no man can disguise or conceal them. There is no danger of deceit now. An intense and pitiless light beats upon every man and every action in this tragic blot of war that is now upon the State. If lobbyists hurry to Washington to attempt to turn what you do in the matter of taxation to their protection or advantage, the light will beat also upon them. There is abundant fuel for the light in the records of the Treasury with regard to profits of every sort. The profiteering that cannot be got at by the restraints of conscience and love of country can be got at by taxation. There is such profiteering now, and the information with regard to it is available and indisputable.

I am advising you to act upon this matter of taxation now, gentlemen, not because I do not know that you can see and interpret the facts and the duty they impose just as well and with as clear a perception of the obligations involved as I can, but because there is a certain solemn satisfaction in sharing with you the responsibilities of such a time. The world never stood in such case before. Men never before had so clear or so moving a vision of duty. I know that you will begrudge the work to be done here by us no more than the men begrudge us theirs who lie in the trenches and sally forth to their death. There is a stimulating comradeship knitting us all together. And this task to which I invite your immediate consideration will be performed under favorable influences if we will look to what the country is thinking and expecting and care nothing at all for what is being said and believed in the lobbies of Washington hotels, where the atmosphere seems to make it possible to believe what is believed nowhere else.

Have you not felt the spirit of the nation rise and its thought become a single and common thought since these eventful days came in which we have been sending our boys to the other side? I think you must read that thought, as I do, to mean this, that the people of this country are not only united in the resolute purpose to win this war, but are ready and willing to bear any burden and undergo any sacrifice that it may be necessary for them to bear in order to win it. We need not be afraid to tax them, if we lay taxes justly. They know that the war must be paid for and that it is they who must pay for it, and if the burden is justly distributed and the sacrifice made a common sacrifice, from which none escapes who can bear it at all, they will carry it cheerfully and with a sort of solemn pride. I have always been proud to be an American, and was never more proud than now, when all that we have said and all that we have foreseen about our people is coming true. The great days have come when the only thing that they ask for or admire is duty, greatly and adequately done; when their only wish for America is that she may share the freedom she enjoys; when a great, compelling sympathy wells up in their hearts for men everywhere who suffer and are oppressed, and when they see at last the high uses for which their wealth has been piled up and their mighty power accumulated, and counting neither blood nor treasure, now that their final day of opportunity has come, rejoice to spend and to be spent through a long night of suffering and terror, in order that they and men everywhere may see the dawn of a day of righteousness and justice and peace. Shall we grow weary when they bid us act?

The President then spoke extemporaneously:

May I add this word, gentlemen? Just as I was leaving the White House I was told that the expected drive on the West front had apparently been begun. You can realize how that solemnized my feeling as I came to you and how it seemed to strengthen the purpose which I have tried to express in these lines.

I have admired the work of this session. The way in which the two houses of Congress have coöperated with the Executive has been generous and admirable, and it is not in any spirit of suggesting duty neglected, but only to remind you of the common cause and the common obligations that I have ventured to come to you today.

By the President of the United States of America.

PROCLAMATIONS

[Drafting of certain Hawaiian Regiments into the Military Service of the United States.]

Whereas, by section one hundred and eleven of an Act of Congress entitled "An Act for making further and more effectual provision for the national defense, and for other purposes," approved by the President on the third day of June, nineteen hundred and seventeen, it is provided that when Congress shall have authorized the use of the armed land forces of the United States, for any purpose requiring the use of troops in excess of those of the Regular Army, the President may draft into the military service of the United States, to serve therein for the period of the war unless sooner discharged, any or all members of the National Guard; and

Whereas, by an Act of Congress entitled "An Act to authorize the President to increase temporarily the military establishment of the United States," approved by the President on the eighteenth day of May, nineteen hundred and seventeen, it is provided "that in view of the existing emergency, which demands the raising of troops in addition to those now available, the President be, and he is hereby, authorized * * * to draft into the military service of the United States, organize, and officer, in accordance with the provisions of section one hundred and eleven of said national defense act * * * any or all members of the National Guard and of the National Guard Reserves, and said members so drafted into the military service of the United States shall serve therein for the period of the existing emergency, unless sooner discharged";

Now, therefore, I, Woodrow Wilson, President of the United States of America, by virtue of the powers conferred upon me by the said Acts of Congress, do hereby draft into the military service of the United States, to serve therein for the period of the existing emergency unless sooner discharged, as of and from the first day of June, nineteen hundred and eighteen, all members of the First and Second Regiments of Infantry of the National Guard of the Territory of Hawaii and all members of the medical personnel of said National Guard lawfully attached to said regiments.

All persons hereby drafted shall, on and from the first day of June, nineteen hundred and eighteen, stand discharged from the militia, and, in accordance with the provisions of said Act of May eighteenth, nineteen hundred and seventeen, shall on and from said date be subject to the laws and regulations governing the Regular Army, except as to promotions, so far as such laws and regulations are applicable to persons whose permanent retention in the military service on the active or retired list is not contemplated by existing law.

The members of each company, battalion and regiment, and of said medical personnel attached thereto, hereby drafted into the military service of the United States shall be embodied in organizations corresponding to those of the Regular Army. The officers of said organizations and staff department who are drafted and whose offices are provided for in like organizations of the Regular Army are hereby appointed officers in the Army of the United States in the arm or department and in the grades in which they now hold commissions as officers of said National Guard, such appointments to be effective, subject to acceptance, on and from the first day of June, nineteen hundred and eighteen, and each of them, subject to such acceptance, is hereby assigned as of said date to the organization in the Army of the United States composed of those who were members of the National Guard of the Territory of Hawaii. The noncommissioned officers of said organizations the members of which are hereby drafted, and all noncommissioned officers of the medical personnel of said National Guard who are hereby drafted, are hereby appointed noncommissioned officers in their present grade in the organizations of the Army composed of said members, or in the corresponding staff department thereof, and shall in each case have the same relative rank as heretofore; and all other enlisted men in said organizations are hereby confirmed in the Army of the United States in the grades and ratings held by them in the National Guard of the Territory of Hawaii in all cases where such grades and ratings correspond to grades and ratings provided for in like organizations of the Regular Army, all such appointments of noncommissioned officers and confirmations of other enlisted men in their grades to be without prejudice to the authority of subordinate commanders in respect to promotions, reductions, and changes in enlisted personnel.

Each of said regiments of said National Guard of the Territory of Hawaii and each organization thereof will, until further orders, bear the same name and designation as was borne by it while a part of the National Guard of the Territory of Hawaii.

In witness whereof I have hereunto set my hand and caused the seal of the United States to be affixed.

Done in the District of Columbia this twenty-eighth day of May, in the year of our Lord one thousand nine hundred and eighteen, and of the independence of the United States of America the one hundred and forty-second.

[SEAL.]

WOODROW WILSON.

By the President:

ROBERT LANSING, *Secretary of State.*

[Registration Day.]

Whereas Congress has enacted and the President has, on the 20th day of May, one thousand nine hundred and eighteen, approved the following Public Resolution:

"*Resolved by the Senate and House of Representatives of the United States of America in Congress assembled,* That during the present emergency all male persons, citizens of the United States, and all male persons residing in the United States, who have, since the fifth day of June, nineteen hundred and seventeen, and on or before the day set for the registration by proclamation by the President, attained the age of twenty-one years, shall be subject to registration in accordance with regulations to be prescribed by the President, and that upon proclamation by the President, stating the time and place of such registration, it shall be the duty of all such persons, except such persons as are exempt from registration under the Act of May eighteenth, nineteen hundred and seventeen, and any Act or Acts amendatory thereof, to present themselves for and submit to registration under the provisions of said Act approved May eighteenth, nineteen hundred and seventeen, and they shall be registered in the same manner and subject to the same requirements and liabilities as those previously registered under the terms of said Act: *Provided,* That those persons registered under the provisions of this Act shall be placed at the bottom of the list of those liable for military service, in the several classes to which they are assigned, under such rules and regulations as the President may prescribe.

SEC. 2. That after the day set under section one hereof for the registration by proclamation by the President at such intervals as the President may from time to time prescribe, the President may require that all male persons, citizens of the United States, and all male persons residing in the United States, who have attained the age of twenty-one years since the last preceding date of registration, and on or before the next day set for the registration by proclamation by the President, except such persons as are exempt from registration under the Act of May eighteenth, nineteen hundred and seventeen, and any Act or Acts amendatory thereof, shall be registered in the same manner and subject to the same requirements and liabilities as those previously registered under the terms of said Act: *Provided,* That students who are preparing for the ministry in recognized theological or divinity schools, and students who are preparing for the practice of medicine and surgery in recognized medical schools, at the time of the approval of this Act shall be exempt from the selective draft prescribed in the Act of May eighteenth, nineteen hundred and seventeen.

Sec. 3. That all such persons when registered shall be liable to military service and to draft under the terms of said Act approved May eighteenth, nineteen hundred and seventeen, under such regulations as the President may prescribe not inconsistent with the terms of said Act.

Sec. 4. That all such persons shall be subject to the terms and provisions and liabilities of said Act approved May eighteenth, nineteen hundred and seventeen, in all respects as if they had been registered under the terms of said Act, and every such person shall be deemed to have notice of the requirements of said Act and of this joint resolution upon the publication of any such proclamation by the President."

And whereas the act of Congress approved May eighteenth, one thousand nine hundred and seventeen, entitled "An act to authorize the President to increase temporarily the Military Establishment of the United States," contains the following provisions:

[Here follow sections 5 and 6 of the act, as quoted on pages 8256, 8257 and 8258.]

Now, therefore, I, Woodrow Wilson, President of the United States, do call upon the governor of each of the several States, the Board of Commissioners of the District of Columbia, and all members of Local Boards and agents thereof appointed under the provisions of said act of Congress approved May 18, 1917, to perform certain duties in the execution of the foregoing law, which duties will be communicated to them directly in the regulations prescribed under the terms of said Public Resolution.

And I do further proclaim and give notice to every person subject to registration in the several States, and in the District of Columbia, in accordance with the above law, that the time and place of such registration shall be between 7 a. m. and 9 p. m. on the 5th of June, 1918, at the office of the Local Board having jurisdiction of the area wherein he permanently resides, or at such other place as shall be designated by public notice by such Local Board.

All male persons, either citizens of the United States or residing in the several States, or in the District of Columbia, who have, since the 5th day of June, 1917, and on or before the 5th of June, 1918, attained their twenty-first birthday, are required to register in accordance with the above law and the regulations prescribed thereunder: *Provided, however,* That the following persons are hereby exempted from registration: Officers and enlisted men of the Regular Army, the Navy, the Marine Corps, and the National Guard and Naval Militia while in the service of the United States, and officers in the Officers' Reserve Corps and enlisted men in the Enlisted Reserve Corps while in active service.

A day for registration in the Territories of Alaska, Hawaii, and Porto Rico will be named in a later proclamation.

As required by the regulations, every Local Board having jurisdiction in a city of 30,000 population or over will promptly cause the mayor thereof to be notified of the place or places designated for registration; every Local Board having jurisdiction in a county, parish, or similar unit will promptly cause the clerk thereof to be notified of the place or places designated for registration, and every Local Board having jurisdiction in a State or Territory, the area of which is divided into divisions for the administration of the act approved May 18, 1917, will promptly cause the clerks of the townships within its division to be notified of the place or places designated for registration.

And I do call upon every mayor, county clerk, or township clerk receiving such notification to have a list of said places of registration posted, and do charge him with the duty of having all persons making inquiry informed of the place or places at which they may register.

Any person who, on account of sickness, will be unable to present himself for registration may apply on or before the day of registration at the office of any Local Board for instructions as to how he may register by agent.

Any person who expects to be absent on the day designated for registration from the jurisdiction of the board in which he permanently resides may register by mail, but his registration card must reach the Local Board having jurisdiction of the area wherein he permanently resides by the day herein named for registration. Any such person should apply as soon as practicable at the office of a Local Board for instructions as to how he may register by mail.

Any person who has no permanent residence must register at the place designated for registration by the Local Board having jurisdic-

15,000 RUSSIAN PRISONERS IN GERMANY

RUSSIAN PRISONERS IN GERMANY.

The preceding picture shows 15,000 Russian prisoners receiving bread in a detention camp at the front, before being sent to the interior. Charges were made on several occasions by the Entente Allies that Germany was mistreating the prisoners whom she had captured, and a considerable amount of evidence was adduced in support of the charge. War prisoners in all of the countries at war are seldom kept in idleness, but are compelled to perform certain work in the country where they are being detained, in order to release more citizens of such country for actual fighting at the front.

tion of the area wherein he may be on the day herein named for registration.

Any person who, on account of absence at sea, or on account of absence without the territorial limits of the United States, may be unable to comply with the regulations pertaining to absentees, shall, within five days after reaching the first United States port, register with his proper Local Board or as provided in the regulations for other absentees.

In witness whereof, I have hereunto set my hand and caused the seal of the United States to be affixed.

Done in the District of Columbia this 20th day of May in the year of our Lord one thousand nine hundred and [SEAL.] eighteen and of the independence of the United States of America, the one hundred and forty-second.

WOODROW WILSON.

By the President:

ROBERT LANSING, *Secretary of State.*

EXECUTIVE ORDER

[Re-distributing duties and establishing new agencies concerned with the Signal Corps and Airplane Divisions of the Army.]

THE WHITE HOUSE, *May 20, 1918.*

By virtue of the authority in me vested as Commander-in-Chief of the Army and by virtue of further authority upon me specifically conferred by "An Act authorizing the President to coordinate or consolidate executive bureaus, agencies, and offices, and for other purposes, in the interest of economy and the more efficient concentration of the Government," approved May 20, 1918, I do hereby make and publish the following order:

I.

The powers heretofore conferred by law or by executive order upon, and the duties and functions heretofore performed by, the Chief Signal Officer of the Army are hereby redistributed as follows:

(1) The Chief Signal Officer of the Army shall have charge, under the direction of the Secretary of War, of all military signal duties, and of books, papers, and devices connected therewith, including telegraph and telephone apparatus and the necessary meteorological instruments for use on target ranges, and other military uses; the construction, repair and operation of military telegraph lines, and the duty of collecting and transmitting information for the Army by telegraph or

otherwise and all other duties usually pertaining to military signaling; and shall perform such other duties as now are or shall hereafter be devolved by law or by Executive Order upon said Chief Signal Officer, which are not connected with the Aviation Section of the Signal Corps or with the purchase, manufacture, maintenance and production of aircraft, and which are not hereinafter conferred, in special or general terms, upon other officers or agencies.

(2) A Director of Military Aeronautics, selected and designated by the Commander-in-Chief of the Army, shall hereafter have charge, under the direction of the Secretary of War, of the Aviation Section of the Signal Corps of the Army, and as such shall be, and he hereby is, charged with the duty of operating and maintaining or supervising the operation and maintenance of all military aircraft, including balloons and airplanes, all appliances pertaining to said aircraft and signaling apparatus of any kind when installed on said aircraft, and of training officers, enlisted men and candidates for aviation service in matters pertaining to military aviation, and shall hereafter perform each and every function heretofore imposed upon and performed by the Chief Signal Officer of the Army in, or in connection with, the Aviation Section of the Signal Corps, except such as pertains to the purchase, manufacture and production of aircraft and aircraft equipment and as is not hereinafter conferred, in special or general terms, upon the Bureau of Aircraft Production; and all airplanes now in use or completed and on hand and all material and parts, and all machinery, tools, appliances and equipment held for use for the maintenance thereof; all lands, buildings, repair shops, warehouses, and all other property, real, personal or mixed, heretofore used by the Signal Corps in, or in connection with, the operation and maintenance of aircraft and the training of officers, enlisted men and candidates for aviation service, or procured and now held for such use by or under the jurisdiction and control of the Signal Corps of the Army; all books, records, files and office equipment heretofore used by the Signal Corps in, or in connection with, such operation, maintenance and training; and the entire personnel of the Signal Corps as at present assigned to, or engaged upon, work in, or in connection with, such operation, maintenance and training, is hereby transferred from the jurisdiction of the Chief Signal Officer and placed under the jurisdiction of the Director of Military Aeronautics; it being the intent hereof to transfer from the jurisdiction of the Chief Signal Officer to the jurisdiction of the said Director of Military Aeronautics every function, power and duty conferred and imposed upon said Director of Military Aeronautics by sub-paragraph (2) of paragraph I hereof, all property of every sort or nature used or procured for use in, or in connection with, the function of the Aviation Section of the Signal Corps placed in charge

of the Director of Military Aeronautics by sub-paragraph (2) of paragraph I hereof, and the entire personnel of the Signal Corps as at present assigned to, or engaged upon, work in, or in connection with, the performance of the functions and duties of the Aviation Section of the Signal Corps placed in charge of the Director of Military Aeronautics by sub-paragraph (2) of paragraph I hereof.

(3) An executive agency, to be known as the Bureau of Aircraft Production, is hereby established, and said agency shall exercise full, complete and exclusive jurisdiction and control over the production of airplanes, airplane engines and aircraft equipment for the use of the Army, and to that end shall forthwith assume control and jurisdiction over all pending Government projects having to do, or connected, with the production of airplanes, airplane engines and aircraft equipment for the Army and heretofore conducted by the Signal Corps of the Army, under the jurisdiction of the Chief Signal Officer; and all material on hand for such production, all unfinished airplanes and airplane engines and all unfinished, unattached, or unassembled aircraft equipment; all lands, buildings, factories, warehouses, machinery, tools and appliances and all other property, real, personal or mixed heretofore used in or in connection with, such production, or procured and now held for such use, by or under the jurisdiction and control of the Signal Corps of the Army; all books, records, files and office equipment used by the said Signal Corps in, or in connection with, such production; all rights under contracts made by the Signal Corps in, or in connection with, such production; and the entire personnel of the Signal Corps as at present assigned to, or engaged upon, work in, or in connection with, such production, are hereby transferred from the jurisdiction of the Signal Corps and placed under the jurisdiction of the Bureau of Aircraft Production; it being the intent hereof to transfer from the jurisdiction of the Signal Corps to the jurisdiction of the said Bureau of Aircraft Production, every function, power and duty connected with said production, all property of every sort or nature used or procured for use in, or in connection with, said production, and the entire personnel of the Signal Corps, as at present assigned to, or engaged upon, work in, or in connection with, such production.

Such person as shall at the time be Chairman of the Aircraft Board created by the Act of Congress approved October 1, 1917, shall also be the executive officer of said Bureau of Aircraft Production, and he shall be, and he hereby is, designated as Director of Aircraft Production, and he shall, under the direction of the Secretary of War, have charge of the activities, personnel, and properties of said bureau.

II.

All unexpended funds of appropriations heretofore made for the Signal Corps of the Army and already specifically allotted for use in connection with the functions of the signal service as defined and limited by subparagraph (1) of paragraph I hereof, shall be and remain under the jurisdiction of the Chief Signal Officer; all such funds already specifically allotted for use in connection with the functions of the Aviation Section of the Signal Corps as defined and limited by subparagraph (2) of paragraph I hereof are hereby transferred to, and placed under the jurisdiction of, the Director of Military Aeronautics for the purpose of meeting the obligations and expenditures authorized by said section; all such funds already specifically allotted for use in connection with the functions hereby bestowed upon the Bureau of Aircraft Production, as defined and limited by subparagraph (3) of paragraph I hereof, are hereby transferred to, and placed under the jurisdiction of, said Director of Aircraft Production for the purpose of meeting the obligations and expenditures authorized by said bureau in carrying out the duties and functions hereby transferred to, and bestowed upon, said bureau; and in so far as such funds have not been already specifically allotted to the different fields of activity of the Signal Corps as heretofore existing, they shall now be allotted by the Secretary of War in such proportions as shall to him seem best intended to meet the requirements of the respective fields of former activity of the Signal Corps and the intention of Congress when making said appropriations; and the funds so allotted by the Secretary of War to meet expenditures in the field of activity of the Aviation Section of the Signal Corps are hereby transferred to, and placed under the jurisdiction of, the Director of Military Aeronautics for the purpose of meeting the obligations and expenditures authorized by said section; and the funds so allotted by the Secretary of War to meet the expenditures in that part of the field of activity of the Signal Corps, which included the functions hereby transferred to the Bureau of Aircraft Production, are hereby transferred to, and placed under the jurisdiction of, the Director of Aircraft Production for the purpose of meeting the obligations and expenditures authorized by said bureau.

III.

This order shall be and remain in full force and effect during the continuance of the present war and for six months after the termination thereof by the proclamation of the treaty of peace, or until theretofore amended, modified or rescinded.

WOODROW WILSON.

By the President:

ROBERT LANSING, *Secretary of State.*

By the President of the United States of America.

A PROCLAMATION

[Copyright—France.]

Whereas it is provided by the Act of Congress of March 4, 1909, entitled "An Act to Amend and Consolidate the Acts Respecting Copyright," that the provisions of said Act, "so far as they secure copyright controlling the parts of instruments serving to reproduce mechanically the musical work, shall include only compositions published and copyrighted after this Act goes into effect, and shall not include the works of a foreign author or composer unless the foreign state or nation of which such author or composer is a citizen or subject grants, either by treaty, convention, agreement, or law, to citizens of the United States similar rights":

And Whereas it is further provided that the copyright secured by the Act shall extend to the work of an author or proprietor who is a citizen or subject of a foreign state or nation, only upon certain conditions set forth in section 8 of said Act, to wit:

(a) When an alien author or proprietor shall be domiciled within the United States at the time of the first publication of his work; or

(b) When the foreign state or nation of which such author or proprietor is a citizen or subject grants, either by treaty, convention, agreement, or law, to citizens of the United States the benefit of copyright on substantially the same basis as to its own citizens, or copyright protection substantially equal to the protection secured to such foreign author under this Act or by treaty; or when such foreign state or nation is a party to an international agreement which provides for reciprocity in the granting of copyright, by the terms of which agreement the United States may, at its pleasure, become a party thereto:

And, Whereas it is also provided by said section that "The existence of the reciprocal conditions aforesaid shall be determined by the President of the United States, by proclamation made from time to time as the purposes of this Act may require":

And Whereas satisfactory official assurance has been given that in France the law now permits to citizens of the United States similar rights to those accorded in section I (e) of the Acts of March 4, 1909:

Now, Therefore, I, Woodrow Wilson, President of the United States of America do declare and proclaim that one of the alternative conditions specified in Section 8 (b) of the Act of March 4, 1909, now exists and is fulfilled in respect to citizens of France, and that the citizens of that country are entitled to all the benefits of section I (e) of the said Act, including "copyright controlling the parts of instruments serving to reproduce mechanically the musical work" in the case of all musical compositions by French composers published and duly registered in the United States on and after the date hereof.

In testimony whereof, I have hereunto set my hand and caused the seal of the United States to be affixed.

Done in the District of Columbia this twenty-fourth day of
[SEAL.]   May, in the year of our Lord one thousand nine hundred and eighteen and of the Independence of the United States of America the one hundred and forty-second.

WOODROW WILSON.

By the President:
ROBERT LANSING, *Secretary of State.*

EXECUTIVE ORDER

[Establishment of War Industries Board.]

THE WHITE HOUSE, *May 28, 1918.*

I hereby establish the War Industries Board as a separate administrative agency to act for me and under my direction. This is the Board which was originally formed by, and subsidiary to, the Council of National Defense under the provisions of "An Act Making Appropriations for the Support of the Army for the Fiscal Year Ending June 30, 1917, and for other purposes," approved August 29, 1916.

The functions, duties and powers of the War Industries Board, as outlined in my letter of March 4, 1918, to Bernard M. Baruch, Esquire, its Chairman, shall be and hereby are continued in full force and effect.

WOODROW WILSON.

The text of the letter mentioned in the above executive order was as follows:

THE WHITE HOUSE, *March 4, 1918.*

MY DEAR MR. BARUCH:

I am writing to ask if you will not accept appointment as Chairman of the War Industries Board, and I am going to take the liberty at the same time of outlining the functions, the constitution, and action of the board as I think they should now be established.

The functions of the Board should be:

1. The creation of new facilities and the disclosing, if necessary the opening up, of new or additional sources of supply.

2. The conversion of existing facilities where necessary to new uses.

3. The studious conservation of resources and facilities by scientific, commercial, and industrial economies.

4. Advice to the several purchasing agencies of the Government with regard to the prices to be paid.

5. The determination, wherever necessary, of priorities of production and of delivery and of the proportions of any given article to be made immediately accessible to the several purchasing agencies when the supply of that article is insufficient, either temporarily or permanently.

6. The making of purchases for the Allies.

The board should be constituted as at present, and should retain, so far as necessary and so far as consistent with the character and purposes of the reorganization, its present advisory agencies, but the ultimate decision of all questions, except the determination of prices, should rest always with the Chairman, the other members acting in a cooperative and advisory capacity. The further organization of advice I will indicate below.

In the determination of priorities of production, when it is not possible to have the full supply of any article that is needed produced at once, the Chairman should be assisted, and so far as practicable guided, by the present priorities organization or its equivalent.

In the determination of priorities of delivery, when they must be determined, he should be assisted when necessary, in addition to the present advisory priorities organization, by the advice and cooperation of a committee constituted for the purpose and consisting of official representatives of the Food Administration, the Fuel Administration, the Railway Administration, the Shipping Board, and the War Trade Board, in order that when a priority of delivery has been determined there may be common, consistent, and concerted action to carry it into effect.

In the determination of prices the Chairman should be governed by the advice of a committee consisting, besides himself, of the members of the board immediately charged with the study of raw materials and of manufactured products, of the Labor member of the board, of the Chairman of the Federal Trade Commission, the Chairman of the Tariff Commission, and the Fuel Administrator.

The Chairman should be constantly and systematically informed of all contracts, purchases, and deliveries, in order that he may have always before him a schematized analysis of the progress of business in the several supply divisions of the Government in all departments.

The duties of the Chairman are:

1. To act for the joint and several benefit of all the supply departments of the Government.

2. To let alone what is being successfully done and interfere as little as possible with the present normal processes of purchase and delivery in the several departments.

3. To guide and assist wherever the need for guidance or assistance may be revealed. For example, in the allocation of contracts, in obtaining access to materials in any way pre-empted, or in the disclosure of the sources of supply.

4. To determine what is to be done when there is any competitive or other conflict of interest between departments in the matter of supplies; for example, when there is not a sufficient immediate supply for all and there must be a decision as to priority of need or delivery, or when there is competition for the same sources of manufacture or supply, or when contracts have not been placed in such a way as to get advantage of the full productive capacity of the country.

5. To see that contracts and deliveries are followed up where such assistance as is indicated under (3) and (4) above has proved to be necessary.

6. To anticipate the prospective needs of the several supply departments of the Government and their feasible adjustment to the industry of the country as far in advance as possible, in order that as definite an outlook and opportunity for planning as possible may be afforded the business men of the country.

In brief, he should act as the general eye of all supply departments in the field of industry.

Cordially and sincerely yours,
WOODROW WILSON.

APPEAL

[For exercise of thrift and purchase of Government War Securities.]

May 29, 1918.

This war is one of nations—not of armies—and all of our 100,000,000 people must be economically and industrially adjusted to war conditions if this nation is to play its full part in the conflict. The problem before us is not primarily a financial problem, but rather a problem of increased production of war essentials, and the saving of the materials and the labor necessary for the support and equipment of our army and our navy. Thoughtless expenditure of money for nonessentials uses up the labor of men, the products of the farm, mines, and factories, and overburdens transportation, all of which must be used to the utmost and at their best for war purposes.

The great results which we seek can be obtained only by the participation of every member of the nation, young and old, in a national concerted thrift movement. I therefore urge that our people everywhere pledge themselves, as suggested by the Secretary of the Treasury, to the practice of thrift; to serve the Government to their utmost in increasing production in all fields necessary to the winning of the war; to conserve food and fuel and useful materials of every kind; to devote their labor only to the most necessary tasks; and to buy only those things which are essential to individual health and efficiency; and that the people, as evidence of their loyalty, invest all that they can save in Liberty Bonds and War Savings Stamps.

The securities issued by the Treasury Department are so many of them within the reach of every one that the door of opportunity in this matter is wide open to all of us. To practice thrift in peace times is a virtue and brings great benefit to the individual at all times; with the desperate need of the civilized world today for materials and labor with which to end the war, the practice of individual thrift is a patriotic duty and a necessity.

I appeal to all who now own either Liberty Bonds or War Savings Stamps to continue to practice economy and thrift and to appeal to all who do not own Government securities to do likewise and purchase them to the extent of their means. The man who buys Government securities transfers the purchasing power of his money to the United States Government until after this war, and to that same degree does not buy in competition with the Government.

I earnestly appeal to every man, woman, and child to pledge themselves on or before the 28th of June to save constantly and to buy as regularly as possible the securities of the Government; and to do this, so far as possible, through membership in war savings societies. The 28th of June ends the special period of enlistment in the great volunteer army of production and saving here at home. May there be none unenlisted on that day!　　WOODROW WILSON.

EXECUTIVE ORDERS

[Vesting authority under Espionage Act with Attorney General.]

THE WHITE HOUSE, *May 31, 1918.*

By virtue of the authority vested in me by the Act approved June 15, 1917, entitled, "An Act to punish acts of interference with the foreign relations, the neutrality, and the foreign commerce of the United States, to punish espionage and better to enforce the criminal laws of the United States, and for other purposes," I hereby vest in the Attorney General all power and authority conferred upon the President by the provisions of sections two and seven of Title VI of said Act, and the Attorney General is hereby authorized and directed to take such steps as may be necessary to administer and execute the same.

WOODROW WILSON.

[Consolidating law activities of Government under Justice Department.]

THE WHITE HOUSE, *May 31, 1918.*

Whereas, in order to avoid confusion in policies, duplication of effort, and conflicting interpretations of the law, unity of control in the administration of the legal affairs of the Federal Government is obviously essential, and has been so recognized by the acts of Congress creating and regulating the Department of Justice;

Now, therefore, I, WOODROW WILSON, President of the United States, by virtue of the authority vested in me as Chief Executive and by the act "authorizing the President to coordinate or consolidate executive bureaus, agencies and offices, and for other purposes, in the interest of economy and the more efficient concentration of the Government," approved May 20, 1918, do hereby order that all law officers of the Government excepting those in the Philippine Islands, including all law officers attached to any executive bureau, agency or office specially created for the prosecution of the existing war, shall "exercise their functions under the supervision and control of the head of the Department of Justice," in like manner as is now provided by law with respect to the Solicitors for the principal Executive Departments and similar officers; that all litigation in which the United States or any Department, executive bureau, agency or office thereof, are engaged shall be conducted under the supervision and control of the head of the Department of Justice; and that any opinion or ruling by the Attorney General upon any question of law arising in any Department, executive bureau, agency or office shall be treated as binding upon all departments, bureaus, agencies or offices therewith concerned. This Order shall not be construed as affecting the jurisdiction exercised under authority of existing law by the Comptroller of the Treasury and the Judge Advocates General of the Army and Navy.

WOODROW WILSON.

By the President of the United States of America.

PROCLAMATIONS

[Certain citizens or subjects of Germany or Austria-Hungary included as "Enemies" for purposes of Trading with the Enemy Act; reports required as to their property.]

Whereas paragraph (c) of Section Two of the Act entitled "An Act To define, regulate, and punish trading with the enemy, and for other purposes," approved October 6, 1917, known as the Trading with the enemy Act, provides that the word "enemy" as used therein shall be deemed to mean for the purpose of such trading and of said Act, in addition to the individuals, partnerships or other bodies of individuals or corporations specified in paragraph (a), and in addition to the Government and political or municipal subdivisions, officers, officials, agents or agencies thereof specified in paragraph (b), of said Section Two, the following:

"Such other individuals, or body or class of individuals, as may be natives, citizens, or subjects of any nation with which the United States is at war, other than citizens of the United States, wherever resident or wherever doing business, as the President, if he shall find the safety of the United States or the successful prosecution of the war shall so require, may, by proclamation, include within the term 'enemy'";

Now, Therefore, I, Woodrow Wilson, President of the United States of America, pursuant to the authority vested in me, and in accordance with the provisions of the said Act of October 6, 1917, known as the Trading with the enemy Act, do hereby find that the safety of the United States and the successful prosecution of the present war require that,

(1) Any woman, wherever resident outside of the United States, who is a citizen or subject of any nation with which the United States is at war and whose husband is either (a) an officer, official or agent of the government of any nation with which the United States is at war, or (b) resident within the territory (including that occupied by the military or naval forces) of any nation with which the United States is at war, or (c) resident outside of the United States and doing business within such territory; and

(2) All citizens or subjects of any nation with which the United States is at war (other than citizens of the United States) who have been or shall hereafer be detained as prisoners of war, or who have been or shall hereafter be interned by any nation which is at war with any nation with which the United States is also at war; and

(3) Such other individuals or body or class of individuals as may be citizens or subjects of any nation with which the United States is at war (other than citizens of the United States) wherever resident outside of the United States, or wherever doing business outside of the United States, who since the beginning of the war have disseminated, or shall hereafter disseminate propaganda calculated to aid the cause of any such nation in such war, or to injure the cause of the United States in such war, or who since the beginning of the war has assisted or shall hereafter assist in plotting or intrigue against the United States, or against any nation which is at war with any nation which is at war also with the United States; and

(4) Such other individuals or body or class of individuals as may be citizens or subjects of any nation with which the United States is at war wherever resident outside of the United States, or wherever doing business outside of the United States, who are or may hereafter be included in a publication issued by the War Trade Board of the United States of America, entitled "Enemy Trading List"; and the term "body or class of individuals" as herein used shall include firms and co-partnerships contained in said enemy trading list of which one or more of the members or partners shall be citizens or subjects of any nation with which the United States is at war; and

(5) Any citizen or subject of any nation with which the United States is at war wherever resident outside of the United States, who has been at any time since August 4, 1914, resident within the territory (including that occupied by the military or naval forces) of any nation with which the United States is at war, shall all be included within the meaning of the word "enemy" for the purposes of the "Trading with the enemy Act" and of such trading; and I do hereby proclaim to all whom it may concern that every such individual or body or class of individuals herein referred to shall be and hereby is included within the meaning of the word "enemy" and shall be deemed to constitute an "enemy" for said purposes.

And by virtue of further authority vested in me by said Act entitled "An Act To define, regulate, and punish trading with the enemy, and for other purposes", approved October 6, 1917, and known as the Trading with the enemy Act, I hereby make the following order, rule and regulation.

I hereby require that, pursuant to the provisions of subsection (a) of section seven of said "Trading with the enemy Act," every corporation incorporated within the United States, and every unincorporated association, or company, or trustee, or trustees within the United States, issuing shares or certificates representing beneficial interests, shall transmit to the Alien Property Custodian a full list of every officer, director, or stockholder known to be, or whom the representative of such corporation, association, company or trustee may have reasonable cause to believe to be, included by the above proclamation within the term "enemy", together with a statement of the amount of stock or shares owned by each such officer, director, or stockholder, or in which he has any interest; and any person in the United States who holds or has or shall hold or have custody or control of money or other property, beneficial or otherwise, alone or jointly with others, of, for, by, on account of or on behalf of, or for the benefit of, and any person within the United States, who is or shall be indebted in any way to, any person included by the above proclamation within the term "enemy", or any person whom he may have reasonable cause to believe to be so included, shall report the fact to the Alien Property Custodian.

Such lists, statements and reports shall be made and transmitted to the Alien Property Custodian, in such form and under such rules and regulations as he may prescribe within thirty days after the date of this order, or within thirty days after money or other property owing or belonging to or held for, by, on account of or on behalf of, or for the benefit of any such "enemy" shall come within the custody or control of the reporter, or within thirty days after any person shall become an "enemy" by virtue of the terms of the above proclamation.

In witness whereof, I have hereunto set my hand and caused the seal of the United States to be affixed.

Done in the District of Columbia this 31st day of May, in the year of our Lord one thousand nine hundred and [SEAL.] eighteen, and of the independence of the United States the one hundred and forty-second.

WOODROW WILSON.

By the President:
ROBERT LANSING, *Secretary of State.*

[Registration Day—Porto Rico.]

[The proclamation opens by quoting the passages quoted in the proclamation on page 8510.]

And whereas, on the twentieth day of May, one thousand nine hundred and eighteen, the President of the United States did issue a proclamation calling upon all persons subject to registration in the several States and in the District of Columbia to register as provided by the aforesaid Public Resolution.

And whereas, in such Proclamation it was provided among other things that

A day for registration in the Territories of Alaska, Hawaii, and Porto Rico will be named in a later proclamation.

Now, Therefore, I, Woodrow Wilson, President of the United States, for the purpose of fixing the date for registration in the Territory of Porto Rico, do hereby set, fix, and establish the fifth day of July, one thousand nine hundred and eighteen, as the date of registration, and I do hereby direct that on such day, between the hours of 7 A. M. and 9 P. M., all male persons herein made subject to registration, do present themselves for the purpose of registration for military purposes, at such places and to be registered by such persons or officials in each municipality as shall be designated and appointed by the Governor of Porto Rico.

All male persons, citizens of the United States residing in Porto Rico, and all other male persons residing in Porto Rico, who have, since the fifth day of July, one thousand nine hundred and seventeen, and on or before the fifth day of July, one thousand nine hundred and eighteen, attained their twenty-first birthday, are required to register, excepting only officers and enlisted men of the Regular Army, the Navy, the Marine Corps, and the National Guard and Naval Militia while in the service of the United States, and officers in the Officers' Reserve Corps and enlisted men in the Enlisted Reserve Corps while in active service.

Any person who, on account of sickness, will be unable to present himself for registration may apply on or before the day of registration at the place designated therefor by the Governor of Porto Rico **for** instructions as to how he may register by agent.

Any person who has no permanent residence must register at the place designated for the registration of persons residing in the area wherein he may be on the day herein named for registration.

Any person who, on account of absence without the Territory of Porto Rico, does not register, shall, within five days after reaching the first port in Porto Rico, register at the proper place designated for registration.

In witness whereof, I have hereunto set my hand and caused the seal of the United States to be affixed.

Done in the District of Columbia this 11th day of June in the year of our Lord one thousand nine hundred and [SEAL.] eighteen and of the independence of the United States of America, the one hundred and forty-second.

WOODROW WILSON.

By the President:

ROBERT LANSING, *Secretary of State.*

STATEMENT

[Urging employers to recruit unskilled labor only through United States Employment Service and asking obedience of labor to the Employment Service's calls.]

June 18, 1918.

For more than a year it has been our pride that not our armies and navies only, but our whole people is engaged in a righteous war. We have said repeatedly that industry plays as essential and honorable a rôle in this great struggle as do our military armaments. We all recognize the truth of this, but we must also see its necessary implications—namely, that industry, doing a vital task for the nation, must receive the support and assistance of the nation.

We must recognize that it is a natural demand—almost a right—of any one serving his country, whether employer or employe, to know that his service is being used in the most effective manner possible. In the case of labor this wholesome desire has been not a little thwarted owing to the changed conditions which war has created in the labor market.

There has been much confusion as to essential products. There has been ignorance of conditions—men have gone hundreds of miles in search of a job and wages which they might have found at their doors. Employers holding Government contracts of the highest importance have competed with holders of similar contracts, and even with the Government itself, and have conducted expensive campaigns for recruiting labor in sections where the supply of labor was already exhausted. California draws its unskilled labor from as far east as Buffalo, and New York from as far west as the Mississippi. Thus labor has been induced to move fruitlessly from one place to another, congesting the railways and losing both time and money.

Such a condition is unfair alike to employer and employe, but most of all to the nation itself, whose existence is threatened by any decrease in its productive power. It is obvious that this situation can be clarified and equalized by a central agency—the United States Employment Service of the Department of Labor, with the counsel of the War Labor Policies Board as the voice of all the industrial agencies of the Government. Such a central agency must have sole direction of all recruiting of civilian workers in war work; and, in taking over this great responsibility, must at the same time have power to assure to essential industry an adequate supply of labor, even to the extent of withdrawing workers from nonessential production. It must also protect labor from insincere and thoughtless appeals made to it under the plea of patriotism and assure it that when it is expected to volunteer in some priority industry, the need is real.

Therefore, I, Woodrow Wilson, President of the United States of America, solemnly urge all employers engaged in war work to refrain after Aug. 1, 1918, from recruiting unskilled labor in any manner except through this central agency. I urge labor to respond as loyally as heretofore to any calls issued by this agency for voluntary enlistment in essential industry. And I ask them both alike to remember that no sacrifice will have been in vain if we are able to prove beyond all question that the highest and best form of efficiency is the spontaneous cooperation of a free people.

EXECUTIVE ORDERS

[Delegating to the United States Shipping Board Emergency Fleet Corporation the powers granted to the President by the Act of Congress amendatory of the emergency shipping legislation, and approved April 22, 1918.]

THE WHITE HOUSE, *June 18, 1918.*

By virtue of authority vested in me by the Act of Congress, entitled "An Act to Amend the emergency shipping fund provisions of the Urgent Deficiency Appropriation Act, approved June fifteenth, nineteen hundred and seventeen, so as to empower the President and his designated agents to take over certain transportation systems for the transportation of shipyard and plant employees, and for other purposes," approved April 22, 1918, I hereby direct that the United States Shipping Board Emergency Fleet Corporation shall have and exercise all power and authority vested in me by said Act.

WOODROW WILSON.

[Assigning authority over war housing program to Secretary of Labor.]

THE WHITE HOUSE, *June 18, 1918.*

By virtue of the authority vested in me by the first section of the Act of Congress entitled "An Act Authorizing the President to coordinate or consolidate executive bureaus, agencies, and offices, and for other purposes, in the interest of economy and the more efficient concentration of the Government", approved May 20, 1918, and by the other acts of Congress hereinafter mentioned, I hereby direct that the Secretary of Labor shall have and exercise all power and authority vested in me by the Act of Congress entitled "An Act to authorize the President to provide housing for War Needs", approved May 16, 1918, and by the Act of Congress entitled "An Act making appropriations to supply additional urgent deficiencies in appropriations for the fiscal year ending June thirtieth, nineteen hundred and eighteen, on account of War expenses and for other purposes," approved June 4, 1918, in so far as the same relates to "Housing for War Needs."

WOODROW WILSON.

By the President of the United States of America.

A PROCLAMATION

[License of Stockyards.]

Whereas, under and by virtue of an Act of Congress entitled "An Act To provide further for the national security and defense by encouraging the production, conserving the supply, and controlling the distribution of food products and fuel", approved by the President on the 10th day of August, 1917, it is provided among other things as follows:

[Here follow the two paragraphs quoted on pages 8322 and 8323.]

And, whereas, it is essential in order to carry into effect the purposes of said Act, and in order to secure an adequate supply and equitable distribution, and to facilitate the movement, of certain necessaries hereafter in this proclamation specified, that the license powers conferred upon the President by said Act be at this time exercised to the extent hereinafter set forth.

Now, therefore, I, Woodrow Wilson, President of the United States of America, by virtue of the powers conferred on me by said Act of Congress, hereby find and determine and by this proclamation do announce, that it is essential, in order to carry into effect the purposes of said Act, to license the importation, storage, and distribution of certain necessaries, to the extent hereinafter specified.

All individuals, partnerships, associations, and corporations engaged in the business of conducting or operating, for compensation or profit, places, establishments, or facilities, commonly known as stockyards, consisting of pens or other enclosures, and their appurtenances, in which live cattle, sheep, swine, or goats are received, held, or kept for sale, feeding, watering, or shipment, and all individuals, partnerships, associations, and corporations, commonly known as commission men, order buyers, traders, speculators, and scalpers, engaged in the business of handling or dealing in live cattle, sheep, swine, or goats in or in connection with such stockyards (except as exempted by said Act of Congress), are hereby required to secure licenses on or before July 25, 1918, which will be issued under such rules and regulations governing the conduct of the business as may be prescribed under said Act.

The Secretary of Agriculture shall carry into effect the provisions of said Act, and shall supervise and direct the exercise of the powers and authority thereby given to the President, as far as the same apply to the said business, and to any and all practices, procedure, and regulations applicable thereto, authorized or required under the provisions of said Act, and in this behalf he shall do and perform such acts and things as may be authorized or required of him from time to time by direction of the President and under such rules and regulations as may be prescribed by the President from time to time. All departments and agencies of the Government are hereby directed to cooperate with the Secretary of Agriculture in the performance of the duties hereinbefore set forth.

Applications for licenses must be made to the Law Department, License Division, United States Food Administration, Washington, D. C., upon forms prepared for that purpose.

Any individual, partnership, association, or corporation, other than as hereinbefore excepted, who shall engage in or carry on any business described herein, without first securing the license required therefor, will be liable to the penalties prescribed by said Act of Congress.

In witness whereof, I have hereunto set my hand and caused the seal of the United States to be affixed.

Done in the District of Columbia, this 18th day of June, in the year of Our Lord One Thousand Nine Hundred and [SEAL.] Eighteen, and of the Independence of the United States of America, the One Hundred and Forty-second.

WOODROW WILSON.

By the President:
ROBERT LANSING, *Secretary of State.*

EXECUTIVE ORDERS

[Food Administration Grain Corporation.]

THE WHITE HOUSE, *June 21, 1918.*

By Section 14 of the Act of Congress of August 10, 1917, entitled "An Act To provide further for the national security and defense by encouraging the production, conserving the supply, and controlling the distribution of food products and fuel", it is provided that whenever the President shall find that an emergency exists requiring stimulation of the production of wheat, and that it is essential that the producers of wheat produced within the United States shall have the benefits of the guarantee provided for in that Section, he shall determine and fix and give public notice of, a guaranteed price for wheat; and that thereupon the Government of the United States guarantees to every producer of wheat that he shall receive under conditions named, a price for wheat not less than such guaranteed price. Under this provision an Executive Proclamation was issued on February 21, 1918, making the necessary findings and fixing guaranteed prices for wheat when delivered at certain specified primary markets.

It is further provided that for the purpose of making any guaranteed price effective under that section, or whenever he deems it essential in order to protect the Government of the United States against material enhancement of its liabilities arising out of any guaranty under this section, the President may in his discretion purchase any wheat for which a guaranteed price shall be fixed under this section, and may hold, transport, or store it, or sell, dispose of, and deliver the same to any citizen of the United States or to any Government engaged in war with any country with which the Government of the United States is or may be at war or to use the same as supplies for any department or agency of the Government of the United States.

It is further provided by Section 11 of said Act of Congress, that the President may from time to time purchase, store, provide storage facilities for, and sell for cash at reasonable prices, wheat, flour, meal, beans and potatoes; and by Section 2 that in carrying out the purposes of such Act, the President may create or use any agency or agencies, and utilize any department or agency of the Government.

Acting under the authority of the foregoing provisions, I hereby designate the Food Administration Grain Corporation, a corporation created in accordance with the provisions of said Act of Congress and Executive Order dated August 14, 1917, as the agency of the United States to carry out and make effective, subject to the control and direction of the United States Food Administrator, the provisions of the guarantee hereinbefore referred to, and to purchase, hold, transport, store, provide storage facilities for, sell, dispose of, and deliver wheat as provided in Sections 11 and 14 of said Act. I further direct that in order to make said guarantee effective and maintain the price of wheat to the grower at not less than the guaranteed basis the said Corporation shall offer and stand ready to purchase, and shall purchase to the full extent of its ability and available funds, all wheat tendered to it by any producer thereof at any primary market named in said Proclamation of February 21, 1918, at the guaranteed price named therein for such market, provided that with the approval of the United States Food Administrator the said Corporation may pay any higher prices than the guaranteed basis for any grade of wheat in any given market, and may extend its offer to purchase to other holders of wheat on such conditions as it sees fit.

I further direct that for such purpose the capital stock of such Corporation be increased to 1,500,000 shares of the par value of $100.00 each; that the United States purchase from time to time at par, so much of the additional capital stock as may be required to supply the necessary capital to enable said Corporation to carry out the provisions of this order, and that none of said additional capital stock shall be sold to any person other than the United States. The United States

Food Administrator is hereby authorized and directed to subscribe for and purchase all or any part of said additional capital stock in the name of and for the use and benefit of the United States, and to pay for the same out of the appropriation of $150,000,000 authorized by Section 19 of the Act of Congress hereinbefore entitled. I further authorize said Corporation to borrow such sums of money, upon the security of wheat or flour owned by it, as may be required to carry out the provisions of this order.

WOODROW WILSON.

[Changing Defensive Sea Area in Chesapeake Bay.]

THE WHITE HOUSE, *June 29, 1918.*

In accordance with the authority vested in me by section forty-four of the act entitled "An act to codify, revise, and amend the penal laws of the United States," approved March fourth, nineteen hundred and nine, as amended by the act "Making appropriations for the naval service for the fiscal year ending June thirtieth, nineteen hundred and eighteen, and for other purposes," approved March fourth, nineteen hundred and seventeen, I, Woodrow Wilson, President of the United States, do order that the defensive sea area at Chesapeake entrance and the defensive sea area at Hampton Roads, established by Executive order under date of April fifth, nineteen hundred and seventeen, be hereby abolished.

And, further, I do order established, subject to the same disclaimer of responsibility for damages inflicted as proclaimed in said order of April fifth, nineteen hundred and seventeen, a defensive sea area, to be maintained until further notification, at the place and within the limits described as follows—that is to say:

Lower Chesapeake:

Outer limit.—Line parallel to that joining Cape Henry Light and Cape Charles Light and 4 nautical miles to eastward thereof, and the lines from Cape Charles Light and from Cape Henry Light perpendicular to this line.

Inner limits.—Line tangent to end of wharf on west side of Old Point Comfort and Fort Wool, and a line running from Back River Light through the Light Vessel marking the southern end of the 35-foot cut known as the Baltimore Channel, thence to the eastern shore of Virginia.

And I do further order that the "Regulations for Carrying into Effect the Executive Order of the President Establishing Defensive Sea Areas," approved by me April 5, 1917, duly promulgated and published, are and shall be considered as of full effect and binding on all persons and vessels within the limits of the defensive sea area hereby established.

The designated points for ships entering and leaving the defensive sea area herein established shall be as follows:

Eastern limit.—Chesapeake Bay main ship channel entrance buoy.

Western limit.—In channel to northwestward of entrance buoy of dredged channel, Elizabeth River.

Northern limit.—Light vessel marking the southern end of the 35-foot cut known as the Baltimore Channel, thence to the eastern shore of Virginia.

WOODROW WILSON.

[Placing All Public Health Activities Under Treasury Department.]

THE WHITE HOUSE, *July 1, 1918.*

Whereas, In order to avoid confusion in policies, duplication of effort, and to bring about more effective results, unity of control in the administration of the public health activities of the Federal Government is obviously essential, and has been so recognized by acts of Congress creating in the Treasury Department a Public Health Service, and specially authorizing such service "to study the diseases of man and the conditions influencing the propagation and spread thereof" and "to cooperate with and aid State and municipal boards of health":

Now, therefore, I, Woodrow Wilson, President of the United States, by virtue of the authority vested in me as Chief Executive, and by the act "authorizing the President to coordinate or consolidate executive bureaus, agencies, and offices, and for other purposes, in the interest of economy and the more efficient concentration of the Government," approved May 20, 1918, do hereby order that all sanitary or public health activities carried on by any executive bureau, agency, or office, especially created for or concerned in the prosecution of the existing war, shall be exercised under the supervision and control of the Secretary of the Treasury.

This order shall not be construed as affecting the jurisdiction exercised under authority of existing law by the Surgeon General of the Navy, and the Provost Marshal General in the performance of health functions which are military in character as distinguished from civil public health duties, or as prohibiting investigations by the Bureau of Labor Statistics of vocational diseases, shop sanitation, and hygiene.

WOODROW WILSON.

INDEPENDENCE DAY ADDRESS

[Delivered at Mt. Vernon, Va., on July 4, 1918, on the Issues Involved in the European War.]

Gentlemen of the Diplomatic Corps and My Fellow-Citizens: I am happy to draw apart with you to this quiet place of old counsel in order to speak a little of the meaning of this day of our nation's independence. The place seems very still and remote. It is as serene and untouched by the hurry of the world as it was in those great days long ago when General Washington was here and held leisurely conference with the men who were to be associated with him in the creation of a nation. From these gentle slopes they looked out upon the world and saw it whole, saw it with the light of the future upon it, saw it with modern eyes that turned away from a past which men of liberated spirits could no longer endure. It is for that reason that we cannot feel, even here, in the immediate presence of this sacred tomb, that this is a place of death. It was a place of achievement. A great promise that was meant for all mankind was here given plan and reality. The associations by which we are here surrounded are the inspiring associations of that noble death which is only a glorious consummation. From this green hillside we also ought to be able to see with comprehending eyes the world that lies around us and conceive anew the purpose that must set men free.

It is significant—significant of their own character and purpose and of the influences they were setting afoot—that Washington and his associates, like the barons at Runnymede, spoke and acted, not for a class, but for a people. It has been left for us to see to it that it shall be understood that they spoke and acted, not for a single people only, but for all mankind. They were thinking, not of themselves and of the material interests which centered in the little groups of landholders and merchants and men of affairs with whom they were accustomed to act, in Virginia and the colonies to the north and south of her, but of a people which wished to be done with classes and special interests and the authority of men whom they had not themselves chosen to rule over them. They entertained no private purpose, desired no peculiar privilege. They were consciously planning that men of every class should be free and America a place to which men out of every nation might resort who wished to share with them the rights and privileges of free men. And we take our cue from them—do we not? We intend what they intended. We here in America believe our participation in this present war to be only the fruitage of what they planted. Our case differs from theirs only in this, that it is our inestimable privilege to concert with men out of every nation who shall make not only the liberties of America secure but the liberties of every other people as well. We are happy in the thought that we are permitted to do what they would have done had they been in our place. There must now be settled, once for all, what was settled for America in the great age upon whose inspiration we draw today. This is surely a fitting place from which calmly to look out upon our task, that we may fortify our spirits for its accomplishment. And this is the appropriate place from which to avow, alike to the friends who look on and to the friends with whom we have the happiness to be associated in action, the faith and purpose with which we act.

This, then, is our conception of the great struggle in which we are engaged. The plot is written plain upon every scene and every act of the supreme tragedy. On the one hand stand the peoples of the world—not only the peoples actually engaged, but many others, also, who suffer under mastery but cannot act; peoples of many races and in every part of the world—the people of stricken Russia still, among the rest, though they are for the moment unorganized and helpless. Opposed to them, masters of many armies, stand an isolated, friendless group of Governments, who speak no common purpose, but only selfish ambitions of their own, by which none can profit but themselves, and whose peoples are fuel in their hands; Governments which fear their people, and yet are for the time being sovereign lords, making every choice for them and disposing of their lives and fortunes as they will, as well as of the lives and fortunes of every people who fall under their power; Governments clothed with the strange trappings and the primitive authority of an age that is altogether alien and hostile to our own. The Past and the Present are in deadly grapple, and the peoples of the world are being done to death between them.

There can be but one issue. The settlement must be final. There can be no compromise. No halfway decision would be tolerable. No halfway decision is conceivable. These are the ends for which the associated peoples of the world are fighting and which must be conceded them before there can be peace:

I.—The destruction of every arbitrary power anywhere that can separately, secretly, and of its single choice disturb the peace of the world; or, if it cannot be presently destroyed, at the least its reduction to virtual impotence.

II.—The settlement of every question, whether of territory, of sovereignty, of economic arrangement, or of political relationship, upon the basis of the free acceptance of that settlement by the people immediately concerned, and not upon the basis of the material interest or advantage of any other nation or people which may desire a different settlement for the sake of its own exterior influence or mastery.

III.—The consent of all nations to be governed in their conduct toward each other by the same principles of honor and of respect for the common law of civilized society that govern the individual citizens of all modern states in their relations with one another; to the end that all promises and covenants may be sacredly observed; no private plots or conspiracies hatched, no selfish injuries wrought with impunity, and a mutual trust established upon the handsome foundation of a mutual respect for right.

IV.—The establishment of an organization of peace which shall make it certain that the combined power of free nations will check every invasion of right and serve to make peace and justice the more secure by affording a definite tribunal of opinion to which all must submit and by which every international readjustment that cannot be amicably agreed upon by the people directly concerned shall be sanctioned.

These great objects can be put into a single sentence. What we seek is the reign of law, based upon the consent of the governed and sustained by the organized opinion of mankind.

These great ends cannot be achieved by debating and seeking to reconcile and accommodate what statesmen may wish, with their projects for balances of power and of national opportunity. They can be realized only by the determination of what the thinking peoples of the world desire, with their longing hope for justice and for social freedom and opportunity.

I can fancy that the air of this place carries the accents of such principles with a peculiar kindness. Here were started forces which the great nation against which they were primarily directed at first regarded as a revolt against its rightful authority, but which it has long since seen to have been a step in the liberation of its own people as well as of the people of the United States; and I stand here now to speak—speak proudly and with confident hope—of the spread of this revolt, this liberation, to the great stage of the world itself! The blinded rulers of Prussia have roused forces they knew little of—forces which, once roused, can never be crushed to earth again; for they have at their heart an inspiration and a purpose which are deathless and of the very stuff of triumph!

ADDRESS TO FELLOW CITIZENS

[Read to Patriotic Meetings Throughout the United States on July 4, 1918.]

You are met, my fellow citizens, to commemorate the signing of that Declaration of Independence which marked the awakening of a new spirit in the lives of nations. Since the birth of our Republic, we have seen this spirit grow. We have heard the demand and watched the struggle for self-government spread and triumph among many peoples. We have come to regard the right to political liberty as the common right of humankind. Year after year, within the security of our borders, we have continued to rejoice in the peaceful increase of freedom and democracy throughout the world. And yet now, suddenly, we are confronted with a menace which endangers everything that we have won and everything that the world has won.

In all its old insolence, with all its ancient cruelty and injustice, military autocracy has again armed itself against the pacific hopes of men. Having suppressed self-government among its own people by an organization maintained in part by falsehood and treachery, it has set out to impose its will upon its neighbors and upon us. One by one, it has compelled every civilized nation in the world either to forego its aspirations or to declare war in their defense. We find ourselves fighting again for our national existence. We are face to face with the necessity of asserting anew the fundamental right of free men to make their own laws and choose their own allegiance, or else permit humanity to become the victim of a ruthless ambition that is determined to destroy what it cannot master.

Against its threat the liberty-loving people of the world have risen and allied themselves. No fear has deterred them, and no bribe of material well-being has held them back. They have made sacrifices such as the world has never known before, and their resistance in the face of death and suffering has proved that the aim which animates the German effort can never hope to rule the spirit of mankind. Against the horror of military conquest, against the emptiness of living in mere bodily contentment, against the desolation of becoming part of a State that knows neither truth nor honor, the world has so revolted that even people long dominated and suppressed by force have now begun to stir and arm themselves.

Centuries of subjugation have not destroyed the racial aspirations of the many distinct peoples of eastern Europe, nor have they accepted the sordid ideals of their political and military masters. They have survived the slow persecutions of peace as well as the agonies of war and now demand recognition for their just claims to autonomy and self-government. Representatives of these races are with you to-day, voicing their loyalty to our ideals and offering their services in the common cause. I ask you, fellow-citizens, to unite with them in making this our Independence Day the first that shall be consecrated to a declaration of independence for all the peoples of the world.

By the President of the United States of America.

A PROCLAMATION

[Taking over Terminal Property of German Steamship Lines.]

Whereas the act of Congress making appropriations to supply urgent deficiencies in appropriations for the fiscal year ending June 30, 1918, and prior fiscal years, on account of war expenses and for other purposes, approved March 28, 1918 (Public No. 109, Sixty-fifth Congress), contains the following provisions:

"The President is authorized to acquire the title to the docks, piers, warehouses, wharves, and terminal equipment and facilities on the Hudson River now owned by the North German Lloyd Dock Company and the Hamburg-American Line Terminal and Navigation Company, two corporations of the State of New Jersey, if he shall deem it necessary for the national security and defense: *Provided,* That if such property can not be procured by purchase, then the President is authorized and empowered to take over for the United States the immediate possession and title thereof. If any such property shall be taken over as aforesaid, the United States shall make just compensation therefor, to be determined by the President. Upon the taking over of said property by the President, as aforesaid, the title to all such property so taken over shall immediately vest in the United States: *Provided, further,* That section 355 of the Revised Statutes of the United States shall not apply to any expenditures herein or hereafter authorized in connection with the property acquired."

Now, therefore, I, Woodrow Wilson, President of the United States of America, pursuant to the authority vested in me by the said act of Congress approved March 28, 1918, do hereby determine and declare that the acquisition of title to the foregoing docks, piers, warehouses, wharves, and terminal equipment and facilities is necessary for the national security and defense, and I do hereby take over for the United States of America the immediate possession and title thereof, including all leaseholds, easements, rights of way, riparian rights, and other rights, estates, and interests therein or appurtenant thereto.

Just compensation for the property hereby taken over will be hereafter determined and paid.

In witness whereof I have hereunto set my hand and caused the seal of the United States to be affixed.

Done in the District of Columbia this 28th day of June, One thousand nine hundred and eighteen, and of the
[SEAL.] Independence of the United States one hundred and forty-two.

WOODROW WILSON.

By the President:

ROBERT LANSING, *Secretary of State.*

EXECUTIVE ORDER

[Transferring Personnel and Records of Federal Trade Commission.]

THE WHITE HOUSE, *July 3, 1918.*

Whereas, In order to avoid duplication of effort and to promote unity and concentration of control in the administration of the provisions of section 25 of the act of Congress approved August 10, 1917, entitled "An act to provide further for the national security and defense by encouraging the production, conserving the supply, and controlling the distribution of food products and fuel," certain activities now being carried on by the Federal Trade Commission relating to the coal industry can, and ought to be carried on by the United States Fuel Administration.

Now, therefore, I, Woodrow Wilson, President of the United States of America, by virtue of the authority vested in me as Chief Executive and, by virtue of the powers conferred on me by the act of Congress, entitled, "An act authorizing the President to coordinate or consolidate executive bureaus, agencies and offices, and for other purposes, in the interest of economy and the more efficient concentration of the Government," approved May 20, 1918, do hereby order and direct:

1. That all records, files, reports, copies of contracts, correspondence, papers and proceedings on file or deposited with the Federal Trade Commission relating to coal or coke, and under and in compliance with the provisions of section 25 of said act approved August 10, 1917, or the orders, rules and regulations of the United States Fuel Administrator (excepting such as relate to costs of coal-mine operations and to general research into the coal industry) be transferred forthwith from the Federal Trade Commission to the United States Fuel Administration.

2. That that part of the personnel of the Federal Trade Commission engaged in such activities hereinabove described and now transferred is hereby detailed or assigned to the United States Fuel Administration.

3. That the books, correspondence, records, and papers in any way referring to transactions of any kind relating to the mining, production, sale, or distribution of coal or coke, and not hereby transferred, shall, at all times, be subject to inspection by the United States Fuel Administrator and by his duly authorized agents, examiners, employees, assistants, and subordinates, together constituting the governmental organization called the United States Fuel Administration.

4. That all persons, partnerships, and corporations engaged in the production or distribution of coal or coke shall promptly furnish, whenever called for, to the United States Fuel Administrator, or his duly authorized agents, examiners, employees, assistants, and subordinates, any data or information relating to the business of such persons, partnerships, or corporations engaged in the production or distribution of coal or coke.

5. That the said United States Fuel Administrator is hereby authorized to procure information in reference to the business of coal and coke producers and distributors in the manner provided for in sec-

tions 6 and 9 of the act of Congress approved September 26, 1914, entitled, "An act to create a Federal Trade Commission, to define its powers and duties, and for other purposes," and said United States Fuel Administration, acting through the United States Fuel Administrator, or his duly authorized agents, examiners, employees, assistants, and subordinates, is hereby authorized and empowered to exercise all the powers granted to the Federal Trade Commission by said act approved September 26, 1914, for the carrying out of the purposes of this order.

This order shall be, and remain, in full force and effect during the continuance of the present war and for six (6) months after the termination thereof by the proclamation of a treaty of peace or until amended, modified, or rescinded.

WOODROW WILSON.

EXECUTIVE ORDER

[Governor of Panama Canal given Espionage Act Powers.]

THE WHITE HOUSE, *July 9, 1918.*

Whereas a national emergency exists of the character contemplated in section 1 under Title II of the act of Congress approved June 15, 1917, commonly known as the espionage act;

Therefore I, Woodrow Wilson, President of the United States of America, by virtue of the powers conferred upon me by the said act of Congress, do hereby authorize the governor of the Panama Canal to exercise, within the territory and waters of the Canal Zone, all the powers mentioned in said section 1, Title II, of said act, to the same extent as is conferred therein on the Secretary of the Treasury with regard to the territorial waters of the United States, and all acts heretofore done by the governor of the Panama Canal or under his authority pursuant to said section of said act are hereby ratified and confirmed.

This order supersedes Executive Order No. 2867, dated May 28, 1918.

WOODROW WILSON.

BY THE PRESIDENT OF THE UNITED STATES OF AMERICA

PROCLAMATIONS

[Registration Days—Alaska.]

[The proclamation opens by quoting the passages quoted on pages 8510 and 8511.]

And whereas, on the twentieth day of May, one thousand nine hundred and eighteen, the President of the United States did issue a

Proclamation calling upon all persons subject to registration in the several States and in the District of Columbia, to register as provided by the aforesaid Public Resolution.

And whereas, in such Proclamation it was provided among other things that

A day for registration in the Territories of Alaska, Hawaii, and Porto Rico will be named in a later proclamation.

Now, Therefore, I, Woodrow Wilson, President of the United States, for the purpose of fixing the time for registration in the Territory of Alaska, do hereby set, fix, and establish the period between 7 A. M. on the second day of July to 9 P. M. on the third day of September (Sundays and legal holidays excepted), one thousand nine hundred and eighteen, as the period of registration, and I do hereby direct that during such period, all male persons herein made subject to registration do present themselves for the purpose of registration at such places and during such hours, and to be registered by such persons or officials in such areas, as shall be designated and appointed by the Governor of the Territory of Alaska.

All male persons, citizens of the United States residing in Alaska, and all other male persons residing in Alaska, who have, since the second day of September, one thousand nine hundred and seventeen, and on or before the third day of September, one thousand nine hundred and eighteen, attained their twenty-first birthday, are required to register, excepting only officers and enlisted men of the Regular Army, the Navy, the Marine Corps, and the National Guard and Naval Militia while in the service of the United States, and officers in the Officers' Reserve Corps and enlisted men in the Enlisted Reserve Corps while in active service.

Any person who, on account of sickness, will be unable to present himself for registration may apply on or before the last day for registration at a place designated therefor by the Governor of Alaska for instructions as to how he may register by agent.

Any person who has no permanent residence must register at the place designated for the registration of persons residing in the area wherein he may be during the period herein named for registration. Any such person who may be in more than one registration area during the period herein named for registration must register at the place designated for the registration of persons residing in one of the areas wherein he may be during such period.

Any person who expects to be absent during the period of registration from the registration area in which he permanently resides, may register by mail, but the registration card must reach the persons or officials appointed to conduct the registration in such area on or before the last day herein named for registration. Any such person should apply as soon as practicable at a place or of an official designated or appointed, respectively, by the Governor of Alaska for instructions as to how he may register by mail.

Any person who, on account of absence without the Territory of Alaska, does not register, shall, within five days after reaching the first port in Alaska, register at the proper place designated for registration, or by mail as provided for other absentees.

In witness whereof, I have hereunto set my hand and caused the seal of the United States to be affixed.

Done in the District of Columbia this 17th day of June in the year of our Lord one thousand nine hundred and eighteen and of the independence of the United States of America, the one hundred and forty-second.

[SEAL]

WOODROW WILSON.

By the President:
ROBERT LANSING, *Secretary of State.*

[Cultivation of Public Lands in the Territory of Hawaii.]

Whereas, by reason of the existence of a state of war it is essential to the national security and defense, for the successful prosecution of the war, and for the support and maintenance of the Army and Navy, to secure an adequate supply of sugar and other food products in the United States, including the Territory of Hawaii;

Now therefore, I, Woodrow Wilson, President of the United States, by virtue of the powers conferred upon me by law, do hereby find and determine, and by this proclamation do announce that it is essential in order to secure such adequate food supply to continue to the fullest extent possible the cultivation of all public lands in the Territory of Hawaii now under cultivation in sugar or other food products; and for the purpose of continuing such cultivation and of maintaining the production of all such food products the Commissioner of Public Lands of the Territory of Hawaii, with the approval of the Governor, is hereby authorized and empowered to enter into all necessary contracts with the lessees of any of said Government lands, the leases of which have expired or which, while this proclamation is in force, will expire, or with any other person, firm, or corporation for the continued cultivation of said lands, until such time as the same shall be occupied and cultivated by homesteaders.

And to further effectuate the purpose of this proclamation, the said Commissioner, with the approval of the Governor, may require of all such homesteaders at the time of entering into their special homestead agreements, a contract which may be incorporated into such special homestead agreement to continue the cultivation of their homesteads, and to reimburse any person or corporation who or which shall have done any cultivation or other work on said land, with the approval of the Commissioner and Governor, for the conservation of the crop thereon, to the amount of the actual cost of such work.

In witness whereof, I have hereunto set my hand and caused the seal of the United States to be affixed.

Done in the District of Columbia this 24th day of June, in the year of our Lord one thousand nine hundred and eighteen, and [SEAL]   of the independence of the United States the one hundred and forty-second.

WOODROW WILSON.

By the President:
ROBERT LANSING, *Secretary of State.*

EXECUTIVE ORDERS

[Gas Experiment Station transferred to control of War Department.]

THE WHITE HOUSE, *25 June, 1918.*

It is hereby ordered that the Experiment Station at American University, Washington, D. C., which station has been established under the supervision of the Bureau of Mines, Interior Department, for the purpose of making gas investigations for the Army, under authority of appropriations made for the Ordnance and Medical Departments of the Army, together with the personnel thereof, be, and the same is hereby, placed under the control of the War Department for operation under the Director of Gas Service of the Army.

WOODROW WILSON.

[Celebration of Bastile Day.]

THE WHITE HOUSE, *July 13, 1918.*

In recognition of the valor, courage and heroism with which the people of France have for nearly four years defended the liberties of the world, it is hereby ordered that the National Flag of France be displayed on all public buildings and vessels of the United States at home and abroad on July 14, 1918, in honor of the French National Holiday—Bastile Day.

WOODROW WILSON.

[Certain sales to be conducted by the Alien Property Custodian.]

THE WHITE HOUSE, *15 July, 1918.*

By virtue of the authority vested in me by "An Act to define, regulate and punish trading with the enemy, and for other purposes," approved October 6, 1917, known as the "Trading with the enemy Act," and the amendment to such Act embodied in "An Act making appropriations to supply urgent deficiencies in appropriations for the fiscal year ending June 30, 1918, and prior fiscal years, on account of war expenses, and for other purposes," approved March 28, 1918, I hereby, in the public interest, make the following determination, order, rule and regulation:

The Alien Property Custodian may sell at private sale, without public or other advertisement, any real property or any right, title, or interest therein of whatsoever kind; ground rents, leaseholds, options on real or personal property, stocks, beneficial interests in stocks, including voting trust certificates, and all other rights appurtenant to the ownership of stock, bonds, negotiable instruments or evidences of indebtedness, seats on stock or other exchanges; in parcels, lots, or quantities having a market value at the time of sale not exceeding Ten Thousand Dollars for each parcel, lot or quantity sold. Any such sale may be conducted at such place and upon such terms and conditions as to the Alien Property Custodian, or his authorized agent, may seem proper.

My reasons for the foregoing determination, order, rule and regulation are:

(*a*) The properties above classified cannot usually be sold to the best advantage at public sale after public or other advertisement.

(*b*) The sales hereby authorized may be made at the time and place of most favorable demand and upon such terms and conditions as may be necessary to secure the best market price.

(*c*) Unnecessary expense, delay and inconvenience may be avoided.

WOODROW WILSON.

[Additional rules and regulations and certain determinations respecting the exercise of the powers and authority and the performance of the duties of the Alien Property Custodian.]

THE WHITE HOUSE, *July 16, 1918.*

By virtue of the authority vested in me by "An Act to define, regulate, and punish trading with the enemy, and for other purposes," approved October 6, 1917, known as the "Trading With the Enemy Act," as amended by "An Act making appropriations to supply urgent deficiencies in appropriations for the fiscal year ending June thirtieth, nineteen hundred and eighteen, and prior fiscal years, on account of war expenses and for other purposes," approved March 28, 1918, I hereby make the following orders, rules and regulations, and determinations.

Definitions

1. The word "person," as used herein, shall be deemed to mean an individual, partnership, association, company, or other unincorporated body of individuals, or corporation or body politic.

2. The word "enemy," as used herein, shall be deemed to mean either an "enemy" or "ally of enemy," as the case may be.

Powers of Management and Administration, Including Sale or Other Disposition

The Alien Property Custodian shall have power, and he is authorized and directed, to hold, manage, administer, protect, preserve, control and sell or otherwise dispose of, in accordance with the following rules and regulations, any and all property other than money which has been or shall be conveyed, transferred, assigned, delivered, and/or paid over to him pursuant to the provisions of the Trading With the Enemy Act as amended and the Executive proclamations and orders issued pursuant thereto, or which has been or shall be required so to be conveyed, transferred, assigned, delivered and/or paid over to him.

1. The Alien Property Custodian shall have the power and authority to do any and all things reasonable and proper in or about the custody, management, administration, protection, preservation and control of any such property according to the nature and character of the property and the attendant circumstances, including (but without limiting the generality of the foregoing) the power and authority to collect all bills, notes, accounts, dividends, interest, rents, royalties, annuities and other receivables, and income and profits and accumulations and distributions of principal or income; to pay all rents, royalties, interest and other accounts and liens or charges; to make repairs, additions and alterations to property, whether real or personal; to rent, lease or otherwise grant the use or right to use or occupy property of any kind; to insure property against loss, and to cancel or surrender insurance policies and collect return premiums and surrender values, and to do any other act or thing with respect to insurance or insurance policies; to grant by lease, license or otherwise, the right to use or other rights under or in respect of patents, copyrights, trade marks, trade secrets and other similar rights; to vote in person or by proxy shares of stock or other beneficial interest in corporations, unincorporated associations, companies or trusts upon any questions at all times and upon all matters upon which any owner of such stock or other beneficial interest shall have the right to vote, including the power and authority to vote for or against and to take part in any sale, dissolution, consolidation, amalgamation or reorganization of any sort, of any such corporation, unincorporated association, company or trust, or of its assets of any part thereof, and to exercise any rights or privileges that may be or become appurtenant to the ownership of such stock or other beneficial interest with like force and effect and under like circumstances in all respects as though the absolute owner thereof; to give any notices and

THE DEVASTATION OF WAR

THE DEVASTATION OF WAR.

The illustration reveals all that was left of the famous church at Péronne, France, after the town had been shelled by the Germans.

file any papers or writings of any kind, proper or necessary for the creation, perfection, protection, liquidation or otherwise in respect of any claims, demands, choses-in-action or other rights of any kind, and to settle, compromise and adjust claims, demands and choses-in-action; to intervene in any suit or proceeding and to file and maintain claims, demands and suits of all kinds in or before, any court, board, commission or other body; to determine and pay all reasonable and proper expenses incurred in or about or with respect of the exercise of any of the powers and authority vested in the Alien Property Custodian or any depositary for him, including expenses that may be incurred in or about securing possession, custody or control of any such property, and including also taxes and other charges heretofore or hereafter lawfully assessed upon or against such property by any body politic; provided that this shall not be construed to require the payment of any stamp or other taxes upon or on account of conveyance, transfer, assignment or delivery of property to the Alien Property Custodian or to any agent, attorney, bailee, nominee or depositary for him; and provided further that this shall not in any way affect the power of the Commissioner of Internal Revenue or any regulations made by him or under his authority.

2. Whenever any such money or other property or any part or parcel thereof is or shall be subject to any claim of lien, charge or incumbrance, or is or shall be held or retained adversely to the Alien Property Custodian or to any requirement with respect to such money or other property made by him, the Alien Property Custodian may compromise or settle such controversy and pay any such claim in any way that he shall decide to be proper and as though he were the absolute owner of the money or other property involved; and he shall have the power and authority to make any payment or payments necessary and to execute and deliver any instruments or writings necessary and proper to effect or evidence the same.

3. Whenever any such property or any part or parcel thereof shall be used or employed in the conduct or other operation of a mine, plant, factory, railroad or other transportation facility, warehouse, mercantile or trading establishment or any sort of a going business or undertaking, the Alien Property Custodian, in addition to the rights, powers and authority elsewhere herein conferred upon him, in respect of the property so used or employed, may continue the conduct or other operation of such business or undertaking; and for such purpose he shall have the right, power and authority to employ and discharge agents, attorneys, servants and other employees; to buy and sell supplies, materials and commodities required or necessary for the conduct of such business, or dealt in or handled thereby, or mined, produced, manufactured or created by it; to take out insurance; to require money owing

by banks, trust companies or other depositaries on special or general deposit to be paid to him or upon his order; to collect debts and other receivables owing to the said business or undertaking or to the former enemy owner or owners thereof and created out of or by the operation of such business or undertaking, and also debts, accounts and other receivables accruing or arising out of the conduct or other operation of such business or undertaking, by the Alien Property Custodian or under his direction or authority; to pay the wages and salaries of agents, attorneys, servants and other employees, and rents, royalties, and other current accounts and liabilities; to intervene in any suit or action pending in any court or before any board, commission or other body, in which such business or undertaking or any of the property or assets thereof shall be involved or concerned and to prosecute or defend, as the case may be; to file, prosecute and maintain in the name of the Alien Property Custodian or otherwise as may be proper, any claim or suit arising out of or based upon transactions had prior or subsequent to the time when such property was conveyed, transferred, assigned, delivered and/or paid over to the Alien Property Custodian or was required so to be, but growing out of the conduct or operation of such business or undertaking or any other use, custody, control or management of any property or assets thereof; and generally to manage, administer, preserve, conduct, operate and control such business or undertaking and any or all parts or parcels and assets thereof as though the absolute owner, either in the name of the Alien Property Custodian or otherwise as he shall determine.

4. The Alien Property Custodian may appoint agents, attorneys, bailees, depositaries and/or managers who, under his direction and control and within the limits of the authority conferred by him, shall be authorized and directed to hold, manage, administer, protect, preserve and otherwise control property conveyed, transferred, assigned, delivered or paid over to him or required so to be, or any part or parcel thereof; and they may be authorized and directed to continue the conduct or other operation of any going business or other undertaking which the Alien Property Custodian himself, as provided elsewhere herein, could continue. Such agents, attorneys, bailees, depositaries and managers shall have and exercise the rights, powers and authority which shall be from time to time conferred upon him or them by the Alien Property Custodian; and such rights, powers and authority may be enlarged, restricted or revoked by the Alien Property Custodian at any time and without giving any notice or reason therefor; and the remuneration of all such agents, attorneys, bailees, depositaries and managers shall be fixed by the Alien Property Custodian and may be increased or reduced at any time.

5. The Alien Property Custodian shall have full power and discre-

tion with respect to property to be sold, and may sell any property or properties as an entirety or in such groups or parcels and at such time or times as he shall determine, and without reference to the previous enemy or ally of enemy ownership thereof. Whenever any such property shall be used or employed in the conduct or other operation of any mine, plant, factory, railroad or other transportation facility, mercantile establishment or any sort of going business or undertaking, the Alien Property Custodian may sell such property as a going business or undertaking and may include not only the tangible property but any and all patents, trade marks, trade names, good will and other intangible rights and assets; and any number of such going businesses or undertakings may be sold together as above specified.

6. Whereas said Trading With the Enemy Act as amended provides that "any property sold, except when sold to the United States, shall be sold only to American citizens at public sale to the highest bidder, after public advertisement of the time and place of sale, which shall be where the property or a major portion thereof is situated, unless the President, stating the reasons therefore in the public interest, shall otherwise determine,"

Now therefore I do thus determine otherwise as follows:

(*a*) Shares of stock or other beneficial interest in a corporation, unincorporated association, company or trust, and claims, receivables and intangibles of all kinds may be advertised and sold wherever the Alien Property Custodian shall determine; and it shall be immaterial whether such shares of stock or other beneficial interest and such claims, receivables and intangibles be represented or evidenced by certificates or instruments or writings of any kind, and whether the Alien Property Custodian shall or shall not have possession or control thereof in the event that the same shall be thus represented or evidenced.

(*b*) Any corporation incorporated within and under the authority of the laws of any state or territory of the United States or of any of its insular possessions shall be allowed to bid at any sale of any such property, but the Alien Property Custodian shall have the right to exclude from bidding at any such sale and/or from purchasing or otherwise acquiring property from him directly or indirectly, any corporation which he shall after investigation determine to be controlled, managed or operated wholly or mainly by or for the account or benefit of a person or persons not a citizen or citizens of the United States or of its insular possessions.

(*c*) The Alien Property Custodian, upon order of the President stating the reasons therefor, shall have the right to reject all bids for any property thus sold and to resell such property at public sale or otherwise as the President may direct; but the Alien

Property Custodian may at or before any sale, by public announcement or by publication, fix a period after the expiration of which the right thus to reject all bids and to resell such property will not be exercised.

My reasons for the foregoing determinations in the public interest are:

(*a*) That such sales may be made at the place of favorable demand and under the best circumstances to secure the market price therefor.

(*b*) That bidders able to purchase and pay for the properties to be sold may be secured.

(*c*) That the powers of sale given to the Alien Property Custodian may be effectively exercised by him.

7. Any property sold by the Alien Property Custodian either at public or private sale may be sold for cash or upon credit; and in the latter event such security for the payment of that portion of the purchase price remaining unpaid may be taken as he shall deem proper in the premises. He shall be authorized to set a minimum or upset price upon any property offered for sale by him; to fix and prescribe the terms and conditions upon which bids will be received; to determine generally and specially qualifications to be met by persons offering to bid; to require deposits from prospective bidders; to determine generally or specially the nature and extent of information concerning and property or properties offered or to be offered for sale which shall be given prospective bidders, and the inspection thereof which shall be allowed; to have made auditor's reports and appraisals of property or properties offered or to be offered for sale; and to make and establish general and special terms and conditions to govern any and all sales to be made by him. Any property or properties thus sold may be sold subject to or free from any or all debts, claims, obligations and liabilities of all kinds created or arising out of or in respect of, any such property or properties or the conduct or other operation of any such business or other undertaking by the Alien Property Custodian or otherwise; and subject to or free from liens, charges or incumbrances; and payment of such debts, claims, obligations, liabilities and liens, charges and incumbrances, and of all expenses of such sale or sales may be made out of the proceeds from such sale or sales, or may be required to be made or assumed by the purchaser, as the Alien Property Custodian shall determine.

8. All costs and expenses incurred by reason of or in respect of, and all claims and demands of every kind, character and description based upon or arising out of, the custody, management, administration, protection, preservation and control of any such property and the conduct or other operation of any such going business or other undertaking and

the sale or other disposition of any such property, shall be limited to and paid or satisfied out of only the property or business or undertaking involved and out of which, on account of which, or in respect of which such cost, expenses, claim or demand shall have been incurred and shall have arisen or been created; provided that whenever such property or the income therefrom or the assets of any such going business or other undertaking shall be insufficient therefor, such cost, expenses, claim or demand shall be charged thereto, but may be paid or satisfied out of money or other property received from, or as the property of, the same enemy. Neither the Alien Property Custodian nor any agent, attorney, bailee, manager or depositary appointed by him shall be liable personally to any one for or on account of anything done or omitted in respect of, or for any debt or other obligation of any kind or character owing, created or growing out of or in any other way arising from, any such property or the custody, management, administration, protection, preservation, control and/or sale or other disposition thereof, and/or from the conduct or other operation of any going business or undertaking; except in the event of intentional injury or fraudulent misconduct by the person attempted to be charged with liability.

9. The Alien Property Custodian and agents, attorneys, bailees, managers and depositaries for him, within the limits of the authority granted by him, shall have power and authority to do any and all things reasonable or proper in or about or in respect to the exercise of any of the powers and authority specifically granted above; and in addition are authorized and directed hereby to manage all such property and to do any act or things in respect thereof or make any disposition thereof or any part thereof by sale or otherwise and exercise any rights or powers which may be or become appurtenant thereto or to the ownership thereof, in like manner as though the Alien Property Custodian were the absolute owner thereof, subject to no limitations or restrictions other than those specifically set forth herein or in said "Trading With the Enemy Act," as amended or any prior Executive orders issued pursuant thereto not in conflict herewith.

Power to Issue Requirements Not Inconsistent with Licenses Granted Under the Authority of the President.

1. Whenever the Alien Property Custodian shall after investigation determine that any money or other property, including any going business or other undertaking, which is being held, managed, used or employed under a license granted by the President, or in the exercise of the power and authority conferred upon the President by said Trading With the Enemy Act as amended, is owing or belonging to or held

for, by, on account of, on behalf of, or for the benefit of any enemy or ally of enemy, and such license provides as one of its terms or conditions that such property shall, upon demand or requirement of the Alien Property Custodian, be conveyed, transferred, assigned, delivered, and/or paid over to him, the Alien Property Custodian may, without the revocation of such license, require that said money or other property or any part or parcel thereof be conveyed, transferred, assigned, delivered or paid over to him; subject, however, to the continued exercise of such license, but under his supervision or under such other supervision as he may prescribe, and for such period of time or until the happening of such event as he shall prescribe. Whenever such money or property or any part thereof, at the time such requirement is made, shall be used or employed in or about the conduct or management of any mine, plant, factory, railroad or other transportation facility, warehouse, mercantile or trading establishment or any sort of a going business or undertaking, the Alien Property Custodian may require that such money or other property and/or the proceeds from the conduct or management of such business be conveyed, transferred, assigned, delivered or paid over to him, subject to the continued exercise of such license and the continued conduct or management of such business or other undertaking as above provided; and he may leave all or such part of the money or other property of such business or other undertaking in the possession of the licensee or the agent or representative of the licensee to be used, disposed of, and accounted for, in the continued exercise of such license. Any requirement made by the Alien Property Custodian pursuant to the provisions hereof shall be subject to modification or change by him at any time prior to the final compliance therewith. Any of such property other than money, including any such going business or undertaking, may be advertised and sold by the Alien Property Custodian, subject to the exercise of any such license, but for the account of the Alien Property Custodian or for the account of the purchaser as the Alien Property Custodian may determine; and until the purchaser of such property shall be placed in the possession thereof or during such other period as the Alien Property Custodian may determine.

Effect upon the Statutory Powers of the Alien Property Custodian and upon Prior Executive Orders

1. Nothing herein contained shall limit or shall be construed to limit, in any way the rights, powers and authority conferred upon the Alien Property Custodian by the "Trading With the Enemy Act" and the amendments thereto and the Executive orders heretofore issued pursuant thereto.

2. All executive orders heretofore made are amended and modified hereby to such an extent as may be necessary to conform with the provisions hereof; but with this exception, all of such orders in force and effect at the time this order is issued are expressly ratified and continued in full force and effect.

WOODROW WILSON.

[Honorably discharged soldiers or sailors to be readmitted to Civil Service.]

THE WHITE HOUSE, *18 July, 1918.*

A person leaving the classified civil service to engage in the military or naval service of the Government during the present war with Germany and who has been honorably discharged may be reinstated in the civil service at any time within five years after his discharge, provided that at the time of reinstatement he has the required fitness to perform the duties of the position in which reinstatement is sought.

WOODROW WILSON.

BY THE PRESIDENT OF THE UNITED STATES OF AMERICA

PROCLAMATIONS

[Possession and Control of Telegraph and Telephone Systems.]

Whereas the Congress of the United States, in the exercise of the constitutional authority vested in them, by joint resolution of the Senate and House of Representatives, bearing date July 16, 1918, resolved:

That the President during the continuance of the present war is authorized and empowered, whenever he shall deem it necessary for the national security or defense, to supervise or to take possession and assume control of any telegraph, telephone, marine cable, or radio system or systems, or any part thereof, and to operate the same in such manner as may be needful or desirable for the duration of the war, which supervision, possession, control, or operation shall not extend beyond the date of the proclamation by the President of the exchange of ratifications of the treaty of peace: Provided, That just compensation shall be made for such supervision, possession, control, or operation, to be determined by the President; and if the amount thereof, so determined by the President, is unsatisfactory to the person entitled to receive the same, such person shall be paid seventy-five per centum of the amount so determined by the President and shall be entitled to sue the United States to recover such further sum as, added to said seventy-five per centum, will make up such amount as will be just compensation therefor, in the manner provided for by section twenty-four, paragraph twenty, and section one hundred and forty-five of the Judicial Code:

Provided further, That nothing in this Act shall be construed to amend, repeal, impair, or affect existing laws or powers of the States in relation to taxation or the lawful police regulations of the several States, except wherein such laws, powers, or regulations may affect the transmission of Government communications, or the issue of stocks and bonds by such system or systems.

And whereas it is deemed necessary for the national security and defense to supervise and to take possession and assume control of all telegraph and telephone systems and to operate the same in such manner as may be needful or desirable;

Now, Therefore, I, Woodrow Wilson, President of the United States, under and by virtue of the powers vested in me by the foregoing resolution, and by virtue of all other powers thereto me enabling, do hereby take possession and assume control and supervision of each and every telegraph and telephone system, and every part thereof, within the jurisdiction of the United States, including all equipment thereof and appurtenances thereto whatsoever and all materials and supplies.

It is hereby directed that the supervision, possession, control, and operation of such telegraph and telephone systems hereby by me undertaken shall be exercised by and through the Postmaster General, Albert S. Burleson. Said Postmaster General may perform the duties hereby and hereunder imposed upon him, so long and to such extent and in such manner as he shall determine, through the owners, managers, boards of directors, receivers, officers, and employees of said telegraph and telephone systems.

Until and except so far as said Postmaster General shall from time to time by general or special orders otherwise provide, the owners, managers, boards of directors, receivers, officers, and employees of the various telegraph and telephone systems shall continue the operation thereof in the usual and ordinary course of the business of said systems, in the names of their respective companies, associations, organizations, owners, or managers, as the case may be.

Regular dividends hitherto declared, and maturing interest upon bonds, debentures, and other obligations, may be paid in due course; and such regular dividends and interest may continue to be paid until and unless the said Postmaster General shall, from time to time, otherwise by general or special orders determine; and, subject to the approval of said Postmaster General, the various telegraph and telephone systems may determine upon and arrange for the renewal and extension of maturing obligations.

By subsequent order of said Postmaster General supervision, possession, control, or operation, may be relinquished in whole or in part to the owners thereof of any telegraph or telephone system or any part thereof supervision, possession, control, or operation of which is hereby assumed or which may be subsequently assumed in whole or in part hereunder.

From and after twelve o'clock midnight on the 31st day of July, 1918, all telegraph and telephone systems included in this order and proclamation shall conclusively be deemed within the possession and control and under the supervision of said Postmaster General without further act or notice.

In witness whereof, I have hereunto set my hand and caused the seal of the United States to be affixed.

Done by the President, in the District of Columbia, this 22nd day of July, in the year of our Lord one thousand nine hundred and eighteen, and of the independence of the United States the one hundred and forty-third.

[SEAL.]

WOODROW WILSON.

By the President:

FRANK L. POLK, *Acting Secretary of State.*

[Possession and Control of the Transportation System of the Boston, Cape Cod and New York Canal Company.]

Whereas the Congress of the United States, in the exercise of the Constitutional authority vested in them, by joint resolution of the Senate and House of Representatives bearing date of April 6, 1917, resolved:

"That the state of war between the United States and the Imperial German Government which has thus been thrust upon the United States is hereby formally declared; and that the President be, and he is hereby, authorized and directed to employ the entire naval and military forces of the United States and the resources of the Government to carry on war against the Imperial German Government; and to bring the conflict to a successful termination all of the resources of the country are hereby pledged by the Congress of the United States;"

And by joint resolution bearing date of December 7, 1917, resolved:

"That a state of war is hereby declared to exist between the United States of America and the Imperial and Royal Austro-Hugarian Government; and that the President be, and he is hereby, authorized and directed to employ the entire naval and military forces of the United States and the resources of the Government to carry on a war against the Imperial and Royal Austro-Hungarian Government; and to bring the conflict to a successful termination all the resources of the country are hereby pledged by the Congress of the United States;"

And whereas it is provided by section 1 of the act approved August

29, 1916, entitled "An act making appropriations for the support of
the Army for the fiscal year ending June 30, 1917, and for other purposes," as follows:

"The President in time of war is empowered, through the Secretary
of War, to take possession and assume control of any system or systems of transportation, or any part thereof, and to utilize the same,
to the exclusion, as far as may be necessary, of all other traffic thereon,
for the transfer or transportation of troops, war material, and equipment, or for such other purposes connected with the emergency as may
be needful or desirable;"

And whereas it has now become necessary in the national defense to
take possession and assume control of certain systems of transportation
and to utilize the same, to the exclusion, as far as may be necessary, of
other than war traffic thereon, for the transportation of troops, war material, and equipment therefor, and for other needful and desirable
purposes connected with the prosecution of the war;

Now, Therefore, I, Woodrow Wilson, President of the United
States, under and by virtue of the powers vested in me by the foregoing resolutions and statute, and by virtue of all other powers thereto
me enabling, do hereby, through Newton D. Baker, Secretary of War,
take possession and assume control at 12:01 A. M. on the twenty-fifth
day of July, 1918, of the following system of transportation and the
appurtenances thereof, to wit; the canal and other property of the
Boston Cape Cod and New York Canal Company, a corporation
organized under the laws of the Commonwealth of Massachusetts,
consisting of a ship canal extending from Cape Cod Bay to Buzzards
Bay in Massachusetts, with all the appurtenances and equipment of
said canal, including all the lands, easements, wharves, docks, buildings, tugs, barges, ships, boats, tackle, appliances, and all other property
of whatsoever kind owned, leased, chartered, controlled or used by the
said corporation in the maintenance and operation of said canal or in
connection with the towage, pilotage, or anchorage of vessels passing
through the same.

To the end that said system of transportation be utilized for the
transfer and transportation of troops, war material, and equipment, to
the exclusion so far as may be necessary of all other traffic thereon;
and that so far as such exclusive use be not necessary or desirable
such system of transportation be operated and utilized in the performance of such other services as the national interest may require and
of the usual and ordinary operation of the said transportation system.

It is hereby directed that the possession, control, operation, and utilization of such transportation system, hereby by me undertaken, shall
be exercised by and through William G. McAdoo, who has been duly

appointed and designated Director General of Railroads. Said Director General may perform the duties imposed upon him, so long and to such extent as he shall determine, through the board of directors, officers, and employees of said corporation; or through such other agents or agencies as he may from time to time appoint. Until and except so far as said Director General shall from time to time by general or special orders otherwise provide, the board of directors, officers, and employees of said corporation shall continue the usual and ordinary operation of said transportation system in the name of said corporation.

Until and except so far as said Director General shall from time to time otherwise by general or special orders determine, such system of transportation shall remain subject to all existing statutes of the United States and to all statutes and orders of regulating commissions of the Commonwealth of Massachusetts; but any orders, general or special, hereafter made by said Director General shall have paramount authority and be obeyed as such.

The Director General shall, as soon as may be after having assumed such possession and control, enter upon negotiations with the said corporation looking to an agreement for just and reasonable compensation for the possession, use and control of its property.

Except with the prior written assent of said Director General, no attachment by mesne process or on execution shall during Federal control be levied on or against any of the property of said corporation or used by said transportation system in the maintenance and operation of said canal while under Federal control; but suits may be brought by and against the said corporation and judgments rendered as hitherto until and except so far as said Director General may, by general or special orders, otherwise determine.

From and after 12:01 A. M., on said twenty-fifth day of July, 1918, the transportation system included in this order and proclamation shall conclusively be deemed within the possession and control of said Director General without further act or notice.

In witness whereof I have hereunto set my hand and caused the seal of the United States to be affixed.

Done by the President, through Newton D. Baker, Secretary of War, in the District of Columbia this 22nd day of July, in the [SEAL.] year of our Lord one thousand nine hundred and eighteen, of the Independence of the United States the one hundred and forty-third.

WOODROW WILSON.

By the President:

FRANK L. POLK, *Acting Secretary of State.*

NEWTON D. BAKER, *Secretary of War.*

ADDRESS TO FELLOW COUNTRYMEN

[Deploring Mob Spirit.]

THE WHITE HOUSE, *July 26, 1918.*

My Fellow Countrymen: I take the liberty of addressing you upon a subject which so vitally affects the honor of the nation and the very character and integrity of our institutions that I trust you will think me justified in speaking very plainly about it.

I allude to the mob spirit which has recently here and there very frequently shown its head among us, not in any single region, but in many and widely separated parts of the country. There have been many lynchings, and every one of them has been a blow at the heart of ordered law and humane justice. No man who loves America, no man who really cares for her fame and honor and character, or who is truly loyal to her institutions, can justify mob action while the courts of justice are open and the governments of the States and the nation are ready and able to do their duty. We are at this very moment fighting lawless passion. Germany has outlawed herself among the nations because she has disregarded the sacred obligations of law and has made lynchers of her armies. Lynchers emulate her disgraceful example. I, for my part, am anxious to see every community in America rise above that level, with pride and a fixed resolution which no man or set of men can afford to despise.

We proudly claim to be the champions of democracy. If we really are, in deed and truth, let us see to it that we do not discredit our own. I say plainly that every American who takes part in the action of a mob or gives it any sort of countenance is no true son of this great democracy, but its betrayer, and does more to discredit her by that single disloyalty to her standards of law and right, than the words of her statesmen or the sacrifices of her heroic boys in the trenches can do to make suffering peoples believe her to be their savior. How shall we commend democracy to the acceptance of other peoples if we disgrace our own by proving that it is, after all, no protection to the weak? Every mob contributes to German lies about the United States what her most gifted liars cannot improve upon by the way of calumny. They can at least say that such things cannot happen in Germany except in times of revolution, when law is swept away!

I therefore very earnestly and solemnly beg that the Governors of all the States, the law officers of every community, and, above all, the men and women of every community in the United States, all who revere America and wish to keep her name without stain or reproach, will co-operate—not passively merely, but actively and watchfully—to make an end of this disgraceful evil. It cannot live where the community does not countenance it.

I have called upon the nation to put its great energy into this war and it has responded—responded with a spirit and a genius for action that has thrilled the world. I now call upon it, upon its men and women everywhere, to see to it that its laws are kept inviolate, its fame untarnished. Let us show our utter contempt for the things that have made this war hideous among the ways of history by showing how those who love liberty and right and justice and are willing to lay down their lives for them upon foreign fields stand ready also to illustrate to all mankind their loyalty to all things at home which they wish to see established everywhere as a blessing and protection to the peoples who have never known the privilege of liberty and self-government. I can never accept any man as a champion of liberty either for ourselves or for the world who does not reverence and obey the laws of our own beloved land, whose laws we ourselves have made. He has adopted the standards of the enemies of his country, whom he affects to despise.

WOODROW WILSON.

EXECUTIVE ORDER

[Amending rules for operation of Panama Canal.]

THE WHITE HOUSE, *July 26, 1918.*

By virtue of the authority vested in me, I hereby establish the following Executive order for the Canal Zone:

Section 1. Paragraph 20 of the Executive order of July 9, 1914, entitled "Rules and regulations for the operation and navigation of the Panama Canal and approaches thereto, including all waters under its jurisdiction," is hereby amended to read as follows:

"20. The captain or master of a vessel in canal waters, except while the vessel is being passed through the locks, shall be charged with the safe handling and proper navigation of the vessel; the pilot is to be considered as being on board solely in an advisory capacity, but masters of vessels must abide by rules and regulations of the canal as interpreted by the pilot. No claim against the Panama Canal for damages on account of injury to a vessel or its cargo while in Canal Zone waters, arising from the operation of the canal (other than the passing of vessels through the locks) shall be allowed unless it shall be determined by the Governor of the Panama Canal that such injury was due to the negligence or want of care on the part of agents or employees of the Panama Canal, and there shall be an appropriation available for the payment of such claim."

Sec. 2. This order shall take effect from and after this date.

WOODROW WILSON.

By the President of the United States of America

A PROCLAMATION

[Giving Shipping Board power over chartering of American vessels and of foreign vessels by Americans, except small craft and vessels in inland or coastwise trade.]

Whereas an act of Congress, approved July 18, 1918, entitled "An act to confer on the President power to prescribe charter rates and freight rates and to requisition vessels, and for other purposes," contains, among others, the following sections conferring authority upon the President:

"Sec. 5. That the President may, by proclamation, require that vessels of the United States of any specified class or description, or in any specified trade or trades, shall not be chartered unless the instrument in which such charter is embodied, and the rates, terms, and conditions thereof are first approved by him. Whenever any vessel is comprised in any such proclamation, it shall be unlawful to make any charter thereof, or comply with or perform any of the rates, terms, or conditions of any charter thereof, or to operate such vessel under any charter, without first obtaining the approval thereof by the President.

"Whenever any charter of such vessel is approved it shall be unlawful, without the approval of the President first obtained, to make any alterations in such charter, or additions thereto, or deletions therefrom, or to make or receive any payment, or do any act with respect to such vessel, except in accordance with such charter.

"Sec. 8. That the President may, by proclamation, extend the provisions of sections 5, 6, and 7, or any of them, to any vessel of foreign nationality under charter to a citizen of the United States or other person subject to the jurisdiction thereof."

"Sec. 10. That the President may, by proclamation, require that no citizen of the United States, or other person subject to the jurisdiction thereof, shall charter any vessel of foreign nationality unless the instrument in which such charter is embodied and the rates, terms, and conditions thereof are first approved by the President. After the making of such proclamation it shall be unlawful for any such citizen or person to make any charter of any such vessel, or comply with or perform any of the rates, terms, or conditions of any charter thereof, or to operate any such vessel under any charter without first obtaining the approval thereof by the President.

"Whenever any such charter is approved it shall be unlawful, without the approval of the President first obtained, to make any alterations in such charter or additions thereto or deletions therefrom, or to make or receive any payment or do any act with respect to such vessel, except in accordance with such charter."

And whereas, section 2 of said act provides as follows:

"Sec. 2. That the President may exercise the power and authority hereby vested in him through such agency or agencies as he shall determine from time to time."

And whereas, the necessities of the war require that the control now exercised over shipping by the United States Shipping Board be made more effective;

Now, therefore, I, Woodrow Wilson, President of the United States of America, acting under authority conferred in section 5 of said act, do proclaim that hereafter vessels of the United States, being full power-driven vessels of 250 tons gross burden or over, or sailing vessels with or without auxiliary power of 50 tons gross burden or over, excepting vessels plying exclusively on the inland rivers and canals of the United States, vessels operating in the Great Lakes or other inland waters, and vessels operating exclusively in the coastwise trade of the United States, shall not hereafter be chartered unless the instrument in which such charter is embodied, and the rates, terms, and conditions thereof are first approved by the President.

Under authority conferred in section 8 of said act, I do further proclaim that the provisions of said section 5, and of this proclamation, shall be, and they are hereby, extended to any vessel of foreign nationality under charter to a citizen of the United States or other person subject to the jurisdiction thereof.

Under authority conferred in section 10 of said act, I do further proclaim that hereafter no citizen of the United States or other person subject to the jurisdiction thereof shall charter any vessel of foreign nationality unless the instrument in which such charter is embodied and the rates, terms, and conditions thereof are first approved by the President.

I do hereby designate the United States Shipping Board as the agency through which shall be exercised all power and authority conferred upon the President in sections 5, 8, and 10 of said act with respect to the classes or descriptions of vessels and the trades specified in this proclamation. Such power and authority may be exercised by said United States Shipping Board through such agents or agencies as it may create or designate.

Nothing contained in this proclamation shall be deemed to withdraw from the United States Shipping Board or the War Trade Board any authority now exercised, directly or indirectly, over foreign or American vessels, by virtue of powers conferred under Title VII of an act entitled "An act to punish acts of interference with the foreign relations, the neutrality, and the foreign commerce of the United

States, to punish espionage, and better to enforce the criminal laws of the United States, and for other purposes," approved June 15, 1917.

In witness whereof, I have hereunto set my hand and caused the seal of the United States to be affixed.

Done in the District of Columbia this 29th day of July, in the year of our Lord one thousand nine hundred and eighteen and [SEAL] of the independence of the United States of America the one hundred and forty-third.

By the President: WOODROW WILSON.

FRANK L. POLK, *Acting Secretary of State.*

EXECUTIVE ORDER

[Supply of petroleum products specifications assigned to Fuel Administration.]

THE WHITE HOUSE, *July 31, 1918.*

Whereas in order to avoid duplication of effort, and in the interest of economy and the more efficient concentration of the Government and for the better utilization of resources and industries, it is desirable that there shall be a standardization of specifications for the supply of petroleum and its products to the United States Government,

Now, therefore, I, Woodrow Wilson, President of the United States, by virtue of the authority vested in me as Chief Executive, and by virtue of the powers conferred on me by the act of Congress, entitled "An act authorizing the President to co-ordinate or consolidate executive bureaus, agencies, and offices, and for other purposes, in the interest of economy and the more efficient concentration of the Government," approved May 20, 1918, do hereby order that the function, power, and duty of preparing and adopting specifications for the supply of petroleum and its products to any and all departments, bureaus, agencies, and offices of the Government be transferred to and exercised by the United States Fuel Administrator. The United States Fuel Administrator shall exercise such functions, powers, and duties through a committee on standardization of petroleum specifications, which shall be composed of the following members:

A chairman, who shall be appointed by the United States Fuel Administrator; one member who shall be appointed by the Secretary of War; one member who shall be appointed by the Secretary of the Navy; one member who shall be appointed by the chairman of the Shipping Board; one member who shall be appointed by the Director General of the Railroad Administration; one member who shall be appointed by the Director of the Bureau of Mines; and one member who shall be appointed by the Director of the Bureau of Standards.

The specifications so prepared and adopted shall be binding upon and govern all departments, bureaus, agencies, and offices of the Government. It shall further be the duty of the United States Fuel Administrator, acting through said Committee on Standardization of Petroleum Specifications, to take all proper means to bring about a standardization of petroleum specifications for the purchases in the United States of the allied Governments.

This order shall be and remain in full force and effect during the continuance of the present war and for six months after the termination thereof by the proclamation of a treaty of peace, or until amended, modified, or rescinded.

WOODROW WILSON.

[Issuance of Passports and Permits to enter or leave the United States.]

Whereas by act of Congress approved the 22d day of May, 1918, entitled "An act to prevent in time of war departure from and entry into the United States contrary to the public safety," it is provided as follows:

"Be it enacted by the Senate and House of Representatives of the United States of America in Congress assembled, That when the United States is at war, if the President shall find that the public safety requires that restrictions and prohibitions in addition to those provided otherwise than by this act be imposed upon the departure of persons from and their entry into the United States, and shall make public proclamation thereof, it shall, until otherwise ordered by the President or Congress, be unlawful—

"(a) For any alien to depart from or enter or attempt to depart from or enter the United States except under such reasonable rules, regulations, and orders, and subject to such limitations and exceptions as the President shall prescribe;

"(b) For any person to transport or attempt to transport from or into the United States another person with knowledge or reasonable cause to believe that the departure or entry of such other person is forbidden by this act;

"(c) For any person knowingly to make any false statement in an application for permission to depart from or enter the United States with intent to induce or secure the granting of such permission either for himself or for another;

"(d) For any person knowingly to furnish or attempt to furnish or assist in furnishing to another a permit or evidence of permission to depart or enter not issued and designed for such other person's use;

"(e) For any person knowingly to use or attempt to use any permit or evidence of permission to depart or enter not issued and designed for his use;

"(f) For any person to forge, counterfeit, mutilate, or alter, or cause or procure to be forged, counterfeited, mutilated, or altered, any permit or evidence of permission to depart from or enter the United States;

"(g) For any person knowingly to use or attempt to use or furnish to another for use any false, forged, counterfeited, mutilated, or altered permit, or evidence of permission, or any permit or evidence of permission which, though originally valid, has become or been made void or invalid.

"Sec. 2. That after such proclamation as is provided for by the preceding section has been made and published and while said proclamation is in force, it shall, except as otherwise provided by the President, and subject to such limitations and exceptions as the President may authorize and prescribe, be unlawful for any citizen of the United States to depart from or enter or attempt to depart from or enter the United States unless he bears a valid passport.

"Sec. 3. That any person who shall willfully violate any of the provisions of this act, or of any order or proclamation of the President promulgate, or of any permit, rule, or regulation issued thereunder, shall, upon conviction, be fined not more than $10,000, or, if a natural person, imprisoned for not more than twenty years, or both; and the officer, director, or agent of any corporation who knowingly participates in such violation shall be punished by like fine or imprisonment, or both; and any vehicle or any vessel, together with its or her appurtenances, equipment, tackle, apparel, and furniture, concerned in any such violation, shall be forfeited to the United States.

"Sec. 4. That the term 'United States' as used in this act includes the Canal Zone and all territory and waters, continental or insular, subject to the jurisdiction of the United States.

"The word 'person' as used herein shall be deemed to mean any individual, partnership, association, company, or other unincorporated body of individuals, or corporation, or body politic."

And whereas other provisions relating to departure from and entry into the United States are contained in section 3, subsection (b), of the trading-with-the-enemy act, approved October 6, 1917, and in section 4067 of the Revised Statutes, as amended by the act of April 16, 1918, and sections 4068, 4069, and 4070 of the Revised Statutes, and in the regulations prescribed in the President's proclamations of April 6, 1917; November 16, 1917; December 11, 1917; and April 19, 1918;

And whereas the act of May 20, 1918, authorizes me to co-ordinate and consolidate executive agencies and bureaus in the interest of economy and more efficient concentration of the Government;

Now, therefore, I, Woodrow Wilson, President of the United States of America, acting under and by virtue of the aforesaid authority vested in me, do hereby find and publicly proclaim and declare that the public safety requires that restrictions and prohibitions in addition to those provided otherwise than by the act of May 22, 1918, above mentioned, shall be imposed upon the departure of persons from and their entry into the United States; and I make the following orders thereunder:

1. No citizen of the United States shall receive a passport entitling him to leave or enter the United States unless it shall affirmatively appear that there are adequate reasons for such departure or entry and that such departure or entry is not prejudicial to the interests of the United States.

2. No alien shall receive permission to depart from or enter the United States unless it shall affirmatively appear that there is reasonable necessity for such departure or entry and that such departure or entry is not prejudicial to the interests of the United States.

3. The provisions of this proclamation and the rules and regulations promulgated in pursuance hereof shall not be held to suspend or supersede in any respect, except as herein expressly provided the President's proclamations of April 6, 1917; November 16, 1917; December 11, 1917, and April 19, 1918, above referred to; nor shall anything contained herein be construed to suspend or supersede any rules or regulations issued under the Chinese-exclusion law or the immigration laws except as herein expressly provided; but the provisions hereof shall, subject to the provisos above mentioned, be regarded as additional to such rules and regulations. Compliance with this proclamation and the rules and regulations promulgated in pursuance hereof shall not exempt any individual from the duty of complying with any statute, proclamation, order, rule, or regulations not referred to herein.

4. I hereby designate the Secretary of State as the official who shall grant, or in whose name shall be granted, permission to aliens to depart from or enter the United States; I reaffirm sections 25, 26, and 27 of the Executive order of October 12, 1917, vesting in the Secretary of State the administration of the provisions of section 3, subsection (b), of the trading with enemy act; I transfer to the Secretary of State the Executive administration of regulations 9 and 10 of the President's proclamation of April 6, 1917; of regulation 15 of the President's proclamation of November 16, 1917, and of regulations 1 and 2 of the President's proclamation of December 1, 1917, and the executive administration of the aforesaid regulations as extended by the President's proclamation of April 19, 1918, said executive administration heretofore having been delegated to the Attorney General under dates of April 6, 1917; November 16, 1917; December 11, 1917, and April 19, 1918. The Rules and Regulations made by the Secretary of the

Treasury, as authorized by Title II, section 1, of the espionage act approved June 15, 1917, and by the Executive order of December 3, 1917, shall be superseded by this proclamation and the rules and regulations promulgated in pursuance hereof in so far as they are inconsistent therewith.

I hereby direct all departments of the Government to co-operate with the Secretary of State in the execution of his duties under this proclamation and the rules and regulations promulgated in pursuance hereof. They shall upon his request make available to him for that purpose the services of their respective officials and agents. The Secretary of the Treasury, the Secretary of War, the Attorney General, the Secretary of the Navy, the Secretary of Commerce, and the Secretary of Labor shall, at the request of the Secretary of State, each appoint a representative to render to the Secretary of State, or his representative, such assistance and advice as he may desire respecting the administration of this proclamation and of the rules and regulations aforesaid.

In witness whereof, I have hereunto set my hand and caused the seal of the United States to be affixed.

Done in the District of Columbia, this eighth day of August, in the year of our Lord one thousand nine hundred and eighteen, [SEAL] and of the independence of the United States, the one hundred and forty-third.

By the President: WOODROW WILSON.

ROBERT LANSING, *Secretary of State.*

BY THE PRESIDENT OF THE UNITED STATES OF AMERICA

PROCLAMATIONS

[Eliminating foreign interests from United States shipping.]

Whereas, an act of Congress, entitled "Shipping act, 1916," approved September 7, 1916, as amended by an act of Congress entitled "An act to amend the act approved September 7, 1916, entitled, 'An act to establish a United States Shipping Board for the purpose of encouraging, developing, and creating a naval auxiliary and naval reserve and a merchant marine to meet the requirements of the commerce of the United States with its territories and possessions and with foreign countries; to regulate carriers by water in the foreign and interstate commerce of the United States; and for other purposes,'" approved July 15, 1918, contains the following provisions:

Sec. 37. That when the United States is at war or during any national emergency, the existence of which is declared by proclamation of the President, it shall be unlawful, without first obtaining the approval of the board:

(a) To transfer or to place under any foreign registry or flag any vessel owned in whole or in part by any person a citizen of the United States or by a corporation organized under the laws of the United States, or of any State, Territory, District, or possession thereof; or

(b) To sell, mortgage, lease, charter, deliver, or in any manner transfer, or agree to sell, mortgage, lease, charter, deliver, or in any manner transfer, to any person not a citizen of the United States (1) any such vessel or any interest therein, or (2) any vessel documented under the laws of the United States, or any interest therein, or (3) any shipyard, dry dock, ship-building or ship-repairing plant or facilities or any interest therein; or

(c) To enter into any contract, agreement, or understanding to construct a vessel within the United States for or to be delivered to any person not a citizen of the United States, without expressly stipulating that such construction shall not begin until after the war or emergency proclaimed by the President has ended; or

(d) To make any agreement, or effect any understanding whereby there is vested in or for the benefit of any person not a citizen of the United States, the controlling interest or a majority of the voting power in a corporation which is organized under the laws of the United States, or of any State, Territory, District, or possession thereof, and which owns any vessel, shipyard, dry dock, or ship-building or ship-repairing plant or facilities; or

(e) To cause or procure any vessel constructed in whole or in part within the United States, which has never cleared for any foreign port, to depart from a port of the United States before it has been documented under the laws of the United States.

And whereas the destruction of maritime tonnage during the present war has rendered it imperative that the American merchant marine be retained under American control and free from alien influence;

Now, therefore, I, Woodrow Wilson, President of the United States of America, acting under authority conferred in me by said act, do hereby proclaim that a state of war and a national emergency within the meaning of said act do now exist, and I do hereby enjoin all persons from doing of the things in said act declared to be unlawful.

For the purposes of said act of Congress, the national emergency herein proclaimed shall be deemed to continue until its termination has been evidenced by a proclamation of the President.

In witness whereof I have hereunto set my hand and caused the seal of the United States to be affixed.

Done in the District of Columbia this 7th day of August, in the year of our Lord one thousand nine hundred and eighteen, and [SEAL.] of the Independence of the United States of America the one hundred and forty-third.

By the President: WOODROW WILSON.

FRANK L. POLK, *Acting Secretary of State.*

APPEAL FOR INCREASED COAL PRODUCTION

THE WHITE HOUSE, *August 9, 1918.*

To All Engaged in Coal Mining:

The existing scarcity of coal is creating a grave danger—in fact, the most serious which confronts us—and calls for prompt and vigorous action on the part of both operators and miners. Without an adequate supply, our war program will be retarded; the effectiveness of our fighting forces in France will be lessened; the lives of our soldiers will be unnecessarily endangered and their hardships increased, and there will be much suffering in many homes throughout the country during the coming Winter.

I am well aware that your ranks have been seriously depleted by the draft, by voluntary enlistment, and by the demands of other essential industries. This handicap can be overcome, however, and sufficient coal can be mined in spite of it, if every one connected with the industry, from the highest official to the youngest boy, will give his best work each day for the full number of work hours.

The operators must be zealous as never before to bring about the highest efficiency of management, to establish the best possible working conditions, and to accord fair treatment to everybody, so that the opportunity to work at his best may be accorded every workman.

The miners should report for work every day unless prevented by unavoidable causes, and should not only stay in the mines the full time, but also see to it that they get more coal than ever before. The other workers in and about the mines should work as regularly and faithfully, so that the work of the miner may not be retarded in any way. This will be especially necessary from this time forward, for your numbers may be further lessened by the draft, which will induct into the army your fair share of those not essential to industry.

Those who are drafted but who are essential will be given deferred classification, and it is their patriotic duty to accept it. And it is the patriotic duty of their friends and neighbors to hold them in high regard for doing so.

The only worker who deserves the condemnation of his community is the one who fails to give his best in this crisis; not the one who accepts deferred classification and works regularly and diligently to increase the coal output.

A great task is to be performed. The operators and their staffs alone cannot do it, nor can the mine workers alone do it; but both parties, working hand in hand, with a grim determination to rid the country of its greatest obstacle to winning the war, can do it.

It is with full confidence that I call upon you to assume the burden of producing an ample supply of coal. You will, I am sure, accept this burden, and will successfully carry it through, and in so doing you will be performing a service just as worthy as service in the trenches, and will win the applause and gratitude of the whole nation.

WOODROW WILSON.

By the President of the United States of America

A PROCLAMATION

[Registration in draft of men reaching age of 21 since June 5, 1918.]

[The proclamation opens by quoting the six sections to be found on pages 8510, 8511, 8256, 8257 and 8258.]

And whereas the last preceding date of registration under the terms of the said public resolution approved May 20, 1918, was June 5, 1918:

Now, therefore, I, Woodrow Wilson, President of the United States, do call upon all male persons, either citizens of the United States or residing in the several States, or in the District of Columbia, who have, since the 5th day of June, 1918, and on or before the 24th day of August, 1918, attained their twenty-first birthday, to register in accordance with the above law and the regulations prescribed thereunder: *Provided, however,* That the following persons are hereby exempted from registration: Officers and enlisted men of the Regular Army, the Navy, the Marine Corps, and the National Guard and Naval Militia while in the service of the United States, and officers in the Officers' Reserve Corps and enlisted men in the Enlisted Reserve Corps while in active service.

And I do further proclaim and give notice to every person subject to registration in the several States, and in the District of Columbia, in accordance with the above law, that the time and place of registration shall be between 7 a. m. and 9 p. m. on the 24th day of August,

1918, at the office of the local board having jurisdiction of the area wherein he permanently resides, or at such other place as shall be designated by public notice by such local board.

And I do call upon the governor of each of the several States, the Board of Commissioners of the District of Columbia, and all members of local boards and agents thereof appointed under the provision of the act of Congress approved May 18, 1917, to perform certain duties in the execution of the foregoing law, which duties have been communicated to them directly in regulations prescribed under the terms of said public resolution.

A day for registration in the Territories of Alaska, Hawaii, and Porto Rico will be named in a later proclamation.

[The proclamation closes with the same words as the proclamation upon pages 8512 and 8513.]

Done in the District of Columbia this 13th day of August in the year of our Lord one thousand nine hundred and eighteen and [SEAL.] of the independence of the United States of America the one hundred and forty-third.

By the President: WOODROW WILSON.

ROBERT LANSING, *Secretary of State.*

LETTER

[Education in War Time.]

THE WHITE HOUSE, *July 31, 1918.*

My Dear Mr. Secretary:

I am pleased to know that despite the unusual burdens imposed upon our people by the war they have maintained their schools and other agencies of education so nearly at their normal efficiency. That this should be continued throughout the war and that, in so far as the draft law will permit, there should be no falling off in attendance in elementary schools, high schools or colleges is a matter of the very greatest importance, affecting both our strength in war and our national welfare and efficiency when the war is over. So long as the war continues there will be constant need of very large numbers of men and women of the highest and most thorough training for war service in many lines. After the war there will be urgent need not only for trained leadership in all lines of industrial, commercial, social and civil life, but for a very high average of intelligence and preparation on the part of all the people. I would therefore urge that the people continue to give generous support to their schools of all grades and that the schools adjust themselves as wisely as possible to the new conditions to the end that no boy or girl shall have less opportunity for education because of the war and that the Nation may be strengthened as it can only be through the right education of all its people. I approve most heartily your plans for making through the Bureau of Education a comprehensive campaign for the support of the schools and for the maintenance of attendance upon them, and trust that you may have the cooperation in this work of the American Council on Education.

Cordially and sincerely yours,
WOODROW WILSON.

Hon. Franklin K. Lane,
  Secretary of the Interior.

EXECUTIVE ORDER

[Amending the Executive Order of October 12th, 1917, to provide for a Representative of the War Industries Board on the War Trade. Board.]

THE WHITE HOUSE, *August 20, 1918.*

By virtue of the authority vested in me by "An Act To define, regulate, and punish Trading with the Enemy and for other purposes," approved October 6, 1917, and by Title VII of the act approved June 15, 1917, entitled "An Act To punish acts of interference with the foreign relations, the neutrality and the foreign commerce of the United States, to punish espionage and better to enforce the criminal laws of the United States and for other purposes," I do hereby amend the Order of October 12th, 1917, vesting power and authority in designated officers and establishing the War Trade Board, composed of representatives, respectively, of the Secretary of State, of the Secretary of the Treasury, of the Secretary of Agriculture, of the Secretary of Commerce, of the Food Administrator, and of the United States Shipping Board, by changing Paragraph I of said Order to read as follows:

"I. I hereby establish a War Trade Board to be composed of representatives, respectively, of the Secretary of State, of the Secretary of the Treasury, of the Secretary of Agriculture, of the Secretary of Commerce, of the Food Administrator, of the United States Shipping Board, and of the War Industries Board."

The Order of October 12th, 1917, as so amended is hereby confirmed and continued, and all orders and proclamations heretofore issued vesting power and authority in the War Trade Board are hereby confirmed and made applicable to the War Trade Board constituted in accordance with this Order.

WOODROW WILSON.

BY THE PRESIDENT OF THE UNITED STATES OF AMERICA

A PROCLAMATION

[Authorizing the Secretary of the Interior to Dispose of Surplus Coal from the Mine Operated by the Alaskan Railroad Commission.]

Whereas, Section 2 of the act of Congress approved October 20, 1914 (38 Stats., 741), authorizes the mining of coal from reserved areas in Alaska under the direction of the President, when necessary, by reason of the insufficient supply, for national protection, or relief from oppressive conditions, and

Whereas, it appears that the available supply of coal for domestic and other uses in the Territory of Alaska is by reason of existing conditions inadequate and insufficient,

Now, therefore, I, Woodrow Wilson, President of the United States of America, under and by virtue of said statute, do hereby authorize and direct the Secretary of the Interior, during the period of the existing war, to sell and dispose of surplus coal taken from the mine now being operated by the Alaskan Railroad Commission, for supplying domestic and other local needs in the Territory.

In witness whereof, I have hereunto set my hand and caused the seal of the United States to be affixed.

Done in the District of Columbia, this 27th day of August, in the year of our Lord one thousand nine hundred and eighteen, [SEAL]   and of the independence of the United States, the one hundred and forty-third.

WOODROW WILSON.

By the President:

ROBERT LANSING, *Secretary of State.*

BY THE PRESIDENT OF THE UNITED STATES OF AMERICA

A PROCLAMATION

[Appointing Day for Registration of all Male Citizens Between the Ages of 18 and 45.]

Whereas Congress has enacted and the President has, on the thirty-first day of August, one thousand nine hundred and eighteen, approved an act amending the act approved May eighteenth, one thousand nine hundred and seventeen;

And whereas said act, as amended, contains the following provisions:

Sec. 5. That all male persons between the ages of eighteen and forty-five, both inclusive, shall be subject to registration in accordance with regulations to be prescribed by the President and upon proclamation by the President or other public notice given by him or by his direction stating the time or times and place or places of any such registration, it shall be the duty of all persons of the designated ages, except officers and enlisted men of the Regular Army; officers and enlisted men of the National Guard while in the service of the United States; officers of the Officers' Reserve Corps and enlisted men in the enlisted Reserve Corps while in the service of the United States; officers and enlisted men of the Navy and Marine Corps; officers and enlisted and enrolled men of the Naval Reserve Force and Marine Corps Reserve while in the service of the United States; officers commissioned in the Army of the United States under the provisions of this act; persons who, prior to any day set for registration by the President hereunder, have registered under the terms of this act or under the terms of the resolution entitled "Joint resolution providing for the registration for military service of all male persons citizens of the United States and all male persons residing in the United States who have, since the fifth day of June, nineteen hundred and seventeen, and on or before the day set for the registration by proclamation by the President, attained the age of twenty-one years, in accordance with such rules and regulations as the President may prescribe under the terms of the act approved May eighteenth, nineteen hundred and seventeen, entitled 'An act to authorize the President to increase temporarily the Military Establishment of the United States,'" approved May twentieth, nineteen hundred and eighteen, whether called for service or not, and diplomatic representatives, technical attaches of foreign embassies and legations, consuls general, consuls, vice consuls, and consular agents of foreign countries, residing in the United States, who are not citizens of the United States, to present themselves for and submit to registration under the provisions of this act; and every such person shall be deemed to have notice of the requirements of this act upon the publication of any such proclamation or any such other public notice as aforesaid given by the President or by his direction and any person who shall willfully fail or refuse to present himself for registration or to submit thereto as herein provided shall be guilty of a misdemeanor and shall, upon conviction in a district court of the United States having jurisdiction thereof, be punished by imprisonment for not more than one year and shall thereupon be duly registered; *Provided,* That in the call of the docket precedence shall be given, in courts trying the same, to the trial of criminal proceedings under this act: *Provided further,* That persons shall be subject to registration as herein provided who shall have attained their eighteenth birthday and who shall not have attained their forty-sixth birthday on or before the day set for the registration in any such proclamation by the President or any such other public notice given by him or by his direction, and all persons so registered shall be and remain subject to draft in the forces hereby authorized unless exempted or excused therefrom as in this act provided: *Provided further,* That the President may at such intervals as he may desire from time to time require all male persons who have attained the age of eighteen years since the last preceding date of registration and on or before the next date set for registration by proclamation by the President, except such persons as are exempt from registration hereunder, to register in the same manner and subject to the same requirements and liabilities as those previously registered under the terms hereof: *And provided further,* That in the case of temporary absence from actual place of legal residence of any person liable to registration as provided herein, such registration may be made by mail under regulations to be prescribed by the President. * * *

Sec. 6. That the President is hereby authorized to utilize the service of any or all departments and any or all officers or agents of the United States and of the several States, Territories, and the District of Columbia, and subdivisions thereof, in the execution of this act, and all officers and agents of the United States and of the several States, Territories and subdivisions thereof, and of the District of Columbia, and all persons designated or appointed under regulations prescribed by the President, whether such appointments are made by the President himself or by the governor or other officer of any State or Territory, to perform any duty in the execution of this act are hereby required to perform such duty as the President shall order or direct, and all such officers and agents and persons so designated or appointed shall hereby have full authority for all acts done by them in the execution of this act by the direction of the President. Correspondence in the execution of this act may be carried in penalty envelopes bearing the frank of the War Department. Any person charged as herein provided with the duty of carrying into effect any of the provisions of this act or the regulations made or directions given thereunder who shall fail or neglect to perform such duty, and any person charged with such duty or having and exercising any authority under said act, regulations, or directions who shall knowingly make or be a party to the making of any false or incorrect registration, physical examination, exemption, enlistment, enrollment, or muster; and any person who shall make or be a party to the making of any false statement or certificate as to the fitness or liability of himself or any other person for service under the provisions of this act, or regulations made by the President thereunder, or otherwise evades or aids another to evade the requirements of this act or of said regulations, or who, in any manner, shall fail or neglect fully to perform any duty required of him in the execution of this act, shall, if not subject to military law, be guilty of a misdemeanor, and upon conviction in the district court of the United States having jurisdiction thereof, be punished by imprisonment for not more than one year, or, if subject to military law, shall be tried by court-martial and suffer such punishment as a court-martial may direct.

Now, therefore, I, Woodrow Wilson, President of the United States, do call upon the governor of each of the several States and Territories, the Board of Commissioners of the District of Columbia, and all members of local boards and agents thereof appointed under the provisions of said act of Congress approved May eighteenth, one thousand nine hundred and seventeen, and all officers and agents of the several States and Territories, of the District of Columbia, and of the counties and municipalities therein, to perform certain duties in the execution of the foregoing law, which duties will be communicated to them directly in regulations of even date herewith.

And I do further proclaim and give notice to every person subject to registration in the several States and in the District of Columbia, in accordance with the above law, that the time and place of such registration shall be between seven a. m. and nine p. m. on Thursday, the twelfth day of September, one thousand nine hundred and eighteen, at a registration place in the precinct wherein he then has his permanent home, or at such other place as shall be designated by public notice by the local board having jurisdiction of the area wherein he then has his permanent home. All male persons in the United States who shall have attained their eighteenth birthday and who shall not have attained their forty-sixth birthday on or before Thursday, the twelfth day of September, one thousand nine hundred and eighteen, the day therein named for registration, are required to register: *Provided, however,* That the following persons are hereby exempted from registration to wit: Persons who, prior to the day herein set for registration, have registered under the terms of the act approved May 18, 1917, or under the terms of the public resolution of Congress approved May 20, 1918, whether called for service or not; officers and enlisted men of the Regular Army; officers commissioned in the Army of the United States, and men of the forces drafted, under the provisions of the act approved May 18, 1917; officers and enlisted men of the National Guard while in the service of the United States; officers of the Officers' Reserve Corps and enlisted men in the Enlisted Reserve Corps while in the service of the United States; officers and enlisted men of the Navy and Marine Corps; officers and enlisted and enrolled men of the Naval Reserve Force and Marine Corps Reserve while in the service of the United States; and diplomatic representatives, technical attaches of foreign embassies and legations, consuls general, consuls, vice consuls, and consular agents of foreign countries, residing in the United States, who are not citizens of the United States.

A day or days for registration in the Territories of Alaska, Hawaii, and Porto Rico will be named in later proclamations.

As required by the regulations, every local board having jurisdiction in a city of 30,000 population or over will promptly cause the mayor thereof to be notified of the place or places designated for registration; every local board having jurisdiction in a county, parish, or similar unit will promptly cause the clerk thereof to be notified of the place or places designated for registration, and every local board having jurisdiction in a State or Territory the area of which is divided into divisions for the administration of the act approved May 18, 1917, will promptly cause the clerks of the townships within its division to be notified of the place or places designated for registration.

And I do call upon every mayor, county clerk, or township clerk receiving such notification to have a list of said places of registration posted, and do charge him with the duty of having all persons making inquiry informed of the place or places at which they may register.

Any person who, on account of sickness, will be unable to present himself for registration may apply on or before the day of registration at the office of any local board for instructions as to how he may register by agent.

Any person who expects to be absent on the day designated for registration from the jurisdiction of the board in which he then permanently resides may register by mail, but his registration card must reach the local board having jurisdiction of the area wherein he then permanently resides by the day herein named for registration. Any such person should apply as soon as practicable at the office of a local board for instructions as to how he may register by mail.

Any person who has no permanent residence must register at the place designated for registration by the local board having jurisdiction of the area wherein he may be on the day herein named for registration.

Any person who, on account of absence at sea, or on account of absence without the territorial limits of the United States, may be unable to comply with the regulations pertaining to absentees, shall, within five days after reaching the United States, register with his proper local board or as provided in the regulations for other absentees.

Fifteen months ago the men of the country from twenty-one to thirty years of age were registered. Three months ago, and again this month, those who have just reached the age of twenty-one were added. It now remains to include all men between the ages of eighteen and forty-five.

This is not a new policy. A century and a quarter ago it was deliberately ordained by those who were then responsible for the safety and defense of the Nation that the duty of military service should rest upon all able-bodied men between the ages of eighteen and forty-five. We now accept and fulfill the obligation which they established, an obligation expressed in our national statutes from that time until now. We solemnly purpose a decisive victory of arms and deliberately devote the larger part of the military man power of the Nation to the accomplishment of that purpose.

The younger men have from the first been ready to go. They have furnished voluntary enlistments out of all proportion to their numbers. Our military authorities regard them as having the highest combatant qualities. Their youthful enthusiasm, their virile eagerness, their gallant spirit of daring make them the admiration of all who see them in action. They covet not only the distinction of serving in this great war but also the inspiring memories which hundreds of thousands of them will cherish through the years to come, of a great duty and a great service for their country and for mankind.

By the men of the older group now called upon, the opportunity now opened to them will be accepted with the calm resolution of those who realize to the full the deep and solemn significance of what they do. Having made a place for themselves in their respective communities, having assumed at home the graver responsibilities of life in many spheres, looking back upon honorable records in civil and industrial life, they will realize as perhaps no others could how entirely their own fortunes and the fortunes of all whom they love are put at stake in this war for right, and will know that the very records they have made render this new duty the commanding duty of their lives. They know how surely this is the Nation's war, how imperatively it demands the mobilization and massing of all our resources of every kind. They will regard this call as the supreme call of their day and will answer it accordingly.

Only a portion of those who register will be called upon to bear arms. Those who are not physically fit will be excused; those exempted by alien allegiance; those who should not be relieved of their present responsibilities; above all, those who can not be spared from the civil and industrial tasks at home upon which the success of our armies depends as much as upon the fighting at the front. But all must be registered in order that the selection for military service may be made intelligently and with full information. This will be our final demonstration of loyalty, democracy, and the will to win, our solemn notice to all the world that we stand absolutely together in a common resolution and purpose. It is the call to duty to which every true man in the country will respond with pride and with the consciousness that in doing so he plays his part in vindication of a great cause at whose summons every true heart offers its supreme service.

In witness whereof I have hereunto set my hand and caused the seal of the United States to be affixed.

Done in the District of Columbia this 31st day of August, in the year of our Lord one thousand nine hundred and eighteen [SEAL.] and of the independence of the United States of America the one hundred and forty-third.

WOODROW WILSON.

By the President:
ROBERT LANSING, *Secretary of State*.

LETTER

[Endorsing Zionist Movement.]

WASHINGTON, D. C., *September 1, 1918.*

MY DEAR RABBI WISE:

I have watched with deep and sincere interest the reconstructive work which the Weizmann commission has done in Palestine at the instance of the British Government, and I welcome an opportunity to express the satisfaction I have felt in the progress of the Zionist movement in the United States and in the allied countries since the declaration by Mr. Balfour, on behalf of the British Government, of Great Britain's approval of the establishment in Palestine of a national home for the Jewish people, and his promise that the British Government would use its best endeavors to facilitate the achievement of that object, with the understanding that nothing would be done to prejudice the civil and religious rights of non-Jewish people in Palestine or the rights and political status enjoyed by Jews in other countries.

I think that all Americans will be deeply moved by the report that even in this time of stress the Weizmann commission has been able to lay the foundation of the Hebrew University at Jerusalem, with the promise that that bears of spiritual rebirth.

Cordially and sincerely yours,

RABBI STEPHEN S. WISE,   WOODROW WILSON.
New York City.

ADDRESS TO FELLOW-CITIZENS

[Labor Day, 1918.]

My Fellow-citizens: Labor Day, 1918, is not like any Labor Day that we have known. Labor Day was always deeply significant with us. Now it is supremely significant. Keenly as we were aware a year ago of the enterprise of life and death upon which the Nation had embarked, we did not perceive its meaning as clearly as we do now. We knew that we were all partners and must stand and strive together, but we did not realize as we do now that we are all enlisted men, members of a single army, of many parts and many tasks, but commanded by a single obligation, our faces set toward a single object. We now know that every tool in every essential industry is a weapon, and a weapon wielded for the same purpose that an Army rifle is wielded—a weapon which if we were to lay down no rifle would be of any use.

And a weapon for what? What is the war for? Why are we enlisted? Why should we be ashamed if we were not enlisted? At first it seemed hardly more than a war of defense against the military aggression of Germany. Belgium had been violated, France invaded, and Germany was afield again, as in 1870 and 1866, to work out her ambitions in Europe; and it was necessary to meet her force with force. But it is clear now that it is much more than a war to alter the balance of power in Europe. Germany, it is now plain, was striking at what free men everywhere desire and must have—the right to determine their own fortunes, to insist upon justice, and to oblige governments to act for them and not for the private and selfish interest of a governing class. It is a war to make the nations and peoples of the world secure against every such power as the German autocracy represents. It is a war of emancipation. Not until it is won can men anywhere live free from constant fear or breathe freely while they go about their daily tasks and know that governments are their servants, not their masters.

This is, therefore, the war of all wars which labor should support and support with all its concentrated power. The world can not be safe, men's lives can not be secure, no man's rights can be confidently and successfully asserted against the rule and mastery of arbitrary groups and special interests, so long as governments like that which, after long premeditation, drew Austria and Germany into this war are permitted to control the destinies and the daily fortunes of men and nations, plotting while honest men work, laying the fires of which innocent men, women, and children are to be the fuel.

You know the nature of this war. It is a war which industry must sustain. The army of laborers at home is as important, as essential,

THE FIRST DAY AT THE CANTONMENT

THE FIRST DAY AT THE CANTONMENT.

The accompanying illustration, taken at Camp Dix, New Jersey, one of the thirty-two major cantonments utilized during the War to train the American Expeditionary Forces, gives an excellent idea of the civilian appearance of the men drafted into the American army, as they appeared upon arrival at camp.

as the army of fighting men in the far fields of actual battle. And the laborer is not only needed as much as the soldier. It is his war. The soldier is his champion and representative. To fail to win would be to imperil everything that the laborer has striven for and held dear since freedom first had its dawn and his struggle for justice began. The soldiers at the front know this. It steels their muscles to think of it. They are crusaders. They are fighting for no selfish advantage for their own Nation. They would despise anyone who fought for the selfish advantage of any nation. They are giving their lives that homes everywhere, as well as the homes they love in America, may be kept sacred and safe, and men everywhere be free as they insist upon being free. They are fighting for the ideals of their own land— great ideals, immortal ideals, ideals which shall light the way for all men to the places where justice is done and men live with lifted heads and emancipated spirits. That is the reason they fight with solemn joy and are invincible.

Let us make this, therefore, a day of fresh comprehension not only of what we are about, and of renewed and clear-eyed resolution, but a day of consecration also, in which we devote ourselves without pause or limit to the great task of setting our own country and the whole world free to render justice to all and of making it impossible for small groups of political rulers anywhere to disturb our peace or the peace of the world or in any way to make tools and puppets of those upon whose consent and upon whose power their own authority and their own very existence depend.

We may count upon each other. The Nation is of a single mind. It is taking counsel with no special class. It is serving no private or single interest. Its own mind has been cleared and fortified by these days which burn the dross away. The light of a new conviction has penetrated to every class amongst us. We realize as we never realized before that we are comrades, dependent on one another, irresistible when united, powerless when divided. And so we join hands to lead the world to a new and better day.

WOODROW WILSON.

By the President of the United States of America

A PROCLAMATION

[Fixing Guaranteed Prices for Wheat.]

[The proclamation opens by quoting the passage quoted on page 8457.]

Now therefore, I, Woodrow Wilson, President of the United States, by virtue of the powers conferred upon me by said Act of Congress, and especially by section 14 thereof, do hereby find that an emergency exists requiring stimulation of the production of wheat, and that it is essential that the producers of wheat produced within the United States shall have the benefits of the guarantee provided for in said section; and, in order to make effective the guarantee by Congress for the crop of nineteen hundred and nineteen and to assure such producers a reasonable profit, I do hereby determine and fix, and give public notice of reasonable guaranteed prices for No. 1 Northern Spring wheat and its equivalents at the respective principal primary markets as follows, to-wit:

New York, New York, Two Dollars and Thirty-nine and a half Cents ($2.39½) per bushel.

Philadelphia, Pennsylvania, Two Dollars and Thirty-nine Cents ($2.39) per bushel.

Baltimore, Maryland, Two Dollars and Thirty-eight and Three-quarter Cents ($2.38¾) per bushel.

Newport News, Virginia, Two Dollars and Thirty-eight and Three-quarter Cents ($2.38¾) per bushel.

Duluth, Minnesota, Two Dollars and Twenty-two and one-half Cents ($2.21½) per bushel.

Minneapolis, Minnesota, Two Dollars and Twenty-one and one-half Cents ($2.21½) per bushel.

Chicago, Illinois, Two Dollars and Twenty-six Cents ($2.26) per bushel.

St. Louis, Missouri, Two Dollars and Twenty-four Cents ($2.24) per bushel.

Kansas City, Missouri, Two Dollars and Eighteen Cents ($2.18) per bushel.

Omaha, Nebraska, Two Dollars and Eighteen Cents ($2.18) per bushel.

New Orleans, Louisiana, Two Dollars and Twenty-eight Cents ($2.28) per bushel.

Galveston, Texas, Two Dollars and Twenty-eight Cents ($2.28) per bushel.

Tacoma, Washington, Two Dollars and Twenty Cents ($2.20) per bushel.

Seattle, Washington, Two Dollars and Twenty Cents ($2.20) per bushel.

Portland, Oregon, Two Dollars and Twenty Cents ($2.20) per bushel.

Astoria, Oregon, Two Dollars and Twenty Cents ($2.20) per bushel.

San Francisco, California, Two Dollars and Twenty Cents ($2.20) per bushel.

Los Angeles, California, Two Dollars and Twenty Cents ($2.20) per bushel.

Salt Lake City, Utah, Two Dollars ($2.00) per bushel.

Great Falls, Montana, Two Dollars ($2.00) per bushel.

Pocatello, Idaho, Two Dollars ($2.00) per bushel.

Spokane, Washington, Two Dollars ($2.00) per bushel.

and that the guaranteed price for the other grades established under the United States Grain Standards Act approved August 11, 1916, based on said price for No. 1 Northern Spring wheat at the respective principal primary markets of the United States above mentioned, will assure the producers of wheat produced within the United States a reasonable profit; the guaranteed prices in the principal primary markets above mentioned being fixed by adopting No. 1 Northern Spring wheat or its equivalents at the principal interior markets, as the basis.

For the purposes of such guaranty only, I hereby fix the guaranteed prices at the respective principal primary markets above mentioned for the following grades of wheat, to-wit: No. 1 Northern Spring, No. 1 Hard Winter, No. 1 Red Winter, No. 1 Durum, No. 1 Hard White. The guaranteed prices at the respective principal primary markets aforesaid of all other grades of wheat established under the United States Grain Standard Act approved August 11, 1916, shall be based on the above guaranteed prices and bear just relation thereto.

The sums thus determined and fixed are guaranteed by the Government of the United States at the respective principal primary markets of the United States above mentioned, to every producer of wheat of any grade so established under the United States Grain Standards Act, upon the condition that said wheat is harvested in the United States during the year 1919, and offered for sale before the first day of June, 1920, to such agent or employee of the United States, or other person as may be hereafter designated, at any one of the above-mentioned cities, which are hereby declared to be the principal primary markets of the United States, and provided that such producer complies with all regulations which may be hereafter promulgated in regard to said guaranty by the President of the United States.

In witness whereof, I have hereunto set my hand and caused the seal of the United States to be affixed.

Done in the District of Columbia, this second day of September, in the year of our Lord one thousand nine hundred and eight-

[SEAL]   een and of the independence of the United States of America the one hundred and forty-third.

WOODROW WILSON.

By the President:

ROBERT LANSING, *Secretary of State.*

MEMORANDUM

[Accompanying Proclamation Fixing Prices of Wheat.]

September 2, 1918.

In issuing today the Government's guaranty of the same price for the 1919 wheat crop that was guaranteed for the 1918 crop I wish it to be understood that in the spring of 1919 I will appoint a disinterested commission, who will secure for me the facts by that time disclosed as to the increased cost of farm labor and supplies, using the three-year prewar average prices of wheat, of labor, and of supply costs as a basis, and that from this information I shall determine whether there should be an increase in price above the present level, and, if so, what advance, in order to maintain for the farmer a good return. Should it then appear that an increase is deserved over the present guaranty, however, it will be applied only to those who have by next harvest already marketed their 1918 wheat.

It is the desire and intention of all departments of the administration to give to the wheat grower a fair and stimulative return in order that the present acreage in wheat may be maintained.

I find a great conflict of opinion among various sections of the country as to the price that should be named as a minimum guaranty. It must be obvious to all, however, that the factors which will make for increased or decreased cost of production of next year's harvest can not be determined until the near approach to the harvest.

In giving a guaranteed price for wheat one year in advance (the only industry guaranteed by the Government) there is involved a considerable national risk. If there should be peace or increased shipping available before the middle of 1920, Europe will naturally supply itself from the large stores of much cheaper wheat now in the Southern Hemisphere; and therefore the Government is undertaking a risk which might in such an event result in a national loss of as much as $500,000,000 through an unsaleable surplus; or, in any event, in maintaining a high level of price to our own people for a long period subsequent to freedom in the world's markets.

Despite this, the desirability of assuring a supply to the world of prime breadstuffs by insuring the farmer against the fluctuations in prices that would result from the uncertainties of the present situation and from the speculation those uncertainties entail, seems to me to make the continuation of the guarantee for another year desirable. On the other hand, it is clear that before increasing this liability by large sums with the risks set forth above, and before increasing the burden of the consumer, the matter should be subjected to searching inquiry at the appropriate time—the time when the pertinent facts will be known.

I feel confident that with this preliminary fixed guarantee, and with the assurance that justice will in any event be done to the grower, he will continue the fine patriotic effort by which he has served the country hitherto; that the Government will have acted prudently; and that the consumer will be satisfied that his interests are not unduly sacrificed, but just and exhaustive consideration given to every element of the matter at the proper time.

WOODROW WILSON.

LETTER

[To Workmen on Strike in Bridgeport, Connecticut.]

THE WHITE HOUSE, *September 13, 1918.*

Gentlemen: I am in receipt of your resolutions of September 6, announcing that you have begun a strike against your employers in Bridgeport, Conn. You are members of the Bridgeport branches of the International Union of Machinists. As such and with the approval of the national officers of your union you signed an agreement to submit the questions as to the terms of your employment to the National War Labor Board and to abide by the award which in accordance with the rules of procedure approved by me might be right.

The members of the board were not able to reach a unanimous conclusion on all the issues presented and, as provided in its constitution, the questions upon which they did not agree were carried before an arbitrator, the unanimous choice of the members of the board.

The arbitrator thus chosen has made an award which more than 90 per cent. of the workers affected accept. You, who constitute less than 10 per cent, refuse to abide by the award, although you are the best paid of the whole body of workers affected and are, therefore, least entitled to press a further increase of wages because of the high cost of living. But whatever the merits of the issue it is closed by the award. Your strike against it is a breach of faith, calculated to reflect on the sincerity of national organized labor in proclaiming its acceptance of the principles and machinery of the National War Labor Board.

If such disregard of the solemn adjudication of a tribunal to which both parties submitted their claims be temporized with, agreements become mere scraps of paper. If errors creep into awards, the proper remedy is submission to the award with an application for re-hearing to the tribunal. But to strike against the award is disloyalty and dishonor.

The Smith & Wesson Company of Springfield, Mass., engaged in Government work, has refused to accept the mediation of the National War Labor Board and has flaunted its rules of decision approved by Presidential proclamation. With my consent the War Department has taken over the plant and business of the company to secure continuity in production and to prevent industrial disturbance.

It is of the highest importance to secure compliance with reasonable rules and procedure for the settlement of industrial disputes. Having exercised a drastic remedy with recalcitrant employers, it is my duty to use means equally well adapted to the end with lawless and faithless employes.

Therefore, I desire that you return to work and abide by the award. If you refuse, each one of you will be barred from employment in any war industry in the community in which the strike occurs for a period of one year. During that time the United States Employment Service will decline to obtain employment for you in any war industry elsewhere in the United States, as well as under the War and Navy Departments, the Shipping Board, the Railway Administration, and all Government agencies, and the Draft Boards will be instructed to reject any claim of exemption based on your alleged usefulness on war production.

Sincerely yours,
WOODROW WILSON.

PROCLAMATIONS

By the President of the United States of America

[License of Stockyards.]

[The Proclamation opens with the same five paragraphs as the Proclamation on page 8528.]

All individuals, partnerships, associations, and corporations (except as exempted by said Act of Congress and except those required to be licensed pursuant to my proclamation dated June 18, 1918, under said Act), engaged in the business of handling, buying, selling, or otherwise dealing in live or dead cattle, sheep, swine, or goats in or in connection with places, establishments, or facilities, commonly known as stockyards, consisting of pens or other inclosures, and their appurtenances, in which cattle, sheep, swine, or goats are received, held, or kept for sale, feeding, watering, or shipment, are hereby required to secure licenses on or before September 19, 1918, which will be issued under such rules and regulations governing the conduct of the business as may be prescribed under said Act.

The Secretary of Agriculture shall carry into effect the provisions of said Act, and shall supervise and direct the exercise of the powers and authority thereby given to the President, as far as the same apply to the said business, including the purchase of live or dead cattle, sheep or swine in or in connection with stockyards, as a part of the business of packing fresh, canned or cured beef, pork or mutton licensed under the provisions of the Proclamation of October 8, 1917, and to any and all practices, procedure, and regulations applicable thereto authorized or required under the provisions of said Act, and in this behalf he shall do and perform such acts and things as may be authorized or required of him from time to time by direction of the President and under such rules and regulations as may be prescribed by the President from time to time. All departments and agencies of the Government are hereby directed to cooperate with the Secretary of Agriculture in the performance of the duties hereinbefore set forth.

Applications for licenses must be made to the law department, license division, United States Food Administration, Washington, D. C., upon forms prepared for that purpose.

Any individual, partnership, association, or corporation, otner than as hereinbefore excepted, who shall engage in or carry on any business described herein, without first securing the license required therefor, will be liable to the penalties prescribed by said Act of Congress.

In witness whereof, I have hereunto set my hand and caused the seal of the United States to be affixed.

Done in the District of Columbia this sixth day of September, in the year of our Lord 1918, and of the independence of [SEAL.] the United States of America, the one hundred and forty-third.

WOODROW WILSON.

By the President:

ROBERT LANSING, *Secretary of State.*

[Prohibiting Manufacture of Malt Liquors.]

Whereas, under and by virtue of an Act of Congress entitled "An Act to provide further for the national security and defense by encouraging the production, conserving the supply, and controlling the distribution of food products and fuel," approved by the President on August 10, 1917, it is provided in Section 15, among other things, as follows:

> "Whenever the President shall find that limitation, regulation, or prohibition of the use of foods, fruits, food materials, or feeds in the production of malt or vinous liquors for beverage purposes, or that reduction of the alcoholic content of any such malt or vinous liquor, is essential, in order to assure an adequate and continuous supply of food, or that the national security and defense will be subserved thereby, he is authorized, from time to time, to prescribe and give public notice of the extent of the limitation, regulation, prohibition, or reduction so necessitated. Whenever such notice shall have been given and shall remain unrevoked, no person shall, after a reasonable time prescribed in such notice, use any foods,

fruits, food materials, or feeds in the production of malt or vinous liquors, or import any such liquors except under license issued by the President and in compliance with rules and regulations determined by him governing the production and importation of such liquors and the alcoholic content thereof."

Now, therefore, I, Woodrow Wilson, President of the United States of America, by virtue of the powers conferred on me by said Act of Congress, do hereby find and determine that it is essential, in order to assure an adequate and continuous supply of food, in order to subserve the national security and defense, and because of the increasing requirements of war industries for the fuel productive capacity of the country, the strain upon transportation to serve such industries, and the shortage of labor caused by the necessity of increasing the armed forces of the United States, that the use of sugar, glucose, corn, rice or any other foods, fruits, food materials and feeds in the production of malt liquors, including near beer, for beverage purposes be prohibited. And by this Proclamation I prescribe and give public notice that on and after October 1st, 1918, no person shall use any sugar, glucose, corn, rice or any other foods, fruits, food materials or feeds, except malt now already made, and hops, in the production of malt liquors, including near beer, for beverage purposes, whether or not such malt liquors contain alcohol, and on and after December 1st, 1918, no person shall use any sugar, glucose, corn, rice or any other foods, fruits, food materials or feeds, including malt, in the production of malt liquors, including near beer, for beverage purposes, whether or not such malt liquors contain alcohol.

In witness whereof I have hereunto set my hand and caused the seal of the United States to be affixed.

Done in the District of Columbia, this sixteenth day of September in the year of our Lord 1918, and of the Independence [SEAL.] of the United States of America the one hundred and forty-third.

WOODROW WILSON.

By the President:
ROBERT LANSING, *Secretary of State.*

[Licensing the Importation, Production, Transportation, and Distribution of Fuel Oil and Natural Gas.]

[The Proclamation opens with the two paragraphs quoted on pages 8322 and 8323.]

And, whereas, it is further provided in said Act as follows:

"That in carrying out the purposes of this act the President is authorized to enter into any voluntary arrangements or agreements, to create and use any agency or agencies."

And, whereas, the President has heretofore designated and appointed Harry A. Garfield United States Fuel Administrator for the purpose of carrying into effect the provisions of said Act, relating to fuel, and has directed that: "Said Fuel Administrator shall supervise, direct, and carry into effect the provisions of said Act and the powers and authority therein given to the President so far as the same apply to fuel as set forth in said Act, and to any and all practices, procedure and regulations authorized under the provisions of said Act applicable to fuel, including the issuance, regulation and revocation under the name of said United States Fuel Administrator of licenses under said Act," and has authorized said Fuel Administrator to employ such assistants and subordinates as may from time to time be deemed by him necessary, said Fuel Administrator and such assistants and subordinates together constituting the governmental organization called the United States Fuel Administration.

And, whereas, it is essential in order to carry into effect the provisions of said Act, and in order to secure an adequate supply and equitable distribution, and to facilitate the movement of certain necessaries hereafter in this proclamation specified, that the license powers conferred upon the President by said Act be at this time exercised to the extent hereinafter set forth,

Now, therefore, I, Woodrow Wilson, President of the United States of America, by virtue of the powers conferred on me by said Act of Congress, hereby find and determine and by this proclamation do announce that it is essential in order to carry into effect the purposes of said Act, to license the importation, manufacture, storage, and distribution of certain necessaries to the extent hereinafter specified:

All persons, firms, corporations, and associations engaged in business as:

(a) Importers of crude oil, fuel oil, gas oil, kerosene or gasoline;

(b) Manufacturers of fuel oil, gas oil, kerosene or gasoline;

(c) Distributors or marketers of crude oil, fuel oil, gas oil, kerosene or gasoline;

(d) Transporters of crude oil, fuel oil, gas oil, kerosene or gasoline (except those specifically exempted by said Act of Congress);

(e) Producers of natural gas who also distribute and market their product;

(f) Distributors or marketers of natural gas;

(g) Transporters of natural gas (except those specifically exempted by said Act of Congress);

excepting, however, retailers of crude oil, fuel oil, gas oil, kerosene, gasoline or natural gas whose gross sales of crude oil, fuel oil, gas oil, kerosene, gasoline and natural gas do not exceed one hundred thousand dollars ($100,000) per annum, are hereby required to secure on or before October 1, 1918, a license, which license will be issued under such rules and regulations governing the conduct of the business as may from time to time be prescribed by the President of the United States, or by the United States Fuel Administrator acting by virtue of the authority heretofore as aforesaid, or hereby, delegated to him by the President.

The United States Fuel Administrator shall supervise, direct, and carry into effect the provisions of said Act and the powers and authority thereby given to the President, as the same applies to crude oil, fuel oil, gas oil, kerosene, gasoline or natural gas, and to any and all practices, procedure and regulations authorized or required under the provisions of said Act, including issuance, regulation, and revocation, in the name of said Fuel Administrator, of licenses under said Act, and in this behalf he shall also do and perform such other acts and things as may be authorized or required of him from time to time by direction of the President, and under such rules and regulations as may be prescribed by the President from time to time.

For all the purposes aforesaid the United States Fuel Administrator may make use of the said governmental organization called the United States Fuel Administration.

Application for licenses must be made to the United States Fuel Administration, Oil Division, Washington, D. C., upon forms approved by the Fuel Administrator for that purpose. The holders of existing licenses issued by the United States Fuel Administration are not required to secure a new license.

Any such person, firm, corporation, or association who, without a license, or whose license shall have been revoked, knowingly engages in or carries on any business for which a license is required under this proclamation, will be liable to the penalties prescribed by said Act of Congress.

In witness whereof, I have hereunto set my hand and caused the seal of the United States to be affixed.

Done in the District of Columbia, this sixteenth day of September, in the year of our Lord 1918, and of the independence [SEAL.] of the United States of America the one hundred and forty-third.

WOODROW WILSON.

By the President:

ROBERT LANSING, *Secretary of State.*

[Registration Days—Alaska, Hawaii and Porto Rico.]

Whereas Congress has enacted and the President has, on the thirty-first day of August, one thousand nine hundred and eighteen, approved an Act amending the Act approved May eighteen, one thousand nine hundred and seventeen,

And whereas said Act, as amended, contains the following provisions:

[Here are quoted the sections quoted on pages 8570, 8571 and 8572.]

And whereas, on the thirty-first day of August, one thousand nine hundred and eighteen, the President of the United States did issue a Proclamation calling upon all persons subject to registration in the several States and in the District of Columbia to register as provided by the aforesaid Act of Congress,

And whereas, in such Proclamation it was provided among other things that "A day or days for registration in the Territories of Alaska, Hawaii, and Porto Rico will be named in a later proclamation,"

Now, therefore, I, Woodrow Wilson, President of the United States, for the purpose of fixing the time for registration in the Territory of Alaska, do hereby set, fix, and establish the period between 7 a. m. on the fifteenth day of October to 9 p. m. on the sixteenth day of December (Sundays and legal holidays excepted), one thousand nine hundred and eighteen, as the period of registration, and I do hereby direct that during such period all male persons herein made subject to registration do present themselves for the purpose of registration at such places and during such hours, and to be registered by such persons or officials in such areas as shall be designated and appointed by the Governor of the Territory of Alaska.

And I do call upon the Governor of Alaska and all members of Local Boards in Alaska and agents thereof appointed under the provisions of said Act of Congress approved May 18, 1917, and all officers and agents of the Territory of Alaska, and of the counties and municipalities therein, to perform certain duties in the execution of the foregoing law, which duties are communicated to them directly in regulations dated August 31, 1918.

[The Proclamation closes with the same passages as the Proclamation on page 8572.]

Any person ordinarily resident in Alaska who, on account of absence at sea, or on account of absence without the Territory of Alaska may be unable to comply with the regulations pertaining to absentees, shall, within five days after reaching Alaska, or other part of the United States, register at the proper place designated for registration, or by mail, as provided for other absentees.

In witness whereof, I have hereunto set my hand and caused the seal of the United States to be affixed.

Done in the District of Columbia this eighteenth day of September
in the year of our Lord 1918, and of the independence
[SEAL.]   of the United States of America, the one hundred and
forty-third.

WOODROW WILSON.

By the President:
ROBERT LANSING, *Secretary of State.*

[The Proclamations appointing October 26, 1918, as the registration day in
Hawaii and Porto Rico were issued on October 7, 1918.]

[Liberty Day.]

Every day the great principles for which we are fighting take fresh
hold upon our thought and purpose and make it clearer what the end
must be and what we must do to achieve it. We now know more certainly than we ever knew before why free men brought the great
nation and government we love into existence, because it grows clearer
and clearer what supreme service it is to be America's privilege to
render to the world. The anniversary of the discovery of America
must therefore have for us in this fateful year a peculiar and thrilling
significance. We should make it a day of ardent re-dedication to the
ideals upon which our government is founded and by which our present
heroic tasks are inspired.

Now, therefore, I, Woodrow Wilson, President of the United States
of America, do appoint Saturday, the 12th day of October, 1918,
as Liberty Day. On that day I request the citizens of every community of the United States, city, town and country-side, to celebrate
the discovery of our country in order to stimulate a generous response
to the Fourth Liberty Loan. Commemorative addresses, pageants,
Harvest Home Festivals, or other demonstrations should be arranged
for in every neighborhood under the general direction of the Secretary of the Treasury and the immediate direction of the Liberty Loan
Committee in cooperation with the United States Bureau of Education and the public school authorities. Let the people's response to
the Fourth Liberty Loan express the measure of their devotion to
the ideals which have guided the country from its discovery until
now, and of their determined purpose to defend them and guarantee
their triumph.

For the purpose of participating in Liberty Day celebrations all
employes of the Federal Government throughout the country whose
services can be spared may be excused on Saturday, the 12th day of
October for the entire day.

In witness whereof, I have hereunto set my hand and caused the
seal of the United States to be affixed.

Done in the District of Columbia this nineteenth day of September
in the year of our Lord 1918, and of the independence
[SEAL.] of the United States of America, the one hundred and
forty-third.

WOODROW WILSON.

By the President:
ROBERT LANSING, *Secretary of State.*

STATEMENTS ON RUSSIA

Toward the end of the summer of 1918, the Bolshevist Government of
Russia adopted a policy of more severe terrorism than had characterized its
rule since November 7, 1917, when the Bolsheviki had overthrown the coalition
moderate Socialist and liberal Government of Kerensky.

The Bolsheviki were the extreme Socialists of Russia, representing the Left
or radical wing of the Social Democratic Party. This party differed from the
other great Socialist party of Russia, the Socialist Revolutionary Party, chiefly
in following in more orthodox fashion the Socialism of Karl Marx, the founder
of modern "scientific" Socialism. This orthodoxy manifested itself primarily in
a determination to establish a Socialist state in Russia before Russia had
passed through the stage of capitalism which the other great Powers of
Europe had reached by the time of the outbreak of the Great War and in a
refusal to cooperate with non-Socialist (bourgeois) elements in the movement
for bettering the condition of the Russian people. The Bolsheviki derive their
name from the Russian word meaning "more," and it was first applied to them
at a convention of the Social Democratic Party in 1903.

After the overthrow of the Tsardom in Russia in March, 1917, the country
fell under a non-Socialist Government headed by Prince Lvoff and Professor
Miliukoff. This was succeeded in the following July by a combination liberal
and moderate Socialist Government, under Alexander F. Kerenski, of the
Right wing of the Socialist Revolutionary Party. The Bolsheviki, under the
leadership of Nikolai Lenin and Leon Trotski, attacked the Kerenski Government chiefly because of its determination to continue the war against the Central Powers and its refusal to distribute the land immediately to the peasants.
On succeeding to power, the Bolsheviki at once proclaimed an armistice with
the Central Powers; and in March, 1918, signed peace with them after Russia
had been invaded by German armies because of the refusal of Lenin and
Trotski to submit to the peace terms demanded by the delegates of the Central Powers at the peace parlies at Brest-Litovsk, Russian Poland. Roumania,
which had been overrun by the Central Powers in the winter of 1916-1917,
joined with Bolshevist Russia in signing the peace of Brest-Litovsk.

Although the Bolsheviki maintained that their Government was but carrying out the orthodox formulae of Socialism, most observers of Bolshevist
Russia insisted that Bolshevism was more akin to Communism than to Socialism. The terrorism and repression with which the following statement of
President Wilson deals reached its climax after an attempt on the life of
Lenin, the head and moving spirit in the Bolshevist Government of Russia, at
a time when the Bolsheviki felt themselves slipping from power; and declined
in their severity after the winter of 1918-1919. The President's statement was
in the form of an order dispatched to American diplomatic representatives
abroad in September, 1918. Its text was as follows:—

This Government is in receipt of information from reliable sources revealing that the peaceable Russian citizens of Moscow, Petrograd, and other cities are suffering from an openly avowed campaign of mass terrorism and are subject to wholesale executions. Thousands of persons have been shot without even a form of trial; ill-administered prisons are filled beyond capacity, and every night scores of Russian citizens are recklessly put to death; and irresponsible bands are venting their brutal passions in the daily massacres of untold innocents.

In view of the earnest desire of the people of the United States to befriend the Russian people and lend them all that is possible of assistance in their struggle to reconstruct their nation upon principles of democracy and self-government, and acting therefore solely in the interest of the Russian people themselves, this Government feels that it cannot be silent or refrain from expressing its horror at this state of terrorism. Furthermore, it believes that in order to check the further increase of the indiscriminate slaughter of Russian citizens all civilized nations should register their abhorrence of such barbarism.

You will inquire, therefore, whether the Government to which you are accredited will be disposed to take some immediate action, which is entirely divorced from the atmosphere of belligerency and the conduct of war, to impress upon the perpetrators of these crimes the aversion with which civilization regards their present wanton acts.

By this time, forces of the Entente Allies and the United States had entered upon a policy of armed intervention in Russia in the hope of restoring the eastern battle-front. Intervention was from two directions,—from the north, along the Murman coast, chiefly by British and American troops; and from Siberia, chiefly by Japanese troops. It was generally believed that intervention in Russia was long opposed by President Wilson, on the grounds that no nation had the right to invade another nation for the purpose of getting at an enemy lying beyond: that if the Bolsheviki should be overthrown, Russia would fall again under a reactionary government; that no matter how subversive the form of government of a country, it must be overthrown by its own subjects, not by outside interference; that the course pursued by Russia was due to at least some extent to the blunders of the Allies; and that the true purpose back of the demand for intervention was to guarantee the debts contracted with other countries, notably France, by the Tsarist governments of Russia and to provide for the economic exploitation of Russia.

On the other hand, the advocates of intervention pointed to the necessity of forestalling Germany in obtaining military supplies dispatched to Russia by the Entente Allies and still stored at the seaports where they had been unloaded; to the betrayal of the Allied cause by the Bolshevist government when it made peace with the Central Powers; to the assertion that the Bolsheviki were in effect, if not in purpose, in sympathy with Germany; to the necessity of aiding some 50,000 Czecho-Slovaks in Russia, who had been prisoners of

war in Russia, who were endeavoring to proceed westward to join the forces
opposed to the Central Powers, but whose progress was being disputed by
Bolshevist troops: and to the ability of Germany to exploit the economic resources of Russia without hindrance unless the Allies and the United States
intervened.

It was generally believed, also, although by the time of the signing of the
peace treaty with Germany there was no official information upon the subject, that President Wilson finally consented to have American troops share
in intervention in Russia in the hope that only by these means would the
United States be able to prevent intervention in Russia from being manipulated
for improper purposes. President Wilson's statement on intervention in Russia, issued through the State Department on August 3, 1918, was as follows:—

In the judgment of the Government of the United States—a judgment arrived at after repeated and very searching considerations of
the whole situation—military intervention in Russia would be more
likely to add to the present sad confusion there than to cure it, and
would injure Russia, rather than help her out of her distresses. Such
military intervention as has been most frequently proposed, even supposing it to be efficacious in its immediate object of delivering an attack upon Germany from the east, would, in its judgment, be more
likely to turn out to be merely a method of making use of Russia than
to be a method of serving her. Her people, if they profited by it at
all, could not profit by it in time to deliver them from their present
desperate difficulties, and their substance would meantime be used to
maintain foreign armies, not to reconstitute their own or to feed their
own men, women and children. We are bending all our energies
now to the purpose, the resolute and confident purpose, of winning
on the western front, and it would, in the judgment of the Government of the United States, be most unwise to divide or dissipate
our forces.

As the Government of the United States sees the present circumstances, therefore, military action is admissible in Russia now only
to render such protection and help as is possible to the Czecho-
Slovaks against the armed Austrian and German prisoners who are
attacking them, and to steady any efforts at self-government or self-
defense in which the Russians themselves may be willing to accept
assistance. Whether from Vladivostok or from Murmansk and Archangel, the only present object for which American troops will be employed will be to guard military stores which may subsequently be
needed by Russian forces and to render such aid as may be acceptable
to the Russians in the organization of their own self-defense.

With such objects in view, the Government of the United States
is now co-operating with the Governments of France and Great Britain
in the neighborhood of Murmansk and Archangel. The United States

and Japan are the only powers which are just now in a position to act in Siberia in sufficient force to accomplish even such modest objects as those that have been outlined. The Government of the United States has, therefore, proposed to the Government of Japan that each of the two Governments send a force of a few thousand men to Vladivostok, with the purpose of co-operating as a single force in the occupation of Vladivostok and in safeguarding, so far as it may, the country to the rear of the westward-moving Czecho-Slovaks, and the Japanese Government has consented.

In taking this action, the Government of the United States wishes to announce to the people of Russia in the most public and solemn manner that it contemplates no interference with the political sovereignty of Russia—not even in the local affairs of the limited areas which her military force may be obliged to occupy—and no impairment of her territorial integrity, either now or hereafter, but that what we are about to do has as its single and only object the rendering of such aid as shall be acceptable to the Russian people themselves in their endeavors to regain control of their own affairs, their own territory, and their own destiny. The Japanese Government, it is understood, will issue a similar assurance.

These plans and purposes of the Government of the United States have been communicated to the Governments of Great Britain, France, and Italy, and those Governments have advised the Department of State that they assent to them in principle. No conclusion that the Government of the United States has arrived at in this important matter is intended, however, as an effort to restrict the actions or interfere with the independent judgment of the Governments with which we are now associated in the war.

It is also the hope and purpose of the Government of the United States to take advantage of the earliest opportunity to send to Siberia a commission of merchants, agricultural experts, labor advisers, Red Cross representatives, and agents of the Young Men's Christian Association accustomed to organizing the best methods of spreading useful information and rendering education help of a modest kind in order in some systematic way to relieve the immediate economic necessities of the people there in every way for which an opportunity may open. The execution of this plan will follow and will not be permitted to embarrass the military assistance rendered to the Czecho-Slovaks.

It is the hope and expectation of the Government of the United States that the Governments with which it is associated will, wherever necessary or possible, lend their active aid in the execution of these military and economic plans.

EXECUTIVE ORDER

[Censorship of Submarine Cables, Telegraph and Telephone Lines.]

THE WHITE HOUSE, *September 26, 1918.*

The Executive Order of April 28, 1917, No. 2604, relating to the censorship of submarine cables, telegraph and telephone lines, is hereby amended to read as follows:

Whereas, the existence of a state of war between the United States and the Imperial German Government makes it essential to the public safety that no communication of a character which would aid the enemy or its allies shall be had,

Therefore, by virtue of the power vested in me under the Constitution and by the Joint Resolution passed by Congress on April 6, 1917, declaring the existence of a state of war, it is ordered that all companies or other persons, owning, controlling or operating telegraph and telephone lines or submarine cables, are hereby prohibited from transmitting messages to points without the United States or to points on or near the Mexican border through which messages may be despatched for the purpose of evading the censorship herein provided, and from delivering messages received from such points, except those permitted under rules and regulations to be established by the Secretary of War for telegraph and telephone lines, and by the Secretary of the Navy for submarine cables.

To these Departments, respectively, is delegated the duty of preparing and enforcing rules and regulations under this order to accomplish the purpose mentioned.

This order shall take effect from date.

WOODROW WILSON.

ADDRESS

[On War Issues and Peace Program. Delivered in the Metropolitan Opera House, New York, on September 27, 1918, on the Opening of the Campaign for the Fourth Liberty Loan.]

My Fellow-Citizens:

I am not here to promote the loan. That will be done—ably and enthusiastically done—by the hundreds of thousands of loyal and tireless men and women who have undertaken to present it to you and to our fellow-citizens throughout the country; and I have not the least doubt of their complete success; for I know their spirit and the spirit of the country. My confidence is confirmed, too, by the thoughtful and experienced co-operation of the bankers here and everywhere, who are lending their invaluable aid and guidance. I have come, rather, to seek an opportunity to present to you some thoughts which I trust will serve to give you, in perhaps fuller measure than before, a vivid sense of the great issues involved, in order that you may appreciate and accept with added enthusiasm the grave significance of the duty of supporting the Government by your men and your means to the utmost point of sacrifice and self-denial. No man or woman who has really taken in what this war means can hesitate to give to the very limit of what he has; and it is my mission here tonight to try to make it clear once more what the war really means. You will need no other stimulation or reminder of your duty.

At every turn of the war we gain a fresh consciousness of what we mean to accomplish by it. When our hope and expectation are most excited we think more definitely than before of the issues that hang upon it and of the purposes which must be realized by means of it. For it has positive and well-defined purposes which we did not determine and which we cannot alter. No statesman or assembly created them; no statesman or assembly can alter them. They have arisen out of the very nature and circumstances of the war. The most that statesmen or assemblies can do is to carry them out or be false to them. They were perhaps not clear at the outset; but they are clear now. The war has lasted more than four years and the whole world has been drawn into it. The common will of mankind has been substituted for the particular purposes of individual states. Individual statesmen may have started the conflict, but neither they nor their opponents can stop it as they please. It has become a peoples' war, and peoples of all sorts and races, of every degree of power and variety of fortune, are involved in its sweeping processes of change and settlement. We came into it when its character had become fully defined and it was plain that no nation could stand apart or be indifferent to its outcome. Its challenge drove to the heart of everything we cared for and lived for. The voice of the war had become clear and gripped our hearts. Our brothers from many lands, as well as our own murdered dead under the sea, were calling to us, and we responded, fiercely and of course.

The air was clear about us. We saw things in their full, convincing proportions as they were; and we have seen them with steady eyes and unchanging comprehension ever since. We accepted the issues of the war as facts, not as any group of men either here or elsewhere had defined them, and we can accept no outcome which does not squarely meet and settle them. Those issues are these:

Shall the military power of any nation or group of nations be suffered to determine the fortunes of peoples over whom they have no right to rule except the right of force?

Shall strong nations be free to wrong weak nations and make them subject to their purpose and interest?

Shall peoples be ruled and dominated, even in their own internal affairs, by arbitrary and irresponsible force or by their own will and choice?

Shall there be a common standard of right and privilege for all peoples and nations or shall the strong do as they will and the weak suffer without redress?

Shall the assertions of right be haphazard and by casual alliance or shall there be a common concert to oblige the observance of common rights?

No man, no group of men, chose these to be the issues of the struggle. They *are* the issues of it; and they must be settled—by no arrangement or compromise or adjustment of interests, but definitely and once for all and with a full and unequivocal acceptance of the principle that the interest of the weakest is as sacred as the interest of the strongest.

This is what we mean when we speak of a permanent peace, if we speak sincerely, intelligently, and with a real knowledge and comprehension of the matter we deal with.

We are all agreed that there can be no peace obtained by any kind of bargain or compromise with the Governments of the Central Empires, because we have dealt with them already and have seen them deal with other Governments that were parties to this struggle, at Brest-Litovsk and Bucharest. They have convinced us that they are without honor and do not intend justice. They observe no covenant, accept no principle but force and their own interest. We cannot "come to terms" with them. They have made it impossible. The German people must by this time be fully aware that we cannot accept the word of those who forced this war upon us. We do not think the same thoughts or speak the same language of agreement.

It is of capital importance that we should also be explicitly agreed that no peace shall be obtained by any kind of compromise or abatement of the principle we have avowed as the principles for which we are fighting. There should exist no doubt about that. I am, therefore, going to take the liberty of speaking with the utmost frankness about the practical implications that are involved in it.

If it be indeed and in truth the common object of the Governments associated against Germany and of the nations whom they govern, as I believe it to be, to achieve by the coming settlements a secure and lasting peace, it will be necessary that all who sit down at the peace table shall come ready and willing to pay the price, the only price, that will procure it; and ready and willing, also, to create in some virile fashion the only instrumentality by which it can be made certain that the agreements of the peace will be honored and fulfilled.

That price is impartial justice in every item of the settlement, no matter whose interest is crossed; and not only impartial justice, but also the satisfaction of the several peoples whose fortunes are dealt with. That indispensable instrumentality is a League of Nations formed under covenants that will be efficacious. Without such an instrumentality, by which the peace of the world can be guaranteed, peace will rest in part upon the word of outlaws, and only upon that word. For Germany will have to redeem her character, not by what happens at the peace table, but by what follows.

And, as I see it, the constitution of that League of Nations and the clear direction of its objects must be a part, is in a sense the most essential part, of the peace settlement itself. It cannot be formed now. If formed now, it would be merely a new alliance confined to the nations associated against a common enemy. It is not likely that it could be formed after the settlement. It is necessary to guarantee the peace; and the peace cannot be guaranteed as an afterthought. The reason, to speak in plain terms again, why it must be guaranteed is that there will be parties to the peace whose promises have proved untrustworthy, and means must be found in connection with the peace settlement itself to remove that source of insecurity. It would be folly to leave the guarantee to the subsequent voluntary action of the Governments we have seen destroy Russia and deceive Roumania.

But these general terms do not disclose the whole matter. Some details are needed to make them sound less like a thesis and more like a practical program. These, then, are some of the particulars, and I state them with greater confidence because I can state them authoritatively as representing this Government's interpretation of its own duty with regard to peace.

First, the impartial justice meted out must involve no discrimination between those to whom we wish to be just and those to whom we do not wish to be just. It must be a justice that plays no favorites and knows no standard but the equal rights of the several peoples concerned;

Second, no special or separate interest of any single nation or any group of nations can be made the basis of any part of the settlement which is not consistent with the common interest of all;

Third, there can be no leagues or alliances or special covenants and understandings within the general and common family of the League of Nations;

Fourth, and more specifically, there can be no special, selfish economic combinations within the League and no employment of any form of economic boycott or exclusion except as the power of economic penalty by exclusion from the markets of the world may be vested in the League of Nations itself as a means of discipline and control;

Fifth, all international agreements and treaties of every kind must be made known in their entirety to the rest of the world.

Special alliances and economic rivalries and hostilities have been the prolific source in the modern world of the plans and passions that produce war. It would be an insincere as well as an insecure peace that did not exclude them in definite and binding terms.

The confidence with which I venture to speak for our people in these matters does not spring from our traditions merely and the well-known principles of international action which we have always professed and followed. In the same sentence in which I say that the United States will enter into no special arrangements or understandings with particular nations let me say also that the United States is prepared to assume its full share of responsibility for the maintenance of the common covenants and understandings upon which peace must henceforth rest. We still read Washington's immortal warning against "entangling alliances" with full comprehension and an answering purpose. But only special and limited alliances entangle; and we recognize and accept the duty of a new day in which we are permitted to hope for a general alliance which will avoid entanglements and clear the air of the world for common understandings and the maintenance of common rights.

I have made this analysis of the international situation which the war has created, not, of course, because I doubted whether the leaders of the great nations and peoples with whom we are associated were of the same mind and entertained a like purpose, but because the air every now and again gets darkened by mists and groundless doubtings and mischievous perversions of counsel and it is necessary once and again to sweep all the irresponsible talk about peace intrigues and weakening morale and doubtful purpose on the part of those in authority utterly, and if need be, unceremoniously, aside and say things in the plainest words that can be found, even when it is only to say over again what has been said before, quite plainly if in less unvarnished terms.

As I have said, neither I nor any other man in governmental authority created or gave form to the issues of this war. I have simply responded to them with such vision as I could command. But I have responded gladly and with a resolution that has grown warmer and more confident as the issues have grown clearer and clearer. It is now plain that they are issues which no man can pervert unless it be willfully. I am bound to fight for them, and happy to fight for them as the time and circumstances have revealed them to me as to all the world. Our enthusiasm for them grows more and more irresistible as they stand out in more and more vivid and unmistakable outline.

And the forces that fight for them draw into closer and closer array, organize their millions into more and more unconquerable might, as they become more and more distinct to the thought and purpose of the peoples engaged. It is the peculiarity of this great war that while statesmen have seemed to cast about for definitions of their purpose and have sometimes seemed to shift their ground and their point of view, the thought of the mass of men, whom statesmen are supposed to instruct and lead, has grown more and more unclouded, more and more certain of what it is that they are fighting for. National purposes have fallen more and more into the background and the common purpose of enlightened mankind has taken their place. The counsels of plain men have become on all hands more simple and straightforward and more unified than the counsels of sophisticated men of affairs, who still retain the impression that they are playing a game of power and playing for high stakes. That is why I have said that this is a peoples' war, not a statesmen's. Statesmen must follow the clarified common thought or be broken.

I take that to be the significance of the fact that assemblies and associations of many kinds made up of plain workaday people have demanded, almost every time they came together, and are still demanding, that the leaders of their Governments declare to them plainly what it is, exactly what it is, that they are seeking in the war, and what they think the items of the final settlement should be. They are not yet satisfied with what they have been told. They still seem to fear that they are getting what they ask for only in statesmen's terms, —only in the terms of territorial arrangements and divisions of power, and not in terms of broad-visioned justice and mercy and peace and the satisfaction of those deep-seated longings of oppressed and distracted men and women and enslaved peoples that seem to them the only things worth fighting a war for that engulfs the world. Perhaps statesmen have not always recognized this changed aspect of the whole world of policy and action. Perhaps they have not always spoken in direct reply to the questions asked because they did not know how searching those questions were and what sort of answers they demanded.

But I, for one, am glad to attempt the answer again and again, in the hope that I may make it clearer and clearer that my one thought is to satisfy those who struggle in the ranks and are, perhaps above all others, entitled to a reply whose meaning no one can have any excuse for misunderstanding, if he understands the language in which it is spoken or can get someone to translate it correctly into his own. And I believe that the leaders of the Governments with which we are associated will speak, as they have occasion, as plainly as I have tried to speak. I hope that they will feel free to say whether they think that I am in any degree mistaken in my interpretation of the issues involved or in my purpose with regard to the means by which a satisfactory settlement of those issues may be obtained. Unity of purpose and of counsel are as imperatively necessary in this war as was unity of command in the battlefield; and with perfect unity of purpose and counsel will come assurance of complete victory. It can be had in no other way. "Peace drives" can be effectively neutralized and silenced only by showing that every victory of the nations associated against Germany brings the nations nearer the sort of peace which will bring security and reassurance to all peoples and make the recurrence of another such struggle of pitiless force and bloodshed forever impossible, and that nothing else can. Germany is constantly intimating the "terms" she will accept; and always finds that the world does not want terms. It wishes the final triumph of justice and fair dealing.

ADDRESS TO SENATE

[Urging the Passage of the Amendment to the Constitution Granting Suffrage to Women. Delivered September 30, 1919.]

The amendment to the federal constitution granting women the right to vote was first introduced in the United States Senate in 1878. In the Senate it was voted upon adversely in 1887. On March 19, 1914, the vote was 35 yeas and 34 nays. In the House of Representatives, the vote in 1915 was 174 yeas and 204 nays. On January 10, 1918, however, the amendment passed the House by a vote of 274 yeas and 136 nays.

By the time of the President's address, the following states had granted women the full right of suffrage:—Wyoming (1869); Colorado (1893); Utah (1896); Idaho (1896); Washington (1910); California (1911); Kansas (1912); Arizona (1912); Oregon (1912); Nevada (1914); Montana (1914); New York (1917). Alaska had granted full suffrage in 1913.

By this time, the following states had granted to women the right of presidential and municipal suffrage:—Illinois (1913); Nebraska (1917); North Dakota (1917); Vermont (1917); Michigan (1917). Arkansas had granted (1917) the right to vote in primaries, which in that state was tantamount to full suffrage. The right to vote in presidential elections only had been granted by Rhode Island in 1917.

By the time of the President's address, women enjoyed the full right to vote in the following:—New Zealand (1893); Australia (1902); Finland (1906); Norway (1907); Iceland (1913); Denmark (1915); the provinces of Manitoba (1916), Alberta (1916), Saskatchewan (1916), British Columbia (1916), Ontario (1917), in Canada; Russia (1917); England, Scotland, Wales and Ireland (1918).

On October 1, 1918, the day following the President's address, the amendment was voted upon in the Senate, with a result of 62 yeas and 34 nays, thus falling two votes short of the two-thirds vote necessary to ratify amendments to the United States Constitution. Most of the opposition to women suffrage in this Senate vote came from the representatives of the Southern states, where there was strong feeling against permitting negro women to vote.

Gentlemen of the Senate:

The unusual circumstances of a world war in which we stand and are judged in the view not only of our own people and our own consciences, but also in the view of all nations and people, will, I hope, justify in your thought, as it does in mine, the message I have come to bring you.

I regard the concurrence of the Senate in the constitutional amendment proposing the extension of the suffrage to women as vitally essential to the successful prosecution of the great war of humanity in which we are engaged. I have come to urge upon you the considerations which have led me to that conclusion. It is not only my privilege, it is also my duty to apprise you of every circumstance and element involved in this momentous struggle which seem to me to affect its very processes and its outcome. It is my duty to win the war and to ask you to remove every obstacle that stands in the way of winning it.

I had assumed that the Senate would concur in the amendment because no disputable principle is involved, but only a question of the method by which the suffrage is to be extended to women.

There is and can be no party issue involved in it. Both of our great national parties are pledged, explicitly pledged, to equality of suffrage for the women of the country. Neither party, therefore, it seems to me, can justify hesitation as to the method of obtaining it, can rightfully hesitate to substitute Federal initiative for State initiative, if the early adoption of this measure is necessary to the successful prosecution of the war, and if the method of State action proposed in the party platforms of 1916 is impracticable, within any reasonable length of time, if practicable at all. And its adoption is, in my judgment, clearly necessary to the successful prosecution of the war and the successful realization of the objects for which the war is being fought.

That judgment I take the liberty of urging upon you with solemn earnestness for reasons which I shall state very frankly and which I shall hope will seem as conclusive to you as they seem to me.

This is a peoples' war, and the peoples' thinking constitutes its atmosphere and morale, not the predilections of the drawing-room or the political considerations of the caucus. If we be indeed democrats, and wish to lead the world to democracy, we can ask other peoples to accept in proof of our sincerity and our ability to lead them whither they wish to be led nothing less persuasive and convincing than our actions.

Our professions will not suffice. Verification must be forthcoming when verification is asked for. And in this case verification is asked for—asked for in this particular matter. You ask by whom? Not through diplomatic channels, not by foreign ministers. Not by the intimations of parliaments. It is asked for by the anxious, expectant, suffering peoples with whom we are dealing and who are willing to put their destinies in some measure in our hands, if they are sure that we wish the same things that they wish.

I do not speak by conjecture. It is not alone the voices of statesmen and of newspapers that reach me and the voices of foolish and intemperate agitators do not reach me at all. Through many, many channels I have been made aware what the plain, struggling, workaday folk are thinking upon whom the chief terror and suffering of this tragic war falls. They are looking to the great, powerful, famous democracy of the West to lead them to the new day for which they have so long waited; and they think, in their logical simplicity, that democracy means that women shall play their part in affairs alongside men and upon an equal footing with them. If we reject measures like this in ignorance or defiance of what a new age has brought forth, of what they have seen, but we have not, they will cease to believe in us; they will cease to follow or to trust us.

They have seen their own Governments accept this interpretation of democracy—seen old Governments like that of Great Britain, which did not profess to be democratic, promise readily and as of course this justice to women, though they had before refused it, the strange revelations of this war having made many things new and plain, to Governments as well as to peoples.

Are we alone to refuse to learn the lesson? Are we alone to ask and take the utmost that our women can give—service and sacrifice of every kind—and still say we do not see what title that gives to them to stand by our sides in the guidance of the affairs of their nation and ours? We have made partners of the women in this war; shall we admit them only to a partnership of sacrifice and suffering and toil and not to a partnership of privilege and right?

This war could not have been fought, either by the other nations engaged or by America, if it had not been for the services of the women—services rendered in every sphere—not merely in the fields of efforts in which we have been accustomed to see them work, but wherever men have worked and upon the very skirts and edges of the battle itself. We shall not only be distrusted but shall deserve to be distrusted if we do not enfranchise them with the fullest possible enfranchisement, as it is now certain that the other great free nations will enfranchise them.

We cannot isolate our thought or action in such a matter from the thought of the rest of the world. We must either conform or deliberately reject what they propose and resign the leadership of liberal minds to others.

The women of America are too noble and too intelligent and too devoted to be slackers whether you give or withhold this thing that is mere justice; but I know the magic it will work in their thoughts and spirits if you give it to them.

I propose it as I would propose to admit soldiers to the suffrage, the men fighting in the field for our liberties and the liberties of the world, were they excluded. The tasks of the women lie at the very heart of the war, and I know how much stronger that heart will beat if you do this just thing and show our women that you trust them as much as you in fact and of necessity depend upon them.

Have I said that the passage of this amendment is a vitally necessary war measure, and do you need further proof? Do you stand in need of the trust of other peoples and of the trust of our own women? Is that trust an asset, or is it not?

I tell you plainly, as the Commander in Chief of our armies and of the gallant men in our fleets, as the present spokesman of this people in our dealings with the men and women throughout the world who are now our partners, as the responsible head of a great Government which stands and is questioned day by day as to its purposes, its principles, its hopes, whether they be serviceable to men everywhere or only to itself, and who must himself answer these questionings, or be shamed, as the guide and director of forces caught in the grip of war, and by the same token in need of every material and spiritual resource this great nation possesses—I tell you plainly that this measure which I urge upon you is vital to the winning of the war and to the energies alike of preparation and of battle.

And not to the winning of the war only. It is vital to the right solution of the great problems which we must settle, and settle immediately when the war is over. We shall need then in our vision of affairs, as we have never needed them before, the sympathy and insight and clear moral instinct of the women of the world.

The problems of that time will strike to the roots of many things that we have not hitherto questioned, and I for one believe that our safety in those questioning days, as well as our comprehension of matters that touch society to the quick will depend upon the direct and authoritative participation of women in our counsels. We shall need their moral sense to preserve what is right and fine and worthy in our system or life, as well as to discover just what it is that ought to be purified and reformed. Without their counselings, we shall be only half wise.

That is my case. This is my appeal. Many may deny its validity, if they choose, but no one can brush aside or answer the arguments upon which it is based. The executive tasks of this war rest upon me. I ask that you lighten them and place in my hands instruments, spiritual instruments, which I do not now possess, which I sorely need, and which I have daily to apologize for not being able to employ.

ARMISTICE NEGOTIATIONS OF THE GREAT WAR

On September 15, 1918, Austria-Hungary addressed to President Wilson a request for a conference to discuss peace. The Central Powers were to direct to President Wilson their communications referring to an armistice because the lofty and thorough character of the American President's pronouncements on the question of war aims and peace terms had made him the unofficial diplomatic leader of the Allies. He had also convinced the Central Powers that his purposes and the purposes of his country were freer from self-seeking and the spirit of revenge, and were more fully directed toward realizing a better world-order in the future instead of perpetuating the hatreds of the past, than were the purposes of the other Allied leaders and countries. The Austro-Hungarian note was merely an indefinite request for a conference, with nothing to indicate that such a conference would be binding.

The answer of the President was as incisive as it was curt, and was dispatched immediately upon the receipt of the Austrian note on September 16:

The Government of the United States feels that there is only one reply which it can make to the suggestion of the Imperial Austro-Hungarian Government. It has repeatedly and with entire candor stated the terms upon which the United States would consider peace, and can and will entertain no proposal for a conference upon a matter concerning which it has made its position and purpose so plain.

Contemporaneously with the Austro-Hungarian peace offer, the German Government officially offered peace to Belgium, with certain concessions, but met with no better success than its ally.

After the end of September, even the official propaganda of the Imperial German Government could no longer restrain the German people from the conviction that their cause was lost. For Bulgaria unconditionally surrendered to the Entente Allies on September 30, and the most docile German "patient Michel" could realize that at last the German war machine had cracked. On this same day, the German Government of Chancellor von Hertling and Foreign Secretary von Hintze resigned, and was succeeded by a Government formed by Prince Max of Baden, with Doctor Solf as the new foreign secretary. At the same time, revolutionary democratizing changes were made in the constitution of the German Empire, with the result that for the first time the Majority or pro-war Socialists officially entered the Government. The Majority Socialist leader, Scheidemann, joined the cabinet, as did the leader of the Catholic Centrists, Erzberger, whose influence for many months had been exerted in favor of moderation and understanding with the Allies.

It was evident that the new Government had taken office only with the understanding that it would enter upon peace negotiations at once, since Austria-Hungary had signally failed in her assignment of opening peace discussions. The world was not surprised, therefore, when on October 5 the German Government of Prince Max addressed the following note (received in Washington on October 6) to President Wilson:

> The German Government requests the President of the United States of America to take steps for the restoration of peace; to notify all belligerents of this request, and to invite them to delegate plenipotentiaries for the purpose of taking up negotiations. The German Government accepts, as a basis for the peace negotiations, the program laid down by the President of the United States in his message to Congress of January 8, 1918, and in his subsequent pronouncements, particularly in his address of September 27, 1918. In order to avoid further bloodshed, the German Government requests you tp bring about the immediate conclusion of a general armistice on land, on water, and in the air.

On the same day, the Austro-Hungarian Government joined with its ally in asking peace, in the following note (received in Washington on October 7):

> The Austro-Hungarian Monarchy, which has waged war always and solely as a defensive war and repeatedly given documentary evidence of its readiness to stop the shedding of blood and to arrive at a just and honorable peace, hereby addresses itself to His Lordship the President of the United States of America and offers to conclude with him and his allies an armistice on every front on land, at sea, and in the air, and to enter immediately upon negotiations for a peace for which the fourteen points in the Message of President Wilson to Congress of January 8, 1918, and the four points contained in President Wilson's address of February 12, 1918, should serve as a foundation and in which the viewpoints declared by President Wilson in his address of September 27, 1918, will also be taken into account.

Before replying directly to the German note, the American Government addressed the following query to the German:

Before making a reply to the request of the Imperial German Government, and in order that that reply shall be as candid and straightforward as the momentous· interests involved require, the President of the United States deems it necessary to assure himself of the exact meaning of the note of the Imperial Chancellor. Does the Imperial Chancellor mean that the Imperial German Government accepts the terms laid down by the President in his address to the Congress of the United States on the 8th of January last and in subsequent addresses, and that its object in entering into discussions would be only to agree upon the practical details of their application?

The President feels bound to say with regard to the suggestion of an armistice that he would not feel at liberty to propose a cessation of arms to the Governments with which the Government of the United States is associated against the Central Powers so long as the armies of those Powers are upon their soil. The good faith of any discussion would manifestly depend upon the consent of the Central Powers immediately to withdraw their forces everywhere from invaded territory.

The President also feels that he is justified in asking whether the Imperial Chancellor is speaking merely for the constituted authorities of the Empire who have so far conducted the war. He deems the answer to these questions vital from every point of view.

The above note was more than a query. It was a subtle but transparent suggestion to the German people as to the requirements which would have to be met by Germany itself before peace should be possible.

The reply of the German Government to the American query was as follows:

In reply to the question of the President of the United States of America the German Government hereby declares:

The German Government has accepted the terms laid down by President Wilson in his address of January the eighth and in subsequent addresses as the foundations of a permanent peace of justice. Consequently, its object in entering into discussions would be only to agree upon practical details of the application of these terms.

The German Government believes that the governments of the Powers associated with the United States also accept the position taken by President Wilson in his addresses.

The German Government, in accordance with the Austro-Hungarian Government, for the purpose of bringing about an armistice declares itself ready to comply with the propositions of the President in regard to evacuation.

The German Government suggests that the President may occasion the meeting of a mixed commission for making the necessary arrangements concerning the evacuation.

The present German Government which has undertaken the responsibility for this step towards peace has been formed by conferences and in agreement with the great majority of the Reichstag. The chancellor, supported in all of his actions by the will of this majority, speaks in the name of the German Government and of the German people.

On October 14, therefore, the following statement was issued by the American Government concerning the German note of October 5:

The unqualified acceptance by the present German Government and by a large majority of the German Reichstag of the terms laid down by the President of the United States of America in his address to the Congress of the United States on the 8th of January, 1918, and in his subsequent addresses justifies the President in making a frank and direct statement of his decision with regard to the communications of the German Government of the 8th and 12th of October, 1918.

It must be clearly understood that the process of evacuation and the conditions of an armistice are matters which must be left to the judgment and advice of the military advisers of the Government of the United States and the Allied Governments, and the President feels it his duty to say that no arrangement can be accepted by the Government of the United States which does not provide absolutely satisfactory safeguards and guarantees of the maintenance of the present military supremacy of the armies of the United States and of the Allies in the field. He feels confident that he can safely assume that this will also be the judgment and decision of the Allied Governments.

The President feels that it is also his duty to add that neither the Government of the United States nor, he is quite sure, the Governments with which the Government of the United States is associated as a belligerent will consent to consider an armistice so long as the armed forces of Germany continue the illegal and inhumane practices which they still persist in. At the very time that the German Government approaches the Government of the United States with proposals of peace its submarines are engaged in sinking passenger ships at sea, and not the ships alone, but the very boats in which their passengers and crews seek to make their way to safety; and in their present enforced withdrawal from Flanders and France the German armies are pursuing a course of wanton destruction which has always been regarded as in direct violation of the rules and practices of civilized warfare. Cities and villages, if not destroyed, are being stripped of all they contain not only, but often of their very inhabitants. The nations associated against Germany can not be expected to agree to a cessation of arms while acts of inhumanity, spoliation, and desolation are being continued which they justly look upon with horror and with burning hearts.

It is necessary also, in order that there may be no possibility of misunderstanding, that the President should very solemnly call the attention of the Government of Germany to the language and plain intent of one of the terms of peace which the German Government has now accepted. It is contained in the address of the President delivered at Mount Vernon on the Fourth of July last. It is as follows: "The destruction of every arbitrary power anywhere that can separately, secretly, and of its single choice disturb the peace of the world; or, if it can not be presently destroyed, at least its reduction to virtual impotency." The power which has hitherto controlled the German nation is of the sort here described. It is within the choice of the German nation to alter it. The President's words just quoted naturally constitute a condition precedent to peace, if peace is to come by the action of the German people themselves. The President feels bound to say that the whole process of peace will, in his judgment, depend upon the definiteness and the satisfactory character of the guarantees which can be given in this fundamental matter. It is indispensable that the Governments associated against Germany should know beyond a peradventure with whom they are dealing.

The President will make a separate reply to the Royal and Imperial Government of Austria-Hungary.

The United States was naturally fully aware that Austria-Hungary was under the complete domination of Germany, and therefore the negotiations with the Austro-Hungarian Government assumed a position secondary to the negotiations with Germany. It was not until October 18 that the following reply was made to the Austro-Hungarian note of October 5:

The President deems it his duty to say to the Austro-Hungarian Government that he can not entertain the present suggestions of that Government because of certain events of utmost importance which, occurring since the delivery of his address of the 8th of January last, have necessarily altered the attitude and responsibility of the Government of the United States. Among the fourteen terms of peace which the President formulated at that time occurred the following:

"X. The people of Austria-Hungary, whose place among the nations we wish to see safeguarded and assured, should be accorded the freest opportunity of autonomous development."

Since that sentence was written and uttered to the Congress of the United States, the Government of the United States has recognized that a state of belligerency exists between the Czecho-Slovaks and the German and Austro-Hungarian Empires and that the Czecho-Slovak National Council is a de facto belligerent government clothed with proper authority to direct the military and political affairs of the Czecho-Slovaks. It has also recognized in the fullest manner the justice of the nationalistic aspirations of the Jugo-Slavs for freedom.

The President is, therefore, no longer at liberty to accept the mere "autonomy" of these peoples as a basis of peace, but is obliged to insist that they, and not he, shall be the judges of what action on the part of the Austro-Hungarian Government will satisfy their aspirations and their conception of their rights and destiny as members of the family of nations.

Under date of October 20, 1918, the German Government, in the following communication, answered the points raised in the American statement of October 14:

In accepting the proposal for an evacuation of the occupied territories, the German Government has started from the assumption that the procedure of this evacuation and of the conditions of an armistice should be left to the judgment of the military advisers, and that the actual standard of power on both sides in the field has to form the basis for arrangements safeguarding and guaranteeing the standard. The German Government suggests to the President to bring about an opportunity for fixing the details. It trusts that the President of the United States will approve of no demand which would be irreconcilable with the honor of the German people, and with opening a way to a peace of justice.

The German Government protests against the reproach of illegal and inhuman actions made against the German land and sea forces, and thereby against the German people. For the covering of a retreat, destructions will always be necessary, and are, in so far, permitted by international law. The German troops are under the strictest instructions to spare private property and to exercise care for the population to the best of their ability. Where transgressions occur in spite of these instructions, the guilty are being punished.

The German Government further denies that the German navy in sinking ships has ever purposely destroyed lifeboats with their passengers. The German Government purposes with regard to all these charges that the facts be cleared up by neutral commissions. In order to avoid anything that might hamper the work of peace the German Government has caused orders to be dispatched to all submarine commanders precluding the torpedoing of passenger ships, without, however, for technical reasons, being able to guarantee that these orders will reach every single submarine at sea before its return.

As the fundamental conditions for peace the President characterizes the destruction of every arbitrary power that can separately, secretly and of its own single choice disturb the peace of the world.

To this the German Government replies: Hitherto the representation of the people in the German Empire has not been endowed with an influence on the formation of the government. The constitution did not provide for a concurrence of the representation of the people in decisions on peace and war. These conditions have just now undergone a fundamental change. The new Government has been formed in complete accord with the wishes of the representation of the people, based on the equal, universal, secret, direct franchise. The leaders of the great parties of the Reichstag are members of this Government.

In the future no government can take or continue in office without possessing the confidence of the majority of the Reichstag. The responsibility of the Chancellor of the empire to the representation of the people is being legally developed and safeguarded.

The first act of the new Government has been to lay before the Reichstag a bill to alter the constitution of the empire so that the consent of the representation of the people is required for decisions on war and peace. The permanence of the new system is, however, guaranteed not only by constitutional safeguards, but also by the unshakable determination of the German people, whose vast majority stands behind these reforms and demands their energetic continuance.

The question of the President, With whom he and the Governments associated against Germany are, dealing? is therefore answered in a clear and unequivocal manner by the statement that the offer of peace and an armistice has come from a Government which, free from arbitrary and irresponsible influence, is supported by the approval of the overwhelming majority of the German people.

On October 23, therefore, the following reply to the original German note on the question of peace was dispatched:

Having received the solemn and explicit assurance of the German Government that it unreservedly accepts the terms of peace laid down in his address to the Congress of the United States on the eighth of

"OVER THE TOP"

"OVER THE TOP."

The camera has caught British "Tommies" as they rushed from the shelter of their own trench across No Man's Land to occupy a German trench which has been made untenable by Allied fire.

January, 1918, and the principles of settlement enunciated in his subsequent addresses, particularly the address of the twenty-seventh of September, and that it desires to discuss the details of their application, and that this wish and purpose emanate, not from those who have hitherto dictated German policy and conducted the present war on Germany's behalf, but from ministers who speak for the majority of the Reichstag and for an overwhelming majority of the German people; and having received also the explicit promise of the present German Government that the humane rules of civilized warfare will be observed both on land and sea by the German armed forces, the President of the United States feels that he can not decline to take up with the Governments with which the Government of the United States is associated the question of an armistice.

He deems it his duty to say again, however, that the only armistice he would feel justified in submitting for consideration would be one which should leave the United States and the powers associated with her in a position to enforce any arrangements that may be entered into and to make a renewal of hostilities on the part of Germany impossible. The President has, therefore, transmitted his correspondence with the present German authorities to the Governments with which the Government of the United States is associated as a belligerent, with the suggestion that, if those Governments are disposed to effect peace upon the terms and principles indicated, their military advisers and the military advisers of the United States be asked to submit to the Governments associated against Germany the necessary terms of such an armistice as will fully protect the interests of the people involved and ensure to the associated Governments the unrestricted power to safeguard and enforce the details of the peace to which the German Government has agreed, provided they deem such an armistice possible from the military point of view. Should such terms of armistice be suggested, their acceptance by Germany will afford the best concrete evidence of her unequivocal acceptance of the terms and principles of peace from which the whole action proceeds.

The President would deem himself lacking in candor did he not point out in the frankest possible terms the reason why extraordinary safeguards must be demanded. Significant and important as the constitutional changes seem to be which are spoken of by the German Foreign Secretary in his note of the 20th of October, it does not appear that the principle of a Government responsible to the German people has yet been fully worked out or that any guarantees either exist or are in contemplation that the alterations of principle and of practice now partially agreed upon will be permanent. Moreover, it does not appear that the heart of the present difficulty has been reached. It may be that future wars have been brought under the control of the

German people, but the present war has not been; and it is with the present war that we are dealing. It is evident that the German people have no means of commanding the acquiescence of the military authorities of the Empire in the popular will; that the power of the King of Prussia to control the policy of the Empire is unimpaired; that the determining initiative still remains with those who have hitherto been the masters of Germany.

Feeling that the whole peace of the world depends now on plain speaking and straightforward action, the President deems it his duty to say, without any attempt to soften what may seem harsh words, that the nations of the world do not and can not trust the word of those who have hitherto been the masters of German policy; and to point out once more that in concluding peace and attempting to undo the infinite injuries and injustices of this war the Government of the United States can not deal with any but veritable representatives of the German people who have been assured of a genuine constitutional standing as the real rulers of Germany. If it must deal with the military masters and the monarchical autocrats of Germany now, or if it is likely to have to deal with them later in regard to the international obligations of the German Empire, it must demand, not peace negotiations, but surrender. Nothing can be gained by leaving this essential thing unsaid.

With all the preliminaries to an armistice thus removed, on October 27 the German Government made the following request for the cessation of hostilities:

The German Government has taken cognizance of the answer of the President of the United States.

The President is aware of the far-reaching changes which have been carried out and are being carried out in the German constitutional structure, and that peace negotiations are being conducted by a people's Government, in whose hands rests, both actually and constitutionally, the power to make the deciding conclusions. The military powers are also subject to it.

The German Government now awaits proposals for an armistice, which shall be the first step toward a just peace, as the President has described it in his proclamation.

On October 28, the following communication was received from the Austro-Hungarian Government in reply to the American note of October 18:

In reply to the note of President Wilson of the nineteenth of this month, addressed to the Austro-Hungarian Government on the question of an armistice and of peace, the Austro-Hungarian Government has the honor to declare that equally with the preceding proclamations of the President, it adheres also to the same point of view contained in the last note upon the rights of the Austro-Hungarian peoples, especially those of the Czecho-Slovaks and the Jugo-Slavs.

Consequently, Austria-Hungary accepting all the conditions the President has laid down for the entry into negotiations for an armistice and peace, no obstacle exists, according to the judgment of the Austro-Hungarian Government, to the beginning of those negotiations.

The Austro-Hungarian Government declares itself ready, in consequence, without awaiting the result of other negotiations, to enter into negotiations upon peace between Austria-Hungary and the States in the opposing group and for an immediate armistice upon all Austro-Hungarian fronts.

It asks President Wilson to be so kind as to begin overtures on this subject.

On October 31, the Secretary of State of the United States dispatched the following note to the Turkish Government:

I did not fail to lay before the President the note which you addressed to him on the 14th instant, and handed to me on that date.

Acting under the instructions of your Government, you enclosed with that note the text of a communication received by the Minister for Foreign Affairs of Spain, from the Chargé d'Affaires of Turkey at Madrid, on October 12, in which the good offices of the Government of Spain were sought to bring to the attention of the President the request of the Imperial Ottoman Government that he take upon himself the task of the reëstablishment of peace, and that he notify all belligerent states of the request and invite them to delegate plenipotentiaries to initiate negotiations; the Imperial Ottoman Government accepting as a basis for the negotiations the programme laid down by the President in his message to Congress of January 8, 1918, and in his subsequent declarations, especially his speech of September 27. It is further requested by the Imperial Ottoman Government that steps be taken for the immediate conclusion of a general armistice on land, on sea, and in the air.

By direction of the President, I have the honor to inform your Excellency that the Government of the United States will bring the communication of the Turkish Chargé d'Affaires to the knowledge of the Governments at war with Turkey.

On October 30, a further statement was received from the German Government, describing in detail the steps which Germany had taken toward democratizing its form of government, but this statement the Government of the United States refused to make public.

On November 4, the following reply to the German request for an armistice was transmitted:

In my note of October 23, 1918, I advised you that the President had transmitted his correspondence with the German authorities to the Governments with which the Government of the United States is associated as a belligerent with the suggestion that, if those Governments were disposed to accept peace upon the terms and principles indicated, their military advisers and the military advisers of the United States be asked to submit to the Governments associated against Germany the necessary terms of such an armistice as would fully protect the interests of the peoples involved and insure the associated Governments the unrestricted power to safeguard and enforce the details of the peace to which the German Government has agreed, provided they deem such an armistice possible from the military point of view.

The President is now in receipt of a memorandum of observations by the Allied Governments on this correspondence, which is as follows:

The Allied Governments have given careful consideration to the correspondence which has passed between the President of the United States and the German Government. Subject to the qualifications which follow, they declare their willingness to make peace with the Government of Germany on the terms of peace laid down in the President's address to Congress of January 8, 1918, and the principles of settlement enunciated in his subsequent addresses.

They must point out, however, that Clause 2, relating to what is usually described as the freedom of the seas, is open to various interpretations, some of which they could not accept. They must, therefore, reserve to themselves complete freedom on this subject when they enter the peace conference.

Further, in the conditions of peace, laid down in his address to Congress of January 8, 1918, the President declared that invaded territories must be restored as well as evacuated and freed. The Allied Governments feel that no doubt ought to be allowed to exist as to what this provision implies. By it they understand that compensation will be made by Germany for all damage done to the civilian population of the Allies and their property by the aggression of Germany by land, by sea, and from the air.

I am instructed by the President to say that he is in agreement with the interpretation set forth in the last paragraph of the memorandum above quoted. I am further instructed by the President to request you to notify the German Government that Marshal Foch has been authorized by the Government of the United States and the Allied Governments to receive properly accredited representatives of the German Government and to communicate to them terms of an armistice.

ROBERT LANSING,
Secretary of State.

On November 7, the German representatives empowered to sign an armistice left for the headquarters of Marshal Foch, where they were received and were given the armistice terms on the following day. The German Government and the German people complained long and bitterly at what they termed the unnecessary and brutal harshness of the armistice terms, so that a delay of a few days ensued before the terms were finally signed. But Germany was helpless, and on November 11, at 5 A. M. French time (11 A. M. Washington time) the document ending the major hostilities of the war was signed. Previously, military defeats had compelled Germany's allies to accept armistice terms amounting to surrender, as follows:—Bulgaria, on September 29; Turkey, on October 31; Austria-Hungary, on November 4.

On November 11, 1918, at one o'clock in the afternoon, the President of the United States announced to Congress and through Congress to the entire country, the official end of the actual major hostilities of the Great War:

Gentlemen of the Congress:

In these anxious times of rapid and stupendous change it will in some degree lighten my sense of responsibility to perform in person the duty of communicating to you some of the larger circumstances of the situation with which it is necessary to deal.

The German authorities who have, at the invitation of the Supreme War Council, been in communication with Marshal Foch have accepted and signed the terms of armistice which he was authorized and instructed to communicate to them. Those terms are as follows:*

One—Cessation of operations by land and in the air six hours after the signature of the armistice.

Two—Immediate evacuation of invaded countries—Belgium, France, Alsace-Lorraine, Luxemburg, so ordered as to be completed within fourteen days from the signature of the armistice. German troops which have not left the above mentioned territories within the period fixed will become prisoners of war. Occupation by the Allied and United States forces jointly will keep pace with evacuation in these areas. All movements of evacuation and occupation will be regulated in accordance with a note annexed to the stated terms.

Three—Repatriation beginning at once and to be completed within fourteen days of all inhabitants of the countries above mentioned, including hostages and persons under trial or convicted.

Four—Surrender in good condition by the German armies of the following equipment: Five thousand guns (two thousand five hundred heavy, two thousand five hundred field). Thirty thousand machine guns. Three thousand minenwerfer. Two thousand aeroplanes (fighters, bombers—firstly D. Seventy-threes and night bombing machines). The above to be delivered *in situ* to the Allies and United States troops in accordance with the detailed conditions laid down in the annexed note.

Five—Evacuation by the German armies of the countries on the

*See page 8620.

left bank of the Rhine. These countries on the left bank of the Rhine shall be administered by the local authorities under the control of the Allied and United States armies of occupation. The occupation of these territories will be determined by Allied and United States garrisons holding the principal crossings of the Rhine, Mayence, Coblenz, Cologne, together with bridgeheads at these points in a thirty kilometer radius on the right bank and by garrisons similarly holding the strategic points of the regions. A neutral zone shall be reserved on the right of the Rhine between the stream and a line drawn parallel to it forty kilometers to the east from the frontier of Holland to the parallel of Gernsheim and as far as practicable a distance of thirty kilometers from the east of stream from this parallel upon Swiss frontier. Evacuation by the enemy of the Rhine lands shall be so ordered as to be completed within a further period of eleven days, in all nineteen days after the signature of the armistice. All movements of evacuation and occupation will be regulated according to the note annexed.

Six—In all territory evacuated by the enemy there shall be no evacuation of inhabitants; no damage or harm shall be done to the persons or property of the inhabitants. No destruction of any kind to be committed. Military establishments of all kinds shall be delivered intact as well as military stores of food, munitions, equipment not removed during the periods fixed for evacuation. Stores of food of all kinds for the civil population, cattle, etc., shall be left *in situ*. Industrial establishments shall not be impaired in any way and their personnel shall not be removed. Roads and means of communication of every kind, railroad, waterways, main roads, bridges, telegraphs, telephones, shall be in no manner impaired.

Seven—All civil and military personnel at present employed on them shall remain. Five thousand locomotives, fifty thousand wagons and ten thousand motor lorries in good working order with all necessary spare parts and fittings shall be delivered to the Associated Powers within the period fixed for the evacuation of Belgium and Luxemburg. The railways of Alsace-Lorraine shall be handed over within the same period, together with all pre-war personnel and material. Further material necessary for the working of railways in the country on the left bank of the Rhine shall be left *in situ*. All stores of coal and material for the up-keep of permanent ways, signals and repair shops to be left entire *in situ* and kept in an efficient state by Germany during the whole period of armistice. All barges taken from the Allies shall be restored to them. A note appended regulates the details of these measures.

Eight—The German command shall be responsible for revealing all mines or delayed-acting fuses disposed on territory evacuated by the German troops and shall assist in their discovery and destruction. The

German command shall also reveal all destructive measures that may have been taken (such as poisoning or polluting of springs, wells, etc.) under penalty of reprisals.

Nine—The right of requisition shall be exercised by the Allied and the United States armies in all occupied territory. The up-keep of the troops of occupation in the Rhine land (excluding Alsace-Lorraine) shall be charged to the German Government.

Ten—An immediate repatriation without reciprocity, according to detailed conditions which shall be fixed, of all Allied and United States prisoners of war. The Allied Powers and the United States shall be able to dispose of these prisoners as they wish.

Eleven—Sick and wounded who cannot be removed from evacuated territory will be cared for by German personnel who will be left on the spot with the medical material required.

Twelve—All German troops at present in any territory which before the war belonged to Russia, Roumania or Turkey shall withdraw within the frontiers of Germany as they existed on August first, 1914.

Thirteen—Evacuation by German troops to begin at once and all German instructors, prisoners, and civilian as well as military agents, now on the territory of Russia (as defined before 1914) to be recalled.

Fourteen—German troops to cease at once all requisitions and seizures and any other undertaking with a view to obtaining supplies intended for Germany in Roumania and Russia (as defined on August first, 1914).

Fifteen—Abandonment of the treaties of Bucharest and Brest-Litovsk and of the supplementary treaties.

Sixteen—The Allies shall have free access to the territories evacuated by the Germans on their eastern frontier either through Danzig or by the Vistula in order to convey supplies to the populations of those territories or for any other purpose.

Seventeen—Unconditional capitulation of all German forces operating in East Africa within one month.

Eighteen—Repatriation, without reciprocity, within a maximum period of one month, in accordance with detailed conditions hereafter to be fixed, of all civilians interned or deported who may be citizens of other Allied or Associated States than those mentioned in clause three, paragraph nineteen, with the reservation that any future claims and demands of the Allies and the United States of America remain unaffected.

Nineteen—The following financial conditions are required: Reparation for damage done. While such armistice lasts no public securities shall be removed by the enemy which can serve as a pledge to the Allies for the recovery or repatriation for war losses. Immediate restitution of the cash deposit in the National Bank of Belgium, and in general immediate return of all documents, specie, stocks, shares, paper money together with plant for the issue thereof, touching public or private interests in the invaded countries. Restitution of the Russian and Roumanian gold yielded to Germany or taken by that Power. This gold to be delivered in trust to the Allies until the signature of peace.

Twenty—Immediate cessation of all hostilities at sea and definite information to be given as to the location and movements of all German ships. Notification to be given to neutrals that freedom of navigation in all territorial waters is given to the naval and mercantile marines of the Allied and Associated Powers, all questions of neutrality being waived.

Twenty-one—All naval and mercantile marine prisoners of war of the Allied and Associated Powers in German hands to be returned without reciprocity.

Twenty-two—Surrender to the Allies and the United States of America of one hundred and sixty German submarines (including all submarine cruisers and mine-laying submarines) with their complete armament and equipment in ports which will be specified by the Allies and the United States of America. All other submarines to be paid off and completely disarmed and placed under the supervision of the Allied Powers and the United States of America.

Twenty-three—The following German surface warships, which shall be designated by the Allies and the United States of America, shall forthwith be disarmed and thereafter interned in neutral ports, or, for the want of them, in Allied ports, to be designated by the Allies and the United States of America and placed under the surveillance of the Allies and the United States of America, only caretakers being left on board, namely: Six battle cruisers, ten battleships, eight light cruisers, including two mine layers, fifty destroyers of the most modern type. All other surface warships (including river craft) are to be concentrated in German naval bases to be designated by the Allies and the United States of America, and are to be paid off and completely disarmed and placed under the supervision of the Allies and the United States of America. All vessels of the auxiliary fleet (trawlers, motor vessels, etc.) are to be disarmed.

Twenty-four—The Allies and the United States of America shall have the right to sweep up all mine fields and obstructions laid by Germany outside German territorial waters, and the positions of these are to be indicated.

Twenty-five—Freedom of access to and from the Baltic to be given to the naval and mercantile marines of the Allied and Associated Powers. To secure this the Allies and the United States of America shall be empowered to occupy all German forts, fortifications, batteries and defense works of all kinds in all the entrances from the Categat into the Baltic, and to sweep up all mines and obstructions within and without German territorial waters without any question of neutrality being raised, and the positions of all such mines and obstructions are to be indicated.

Twenty-six—The existing blockade conditions set up by the Allies and Associated Powers are to remain unchanged and all German merchant ships found at sea are to remain liable to capture.

Twenty-seven—All naval aircraft are to be concentrated and immobilized in German bases to be specified by the Allies and the United States of America.

Twenty-eight—In evacuating the Belgian coasts and ports, Germany shall abandon all merchant ships, tugs, lighters, cranes and all other harbor materials, all materials for inland navigation, all aircraft and all materials and stores, all arms and armaments, and all stores and apparatus of all kinds.

Twenty-nine—All Black Sea ports are to be evacuated by Germany; all Russian war vessels of all descriptions seized by Germany in the Black Sea are to be handed over to the Allies and the United States of America; all neutral merchant vessels seized are to be released; all warlike and other materials of all kinds seized in those ports are to be returned and German materials as specified in clause twenty-eight are to be abandoned.

Thirty—All merchant vessels in German hands belonging to the Allied and Associated Powers are to be restored in ports to be specified by the Allies and the United States of America without reciprocity.

Thirty-one—No destruction of ships or of materials to be permitted before evacuation, surrender or restoration.

Thirty-two—The German Government shall formally notify the neutral Governments of the world, and particularly the Governments of Norway, Sweden, Denmark and Holland, that all restrictions placed on the trading of their vessels with the Allied and Associated countries, whether by the German Government or by private German interests, and whether in return for specific concessions such as the export of shipbuilding materials or not, are immediately canceled.

Thirty-three—No transfers of German merchant shipping of any description to any neutral flag are to take place after signature of the armistice.

Thirty-four—The duration of the armistice is to be thirty days, with option to extend. During this period, on failure of execution of any of the above clauses, the armistice may be denounced by one of the contracting parties on forty-eight hours' previous notice.

Thirty-five—This armistice to be accepted or refused by Germany within seventy-two hours of notification.

The war thus comes to an end; for, having accepted these terms of armistice, it will be impossible for the German command to renew it.

It is not now possible to assess the consequences of this great consummation. We know only that this tragical war, whose consuming flames swept from one nation to another until all the world was on fire, is at an end and that it was the privilege of our people to enter it at its most critical juncture in such fashion and in such force as to contribute in a way of which we are all deeply proud to the great result. We know, too, that the object of the war is attained, the object upon which all free men had set their hearts; and attained with a sweeping completeness which even now we do not realize. Armed imperialism such as the men conceived who were but yesterday the masters of German is at an end, its illicit ambitions engulfed in black disaster. Who will now seek to revive it? The arbitrary power of the military caste of Germany which once could secretly and of its own single choice disturb the peace of the world is discredited and destroyed. And more than that—much more than that—has been accomplished. The great nations which associated themselves to destroy it have now definitely united in the common purpose to set up such a peace as will satisfy the longing of the whole world for disinterested justice, embodied in settlements which are based upon something much better and much more lasting than the selfish competitive interests of powerful states. There is no longer conjecture as to the objects the victors have in mind. They have a mind in the matter not only, but a heart also. Their avowed and concerted purpose is to satisfy and protect the weak as well as to accord their just rights to the strong.

The humane temper and intention of the victorious Governments has already been manifested in a very practical way. Their representatives in the Supreme War Council at Versailles have by unanimous resolution assured the peoples of the Central Empires that everything that is possible in the circumstances will be done to supply them with food and relieve the distressing want that is in so many places threatening their very lives; and steps are to be taken immediately to organize these efforts at relief in the same systematic manner that they were organized in the case of Belgium. By the use of the idle tonnage of the Central Empires it ought presently to be possible to lift the fear of utter misery from their oppressed populations and set their minds and energies free for the great and hazardous tasks of political reconstruction which now face them on every hand. Hunger does not breed reform; it breeds madness and all the ugly distempers that make an ordered life impossible.

For with the fall of the ancient governments which rested like an incubus upon the peoples of the Central Empires has come political change not merely, but revolution; and revolution which seems as yet to assume no final and ordered form but to run from one fluid change to another, until thoughtful men are forced to ask themselves, With what governments, and of what sort, are we about to deal in the making of the covenants of peace? With what authority will they meet us, and with what assurance that their authority will abide and sustain securely the international arrangements into which we are about to enter? There is here matter for no small anxiety and misgiving. When peace is made, upon whose promises and engagements besides our own is it to rest?

Let us be perfectly frank with ourselves and admit that these questions cannot be satisfactorily answered now or at once. But the moral is not that there is little hope of an early answer that will suffice. It is only that we must be patient and helpful and mindful above all of the great hope and confidence that lie at the head of what is taking place. Excesses accomplish nothing. Unhappy Russia has furnished abundant recent proof of that. Disorder immediately defeats itself. If excesses should occur, if disorder should for a time raise its head, a sober second thought will follow and a day of constructive action, if we help and do not hinder.

The present and all that it holds belong to the nations and the peoples who preserve their self-control and the orderly processes of their governments; the future to those who prove themselves the true friends of mankind. To conquer with arms is to make only a temporary conquest; to conquer the world by earning its esteem is to make permanent conquest. I am confident that the nations that have learned the discipline of freedom and that have settled with self-possession to its ordered practice are now about to make conquest of the world by the sheer power of example and of friendly helpfulness.

The peoples who have but just come out from under the yoke of arbitrary government and who are now coming at last into their freedom will never find the treasures of liberty they are in search of if they look for them by the light of the torch. They will find that every pathway that is stained with the blood of their own brothers leads to the wilderness, not to the seat of their hope. They are now face to face with their initial test. We must hold the light steady until they find themselves. And in the meantime, if it be possible, we must establish a peace that will justly define their place among the nations, remove all fear of their neighbors and of their former masters, and enable them to live in security and contentment when they have set their own affairs in order. I, for one, do not doubt their purpose or their capacity. There are some happy signs that they know and will choose the way of self-control and peaceful accommodation. If they do, we shall put our aid at their disposal in every way that we can.

If they do not, we must await with patience and sympathy the awakening and recovery that will assuredly come at last.

After the President had delivered the above address, it was announced that the terms of the armistice as given him had been changed immediately before signing, and too late to be transmitted to him before he addressed Congress. The significance of the changes is noted below.

Article Three, fifteen days instead of fourteen are allowed for the repatriation, beginning at once, of all the inhabitants removed from invaded countries, including hostages and persons under trial or convicted.

Article Four, providing for the surrender of munitions and equipment, reduces the number of machine guns to be delivered from 30,000 to 25,000, the number of aeroplanes from 2,000 to 1,700.

Article Five, providing for the evacuation by the Germans of the countries on the left bank of the Rhine, stipulates that these countries shall be administered by "the local troops of occupation," instead of by the local authorities under the control of the Allied and United States armies, and the occupation is to be "carried out by" instead of "determined by" Allied and United States garrisons holding strategic points and the principal crossings of the Rhine. Thirteen days instead of twenty-five are allowed for completion of the evacuation.

Article Six, providing that no damage or harm shall be done to persons and property in territory exacuated by the Germans, has a sentence added specifically stipulating that "no person shall be prosecuted for offences of participation in war measures prior to the signing of the armistice."

Article Seven, providing for the abandonment or delivery in good order to the Associated Powers of all roads and means of communication and transportation in evacuated territory, calls for 150,000 wagons (railroad cars), instead of 50,000; 5,000 motor lorries, instead of 10,000, and requires that all civil and military personnel at present employed on such means of communication and transportation, including waterways, shall remain. Thirty-one, instead of twenty-five, days are allowed for handing over the material. Thirty-six days are allowed for the handing over of the railways of Alsace-Lorraine, together with the pre-war personnel.

Article Eight, forty-eight hours is given the German command to reveal destructive measures, such as polluted springs and wells, and to reveal and assist in discovering and destroying mines or delayed action fuses on evacuated territory. No time limit was fixed originally.

Article Nine, providing for the right of requisition by the United States and Allied armies in occupied territory, has the clause added: "Subject to regulation of accounts with those whom it may concern."

Article Ten, providing for the repatriation without reciprocity of all Allied and United States prisoners of war, including persons under trial or convicted, has the following added: "This condition annuls the previous conventions on the subject of the exchange of prisoners of war, including the one of July, 1918, in course of ratification. However, the repatriation of German prisoners of war interned in Holland and in Switzerland shall continue as before. The repatriation of German prisoners of war shall be regulated at the conclusion of the preliminaries of peace."

Article Twelve, providing for the withdrawal of German troops from territory which belonged before the war to Russia, Roumania and Turkey, is rewritten. Territory which belonged to Austria-Hungary is added to that from which the Germans must withdraw immediately, and as to territory which belonged to Russia, it is provided that the German troops now there shall withdraw within the frontiers of Germany "as soon as the Allies, taking into account the internal situation of those territories, shall decide that the time for this has come."

Article Fifteen, "renunciation" is substituted for "abandonment" in stipulating that the treaties of Bucharest and Brest-Litovsk are nullified.

Article Sixteen, providing free access for the Allies into territory evacuated through the German Eastern frontier, is changed so as to declare such access is for the purpose of conveying supplies to the populations "and for the purpose of maintaining order," instead of "or for any other purpose."

Article Seventeen, originally providing for the "unconditional capitulation" within one month of all German forces operating in East Africa, is replaced by a clause requiring only "evacuation by all German forces operating in East Africa within a period to be fixed by the Allies."

Article Eighteen, providing for the repatriation of all civilians belonging to the Allies or Associated Powers other than those enumerated in Article Three, is amended to eliminate a reservation that any future claims or demands by the Allies and the United States shall remain unaffected.

Article Twenty-two, providing for the surrender of 160 German submarines, is changed to read "all submarines now existing," with the added stipulation that "those which cannot take the sea shall be disarmed of material and personnel, and shall remain under the supervision of the Allies and the United States." Further provisions are added requiring that all the conditions of the article shall be carried into effect within fourteen days; that submarines ready for sea shall be prepared to leave German ports immediately upon orders by wireless, and the remainder at the earliest possible moment.

Article Twenty-three, providing for the disposition of German surface warships, has additional clauses requiring that vessels designated for internment shall be ready to leave German ports within seven days, upon directions by wireless, and that the military armament of all vessels of the auxiliary fleet shall be put on shore.

Article Twenty-six, providing that the Allied blockade remains unchanged, has this sentence added: "The Allies and the United States should give consideration to the provisioning of Germany during the armistice to the extent recognized as necessary."

Article Twenty-eight, providing conditions of evacuation of the Belgian coast (from which the Germans actually had been driven before the armistice was signed), was changed in minor particulars.

Article Thirty-four, providing that the duration of the armistice shall be thirty days, and that if its clauses are not carried into execution it may be renounced upon forty-eight hours' warning, has the following added:

"It is understood that the execution of Article Three and Eighteen shall not warrant the denunciation of the armistice on the ground of insufficient execution within a period fixed, except in the case of bad faith in carrying them into execution. In order to assure the execution of this convention under the best conditions, the principle of a permanent international armistice commission is admitted."

MESSAGES EXCHANGED AT SIGNING OF ARMISTICE

[Between President Wilson and Secretary of State Lansing and Heads of Nations Associated with the United States in the War.]

November 12, 1918.

M. Stephen Pichon,
    Minister of Foreign Affairs, Paris.

At this supreme moment in the history of your nation, when a complete victory has been won over the most formidable of enemies, I desire to extend to you personally and on behalf of my Government the most heartfelt congratulations of the American people and a sincere expression of the joy and admiration with which they are inspired by the valor of your armies and the steadfastness of your people.

LANSING.

Paris, *November 13, 1918.*

Mr. Robert Lansing,
    Secretary of State, Washington.

I am deeply touched with your telegram. The share of America in the victory you are celebrating is so great that never will any Frenchman forget it. In the run of history, the ancient alliance of our two countries was once more sealed by brotherhood in arms. The Americans and French are united in these days of rejoicing as they were in the days of fighting. I beg you to convey to the Federal Government the thanks of France and of the Government of the Republic and to accept for yourself who always evinced so much sympathy with my country my sentiments of cordial friendship.

S. PICHON.

November 12, 1918.

Right Honorable Arthur J. Balfour,
    Secretary of State for Foreign Affairs, London:

At the moment when innumerable difficulties have been surmounted and final and complete victory has been achieved, I desire to express to you the deep joy felt by the Government and people of this country and their admiration for the steadfastness, energy, and valor of the British nation throughout this momentous struggle.

ROBERT LANSING,
Secretary of State.

London, *November 13, 1918.*

Secretary of State, Washington:

Your generous message has given the utmost satisfaction to His Majesty's Government, and it will be read with profound appreciation throughout the British Empire. We are proud to think that in the cause of international freedom we, like our allies, have worked and suffered, fought and conquered side by side with the people of your great country. May this unity of ideals bind us ever closer together through all the generations to whom the great war will be no more than an ancient and glorious memory.

BALFOUR.

THE WHITE HOUSE, November 11, 1918.

His Majesty, Vittorio Emanuele,
    King of Italy, Rome.

In the name of the people of the United States and in my own I extend hearty congratulations on this, Your Majesty's natal day, which happily is also a golden day for the world's peace and security, marking as it does the crowning point of the successful struggle of civilization against savagery. Well may the Italian people rejoice in the removal of danger and menace for the future and welcome the complete victory to which their valor and fidelity have so gloriously contributed. Such victories as this win their own just rewards in that they bring home to the victors a realizing sense of their responsibility to see to it that their sacrifices in the cause of the right shall assure for all time a new era of liberty, justice, and prosperity for the peoples of the earth.

WOODROW WILSON.

ROME QUIRINALE, November 16, 1918.

President Wilson,
    Washington, D. C.

I sincerely thank you for the cordial expression you were pleased to send me in the name of the American people also on the occasion of my birthday. I fully appreciate the noble word with which you kindly greeted our victory. Italy, having worshipped right in the world and revived national unity in the name of the principles of freedom, will adhere to those ideals for which it carried on the bitter struggle now ended by well-deserved triumph.

VITTORIO EMANUELE.

ROME, November 16, 1918.

His Excellency, the President, Woodrow Wilson,
    Washington, D. C.:

With a joyful heart I salute the strong people of the United States of America in this era which marks for the liberated democracies the triumph of the ideals for which the great American Nation under your will and firm guidance, Mr. President, took up arms on the side of the peoples fighting for their independence and a more civilized future for all mankind. In the name of the people and soldiers of Italy I express to you and your noble Nation the sentiments of earnest admiration and the fervent wish that the memory of the battles fought together may enhance the ties of lasting friendship between our peoples.

                                        VITTORIO EMANUELE.

November 20, 1918.

His Majesty Vittorio Emanuele, King of Italy, Rome, Italy:

Your Majesty's message of congratulation has given the deepest pleasure. I think that it is a cause for particular pride on the part of the people of the United States that they should have been able at the right time to assist in the great struggle in which Italy has so distinguished herself, and I am sure that I speak their heart in thanking Your Majesty with sincerest warmth for your message and in sending in return the heartfelt salutations of our own people.

                                        WOODROW WILSON.

TOKYO, *November 13, 1918.*

The President of the United States, Washington:

At this juncture when the definite signature of an armistice has set the seal of success on the efforts of the Allied arms I can not forebear telegraphing to you the delight with which I share the satisfaction you must experience at this splendid vindication of the unconquerable persistence displayed by the Allies in working together for the attainment of their great end. I would add a special note of admiration shared by all my people for the gallant alacrity and whole-hearted efficiency with which the American people entered the arena and thereby so decisively contributed to the magnificent triumph.

                                        YOSHIHITO.

THE WHITE HOUSE, *November 15, 1918.*

His Imperial Majesty Yoshihito, Emperor of Japan, Tokyo:

Your Majesty's message has given us the sincerest pleasure, and I wish in reply to express to you the satisfaction which the people of the United States have felt in being associated with the gallant people of Japan in fighting for the cause of practical justice and genuine liberation of the world from the influence of selfish national policy.

                                        WOODROW WILSON.

TOKYO.

Honorable Robert Lansing, Secretary of State, Washington:

Accept my heartiest and warmest congratulations on the triumphant conclusion of an armistice which, we trust, will lead to a peace glorious for the forces of human civilization and fraught with happiness to the world. Such a fruition of the prolonged struggle will not have been too dearly purchased by all the precious lives of whose suffering and sacrifice we think with one universal pride to-day.

UCHIDA.

November 15, 1918.

His Excellency Viscount Uchida,

Minister for Foreign Affairs, Tokyo, Japan:

I appreciate highly your telegram of congratulation on the triumph of the united strength of human civilization over the baneful forces which aimed to rule the world for themselves alone.

The difficulties which beset us have been overcome. The enemy has been vanquished, and unified as we are by the common ideals for which we have fought, and by the teachings of the trials and sufferings which we have shared, we can now turn with hopeful confidence to the work which remains to be done.

ROBERT LANSING,
Secretary of State.

PEKING, *November 13, 1918.*

His Excellency President Woodrow Wilson, Washington:

The people of China learn with great joy that the terms of the armistice have been accepted by Germany. Thus the cause of justice and freedom has been vindicated and its final triumph has been won by the allied arms. On behalf of my Government and the people of China I hasten hereby to offer to your excellency, and, through you, to the people of the United States, my hearty congratulations and to express my confidence that at the peace conference, which no doubt will soon follow, the delegates of our two countries will continue to work hand in hand for the cause of freedom, justice, and fair dealing.

HSU SHIHCHANG.

THE WHITE HOUSE, *November 15, 1918.*

His Excellency Hsu Shihchang, President of China,

Peking, China:

Please accept my warmest thanks for your message. I know how ardently and sincerely the people of China are engaged on the side of justice and freedom, and it is delightful to feel the influence of their supporting sentiment in these days when the purpose of the whole world must be turned to justice and lasting peace.

WOODROW WILSON.

PANAMA, *November 11, 1918.*

His Excellency President Wilson, Washington:

Allow me to congratulate your excellency and every American for the brilliant victory obtained by the Allied cause with the signing by Germany of the armistice as the prelude of the final crushing of Prussian militarism and triumph of true democracy.

With the assurance of my highest consideration.

BELISARIO PORRAS.

THE WHITE HOUSE, *November 13, 1918.*

Honorable Belisario Porras, President Republic of Panama,
    Panama:

I greatly appreciate your excellency's generous message of yesterday and send my warmest greetings to the people of Panama in this time of triumph and relief.

WOODROW WILSON.

GUATEMALA, *November 14, 1918.*

Honorable Secretary of State, Washington:

The Government and people of Guatemala most enthusiastically celebrate the splendid victory won by the United States and other Allied nations in the noble struggle for justice and liberty. I have the honor in their name to offer to your excellency, the Government, and people of your friendly nation the most sincere felicitations and the sentiments of sympathy and admiration of Guatemala.

G. AGUIRRE,
            Minister of Foreign Relations.

November 16, 1918.

His Excellency G. Aguirre, Minister for Foreign Affairs,
    Guatemala:

I appreciate highly your excellency's telegram giving expression to the joy felt in common by the Government and people of Guatemala and the Government and people of the United States over the armistice with Austria. We have now still greater grounds for rejoicing and the mutual interchange of congratulations, for final victory has been won and we can now look forward with confidence to the attainment of the high ideals which have been the inspiration of the powers which opposed the military autocracy of Germany.

ROBERT LANSING,
            Secretary of State.

ADDRESSES TO FELLOW-COUNTRYMEN

[Fourth Liberty Loan.]

THE WHITE HOUSE, *October 10, 1919.*

Recent events have enhanced, not lessened, the importance of this loan, and I hope that my fellow-countrymen will let me say this to them very frankly. The best thing that could happen would be that the loan should not only be fully subscribed, but very greatly over-subscribed. We are in the midst of the greatest exercise of the power of this country that has ever been witnessed or forecast, and a single day of relaxation in that effort would be of tragical damage alike to ourselves and to the rest of the world. Nothing has happened which makes it safe or possible to do anything but push our effort to the utmost. The time is critical, and the response must be complete.

WOODROW WILSON.

THE WHITE HOUSE, *October 14, 1919.*

The reply of the German Government to my note of inquiry dated October 8 gives occasion for me to say to my fellow countrymen that neither that reply nor any other recent events have in any way diminished the vital importance of the Liberty Loan. Relaxation now, hesitation now, would mean defeat when victory seems to be in sight; would mean years of war instead of peace upon our own terms.

I earnestly request every patriotic American to leave to the Governments of the United States and of the Allies the momentous discussions initiated by Germany and to remember that, for each man, his duty is to strengthen the hands of these Governments and to do it in the most important way now immediately presented—by subscribing to the utmost of his ability for bonds of the Fourth Liberty Loan. That loan must be successful. I am sure that the American people will not fail to see their duty and make it successful.

WOODROW WILSON.

[Asking Election of Democratic Congress in 1918.]

THE WHITE HOUSE, *October 25, 1918.*

My Fellow Countrymen—The Congressional elections are at hand. They occur in the most critical period our country has ever faced, or is likely to face in our time. If you have approved of my leadership, and wish me to continue to be your unembarrassed spokesman in affairs at home and abroad, I earnestly beg that you will express yourselves unmistakably to that effect by returning a Democratic majority to both the Senate and the House of Representatives.

I am your servant and will accept your judgment without cavil, but my power to administer the great trust assigned me by the Constitution would be seriously impaired should your judgment be adverse, and I must frankly tell you so because so many critical issues depend upon your verdict. No scruple of taste must in grim times like these be allowed to stand in the way of speaking the plain truth.

I have no thought of suggesting that any political party is paramount in matters of patriotism. I feel too deeply the sacrifices which have been made in this war by all our citizens, irrespective of party affiliations, to harbor such an idea. I mean only that the difficulties and delicacies of our present task are of a sort that makes it imperatively necessary that the nation should give its undivided support to the Government under a unified leadership, and that a Republican Congress would divide the leadership.

The leaders of the minority in the present Congress have unquestionably been pro-war, but they have been anti-Administration. At almost every turn since we entered the war they have sought to take the choice of policy and the conduct of the war out of my hands and put it under the control of instrumentalities of their own choosing.

This is no time either for divided council or for divided leadership. Unity of command is as necessary now in civil action as it is upon the field of battle. If the control of the House and the Senate should be taken away from the party now in power, an opposing majority could assume control of legislation and oblige all action to be taken amid contest and obstruction.

The return of a Republican majority to either house of the Congress would, moreover, be interpretative on the other side of the water as a repudiation of my leadership. Spokesmen of the Republican party are urging you to elect a Republican Congress in order to back up and support the President, but even if they should in this impose upon some credulous voters on this side of the water, they would impose on no one on the other side. It is well understood there as well as here that Republican leaders desire not so much to support the President as to control him.

The peoples of the Allied countries with whom we are associated against Germany are quite familiar with the significance of elections. They would find it very difficult to believe that the voters of the United States had chosen to support their President by electing to the Congress a majority controlled by those who are not, in fact, in sympathy with the attitude and action of the Administration.

I need not tell you, my fellow countrymen, that I am asking your support not for my own sake or for the sake of a political party, but for the sake of the nation itself in order that its inward duty of purpose may be evident to all the world. In ordinary times I would not feel at liberty to make such an appeal to you. In ordinary times divided counsel can be endured without permanent hurt to the country. But these are not ordinary times.

If in these critical days it is your wish to sustain me with undivided minds, I beg that you will say so in a way which it will not be possible to misunderstand, either here at home or among our associates on the other side of the sea. I submit my difficulties and my hopes to you.

LETTER

[To Senator Simmons, Discussing the "Economic Barriers" Phrase in the Address of January 8, 1918, and Denying Implication of Free Trade.]

WASHINGTON, D. C., *October 28, 1918.*

Dear Senator:

I am glad to respond to the question addressed to me by your letter of October 26. The words I used in my address to the Congress of January 8, 1918, were: "The removal, so far as possible, of all economic barriers and the establishment of an equality of trade conditions among all the nations consenting to the peace and associating themselves for its maintenance."

I, of course, meant to suggest no restriction upon the free determination by any nation of its own economic policy, but only that, whatever tariff any nation might deem necessary for its own economic service, be that tariff high or low, it should apply equally to all foreign nations; in other words, that there should be no discriminations against some nations that did not apply to others. This leaves every nation free to determine for itself its own internal policies and limits only its right to compound these policies of hostile discriminations between one nation and another. Weapons of economic discipline and punishment should be left to the joint action of Allied nations for the purpose of punishing those who will not submit to a general programme of justice and equality.

The experiences of the past among nations have taught us that the attempt by one nation to punish another by exclusive and discriminatory trade agreements has been a prolific breeder of that kind of antagonism which oftentimes results in war, and that if a permanent peace is to be established among nations every obstacle that has stood in the way of international friendship should be cast aside. It was with that fundamental purpose in mind that I announced this principle in my address of January 8. To pervert this great principle for partisan purposes, and to inject the bogey of free trade, which is not involved at all, is to attempt to divert the mind of the nation from the broad and humane principle of a durable peace by introducing an internal question of quite another kind. American business has in the past been unaffected by a policy of the kind suggested and it has nothing to fear now from a policy of simply international justice. It is indeed lamentable that the momentous issues of this solemn hour should be seized upon in an effort to bend them to partisan service. To the initiated and discerning, the motive is transparent and the attempt fails.

Sincerely yours,
WOODROW WILSON.

BY THE PRESIDENT OF THE UNITED STATES OF AMERICA

PROCLAMATIONS

[Possession and Control of Marine Cable Systems.]

Whereas the Congress of the United States, in the exercise of the constitutional authority vested in them, by joint resolution of the Senate and House of Representatives, bearing date July 16, 1918, resolved:

> That the President during the continuance of the present war is authorized and empowered, whenever he shall deem it necessary for the national security or defense, to supervise or take possession and assume control of any telegraph, telephone, marine cable, or radio system or systems, or any part thereof, and to operate the same in such manner as may be needful or desirable for the duration of the war, which supervision, possession, control, or operation shall not extend beyond the date of the proclamation by the President of the exchange of ratifications of the treaty of peace: Provided, That just compensation shall be made for such supervision, possession, control, or operation, to be determined by the President; and if the amount thereof, so determined by the President, is unsatisfactory to the person entitled to receive the same, such person shall be paid seventy-five per centum of the amount so determined by the President and shall be entitled to sue the United States to recover such further sum as, added to said seventy-five per centum, will make up such amount as will be just compensation therefor, in the manner provided for by section twenty-four, paragraph twenty, and section one hundred and forty-five of the Judicial Code: Provided further, That nothing in this Act shall be construed to amend, repeal, impair or affect existing laws or powers of the several States in relation to taxation or the lawful police regulations of the several States except wherein such laws, powers or regulations may affect the transmission of Government communications, or the issue of stocks and bonds by such system or systems.

And whereas it is deemed necessary for the national security and defense to supervise and to take possession and assume control of all marine cable systems and to operate the same in such manner as may be needful or desirable:

Now, therefore, I, Woodrow Wilson, President of the United States, under and by virtue of the powers vested in me by the foregoing resolution, and by virtue of all other powers thereto me enabling, do hereby take possession and assume control and supervision of each and every marine cable system and every part thereof owned or controlled and operated by any company or companies organized and existing under the laws of the United States, or any State thereof, including all equipment thereof and appurtenances thereto, whatsoever, and all materials and supplies.

It is hereby directed that the supervision, possession, control, and operation of such marine cable systems hereby by me undertaken shall be exercised by and through the Postmaster General, Albert S. Burleson. Said Postmaster General may perform the duties hereby and hereunder imposed upon him, so long and to such extent and in such manner as he shall determine, through the owners, managers, boards of directors, receivers, officers, and employees of said marine cable systems.

Until and except so far as said Postmaster General shall from time to time by general or special orders otherwise provide, the owners, managers, boards of directors, receivers, officers, and employees, of the various marine cable systems shall continue the operation thereof in the usual and ordinary course of the business of said systems in the names of their respective companies, associations, organizations, owners, or managers, as the case may be.

Regular dividends hitherto declared and maturing interest upon bonds, debentures and other obligations may be paid in due course and such regular dividends and interest may continue to be paid until and unless the said Postmaster General shall, from time to time, otherwise by general or special orders determine; and, subject to the approval of said Postmaster General, the various marine cable systems may determine upon and arrange for the renewal and extension of maturing obligations.

From and after twelve o'clock midnight on the second day of November, 1918, all marine cable systems included in this order and proclamation shall conclusively be deemed within the possession and control and under the supervision of said Postmaster General without further act or notice.

In witness whereof, I have hereunto set my hand and caused the seal of the United States to be affixed.

Done by the President, in the District of Columbia, this second day of November in the year of our Lord one thousand nine [SEAL.] hundred and eighteen and of the independence of the United States the one hundred and forty-third.

WOODOW WILSON.

By the President:

ROBERT LANSING, *Secretary of State.*

[Possession and Control of the American Railway Express Company.]

Whereas the organizations for the conduct of the express business over numerous systems of transportation which have been duly placed under Federal control, and pertaining to such systems of transportation, have been consolidated into the American Railway Express Company, which has been made the sole agent of the Government for conducting the express business, with the result that the entire transportation system of said express company has been necessarily in substance and effect placed under Federal control, and

Whereas it is desirable, in order to administer to the best advantage the transportation business and operations of the American Railway Express System, to make it specifically clear by this proclamation that the President has the possession, use, control, and operation of the entire transportation system of the American Railway Express Company,

Now, therefore, I, Woodrow Wilson, President of the United States, under and by virtue of the powers vested in me by law, do hereby, through Newton D. Baker, Secretary of War, take possession and assume control at 12 o'clock noon on the eighteenth day of November, 1918, of that certain system of transportation called the American Railway Express Company, and all of its appurtenances and property of every kind of nature, directly or indirectly owned, leased, chartered, controlled, or used in the conduct of, or in connection with, its express business.

It is hereby further directed that the possession, control, operation, and utilization of said express transportation system hereby by me undertaken shall be exercised by and through William G. McAdoo, heretofore appointed Director General of Railroads, with all the powers conferred upon him by the said proclamations of December 26, 1917, and March 29, 1918, respectively, together with all and singular the powers conferred upon the President by the Act of Congress entitled, "An Act to provide for the operation of transportation systems while under Federal control, for the just compensation of their owners, and for other purposes," approved March 21, 1918.

The said Director General of Railroads may perform the duties hereby imposed upon him, so long and to such an extent as he shall determine, through the board of directors, officers, and employees of the said American Railway Express Company, under the contract already made, and dated the twenty-sixth day of June, 1918, between the said Director General of Railroads and said American Railway Express Company, and until and except so far as said Director General shall from time to time by general or special orders otherwise provide, the board of directors, officers, and employees of said company shall continue the operation thereof in the usual and ordinary course under such contract.

From and after 12 o'clock noon on said eighteenth of November, 1918, the said transportation system shall conclusively be deemed within the possession and control of said Director General without further act or notice.

In witness whereof I have hereunto set my hand and caused the seal of the United States to be affixed.

Done by the President, through Newton D. Baker, Secretary of War, in the District of Columbia, this sixteenth day of [SEAL.] November, in the year of our Lord, 1918, and of the independence of the United States the one hundred and forty-third.

WOODROW WILSON.

By the President:

ROBERT LANSING, *Secretary of State.*

[Thanksgiving.]

It has long been our custom to turn in the autumn of the year in praise and thanksgiving to Almighty God for His many blessings and mercies to us as a nation. This year we have special and moving cause to be grateful and to rejoice. God has in His good pleasure given us peace. It has not come as a mere cessation of arms, a relief from the strain and tragedy of war. It has come as a great triumph of Right. Complete victory has brought us, not peace alone, but the confident promise of a new day as well, in which justice shall replace force and jealous intrigue among the nations. Our gallant armies have participated in a triumph which is not marred or stained by any purpose of selfish aggression. In a righteous cause they have won immortal glory and have nobly served their nation in serving mankind. God has indeed been gracious. We have cause for such rejoicing as revives and strengthens in us all the best traditions of our national history. A new day shines about us, in which our hearts take new courage and look forward with new hope to new and greater duties.

While we render thanks for these things, let us not forget to seek the Divine guidance in the performance of those duties, and Divine mercy and forgiveness for all errors of act or purpose, and pray that in all that we do we shall strengthen the ties of friendship and mutual respect upon which we must assist to build the new structure of peace and good-will among the nations.

Wherefore, I, Woodrow Wilson, President of the United States of America, do hereby designate Thursday, the twenty-eighth day of

November next, as a day of thanksgiving and prayer, and invite the people throughout the land to cease upon that day from their ordinary occupations and in their several homes and places of worship to render thanks to God, the Ruler of nations.

In witness whereof I have hereunto set my hand and caused the seal of the United States to be affixed.

Done in the District of Columbia this sixteenth day of November, in the year of our Lord, one thousand nine hundred and [SEAL.] eighteen and of the independence of the United States of America the one hundred and forty-third.

WOODROW WILSON.

By the President:

ROBERT LANSING, *Secretary of State.*

EXECUTIVE ORDER

[Excepting Certain Persons from the Classification of "Alien Enemy" for the Purpose of Permitting Them to Apply for Naturalization.]

THE WHITE HOUSE, *November 26, 1918.*

Whereas, the Act of Congress approved May 9, 1918, entitled "An Act to amend the naturalization laws and to repeal certain sections of the Revised Statutes of the United States and other laws relating to naturalization, and for other purposes," provided in part as follows:

"Eleventh. No alien who is a native, citizen, subject, or denizen of any country, State, or sovereignty with which the United States is at war shall be admitted to become a citizen of the United States unless he made his declaration of intention not less than two nor more than seven years prior to the existence of the state of war, or was at that time entitled to become a citizen of the United States, without making a declaration of intention, or unless his petition for naturalization shall then be pending and is otherwise entitled to admission, notwithstanding he shall be an alien enemy at the time and in the manner prescribed by the laws passed upon that subject: *Provided,* That no alien embraced within this subdivision shall have his petition for naturalization called for a hearing, or heard, except after ninety days' notice given by the clerk of the court to the Commissioner or Deputy Commissioner of Naturalization to be present, and the petition shall be given no final hearing except in open court and after such notice to the representative of the Government from the Bureau of Naturalization, whose objection shall cause the petition to be continued from time to time for so long as the Government may require: *Provided, however,* that nothing herein contained shall be taken or construed to interfere with or prevent the apprehension and removal, agreeably to law, of any alien enemy at any time previous to the actual naturalization of such alien; and section twenty-one hundred and seventy-one of the Revised Statutes of the United States is hereby repealed: *Provided further,* That the President of the United States may, in his discretion, upon investigation and report by the Department of Justice fully establishing the loyalty of any alien enemy not included in the foregoing exemption, except such alien enemy from the classification of alien enemy, and thereupon he shall have the privilege of applying for naturalization; etc."

Now, therefore, for the purpose defined in said section, in the exercise of the discretion so vested in me, I do hereby direct that there be excepted from the classification of "alien enemy" all persons whom, after investigation and report by the Department of Justice, the Attorney General shall from time to time certify to the Secretary of Labor as persons loyal to the United States.

WOODROW WILSON.

TELEGRAMS

[To Governor of California, Concerning the "Mooney Case." Made Public November 28, 1918.]

On July 22, 1916, a parade was being held in San Francisco to promote the movement to increase the preparedness of the United States for war. Early in the progress of the parade, a bomb was exploded in one of the city's side streets which was filled with spectators and paraders. Six persons were killed instantaneously and several of the forty wounded died later as a result of the outrage. At that time, the pacifists were strongly opposing the movement for preparedness, but the arrests made after investigation were not made in the camp of the pacifists, but in the camp of radical labor. Soon after the explosion, Thomas J. Mooney and his wife, Rena Mooney, Warren K. Billings, Israel Weinberg and Edward D. Nolan were charged with the crime. Mooney, who was the centre of the case, was a well-known radical labor leader of the Pacific Coast. He had been identified with anarchists and was an ardent follower of the principles of "direct action" or syndicalism. His defenders claimed that because of his views and his activities in behalf of Labor the property interests of San Francisco had wilfully used the bomb outrage as a pretext for getting rid of him and for discrediting the entire labor movement.

Billings was tried first, was found guilty, and was sentenced to life imprisonment. Mooney was tried in January, 1917, and was convicted in the following month of murder in the first degree, largely on the testimony of a witness named Oxman. Mooney's defenders later brought forward testimony to prove that Oxman had suborned perjury, and a change in the evidence later resulted in the acquittal of Mrs. Mooney and Weinberg, and Nolan was not brought to trial. A Federal investigating commission appointed by the President recommended in January, 1918, that Mooney be given another trial, on the ground that there was evidence to prove that Mooney had been the victim of a conspiracy, that he had suffered from the intensity of feeling in San Francisco as a result of the bomb explosion, and that new information of an important character bearing on the case had been brought to light since his conviction.

The Mooney Case soon assumed an international importance. For radicals from the United States emigrating to Russia soon after the Russian Revolution of March, 1917, brought the Mooney Case to the attention of Russia, with the result of weakening in Russia the reputation of the United States as the home of justice and democracy. Indeed, interest in the Mooney Case in most sections of the United States came by way of Europe, with the news that mass-meetings were being held in Europe to procure the release of "Tom Muni." The United States at that time was exerting great pressure to prove to Russia that the cause of the Entente Allies in the European War was holier than the cause of the Central Powers; and President Wilson's hand in international negotiations was so weakened by the effect of the Mooney Case on Europe as to cause him to interfere in the case.

Without being granted a new trial, Mooney's sentence was commuted by the Governor of California, on November 28, 1918, to life imprisonment.

THE WHITE HOUSE, *March 27, 1918.*

Governor William D. Stephens, Sacramento, Cal:

With very great respect I take the liberty of saying to you that if you could see your way to commute the sentence of Mooney it would have a most heartfelt effect upon certain international affairs which his execution would greatly complicate.

THE WHITE HOUSE, *June 4, 1918.*

Hon. William D. Stephens, Sacramento, Cal.:

I beg that you will believe that I am moved only by a sense of public duty and of consciousness of the many and complicated interests involved when I again most respectfully suggest a commutation of the death sentence imposed upon Mooney. I would not venture again to call your attention to this case did I not know the international significance which attaches to it.

WOODROW WILSON.

BY THE PRESIDENT OF THE UNITED STATES OF AMERICA

PROCLAMATIONS

[Relief in the Near East.]

THE WHITE HOUSE, *November 29, 1918.*

For more than three years American philanthropy has been a large factor in keeping alive Armenian, Syrian, Greek and other exiles and refugees of Western Asia.

On two former occasions I have appealed to the American people in behalf of these homeless sufferers, whom the vicissitudes of war and massacre had brought to the extremest need.

The response has been most generous, but now the period of rehabilitation is at hand. Vastly larger sums will be required to restore these once prosperous, but now impoverished, refugees to their former homes than were required merely to sustain life in their desert exile.

It is estimated that about 4,000,000 Armenian, Syrian, Greek and other war sufferers in the Near East will require outside help to sustain them through the winter. Many of them are now hundreds of miles from their home land. The vast majority of them are helpless women and children, including 400,000 orphans.

The American Committee for Relief in the Near East is appealing for a minimum of $30,000,000 to be subscribed January 12, 1919, with which to meet the most urgent needs of these people.

I, therefore, again call upon the people of the United States to make even more generous contributions than they have made heretofore to sustain through the winter months those, who, through no fault of their own, have been left in a starving, shelterless condition, and to help re-establish these ancient and sorely oppressed people in their former homes on a self-supporting basis.

WOODROW WILSON.

SIXTH ANNUAL ADDRESS

[Delivered to Joint Session of Congress, December 2, 1918.]

Gentlemen of the Congress: The year that has elapsed since I last stood before you to fulfil my constitutional duty to give to the Congress from time to time information on the state of the Union has been so crowded with great events, great processes, and great results that I cannot hope to give you an adequate picture of its transactions or of the far-reaching changes which have been wrought in the life of our nation and of the world. You have yourselves witnessed these things, as I have. It is too soon to assess them; and we who stand in the midst of them and are part of them are less qualified than men of another generation will be to say what they mean, or even what they have been. But some great outstanding facts are unmistakable and constitute, in a sense, part of the public business with which it is our duty to deal. To state them is to set the stage for the legislative and executive action which must grow out of them and which we have yet to shape and determine.

A year ago we had sent 145,918 men overseas. Since then we have sent 1,950,513, an average of 162,542 each month, the number in fact rising, in May last, to 245,951, in June to 278,760, in July to 307,182, and continuing to reach similar figures in August and September,— in August 289,570 and in September 257,438. No such movement of troops ever took place before, across three thousand miles of sea, followed by adequate equipment and supplies, and carried safely through extraordinary dangers of attack,—dangers which were alike strange and infinitely difficult to guard against. In all this movement only seven hundred and fifty-eight men were lost by enemy attack,—six hundred and thirty of whom were upon a single English transport which was sunk near the Orkney Islands.

I need not tell you what lay back of this great movement of men and material. It is not invidious to say that back of it lay a supporting organization of the industries of the country and of all its productive activities more complete, more thorough in method and effective in result, more spirited and unanimous in purpose and effort than any other great belligerent had been able to effect. We profited greatly by the experience of the nations which had already been engaged for nearly three years in the exigent and exacting business, their every resource and every executive proficiency taxed to the utmost. We were their pupils. But we learned quickly and acted with a promptness and a readiness of cooperation that justify our great pride that we were able to serve the world with unparalleled energy and quick accomplishment.

But it is not the physical scale and executive efficiency of preparation, supply, equipment and despatch that I would dwell upon, but the mettle and quality of the officers and men we sent over and of the sailors who kept the seas, and the spirit of the nation that stood behind them. No soldiers or sailors ever proved themselves more quickly ready for the test of battle or acquitted themselves with more splendid courage and achievement when put to the test. Those of us who played some part in directing the great processes by which the war was pushed irresistibly forward to the final triumph may now forget all that and delight our thoughts with the story of what our men did. Their officers understood the grim and exacting task they had undertaken and performed it with an audacity, efficiency, and unhesitating courage that touch the story of convoy and battle with imperishable distinction at every turn, whether the enterprise were great or small, —from their great chiefs, Pershing and Sims, down to the youngest lieutenant; and their men were worthy of them,—such men as hardly need to be commanded, and go to their terrible adventure blithely and with the quick intelligence of those who know just what it is they would accomplish. I am proud to be the fellow-countryman of men of such stuff and valor. Those of us who stayed at home did our duty; the war could not have been won or the gallant men who fought it given their opportunity to win it otherwise; but for many a long day we shall think ourselves "accurs'd we were not there, and hold our manhoods cheap while any speaks that fought" with these at St. Mihiel or Thierry. The memory of those days of triumphant battle will go with these fortunate men to their graves; and each will have his favorite memory. "Old men forget; yet all shall be forgot, but he'll remember with advantages what feats he did that day!"

What we all thank God for with deepest gratitude is that our men went in force into the line of battle just at the critical moment when the whole fate of the world seemed to hang in the balance and threw their fresh strength into the ranks of freedom in time to turn the whole tide and sweep of the fateful struggle,—turn it once for all, so that thenceforth it was back, back, back for their enemies, always back, never again forward! After that it was only a scant four months before the commanders of the Central Empires knew themselves beaten; and now their very empires are in liquidation!

And throughout it all how fine the spirit of the nation was: what unity of purpose, what untiring zeal! What elevation of purpose ran through all its splendid display of strength, its untiring accomplishment! I have said that those of us who stayed at home to do the work of organization and supply will always wish that we had been with the men whom we sustained by our labor; but we can never be ashamed. It has been an inspiring thing to be here in the midst of fine men who had turned aside from every private interest of their own and devoted the whole of their trained capacity to the tasks that supplied the sinews of the whole great undertaking! The patriotism, the unselfishness, the thoroughgoing devotion and distinguished capacity that marked their toilsome labors, day after day, month after month, have made them fit mates and comrades of the men in the trenches and on the sea. And not the men here in Washington only. They have but directed the vast achievement. Throughout innumerable factories, upon innumerable farms, in the depths of coal mines and iron mines and copper mines, wherever the stuffs of industry were to be obtained and prepared, in the shipyards, on the railways, at the docks, on the sea, in every labor that was needed to sustain the battle lines, men have vied with each other to do their part and do it well. They can look any man-at-arms in the face, and say, We also strove to win and gave the best that was in us to make our fleets and armies sure of their triumph!

And what shall we say of the women,—of their instant intelligence, quickening every task that they touched; their capacity for organization and cooperation, which gave their action discipline and enhanced the effectiveness of everything they attempted; their aptitude at tasks to which they had never before set their hands; their utter self-sacrifice alike in what they did and in what they gave? Their contribution to the great result is beyond appraisal. They have added a new lustre to the annals of American womanhood.

The least tribute we can pay them is to make them the equals of men in political rights as they have proved themselves their equals in every field of practical work they have entered, whether for themselves or for their country. These great days of completed achievement would be sadly marred were we to omit that act of justice. Besides the immense practical services they have rendered the women of the country have been the moving spirits in the systematic economies by which our people have voluntarily assisted to supply the suffering peoples of the world and the armies upon every front with food and everything else that we had that might serve the common cause. The details of such a story can never be fully written, but we carry them at our hearts and thank God that we can say that we are the kinsmen of such.

And now we are sure of the great triumph for which every sacrifice was made. It has come, come in its completeness, and with the pride and inspiration of these days of achievement quick within us, we turn to the tasks of peace again,—a peace secure against the violence of irresponsible monarchs and ambitious military coteries and made ready for a new order, for new foundations of justice and fair dealing.

We are about to give order and organization to this peace not only for ourselves but for the other peoples of the world as well, so far as they will suffer us to serve them. It is international justice that we seek, not domestic safety merely. Our thoughts have dwelt of late upon Europe, upon Asia, upon the near and the far East, very little upon the acts of peace and accommodation that wait to be performed at our own doors. While we are adjusting our relations with the rest of the world is it not of capital importance that we should clear away all grounds of misunderstanding with our immediate neighbors and give proof of the friendship we really feel? I hope that the members of the Senate will permit me to speak once more of the unratified treaty of friendship and adjustment with the Republic of Colombia. I very earnestly urge upon them an early and favorable action upon that vital matter. I believe that they will feel, with me, that the stage of affairs is now set for such action as will be not only just but generous and in the spirit of the new age upon which we have so happily entered.

So far as our domestic affairs are concerned the problem of our return to peace is a problem of economic and industrial readjustment. That problem is less serious for us than it may turn out to be for the nations which have suffered the disarrangements and the losses of war longer than we. Our people, moreover, do not wait to be coached and led. They know their own business, are quick and resourceful at every readjustment, definite in purpose, and self-reliant in action. Any leading strings we might seek to put them in would speedily become hopelessly tangled because they would pay no attention to them and go their own way. All that we can do as their legislative and executive servants is to mediate the process of change here, there, and elsewhere as we may. I have heard much counsel as to the plans that should be formed and personally conducted to a happy consummation, but from no quarter have I seen any general scheme

LAUNCHING A WAR TRANSPORT

LAUNCHING A WAR TRANSPORT.

No effort of the United States was of greater value in the final defeat of the Central Powers than shipbuilding. Throughout 1918 and 1919 the German submarine warfare was seriously threatening the ability of the Entente Allies to continue the war; and the presence of American soldiers in large numbers upon the battlefields of Europe was contingent upon the existence of a fleet of transports large enough, not only to carry them across the seas, but also to carry abundant supplies to them despite the activities of the German underseas craft. In the illustration one of the largest transports built for the Army service is seen leaving the ways at Hog Island, the monster shipbuilding plant near Philadelphia erected by the United States during her participation in the War.

of "reconstruction" emerge which I thought it likely we could force our spirited business men and self-reliant laborers to accept with due pliancy and obedience.

While the war lasted we set up many agencies by which to direct the industries of the country in the services it was necessary for them to render, by which to make sure of an abundant supply of the materials needed, by which to check undertakings that could for the time be dispensed with and stimulate those that were most serviceable in war, by which to gain for the purchasing departments of the Government a certain control over the prices of essential articles and materials, by which to restrain trade with alien enemies, make the most of the available shipping, and systematize financial transactions, both public and private, so that there would be no unnecessary conflict or confusion,—by which, in short, to put every material energy of the country in harness to draw the common load and make of us one team in the accomplishment of a great task. But the moment we knew the armistice to have been signed we took the harness off. Raw materials upon which the Government had kept its hand for fear there should not be enough for the industries that supplied the armies have been released and put into the general market again. Great industrial plants whose whole output and machinery had been taken over for the uses of the Government have been set free to return to the uses to which they were put before the war. It has not been possible to remove so readily or so quickly the control of foodstuffs and of shipping, because the world has still to be fed from our granaries and the ships are still needed to send supplies to our men overseas and to bring the men back as fast as the disturbed conditions on the other side of the water permit; but even there restraints are being relaxed as much as possible and more and more as the weeks go by.

Never before have there been agencies in existence in this country which knew so much of the field of supply, of labor, and of industry as the War Industries Board, the War Trade Board, the Labor Department, the Food Administration, and the Fuel Administration have known since their labors became thoroughly systematized; and they have not been isolated agencies; they have been directed by men who represented the permanent Departments of the Government and so have been the centres of unified and cooperative action. It has been the policy of the Executive, therefore, since the armistice was assured (which is in effect a complete submission of the enemy) to put the knowledge of these bodies at the disposal of the business men of the country and to offer their intelligent mediation at every point and in every matter where it was desired. It is surprising how fast the process of return to a peace footing has moved in the three weeks since the fighting stopped. It promises to outrun any inquiry that may be instituted and any aid that may be offered. It will not be easy to direct it any better than it will direct itself. The American business man is of quick initiative.

The ordinary and normal processes of private initiative will not, however, provide immediate employment for all of the men of our returning armies. Those who are of trained capacity, those who are skilled workmen, those who have acquired familiarity with established businesses, those who are ready and willing to go to the farms, all those whose aptitudes are known or will be sought out by employers will find no difficulty, it is safe to say, in finding place and employment. But there will be others who will be at a loss where to gain a livelihood unless pains are taken to guide them and put them in the way of work. There will be a large floating residuum of labor which should not be left wholly to shift for itself. It seems to me important, therefore, that the development of public works of every sort should be promptly resumed, in order that opportunities should be created for unskilled labor in particular, and that plans should be made for such developments of our unused lands and our natural resources as we have hitherto lacked stimulation to undertake.

I particularly direct your attention to the very practical plans which the Secretary of the Interior has developed in his annual report and before your Committees for the reclamation of arid, swamp, and cut-over lands which might, if the States were willing and able to co-operate, redeem some three hundred million acres of land for cultivation. There are said to be fifteen or twenty million acres of land in the West, at present arid, for whose reclamation water is available, if properly conserved. There are about two hundred and thirty million acres from which the forests have been cut but which have never yet been cleared for the plow and which lie waste and desolate. These lie scattered all over the Union. And there are nearly eighty million acres of land that lie under swamps or subject to periodical overflow or too wet for anything but grazing, which it is perfectly feasible to drain and protect and redeem. The Congress can at once direct thousands of the returning soldiers to the reclamation of the arid lands which it has already undertaken, if it will but enlarge the plans and appropriations which it has entrusted to the Department of the Interior. It is possible in dealing with our unused land to effect a great rural and agricultural development which will afford the best sort of opportunity to men who want to help themselves; and the Secretary of the Interior has thought the possible methods out in a way which is worthy of your most friendly attention.

I have spoken of the control which must yet for a while, perhaps for a long while, be exercised over shipping because of the priority of service to which our forces overseas are entitled and which should also be accorded the shipments which are to save recently liberated peoples from starvation and many devasted regions from permanent ruin. May I not say a special word about the needs of Belgium and northern France? No sums of money paid by way of indemnity will serve of themselves to save them from hopeless disadvantage for years to come. Something more must be done than merely find the money. If they had money and raw materials in abundance to-morrow they could not resume their place in the industry of the world to-morrow,—the very important place they held before the flame of war swept across them. Many of their factories are razed to the ground. Much of their machinery is destroyed or has been taken away. Their people are scattered and many of their best workmen are dead. Their markets will be taken by others, if they are not in some special way assisted to rebuild their factories and replace their lost instruments of manufacture. They should not be left to the vicissitudes of the sharp competition for materials and for industrial facilities which is now to set in. I hope, therefore, that the Congress will not be unwilling, if it should become necessary, to grant to some such agency as the War Trade Board the right to establish priorities of export and supply for the benefit of these people whom we have been so happy to assist in saving from the German terror and whom we must not now thoughtlessly leave to shift for themselves in a pitiless competitive market.

For the steadying and facilitation of our own domestic business readjustments nothing is more important than the immediate determination of the taxes that are to be levied for 1918, 1919, and 1920. As much of the burden of taxation must be lifted from business as sound methods of financing the Government will permit, and those who conduct the great essential industries of the country must be told as exactly as possible what obligations to the Government they will be expected to meet in the years immediately ahead of them. It will be of serious consequence to the country to delay removing all uncertainties in this matter a single day longer than the right processes of debate justify. It is idle to talk of successful and confident business reconstruction before those uncertainties are resolved.

If the war had continued it would have been necessary to raise at least eight billion dollars by taxation payable in the year 1919; but the war has ended and I agree with the Secretary of the Treasury that it will be safe to reduce the amount to six billions. An immediate rapid decline in the expenses of the Government is not to be looked for. Contracts made for war supplies will, indeed, be rapidly cancelled and liquidated, but their immediate liquidation will make heavy drains on the Treasury for the months just ahead of us. The maintenance of our forces on the other side of the sea is still necessary. A considerable proportion of those forces must remain in Europe during the period of occupation, and those which are brought home will be transported and demobilized at heavy expense for months to come. The interest on our war debt must of course be paid and provision made for the retirement of the obligations of the Government which represent it. But these demands will of course fall much below what a continuation of military operations would have entailed and six billions should suffice to supply a sound foundation for the financial operations of the year.

I entirely concur with the Secretary of the Treasury in recommending that the two billions needed in addition to the four billions provided by existing law be obtained from the profits which have accrued and shall accrue from war contracts and distinctively war business, but that these taxes be confined to the war profits accruing in 1918, or in 1919 from business originating in war contracts. I urge your acceptance of his recommendation that provision be made now, not subsequently, that the taxes to be paid in 1920 should be reduced from six to four billions. Any arrangements less definite than these would add elements of doubt and confusion to the critical period of industrial readjustment through which the country must now immediately pass, and which no true friend of the nation's essential business interests can afford to be responsible for creating or prolonging. Clearly determined conditions, clearly and simply charted, are indispensable to the economic revival and rapid industrial development which may confidently be expected if we act now and sweep all interrogation points away.

I take it for granted that the Congress will carry out the naval programme which was undertaken before we entered the war. The Secretary of the Navy has submitted to your Committees for authorization that part of the programme which covers the building plans of the next three years. These plans have been prepared along the lines and in accordance with the policy which the Congress established, not under the exceptional conditions of the war, but with the intention of adhering to a definite method of development for the navy. I earnestly recommend the uninterrupted pursuit of that policy. It would clearly be unwise for us to attempt to adjust our programmes to a future world policy as yet undetermined.

The question which causes me the greatest concern is the question of the policy to be adopted towards the railroads. I frankly turn to you for counsel upon it. I have no confident judgment of my own. I do not see how any thoughtful man can have who knows anything of the complexity of the problem. It is a problem which must be studied, studied immediately, and studied without bias or prejudice.

Nothing can be gained by becoming partisans of any particular plan of settlement.

It was necessary that the administration of the railways should be taken over by the Government so long as the war lasted. It would have been impossible otherwise to establish and carry through under a single direction the necessary priorities of shipment. It would have been impossible otherwise to combine maximum production at the factories and mines and farms with the maximum possible car supply to take the products to the ports and markets; impossible to route troop shipments and freight shipments without regard to the advantage or disadvantage of the roads employed; impossible to subordinate, when necessary, all questions of convenience to the public necessity; impossible to give the necessary financial support to the roads from the public treasury. But all these necessities have now been served, and the question is, What is best for the railroads and for the public in the future?

Exceptional circumstances and exceptional methods of administration were not needed to convince us that the railroads were not equal to the immense tasks of transportation imposed upon them by the rapid and continuous development of the industries of the country. We knew that already. And we knew that they were unequal to it partly because their full cooperation was rendered impossible by law and their competition made obligatory, so that it has been impossible to assign to them severally the traffic which could best be carried by their respective lines in the interest of expedition and national economy.

We may hope, I believe, for the formal conclusion of the war by treaty by the time Spring has come. The twenty-one months to which the present control of the railways is limited after formal proclamation of peace shall have been made will run at the farthest, I take it for granted, only to the January of 1921. The full equipment of the railways which the federal administration had planned could not be completed within any such period. The present law does not permit the use of the revenues of the several roads for the execution of such plans except by formal contract with their directors, some of whom will consent while some will not, and therefore does not afford sufficient authority to undertake improvements upon the scale upon which it would be necessary to undertake them. Every approach to this difficult subject-matter of decision brings us face to face, therefore, with this unanswered question: What is it right that we should do with the railroads, in the interest of the public and in fairness to their owners?

Let me say at once that I have no answer ready. The only thing that is perfectly clear to me is that it is not fair either to the public or to the owners of the railroads to leave the question unanswered and that it will presently become my duty to relinquish control of the roads, even before the expiration of the statutory period, unless there should appear some clear prospect in the meantime of a legislative solution. Their release would at least produce one element of a solution, namely certainty and a quick stimulation of private initiative.

I believe that it will be serviceable for me to set forth as explicitly as possible the alternative courses that lie open to our choice. We can simply release the roads and go back to the old conditions of private management, unrestricted competition, and multiform regulation by both state and federal authorities; or we can go to the opposite extreme and establish complete government control, accompanied, if necessary, by actual government ownership; or we can adopt an intermediate course of modified private control, under a more unified and affirmative public regulation and under such alterations of the law as will permit wasteful competition to be avoided and a considerable degree of unification of administration to be effected, as, for example, by regional corporations under which the railways of definable areas would be in effect combined in single systems.

The one conclusion that I am ready to state with confidence is that it would be a disservice alike to the country and to the owners of the railroads to return to the old conditions unmodified. Those are conditions of restraint without development. There is nothing affirmative or helpful about them. What the country chiefly needs is that all its means of transportation should be developed, its railways, its waterways, its highways, and its countryside roads. Some new element of policy, therefore, is absolutely necessary,—necessary for the service of the public, necessary for the release of credit to those who are administering the railways, necessary for the protection of their security holders. The old policy may be changed much or little, but surely it cannot wisely be left as it was. I hope that the Congress will have a complete and impartial study of the whole problem instituted at once and prosecuted as rapidly as possible. I stand ready and anxious to release the roads from the present control and I must do so at a very early date if by waiting until the statutory limit of time is reached I shall be merely prolonging the period of doubt and uncertainty which is hurtful to every interest concerned.

I welcome this occasion to announce to the Congress my purpose to join in Paris the representatives of the governments with which we have been associated in the war against the Central Empires for the purpose of discussing with them the main features of the treaty of peace. I realize the great inconveniences that will attend my leaving the country, particularly at this time, but the conclusion that it was my paramount duty to go has been forced upon me by considerations which I hope will seem as conclusive to you as they have seemed to me.

The Allied governments have accepted the bases of peace which I outlined to the Congress on the eighth of January last, as the Central Empires also have, and very reasonably desire my personal counsel in their interpretation and application, and it is highly desirable that I should give it in order that the sincere desire of our Government to contribute without selfish purpose of any kind to settlements that will be of common benefit to all the nations concerned may be made fully manifest. The peace settlements which are now to be agreed upon are of transcendent importance both to us and to the rest of the world, and I know of no business or interest which should take precedence of them. The gallant men of our armed forces on land and sea have consciously fought for the ideals which they knew to be the ideals of their country; I have sought to express those ideals; they have accepted my statements of them as the substance of their own thought and purpose, as the associated governments have accepted them; I owe it to them to see to it, so far as in me lies, that no false or mistaken interpretation is put upon them, and no possible effort omitted to realize them. It is now my duty to play my full part in making good what they offered their life's blood to obtain. I can think of no call to service which could transcend this.

I shall be in close touch with you and with affairs on this side the water, and you will know all that I do. At my request, the French and English governments have absolutely removed the censorship of cable news which until within a fortnight they had maintained and there is now no censorship whatever exercised at this end except upon attempted trade communications with enemy countries. It has been necessary to keep an open wire constantly available between Paris and the Department of State and another between France and the Department of War. In order that this might be done with the least possible interference with the other uses of the cables, I have temporarily taken over the control of both cables in order that they may be used as a single system. I did so at the advice of the most experienced cable officials, and I hope that the results will justify my hope that the news of the next few months may pass with the utmost freedom and with the least possible delay from each side of the sea to the other.

May I not hope, Gentlemen of the Congress, that in the delicate tasks I shall have to perform on the other side of the sea, in my efforts truly and faithfully to interpret the principles and purposes of the country we love, I may have the encouragement and the added strength of your united support? I realize the magnitude and difficulty of the duty I am undertaking; I am poignantly aware of its grave responsibilities. I am the servant of the nation. I can have no private thought or purpose of my own in performing such an errand. I go to give the best that is in me to the common settlements which I must now assist in arriving at in conference with the other working heads of the associated governments. I shall count upon your friendly countenance and encouragement. I shall not be inaccessible. The cables and the wireless will render me available for any counsel or service you may desire of me, and I shall be happy in the thought that I am constantly in touch with the weighty matters of domestic policy with which we shall have to deal. I shall make my absence as brief as possible and shall hope to return with the happy assurance that it has been possible to translate into action the great ideals for which America has striven.

APPEAL

[For Support of the American Red Cross. Made Public on December 8, 1918.]

To the American People:

One year ago twenty-two million Americans, by enrolling as members of the Red Cross at Christmas time, sent to the men who were fighting our battles overseas a stimulating message of cheer and goodwill. They made it clear that our people were of their own free choice united with their Government in the determination not only to wage war with the instruments of destruction, but also by every means in their power to repay the ravages of the invader and sustain and renew the spirit of the army and of the homes which they represented. The friends of the American Red Cross in Italy, Belgium, and France have told, and will tell again, the story of how the Red Cross workers restored morale in the hospitals, in the camps, and at the cantonments, and we ought to be very proud that we have been permitted to be of service to those whose sufferings and whose glory are the heritage of humanity.

Now, by God's grace, the Red Cross Christmas message of 1918 is to be a message of peace as well as a message of good-will. But peace does not mean that we can fold our hands. It means further sacrifice. We must prove conclusively to an attentive world that America is permanently aroused to the needs of the new era, our old indifference gone forever.

The exact nature of the future service of the Red Cross will depend upon the program of the associated governments, but there is immediate need today for every heartening word and for every helpful service. We must not forget that our soldiers and our sailors are still under orders, and still have duties to perform of the highest consequence, and that the Red Cross Christmas membership means a great deal to them. The people of the saddened lands, moreover, returning home today where there are no homes, must have the assurance that the hearts of our people are with them in the dark and doubtful days ahead. Let us, so far as we can, help them back to faith in mercy and in future happiness.

As President of the Red Cross, conscious in this great hour of the value of such a message from the American people, I should be glad if every American would join the Red Cross for 1919, and thus send forth to the whole human family the Christmas greeting for which it waits and for which it stands in greatest need.

WOODROW WILSON.

PRESIDENT WILSON S TRIP TO EUROPE

On November 18, 1918, after several weeks of rumor that the President would himself go to Europe to participate in the formal and informal peace conferences incident upon the ending of the European War, the following announcement was issued from the White House:—

The President expects to sail for France immediately after the opening of the regular session of Congress, for the purpose of taking part in the discussion and settlement of the main features of the treaty of peace.

It is not likely that it will be possible for him to remain throughout the sessions of the formal peace conference, but his presence at the outset is necessary in order to obviate the manifest disadvantages of discussion by cable in determining the greater outlines of the final treaty, about which he must necessarily be consulted.

He will, of course, be accompanied by delegates who will sit as the representatives of the United States throughout the conference. The names of the delegates will be presently announced.

In the President's annual message to Congress on December 2, 1918, he announced to that body his intention to sail for Europe. (See page 8646.)

The visit thus announced by the President was the first ever made to European shores by a President of the United States during his incumbency of office, although President Roosevelt and President Taft had left Continental United States to visit Panama and Cuba. The President was accompanied abroad by Mrs. Wilson and her mother and by a large personal and official staff, including a number of those who had been in positions of high power in administering the war program of the country. Two other of the five peace delegates of the United States accompanied the President—Secretary of State Robert Lansing and Henry White, former ambassador to France and Italy; the other two—General Tasker H. Bliss, formerly Chief of Staff and Military Representative of the United States on the Inter-Allied War Council, and Mr.

Edward M. House, long the President's most trusted adviser—joining the Presidential party in France.

The voyage was made on the *George Washington,* one of the German ships taken over by the United States when the United States entered the war, to be put into use as a naval transport. The *George Washington* sailed from Hoboken at 10 A. M. on December 4, escorted on the entire trip to Europe by the battleship *Pennsylvania* and several torpedo boat destroyers. The route was the southerly one rounding the Azores.

President Wilson and his party landed at Brest, France, at 1 P. M. on December 13, leaving for Paris three hours later, and arriving there at 6:15 P. M. Everywhere the President was greeted with jubilation and honors such as all observers agreed had never before been paid a foreign visitor. Especially among the great masses of the people was the President popular, and the evidence was undeniable that he was looked upon everywhere in Europe as the most potent and invigorating force making for honorable, democratic and lasting terms of peace, primarily because of his project for a League of Nations.

While in France, President Wilson was the guest of honor at a number of formal state functions, but his time was occupied chiefly with private conferences with Allied leaders and statesmen. In Paris, he conferred at length not only with Premier Clemenceau, President Poincaré and Foreign Minister Pichon of France, but also with King Victor Emmanuel, Premier Orlando and Foreign Minister Sonnino of Italy and Premier Venizelos of Greece. The President's public utterances laid emphasis upon the necessity for the organization of a League of Nations, but otherwise were guarded and formal. At a luncheon tendered him on December 14 by President Poincaré he responded to a toast as follows:—

Mr. President: I am deeply indebted to you for your gracious greeting. It is very delightful to find myself in France and to feel the quick contact of sympathy and unaffected friendship between the representatives of the United States and the representatives of France.

You have been very generous in what you were pleased to say about myself, but I feel that what I have said and what I have tried to do has been said and done only in an attempt to speak the thought of the people of the United States truly, and to carry that thought out in action.

From the first, the thought of the people of the United States turned toward something more than the mere winning of this war. It turned to the establishment of eternal principles of right and justice. It realized that merely to win the war was not enough; that it must be won in such a way and the questions raised by it settled in such a way as to insure the future peace of the world and lay the foundations for the freedom and happiness of its many peoples and nations.

Never before has war worn so terrible a visage or exhibited more grossly the debasing influence of illicit ambitions. I am sure that I shall look upon the ruin wrought by the armies of the Central Empires with the same repulsion and deep indignation that they stir in the hearts of the men of France and Belgium, and I appreciate, as you do, sir, the necessity of such action in the final settlement of the issues of the war as will not only rebuke such acts of terror and spoliation, but make men everywhere aware that they cannot be ventured upon without the certainty of just punishment.

I know with what ardor and enthusiasm the soldiers and sailors of the United States have given the best that was in them to this war of redemption. They have expressed the true spirit of America. They believe their ideals to be acceptable to free peoples everywhere, and are rejoiced to have played the part they have played in giving reality to those ideals in co-operation with the armies of the Allies. We are proud of the part they have played, and we are happy that they should have been associated with such comrades in a common cause.

It is with peculiar feeling, Mr. President, that I find myself in France joining with you in rejoicing over the victory that has been won. The ties that bind France and the United States are peculiarly close. I do not know in what other comradeship we could have fought with more zest or enthusiasm. It will daily be a matter of pleasure for me to be brought into consultation with the statesmen of France and her allies in concerting the measures by which we may secure permanence for these happy relations of friendship and co-operation, and secure for the world at large such safety and freedom in its life as can be secured only by the constant association and co-operation of friends.

I greet you not only with deep personal respect, but as the representative of the great people of France, and beg to bring you the greetings of another great people to whom the fortunes of France are of profound and lasting interest.

I raise my glass to the health of the President of the French Republic and to Mme. Poincaré and the prosperity of France.

An address by the President in France which created great interest was that delivered at the Sorbonne (University of Paris), on December 21, after receiving the honorary degree of doctor of laws:—

I feel very keenly the distinguished honor which has been conferred upon me by the great University of Paris, and it is very delightful to me also to have the honor of being introduced into the great company of scholars whose life and fame have made the history of the University of Paris a thing admirable among men of cultivation in all parts of the world.

By what you have said, Sir, of the theory of education which has been followed in France and which I have tried to promote in the United States, I am tempted to venture upon a favorite theme. I have always thought that the chief object of education was to awaken the spirit, and that, inasmuch as a literature whenever it has touched its great and higher notes was an expression of the spirit of mankind, the best induction into education was to feel the pulses of humanity which had beaten from age to age through the universities of men who had penetrated to the secrets of the human spirit.

And I agree with the intimation which has been conveyed today that the terrible war through which we have just passed has not been only a war between nations, but that it has been also a war between systems of culture—the one system the aggressive system, using science without conscience, stripping learning of its moral restraints, and using every faculty of the human mind to do wrong to the whole race; the other system reminiscent of the high traditions of men, reminiscent of all these struggles, some of them obscure, but others clearly revealed in history, of men of indomitable spirit everywhere struggling toward the right and seeking above all things else to be free.

The triumph of freedom in this war means that that spirit shall now dominate the world. There is a great wave of moral force moving through the world, and every man who opposes himself to that wave will go down in disgrace.

The task of those who are gathered here, or will presently be gathered here, to make the settlements of this peace, is greatly simplified by the fact that they are the masters of no one; they are the servants of mankind. And if we do not heed the mandates of mankind we shall make ourselves the most conspicuous and deserved failures in the history of the world.

My conception of the League of Nations is just this—that it shall operate as the organized moral force of men throughout the world, and that whenever or wherever wrong and aggression are planned or contemplated, this searching light of conscience will be turned upon them, and men everywhere will ask, "What are the purposes that you hold in your heart against the fortunes of the world?"

Just a little exposure will settle most questions. If the Central Powers had dared to discuss the purposes of this war for a single fortnight, it never would have happened; and if, as should be, they were forced to discuss it for a year, the war would have been inconceivable.

So I feel that war is, as has been said more than once today, intimately related with the university spirit. The university spirit is intolerant of all the things that put the human mind under restraint. It is intolerant of everything that seeks to retard the advancement of ideals, the acceptance of the truth, the purification of life; and every university man can ally himself with the forces of the present time with the feeling that now at last the spirit of truth, the spirit to which universities have devoted themselves, has prevailed and is triumphant.

If there is one point of pride that I venture to entertain, it is that it has been my private privilege in some measure to interpret the university spirit in the public life of a great nation, and I feel that in honoring me today in this unusual and conspicuous manner you have first of all honored the people whom I represent. The spirit that I try to express I know to be their spirit and in proportion as I serve them I believe that I advance the cause of freedom.

I, as before, wish to thank you, Sir, from the bottom of my heart for a distinction which has in a singular way crowned my academic career.

On December 24, President Wilson left Paris to spend Christmas with American troops on the battle-front. His address to them on December 25 was as follows:—

General Pershing and Fellow-Comrades: I wish that I could give to each one of you the message that I know you are longing to receive from those at home who love you. I cannot do that, but I can tell you how every one has put his heart into it. So you have done your duty, and something more. You have done your duty, and you have done it with a spirit which gave it distinction and glory.

And now we are to hail the fruits of everything. You conquered, when you came over, what you came over for, and you have done what it was appointed for you to do. I know what you expected of me. Some time ago a gentleman from one of the countries with which we are associated was discussing with me the moral aspects of this war, and I said that if we did not insist upon the high purpose which we have accomplished the end would not be justified.

Everybody at home is proud of you and has followed every movement of this great army with confidence and affection. The whole people of the United States are now waiting to welcome you home with an acclaim which probably has never greeted any other army, because our country is like this country—we have been so proud of the stand taken, of the purpose for which this war was entered by the United States.

You knew what we expected of you, and you did it. I know what you and the people at home expected of me, and I am happy to say, my fellow-countrymen, that I do not find in the hearts of the great leaders with whom it is my privilege now to co-operate any difference of principle or of fundamental purpose.

It happened that it was the privilege of America to present the chart for peace, and now the process of settlement has been rendered comparatively simple by the fact that all the nations concerned have accepted that chart, and the application of these principles laid down there will be their application. The world will now know that the nations that fought this war, as well as the soldiers who represented them, are ready to make good—make good not only in the assertion of their own interests, but make good in the establishment of peace upon the permanent foundation of right and of justice.

Because this is not a war in which the soldiers of the free nations have obeyed masters. You have commanders, but you have no masters. Your very commanders represent you in representing the nation of which you constitute so distinguished a part. And everybody concerned in the settlement knows that it must be a people's peace and that nothing must be done in the settlement of the issues of the war which is not as handsome as the great achievements of the armies of the United States and the Allies.

It is difficult, very difficult, men, in any formal speech like this to show you my real heart. You men probably do not realize with what anxious attention and care we have followed every step you have advanced and how proud we are that every step was in advance, and not in retreat; that every time you set your face in any direction you kept your face in that direction. A thrill has gone through my heart, as it has gone through the hearts of every American, with almost every gun that was fired and every stroke that was struck in the gallant fighting that you have done; and there has been only one regret in America, and that was the regret that every man there felt that he was not there in France, too.

It has been a hard thing to perform the tasks in the United States; it has been a hard thing to take part in directing what you did without coming over and helping you to do it. It has taken a lot of moral courage to stay at home. But we are proud to back you up everywhere that it was possible to back you up. And now I am happy to find what splendid names you have made for yourselves among the civilian population of France, as well as among your comrades in the armies of the French, and it is a fine testimony to you men that these people like you and love you and trust you, and the finest part of it all is that you deserve their trust.

I feel a comradeship with you today which is delightful, as I look down upon these undisturbed fields and think of the terrible scenes through which you have gone and realize how the quiet of peace, the tranquillity of settled hopes has descended upon us. And, while it is hard far away from home, confidentially, to bid you a Merry Christmas, I can, I think, confidentially, promise you a Happy New Year, and I can from the bottom of my heart say, God bless you.

On December 25, President Wilson reviewed 10,000 American troops at Chaumont, leaving the following day for England. He landed at Dover on December 26, leaving immediately for London, where he was received with honors mingled with veneration which indicated that he was firmly entrenched in the hearts of the mass of the English people as of the French. The text of his response to the toast proposed to him by King George V of England at a welcoming banquet at Windsor Castle on December 27 is as follows:—

Your Majesty: I am deeply complimented by the gracious words which you have uttered. The welcome which you have given me and Mrs. Wilson has been so warm, so natural, so evidently from the heart, that we have been more than pleased. We have been touched by it, and I believe that I correctly interpret that welcome as embodying not only your own generous spirit toward us personally, but also as expressing for yourself and the great nation over which you preside that same feeling for my people, for the people of the United States.

For you and I, Sir—I temporarily—embody the spirit of two great nations, and whatever strength I have and whatever authority, I possess it only so long and so far as I express the spirit and purpose of the American people.

Every influence that the American people have over the affairs of the world is measured by their sympathy with the aspirations of free-men everywhere.

America does love freedom, and I believe that she loves freedom un-selfishly. But if she does not she will not and cannot help the influence to which she justly aspires.

I have had the privilege, Sir, of conferring with the leaders of your own Government and with the spokesmen of the Governments of France and of Italy, and I am glad to say that I have the same con-ceptions that they have of the significance and scope of the duty on which we have met.

We have used great words, all of us have used the great words "Right" and "Justice," and now we are to prove whether or not we understand these words, and how they are to be applied to the particu-lar settlements which must conclude this war. And we must not only understand them, but we must have the courage to act upon our under-standing.

Yet, after I have uttered the word "Courage," it comes into my mind that it would take more courage to resist the great moral tide now running in the world than to yield to it, than to obey it.

There is a great tide running in the hearts of men. The hearts of men have never beaten so singularly in unison before. Men have never before been so conscious of their brotherhood. Men have never before realized how little difference there was between right and justice in one latitude and in another, under one sovereignty and under another.

And it will be our high privilege, I believe, Sir, not only to apply the moral judgment of the world to the particular settlements which we shall attempt, but also to organize the moral force of the world to preserve those settlements, to steady the forces of mankind, and to make the right and the justice to which great nations like our own have devoted themselves, the predominant and controlling force of the world.

There is something inspiring in knowing that this is the errand that we have come on. Nothing less than this would have justified me in leaving the important tasks which fall upon me upon the other side of the sea—nothing but the consciousness that nothing else compares with this in dignity and importance.

Therefore, it is the more delightful to find myself in the company of a body of men united in ideal and purpose, and to feel that I am privileged to unite my thoughts with yours in carrying forward these standards which we are so proud to hold so high and to defend.

May I not, Sir, with a feeling of profound sincerity and friendship and sympathy propose your health and the health of the Queen and the prosperity of Great Britain?

On Saturday, December 28, President Wilson delivered the following address in the Guildhall of London:—

Mr. Lord Mayor—We have come upon times when ceremonies like this have a new significance which most impresses me as I stand here. The address which I have just heard is most generously and graciously conceived, and the delightful accent of sincerity in it seems like a part of that voice of counsel which is now everywhere to be heard.

I feel that a distinguished honor has been conferred upon me by this reception, and I beg to assure you, sir, and your associates of my very profound appreciation, but I know that I am only part of what I may call a great body of circumstances.

I do not believe that it was fancy on my part that I heard in the voice of welcome uttered in the streets of this great city and in the streets of Paris something more than a personal welcome. It seemed to me that I heard the voice of one people speaking to another people, and it was a voice in which one could distinguish a singular combination of emotions.

There was surely there the deep gratefulness that the fighting was over. There was the pride that the fighting had had such a culmination. There was that sort of gratitude that the nations engaged had produced such men as the soldiers of Great Britain and of the United States and of France and of Italy—men whose prowess and achievements they had witnessed with rising admiration as they moved from culmination to culmination.

But there was something more in it, the consciousness that the business is not yet done, the consciousness that it now rests upon others to see that those lives were not lost in vain.

I have not yet been to the actual battlefields, but I have been with many of the men who have fought the battles, and the other day I had the pleasure of being present at a session of the French Academy when they admitted Marshal Joffre to their membership.

That sturdy, serene soldier stood and uttered, not the words of triumph, but the simple words of affection for his soldiers and the conviction which he summed up in a sentence which I will not try accurately to quote, but reproduce in its spirit. It was that France must always remember that the small and the weak could never live free in the world unless the strong and the great always put their power and their strength in the service of right.

That is the afterthought—the thought that something must be done now; not only to make the just settlements—that, of course—but to see that the settlements remain and are observed and that honor and justice prevail in the world.

And, as I have conversed with the soldiers, I have been more and more aware that they fought for something that not all of them had defined, but which all of them recognized the moment you stated it to them.

They fought to do away with an old order and to establish a new one, and the center and characteristic of the old order was that unstable thing which we used to call the "balance of power," a thing in which the balance was determined by the sword which was thrown in on the one side or the other, a balance which was determined by the unstable equilibrium of competitive interests, a balance which was maintained by jealous watchfulness and an antagonism of interests which, though it was generally latent, was always deep-seated.

The men who have fought in this war have been the men from the free nations who are determined that that sort of thing should end now and forever. It is very interesting to me to observe how from every quarter, from every sort of mind, from every concert of counsel, there comes the suggestion that there must now be not a balance of power, not one powerful group of nations set up against another, but a single, overwhelming, powerful group of nations, who shall be the trust of the peace of the world.

It has been delightful in my conferences with the leaders of your Government to find how our minds moved along exactly the same line, and how our thought was always that the key to the peace was the guarantee of the peace, not the items of it; that the items would be worthless unless there stood back of them a permanent concert of power for their maintenance. That is the most reassuring thing that has ever happened in the world.

When this war began the thought of a League of Nations was indulgently considered as the interesting thought of closeted students.

It was thought of as one of those things that it was right to characterize by a name which, as a university man, I have always resented. It was said to be academic, as if that in itself were a condemnation—something that men could think about but never get. Now we find the practical leading minds of the world determined to get it.

No such sudden and potent union of purpose has ever been witnessed in the world before. Do you wonder, therefore, gentlemen, that, in common with those who represent you, I am eager to get at the business and write the sentences down? And that I am particularly happy that the ground is cleared and the foundations laid? For we have already accepted the same body of principles.

Those principles are clearly and definitely enough stated to make their application a matter which should afford no fundamental difficulty.

And back of us is that imperative yearning of the world to have all disturbing questions quieted, to have all threats against peace silenced, to have just men everywhere come together for a common object. The peoples of the world want peace and they want it now, not merely by conquest or arms but by agreement of mind.

It was this incomparably great object that brought me overseas. It has never before been deemed excusable for a President of the United States to leave the territory of the United States, but I know that I have the support of the judgment of my colleagues in the government of the United States in saying that it was my paramount duty to turn away even from the imperative tasks at home to lend such counsel and aid as I could to this great, may I not say final, enterprise of humanity.

On Sunday, December 29, President Wilson visited the girlhood home of his mother in Carlisle, England, where he gave a few remarks at the services in the church of which his grandfather had been minister.

On December 30, President Wilson was given the freedom of the city of Manchester, upon which occasion he delivered the following address:—

My Lord Mayor, Ladies and Gentlemen, perhaps I may be permitted to add *Fellow-Citizens*—You have made me feel in a way that is deeply delightful the generous welcome which you have accorded me, and back of it I know there lies the same sort of feeling for the great people whom I have the privilege of representing.

There is a feeling of cordiality, fraternity and friendship between the two great nations, and as I have gone from place to place and been made everywhere to feel the pulse of sympathy that is now beating between us I have been led to some very serious thoughts as to what the basis of it all is. For I think you will agree with me that friendship is not a mere sentiment—patriotism is not a mere sentiment. It is based upon a principle, upon the principle that leads a man to give more than he demands.

Similarly, friendship is based not merely upon affection, but upon common service. The man is not your friend who is not willing to serve you, and you are not his friend unless you are willing to serve him. And out of that impulse of common interest and desire of common service arises that noble feeling which we consecrate as friendship.

And so it does seem to me that the theme that we must have in our minds now in this great day of settlement is the theme of common interest and the determination of what it is that is our common interest. You know that heretofore the world has been governed, or at any rate the attempt has been made to govern it, by partnerships of interest, and that they have broken down. Interest does not bind men together. Interest separates men. For, the moment there is the slightest departure from the nice adjustment of interests, then jealousies begin to spring up. There is only one thing that can bind peoples together, and that is common devotion to right.

Ever since the history of liberty began men have talked about their rights, and it has taken several hundred years to make them perceive that the principal condition of right is duty, and that unless a man performs his full duty he is entitled to no right. It is a fine co-relation of the influence of duty that right is the equipoise and balance of society.

And so, when we analyze the present situation and the future that we now have to mold and control, it seems to me there is no other thought than that that can guide us. You know that the United States has always felt from the very beginning of her story that she must keep herself separate from any kind of connection with European politics. I want to say very frankly to you that she is not now interested in European politics, but she is interested in the partnership of right between America and Europe. If the future had nothing for us but a new attempt to keep the world at a right poise by a balance of power the United States would take no interest, because she will join no combination of power which is not a combination of all of us. She is not interested merely in the peace of Europe, but in the peace of the world.

Therefore it seems to me that in the settlement which is just ahead of us something more delicate and difficult than was ever attempted before has to be accomplished—a genuine concert of mind and of purpose. But, while it is difficult, there is an element present that makes it easy. Never before in the history of the world, I believe, has there been such a keen international consciousness as there is now.

There is a great voice of humanity abroad in the world just now which he who cannot hear is deaf. There is a great compulsion of the common conscience now in existence which if any statesman resist, will gain for him the most uneviable eminence in history. We are not obeying the mandate of parties or of politics. We are obeying the mandate of humanity.

That is the reason why it seems to me that the things that are most often in our minds are the least significant. I am not hopeful that the individual items of the settlement which we are about to attempt will be altogether satisfactory. One has only to apply his mind to any one of the questions of boundary and of altered sovereignty and of racial aspirations to do something more than conjecture that there is no man and no body of men who know just how they ought to be settled; and yet if we are to make unsatisfactory settlements we must see to it that they are rendered more and more satisfactory by the subsequent adjustments which are made possible. We must provide the machinery for readjustments in order that we have the machinery of good-will and friendship.

Friendship must have a machinery. If I cannot correspond with you, if I cannot learn your minds, if I cannot co-operate with you, I cannot be your friend; and if the world is to remain a body of friends, it must have the means of friendship, the means of constant friendly intercourse, the means for constant watchfulness over the common interests.

That makes it necessary to make some great effort to have with one another an easy and constant method of conference, so that troubles may be taken when they are little and not allowed to grow until they are big. I never thought I had a big difference with a man that I did not find when I came into conference with him that, after all, it was rather a little difference, and that if we were frank with one another and did not too much stand upon that great enemy of mankind which is called pride, we could come together.

It is the wish to come together that is more than half of the process. It is a doctrine which ought to be easy of comprehension in a great commercial centre like this. You cannot trade with a man who suspects you. You cannot establish commercial and industrial relations with those who do not trust you. Good-will is the forerunner of trade. Good-will is the foundation of trade, and trade is the great amicable instrument of the world on that account.

I felt, before I came here, at home in Manchester, because Manchester has so many of the characteristics of our great American cities. I was reminded of an anecdote of a humorous fellow-countryman of mine who was sitting at luncheon in his club one day when a man whom he did not like particularly came up and slapped him on the shoulders and said:

"Hello, Ollie! How are you?"

He looked at him coldly and said:

"I don't know your face, and I don't know your name, but your manners are very familiar."

I don't know your name, but your manners are very familiar, and very delightfully familiar, so that I felt that in the community of interest and understanding which is established in great currents of trade we are enabled to see international processes perhaps better than they can be seen by others. I take it I am not far from right in supposing that is the reason why Manchester has been the centre of the great forward-looking sentiments of men who had the instincts of large planning, not merely for the city itself, but for the Kingdom and the Empire and the world. And with that outlook we can be sure we can go shoulder and shoulder together.

I wish it were possible for us to do something like some of my very stern ancestors did, for among my ancestors are those very determined persons who were known as the Covenanters. I wish we could, not for Great Britain and the United States, but for France, for Italy and the world, enter into a great League and Covenant declaring ourselves first of all friends of mankind and uniting ourselves together for the maintenance of the triumph of right.

Mr. Wilson left England on December 31, spending the following day in Paris, and arriving in Italy on January 2, 1919. He reached Rome on the morning of January 3, where he was received with the highest honors and enthusiasm. The text of his address on January 3 to the Italian Chamber of Deputies is as follows:—

Your Majesty and Mr. President of the Chamber—You are bestowing upon me an unprecedented honor, which I accept because I believe that it is extended to me as the representative of the great people for whom I speak. And I am going to take this first opportunity to say how entirely the heart of the American people has been with the great people of Italy.

We have seemed, no doubt, indifferent at times, to look from a great distance, but our hearts have never been far away. All sorts of ties have long bound the people of our America to the people of Italy, and when the people of the United States, knowing this people, have witnessed its sufferings, its sacrifices, its heroic actions upon the battlefield, and its heroic endurance at home—its steadfast endurance at home touching us more nearly to the quick even than its heroic action on the battlefield—we have been bound by a new tie of profound admiration.

Then, back of it all, and through it all, running like the golden thread that wove it together, was our knowledge that the people of Italy had gone into this war for the same exalted principle of right and justice that moved our own people. And so I welcome this opportunity of conveying to you the heartfelt greetings of the people of the United States.

But we cannot stand in the shadow of this war without knowing there are things which are in some senses more difficult than those we have undertaken, because, while it is easy to speak of right and justice, it is sometimes difficult to work them out in practice, and there will be required a purity of motives and disinterestedness of object which the world has never witnessed before in the councils of nations.

It is for that reason that it seems to me you will forgive me if I lay some of the elements of the new situation before you for a moment. The distinguishing fact of this war is that great empires have gone to pieces. And the characteristics of those empires are that they held different peoples reluctantly together under the coercion of force and the guidance of intrigue.

The great difficulty among such States as those of the Balkans has been that they were always accessible to secret influence; that they were always being penetrated by intrigue of some sort or another, that north of them lay disturbed populations which were held together not by sympathy and friendship, but by the coercive force of a military power.

Now the intrigue is checked, and the bonds are broken, and what we are going to provide is a new cement to hold the people together. They have not been accustomed to being independent. They must now be independent.

I am sure that you recognize the principle as I do—that it is not our privilege to say what sort of a Government they should set up. But we are friends of those people, and it is our duty as their friends to see to it that some kind of protection is thrown around them—something supplied which will hold them together.

There is only one thing that holds nations together, if you exclude force, and that is friendship and good-will. The only thing that binds men together is friendship, and by the same token the only thing that binds nations together is friendship. Therefore our task at Paris is to organize the friendship of the world—to see to it that all the moral forces that make for right and justice and liberty are united and are given a vital organization to which the peoples of the world will readily and gladly respond.

In other words, our task is no less colossal than this: To set up a new international psychology; to have a new real atmosphere. I am happy to say that, in my dealings with the distinguished gentlemen who lead your nation, and those who lead France and England, I feel that atmosphere gathering, that desire to do justice, that desire to establish friendliness, that desire to make peace rest upon right; and with this common purpose no obstacles need be formidable.

The only use of an obstacle is to be overcome. All that an obstacle does with brave men is not to frighten them, but to challenge them. So that it ought to be our pride to overcome everything that stands in the way.

We know that there cannot be another balance of power. That has been tried and found wanting, for the best of all reasons that it does not stay balanced inside itself, and a weight which does not hold together cannot constitute a makeweight in the affairs of men.

Therefore there must be something substituted for the balance of power, and I am happy to find everywhere in the air of these great nations the conception that that thing must be a thoroughly united League of Nations.

What men once considered theoretical and idealistic turns out to be practical and necessary. We stand at the opening of a new age in which a new statesmanship will, I am confident, lift mankind to new levels of endeavor and achievement.

While in Rome, President Wilson conferred again with the leaders of the Italian Government and with emissaries from the Jugo-Slavs and other nationalities on the Balkan peninsula, whose claims were in dispute with the claims of Italy to territory along the east coast of the Adriatic, which had been assigned Italy by secret treaty with the Entente Allies in 1915, just before Italy entered the war. On January 5, President Wilson paid a formal visit to the Pope in the Vatican, later visiting a delegation of the Protestant bodies in Rome. On the following day, he left for France, stopping to deliver addresses and receiving marked honors at Genoa, Turin and Milan.

His remarks at the statue of Columbus at Genoa on January 6 were as follows:—

Standing in front of this monument, Sir, I fully recognize the significance of what you have said. Columbus did do a service to mankind in discovering America and it is America's pleasure and America's pride that she has been able to show that it was a service to mankind to open that great continent to settlement, the settlement of a free people, of a people free because they are free to desire to see other peoples free and to share their liberty with the people of the world. It is for this reason no doubt, besides his fine spirit of adventure, that Columbus will always be remembered and honored, not only here in the land of his birth, but throughout the world, as the man who led the way to those fields of freedom which, planted with a great seed, have now sprung up to the fructification of the world.

ADDRESS TO PEACE CONFERENCE

[At First Formal Session of Allied and Associated Nations, Paris, France, *January 18, 1919*, Proposing Premier Georges Clemenceau of France as the Permanent Chairman of the Conference.]

Mr. Chairman—It gives me great pleasure to propose as permanent chairman of the conference M. Clemenceau, the President of the council.

I would do this as a matter of custom. I would do this as a tribute to the French Republic. But I wish to do it as something more than that. I wish to do it as a tribute to the man.

France deserves the precedence not only because we are meeting at her capital, and because she has undergone some of the most tragical suffering of the war, but also because her capital, her ancient and beautiful capital, has so often been the centre of conferences of this sort on which the fortunes of large parts of the world turned.

It is a very delightful thought that the history of the world, which has so often centred here, will now be crowned by the achievements of this conference—because there is a sense in which this is the supreme conference of the history of mankind.

More nations are represented here than were ever represented in such a conference before. The fortunes of all peoples are involved. A great war is ended, which seemed about to bring a universal cataclysm. The danger is passed. A victory has been won for mankind, and it is delightful that we should be able to record these great results in this place.

But it is more delightful to honor France because we can honor her in the person of so distinguished a servant. We have all felt in our participation in the struggles of this war the fine steadfastness which characterized the leadership of the French in the hands of M. Clemenceau. We have learned to admire him, and those of us who have been associated with him have acquired a genuine affection for him.

Moreover, those of us who have been in these recent days in constant consultation with him know how warmly his purpose is set toward the goal of achievement to which all our faces are turned. He feels as we feel, as I have no doubt everybody in this room feels, that we are trusted to do a great thing, to do it in the highest spirit of friendship and accommodation, and to do it as promptly as possible in order that the hearts of men may have fear lifted from them, and that they may return to those purposes of life which will bring them happiness and contentment and prosperity.

Knowing his brotherhood of heart in these great matters, it affords me a personal pleasure to propose that M. Clemenceau shall be the permanent Chairman of this conference.

THE LEAGUE OF NATIONS

President Wilson's remarks on opening the discussion in the Peace Conference on the project for a league of nations on January 25, 1919 were as follows:

Mr. Chairman:

I consider it a distinguished privilege to be permitted to open the
discussion in this conference on the League of Nations. We have
assembled for two purposes, to make the present settlements which
have been rendered necessary by this war, and also to secure the
peace of the world, not only by the present settlements but by the
arrangements we shall make at this conference for its maintenance.
The League of Nations seems to me to be necessary for both of these
purposes. There are many complicated questions connected with the
present settlements which perhaps cannot be successfully worked out
to an ultimate issue by the decisions we shall arrive at here. I can
easily conceive that many of these settlements will need subsequent
reconsideration, that many of the decisions we make shall need subsequent alteration in some degree; for, if I may judge by my own
study of some of these questions, they are not susceptible of confident
judgments at present.

It is, therefore, necessary that we should set up some machinery by
which the work of this conference should be rendered complete. We
have assembled here for the purpose of doing very much more than
making the present settlements. We are assembled under very peculiar conditions of world opinion. I may say without straining the
point that we are not representatives of governments, but representatives of peoples. It will not suffice to satisfy governmental circles
anywhere. It is necessary that we should satisfy the opinion of mankind. The burdens of this war have fallen in an unusual degree upon
the whole population of the countries involved. I do not need to
draw for you the picture of how the burden has been thrown back
from the front upon the older men, upon the women, upon the children, upon the homes of the civilized world, and how the real strain
of the war has come where the eye of government could not reach,
but where the heart of humanity beats. We are bidden by these people to make a peace which will make them secure. We are bidden by
these people to see to it that this strain does not come upon them
again, and I venture to say that it has been possible for them to bear
this strain because they hoped that those who represented them could
get together after this war and make such another sacrifice unnecessary.

It is a solemn obligation on our part, therefore, to make permanent
arrangements that justice shall be rendered and peace maintained.
This is the central object of our meeting. Settlements may be tem-

porary, but the action of the nations in the interest of peace and justice must be permanent. We can set up permanent processes. We may not be able to set up permanent decisions. Therefore, it seems to me that we must take, so far as we can, a picture of the world into our minds. Is it not a startling circumstance, for one thing, that the great discoveries of science, that the quiet studies of men in laboratories, that the thoughtful developments which have taken place in quiet lecture rooms, have now been turned to the destruction of civilization? The powers of destruction have not so much multiplied as gained facility. The enemy whom we have just overcome had at his seats of learning some of the principal centers of scientific study and discovery, and he used them in order to make destruction sudden and complete; and only the watchful, continuous cooperation of men can see to it that science as well as armed men is kept within the harness of civilization.

In a sense the United States is less interested in this subject than the other nations here assembled. With her great territory and her extensive sea borders, it is less likely that the United States should suffer from the attack of enemies than that many of the other nations here should suffer; and the ardor of the United States—for it is a very deep and genuine ardor—for the society of nations is not an ardor springing out of fear or apprehension, but an ardor springing out of the ideals which have come to consciousness in this war. In coming into this war the United States never for a moment thought that she was intervening in the politics of Europe or the politics of Asia or the politics of any part of the world. Her thought was that all the world had now become conscious that there was a single cause which turned upon the issues of this war. That was the cause of justice and of liberty for men of every kind and place. Therefore, the United States should feel that its part in this war had been played in vain if there ensued upon it merely a body of European settlements. It would feel that it could not take part in guaranteeing those European settlements unless that guaranty involved the continuous superintendence of the peace of the world by the associated nations of the world.

Therefore, it seems to me that we must concert our best judgment in order to make this League of Nations a vital thing—not merely a formal thing, not an occasional thing, not a thing sometimes called into life to meet an exigency, but always functioning in watchful attendance upon the interests of the nations—and that its continuity should be a vital continuity; that it should have functions that are continuing functions and that do not permit an intermission of its watchfulness and of its labor; that it should be the eye of the nations to keep watch upon the common interest, an eye that does not slumber, an eye that is everywhere watchful and attentive.

And if we do not make it vital, what shall we do? We shall disappoint the expectations of the peoples. This is what their thought centers upon. I have had the very delightful experience of visiting several nations since I came to this side of the water, and every time the voice of the body of the people reaches me through any representative, at the front of its plea stood the hope for the League of Nations. Gentlemen, the select classes of mankind are no longer the governors of mankind. The fortunes of mankind are now in the hands of the plain people of the whole world. Satisfy them, and you have justified their confidence not only but established peace. Fail to satisfy them, and no arrangement that you can make will either set up or steady the peace of the world.

You can imagine, gentlemen, I dare say, the sentiments and the purpose with which the representatives of the United States support this great project for a League of Nations. We regard it as the keystone of the whole program which expressed our purposes and ideals in this war and which the associated nations have accepted as the basis of the settlement. If we returned to the United States without having made every effort in our power to realize this program, we should return to meet the merited scorn of our fellow citizens. For they are a body that constitutes a great democracy. They expect their leaders to speak their thoughts and no private purpose of their own. They expect their representatives to be their servants. We have no choice but to obey their mandate. But it is with the greatest enthusiasm and pleasure that we accept that mandate; and because this is the keystone of the whole fabric, we have pledged our every purpose to it, as we have to every item of the fabric. We would not dare abate a single part of the program which constitutes our instruction. We would not dare compromise upon any matter as the champion of this thing—this peace of the world, this attitude of justice, this principle that we are the masters of no people but are here to see that every people in the world shall choose its own masters and govern its own destinies, not as we wish but as it wishes. We are here to see, in short, that the very foundations of this war are swept away. Those foundations were the private choice of small coteries of civil rulers and military staffs. Those foundations were the aggression of great powers upon the small. Those foundations were the holding together of empires of unwilling subjects by the duress of arms. Those foundations were the power of small bodies of men to work their will upon mankind and use them as pawns in a game. And nothing less than the emancipation of the world from these things will accomplish peace.

You can see that the representatives of the United States are, therefore, never put to the embarrassment of choosing a way of expediency, because they have laid down for them the unalterable lines of principle. And, thank God, those lines have been accepted as the lines of settlement by all the high-minded men who have had to do with the beginnings of this great business.

I hope, Mr. Chairman, that when it is known, as I feel confident it will be known, that we have adopted the principle of the League of Nations and mean to work out that principle in effective action, we shall by that single thing have lifted a great part of the load of anxiety from the hearts of men everywhere. We stand in a peculiar case. As I go about the streets here I see everywhere the American uniform. Those men came into the war after we had uttered our purposes. They came as crusaders, not merely to win a war, but to win a cause; and I am responsible to them, for it fell to me to formulate the purposes for which I asked them to fight, and I, like them, must be a crusader for these things, whatever it costs and whatever it may be necessary to do, in honor, to accomplish the object for which they fought. I have been glad to find from day to day that there is no question of our standing alone in this matter, for there are champions of this cause upon every hand. I am merely avowing this in order that you may understand why, perhaps, it fell to us, who are disengaged from the politics of this great continent and of the Orient, to suggest that this was the keystone of the arch and why it occurred to the generous mind of our president to call upon me to open this debate. It is not because we alone represent this idea, but because it is our privilege to associate ourselves with you in representing it.

I have only tried in what I have said to give you the fountains of the enthusiasm which is within us for this thing, for those fountains spring, it seems to me, from all the ancient wrongs and sympathies of mankind, and the very pulse of the world seems to beat to the surface in this enterprise.

The formation of a league of nations, like most questions of front-rank importance at the Peace Conference, was referred to a special committee created for the purpose of considering the question and of reporting its deliberations back to the Peace Conference. In this committee, President Wilson was the guiding spirit, although the final text of the Covenant of the League shows more traces of the British preliminary draft, as elaborated by Lord Robert Cecil, of England, and General Smuts, of South Africa, than of the American preliminary draft. It was no secret that of the five great powers who were supreme at the Peace Conference, France, Japan and Italy were less enthusiastic about the formation of a league of nations than the United States and Great Britain; and that the final text of the Covenant was in essence an Anglo-American product. On submitting to the Peace Conference, on February 14,

1919, the text of the Covenant as at first drafted, President Wilson's address was as follows:

MR. CHAIRMAN:

I have the honor and as I esteem it the very great privilege of reporting in the name of the commission constituted by this conference on the formulation of a plan for the League of Nations. I am happy to say that it is a unanimous report, a unanimous report from the representatives of fourteen nations—the United States, Great Britain, France, Italy, Japan, Belgium, Brazil, China, Czecho-Slovakia, Greece, Poland, Portugal, Roumania, and Serbia. I think it will be serviceable and interesting if I, with your permission, read the document as the only report we have to make.

[The President then read the text of the Covenant.*]

It gives me pleasure to add to this formal reading of the result of our labors that the character of the discussion which occurred at the sittings of the commission was not only of the most constructive but of the most encouraging sort. It was obvious throughout our discussions that, although there were subjects upon which there were individual differences of judgment, with regard to the method by which our objects should be obtained, there was practically at no point any serious difference of opinion or motive as to the objects which we were seeking. Indeed, while these debates were not made the opportunity for the expression of enthusiasms and sentiments, I think the other members of the commission will agree with me that there was an undertone of high resolve and of enthusiasm for the thing we were trying to do, which was heartening throughout every meeting; because we felt that in a way this conference had entrusted to us the expression of one of its highest and most important purposes, to see to it that the concord of the world in the future with regard to the objects of justice should not be subject to doubt or uncertainty; that the cooperation of the great body of nations should be assured from the first in the maintenance of peace upon the terms of honor and of the strict regard for international obligation. The compulsion of that task was constantly upon us, and at no point was there shown the slightest desire to do anything but suggest the best means to accomplish that great object. There is very great significance, therefore, in the fact that the result was reached unanimously. Fourteen nations were represented, among them all of those powers which for convenience we have called the great powers, and among the rest a representation of the greatest variety of circumstance and interest. So that I think we are justified in saying that it was a representative group of the members of this great conference. The signifi-

*See page 8681.

cance of the result, therefore, has that deepest of all meanings, the union of wills in a common purpose, a union of wills which can not be resisted, and which I dare say no nation will run the risk of attempting to resist.

Now, as to the character of the document. While it has consumed some time to read this document, I think you will see at once that it is, after all, very simple, and in nothing so simple as in the structure which it suggests for the League of Nations—a body of delegates, an executive council, and a permanent secretariat. When it came to the question of determining the character of the representation in the body of delegates, we were all aware of a feeling which is current throughout the world. Inasmuch as I am stating it in the presence of official representatives of the various Governments here present, including myself, I may say that there is a universal feeling that the world can not rest satisfied with merely official guidance. There reached us through many channels the feeling that if the deliberative body of the League was merely to be a body of officials representing the various Governments, the peoples of the world would not be sure that some of the mistakes which preoccupied officials had admittedly made might not be repeated. It was impossible to conceive a method or an assembly so large and various as to be really representative of the great body of the peoples of the world, because, as I roughly reckon it, we represent as we sit around this table more than twelve hundred million people. You can not have a representative assembly of twelve hundred million people, but if you leave it to each Government to have, if it pleases, one or two or three representatives, though only a single vote, it may vary its representation from time to time not only, but it may originate the choice of its several representatives, if it should have several, in different ways. Therefore, we thought that this was a proper and a very prudent concession to the practically universal opinion of plain men everywhere that they wanted the door left open to a variety of representation instead of being confined to a single official body with which they might or might not find themselves in sympathy.

And you will notice that this body has unlimited rights of discussion—I mean of discussion of anything that falls within the field of international relationship—and that it is specially agreed that war or international misunderstandings or anything that may lead to friction and trouble is everybody's business, because it may affect the peace of the world. And in order to safeguard the popular power so far as we could of this representative body it is provided, you will notice, that when a subject is submitted, not to arbitration, but to discussion by the executive council, it can upon the initiative of either one of the parties to the dispute be drawn out of the executive council onto the larger forum of the general body of delegates, because throughout this instrument we are depending primarily and chiefly upon one great force, and that is the moral force of the public opinion of the world—the cleansing and clarifying and compelling influences of publicity—so that intrigues can no longer have their coverts, so that designs that are sinister can at any time be drawn into the open, so that those things that are destroyed by the light may be properly destroyed by the overwhelming light of the universal expression of the condemnation of the world.

Armed force is in the background in this program, but it *is* in the background, and if the moral force of the world will not suffice, the physical force of the world shall. But that is the last resort, because this is intended as a constitution of peace, not as a league of war.

The simplicity of the document seems to me to be one of its chief virtues, because, speaking for myself, I was unable to forsee the variety of circumstances with which this League would have to deal. I was unable, therefore, to plan all the machinery that might be necessary to meet differing and unexpected contingencies. Therefore, I should say of this document that it is not a straitjacket, but a vehicle of life. A living thing is born, and we must see to it that the clothes we put upon it do not hamper it—a vehicle of power, but a vehicle in which power may be varied at the discretion of those who exercise it and in accordance with the changing circumstances of the time. And yet, while it is elastic, while it is general in its terms, it is definite in the one thing that we were called upon to make definite. It is a definite guarantee of peace. It is a definite guarantee by word against aggression. It is a definite guarantee against the things which have just come near bringing the whole structure of civilization into ruin. Its purposes do not for a moment lie vague. Its purposes are declared and its powers made unmistakable.

It is not in contemplation that this should be merely a League to secure the peace of the world. It is a League which can be used for cooperation in any international matter. That is the significance of the provision introduced concerning labor. There are many ameliorations of labor conditions which can be affected by conference and discussion. I anticipate that there will be a very great usefulness in the bureau of labor which it is contemplated shall be set up by the League. While men and women and children who work have been in the background through long ages, and sometimes seemed to be forgotten, while Governments have had their watchful and suspicious eyes upon the maneuvers of one another, while the thought of statesmen has been about structural action and the large transactions of commerce and of finance, now, if I may believe the picture which I see, there comes into the foreground the great body of the laboring people of the world, the men and women and children upon whom the great burden of sustaining the world must from day to day fall, whether we wish it to do so or not; people who go to bed tired and wake up without the stimulation of lively hope. These people will be drawn into the field of international consultation and help, and will be among the wards of the combined Governments of the world. There is, I take leave to say, a very great step in advance in the mere conception of that.

Then, as you will notice, there is an imperative article concerning the publicity of all international agreements. Henceforth no member of the League can claim any agreement valid which it has not registered with the secretary general, in whose office, of course, it will be subject to the examination of anybody representing a member of the League. And the duty is laid upon the secretary general to publish every document of that sort at the earliest possible time. I suppose most persons who have not been conversant with the business of foreign offices do not realize how many hundreds of these agreements are made in a single year, and how difficult it might be to publish the more unimportant of them immediately—how uninteresting it would be to most of the world to publish them immediately—but even they must be published just so soon as it is possible for the secretary general to publish them.

Then there is a feature about this Covenant which to my mind is one of the greatest and most satisfactory advances that have been made. We are done with annexations of helpless people, meant in some instances by some powers to be used merely for exploitation. We recognize in the most solemn manner that the helpless and undeveloped peoples of the world, being in that condition, put an obligation upon us to look after their interests primarily before we use them for our interest; and that in all cases of this sort hereafter it shall be the duty of the League to see that the nations who are assigned as the tutors and advisers and directors of those peoples shall look to their interest and to their development before they look to the interests and material desires of the mandatory nation itself. There has been no greater advance than this, gentlemen. If you look back upon the history of the world you will see how helpless peoples have too often been a prey to powers that had no conscience in the matter. It has been one of the many distressing revelations of recent years that the great power which has just been happily defeated put intolerable burdens and injustices upon the helpless people of some of the colonies which it annexed to itself; that its interest was rather their extermination than their development; that the desire was to possess their land for European purposes, and not to enjoy their confidence in order that mankind might be lifted in those places to the

AN ABANDONED "TANK"

AN ABANDONED "TANK."

The caterpillar tractor, or "tank," shown in the foreground has been rendered "hors de combat" and has been abandoned in a trench. On the tank may be seen the variegated paint designs (camouflage) used for the purpose of confusing the enemy as to the exact outlines of the machine and the exact direction in which it is moving. The illustration gives an excellent idea of the appearance of a trench after it has been mercilessly pounded by fire and of the transformation of the once fair lands of northern France and Belgium into a desert by the mutilations of modern war. At the extreme right may be discerned the body of one who made the supreme sacrifice and in the background other tanks are advancing upon the enemy.

next higher level. Now, the world, expressing its conscience in law, says there is an end of that. Our consciences shall be applied to this thing. States will be picked out which have already shown that they can exercise a conscience in this matter, and under their tutelage the helpless peoples of the world will come into a new light and into a new hope.

So I think I can say of this document that it is at one and the same time a practical document and a humane document. There is a pulse of sympathy in it. There is a compulsion of conscience throughout it. It is practical, and yet it is intended to purify, to rectify, to elevate. And I want to say that, so far as my observation instructs me, this is in one sense a belated document. I believe that the conscience of the world has long been prepared to express itself in some such way. We are not just now discovering our sympathy for these people and our interest in them. We are simply expressing it, for it has long been felt, and in the administration of the affairs of more than one of the great States represented here—so far as I know, of all the great States that are represented here—that humane impulse has already expressed itself in their dealings with their colonies whose peoples were yet at a low stage of civilization. We have had many instances of colonies lifted into the sphere of complete self-government. This is not the discovery of a principle. It is the universal application of a principle. It is the agreement of the great nations which have tried to live by these standards in their separate administrations to unite in seeing that their common force and their common thought and intelligence are lent to this great and humane enterprise. I think it is an occasion, therefore, for the most profound satisfaction that this humane decision should have been reached in a matter for which the world has long been waiting and until a very recent period thought that it was still too early to hope.

Many terrible things have come out of this war, gentlemen, but some very beautiful things have come out of it. Wrong has been defeated, but the rest of the world has been more conscious than it ever was before of the majesty of right. People that were suspicious of one another can now live as friends and comrades in a single family, and desire to do so. The miasma of distrust, of intrigue, is cleared away. Men are looking eye to eye and saying, "We are brothers and have a common purpose. We did not realize it before, but now we do realize it, and this is our covenant of fraternity and of friendship."

The complete text of the League of Nations, as finally adopted by the Paris Conference, was as follows:

In order to promote international co-operation and to achieve international peace and security, by the acceptance of obligations not to resort to war, by the prescription of open, just and honorable relations between nations, by the firm establishment of the understandings of international law as to actual rule of conduct among governments, and by the maintenance of justice and a scrupulous respect for all treaty obligations in the dealings of organized peoples with one another, the high contracting parties agree to this Covenant of the League of Nations.

Article One—The original members of the League of Nations shall be those of the signatories which are named in the annex to this Covenant and also such of those other States named in the annex as shall accede without reservation to this Covenant. Such accessions shall be effected by a declaration deposited with the Secretariat within two months of the coming into force of the Covenant. Notice thereof shall be sent to all other members of the League.

Any fully self-governing state, dominion or colony not named in the annex, may become a member of the League of Nations if its admission is agreed to by two-thirds of the assembly, provided that it shall give effective guarantees of its sincere intention to observe its international obligations, and shall accept such regulations as may be prescribed by the League in regard to its military and naval forces and armaments.

Any member of the League may, after two years' notice of its intention so to do, withdraw from the League, provided that all its international obligations and all its obligations under this Covenant shall have been fulfilled at the time of its withdrawal.

Article Two—The action of the League under this Covenant shall be effected through the instrumentality of an assembly and a council, with a permanent secretariat.

Article Three—The assembly shall consist of representatives of the members of the League.

The assembly shall meet at stated intervals and from time to time as occasion may require, at the seat of the League, or at such other place as may be decided upon.

The assembly may deal at its meetings with any matter within the sphere of action of the League or affecting the peace of the world.

At meetings of the assembly, each member of the League shall have one vote, and may have not more than three representatives.

Article Four—The council shall consist of representatives of the United States of America, of the British Empire, of France, of Italy, and of Japan, together with representatives of four other members of the League. These four members of the League shall be selected by the assembly from time to time in its discretion. Until the appointment of the representatives of the four members of the League first selected by the assembly, representatives of——* shall be members of the council.

With the approval of the majority of the assembly, the council may name additional members of the League whose representatives shall always be members of the council; the council with like approval may increase the number of members of the League to be selected by the assembly for representation on the council.

The council shall meet from time to time as occasion may require, and at least once a year, at the seat of the League, or at other places as may be decided upon.

The council may deal at its meetings with any matter within the sphere of action of the League or affecting the peace of the world.

Any member of the League not represented on the council shall be invited to send a representative to sit as a member at any meeting of the council during

*See page 8683.

the consideration of matters specially affecting the interests of that member of the League.

At meetings of the council, each member of the League represented on the council shall have one vote, and may have not more than one representative.

Article Five—Except where otherwise expressly provided in this Covenant or by the terms of this treaty, decisions at any meeting of the assembly or of the council shall require the agreement of all the members of the League represented at the meeting.

All matters of procedure at meetings of the assembly or of the council, the appointment of committees to investigate particular matters, shall be regulated by the assembly or by the council and may be decided by a majority of the members of the League represented at the meeting.

The first meeting of the assembly and the first meeting at the council shall be summoned by the President of the United States of America.

Article Six—The permanent secretariat shall be established at the seat of the League. The secretariat shall comprise a secretariat general and such secretaries and staff as may be required.

The first secretary general shall be the person named in the annex; thereafter the secretary general shall be appointed by the council with the approval of the majority of the assembly.

The secretariat and the staff of the secretariat shall be appointed by the secretary general with the approval of the council.

The secretary general shall act in that capacity at all meetings of the assembly and of the council.

The expenses of the secretariat shall be borne by the members of the League in accordance with the apportionment of the expenses of the International Bureau of the Universal Postal Union.

Article Seven—The seat of the League is established at Geneva.

The council may at any time decide that the seat of the League shall be established elsewhere.

All positions under or in connection with the League, including the secretariat, shall be open equally to men and women.

Representatives of the members of the League and officials of the League when engaged on the business of the League shall enjoy diplomatic privileges and immunities.

The buildings and other property occupied by the League or its officials or by representatives attending its meetings shall be inviolable.

Article Eight—The members of the League recognize that the maintenance of peace requires the reduction of national armaments to the lowest point consistent with national safety and the enforcement by the common action of international obligations.

The council, taking account of the geographical situation and circumstances of each state, shall formulate plans for such reduction for the consideration and action of the several governments.

Such plans shall be subject to reconsideration and revision at least every ten years.

After these plans shall have been adopted by the several governments, limits of armaments therein fixed shall not be exceeded without the concurrence of the council.

The members of the League agree that the manufacture by private enterprise of munitions and implements of war is open to grave objections. The council shall advise how the evil effects attendant upon such manufacture can be prevented, due regard being had to the necessities of those members of the League which are not able to manufacture the munitions and implements of war necessary for their safety.

The members of the League undertake to interchange full and frank information as to the scale of their armaments, their military and naval programs and the condition of such of their industries as are adaptable to war-like purposes.

Article Nine—A permanent commission shall be constituted to advise the council on the execution of the provisions of Article One and Eight and on military and naval questions generally.

Article Ten—The members of the League undertake to respect and preserve as against external aggression the territorial integrity and existing political independence of all members of the League. In case of any such aggression or in case of any threat or danger of such aggression, the council shall advise upon the means by which this obligation shall be fulfilled.

Article Eleven—Any war or threat of war, whether immediately affecting any of the members of the League or not, is hereby declared a matter of concern to the whole League, and the League shall take any action that may be deemed wise and effectual to safeguard the peace of nations. In case any such emergency should arise, the secretary general shall, on the request of any member of the League, forthwith summon a meeting of the council.

It is also declared to be the fundamental right of each member of the League to bring to the attention of the assembly or of the council any circumstance whatever affecting international relations which threatens to disturb either the peace or the good understanding between nations upon which peace depends.

Article Twelve—The members of the League agree that if there should arise between them any dispute likely to lead to a rupture, they will submit the matter either to arbitration or to inquiry by the council, and they agree in no case to resort to war until three months after the award by the arbitrators or the report of the council.

In any case under this article the award of the arbitrators shall be made within a reasonable time, and the report of the council shall be made within six months after the submission of the dispute.

Article Thirteen—The members of the League agree that whenever any dispute shall arise between them which they recognize to be suitable for submission to arbitration and which cannot be satisfactorily settled by diplomacy, they will submit the whole subject matter to arbitration. Disputes as to the interpretation of a treaty, as to any question of international law, as to the existence of any fact which if established would constitute a breach of any international obligation, or as to the extent and nature of the reparation to be made for any such breach, are declared to be among those which are generally suitable for submission to arbitration. For the consideration of any such dispute the court of arbitration to which the case is referred shall be the court agreed on by the parties to the dispute or stipulated in any convention existing between them.

The members of the League agree that they will carry out in full good faith any award that may be rendered and that they will not resort to war against a member of the League which complies therewith. In the event of any failure to carry out such an award, the council shall propose what steps should be taken to give effect thereto.

Article Fourteen—The council shall formulate and submit to the members of the League for adoption plans for the establishment of a permanent court of international justice. The court shall be competent to hear and determine any dispute of an international character which the parties thereto submit to it. The court may also give an advisory opinion upon any dispute or question referred to it by the council or by the assembly.

Article Fifteen—If there should arise between members of the League any dispute likely to lead to a rupture, which is not submitted to arbitration as above, the members of the League agree that they will submit the matter to the council. Any party to the dispute may effect such submission by giving notice of the existence of the dispute to the secretary general, who will make all necessary arrangements for a full investigation and consideration thereof. For this purpose the parties to the dispute will communicate to the secretary general, as promptly as possible, statements of their case, all the relevant facts and papers; the council may forthwith direct the publication thereof.

The council shall endeavor to effect a settlement of any dispute, and if such efforts are successful, a statement shall be made public giving such facts and explanations regarding the dispute and terms of settlement thereof as the council may deem appropriate.

If the dispute is not thus settled, the council either unanimously or by a majority vote shall make and publish a report containing a statement of the facts of the dispute and the recommendations which are deemed just and proper in regard thereto.

Any member of the League represented on the council may make public a statement of the facts of the dispute and of its conclusions regarding the same.

If a report by the council is unanimously agreed to by the members thereof other than the representatives of one or more of the parties to the dispute, the members of the League agree that they will not go to war with any party to the dispute which complies with the recommendations of the report.

If the council fails to reach a report which is unanimously agreed to by the members thereof, other than the representatives of one or more of the parties to the dispute, the members of the league reserve to themselves the right to take such action as they shall consider necessary for the maintenance of right and justice.

If the dispute between the parties is claimed by one of them, and is found by the council, to arise out of a matter which by international law is solely within the domestic jurisdiction of that party, the council shall so report, and shall make no recommendation as to its settlement.

The council may in any case under this article refer the dispute to the assembly. The dispute shall be so referred at the request of either party to the dispute provided that such request be made within fourteen days after the submission of the dispute to the council.

In any case referred to the assembly all the provisions of Article Twelve relating to the action and powers of the council shall apply to the action and powers of the assembly, provided that a report made by the assembly, if concurred in by the representatives of those members of the League represented on the council and of a majority of the other members of the League, exclusive in each case of the representatives of the parties to the dispute, shall have the same force as a report by the council concurred in by all the members thereof other than the representatives of one or more of the parties to the dispute.

Article Sixteen—Should any member of the League resort to war in disregard of its covenants under Articles Twelve, Thirteen or Fifteen, it shall ipso facto be deemed to have committed an act of war against all other members of the League, which hereby undertake immediately to subject it to the severance of all trade or financial relations, the prohibition of all intercourse between their nationals and the nationals of the Covenant-breaking state and the prevention of all financial, commercial, or personal intercourse between the nationals of the Covenant-breaking state and the nationals of any other state, whether a member of the League or not.

It shall be the duty of the council in such case to recommend to the several governments concerned what effective military or naval forces the members of the League shall severally contribute to the armaments of forces to be used to protect the covenants of the League.

The members of the League agree, further, that they will mutually support one another in the financial and economic measures which are taken under this article, in order to minimize the loss and inconvenience resulting from the above measures, and that they will mutually support one another in resisting any special measures aimed at one of their number by the Covenant-breaking state, and that they will take the necessary steps to afford passage through their territory to the forces of any of the members of the League which are co-operating to protect the covenants of the League.

Any member of the League which has violated any Covenant of the League may be declared to be no longer a member of the League by a vote of the council concurred in by the representatives of all the other members of the League represented thereon.

Article Seventeen—In the event of a dispute between a member of the League and a state which is not a member of the League, or between states not members of the League, the state or states not members of the League shall be invited to accept the obligations of membership in the League for the purposes of such dispute, upon such conditions as the council may deem just. If such invitation is accepted, the provisions of Articles Twelve to Sixteen inclusive shall be applied with such modifications as may be deemed necessary by the council.

Upon such invitation being given, the council shall immediately institute an inquiry into the circumstances of the dispute and recommend such action as may seem best and most effectual in the circumstances.

If a state so invited shall refuse to accept the obligations of membership in the League for the purposes of such dispute, and shall resort to war against a member of the League, the provisions of Article Sixteen shall be applicable as against the state taking such action.

If both parties to the dispute, when so invited, refuse to accept the obligations of membership in the League for the purpose of such dispute, the council may take such measures and make such recommendations as will prevent hostilities and will result in the settlement of the dispute.

Article Eighteen—Every convention or international engagement entered into henceforward by any member of the League, shall be forthwith registered with the secretariat and shall as soon as possible be published by it. No such treaty or international engagement shall be binding until so registered.

Article Nineteen—The assembly may from time to time advise the reconsideration by members of the League of treaties which have become inapplicable, and the consideration of international conditions whose continuance might endanger the peace of the world.

Article Twenty—The members of the League severally agree that this Covenant is accepted as abrogating all obligations or understandings inter se which are inconsistent with the terms thereof, and solemnly undertake that they will not hereafter enter into any engagements inconsistent with the terms thereof.

In case a member of the League shall, before becoming a member of the League, have undertaken any obligations inconsistent with the terms of this Covenant, it shall be the duty of such member to take immediate steps to procure its release from such obligations.

Article Twenty-One—Nothing in this Covenant shall be deemed to affect the validity of international engagements such as treaties of arbitration or regional understandings like the Monroe Doctrine for securing the maintenance of peace.

Article Twenty-Two—To those colonies and territories which as a consequence of the late war have ceased to be under the sovereignty of the states which formerly governed them and which are inhabited by peoples not yet able to stand by themselves under the strenuous conditions of the modern world, there should be applied the principle that the well-being and development of such peoples form a sacred trust of civilization and that securities for the performance of this trust should be embodied in this covenant.

The best method of giving practicable effect to this principle is that the tutelage of such peoples be entrusted to advanced nations who, by reasons of their resources, their experience or their geographical position, can best undertake this responsibility, and who are willing to accept it, and that this tutelage should be exercised by them as mandatories on behalf of the League.

The character of the mandate must differ according to the stage of the development of the people, the geographical situation of the territory, its economic condition and other similar circumstances.

Certain communities formerly belonging to the Turkish Empire have reached a stage of development where their existence as independent nations can be provisionally recognized subject to the rendering of administrative advice and assistance by a mandatory until such time as they are able to stand alone. The wishes of these communities must be a principal consideration in the selection of the mandatory.

Other peoples, especially those of Central Africa, are at such a stage that the mandatory must be responsible for the administration of the territory under conditions which will guarantee freedom of conscience or religion subject only to the maintenance of public order and morals, the prohibition of abuses such as the slave trade, the arms traffic and the liquor traffic and the prevention of the establishment of fortifications or military and naval bases and of military training of the natives for other than police purposes and the defense of territory, and will also secure equal opportunities for the trade and commerce of other members of the League.

There are territories, such as Southwest Africa and certain of the South Pacific islands, which, owing to the sparseness of their population, or their small size or their remoteness from the centres of civilization or their geographical contiguity to the territory of the mandatory and other circumstances, can be best administered under the laws of the mandatory as integral portions of its territory, subject to the safeguards above mentioned in the interests of the indigenous population. In every case of mandate, the mandatory shall render to the council an annual report in reference to the territory committed to its charge.

The degree of authority, control or administration to be exercised by the mandatory shall, if not previously agreed upon by the member of the League, be explicitly defined in each case by the council.

A permanent commission shall be constituted to receive and examine the annual reports of the mandatories and to advise the council on all matters relating to the observance of the mandates.

Article Twenty-Three—Subject to and in accordance with the provisions of international conventions existing or hereafter to be agreed upon, the members of the League (a) will endeavor to secure and maintain fair and humane conditions of labor for men, women and children both in their own countries and in all countries to which their commercial and industrial relations extend, and for that purpose will establish and maintain the necessary international organizations; (b) undertake to secure just treatment of the native inhabitants of territories under their control; (c) will entrust the League with the general supervision over the execution of agreements with regard to the traffic in women and children, and the traffic in opium and other dangerous drugs; (d) will entrust the League with the general supervision of the trade in arms and ammunition with the countries in which the control of this traffic is necessary in the common interests; (e) will make provisions to secure and maintain freedom of communication and of transit and equitable treatment for the commerce of all members of the League. In this connection the special necessities of the regions devastated during the war of 1914-1918 shall be borne in mind; (f) will endeavor to take steps in matters of international concern for the prevention and control of disease.

Article Twenty-Four—There shall be placed under the direction of the League all international bureaus already established by general treaties if the parties to such treaties consent. All such international bureaus and commissions for the regulation of matters of international interest hereafter constituted shall be placed under the direction of the League.

In all matters of international interest which are regulated by general conventions but which are not placed under the control of international bureaus or commissions, the secretariat of the League shall, subject to the consent of the council and if desired by the parties, collect and distribute all relevant information and shall render any other assistance which may be necessary or desirable.

The council may include as part of the expenses of the secretariat the expenses of any bureau or commission which is placed under the direction of the League.

Article Twenty-Five—The members of the League agree to encourage and promote the establishment and co-operation of duly authorized voluntary national Red Cross organizations having as purposes improvement of health, the prevention of disease and the mitigation of suffering throughout the world.

Article Twenty-Six—Amendments to this Covenant will take effect when ratified by the members of the League whose representatives compose the council and by a majority of the members of the League whose representatives compose the assembly.

No such amendment shall bind any member of the League which signifies its dissent therefrom, but in that case it shall cease to be a member of the League.

Original members of the League of Nations—
    Signatories of the Treaty of Peace:
    United States of America, Belgium, Bolivia, Brazil, British Empire, Canada, Australia, South Africa, New Zealand, India, China, Cuba, Czecho-Slovakia, Ecuador, France, Greece, Guatemala, Haiti, Hedjaz, Honduras, Italy, Japan,

Liberia, Nicaragua, Panama, Peru, Poland, Portugal, Roumania, Servia, Siam, Uruguay.

States invited to accede to the Covenant:

Argentine Republic, Chile, Columbia, Denmark, Netherlands, Norway, Paraguay, Persia, Salvador, Spain, Sweden, Switzerland, Venezuela.

The above final text of the Covenant of the League of Nations is different in a number of respects from the first draft of the Covenant, as adopted on February 14. The first draft called forth a storm of protest, with the result that changes were made. The changes are succinctly indicated by the following address of President Wilson to the Peace Conference on April 28, when the final draft of the Covenant was adopted:

MR. CHAIRMAN: When the text of the Covenant of the League of Nations was laid before you I had the honor of reading the Covenant in extenso. I will not detain you to-day to read the Covenant as it has now been altered, but will merely take the liberty of explaining to you some of the alterations that have been made.

The report of the commission has been circulated. You yourselves have in hand the text of the Covenant, and will no doubt have noticed that most of the changes that have been made are mere changes of phraseology, not changes of substance, and that, besides that, most of the changes are intended to clarify the document, or, rather, to make explicit what we all have assumed was implicit in the document as it was originally presented to you. But I shall take the liberty of calling your attention to the new features, such as they are. Some of them are considerable, the rest trivial.

The first paragraph of Article I is new. In view of the insertion of the Covenant in the peace treaty, specific provision as to the signatories of the treaty, who would become members of the League, and also as to neutral states to be invited to accede to the Covenant, were obviously necessary. The paragraph also provides for the method by which a neutral state may accede to the Covenant.

The third paragraph of Article I is new, providing for the withdrawal of any member of the League on a notice given of two years.

The second paragraph of Article IV is new, providing for a possible increase in the council, should other powers be added to the League of Nations whose present accession is not anticipated.

The two last paragraphs of Article IV are new, providing specifically for one vote for each member of the League in the council, which was understood before, and providing also for one representative of each member of the League.

The first paragraph of Article V is new, expressly incorporating the provision as to the unanimity of voting, which was at first taken for granted.

The second paragraph of Article VI has had added to it that a majority of the assembly must approve the appointment of the secretary general.

The first paragraph of Article VII names Geneva as the seat of the League and is followed by a second paragraph which gives the council power to establish the seat of the League elsewhere should it subsequently deem it necessary.

The third paragraph of Article VII is new, establishing equality of employment of men and women, that is to say, by the League.

The second paragraph of Article VIII is new, inasmuch as it undertakes to give instances of disputes which are generally suitable for submission to arbitration, instances of what have latterly been called "justiciable" questions.

The eighth paragraph of Article XV is new. This is the amendment regarding domestic jurisdiction, that where the council finds that a question arising out of an international dispute affects matters which are clearly under the domestic jurisdiction of one or other of the parties it is to report to that effect and make no recommendation.

The last paragraph of Article XVI is new, providing for expulsion from the League in certain extraordinary circumstances.

Article XXI is new.

The second paragraph of Article XXII inserts the words with regard to mandatories: "and who are willing to accept it," thus explicitly introducing the principle that a mandate cannot be forced upon a nation unwilling to accept it.

Article XXIII is a combination of several former articles and also contains the following: A clause providing for the just treatment of aborigines; a clause looking toward a prevention of the white slave traffic and the traffic in opium, and a clause looking toward progress in international prevention and control of disease.

Article XXV specifically mentions the Red Cross as one of the international organizations which are to connect their work with the work of the League.

Article XXVI permits the amendment of the Covenant by a majority of the states composing the assembly, instead of three-fourths of the states, though it does not change the requirements in that matter with regard to the vote in the council.

The second paragraph of Article XXVI also is new, and was added at the request of the Brazilian delegation, in order to avoid certain constitutional difficulties. It permits any member of the League to dissent from an amendment, the effect of such dissent being withdrawal from the League.

And the annex is added giving the names of the signatories of the treaty, who becomes members, and the names of the states invited to accede to the Covenant. These are all the changes, I believe, which are of moment.

Mr. President, I take the opportunity to move the following resolutions in order to carry out the provisions of the Covenant. You will notice that the Covenant provides that the first secretary-general shall be chosen by this conference. It also provides that the first choice of the four member states who are to be added to the five great Powers on the council is left to this conference.

I move, therefore, that the first secretary general of the council shall be the Honorable Sir James Eric Drummond, and, second, that until such time as the assembly shall have selected the first four members of the League to be represented on the council in accordance with Article IV of the Covenant representatives of Belgium, Brazil, Greece and Spain shall be members; and, third, that the powers to be represented on the council of the League of Nations are requested to name representatives who shall form a committee of nine to prepare plans for the organization of the League and for the establishment of the seat of the League and to make arrangements and to prepare the agenda for the first meeting of the assembly, this committee to report both to the council and to the assembly of the League.

I think it not necessary to call your attention to other matters we have previously discussed—the capital significance of this Covenant, the hopes which are entertained as to the effect it will have upon steadying the affairs of the world, and the obvious necessity that there should be a concert of the free nations of the world to maintain justice in international relations, the relations between people and between the nations of the world.

If Baron Makino will pardon me for introducing a matter which I absentmindedly overlooked, it is necessary for me to propose the alteration of several words in the first line of Article V. Let me say that in several parts of the treaty, of which this Covenant will form a part, certain duties are assigned to the council of the League of Nations. In some instances it is provided that the action they shall take shall be by a majority vote. It is therefore necessary to make the Covenant conform with the other portions of the treaty by adding these words. I will read the first line and add the words:

"Except where otherwise expressly provided in this Covenant, or by the terms of this treaty, decisions at any meeting of the assembly or of the council shall require the agreement of all the members of the League represented at the meeting."

"Except where otherwise expressly provided in this Covenant" is the present reading, and I move the addition "or by the terms of this treaty." With that addition, I move the adoption of the Covenant.

CABLEGRAMS

[To the Secretary of the Treasury, Transmitted Through the Secretary of State, Requesting Appropriation for Food Relief in Europe.]

January 4, 1919.

Extended investigation and consideration of the food situation in certain parts of Europe disclose that especially the urban populations in certain areas are not only facing absolute starvation during the coming winter, but that many of these populations are unable to find immediate resources with which to purchase their food. These regions have been so subjected to destruction by war, not only of their foodstuffs but of their financial resources and their power of production and export, that they are utterly incapable of finding any resources that can be converted into international exchange for food purchases. While the Secretary of the Treasury can accept obligations of certain governments and through these measures their situations can be cared for temporarily, there are still other areas through eastern and southern Europe where such arrangements can not be made. This applies more particularly to the liberated peoples of Austria, Turkey, Poland, and western Russia. In these countries freedom and government will slowly emerge from the chaos and require our every assistance.

The total shipments of foodstuffs from the United States to all parts of Europe during the next seven months will be likely to exceed one and one-half billion dollars, and from our abundance we can surely afford to offer succor to those countries destitute of resources or credit. The minimum sums upon which this work can be carried on for the next six months in the countries above mentioned will amount to at least $100,000,000 for such services and supplies as we can render, and even this sum contemplates the finding of resources by so much of the population as can do so and as much assistance as can be given by the Allied governments. The high mission of the American people to find a remedy for starvation and absolute anarchy renders it necessary that we should undertake the most liberal assistance to these destitute regions.

The situation is one of extreme urgency, for foodstuffs must be placed in certain localities within the next fifteen to thirty days if human life and order are to be preserved. I, therefore, request that you ask Congress to make available to me an immediate appropriation of $100,000,000 for the broad purpose of providing foodstuffs and other urgent supplies, for the transportation, distribution, and administration thereof to such populations in Europe, outside of Germany, as may be determined upon by me from time to time as necessary. I wish to appeal to the great sense of charity and good will of the American people toward the suffering, and to place this act upon a primarily humanitarian basis of the first magnitude. While the sum of money is in itself large, it is so small compared with the expenditures we have undertaken in the hope of bettering the world, that it becomes a mere pittance compared to the results that will be obtained from it, and the lasting effect that will remain in the United States through an act of such broad humanity and statesmanlike influence.

[To Chairmen of the Congressional Committees on Appropriations, Asking Passage of Bill Providing for Food Relief.]

January 13, 1919.

I cannot too earnestly or solemnly urge upon the Congress the appropriation for which Mr. Hoover has asked for the administration of food relief. Food relief is now the key to the whole European situation and to the solutions of peace; Bolshevism is steadily advancing westward, is poisoning Germany. It cannot be stopped by force, but it can be stopped by food, and all the leaders with whom I am in conference agree that concerted action in this matter is of immediate and vital importance.

The money will not be spent for food for Germany itself, because Germany can buy its food; but it will be spent for financing the movement of food to our real friends in Poland and to the people of the liberated units of the Austro-Hungarian empire and to our associates in the Balkans. I beg that you will present this matter with all possible urgency and force to the Congress.

I do not see how we can find definite powers with whom to conclude peace unless this means of stemming the tide of anarchism be employed.

By the President of the United States of America

PROCLAMATIONS

[Announcing the Death of Ex-President Theodore Roosevelt.]

To the People of the United States:

It becomes my sad duty to announce officially the death of Theodore Roosevelt, President of the United States from September 14, 1901 to March 4, 1909, which occurred at his home at Sagamore Hill, Oyster Bay, New York, at 4:15 o'clock in the morning of January 6, 1919. In his death the United States has lost one of its most distinguished and patriotic citizens, who had endeared himself to the people by his strenuous devotion to their interests and to the public interests of his country.

As President of the Police Board of his native city, as Member of the Legislature and Governor of his State, as Civil Service Commissioner, as Assistant Secretary of the Navy, as Vice-President and as President of the United States, he displayed administrative powers of a signal order and conducted the affairs of these various offices with a concentration of effort and a watchful care which permitted no divergence from the line of duty he had definitely set for himself.

In the War with Spain, he displayed singular initiative and energy and distinguished himself among the commanders of the army in the field. As President he awoke the Nation to the dangers of private control which lurked in our financial and industrial systems. It was by thus arresting the attention and stimulating the purpose of the country that he opened the way for subsequent necessary and beneficent reforms.

His private life was characterized by a simplicity, a virtue and an affection worthy of all admiration and emulation by the people of America.

In testimony of the respect in which his memory is held by the Government and people of the United States, I do hereby direct that the flags of the White House and the several Departmental Buildings be displayed at half staff for a period of thirty days, and that suitable military and naval honors under orders of the Secretaries of War and of the Navy may be rendered on the day of the funeral.

Done this seventh day of January, in the year of Our Lord one thousand nine hundred and nineteen, and of the Independ-
[SEAL.]   ence of the United States of America the one hundred and forty-third.

                                    WOODROW WILSON.

By the President:

ROBERT LANSING, *Secretary of State.*

[Appointing Walker D. Hines Director General of Railroads.]

Whereas, by the proclamation dated December 26, 1917, taking over each and every system of transportation and the appurtenances thereof located wholly or in part within the boundaries of the continental United States, it was provided "that the possession, control, operation, and utilization of such transportation systems hereby by me undertaken shall be exercised by and through William G. McAdoo, who is hereby appointed and designated Director General of Railroads;" and

Whereas, by a subsequent proclamation dated April 11, 1918, certain other systems of transportation were taken under Federal control; and

Whereas, the said William G. McAdoo, Director General of Railroads as aforesaid, has tendered his resignation which has been duly accepted:

Now, therefore, I, Woodrow Wilson, President of the United States, under and by virtue of the powers and authority vested in me by law affecting the Federal control of railroads and systems of transportation, and of all powers me hereto enabling, do hereby appoint Walker D. Hines, of New York, Director General of Railroads, and authorize him, either personally or through such divisions, agencies, or persons as he may appoint, in his own name or in the name of such divisions, agencies, or persons, or in the name of the President, to agree with the carriers or any of them or with any other person in interest, upon the amount of compensation to be paid pursuant to law, and to sign, seal, and deliver in his own name or in the name of the President or in the name of the United States of America such agreements as may be necessary and expedient with the carriers or other persons in interest respecting compensation, or any other matter concerning which it may be necessary or expedient to deal, and to make any and all contracts, agreements, or obligations necessary or expedient and to issue any and all orders which may in any way be found necessary and expedient in connection with the Federal control of such systems of transportation, railroads, or inland waterways, as fully in all respects as the President is authorized to do, and generally to do and perform all and singular all acts and things and to exercise all and singular the powers and duties in relation to such Federal control as the President is by law empowered to do and perform.

In witness whereof, I have hereunto set my hand and caused the seal of the United States to be affixed.

Done this tenth day of January, in the year of our Lord one thousand nine hundred and nineteen, and of the Independence [SEAL.] of the United States of America the one hundred and forty-third.

WOODROW WILSON.

By the President:

FRANK L. POLK, *Acting Secretary of State*

[Permitting the Use of Grain in the Manufacture of Non-Intoxicating Beverages.]

Whereas, under and by virtue of an act of Congress entitled "An Act to Provide further for the National Security and Defense by encouraging the production, conserving the supply, and controlling the distribution of food products and fuel," approved August 10, 1917, the President, on the 16th day of September, 1918, made the following proclamation:

[Here follows the Proclamation to be found on pages 8583-4.]

And whereas the prohibition of the use of grain in the manufacture of beverages which are not intoxicating has been found by the President to be no longer essential in order to assure an adequate and continuous supply of food:

Now, therefore, I do hereby modify the aforesaid proclamation made on the 16th day of September, 1918, to the extent of permitting the use of grain in the manufacture of beverages which are not intoxicating.

In witness whereof, I have hereunto set my hand and caused the seal of the United States to be affixed.

Done this thirteenth day of January in the year of our Lord one thousand nine hundred and nineteen, and of the Independ-
[SEAL]   ence of the United States of America the one hundred and forty-third.

WOODROW WILSON.

By the President:
ROBERT LANSING, *Secretary of State.*

PROCLAMATION

[Announcing Prohibition Amendment to United States Constitution.]

To All to whom These Presents Shall Come, Greeting:

Know ye, that the Congress of the United States, at the second session of the Sixty-fifth Congress begun at Washington on the third day of December in the year one thousand nine hundred and seventeen, passed a resolution in the words and figures following, to wit:

"Joint resolution, proposing an amendment to the Constitution of the United States:

Resolved, by the Senate and House of Representatives of the United States of America in Congress Assembled (two-thirds of each House concurring therein), That the following amendment to the Constitution be, and hereby is, proposed to the states, to become valid as a part of the Constitution when ratified by the legislatures of the several states as provided by the Constitution:

Section 1. After one year from the ratification of this article the manufacture, sale or transportation of intoxicating liquors within, the importation thereof into, or the exportation thereof from the United States and all territory subject to the jurisdiction thereof for beverage purposes is hereby prohibited.

Section 2. The Congress and the several states shall have concurrent power to enforce this article by appropriate legislation.

Section 3. This article shall be inoperative unless it shall have been ratified as an amendment to the Constitution by the legislatures of the several states, as provided in the Constitution, within seven years from the date of the submission hereof to the states by the Congress."

And, further, that it appears from official documents on file in this department that the amendment to the Constitution of the United States proposed as aforesaid has been ratified by the legislatures of the states of Alabama, Arizona, California, Colorado, Delaware, Florida, Georgia, Idaho, Illinois, Indiana, Kansas, Kentucky, Louisiana, Maine, Maryland, Massachusetts, Michigan, Minnesota, Mississippi, Montana, Nebraska, New Hampshire, North Carolina, North Dakota, Ohio, Oklahoma, Oregon, South Dakota, South Carolina, Texas, Utah, Virginia, Washington, West Virginia, Wisconsin and Wyoming.

And further, that the states whose legislatures have so ratified the said proposed amendment constitute three-fourths of the whole number of states in the United States;

Now, therefore, be it known that I, Frank L. Polk, Acting Secretary of State of the United States, by virtue and in pursuance of Section 205 of the Revised Statutes of the United States, do hereby certify that the amendment aforesaid has become valid to all intents and purposes as a part of the Constitution of the United States.

In testimony whereof I have hereunto set my hand and caused the seal of the Department of State to be affixed.

Done at the City of Washington this 29th day of January in the year of our Lord one thousand nine hundred and nineteen.

FRANK L. POLK, *Acting Secretary of State.*

MESSAGE

[From Secretary of State Lansing to Premier Paderewski, of Poland, Announcing Recognition of Poland.]

January 29, 1919.

The President of the United States directs me to extend to you as Foreign Minister and Secretary of Foreign Affairs of the provisional Polish Government its sincere wishes for your success in the high office which you have assumed and his earnest hope that the Government of which you are a part will bring prosperity to the republic of Poland.

It is my privilege to extend to you at this time my personal greetings and officially to assure you that it will be a source of gratification to enter into official relations with you at the earliest opportunity. To render to your country such aid as is possible at this time as it enters upon a new cycle of independent life will be in due accord with that spirit of friendliness which has in the past animated the American people in their relations with your countrymen.

EXECUTIVE ORDER

[Placing Administration of Food Relief for Europe Under Herbert Hoover and American Relief Administration.]

THE WHITE HOUSE, *February 24, 1919.*

In pursuance of an Act entitled "An Act providing for the relief of such populations in Europe and countries contiguous thereto outside of Germany, German Austria, Hungary, Bulgaria and Turkey, as may be determined upon by the President as necessary," approved February 24, 1919, I hereby direct that the furnishing of foodstuffs and other urgent supplies and the transportation, distributing and administration thereof, provided for in said Act, shall be conducted under the direction of Herbert Hoover, who is hereby appointed Director General of the American Relief Administration with full power to determine to which of the populations named in said Act the supplies shall be furnished and in what quantities, and further to arrange for reimbursement so far as possible as in said Act provided.

He is hereby authorized to establish the American Relief Administration for the purpose of carrying out the provisions of said Act and to employ such persons and incur such expenses as may be necessary for such purpose, to disburse all sums appropriated under the aforesaid Act or appoint a disbursing officer with that power; and particularly to employ the Food Administration Grain Corporation, organized under the provisions of the Food Control Act of August 10, 1917, as an agency for the purchase, transportation and distribution of foodstuffs and supplies to the populations requiring relief.

He is hereby further authorized in the carrying out of the aforesaid Act of February twenty-fourth, 1919 to contract with the Food Administration Grain Corporation or any other person or corporation, that such person or corporation shall carry stocks of food in transit to Europe, and at points in Europe, in such quantities as may be agreed upon and as are required to meet relief needs, and that there shall be paid to such person or corporation in advance from the appropriation made in the aforesaid Act of February twenty-fourth, 1919, any sums which may be required for the purchase and transportation of foodstuffs and maintenance of stocks.

WOODROW WILSON.

ADDRESS

On February 24, 1919, President Wilson landed in Boston, returning from the Peace Conference at Paris in order to be present at the closing days of the last session of the Sixty-Fifth Congress. He left the shores of the United States for Europe again on March 6, 1919. His address on arriving at Boston was as follows:

Governor Coolidge, Mr. Mayor, Fellow-Citizens:—I wonder if you are half as glad to see me as I am to see you. It warms my heart to see a great body of my fellow-citizens again, because, in some respects, during the recent months I have been very lonely indeed without your comradeship and counsel; and I tried at every step of the work which fell to me to recall what I was sure would be your counsel with regard to the great matters which were under consideration.

I do not want you to think that I have not been appreciative of the extraordinarily generous reception which was given to me on the other side in saying that it makes me very happy to get home again. I do not mean to say that I was not very deeply touched by the cries that came from the great crowds on the other side. But I want to say to you in all honesty that I felt them to be a call of greeting to you rather than to me.

I did not feel that the greeting was personal. I had in my heart the over-crowning pride of being your representative and of receiving the plaudits of men everywhere who felt that your hearts beat with theirs in the cause of liberty. There was no mistaking the tone in the voices of those great crowds. It was not a tone of mere greeting, it was not a tone of mere generous welcome; it was the calling of comrade to comrade, the cries that come from men who say, "We have waited for this day, when the friends of liberty should come across the sea and shake hands with us, to see that a new world was constructed upon a new basis and foundation of justice and right."

I can't tell you the inspiration that came from the sentiments that came out of those simple voices of the crowd. And the proudest thing I have to report to you is that this great country of ours is trusted throughout the world.

I have not come to report the proceedings or the results of the proceedings of the Peace Conference; that would be premature. I can say that I have received very happy impressions from this conference; the impression that, while there are many differences of judgment, while there are some divergences of object, there is, nevertheless, a common spirit and a common realization of the necessity of setting up new standards of right in the world.

Because the men who are in conference in Paris realize as keenly as any American can realize that they are not the masters of their people; that they are the servants of their people, and that the spirit of their people has awakened to a new purpose and a new conception of their power to realize that purpose, and that no man dare go home from that conference and report anything less noble than was expected of it.

The conference seems to you to go slowly; from day to day in Paris it seems to go slowly; but I wonder if you realize the complexity of the task which it has undertaken. It seems as if the settlements of this war affect, and affect directly, every great, and I sometimes think every small, nation in the world, and no one decision can prudently be made which is not properly linked in with the great series of other decisions which must accompany it, and it must be reckoned in with the final result if the real quality and character of that result is to be properly judged.

What we are doing is to hear the whole case; hear it from the mouths of the men most interested; hear it from those who are officially commissioned to state it; hear the rival claims; hear the claims that affect new nationalities, that affect new areas of the world, that affect new commercial and economic connections that have been established by the great world war through which we have gone. And I have been struck by the moderateness of those who have represented national claims. I can testify that I have nowhere seen the gleam of passion. I have seen earnestness, I have seen tears come to the eyes of men who plead for downtrodden people whom they were privileged to speak for; but they were not the tears of anguish, they were the tears of ardent hope.

And I don't see how any man can fail to have been subdued by these pleas, subdued to this feeling, that he was not there to assert an individual judgment of his own but to try to assist the cause of humanity.

And, in the midst of it all, every interest seeks out, first of all, when it reaches Paris, the representatives of the United States. Why? Because—and I think I am stating the most wonderful fact in history—because there is no nation in Europe that suspects the motives of the United States.

Was there ever so wonderful a thing seen before? Was there ever so moving a thing? Was there ever any fact that so bound the nation that had won that esteem forever to deserve it?

I would not have you understand that the great men who represent the other nations there in conference are disesteemed by those who know them. Quite the contrary. But you understand that the nations of Europe have again and again clashed with one another in competitive interest. It is impossible for men to forget those sharp issues that were drawn between them in times past. It is impossible for men to believe that all ambitions have all of a sudden been foregone. They remember territory that was coveted; they remember rights that it was attempted to extort; they remember political ambitions which it was attempted to realize, and, while they believe that men have come into a different temper, they cannot forget these things, and so they do not resort to one another for a dispassionate view of the matters in controversy. They resort to that nation which has won the enviable distinction of being regarded as the friend of mankind.

Whenever it is desired to send a small force of soldiers to occupy a piece of territory where it is thought nobody else will be welcome, they ask for American soldiers. And where other soldiers would be looked upon with suspicion and perhaps met with resistance, the American soldier is welcomed with acclaim.

I have had so many grounds for pride on the other side of the water that I am very thankful that they are not grounds for personal pride, but for national pride. If they were grounds for personal pride, I'd be the most stuck-up man in the world.

And it has been an infinite pleasure to me to see those gallant soldiers of ours, of whom the Constitution of the United States made me the proud commander. You may be proud of the 26th Division, but I commanded the 26th Division, and see what they did under my direction! And everybody praises the American soldier, with the feeling that in praising him he is subtracting from the credit of no one else.

I have been searching for the fundamental fact that converted Europe to believe in us. Before this war, Europe did not believe in us as she does now. She did not believe in us throughout the first three years of the war. She seems really to have believed that we were holding off because we thought we could make more by staying out than by going in. And, all of a sudden, in a short eighteen months, the whole verdict is reversed. There can be but one explanation for it. They saw what we did—that, without making a single claim, we put all our men and all our means at the disposal of those who were fighting for their homes, in the first instance, but also for a cause, the cause of human rights and justice, and that we went in, not to support their national claims, but to support the great cause which they held in common. And when they saw that America not only held ideals, but acted ideals, they were converted to America and became firm partisans of those ideals.

I met a group of scholars when I was in Paris—some gentlemen from one of the Greek universities who had come to see me, and in whose presence, or rather in the presence of whose traditions of learning, I felt very young indeed. I told them that I had one of the delightful revenges that sometimes come to a man. All my life I had heard men speak with a sort of condescension of ideals and of idealists, and particularly those separated, encloistered persons whom they choose to term academic, who were in the habit of uttering ideals in the free atmosphere, when they clash with nobody in particular.

And I said I have had this sweet revenge: speaking with perfect frankness, in the name of the people of the United States, I have uttered as the objects of this great war ideals, and nothing but ideals, and the war has been won by that inspiration. Men were fighting with tense muscles and lowered heads until they came to realize those things, feeling they were fighting for their lives and their country, and when these accents of what it was all about reached them from America, they lifted their heads, they raised their eyes to heaven, when they saw men in khaki coming across the sea in the spirit of crusaders, and they found that these were strange men, reckless of danger not only, but reckless because they seemed to see something that made that danger worth while. Men have testified to me in Europe that our men were possessed by something that they could only call a religious fervor. They were not like any of the other soldiers. They had a vision, they had a dream, and they were fighting in the dream, and, fighting in the dream, they turned the whole tide of battle, and it never came back.

One of our American humorists, meeting the criticism that American soldiers were not trained long enough, said: "It takes only half as long to train an American soldier as any other, because you only have to train him to go one way." And he did only go one way, and he never came back until he could do it when he pleased.

And now do you realize that this confidence we have established throughout the world imposes a burden upon us, if you choose to call it a burden? It is one of those burdens which any nation ought to be proud to carry. Any man who resists the present tides that run in the world will find himself thrown upon a shore so high and barren that it will seem as if he had been separated from his human kind forever.

The Europe that I left the other day was full of something that it had never felt fill its heart so full before. It was full of hope. The Europe of the second year of the war, the Europe of the third year of the war, was sinking to a sort of stubborn desperation. They did not see any great thing to be achieved, even when the war should be won. They hoped there would be some salvage; they hoped that they could clear their territories of invading armies; they hoped they could set up their homes and start their industries afresh. But they thought it would simply be the resumption of the old life that Europe had led—led in fear, led in anxiety, led in constant suspicious watchfulness. They never dreamed that it would be a Europe of settled peace and of justified hope.

And now these ideals have wrought this new magic, that all the peoples of Europe are buoyed up and confident in the spirit of hope, because they believe that we are at the eve of a new age in the world, when nations will understand one another, when nations will support one another in every just cause, when nations will unite every moral and every physical strength to see that the right shall prevail.

If America were at this juncture to fail the world, what would come of it? I do not mean any disrespect to any other great people when I say that America is the hope of the world; and if she does not justify that hope, the results are unthinkable. Men will be thrown back upon the bitterness of disappointment not only, but the bitterness of despair. All nations will be set up as hostile camps again; the men at the Peace Conference will go home with their heads upon their breasts, knowing that they have failed—for they were bidden not to come home from there until they did something more than sign a treaty of peace.

Suppose we sign the treaty of peace and that it is the most satisfactory treaty of peace that the confusing elements of the modern world will afford, and go home and think about our labors, we will know that we have left written upon the historic table at Versailles, upon which Vergennes and Benjamin Franklin wrote their names, nothing but a modern scrap of paper; no nations united to defend it, no great forces combined to make it good, no assurance given to the downtrodden and fearful people of the world that they shall be safe.

Any man who thinks that America will take part in giving the world any such rebuff and disappointment as that does not know America. I invite him to test the sentiments of the nation. We set this nation up to make men free, and we did not confine our conception and purpose to America, and now we will make men free. If we did not do that, the fame of America would be gone, and all her powers would be dissipated. She then would have to keep her power for those narrow, selfish, provincial purposes which seem so dear to some minds that have no sweep beyond the nearest horizon.

I should welcome no sweeter challenge than that. I have fighting blood in me, and it is sometimes a delight to let it have scope, but if it is a challenge on this occasion it will be an indulgence. Think of the picture, think of the utter blackness that would fall on the world. America has failed! America made a little essay at generosity, and then withdrew. America said, "We are your friends," but it was only for today, not for tomorrow. America said, "Here is our power to vindicate right," and then the next day said, "Let right take care of itself, and we will take care of ourselves." America said, "We set up a light to lead men along the paths of liberty, but we have lowered it; it is intended only to light our own path." We set up a great ideal of liberty, and then we said: "Liberty is a thing that you must win for yourself. Do not call upon us."

And think of the world that we would leave. Do you realize how many new nations are going to be set up in the presence of old and powerful nations in Europe, and left there, if left by us, without a disinterested friend?

Do you believe in the Polish cause, as I do? Are you going to set up Poland, immature, inexperienced, as yet unorganized, and leave her with a circle of armies around her? Do you believe in the aspiration of the Czecho-Slovaks and the Jugo-Slavs, as I do? Do you know how many powers would be quick to pounce upon them if there were not the guarantees of the world behind their liberty?

Have you thought of the sufferings of Armenia? You poured out your money to help succor the Armenians after they suffered; now set your strength so that they shall never suffer again.

The arrangements of the present peace cannot stand a generation unless they are guaranteed by the united forces of the civilized world. And, if we do not guarantee them, can you not see the picture? Your hearts have instructed you where the burden of this war fell. It did not fall upon the national treasuries, it did not fall upon the instruments of administration, it did not fall upon the resources of the nation. It fell upon the victims' homes everywhere—where women were toiling in the hope that their men would come back.

When I think of the homes upon which dull despair would settle were this great hope disappointed, I should wish for my part never to have had America play any part whatever in this attempt to emancipate the world. But I talk as if there were any question. I have no more doubt of the verdict of America in this matter than I have doubt of the blood that is in me.

And so, my fellow-citizens, I have come back to report progress, and I do not believe that the progress is going to stop short of the goal. The nations of the world have set their heads now to do a great thing and they are not going to slacken their purpose. And when I speak of the nations of the world I do not speak of the Governments of the world. I speak of the peoples who constitute the nations of the world. They are in the saddle and they are going to see to it that, if their present Governments do not do their will, some other Governments shall. And the secret is out and the present Governments know it.

There is a great deal of harmony to be got out of common knowledge. There is a great deal of sympathy to be got out of living in the same atmosphere, and except for the differences of language, which puzzled my American ear very sadly, I could have believed I was at home, in France, or in Italy, or in England, when I was on the streets, when I was in the presence of the crowds, when I was in great halls where men were gathered together irrespective of class. I did not feel quite as much at home there as I do here, but I felt that, now, at any rate, after this storm of war had cleared the air, men were seeing eye to eye everywhere and that these were the kind of folks who would understand what the kind of folks at home would understand and that they were thinking the same things.

I feel about you as I am reminded of a story of that excellent witness and good artist, Oliver Herford, who one day, sitting at luncheon at his club, was slapped vigorously on the back by a man whom he did not know very well. He said: "Oliver, old boy, how are you?" He looked at him rather coldly. He said: "I don't know your name, I don't know your face, but your manners are very familiar." And I must say that your manners are very familiar, and, let me add, very delightful.

It is a great comfort, for one thing, to realize that you all understand the language I am speaking. A friend of mine said that to talk through an interpreter was like witnessing the compound fracture of an idea. But the beauty of it is that, whatever the impediments of the channel of communication, the idea is the same, it gets registered, and it gets registered in responsive hearts and receptive purposes.

I have come back for a strenuous attempt to transact business for a little while in America, but I have really come back to say to you, in all soberness and honesty, that I have been trying my best to speak your thoughts.

When I sample myself, I think I find that I am a typical American, and, if I sample deep enough and get down to what is probably the true stuff of a man, then I have hope that it is part of the stuff that is like the other fellow's at home. And, therefore, probing deep in my heart and trying to see the things that are right, without regard to the things that may be debated as expedient, I feel that I am interpreting the purpose and the thought of America; and in loving America I find I have joined the great majority of my fellow-men throughout the world.

STATEMENT

The Sixty-Fifth Congress adjourned on March 4, 1919, without passing certain pressing legislation, including appropriation bills. This action was obviously taken in the hope of compelling the President to call the Sixty-Sixth Congress in special session in the immediate future. Upon the adjournment of Congress, President Wilson issued the following statement:

A group of men in the Senate have deliberately chosen to embarrass the administration of the Government, to imperil the financial interests of the railways systems of the country, and to make arbitrary use of powers intended to be employed in the interests of the people.

It is plainly my present duty to attend the Peace Conference in Paris. It is also my duty to be in close contact with the public business during a session of the Congress. I must make my choice between these two duties, and I confidently hope that the people of the country will think that I am making the right choice. It is not in the interest of the right conduct of public affairs that I should call the Congress in special session while it is impossible for me to be in Washington, because of a more pressing duty elsewhere, to co-operate with the Houses.

I take it for granted that the men who have obstructed and prevented the passage of necessary legislation have taken all of this into consideration and are willing to assume the responsibility of the impaired efficiency of the Government and the embarrassed finances of the country during the time of my enforced absence.

BY THE PRESIDENT OF THE UNITED STATES OF AMERICA

A PROCLAMATION

[Amending Proclamation of September 16, 1918, Prohibiting Manufacture of Malt Liquors.]

Whereas, under and by virtue of an act of Congress entitled "An Act to provide further for the national security and defence by encouraging the production, conserving the supply, and controlling the distribution of food products and fuel, approved August 10, 1917, the President, on the 16th day of September, 1918, made a proclamation, containing the following prohibition:

"I prescribe and give public notice that on and after October 1, 1918, no person shall use any sugar, glucose, corn, rice, or any other foods, fruits, food materials or feeds, except hops and malt now already made, in the production of malt liquors, including near beer, for beverage purposes, whether or not such malt liquors contain alcohol, and on and after December 1, 1918, no person shall use any sugar, glucose, corn, rice, or any other foods, fruits, food materials or feeds, including malt, in the production of malt liquors, including near beer, for beverage purposes, whether or not such malt liquors contain alcohol."

And whereas the President, under authority of the said act of August 10, 1917, by further proclamation dated January 30, 1919, modified the said proclamation of September 16, 1918, so as to permit the use of grain in the manufacture of beverages which are not intoxicating, such proclamation providing as follows:

"Whereas the prohibition of the use of grain in the manufacture of beverages which are not intoxicating has been found by the President to be no longer essential in order to assure an adequate and continuous supply of food:

Now, therefore, I do hereby modify the aforesaid proclamation made on the sixteenth day of September, 1918, to the extent of permitting the use of grain in the manufacture of beverages which are not intoxicating."

And whereas for the production from a cereal base of a nonintoxicating beverage, which shall be nutritious and palatable, food products other than grains, of which there is now an adequate supply, but of which the use for such purposes is prohibited by the aforesaid proclamation of September 16, 1918, are required:

Now, therefore, I, Woodrow Wilson, President of the United States of America, do hereby amend the aforesaid proclamation of September 16, 1918, by inserting in the first sentence of the prohibiting paragraph, after the words, "production of" the word "intoxicating" and by striking out of the same sentence the words "including near beer"; and by inserting in the succeeding sentence in both places where the phrase "production of malt liquors" occurs, after the words, "production of" the word "intoxicating", and striking out the phrases "including near beer" and "whether or not such malt liquors contain alcohol" in both places in that sentence where these phrases occur, so that as amended the prohibitory provisions of said proclamation shall read as follows:

"That the use of sugar, glucose, corn, rice, or any other foods, fruits, food materials and feeds in the production of intoxicating malt liquors for beverage purposes be prohibited. And by this Proclamation I prescribe and give public notice that on and after October 1, 1918, no person shall use any sugar, glucose, corn, rice, or any other foods, fruits, food materials or feeds, except hops and malt now already made, in the production of intoxicating malt liquors, for beverage purposes, and on and after December 1, 1918, no person shall use any sugar, glucose, corn, rice or any other foods, fruits, food materials or feeds, including malt, in the production of intoxicating malt liquors, for beverage purposes, whether or not such malt liquors contain alcohol."

and the aforesaid proclamation of September 16, 1918, as thus amended, shall remain in full force and effect.

In witness whereof, I have hereunto set my hand and caused the seal of the United States to be affixed.

Done this 4th day of March in the year of our Lord one thousand nine hundred and nineteen, and of the independence [SEAL.] of the United States of America the one hundred and forty-third.

WOODROW WILSON.

By the President:

FRANK L. POLK, *Acting Secretary of State.*

EXECUTIVE ORDERS

[Amendments to the Civil Service Rules, Concerning Especially Veterans of the Great War.]

THE WHITE HOUSE, *16 April 1919.*

Section 1, Civil Service Rule IX, is amended to read as follows:

1. A person separated without delinquency or misconduct from a competitive position or from a position which he entered by transfer or promotion from a competitive position or to accept another appointment in the executive civil service may be reinstated subject to the following limitations:

(a) Unless otherwise provided hereinafter a person may be reinstated only to the department or independent government establishment from which separated and upon requisition made within one year from the date of his separation.

(b) A person who served in the Civil War or the War with Spain and was honorably discharged or his widow or an army nurse of either war, separated therefore from the competitive classified service, may be reinstated in the department or independent establishment from which separated without time limit. If hereafter separated, reinstatement may be made within five years from the date of separation.

(c) A soldier, sailor, marine, or army nurse of the War with Germany formerly in the competitive classified service may be reinstated in any part of the competitive classified service within five years from the date of honorable discharge from the military service if he has the required fitness to perform the duties of the position to which his reinstatement is sought.

(d) The widow of a veteran of the War with Germany formerly in the competitive classified service who was the wife of such veteran while he was in the military service may be reinstated in any part of the competitive classified service within five years from the date of termination of her husband's military service by death or honorable discharge.

(e) No person in any of the foregoing groups may be reinstated to a position requiring an examination different from that required in the position from which he was separated without passing an appropriate examination.

Section 2 of Rule IX remains unchanged.

The Executive Order of July 18, 1918, providing for the reinstatement of government employees who left the classified civil service to enter the military or naval service during the War with Germany, and the Executive Order of February 7, 1919, amending section 1 of

Civil Service Rule IX (erroneously referred to as Rule XI) are hereby revoked.

This Executive Order is recommended by the Civil Service Commission to harmonize and consolidate provisions relating to the reinstatement of veterans, their widows, and army nurses.

WOODROW WILSON.

The White House, *16 April 1919.*

Civil Service Rule V is hereby amended by the addition to the following proviso to clause (b) of section 4:

> Provided, that the Commission may, in its discretion, exempt from the physical requirements established for any position a disabled and honorably discharged soldier, sailor, or marine upon the certification of the Federal Board for Vocational Education that he has been specially trained for and has passed a practical test demonstrating his physical ability to perform the duties of the class of positions in which employment is sought.

> As amended section 4 will read:

> The Commission may refuse to examine an applicant or to certify an eligible for any of the following reasons: (a) Dismissal from the service for delinquency or misconduct within one year next preceding the date of his application; (b) physical or mental unfitness for the position for which he applies: Provided, that the Commission may, in its discretion, exempt from the physical requirements established for any position a disabled and honorably discharged soldier, sailor, or marine upon the certification of the Federal Board for Vocational Education that he has been specially trained for and has passed a practical test demonstrating his physical ability to perform the duties of the class of positions in which employment is sought; (c) criminal, infamous, dishonest, immoral, or notoriously disgraceful conduct; (d) intentionally making a false statement in any material fact, or practicing any deception or fraud in securing examination, registration, certification, or appointment; (e) refusal to furnish testimony as required by Rule XIV; (f) the habitual use of intoxicating beverages to excess. Any of the last five foregoing disqualifications shall also be good cause for removal from the service.

This amendment is recommended by the Civil Service Commission after consultation with officials of the Federal Board for Vocational Education and the United States Employees' Compensation Commission.

WOODROW WILSON.

APPEAL

[For Success of Victory Liberty Loan.]

April 19, 1919.

For two anxious years the American people have striven to fulfill the task of saving our civilization. By the exertion of unmeasured power they have quickly won the victory, without which they would have remained in the field until the last resource had been exhausted.

Bringing to the contest a strength of spirit made doubly strong by the righteousness of their cause, they devoted themselves unswervingly to the prosecution of their undertaking, in the full knowledge that no conquest lay in their path excepting the conquest of right.

Today the world stands freed from the threat of militarism, which has so long weighed upon the spirit and the labor of peaceful nations. But as yet we stand only at the threshold of happier times. To enter, we must fulfill to the utmost the engagements we have made. The Victory Liberty Loan is the indispensable means.

Two years ago we pledged our lives and fortunes to the cause for which we have fought. Sixty thousand of our strongest sons have redeemed for us that pledge of blood. To redeem in full faith the promise of this sacrifice, we now must give this new evidence of our purpose.

WOODROW WILSON.

STATEMENT ON THE DISPOSITION OF FIUME

One of the most difficult problems before the Peace Conference of Paris was concerned with the disposition of the sea-port of Fiume, on the Istrian Peninsula, on the northeast shore of the Adriatic. As will be seen below, Italy had entered the Great War with a secret understanding with France and Great Britain whereby as a result of victory over the Central Powers Italy was to acquire not only those portions of the Trentino and the land around Trieste which was inhabited chiefly by Italians, but also certain portions of the Austrian Tyrol, parts of the northeast Adriatic shore and some islands in the Adriatic in which the Italian nationality could hardly be said to be in the ascendancy. However, Fiume was not granted to Italy in this secret arrangement.

The nationality of the inhabitants of Fiume was sharply disputed at the Peace Conference. Neutral investigations, on the whole, tended to show that although Fiume proper was inhabited chiefly by Italians, yet the adjacent suburb, larger and industrially more important than Fiume, was inhabited so preponderantly by South (Jugo) Slavs as to make the whole a city of South Slavic nationality. President Wilson's statement regarding Fiume was issued on April 23, 1919. It was the only occasion at the Conference when he publicly and openly appealed to the people over the heads of the diplomats. However, it was commonly understood that Wilson was supported in his stand by Premiers Clemenceau, of France, and Lloyd-George, of Great Britain. The immediate effect of the statement was the temporary withdrawal of the Italian delegation to the Peace Conference.

In view of the capital importance of the questions affected, and in order to throw all possible light upon what is involved in their settlement, I hope that the following statement will contribute to the final formation of opinion and to a satisfactory solution:

When Italy entered the war she entered upon the basis of a definite private understanding with Great Britain and France, now known as the Pact of London. Since that time the whole face of circumstances has been altered. Many other powers, great and small, have entered the struggle, with no knowledge of that private understanding.

The Austro-Hungarian Empire, then the enemy of Europe, and at whose expense the Pact of London was to be kept in the event of victory, has gone to pieces and no longer exists. Not only that, but the several parts of that empire, it is agreed now by Italy and all her associates, are to be erected into independent States and associated in a League of Nations, not with those who were recently our enemies, but with Italy herself and the powers that stood with Italy in the great war for liberty.

We are to establish their liberty as well as our own. They are to be among the smaller States whose interests are henceforth to be safeguarded as scrupulously as the interests of the most powerful States.

The war was ended, moreover, by proposing to Germany an armistice and peace which should be founded on certain clearly-defined principles which set up a new order of right and justice. Upon those principles the peace with Germany has been conceived, not only, but formulated. Upon those principles it will be executed.

We cannot ask the great body of powers to propose and effect peace with Austria and establish a new basis of independence and right in the States which originally constituted the Austro-Hungarian Empire and in the States of the Balkan group on principles of another kind. We must apply the same principles to the settlement of Europe in those quarters that we have applied in the peace with Germany. It was upon the explicit avowal of those principles that the initiative for peace was taken. It is upon them that the whole structure of peace must rest.

If those principles are to be adhered to, Fiume must serve as the outlet of the commerce, not of Italy, but of the land to the north and northeast of that port, Hungary, Bohemia, Rumania, and the States of the new Jugo-Slav group. To assign Fiume to Italy would be to create the feeling that we have deliberately put the port upon which all those countries chiefly depend for their access to the Mediterranean in the hands of a power of which it did not form an integral part and whose sovereignty, if set up there, must inevitably seem foreign, not domestic or identified with the commercial and industrial life of the regions which the port must serve. It is for that reason, no doubt, that Fiume was not included in the Pact of London, but there definitely assigned to the Croatians.

And the reason why the line of the Pact of London swept about many of the islands of the eastern coast of the Adriatic and around the portion of the Dalmatian coast which lies most open to that sea was not only that here and there on those islands, and here and there on that coast, there are bodies of people of Italian blood and connection, but also, and no doubt chiefly, because it was felt that it was necessary for Italy to have a foothold amidst the channels of the eastern Adriatic in order that she might make her own coasts safe against the naval aggression of Austria-Hungary.

But Austria-Hungary no longer exists. It is proposed that the fortifications which the Austrian Government constructed there shall be razed and permanently destroyed.

It is part also of the new plan of European order which centres in the League of Nations that the new States erected there shall accept a limitation of armaments which puts aggression out of the question. There can be no fear of the unfair treatment of groups of Italian people there, because adequate guarantees will be given, under international sanction, of the equal and equitable treatment of all racial or national minorities.

In brief, every question associated with this settlement wears a new aspect—a new aspect given it by the very victory for right for which Italy has made the supreme sacrifice of blood and treasure. Italy, along with the four other great powers, has become one of the chief trustees of the new order which she has played so honorable a part in establishing.

And on the north and northeast her natural frontiers are completely restored, along the whole sweep of the Alps from northwest to southeast to the very end of the Istrian Peninsula, including all the great watershed within which Trieste and Pola lie, and all the fair regions whose face nature has turned toward the great peninsula upon which the historic life of the Latin people has been worked out through centuries of famous story ever since Rome was first set upon her seven hills.

Her ancient unity is restored. Her lines are extended to the great walls which are her natural defense. It is within her choice to be surrounded by friends; to exhibit to the newly liberated peoples across the Adriatic that noblest quality of greatness, magnanimity, friendly generosity, the preference of justice over interest.

The nations associated with her, the nations that knew nothing of the Pact of London or of any other special understanding that lies at the beginning of this great struggle, and who have made their supreme sacrifice also in the interest, not of national advantage or defense, but

Photo from Western Newspaper Union

THE LARGEST AIRPLANE, 1919

THE LARGEST AIRPLANE, 1919.

The plane in the accompanying photograph, put into service early in 1919, at the time of its completion was the largest heavier-than-air machine in the world. It was used in the transport service of the United States for the detection of enemy submarines.

of the settled peace of the world, are now united with her older associates in urging her to assume a leadership which cannot be mistaken in the new order of Europe.

America is Italy's friend. Her people are drawn, millions strong, from Italy's own fair countrysides. She is linked in blood, as well as in affection, with the Italian people. Such ties can never be broken. And America was privileged, by the generous commission of her associates in the war, to initiate the peace we are about to consummate— to initiate it upon terms which she had herself formulated and in which I was her spokesman.

The compulsion is upon her to square every decision she takes a part in with those principles. She can do nothing else. She trusts Italy, and in her trust believes that Italy will ask nothing of her that cannot be made unmistakably consistent with those sacred obligations.

Interests are not now in question, but the rights of peoples, of States new and old, of liberated peoples and peoples whose rulers have never accounted them worthy of a right; above all, the right of the world to peace and to such settlements of interest as shall make peace secure.

These, and these only, are the principles for which America has fought. These, and these only, are the principles upon which she can consent to make peace. Only upon these principles, she hopes and believes, will the people of Italy ask her to make peace.

Explanatory Statement

There is no question to which I have given more careful or anxious thought than I have given to this, because in common with all my colleagues it is my earnest desire to see the utmost justice done to Italy.

Throughout my consideration of it, however, I have felt that there was one matter in which I had no choice and could wish to have none. I felt bound to square every conclusion that I should reach as accurately as possible with the fourteen principles of peace which I set forth in my address to the Congress of the United States on the 8th of January, 1918, and in subsequent addresses.

These fourteen points and the principles laid down in the subsequent addresses were formally adopted with only a single reservation by the powers associated against Germany and will constitute the basis of peace with Germany. I do not feel at liberty to suggest one basis for peace with Germany and another for peace with Austria.

It will be remembered that in reply to a communication from the Austrian government offering to enter into negotiations for an armistice and peace on the basis of the fourteen points to which I have alluded I said that there was one matter to which those points no longer applied. They had demanded autonomy for the several states which had constituted parts of the Austro-Hungarian Empire, and I pointed out that it must now be left to the choice of the people of these several countries what their destinies and political relations should be.

They have chosen with the sympathy of the whole world to be set up as independent states. Their complete separation from Austria and the complete dissolution of the Austro-Hungarian Empire has given a new aspect and significance to the settlements which may be effected with regard at any rate to the eastern boundaries of Italy.

Personally, I am quite willing that Italy should be accorded along the whole front of her northern frontier, and wherever she comes into contact with Austrian territory, all that was accorded her in the so-called Pact of London, but I am of the clear opinion that the Pact of London can no longer apply to the settlement of her eastern bounaaries.

The line drawn in the Pact of London was conceived for the purpose of establishing an absolutely adequate frontier of safety for Italy against any possible hostility or aggression on the part of Austria. But Austria-Hungary no longer exists. These eastern frontiers will touch countries stripped of the military and naval power of Austria, settled in independence of Austria and organized for the purpose of satisfying legitimate national aspirations, and created states not hostile to the new European order, but arising out of it, interested in its maintenance, dependent upon the cultivation of friendships and bound to a common policy of peace and accommodation by the covenant of the League of Nations.

It is with these facts in mind that I have approached the Adriatic question. It is commonly agreed, and I very heartily adhere to the agreement, that the ports of Trieste and Pola, and with them the greater part of the Istrian Peninsula, should be ceded to Italy, her eastern frontier running along the natural strategic line established by the physical conformation of the country—a line which it has been attempted to draw with some degree of accuracy on the attached map.

Within this line on the Italian side will lie considerable bodies of non-Italian population, but their fortunes are so naturally linked by the nature of the country itself with the rest of the Italian people that I think their inclusion is fully justified.

There would be no justification in my judgment in including Fiume, or any part of the coastline to the south of Fiume, within the boundaries of the Italian Kingdom. Fiume is by situation and by all the circumstances of its development not an Italian but an international port, serving the countries to the east and north of the Gulf of Fiume.

Just because it is an international port and cannot with justice be subordinated to any one sovereignty, it is my clear judgment that it should enjoy a very considerable degree of genuine autonomy, and while it should be included, no doubt, within the customs system of the new Jugo-Slavic state, it should nevertheless be left free in its own interest, and in the interest of the states lying about it, to devote itself to the service of the commerce which naturally and inevitably seeks an outlet or inlet at its port.

The states which it serves will be new states. They will have complete confidence in their access to an outlet on the sea. The friendship and the connections of the future will largely depend upon such an arrangement as I have suggested, and friendship, coöperation and freedom of action must underly every arrangement of peace if peace is to be lasting.

I believe there will be a common agreement that the island of Lissa should be ceded to Italy, and that she should retain the port of Volpna. I believe that it will be generally agreed that the fortifications which the Austrian Government established upon the islands near the eastern coast of the Adriatic should be permanently dispensed with under international guarantee, and that the disarmament which is to be arranged under the League of Nations should limit the states on the eastern coast of the Adriatic to only such minor naval forces as are necessary for policing the waters of the islands and the coast. These are the conclusions which I am forced to by compulsion of the understandings which underlie the whole initiation of the present peace.

No other conclusions seem to be acceptable to being rendered concise with these understandings. They were understandings accepted by the whole world and bear with peculiar compulsion upon the United States, because the privilege was accorded her of taking the initiative of bringing about the negotiations for peace, and her plans underlie the whole difficult business.

And certainly Italy obtains under such a settlement the great historic object which her people have so long had in mind. The historic wrongs inflicted upon her by Austria-Hungary and by a long series of unjust transactions, which I hope will before long sink out of the memory of man, are completely redressed. Nothing is denied her which will complete her national unity.

Here and there upon the islands of the Adriatic and upon the eastern coast of that sea there are settlements containing large Italian elements of population, but the pledge under which the new states enter the family of nations will abundantly safeguard the liberty, the development and all the just rights of national and racial minorities, and back of these safeguards will always lie the watchful authority of the League of Nations. And at the very outset we shall have avoided the fatal error of making Italy's nearest neighbors on her east her enemies and nursing just such a sense of injustice as has disturbed the peace of Europe for generations together and played no small part in bringing on the terrible conflict through which we have just passed.

BY THE PRESIDENT OF THE UNITED STATES OF AMERICA

PROCLAMATIONS

[Boy Scout Week.]

The Boy Scouts of America have rendered notable service to the Nation during the world war. They have done effective work in the Liberty Loan and War Savings campaigns, in discovering and reporting upon the black walnut supply, in coöperating with the Red Cross and other war work agencies, in acting as despatch bearers for the Committee on Public Information, and in other important fields. The Boy Scouts have not only demonstrated their worth to the Nation, but have also materially contributed to a deeper appreciation by the American people of the higher conceptions of patriotism and good citizenship.

The Boy Scout movement should not only be preserved, but strengthened. It deserves the support of all public-spirited citizens. The available means for the Boy Scout movement have thus far sufficed for the organization and training of only a small proportion of the boys of the country. There are approximately 10,000,000 boys in the United States between the ages of twelve and twenty-one. Of these only 375,000 are enrolled as members of the Boy Scouts of America.

America cannot acquit herself commensurately with her power and influence in the great period now facing her and the world unless the boys of America are given better opportunities than heretofore to prepare themselves for the responsibilities of citizenship.

Every nation depends for its future upon the proper training and development of its youth. The American boy must have the best training and discipline our great democracy can provide if America is to maintain her ideals, her standards, and her influence in the world.

The plan, therefore, for a Boy Scout week during which a universal appeal will be made to all Americans to supply the means to put the Boy Scouts of America in a position to carry forward effectively and continuously the splendid work they are doing for the youth of America should have the unreserved support of the Nation.

Therefore, I, Woodrow Wilson, President of the United States of America, do hereby recommend that the period beginning Sunday, June 8th, to Flag Day, June 14th, be observed as Boy Scout Week through the United States for the purpose of strengthening the work of the Boy Scouts of America.

I earnestly recommend that, in every community, a Citizens' Committee, under the leadership of a National Citizens' Committee, be organized to coöperate in carrying out a program for a definite recognition of the effective services rendered by the Boy Scouts of America; for a survey of the facts relating to the boyhood of each community, in order that with the coöperation of churches, schools and other organizations definitely engaged in work for boys, adequate provision may be made for extending the Boy Scout program to a larger proportion of American boyhood.

The Boy Scout movement offers unusual opportunity for volunteer service. It needs men to act as committeemen and as leaders of groups of boys. I hope that all who can will enlist for such personal service, enroll as associate members and give all possible financial assistance to this worthy organization of American boyhood. Anything that is done to increase the effectiveness of the Boy Scouts of America will be a genuine contribution to the welfare of the Nation.

In witness whereof I have hereunto set my hand and caused the seal of the United States to be affixed.

Done this first day of May in the year of our Lord one thousand nine hundred and nineteen and of the independence of the [SEAL.] United States of America the one hundred and forty-third.

WOODROW WILSON.

By the President:

ROBERT LANSING, *Secretary of State.*

[Extra Session of Congress, 1919.]

Whereas public interests require that the Congress of the United States should be convened in extra session at twelve o'clock, noon, on the nineteenth day of May, 1919, to receive such communication as may be made by the Executive:

Now, therefore, I, Woodrow Wilson, President of the United States of America, do hereby proclaim and declare that an extraordinary occasion requires the Congress of the United States to convene in extra session at the Capitol in the District of Columbia on the nineteenth day of May, 1919, at twelve o'clock, noon, of which all persons who shall at that time be entitled to act as members thereof are hereby required to take notice.

Given under my hand and the Seal of the United States of America the seventh day of May in the year of our Lord one thousand nine hundred and nineteen, and of the Independence of [SEAL.] the United States the one hundred and forty-third.

WOODROW WILSON.

By the President:

ROBERT LANSING, *Secretary of State.*

EXECUTIVE ORDER

[United States Wheat Director.]

THE WHITE HOUSE, *May 14, 1919.*

I, Woodrow Wilson, President of the United States of America, pursuant to an act of Congress entitled "An Act to provide further for the National Security and Defense by encouraging the production, conserving the supply and controlling the distribution of food products and fuel," approved August 10th, 1917, and an act of Congress entitled "An Act to enable the President to carry out the price guarantees made to producers of wheat of the crops of 1918 and 1919 and to protect the United States against undue enhancement of its liabilities thereunder," approved March 4th, 1919, and by virtue of the authority vested in me by said acts of Congress and each of them, as well as by virtue of any and all other acts of Congress conferring authority upon me in the premises, do hereby authorize, order and direct as follows:

The executive administration of the provisions of the above acts insofar as they apply to the wheat and its product of the crop of 1919 and the guarantees made to producers thereof and the protection of the United States against undue enhancement of its liabilities thereunder is hereby vested in a person to be designated and called the United States Wheat Director, and I hereby appoint Julius H. Barnes as such United States Wheat Director to act as such during the pleasure of the President. I hereby authorize and direct the United States Wheat Director to take such measures, adopt such administrative procedure, enter into such arrangements or agreements, withhold, refuse, issue, suspend and revoke such licenses and make such requisitions, orders, rules and regulations not inconsistent with law as he may from time to time deem necessary and proper for the purpose of such executive administration or as may be required in order to carry into effect this order or any orders and proclamations hereafter issued by me under the aforesaid acts or either of them in connection with such executive administration for such purpose. I vest in the United States Wheat Director all power and authority conferred upon me under the provisions of said acts applicable thereto. The United States Wheat Director shall have authority to employ and make use of the services of such agents, assistants and employees as he may deem necessary and as may be selected by him for service in connection with said executive administration with the consent and approval of the President and under such rules and regulations as may from time to time be prescribed. He shall also have authority to make use of the services of legal counsel and employ and fix the compensation of such counsel as may from time to time be deemed by him necessary for the purpose of aiding him in such executive administration and in carrying the provisions of said acts into effect.

I further find it essential and hereby direct that in order to carry out the guarantees made to producers of the wheat of the crop of 1919, and to protect the United States against undue enhancement of its liabilities thereunder, the United States Wheat Director utilize the services of the Food Administration Grain Corporation as an agency of the United States; and to that end I authorize the Food Administration Grain Corporation to buy and sell wheat of the crop of 1918 after June 1st, 1919, and I further authorize the Food Administration Grain Corporation, subject to the approval of the United States Wheat Director, to buy or contract for the purchase of wheat of the 1919 crop at places designated for the delivery of the same by the President's proclamation or at such other places as the United States Wheat Director may designate, for cash at the said guaranteed prices. And the said Food Administration Grain Corporation with the approval of the United States Wheat Director is thereafter authorized to buy or contract for the purchase of, for cash, or sell, consign or contract for the sale of, for cash or on credit, wheat of the said crops and flour produced therefrom at said guaranteed prices or at such other prices and on such terms or conditions as the United States Wheat Director may deem necessary or expedient. And said Food Administration Grain Corporation is authorized to borrow such sums of money, to enter into such voluntary agreements, to make such arrangements, and to do and perform such acts and things as may be necessary in order to make such guaranteed price effective and to carry out the purposes of said acts.

Inasmuch as the Food Administration Grain Corporation was formed as an agency of the United States in connection with the United States Food Administration activities under the control and direction of the United States Food Administration and since its functions will be substantially complete on June 30th, 1919, I hereby direct that the Food Administration Grain Corporation close its books on June 30, 1919, and make a complete report as of said date. And, further, that upon said date or as soon thereafter as may be practicable it shall take the proper steps to change its corporate name from Food Administration Grain Corporation to United States Grain Corporation, under which title it shall perform such duties as hereinbefore provided or as I may hereafter direct.

I further direct that Julius H. Barnes act as a director and as an executive officer of said corporation and that the other directors and executive officers of said corporations be selected by Julius H. Barnes with the approval of the President.

I further direct that the authorized capital stock of said corporation be increased from 1,500,000 to 5,000,000 shares of the par value of one hundred dollars each, and that the United States purchase from time to time at par so much of the additional capital stock as may be required to supply the necessary capital to enable said corporation to carry out the provisions of this order and that none of said additional stock shall be held by any person other than the United States. The United States Wheat Director is hereby authorized and directed to subscribe for and purchase at any time or from time to time all or any part of said additional capital stock in the name of and for the use and benefit of the United States and to pay for the same out of the appropriation of one billion dollars which is provided for in Section 8 of the foregoing act of Congress approved March 4th, 1919, and I direct the United States Treasurer to honor the requisition of the United States Wheat Director in this respect.

I further direct that all departments and established agencies of the Government coöperate with the United States Wheat Director in the performance of his duty as hereinbefore set forth and to give the United States Wheat Director such support and assistance as may be requisite or expedient to enable him to perform his said duties and avoid duplication of effort and expenditure of funds.

WOODROW WILSON.

MESSAGE TO CONGRESS

On the assembling of the Sixty-Sixth Congress in extraordinary session on May 20, 1919, the following message from President Wilson, in France, was read. This occasion was the first on which a message of length had been sent by a President to Congress by means of cable.

Gentlemen of the Congress:

I deeply regret my inability to be present at the opening of the extraordinary session of the Congress. It still seems to be my duty to take part in the counsels of the peace conference and contribute what I can to the solution of the innumerable questions to whose settlement it has had to address itself. For they are questions which affect the peace of the whole world and from them, therefore, the United States cannot stand apart.

I deemed it my duty to call the Congress together at this time because it was not wise to postpone longer the provisions which must be made for the support of the Government. Many of the appropriations which are absolutely necessary for the maintenance of the Government and the fulfillment of its varied obligations for the fiscal year 1919-1920 have not yet been made. The end of the present fiscal year is at hand, and action upon these appropriations can no longer be prudently delayed. It is necessary, therefore, that I should immediately call your attention to this critical need. It is hardly necessary for me to urge that it may receive your prompt attention.

I shall take the liberty of addressing you on my return on the subjects which have most engrossed our attention and the attention of the world during these last anxious months, since the armistice of last November was signed, the international settlements which must form the subject matter of the present treaties of peace and of our national action in the immediate future. It would be premature to discuss them or to express a judgment about them before they are brought to their complete formulation by the agreements which are now being sought at the table of the conference. I shall hope to lay them before you in their many aspects so soon as arrangements have been reached.

I hesitate to venture any opinion or press any recommendation with regard to domestic legislation while absent from the United States and out of daily touch with intimate sources of information and counsel. I am conscious that I need, after so long an absence from Washington, to seek the advice of those who have remained in constant contact with domestic problems and who have known them close at hand from day to day; and I trust that it will very soon be possible for me to do so. But there are several questions pressing for consideration to which I feel that I may and, indeed, must, even now direct your attention, if only in general terms. In speaking of them I shall, I dare say, be doing little more than speak your own thoughts. I hope that I shall speak your own judgment also.

The question which stands at the front of all others in every country amidst the present great awakening is the question of labor; and perhaps I can speak of it with as great advantage while engrossed in the consideration of interests which affect all countries alike as I could at home and amidst the interests which naturally most affect my thought, because they are the interests of our own people.

By the question of labor I do not mean the question of efficient industrial production, the question of how labor is to be obtained and made effective in the great process of sustaining populations and winning success amidst commercial and industrial rivalries. I mean that much greater and more vital question: How are the men and women who do the daily labor of the world to obtain progressive improvement in the conditions of their labor, to be made happier, and to be served better by the communities and the industries which their labor sustains and advances? How are they to be given their right advantage as citizens and human beings?

We cannot go any further in our present direction. We have already gone too far. We cannot live our right life as a nation or achieve our proper success as an industrial community if capital and labor are to continue to be antagonistic instead of being partners; if they are to continue to distrust one another and contrive how they can get the better of one another, or what perhaps amounts to the same thing, calculate by what form and degree of coercion they can manage to extort on the one hand work enough to make enterprise profitable, on the other justice and fair treatment enough to make life tolerable. That bad road has turned out a blind alley. It is no thoroughfare to real prosperity. We must find another, leading in another direction and to a very different destination. It must lead not merely to accommodation but also to a genuine coöperation and partnership based upon a real community of interest and participation in control.

There is now, in fact, a real community of interest between capital and labor, but it has never been made evident in action. It can be made operative and manifest only in a new organization of industry. The genius of our business men and the sound practical sense of our workers can certainly work such a partnership out when once they realize exactly what it is that they seek and sincerely adopt a common purpose with regard to it.

Labor legislation lies, of course, chiefly with the states; but the new spirit and method of organization which must be effected are not to be brought about by legislation so much as by the common counsel and voluntary coöperation of capitalist, manager, and workman. Legislation can go only a very little way in commanding what shall be done. The organization of industry is a matter of corporate and individual initiative and of practical business arrangement. Those who really desire a new relationship between capital and labor can readily find a way to bring it about; and perhaps Federal legislation can help more than state legislation could.

The object of all reform in this essential matter must be the genuine democratization of industry, based upon a full recognition of the right of those who work, in whatever rank, to participate in some organic way in every decision which directly affects their welfare or the part they are to play in industry. Some positive legislation is practicable. The Congress has already shown the way to one reform which should be world-wide, by establishing the eight-hour day as the standard day in every field of labor over which it can exercise control. It has sought to find the way to prevent child labor, and will, I hope and believe, presently find it. It has served the whole country by leading the way in developing the means of preserving and safeguarding life and health in dangerous industries. It can now help in the difficult task of giving a new form and spirit to industrial organization by coordinating the several agencies of conciliation and adjustment which have been brought into existence by the difficulties and mistaken policies of the present management of industry, and by setting up and

developing new Federal agencies of advice and information which may
serve as a clearing house for the best experiments and the best
thought on this great matter, upon which every thinking man must be
aware that the future development of society directly depends.

Agencies of international counsel and suggestion are presently to
be created in connection with the League of Nations in this very field;
but it is national action and the enlightened policy of individuals, corporations and societies within each nation that must bring about the
actual reforms. The members of the committees on labor in the two
houses will hardly need suggestions from me as to what means they
shall seek to make the Federal Government the agent of the whole
nation in pointing out and, if need be, guiding the process of reorganization and reform.

I am sure that it is not necessary for me to remind you that there
is one immediate and very practical question of labor that we should
meet in the most liberal spirit. We must see to it that our returning
soldiers are assisted in every practicable way to find the places for
which they are fitted in the daily work of the country. This can be
done by developing and maintaining upon an adequate scale the admirable organization created by the Department of Labor for placing
men seeking work; and it can also be done, in at least one very great
field, by creating new opportunities for individual enterprise.

The Secretary of the Interior has pointed out the way by which
returning soldiers may be helped to find and take up land in the
hitherto undeveloped regions of the country, which the Federal Government has already prepared or can readily prepare for cultivation,
and also on many of the cut over or neglected areas which lie within
the limits of the older states; and I once more take the liberty of
recommending very urgently that his plans shall receive the immediate
support of the Congress.

Peculiar and very stimulating conditions await our commerce and
industrial enterprise in the immediate future. Unusual opportunities
will presently present themselves to our merchants and producers in
foreign markets, and large fields of profitable investment will be
opened to our free capital. But it is not only of that that I am thinking;
it is not chiefly of that that I am thinking. Many great industries
prostrated by the war wait to be rehabilitated, in many parts of the
world where what will be lacking is not brains or willing hands or
organizing capacity or experienced skill, but machinery and raw materials and capital.

I believe that our business men, our merchants, our manufacturers,
and our capitalists, will have the vision to see that prosperity in one
part of the world ministers to prosperity everywhere. That there is
in a very true sense a solidarity of interest throughout the world of

enterprise, and that our dealings with the countries that have need of our products and our money will teach them to deem us more than ever friends whose necessities we seek in the right way to serve.

Our new merchant ships, which have in some quarters been feared as destructive rivals, may prove helpful rivals, rather, and common servants, very much needed and very welcome. Our great shipyards, new and old, will be so opened to the use of the world that they will prove immensely serviceable to every maritime people in restoring, much more rapidly than would otherwise have been possible, the tonnage wantonly destroyed in the war.

I have only to suggest that there are many points at which we can facilitate American enterprise in foreign trade by opportune legislation and make it easy for American merchants to go where they will be welcomed as friends rather than as dreaded antagonists. America has a great and honorable service to perform in bringing the commercial and industrial undertakings of the world back to their old scope and swing again, and putting a solid structure of credit under them. All our legislation should be friendly to such plans and purposes.

The credit and enterprise alike will be quickened by timely and helpful legislation with regard to taxation. I hope that the Congress will find it possible to undertake an early reconsideration of Federal taxes in order to make our system of taxation more simple and easy of administration and the taxes themselves as little burdensome as they can be made and yet sufficient to support the Government and meet all its obligations. The figures to which those obligations have arisen are very great indeed, but they are not so great as to make it difficult for the nation to meet them, and meet them perhaps in a single generation, by taxes which will neither crush nor discourage. These are not so great as they seem, not so great as the immense sums we have had to borrow, added to the immense sums we have had to raise by taxation, would seem to indicate; for a very large proportion of those sums were raised in order that they might be loaned to the governments with which we were associated in the war, and those loans will, of course, constitute assets, not liabilities, and will not have to be taken care of by our taxpayers.

The main thing we shall have to care for is that our taxation shall rest as lightly as possible on the productive resources of the country, that its rates shall be stable, and that it shall be constant in its revenue yielding power. We have found the main sources from which it must be drawn. I take it for granted that its mainstays will henceforth be the income tax, the excess profits tax, and the estate tax. All these can so be adjusted to yield constant and adequate returns, and yet not constitute a too grievous burden on the taxpayers.

A revision of the income tax has already been provided for by the act of 1918, but I think you will find that further changes can be made to advantage both in the rates of the tax and in the method of collection. The excess profits tax need not long be maintained at the rates which were necessary while the enormous expenses of the war had to be borne; but it should be made the basis of a permanent system which will reach undue profits without discouraging the enterprise and activity of our business men. The tax on inheritances ought, no doubt, to be reconsidered in its relation to the fiscal systems of the several States, but it certainly ought to remain a permanent part of the fiscal system of the Federal Government also.

Many of the minor taxes provided for in the revenue legislation of 1917 and 1918, though no doubt made necessary by the pressing necessities of the war time, can hardly find sufficient justification under the easier circumstances of peace and can now happily be got rid of. Among these, I hope you will agree, are the excises upon various manufactures and the taxes upon retail sales. They are unequal in the incidence on different industries and on different individuals. Their collection is difficult and expensive. Those which are levied upon articles sold at retail are largely evaded by the readjustment of retail prices.

On the other hand, I should assume that it is expedient to maintain a considerable range of indirect taxes, and the fact that alcoholic liquors will presently no longer afford a source of revenue by taxation makes it the more necessary that the field should be carefully restudied in order that equivalent sources of revenue may be found which it will be legitimate, and not burdensome, to draw upon. But you have at hand in the Treasury Department many experts who can advise you upon the matters much better than I can. I can only suggest the lines of a permanent and workable system, and the placing of the taxes where they will least hamper the life of the people.

There is, fortunately, no occasion for undertaking in the immediate future any general revision of our system of import duties. No serious danger of foreign competition now threatens American industries. Our country has emerged from the war less disturbed and less weakened than any of the European countries which are our competitors in manufacture. Their industrial establishments have been subjected to greater strain than ours, their labor force to a more serious disorganization, and this is clearly not the time to seek an organized advantage.

The work of mere reconstruction will, I am afraid, tax the capacity and the resources of their people for years to come. So far from there being any danger or need of accentuated foreign competition, it is likely that the conditions of the next few years will greatly facilitate the marketing of American manufactures abroad. Least of all should we depart from the policy adopted in the Tariff Act of 1913 of permitting the free entry into the United States of the raw materials needed to supplement and enrich our own abundant supplies.

Nevertheless, there are parts of our tariff system which need prompt attention. The experiences of the war have made it plain that in some cases too great reliance on foreign supply is dangerous, and that in determining certain parts of our tariff policy domestic considerations must be borne in mind which are political as well as economic. Among the industries to which special consideration should be given is that of the manufacture of dyestuffs and related chemicals. Our complete dependence upon German supplies before the war made the interruption of trade a cause of exceptional economic disturbance. The close relations between the manufacture of dyestuffs on the one hand and of explosives and poisonous gases on the other, moreover, has given the industry an exceptional significance and value.

Although the United States will gladly and unhesitatingly join in the program of international disarmament, it will, nevertheless, be a policy of obvious prudence to make certain of the successful maintenance of many strong and well equipped chemical plants. German chemical industry, with which we will be brought into competition, was and may well be again a thoroughly knit monopoly, capable of exercising a competition of a peculiarly insidious and dangerous kind.

The United States should, moreover, have the means of properly protecting itself whenever our trade is discriminated against by foreign nations, in order that we may be assured of that equality of treatment which we hope to accord and to promote the world over. Our tariff laws as they now stand provide no weapon of retaliation in case other governments should enact legislation unequal in its bearing on our products as compared with the products of other countries. Though we are as far as possible from desiring to enter upon any course of retaliation, we must frankly face the fact that hostile legislation by other nations is not beyond the range of possibility and that it may have to be met by counter-legislation.

This subject has fortunately been exhaustively investigated by the United States Tariff Commission. A recent report of that Commission has shown very clearly what we lack and that we ought to have the instruments necessary for the assurance of equal and equitable treatment. The attention of the Congress has been called to this matter on past occasions, and the past measures which are now recommended by the Tariff Commission are substantially the same that have been suggested by previous administrations. I recommend that this phase of the tariff question receive the early attention of the Congress.

Will you not permit me, turning from these matters, to speak once more and very earnestly of the proposed amendment to the Constitution which would extend the suffrage to women and which passed the House of Representatives at the last session of the Congress? It seems to me that every consideration of justice and of public advantage calls for the immediate adoption of that amendment and its submission forthwith to the Legislatures of the several States.

Throughout all the world this long delayed extension of the suffrage is looked for; in the United States, longer, I believe, than anywhere else. The necessity for it, and the immense advantage of it to the national life, has been urged and debated by women and men who saw the need for it and urged the policy of it when it required steadfast courage to be so much beforehand with the common conviction; and I, for one, covet for our country the distinction of being among the first to act in a great reform.

The telegraph and telephone lines will of course be returned to their owners so soon as the retransfer can be effected without administrative confusion, so soon, that is, as the change can be made with least possible inconvenience to the public and to the owners themselves. The railroads will be handed over to their owners at the end of the calendar year; if I were in immediate contact with the administrative questions which must govern the retransfer of the telegraph and telephone lines, I could name the exact date for their return also.

Until I am in direct contact with the practical questions involved I can only suggest that in the case of the telegraphs and telephones as in the case of the railways, it is clearly desirable in the public interest that some legislation should be considered which may tend to make of these indispensable instrumentalities of our modern life a uniform and co-ordinated system which will afford those who use them as complete and certain means of communication with all parts of the country as has so long been afforded by the postal system of the government, and at rates as uniform and intelligible. Expert advice is, of course, available in this very practical matter, and the public interest is manifest.

Neither the telegraph nor the telephone service of the country can be said to be in any sense a national system. There are many confusions and inconsistencies of rates. The scientific means by which communication by such instrumentalities could be rendered more thorough and satisfactory has not been made full use of. An exhaustive study of the whole question of electrical communication and of the means by which the central authority of the nation can be used to unify and improve it, if undertaken by the appropriate committees of the Congress, would certainly result indirectly even if not directly in a great public benefit.

The demobilization of the military forces of the country has progressed to such a point that it seems to me entirely safe now to remove the ban upon the manufacture and sale of wines and beers, but I am advised that without further legislation I have not the legal authority to remove the present restrictions. I therefore recommend that the act approved November 21, 1918, entitled "An act to enable the Secretary of Agriculture to carry out, during the fiscal year ending June 30, 1919, the purpose of the act entitled 'An act to provide further for the national security and defense by stimulating agriculture and facilitating the distribution of agricultural products,' and for other purposes" be amended or repealed in so far as it applies to wines and beers.

I sincerely trust that I shall very soon be at my post in Washington again to report upon the matters which made my presence at the peace table apparently imperative, and to put myself at the service of the Congress in every matter of administration or counsel that may seem to demand executive action or advice.

WOODROW WILSON.

MEMORIAL DAY ADDRESS

[Delivered on May 30, 1919, among the Graves of American Soldiers in Suresnes Cemetery, near Paris, France.]

Mr. Ambassador, Ladies and Gentlemen, Fellow-Countrymen:

No one with a heart in his breast, no American, no lover of humanity, can stand in the presence of these graves without the most profound emotion. These men who lie here are men of a unique breed. Their like has not been seen since the far days of Crusades. Never before have men crossed the seas to a foreign land to fight for a cause of humanity which they did not pretend was particularly their own, but knew was the cause of humanity and of mankind.

And when they came, they found comrades for their courage and their devotion. They found armies of liberty already in the field— men who, though they had gone through three years of fiery trial, seemed only to be just discovering, not for a moment losing, the high temper of the great affair, men seasoned in the bloody service of liberty. Joining hands with these, the men of America gave that greatest of all gifts, the gift of life and the gift of spirit.

It will always be a treasured memory on the part of those who knew and loved these men that the testimony of everybody who saw them in the field of action was borne to their unflinching courage, their ardor to the point of audacity, their full consciousness of the high cause they had come to serve, and their constant vision of the issue.

It is delightful to learn from those who saw these men fight, and saw them waiting in the trenches for the summons to the fight, that they had a touch of the high spirit of religion, that they knew they were exhibiting a spirit as well as a physical might, and those of us who know and love America know that they were discovering to the whole world the true spirit and devotion of their motherland. It was America who came in the person of these men, and who will forever be grateful that she was so represented.

And it is the more delightful to entertain these thoughts because we know that these men, though buried in a foreign land, are not buried in an alien soil. They are at home, sleeping with the spirits of those who thought the same thoughts and entertained the same aspirations. The noble women of Suresnes have given evidence of the loving sense with which they received these dead as their own, for they have cared for their graves, they have made it their interest, their loving interest, to see that there was no hour of neglect, and that constantly through all the months that have gone by the mothers at home should know that there were mothers here who remembered and honored their dead.

You have just heard in the beautiful letter from M. Clemenceau what I believe to be the real message of France to us on a day like this—a message of genuine comradeship, a message of genuine sympathy, and I have no doubt that if our British comrades were here they would speak in the same spirit and in the same language. For the beauty of this war is that it has brought a new partnership, and a new comradeship, and a new understanding into the field of the effort of the nation.

But it would be no profit to us to eulogize these illustrious dead if we did not take to heart the lesson which they have taught us. They are dead; they have done their utmost to show their devotion to a great cause, and they have left us to see to it that that cause shall not be betrayed, whether in war or peace.

It is our privilege and our high duty to consecrate ourselves afresh on a day like this to the objects for which they fought. It is not necessary that I should rehearse to you what these objects were.

These men did not come across the sea merely to defeat Germany and her associated powers in the war. They came to defeat forever the things for which the Central Powers stood, the sort of power they meant to assert in the world, the arrogant, selfish domination which they meant to establish; and they came, moreover, to see to it that there should never be a war like this again. It is for us, particularly for us who are civilized, to use our proper weapons of counsel and agreement to see to it that there never is such a war again. The nation that should now fling out of this common concord of counsel would betray the human race.

So it is our duty to take and maintain the safeguards which will see to it that the mothers of America, and the mothers of France and England and Italy and Belgium, and all other suffering nations, should never be called upon for this sacrifice again. This can be done. It must be done. And it will be done.

The things that these men left us, though they did not in their counsels conceive it, is the great instrument which we have just erected in the League of Nations. The League of Nations is the Covenant of Government that these men shall not have died in vain.

I like to think that the dust of those sons of America who were privileged to be buried in their mother country will mingle with the dust of the men who fought for the preservation of the Union, and that as those men gave their lives in order that America might be united, these men have given their lives in order that the world might be united. Those men gave their lives in order to secure the freedom of a nation. These men have given theirs in order to secure the freedom of mankind; and I look forward to an age when it will be just as impossible to regret the results of their labor as it is now impossible to regret the result of the labor of those men who fought for the union of the States. I look for the time when every man who now puts his counsel against the united service of mankind under the League of Nations will be just as ashamed of it as if he now regretted the union of the States.

You are aware, as I am aware, that the airs of an older day are beginning to stir again, that the standards of an old order are trying to assert themselves again. There is here and there an attempt to insert into the counsel of statesmen the old reckoning of selfishness and bargaining and national advantage which were the roots of this war, and any man who counsels these things advocates a renewal of the sacrifice which these men have made, for if this is not the final battle for right, there will be another that will be final.

Let these gentlemen who suppose that it is possible for them to accomplish this return to an order of which we are ashamed, and that we are ready to forget, realize they cannot accomplish it. The peoples of the world are awake and the peoples of the world are in the saddle. Private counsels of statesmen cannot now and cannot hereafter determine the destinies of nations. If we are not the servants of the opinion of mankind, we are of all men the littlest, the most contemptible, the least gifted with vision. If we do not know courage we cannot accomplish our purpose; and this age is an age which looks forward, not backward; which rejects the standard of national selfishness that once governed the counsels of nations, and demands that they shall give way to a new order of things in which only the question will be "Is it right?" "Is it just?" "Is it in the interest of mankind?"

This is a challenge that no previous generation ever dared to give ear to. So many things have happened, and they have happened so fast in the last four years that I do not think many of us realize what it is that has happened. Think how impossible it would have been to get a body of responsible statesmen seriously to entertain the idea of the organization of a League of Nations four years ago! And think of the change that has taken place!

I was told before I came to France that there would be confusion of counsels about this thing, and I found unity of counsel. I was told that there would be opposition, and I found union of action. I found the statesmen with whom I was about to deal united in the idea that we must have a League of Nations; that we could not merely make a peace settlement and then leave it to make itself effectual, but that we must conceive some common organization by which we should give our common faith that this peace would be maintained, and the conclusions at which we had arrived should be made as secure as the united counsels of all the great nations that fought against Germany could make them. We have listened to the challenge, and that is the proof that there shall never be a war like this again.

Ladies and gentlemen, we all believe, I hope, that the spirits of these men are not buried with their bones. Their spirits live. I hope—I believe—that their spirits are present with us at this hour. I hope that I feel the compulsion of their presence. I hope that I realize the significance of their presence. Think, soldiers, of those comrades of yours who are gone. If they were here what would they say? They would not remember what you are talking about today. They would remember America, which they left with their high hope and purpose. They would remember the terrible field of battle. They would remember what they constantly recalled in times of danger, what they had come for, and how worth while it was to give their lives for it.

And they would say, "Forget all the little circumstances of the day. Be ashamed of the jealousies that divide you. We command you in the name of those who, like ourselves, have died to bring the counsels of men together; and we remind you what America said she was born for. She was born, she said, to show mankind the way to liberty. She was born to make this great gift a common gift. She was born to show men the way of experience by which they might realize this gift and maintain it; and we readjure you, in the name of all the great traditions of America, to make yourselves soldiers now once for all in this common cause, where we need wear no uniform except the uniform of the heart, clothing ourselves with the principles of right and saying to men everywhere, 'You are our brothers and we invite you into the comradeship of liberty and of peace.' "

Let us go away hearing these unspoken mandates of our dead comrades.

If I may speak a personal word, I beg you to realize the compulsion that I myself feel that I am under. By the Constitution of our great country, I was the commander-in-chief of these men. I advised the Congress to declare that a state of war existed. I sent these lads over here to die. Shall I—can I—ever speak a word of counsel which is inconsistent with the assurances I gave them when they came over? It is inconceivable.

There is something better, if possible, that a man can give than his life, and that is his living spirit to a service that is not easy, to resist counsels that are hard to resist, to stand against purposes that are difficult to stand against, and to say, "Here stand I, consecrated in the spirit of the men who were once my comrades, and who are now gone, and who left me under eternal bonds of fidelity."

EXECUTIVE ORDER

[Consolidating Present Collection Districts and Creating New Districts.]

THE WHITE HOUSE, *June 29, 1919.*

The attached Executive Order abolishes 10 Internal Revenue Collection Districts, consolidating them with other Districts—and creates 10 new Districts in states which do not now have separate Collection Districts. This leaves the number of Districts the same as at present—64. It gives each state, with the single exception of Nevada, at least one separate Collection District of its own.

With the number of tax returns increasing from 400,000 ten years ago to over 15,000,000 for 1919, with the many complicated tax laws requiring so much personal explanation and service, the old order of Internal Revenue policy based on conditions existing many years ago no longer legitimately performs its expected functions. It has become imperative that each state have its own revenue service and that as rapidly as possible the head collection offices be decentralized so that they shall become clearing and accounting places for Washington, and thus permit the opening of permanent personal service division headquarters in every important city.

This program is designed to accomplish this by creating new state districts, by abolishing districts where changed revenue conditions logically permit such action and by opening up in such consolidated districts the personal service division headquarters more efficiently to serve taxpayers.

The following changes are provided for, effective as of August, 1, 1919.

Illinois—The 5th, (Peoria) Collection District is combined with the 1st, (Chicago) District, with headquarters at Chicago, and the 13th, (East St. Louis) District is combined with the 8th, (Springfield) District, with headquarters at Springfield. This reduces the number of Collection Districts in Illinois from four to two, and affords opportunity for extending the service by the opening of Division headquarters in the cities of Joliet, Aurora, Rockford, Peoria, Rock Island, East St. Louis, Cairo, Danville, Decatur, Bloomington, and Centralia.

Indiana—The 7th, (Terre Haute) Collection District is combined with the 6th, (Indianapolis) District, with headquarters at Indianapolis. This makes but one district for the entire state and affords opportunity for extending the service by the opening of Division headquarters in the cities of Terre Haute, Evansville, Gary, South Bend, Fort Wayne, Muncie, Logansport, Lafayette, New Albany, Bedford and Columbus.

Kentucky—The 2d, (Owensboro) 6th, (Covington) 7th, (Lexington) and 8th, (Danville) Collection Districts are combined with the 5th (Louisville) District, with headquarters at Louisville. This eliminates four Collection Districts, leaving but one District for the entire state and affords opportunity for extending the service by the opening of Division headquarters in the cities of Covington, Lexington, Danville, Owensboro, Paducah, Bowling Green, Middlesboro and Ashland.

North Carolina—The 5th, (Statesville) Collection District is combined with the 4th, (Raleigh) District, with headquarters at Raleigh, making but one District for the entire state and affords opportunity for extending the service by the opening of Division headquarters in the cities of Asheville, Charlotte, Wilmington, Statesville and Washington.

Pennsylvania—The 9th, (Lancaster) Collection District is combined with the 1st, (Philadelphia) District, with headquarters at Philadelphia. This reduces the number of Collection Districts in Pennsylvania from four to three, the 12th, (Scranton) District and the 23d, (Pittsburgh) District remaining the same as at present, and affords opportunity for extending the service by the opening of Division headquarters in the cities of Chester, Lancaster, Reading, Harrisburg, York, Altoona, Allentown, Norristown and Pottsville.

Wisconsin—The 1st, (Milwaukee) Collection District is combined with the 2d, (Madison) District, with headquarters at Milwaukee, making but one District for the entire state and affords opportunity for extending the service by opening of Division headquarters in the cities of Madison, LaCrosse, Eau-Clair, Superior, Wausaw, Green Bay, Oshkosh, Sheboygan and Racine.

(To take effect upon qualification of Collectors for new Districts.)

Alabama and Mississippi—Separate Collection Districts are created for the states of Alabama and Mississippi, which now comprise the one District of Alabama. Collectors' offices will be located at Birmingham, Alabama, and Jackson, Mississippi.

Arizona and New Mexico—Separate Collection Districts are created for the states of Arizona and New Mexico, which now comprise the one District of New Mexico. Collectors' offices will be located at Phoenix, Arizona, and Albuquerque, New Mexico.

Colorado and Wyoming—Separate Collection Districts are created for the states of Colorado and Wyoming, which now comprise the one District of Colorado. Collectors' offices will be located at Denver, Colorado, and Cheyenne, Wyoming.

Connecticut and Rhode Island—Separate Collection Districts are created for the states of Connecticut and Rhode Island, which now comprise the one District of Connecticut. Collectors' offices will be located at Hartford, Connecticut, and Providence, Rhode Island.

Maryland and Delaware—Separate Collection Districts are created for the states of Maryland and Delaware, which now comprise the one District of Maryland. Collectors' offices will be located at Baltimore, Maryland, and Wilmington, Delaware.

Montana, Idaho and Utah—Separate Collection Districts are created for the states of Montana, Idaho and Utah, which now comprise the one District of Montana. Collectors' offices will be located at Helena, Montana, Boise, Idaho, and Salt Lake City, Utah.

Maine, New Hampshire and Vermont—Separate Collection Districts are created for the states of Maine, New Hampshire and Vermont, which now comprise the one District of New Hampshire. Collectors' offices will be located at Portland, Maine, Burlington, Vermont, and Manchester, New Hampshire, this office being moved from Portsmouth to Manchester.

North Dakota and South Dakota—Separate Collection Districts are created for the states of North Dakota and South Dakota, which now comprise the one District of North and South Dakota. Collectors' offices will be located at Fargo, North Dakota, and Aberdeen, South Dakota.

WOODROW WILSON.

ADDRESS TO FELLOW-COUNTRYMEN

[Announcing the signing of the peace treaty with Germany at Versailles, France. The message was cabled from France on June 28, 1919.]

My Fellow Countrymen: The treaty of peace has been signed. If it is ratified and acted upon in full and sincere execution of its terms it will furnish the charter for a new order of affairs in the world.

It is a severe treaty in the duties and penalties it imposes upon Germany, but it is severe only because great wrongs done by Germany are to be righted and repaired.

It imposes nothing that Germany cannot do; and she can regain her rightful standing in the world by the prompt and honorable fulfillment of its terms. And it is much more than a treaty of peace with Germany. It liberates great peoples who have never before been able to find the way to liberty. It ends, once for all, an old and intolerable order under which small groups of selfish men could use the peoples of great empires to serve their own ambition for power and dominion.

It associates the free governments of the world in a permanent league in which they are pledged to use their united power to maintain peace by maintaining right and justice.

It makes international law a reality supported by imperative sanctions. It does away with the right of conquest and rejects the policy of annexation and substitutes a new order under which backward nations—populations which have not yet come to political consciousness—and peoples who are ready for independence but not yet quite prepared to dispense with protection and guidance—shall no more be subjected to the domination and exploitation of a stronger nation, but shall be put under the friendly direction and afforded the helpful assistance of governments which undertake to be responsible to the opinion of mankind in the execution of their task by accepting the direction of the League of Nations.

It recognizes the inalienable rights of nationality; the rights of minorities and the sanctity of religious belief and practice. It lays the basis for conventions which shall free the commercial intercourse of the world from unjust and vexatious restrictions and for every sort of international co-operation that will serve to cleanse the life of the world and facilitate its common action in beneficent service of every kind. It furnishes guarantees such as were never given or even contemplated before for the fair treatment of all who labor at the daily tasks of the world. It is for this reason that I have spoken of it as a great charter for a new order of affairs. There is ground here for deep satisfaction, universal reassurance, and confident hope.

WOODROW WILSON.

ADDRESS TO THE SENATE

[President Wilson left France on June 29, 1919, reaching the United States on July 8. On July 10 he addressed the Senate on the peace treaty, as follows:]

Gentlemen of the Senate:

The treaty of peace with Germany was signed at Versailles on the twenty-eighth of June. I avail myself of the earliest opportunity to lay the treaty before you for ratification and to inform you with regard to the work of the conference by which that treaty was formulated.

The treaty constitutes nothing less than a world settlement. It would not be possible for me either to summarize or to construe its manifold provisions in an address which must of necessity be something less than a treatise. My services and all the information I possess will be at your disposal and at the disposal of your Committee on Foreign Relations at any time, either informally or in session, as you may prefer; and I hope that you will not hesitate to make use of them. I shall at this time, prior to your own study of the document, attempt only a general characterization of its scope and purpose.

In one sense, no doubt, there is no need that I should report to you what was attempted and done at Paris. You have been daily cognizant of what was going on there,—of the problems with which the Peace Conference had to deal and of the difficulty of laying down straight lines of settlement anywhere on a field on which the old lines of international relationship and the new alike, followed so intricate a pattern and were for the most part cut so deep by historical circumstances which dominated action even where it would have been best to ignore or reverse them. The cross currents of politics and of interest must have been evident to you. It would be presuming in me to attempt to explain the questions which arose or the many diverse elements that entered into them. I shall attempt something less ambitious than that and more clearly suggested by my duty to report to the Congress the part it seemed necessary for my colleagues and me to play as the representatives of the Government of the United States.

That part was dictated by the role America had played in the war and by the expectations that had been created in the minds of the peoples with whom we had associated ourselves in that great struggle.

The United States entered the war upon a different footing from every other nation except our associates on this side the sea. We entered it, not because our material interests were directly threatened or because any special treaty obligations to which we were parties had been involved, but only because we saw the supremacy, and even the validity, of right everywhere put in jeopardy and free government likely to be everywhere imperiled by the intolerable aggression of a power which respected neither right nor obligation and whose very system of government flouted the rights of the citizen as against the autocratic authority of his governors. And in the settlement of the peace we have sought no special reparation for ourselves, but only the restoration of right and the assurance of liberty everywhere that the effects of the settlement were to be felt. We entered the war as the disinterested champions of right and we interested ourselves in the terms of the peace in no other capacity.

The hopes of the nations allied against the Central Powers were at a very low ebb when our soldiers began to pour across the sea. There was everywhere amongst them, except in their stoutest spirits, a sombre foreboding of disaster. The war ended in November, eight months ago, but you have only to recall what was feared in midsummer last, four short months before the armistice, to realize what it was that our timely aid accomplished alike for their morale and their physical safety. That first, never-to-forgotten action at Château-

Thierry had already taken place. Our redoubtable soldiers and marines had already closed the gap the enemy had succeeded in opening for their advance upon Paris,—had already turned the tide of battle back towards the frontiers of France and begun the rout that was to save Europe and the world. Thereafter the Germans were to be always forced back, back, were never to thrust successfully forward again. And yet there was no confident hope. Anxious men and women, leading spirits of France, attended the celebration of the Fourth of July last year in Paris out of generous courtesy,—with no heart for festivity, little zest for hope. But they came away with something new at their hearts; they have themselves told us so. The mere sight of our men,—of their vigour, of the confidence that showed itself in every movement of their stalwart figures and every turn of their swinging march, in their steady comprehending eyes and easy discipline, in the indomitable air that added spirit to everything they did,—made everyone who saw them that memorable day realize that something had happened that was much more than a mere incident in the fighting, something very different from the mere arrival of fresh troops. A great moral force had flung itself into the struggle. The fine physical force of those spirited men spoke of something more than bodily vigor. They carried the great ideals of a free people at their hearts and with that vision were unconquerable. Their very presence brought reassurance; their fighting made victory certain.

They were recognized as crusaders, and as their thousands swelled to millions their strength was seen to mean salvation. And they were fit men to carry such a hope and make good the assurance it forecast. Finer men never went into battle; and their officers were worthy of them. This is not the occasion upon which to utter a eulogy of the armies America sent to France, but perhaps, since I am speaking of their mission, I may speak also of the pride I shared with every American who saw or dealt with them there. They were the sort of men America would wish to be represented by, the sort of men every American would wish to claim as fellow-countrymen and comrades in a great cause. They were terrible in battle, and gentle and helpful out of it, remembering the mothers and the sisters, the wives and the little children at home. They were free men under arms, not forgetting their ideals of duty in the midst of tasks of violence. I am proud to have had the privilege of being associated with them and of calling myself their leader.

But I speak now of what they meant to the men by whose sides they fought and to the people with whom they mingled with such utter simplicity, as friends who asked only to be of service. They were for all the visible embodiment of America. What they did made America and all that she stood for a living reality in the thoughts not only of the people of France but also of tens of millions of men and women throughout all the toiling nations of a world standing everywhere in peril of its freedom and of the loss of everything it held dear, in deadly fear that its bonds were never to be loosed, its hopes forever to be mocked and disappointed.

And the compulsion of what they stood for was upon us who represented America at the peace table. It was our duty to see to it that every decision we took part in contributed, so far as we were able to influence it, to quiet the fears and realize the hopes of the peoples who had been living in that shadow, the nations that had come by our assistance to their freedom. It was our duty to do everything that it was within our power to do to make the triumph of freedom and of right a lasting triumph in the assurance of which men might everywhere live without fear.

Old entanglements of every kind stood in the way,—promises which Governments had made to one another in the days when might and right were confused and the power of the victor was without restraint. Engagements which contemplated any dispositions of territory, any extensions of sovereignty that might seem to be to the interest of those who had the power to insist upon them, had been entered into without thought of what the peoples concerned might wish or profit by; and these could not always be honorably brushed aside. It was not easy to graft the new order of ideas on the old, and some of the fruits of the grafting may, I fear, for a time be bitter. But, with very few exceptions, the men who sat with us at the peace table desired as sincerely as we did to get away from the bad influences, the illegitimate purposes, the demoralizing ambitions, the international counsels and expedients out of which the sinister designs of Germany had sprung as a natural growth.

It had been our privilege to formulate the principles which were accepted as the basis of the peace, but they had been accepted, not because we had come in to hasten and assure the victory and insisted upon them, but because they were readily acceded to as the principles to which honorable and enlightened minds everywhere had been bred. They spoke the conscience of the world as well as the conscience of America, and I am happy to pay my tribute of respect and gratitude to the able, forward-looking men with whom it was my privilege to co-operate for their unfailing spirit of co-operation, their constant effort to accommodate the interests they represented to the principles we were all agreed upon. The difficulties, which were many, lay in the circumstances, not often in the men. Almost without exception the men who led had caught the true and full vision of the problem of peace as an indivisible whole, a problem, not of mere adjustments of interests, but of justice and right action.

The atmosphere in which the Conference worked seemed created, not by the ambitions of strong governments, but by the hopes and aspirations of small nations and of peoples hitherto under bondage to the power that victory had shattered and destroyed. Two great empires had been forced into political bankruptcy, and we were the receivers. Our task was not only to make peace with the Central Empires and remedy the wrongs their armies had done. The Central Empires had lived in open violation of many of the very rights for which the war had been fought, dominating alien peoples over whom they had no natural right to rule, enforcing, not obedience, but veritable bondage, exploiting those who were weak for the benefit of those who were masters and overlords only by force of arms. There could be no peace until the whole order of central Europe was set right.

That meant that new nations were to be created,—Poland, Czecho-Slovakia, Hungary itself. No part of ancient Poland had ever in any true sense become a part of Germany, or of Austria, or of Russia. Bohemia was alien in every thought and hope to the monarchy of which she had so long been an artificial part; and the uneasy partnership between Austria and Hungary had been one rather of interest than of kinship or sympathy. The Slavs whom Austria had chosen to force into her empire on the south were kept to their obedience by nothing but fear. Their hearts were with their kinsmen in the Balkans. These were all arrangements of power, not arrangements of natural union or association. It was the imperative task of those who would make peace and make it intelligently to establish a new order which would rest upon the free choice of peoples rather than upon the arbitrary authority of Hapsburgs or Hohenzollerns.

More than that, great populations bound by sympathy and actual kin to Rumania were also linked against their will to the conglomerate Austro-Hungarian monarchy or to other alien sovereignties, and it was part of the task of peace to make a new Rumania as well as a new Slavic state clustering about Serbia.

And no natural frontiers could be found to these new fields of adjustment and redemption. It was necessary to look constantly forward to other related tasks. The German colonies were to be disposed of. They had not been governed; they had been exploited merely, without thought of the interest or even the ordinary human rights of their inhabitants.

The Turkish Empire, moreover, had fallen apart, as the Austro-Hungarian had. It had never had any real unity. It had been held together only by pitiless, inhuman force. Its peoples cried aloud for release, for succor from unspeakable distress, for all that the new day of hope seemed at last to bring within its dawn. Peoples hitherto in utter darkness were to be led out into the same light and given at last a helping hand. Undeveloped peoples and peoples ready for recognition but not yet ready to assume the full responsibilities of statehood were to be given adequate guarantees of friendly protection, guidance, and assistance.

And out of the execution of these great enterprises of liberty sprang opportunities to attempt what statesmen had never found the way before to do; an opportunity to throw safeguards about the rights of racial, national, and religious minorities by solemn international covenant; an opportunity to limit and regulate military establishments where they were most likely to be mischievous; an opportunity to effect a complete and systematic internationalization of waterways and railways which were necessary to the free economic life of more than one nation and to clear many of the normal channels of commerce of unfair obstructions of law or of privilege; and the very welcome opportunity to secure for labor the concerted protection of definite international pledges of principle and practice.

These were not tasks which the Conference looked about it to find and went out of its way to perform. They were inseparable from the settlements of peace. They were thrust upon it by circumstances which could not be overlooked. The war had created them. In all quarters of the world old established relationships had been disturbed or broken and affairs were at loose ends, needing to be mended or united again, but could not be made what they were before. They had to be set right by applying some uniform principle of justice or enlightened expediency. And they could not be adjusted by merely prescribing in a treaty what should be done. New states were to be set up which could not hope to live through their first period of weakness without assured support by the great nations that had consented to their creation and won for them their independence. Ill governed colonies could not be put in the hands of governments which were to act as trustees for their people and not as their masters if there was to be no common authority among the nations to which they were to be responsible in the execution of their trust. Future international conventions with regard to the control of waterways, with regard to illicit traffic of many kinds, in arms or in deadly drugs, or with regard to the adjustment of many varying international administrative arrangements could not be assured if the treaty were to provide no permanent common international agency, if its execution in such matters were to be left to the slow and uncertain processes of co-operation by ordinary methods of negotiation. If the Peace Conference itself was to be the end of co-operative authority and common counsel among the governments to which the world was looking to enforce justice and give pledges of an enduring settlement, regions like the Sarre basin could not be put under a temporary administrative regime which did not involve a transfer of political sovereignty and which contemplated a final determination of its political connections by popular vote to be taken at a distant date; no free city like Danzig could be created which was, under elaborate international guarantees, to accept exceptional obligations with regard to the use of its port and exceptional relations with a State of which it was not to form a part; properly safeguarded plebescites could not be provided for where populations were at some future date to make choice what sovereignty they would live under; no certain and uniform method of arbitration could be secured for the settlement of anticipated difficulties of final decision with regard to many matters dealt with in the treaty itself; the long-continued supervision of the task of reparation which Germany was to undertake to complete within the next generation might entirely break down; the reconsideration and revision of administrative arrangements and restrictions which the treaty prescribed but which it was recognized might not prove of lasting advantage or entirely fair if too long enforced would be impracticable. The promises governments were making to one another about the way in which labor was to be dealt with, by law not only but in fact as well, would remain a mere humane thesis if there was to be no common tribunal of opinion and judgment to which liberal statesmen could resort for the influences which alone might secure their redemption. A league of free nations had become a practical necessity. Examine the treaty of peace and you will find that everywhere throughout its manifold provisions its framers have felt obliged to turn to the League of Nations as an indispensable instrumentality for the maintenance of the new order it has been their purpose to set up in the world,—the world of civilized men.

That there should be a league of nations to steady the counsels and maintain the peaceful understandings of the world, to make, not treaties alone, but the accepted principles of international law as well, the actual rule of conduct among the governments of the world, had been one of the agreements accepted from the first as the basis of peace with the Central Powers. The statesmen of all the belligerent countries were agreed that such a league must be created to sustain the settlements that were to be effected. But at first I think there was a feeling among some of them that, while it must be attempted, the formation of such a league was perhaps a counsel of perfection which practical men, long experienced in the world of affairs, must agree to very cautiously and with many misgivings. It was only as the difficult work of arranging an all-but-universal adjustment of the world's affairs advanced from day to day from one stage of conference to another that it became evident to them that what they were seeking would be little more than something written upon paper, to be interpreted and applied by such methods as the chances of politics might make available if they did not provide a means of common counsel which all were obliged to accept, a common authority whose decisions would be recognized as decisions which all must respect.

And so the most practical, the most skeptical among them turned more and more to the League as the authority through which international action was to be secured, the authority without which, as they had come to see it, it would be difficult to give assured effect either to this treaty or to any other international undersanding upon which they were to depend for the maintenance of peace. The fact that the Covenant of the League was the first substantive part of the treaty to be worked out and agreed upon, while all else was in solution, helped to make the formulation of the rest easier. The Conference was, after all, not to be ephemeral. The concert of nations was to continue, under a definite Covenant which had been agreed upon and which all were convinced was workable. They could go forward with confidence to make arrangements intended to be permanent. The most practical of the conferees were at last the most ready to refer to the League of Nations the superintendence of all interests which did not admit of immediate determination, of all administrative problems which were to require a continuing oversight. What had seemed a counsel of perfection had come to seem a plain counsel of necessity. The League of Nations was the practical statesman's hope of success in many of the most difficult things he was attempting.

And it had validated itself in the thought of every member of the Conference as something much bigger, much greater every way, than a mere instrument for carrying out the provisions of a particular treaty. It was universally recognized that all the peoples of the world demanded of the Conference that it should create such a continuing concert of free nations as would make wars of aggression and spoilation such as this that has just ended forever impossible. A cry had gone out from every home in every stricken land from which sons and brothers and fathers had gone forth to the great sacrifice that such a sacrifice should never again be exacted. It was manifest why it had been exacted. It had been exacted because one nation desired dominion and other nations had known no means of defense except armaments and alliances. War had lain at the heart of every arrangement of the Europe,—of every arrangement of the world,— that preceded the war. Restive peoples had been told that fleets and armies, which they toiled to sustain, meant peace; and they now knew that they had been lied to: that fleets and armies had been maintained to promote national ambitions and meant war. They knew that no old policy meant anything else but force, force,—always force. And they knew that it was intolerable. Every true heart in the world, and every enlightened judgment demanded that, at whatever cost of independent action, every government that took thought for its people or for justice or for ordered freedom should lend itself to a new purpose and utterly destroy the old order of international politics. Statesmen might see difficulties, but the people could see none and could brook no denial. A war in which they had been bled white to beat the terror that lay concealed in every Balance of Power must not end in a mere victory of arms and a new balance. The monster that had resorted to arms must be put in chains that could not be broken. The united power of free nations must put a stop to aggression, and the world must be given peace. If there was not the will or the intelligence to accomplish that now, there must be another and a final war and the world must be swept clean of every power that could renew the terror. The League of Nations was not merely an instrument to adjust and remedy old wrongs under a new treaty of peace; it was the only hope for mankind. Again and again had the demon of war been cast out of the house of the peoples and the house swept clean by a treaty of peace; only to prepare a time when he would enter in again with spirits worse than himself. The house must now be given a tenant who could hold it against all such. Convenient, indeed indispensable, as statesmen found the newly planned League of Nations to be for the execution of present plans of peace and reparation, they saw it in a new aspect before their work was finished. They saw it as the main object of the peace, as the only thing that could complete it or make it worth while. They saw it as the hope of the world, and that hope they did not dare to disappoint. Shall we or any other free people hesitate to accept this great duty? Dare we reject it and break the heart of the world?

And so the result of the Conference of Peace, so far as Germany is concerned, stands complete. The difficulties encountered were very many. Sometimes they seemed insuperable. It was impossible to accommodate the interests of so great a body of nations,—interests which directly or indirectly affected almost every nation in the world,—without many minor compromises. The treaty, as a result, is not exactly what we would have written. It is probably not what any one of the national delegations would have written. But results were worked out which on the whole bear test. I think that it will be found that the compromises which were accepted as inevitable nowhere cut to the heart of any principle. The work of the Conference squares, as a whole, with the principles agreed upon as the basis of the peace as well as with the practical possibilities of the international situations which had to be faced and dealt with as facts.

I shall presently have occasion to lay before you a special treaty with France, whose object is the temporary protection of France from unprovoked aggression by the Power with whom this treaty of peace has been negotiated. Its terms link it with this treaty. I take the liberty, however, of reserving it for special explication on another occasion.

The role which America was to play in the Conference seemed determined, as I have said, before my colleagues and I got to Paris,—determined by the universal expectations of the nations whose representatives, drawn from all quarters of the globe, we were to deal with. It was universally recognized that America had entered the war to promote no private or peculiar interest of her own but only as the champion of rights which she was glad to share with free men and lovers of justice everywhere. We had formulated the principles upon which the settlement was to be made,—the principles upon which the armistice had been agreed to and the parleys of peace undertaken,—and no one doubted that our desire was to see the treaty of peace formulated along the actual lines of those principles,—and desired nothing else. We were welcomed as disinterested friends. We were resorted to as arbiters in many a difficult matter. It was recognized that our material aid would be indispensable in the days to come, when industry and credit would have to be brought back to their normal operation again and communities beaten to the ground assisted to their feet once more, and it was taken for granted, I am proud to say, that we would play the helpful friend in these things as in all others without prejudice or favor. We were generously accepted as the unaffected champions of what was right. It was a very responsible role to play; but I am happy to report that the fine group of Americans who helped with their expert advice in each part of the varied settlements sought in every transaction to justify the high confidence reposed in them.

And that confidence, it seems to me, is the measure of our opportunity and of our duty in the days to come, in which the new hope of the peoples of the world is to be fulfilled or disappointed. The fact that America is the friend of the nations, whether they be rivals or associates, is no new fact; it is only the discovery of it by the rest of the world that is new.

America may be said to have just reached her majority as a world power. It was almost exactly twenty-one years ago that the results of the war with Spain put us unexpectedly in possession of rich islands on the other side of the world and brought us into association with other governments in the control of the West Indies. It was regarded as a sinister and ominous thing by the statesmen of more than one European chancellory that we should have extended our power beyond the confines of our continental dominions. They were accustomed to think of new neighbors as a new menace, of rivals as

WAR TRAINING AT AN AMERICAN UNIVERSITY

WAR TRAINING AT AN AMERICAN UNIVERSITY.

American colleges and universities were in the forefront of the institutions used to train American youth for the purposes of war. The illustration shows a section of the student body of Harvard University, members of the Reserve Officers' Training Corps, drilling upon the grounds of the University.

watchful enemies. There were persons amongst us at home who looked with deep disapproval and avowed anxiety on such extensions of our national authority over distant islands and over peoples whom they feared we might exploit, not serve and assist. But we have not exploited them. We have been their friends and have sought to serve them. And our dominion has been a menace to no other nation. We redeemed our honor to the utmost in our dealings with Cuba. She is weak but absolutely free; and it is her trust in us that makes her free. Weak peoples everywhere stand ready to give us any authority among them that will assure them a like friendly oversight and direction. They know that there is no ground for fear in receiving us as their mentors and guides. Our isolation was ended twenty years ago; and now fear of us is ended also, our counsel and association sought after and desired. There can be no question of our ceasing to be a world power. The only question is whether we can refuse the moral leadership that is offered us, whether we shall accept or reject the confidence of the world.

The war and the Conference of Peace now sitting in Paris seem to me to have answered that question. Our participation in the war established our position among the nations and nothing but our own mistaken action can alter it. It was not an accident or a matter of sudden choice that we are no longer isolated and devoted to a policy which has only our own interest and advantage for its object. It was our duty to go in, if we were indeed the champions of liberty and of right. We answered to the call of duty in a way so spirited, so utterly without thought of what we spent of blood or treasure, so effective, so worthy of the admiration of true men everywhere, so wrought out of the stuff of all that was heroic, that the whole world saw at last, in the flesh, in noble action, a great ideal asserted and vindicated, by a nation they had deemed material and now found to be compact of the spiritual forces that must free men of every nation from every unworthy bondage. It is thus that a new role and a new responsibility have come to this great nation that we honor and which we would all wish to lift to yet higher levels of service and achievement.

The stage is set, the destiny disclosed. It has come about by no plan of our conceiving, but by the hand of God who led us into this way. We cannot turn back. We can only go forward, with lifted eyes and freshened spirit, to follow the vision. It was of this that we dreamed at our birth. America shall in truth show the way. The light streams upon the path ahead, and nowhere else.

THE TREATY WITH GERMANY

The preamble names as parties of the one part the United States, the British Empire, France, Italy, and Japan, described as the Five Allied and

Associated Powers, and Belgium, Bolivia, Brazil, China, Cuba, Ecuador, Greece, Guatemala, Haiti, the Hedjaz, Honduras, Liberia, Nicaragua, Panama, Peru, Poland, Portugal, Roumania, Serbia, Siam, Czecho-Slovakia, and Uruguay, who with the five above are described as the allied and associated powers, and on the other part, Germany.

It states that: bearing in mind that on the request of the then Imperial German Government an armistice was granted on November 11, 1918, by the principal allied and associated powers in order that a treaty of peace might be concluded with her, and whereas the allied and associated powers, being equally desirous that the war in which they were successively involved directly or indirectly and which originated in the declaration of war by Austria-Hungary on July 28, 1914, against Servia, the declaration of war by Germany against Russia on August 1, 1914, and against France on August 3, 1914, and in the invasion of Belgium, should be replaced by firm, just, and durable peace, the plenipotentiaries (having communicated their full powers found in good and due form) have agreed as follows:

From the coming into force of the present treaty the state of war will terminate. From the moment and subject to the provisions of this treaty, official relations with Germany, and with each of the German States, will be resumed by the allied and associated powers.

SECTION I—LEAGUE OF NATIONS. The Covenant of the League of Nations constitutes Section I of the peace treaty, which places upon the League many specific, in addition to its general, duties. It may question Germany at any time for a violation of the neutralized zone east of the Rhine as a threat against the world's peace. It will appoint three of the five members of the Sarre Commission, oversee its regime, and carry out the plebiscite. It will appoint the High Commissioner of Danzig, guarantee the independence of the free city, and arrange for treaties between Danzig and Germany and Poland. It will work out the mandatory system to be applied to the former German colonies, and act as a final court in part of the plebiscites of the Belgian-German frontier, and in disputes as to the Kiel Canal, and decide certain of the economic and financial problems. An International Conference on Labor is to be held in October under its direction, and another on the international control of ports, waterways, and railways is foreshadowed.

SECTION II—BOUNDARIES OF GERMANY. Germany cedes to France Alsace-Lorraine, 5,600 square miles to the southwest, and to Belgium two small districts between Luxemburg and Holland, totaling 382 square miles. She also cedes to Poland the southeastern tip of Silesia beyond and including Oppeln, most of Posen, and West Prussia, 27,686 square miles, East Prussia being isolated from the main body by a part of Poland. She loses sovereignty over the northeastern tip of East Prussia, 40 square miles north of the river Memel, and the internationalized areas about Danzig, 729 square miles, and the Basin of the Sarre, 738 square miles, between the western border of the Rhenish Palatinate of Bavaria and the southeast corner of Luxemburg. The Danzig area consists of the V between the Nogat and Vistula Rivers made a W by the addition of a similar V on the west, including the city of Danzig. The southeastern third of East Prussia and the area between East Prussia and the Vistula north of latitude 53 degrees 3 minutes is to have its nationality determined by popular vote, 5,785 square miles, as is to be the case in part of Schleswig, 2,787 square miles.

SECTION III—*Belgium.* Germany is to consent to the abrogation of the treaties of 1839, by which Belgium was established as a neutral State, and to agree in advance to any convention with which the allied and associated Powers may determine to replace them. She is to recognize the full sovereignty of Belgium over the contested territory of Moresnet and over part of Prussian Moresnet, and to renounce in favor of Belgium all rights over the circles of Eupen and Malmedy, the inhabitants of which are to be entitled within six months to protest against this change of sovereignty either in whole or in part, the final decision to be reserved to the League of Nations. A commission is to settle the details of the frontier, and various regulations for change of nationality are laid down.

Luxemburg. Germany renounces her various treaties and conventions with the Grand Duchy of Luxemburg, recognizes that it ceased to be a part of the German Zollverein from January first, last, renounces all right of exploitation of the railroads, adheres to the abrogation of its neutrality, and accepts in advance any international agreement as to it reached by the allied and associated powers.

Left Bank of the Rhine. As provided in the military clauses, Germany will not maintain any fortifications or armed forces less than fifty kilometers to the east of the Rhine, hold any manoeuvres, nor maintain any works to facilitate mobilization. In case of violation, "she shall be regarded as committing a hostile act against the Powers who sign the present treaty and as intending to disturb the peace of the world." "By virtue of the present treaty, Germany shall be bound to respond to any request for an explanation which the Council of the League of Nations may think it necessary to address to her."

Alsace-Lorraine. After recognition of the moral obligation to repair the wrong done in 1871 by Germany to France and the people of Alsace-Lorraine, the territories ceded to Germany by the Treaty of Frankfort are restored to France with their frontiers as before 1871, to date from the signing of the armistice, and to be free of all public debts.

Citizenship is regulated by detailed provisions distinguishing those who are immediately restored to full French citizenship, those who have to make formal applications therefor, and those for whom naturalization is open after three years. The last named class includes German residents in Alsace-Lorraine, as distinguished from those who acquire the position of Alsace-Lorrainers as defined in the treaty. All public property and all private property of German ex-sovereigns passes to France without payment or credit. France is substituted for Germany as regards ownership of the railroads and rights over concessions of tramway. The Rhine bridges pass to France with the obligation for their upkeep.

For five years manufactured products of Alsace-Lorraine will be admitted to Germany free of duty to a total amount not exceeding in any year the average of the three years preceding the war and textile materials may be imported from Germany to Alsace-Lorraine and re-exported free of duty. Contracts for electric power from the right bank must be continued for ten years. For seven years, with possible extension to ten, the ports of Kehl and Strassbourg shall be administered as a single unit by a French administrator appointed and supervised by the Central Rhine Commission. Property rights will be safeguarded in both ports and equality of treatment as respects traffic assured the nationals, vessels, and goods of every country.

Contracts between Alsace-Lorraine and Germans are maintained save for France's right to annul on grounds of public interest. Judgments of courts hold in certain classes of cases while in others a judicial exequatur is first required. Political condemnations during the war are null and void and the obligation to repay war fines is established as in other parts of allied territory.

Various clauses adjust the general provisions of the treaty to special conditions of Alsace-Lorraine, certain matters of execution being left to conventions to be made between France and Germany.

The Sarre. In compensation for the destruction of coal mines in Northern France and as payment on account of reparation, Germany cedes to France full ownership of the coal mines of the Sarre Basin with their subsidiaries, accessories and facilities. Their value will be estimated by the Reparation Commission and credited against that account. The French rights will be governed by German law in force at the armistice excepting war legislation, France replacing the present owners, whom Germany undertakes to indemnify. France will continue to furnish the present proportion of coal for local needs and contribute in just proportion to local taxes. The basin extends from the frontier of Lorraine as re-annexed to France north as far as Stwendel including on the west the valley of the Sarre as far as Sarre Holzbach and on the east the town of Homburg.

In order to secure the rights and welfare of the population and guarantee to France entire freedom in working the mines the territory will be governed by a commission appointed by the League of Nations and consisting of five members, one French, one a native inhabitant of the Sarre, and three representing three different countries other than France and Germany. The League will appoint a member of the Commission as Chairman to act as executive of the commission. The commission will have all powers of government formerly belonging to the German Empire, Prussia and Bavaria, will administer the railroads and other public services and have full power to interpret the treaty clauses. The local courts will continue, but subject to the Commission. Existing German legislation will remain the basis of the law, but the Commission may make modification after consulting a local representative assembly which it will organize. It will have the taxing power but for local purposes only. New taxes must be approved by this assembly. Labor legislation will consider the wishes of the local labor organizations and the labor program of the League. French and other labor may be freely utilized, the former being free to belong to French unions. All rights acquired as to pensions and social insurance will be maintained by Germany and the Sarre Commission.

There will be no military service but only a local gendarmerie to preserve order. The people will preserve their local assemblies, religious liberties, schools, and language, but may vote only for local assemblies. They will keep their present nationality except so far as individuals may change it. Those wishing to leave will have every facility with respect to their property. The territory will form part of the French customs system, with no export tax on coal and metallurgical products going to Germany nor on German products entering the basin and for five years no import duties on products of the basin going to Germany or German products coming into the basin. For local consumption French money may circulate without restriction.

After fifteen years a plebiscite will be held by communes to ascertain the desires of the population as to continuance of the existing regime under the League of Nations, union with France or union with Germany. The right to vote will belong to all inhabitants over twenty resident therein at the signature. Taking into account the opinions thus expressed the League will decide the ultimate sovereignty. In any portion restored to Germany the German Government must buy out the French mines at an appraised valuation. If the price is not paid within six months thereafter this portion passes finally to France. If Germany buys back the mines the League will determine how much of the coal shall be annually sold to France.

SECTION IV—*German Austria.* "Germany recognizes the total independence of German Austria in the boundaries traced."

Czecho-Slovakia. Germany recognizes the entire independence of the Czecho-Slovak State, including the autonomous territory of the Ruthenians south of the Carpathians, and accepts the frontiers of this State as to be determined, which in the case of the German frontier shall follow the frontier of Bohemia in 1914. The usual stipulations as to acquisition and change of nationality follow.

Poland. Germany cedes to Poland the greater part of Upper Silesia, Posen and the province of West Prussia on the left bank of the Vistula. A field Boundary Commission of seven, five representing the allied and associated powers and one each representing Poland and Germany, shall be constituted within fifteen days of the peace to delimit this boundary. Such special provisions as are necessary to protect racial, linguistic or religious minorities and to protect freedom of transit and equitable treatment of commerce of other nations shall be laid down in a subsequent treaty between the principal allied and associated powers and Poland.

East Prussia. The southern and the eastern frontier of East Prussia as touching Poland is to be fixed by plebiscites, the first in the regency of Allenstein between the southern frontier of East Prussia and the northern frontier, or Regierungsbezirk Allenstein, from where it meets the boundary between East and West Prussia to its junction with the boundary between the circles of Oletsko and Augersburg, thence the northern boundary of Oletsko to its junction with the present frontier, and the second in the area comprising the circles of Stuhm and Rosenburg and the parts of the circles of Marienburg and Marienwerder east of the Vistula.

In each case German troops and authorities will move out within fifteen days of the peace, and the territories of five members appointed by the principal allied and associated powers, with the particular duty of arranging for a free, fair and secret vote. The commission will report the results of the plebiscites to the powers with a recommendation for the boundary, and will terminate its work as soon as the boundary has been laid down and the new authorities set up.

The principal allied and associated powers will draw up regulations assuring East Prussia full and equitable access to and use of the Vistula. A subsequent convention, of which the terms will be fixed by the principal allied and associated powers, will be entered into between Poland, Germany and Danzig, to assure suitable railroad communication across German territory on the right bank of the Vistula between Poland and Danzig, while Poland shall grant free passage from East Prussia to Germany.

Danzig. Danzig and the district immediately about it is to be constituted into the "free city of Danzig" under the guarantee of the League of Nations. A high commissioner appointed by the League and President of Danzig shall draw up a constitution in agreement with the duly appointed representatives of the city, and shall deal in the first instance with all differences arising between the city and Poland. The actual boundaries of the city shall be delimited by a commission appointed within six months from the peace and to include three representatives chosen by the allied and associated powers, and one each by Germany and Poland.

A convention, the terms of which shall be fixed by the principal allied and associated powers, shall be concluded between Poland and Danzig, which shall include Danzig within the Polish customs frontiers, through a free area in the port; insure to Poland the free use of all the city's waterways, docks and other port facilities, the control and administration of the Vistula and the whole through railway system within the city, and postal, telegraphic and telephonic communication between Poland and Danzig; provide against discrimination against Poles within the city, and place its foreign relations and the diplomatic protection of its citizens abroad in charge of Poland.

Denmark. The frontier between Germany and Denmark will be fixed by the self-determination of the population. Ten days from the peace German troops and authorities shall evacuate the region north of the line running from the mouth of the Schlef, south of Kappel, Schleswig, and Friedrichstadt along the Eider to the North Sea south of Tonning; the Workmen's and Soldiers' Councils shall be dissolved, and the territory administered by an international commission of five, of whom Norway and Sweden shall be invited to name two.

The commission shall insure a free and secret vote in three zones. That between the German-Danish frontier and a line running south of the Island of Alsen, north of Flensburg, and south of Tondern to the North Sea north of the Island of Sylt, will vote as a union within three weeks after the evacuation. Within five weeks after this vote the second zone, whose southern boundary runs from the North Sea south of the Island of Fehr to the Baltic south of Sygum, will vote by communes. Two weeks after that vote the third zone running to the limit of evacuation will also vote by communes. The international commission will then draw a new frontier on the basis of these plebiscites and with due regard for geographical and economic conditions. Germany will renounce all sovereignty over territories north of this line in favor of the Associated Governments, who will hand them over to Denmark.

Helgoland. The fortifications, military establishments, and harbors of the Islands of Helgoland and Dune are to be destroyed under the supervision of the Allies by German labor and at Germany's expense. They may not be reconstructed, nor any similar fortification built in the future.

Russia. Germany agrees to respect as permanent and inalienable the independence of all territories which were part of the former Russian Empire, to accept the abrogation of the Brest-Litovsk and other treaties entered into with the Maximalist Government of Russia, to recognize the full force of all treaties entered into by the allied and associated powers with States which were a part of the former Russian Empire, and to recognize the frontiers as determined thereon. The allied and associated powers formally reserve the right of Russia to obtain restitution and reparation on the principles of the present treaty.

Section V—German Rights Outside Europe. Outside Europe, Germany renounces all rights, titles, and privileges as to her own or her allies' territories to all the allied and associated powers, and undertakes to accept whatever measures are taken by the five allied powers in relation thereto.

Colonies and Overseas Possessions. Germany renounces in favor of the allied and associated powers her overseas possessions with all rights and titles therein. All movable and immovable property belonging to the German Empire, or to any German State, shall pass to the Government exercising authority therein. These Governments may make whatever provisions seem suitable for the repatriation of German nationals and as to the conditions on which German subjects of European origin shall reside, hold property, or carry on business. Germany undertakes to pay reparation for damages suffered by French nationals in Kamerun or its frontier zone through the acts of German civil and military authorities and of individual Germans from the 1st of January, 1900, to the 1st of August, 1914. Germany renounces all rights under the convention of the 4th of November, 1911, and the 29th of September, 1912, and undertakes to pay to France in accordance with an estimate presented and approved by the Repatriation Commission all deposits, credits, advances, etc., thereby secured. Germany undertakes to accept and observe any provisions by the allied and associated powers as to the trade in arms and spirits in Africa as well as to the General Act of Berlin of 1885 and the General Act of Brussels in 1890. Diplomatic protection to inhabitants of former German colonies is to be given by the Governments exercising authority.

China. Germany renounces in favor of China all privileges and indemnities resulting from the Boxer Protocol of 1901, and all buildings, wharves, barracks for munitions of warships, wireless plants, and other public property except diplomatic or consular establishments in the German concessions of Tientsin and Hankow and in other Chinese territory except Kiao-Chau and agrees to return to China at her own expense all the astronomical instruments seized in 1900 and 1901. China will, however, take no measures for disposal of German property in the legation quarter at Peking without the consent of the Powers signatory to the Boxer Protocol.

Germany accepts the abrogation of the concessions at Hankow and Tientsin, China agreeing to open them to international use. Germany renounces all claims against China or any allied and associated Government for the internment or repatriation of her citizens in China and for the seizure or liquidation of German interests there since August 14, 1917. She renounces in favor of Great Britain her State property in the British concession at Canton and of France and China jointly the property of the German school in the French concession at Shanghai.

Siam. Germany recognizes that all agreements between herself and Siam, including the right of extra-territoriality, ceased July 22, 1917. All German public property, except consular and diplomatic premises, passes without compensation to Siam. German private property is to be dealt with in accordance with the economic clauses. Germany waives all claims against Siam for the seizure and condemnation of her ships, liquidation of her property, or internment of her nationals.

Liberia. Germany renounces all rights under the international arrangements of 1911 and 1912 regarding Liberia, more particularly the right to nominate a receiver of the customs, and disinterests herself in any further negotiations for the rehabilitation of Liberia. She regards as abrogated all commercial treaties and agreements between herself and Liberia and recognizes Liberia's right to determine the status and condition of the re-establishment of Germans in Liberia.

Morocco. Germany renounces all her rights, titles, and privileges under the Act of Algeciras and the Franco-German agreements of 1909 and 1911, and under all treaties and arrangements with the Sherifian Empire. She undertakes not to intervene in any negotiations as to Morocco between France and other Powers, accepts all the consequences of the French protectorate and renounces the capitulations; the Sherifian Government shall have complete liberty of action in regard to German nationals, and all German protected persons shall be subject to the common law. All movable and immovable German property, including mining rights, may be sold at public auction, the proceeds to be paid to the Sherifian Government and deducted from the reparation account. Germany is also required to relinquish her interests in the State Bank of Morocco. All Moroccan goods entering Germany shall have the same privilege as French goods.

Egypt. Germany recognizes the British Protectorate over Egypt declared on December 18, 1914, and renounces as from August 1, 1914 the capitulation and all the treaties, agreements, etc., concluded by her with Egypt. She undertakes not to intervene in any negotiations about Egypt between Great Britain and other Powers. There are provisions for jurisdiction over German nationals and property and for German consent to any changes which may be made in relation to the Commission of Public Debt. Germany consents to the transfer to Great Britain of the powers given to the late Sultan of Turkey for securing the free navigation of the Suez Canal. Arrangements for property belonging to German nationals in Egypt are made similar to those in the case of Morocco and other countries. Anglo-Egyptian goods entering Germany shall enjoy the same treatment as British goods.

Turkey and Bulgaria. Germany accepts all arrangements which the Allied and Associated Powers make with Turkey and Bulgaria with reference to any rights, privileges or interests claimed in those countries by Germany or her nationals and not dealt with elsewhere.

Shantung. Germany cedes to Japan all rights, titles, and privileges, notably as to Kiao-Chau, and the railroads, mines, and cables acquired by her treaty with China of March 6, 1897, by and other agreements as to Shantung. All German rights to the railroad from Tsing-tao to Tsinan-fu, including all facilities and mining rights and rights of exploitation, pass equally to Japan, and the cables from Tsing-tao to Shanghai and Che-foo, the cables free of all charges. All German State property, movable and immovable, in Kiao-Chau is acquired by Japan free of all charges.

SECTION VI—MILITARY, NAVAL AND AIR—*Military Forces.* The demobilization of the German Army must take place within two months of the peace. Its strength may not exceed 100,000, including 4,000 officers, with not over seven divisions of infantry and three of cavalry, and to be devoted exclusively to maintenance of internal order and control of frontiers. Divisions may not be grouped under more than two army corps headquarters staffs. The German General Staff is abolished. The army administrative service, consisting of civilian personnel not included in the number of effectives, is reduced to one-tenth the toal in the 1913 budget. Employes of the German States, such as customs officers, first guards, and coast guards, may not exceed the number in 1913. Gendarmes and local police may be increased only in accordance with the growth of population. None of these may be assembled for military training.

Armaments. All establishments for the manufacturing, preparation, storage, or design of arms and munitions of war, except those specifically excepted, must be closed within three months of the peace, and their personnel dismissed. The exact amount of armament and munitions allowed Germany is laid down in detail tables, all in excess to be surrendered or rendered useless. The manufacture or importation of asphyxiating, poisonous, or other gases and all analogous liquids is forbidden as well as the importation of arms, munitions, and war materials. Germany may not manufacture such materials for foreign governments.

Conscription. Conscription is abolished in Germany. The enlisted personnel must be maintained by voluntary enlistment for terms of twelve consecutive years, the number of discharges before the expiration of that term not in any year to exceed 5 per cent of the total effectives. Officers remaining in the service must agree to serve to the age of 45 years, and newly appointed officers must agree to serve actively for twenty-five years.

No military schools except those absolutely indispensable for the units allowed shall exist in Germany two months after the peace. No associations such as societies of discharged soldiers, shooting or touring clubs, educational establishments or universities may occupy themselves with military matters. All measures of molibilization are forbidden.

Fortresses. All fortified works, fortresses, and field works situated in German territory within a zone of fifty kilometers east of the Rhine will be dismantled within three months. The construction of any new fortifications there is forbidden. The fortified works on the southern and eastern frontiers, however, may remain.

Control. Inter-Allied commissions of control will see to the execution of the provisions for which a time limit is set, the maximum named being three months. They may establish headquarters at the German seat of Government and go to any part of Germany desired. Germany must give them complete facilities, pay their expenses, and also the expenses of execution of the treaty, including the labor and material necessary in demolition, destruction or surrender of war equipment.

Naval. The German navy must be demobilized within a period of two months after the peace. Germany will be allowed 6 small battleships, 6 light cruisers, 12 destroyers, 12 torpedo boats, and no submarines, either military or commercial, with a personnel of 15,000 men, including officers, and no reserve force of any character. Conscription is abolished, only voluntary service being permitted, with a minimum period of 25 years' service for officers and 12 for men. No member of the German mercantile marine will be permitted any naval training.

All German vessels of war in foreign ports and the German high seas fleet interned at Scapa Flow will be surrendered, the final disposition of these ships to be decided upon by the allied and associated powers. Germany must surrender 42 modern destroyers, 50 modern torpedo boats, and all submarines, with their salvage vessels. All war vessels under construction, including submarines, must be broken up. War vessels not otherwise provided for are to be placed in reserve, or used for commercial purposes. Replacement of ships except those lost can take place only at the end of 20 years for battleships and 15 years for destroyers. The largest armored ship Germany will be permitted will be 10,000 tons.

Germany is required to sweep up the mines in the North Sea and the Baltic Sea, as decided upon by the Allies. All German fortifications in the Baltic, defending the passages through the belts, must be demolished. Other coasts defenses are permitted, but the number and calibre of the guns must not be increased.

Wireless. During a period of three months after the peace German high power wireless stations at Nauen, Hanover, and Berlin will not be permitted to send any message except for commercial purposes, and under supervision of the allied and associated Governments, nor may any more such stations be constructed.

Cables. Germany renounces all title to specified cables, the value of such as were privately owned being credited to her against reparation indebtedness.

Germany will be allowed to repair German submarine cables which have been cut but are not being utilized by the allied powers, and also portions of cables which, after having been cut, have been removed, or are at any rate not being utilized by any one of the allied and associated powers. In such cases the cables, or portions of cables, removed or utilized remain the property of the allied and associated powers, and accordingly fourteen cables or parts of cables are specified which will not be restored to Germany.

Air. The armed forces of Germany must not include any military or naval air forces except for not over 100 unarmed seaplanes to be retained till October 1 to search for submarine mines. No dirigibles shall be kept. The entire air personnel is to be demobilized within two months, except for 1,000 officers and men retained till October. No aviation grounds or dirigible sheds are to be allowed within 150 kilometers of the Rhine, on the eastern or southern frontiers, existing installations within these limits to be destroyed. The manufacture of aircraft and parts of aircraft is forbidden for six months. All military and naval aeronautical material under a most exhaustive definition must be surrendered within three months, except for the 100 seaplanes already specified.

Prisoners of War. The repatriation of German prisoners and interned civilians is to be carried out without delay and at Germany's expense by a commission composed of representatives of the Allies and Germany. Those under sentence for offenses against discipline are to be repatriated without regard to the completion of their sentences. Until Germany has surrendered persons guilty of offenses against the laws and customs of war, the Allies have the right to retain selected German officers. The Allies may deal at their own discretion with German nationals who do not desire to be repatriated, all repatriation being conditional on the immediate release of any allied subjects still in Germany. Germany is to accord facilities to commissions of inquiry in collecting information in regard to missing prisoners of war and of imposing penalties on German officials who have concealed allied nationals. Germany is to restore all property belonging to allied prisoners. There is to be a reciprocal exchange of information as to dead prisoners and their graves.

Graves. Both parties will respect and maintain the graves of soldiers and sailors buried on their territories, agree to recognize and assist any commission charged by any allied or associated Government with identifying, registering, maintaining or erecting suitable monuments over the graves, and to afford to each other all facilities for the repatriation of the remains of their soldiers.

SECTION VII—RESPONSIBILITIES. "The allied and associated powers publicly arraign William II of Hohenzollern, formerly German Emperor, not for an offense against criminal law, but for a supreme offense against international morality and the sanctity of treaties."

The ex-Emperor's surrender is to be requested of Holland and a special tribunal set up, composed of one judge from each of the five great powers, with full guarantee of the right of defense. It is to be guided "by the highest motives of international policy with a view of vindicating the solemn obligations of international undertakings and the validity of international morality," and will fix the punishment it feels should be imposed.

Persons accused of having committed acts in violation of the laws and customs of war are to be tried and punished by military tribunals under military law. If the charges affect nationals of only one State, they will be tried before a tribunal of that State; if they affect nationals of several States, they will be tried before joint tribunals of the States concerned. Germany shall hand over to the associated Governments, either jointly or severally, all persons so accused and all documents and information necessary to insure full knowledge of the incriminating acts, the discovery of the offenders, and the just appreciation of the responsibility. The Judge presiding will be entitled to name his own counsel.

SECTION VIII—REPARATION AND RESTITUTION. "The allied and associated Governments affirm, and Germany accepts, the responsibility of herself and her allies for causing all the loss and damage to which the allied and associated Governments and their nationals have been subjected as a consequence of the war imposed upon them by the aggression of Germany and her allies."

The total obligation of Germany to pay as defined in the category of damages is to be determined and notified to her after a fair hearing, and not later than May 1, 1921, by an interallied Reparation Commission.

At the same time a schedule of payments to discharge the obligation within thirty years shall be presented. These payments are subject to postponement in certain contingencies. Germany irrevocably recognizes the full authority of this commission, agrees to supply it with all the necessary information and to pass legislation to effectuate its findings. She further agrees to restore to the allies cash and certain articles which can be identified.

As an immediate step toward restoration Germany shall pay within two years one thousand million pounds sterling in either gold, goods, ships, or other specific forms of payment—this sum being included in, and not additional to, the first thousand million bond issue referred to below, with the understanding that certain expenses, such as those of the armies of occupation and payments for food and raw materials, may be deducted at the discretion of the Allies.

Germany further binds herself to repay all sums borrowed by Belgium from her allies as a result of Germany's violation of the treaty of 1839 up to November 11, 1918, and for this purpose will issue at once and hand over to the Reparation Commission 5 per cent gold bonds falling due in 1926.

While the allied and associated Governments recognize that the resources of Germany are not adequate, after taking into account permanent diminution of such resources which will result from other treaty claims, to make complete reparation for all such loss and damages, they require her to make compensation for all damages caused to civilians under seven main categories:

(*a*) Damages by personal injury to civilians caused by acts of war, directly or indirectly, including bombardment from the air.

(*b*) Damages caused by civilians, including exposure at sea, resulting from acts of cruelty ordered by the enemy, and to civilians in the occupied territories.

(*c*) Damages caused by maltreatment of prisoners.

(*d*) Damages to the Allied peoples represented by pensions and separation allowances, capitalized at the signature of this treaty.

(*e*) Damages to property other than naval or military materials.

(*f*) Damages to civilians by being forced to labor.

(*g*) Damages in the form of levies or fines imposed by the enemy.

In periodically estimating Germany's capacity to pay, the Reparation Commission shall examine the German system of taxation, first to the end that the sums for reparation which Germany is required to pay shall become a charge upon all her revenues prior to that for the service or discharge of any domestic loan; and secondly, so as to satisfy itself that in general the German scheme of taxation is fully as heavy proportionately as that of any of the powers represented on the commission.

The measures which the allied and associated powers shall have the right to take, in case of voluntary default by Germany, and which Germany agrees not to regard as acts of war, may include economic and financial prohibitions and reprisals and in general such other measures as the respective Governments may determine to be necessary in the circumstances.

The commission shall consist of one representative each of the United States, Great Britain, France, Italy and Belgium, a representative of Servia or Japan taking the place of the Belgian representative when the interests of either country are particularly affected, with all other allied powers entitled, when their claims are under consideration, to the right of representation without voting power. It shall permit Germany to give evidence regarding her capacity to pay, and shall assure her a just opportunity to be heard. It shall make its permanent headquarters at Paris, establish its own procedure and personnel; have general control of the whole reparation problem; and become the exclusive agency of the Allies for receiving, holding, selling, and distributing reparation payments. Majority vote shall prevail, except that unanimity is required on questions involving the sovereignty of any of the Allies, the cancellation of all or part of Germany's obligations, the time and manner of selling, distributing, and negotiating bonds issued by Germany, and postponement between 1921 and 1926 of annual payments beyond 1930 and any postponement after 1926 for a period of more than three years of the application of a different method of measuring damage than in a similar former case, and the interpretation of provisions. Withdrawal from representation is permitted on twelve months' notice.

The Commission may require Germany to give from time to time by way of guarantee, issues of bonds or other obligations to cover such claims as are not otherwise satisfied. In this connection and on account of the total amount of claims, bond issues are presently to be required of Germany in acknowledgment of its debt as follows: 20,000,000,000 marks gold, payable not later than May 1, 1921, without interest; 40,000,000,000 marks gold bearing 2½ per cent interest between 1921 and 1926, and thereafter 5 per cent, with a 1 per cent sinking fund payment beginning 1926; and an undertaking to deliver 40,000,000,-000 marks gold bonds bearing interest at 5 per cent, under terms to be fixed by the Commission.

Interest on Germany's debt will be 5 per cent, unless otherwise determined by the Commission in the future, and payments that are not made in gold may "be accepted by the Commission in the form of properties, commodities, businesses, rights, concessions, etc." Certificates of beneficial interest, representing either bonds or goods delivered by Germany, may be issued by the Commission to the interested Powers, no Power being entitled, however, to have its certificates divided into more than five pieces. As bonds are distributed and pass from the control of the Commission, an amount of Germany's debt equivalent to their par value is to be considered as liquidated.

Shipping. The German Government recognizes the right of the Allies to the replacement, ton for ton and class for class, of all merchant ships and fishing boats lost or damaged owing to the war, and agrees to cede to the Allies all German merchant ships of 1,600 tons gross and upward; one-half of her ships between 1,600 and 1,000 tons gross, and one-quarter of her steam trawlers and other fishing boats. These ships are to be delivered within two months to the

Reparations Commission together with documents of title evidencing the transfer of the ships free from encumbrance.

"As an additional part of reparation," the German Government further agrees to build merchant ships for the account of the Allies to the amount of not exceeding 200,000 tons gross annually during the next five years.

All ships used for inland navigation taken by Germany from the Allies are to be restored within two months, the amount of loss not covered by such restitution to be made up by the cession of the German river fleet up to 20 per cent thereof.

Dyestuffs and Chemical Drugs. In order to effect payment by deliveries in kind, Germany is required, for a limited number of years, varying in the case of each, to deliver coal, coal-tar products, dyestuffs and chemical drugs, in specific amounts to the Reparations Commission. The Commission may so modify the conditions of delivery as not to interfere unduly with Germany's industrial requirements. The deliveries of coal are based largely upon the principle of making good diminutions in the production of the Allied countries resulting from the war.

Germany accords option to the Commission on dyestuffs and chemical drugs, including quinine, up to 50 per cent of the total stock in Germany at the time the treaty comes into force, and similar option during each six months to the end of 1924 up to 25 per cent of the previous six months' output.

Devastated Areas. Germany undertakes to devote her economic resources directly to the physical restoration of the invaded areas. The Reparations Commission is authorized to require Germany to replace the destroyed articles by the delivery of animals, machinery, etc., existing in Germany, and to manufacture materials required for reconstruction purposes; all with due consideration for Germany's essential domestic requirements.

Germany is to deliver annually for ten years to France coal equivalent to the difference between the annual pre-war output of the Nord and Pas de Calais mines and the annual production during the above ten-year period. Germany further gives options over ten years for delivery of 7,000,000 tons of coal per year to France in addition to the above, of 8,000,000 tons to Belgium and of an amount rising from 4,500,000 tons in 1919 to 1920 to 8,500,000 in 1923 to 1924 to Italy at prices to be fixed as prescribed in the treaty. Coke may be taken in place of coal in the ration of three tons to four. Provision is also made for delivery to France over three years of benzol, coal tar, and of ammonia. The Commission has powers to postpone or annul the above deliveries should they interfere unduly with the industrial requirements of Germany.

Germany is to restore within six months the Koran of the Caliph Othman, formerly at Medina, to the King of the Hedjaz, and the skull of the Sultan Okwawa, formerly in German East Africa, to his Britannic Majesty's Government.

The German Government is also to restore to the French Government certain papers taken by the German authorities in 1870, belonging then to M. Reuher, and to restore the French flags taken during the war of 1870 and 1871.

As reparation for the destruction of the Library of Louvain Germany is to hand over manuscripts, early printed books, prints, etc., to the equivalent of those destroyed.

In addition to the above Germany is to hand over to Belgium wings, now in Berlin, belonging to the altar-piece of "The Adoration of the Lambs," by Hubert and Jan van Eyck, the center of which is now in the Church of St.

Bavon at Ghent, and the wings, now in Berlin and Munich, of the altar-piece of "The Last Supper," by Dirk Bouts, the center of which belongs to the Church of St. Peter at Louvain.

Finance. Powers to which German territory is ceded will assume a certain portion of the German pre-war debt, the amount to be fixed by the Reparations Commission on the basis of the ratio between the revenue of the ceded territory and Germany's total revenues for the three years preceding the war. In view, however, of the special circumstances under which Alsace-Lorraine was separated from France in 1871, when Germany refused to accept any part of the French public debt, France will not assume any part of Germany's pre-war debt there, nor will Poland share in certain German debts incurred for the oppression of Poland. If the value of the German public property in ceded territory exceeds the amount of debt assumed, the States to which property is ceded will give credit on reparation for the excess, with the exception of Alsace-Lorraine. Mandatory powers will not assume any German debts or give any credit for German Government property. Germany renounces all right of representation on, or control of State banks, commissions, or other similar international financial and economic organizations.

Germany is required to pay the total cost of the armies of occupation from the date of the armistice so long as they are maintained in German territory, this cost to be a first charge on her resources. The cost of reparation is the next charge, after making such provisions for payments for imports as the Allies may deem necessary.

Germany is to deliver to the allied and associated powers all sums deposited in Germany by Turkey and Austria-Hungary in connection with the financial support extended by her to them during the war, and to transfer to the Allies all claims against Austria-Hungary, Bulgaria, or Turkey in connection with agreements made during the war. Germany confirms the renunciation of the Treaties of Bucharest and Brest-Litovsk.

On the request of the Reparation Commission, Germany will expropriate any rights or interests of her nationals in public utilities in ceded territories or those administered by mandatories, and in Turkey, China, Russia, Austria-Hungary, and Bulgaria, and transfer them to the Reparations Commission, which will credit her with their value. Germany guarantees to repay to Brazil the fund arising from the sale of Sao Paulo coffee which she refused to allow Brazil to withdraw from Germany.

Section IX. This section provides for the enforcement of the international legislation against the opium trade and the safeguarding of the activities of the religious missions in the ceded territory, Germany renouncing all claims concerning such missions.

Section X—Economic Clauses—*Customs.* For a period of six months Germany shall impose no tariff duties higher than the lowest in force in 1914, and for certain agricultural products, wines, vegetable oils, artificial silk, and washed or scoured wool this restriction obtains for two and a half years more. For five years, unless further extended by the League of Nations, Germany must give most favored nation treatment to the allied and associated powers. She shall impose no customs tariff for five years on goods originating in Alsace-Lorraine; and for three years on goods originating in former German territory ceded to Poland with the right of observation of a similar exception for Luxemburg.

Shipping. Shipping of the allied and associated powers shall for five years and thereafter under condition of reciprocity, unless the League of Nations otherwise decides, enjoy the same right in German ports as German vessels, and have most favored nation treatment in fishing, coasting trade, and towage even in territorial waters. Ships of a country having no seacoast may be registered at some one place within its territory.

Unfair Competition. Germany undertakes to give the trade of the allied and associated powers adequate safeguards against unfair competition, and in particular to suppress the use of false wrappings and markings, and on condition of reciprocity to respect the laws and judicial decisions of allied and associated States in respect of regional appellations of wines and spirits.

Treatment of Nationals. Germany shall impose no exceptional taxes or restrictions upon the nationals of allied and associated States for a period of five years and, unless the League of Nations acts, for an additional five years German nationality shall not continue to attach to a person who has become a national of an allied or associated State.

Multilateral Conventions. Some forty multilateral conventions are renewed between Germany and the allied and associated powers, but special conditions are attached to Germany's readmission to several. As to postal and telegraphic conventions Germany must not refuse to make reciprocal agreements with the new States. She must agree as respects the radio-telegraphic convention to provisional rules to be communicated to her, and adhere to the new convention when formulated. In the North Sea fisheries and North Sea liquor traffic convention, rights of inspection and police over Allied and associated fishing boats shall be exercised for at least five years only by vessels of these Powers. As to the international railway union she shall adhere to the new convention when formulated. China, as to the Chinese customs tariff arrangement of 1905 regarding Whangpoo, and the Boxer indemnity of 1901; France, Portugal, and Roumania, as to The Hague Convention of 1903, relating to civil procedure, and Great Britain and the United States as to Article III of the Samoan Treaty of 1899, are relieved of all obligations toward Germany.

Bilateral Treaties. Each allied and associated State may renew any treaty with Germany in so far as consistent with the peace treaty by giving notice within six months. Treaties entered into by Germany since August 1, 1914, with other enemy States, and before or since that date with Roumania, Russia, and governments representing parts of Russia are abrogated, and concessions granted under pressure by Russia to German subjects are annulled. The allied and associated States are to enjoy most favored nation treatment under treaties entered into by Germany and other enemy States before August 1, 1914, and under treaties entered into by Germany and neutral States during the war.

Pre-War Debts. A system of clearing houses is to be created within three months, one in Germany and one in each allied and associated State which adopts the plan for the payment of pre-war debts, including those arising from contracts suspended by the war. For the adjustment of the proceeds of the liquidation of enemy property and the settlement of other obligations each participating State assumes responsibility for the payment of all debts owing by its nationals to nationals of the enemy States, except in cases of pre-war insolvency of the debtor. The proceeds of the sale of private enemy property in each participating State may be used to pay the debts owed to the nationals of that State, direct payment from debtor to creditor and all communications relating thereto being prohibited. Disputes may be settled by arbitration by the courts of the debtor country, or by the mixed arbitral tribunal. Any ally or associated power may, however, decline to participate in this system by giving Germany six months' notice.

Enemy Property. Germany shall restore or pay for all private enemy property seized or damaged by her, the amount of damages to be fixed by the mixed arbitral tribunal. The allied and associated States may liquidate German private property within their territories as compensation for property of their nationals not restored or paid for by Germany. For debts owed to their nationals by German nationals and for other claims against Germany, Germany is to compensate its nationals for such losses and to deliver within six months all documents relating to property held by its nationals in allied and associated States. All war legislation as to enemy property rights and interests is confirmed and all claims by Germany against the allied or associated Governments for acts under exceptional war measures abandoned.

Pre-war contracts between allied and associated nationals excepting the United States, Japan, and Brazil and German nationals are cancelled except for debts for accounts already performed.

Agreements. For the transfer of property where the property had already passed, leases of land and houses, contracts of mortgages, pledge or lien, mining concessions, contracts with governments and insurance contracts, mixed arbitral tribunals shall be established of three members, one chosen by Germany, one by the allied and associated States and the third by agreement, or, failing which, by the President of Switzerland. They shall have jurisdiction over all disputes as to contracts concluded before the present peace treaty.

Fire insurance contracts are not considered dissolved by the war, even if premiums have not been paid, but lapse at the date of the first annual premium falling due three months after the peace. Life insurance contracts may be restored by payments of accumulated premiums with interest, sums falling due on such contracts during the war to be recoverable with interest. Marine insurance contracts are dissolved by the outbreak of war except where the risk insured against had already been incurred. Where the risk had not attached, premiums paid are recoverable, otherwise premiums due and sums due on losses are recoverable. Reinsurance treaties are abrogated unless invasion has made it impossible for the reinsured to find another reinsurer. Any allied or associated power, however, may cancel all the contracts running between its nationals and a German life insurance company, the latter being obligated to hand over the proportion of its assets attributable to such policies.

Industrial Property. Rights as to industrial, literary, and artistic property are re-established. The special war measures of the allied and associated powers are ratified and the right reserved to impose conditions on the use of German patents and copyrights when in the public interests. Except as between the United States and Germany, pre-war licenses and rights to sue for infringements committed during the war are cancelled.

Section XI—Aerial Navigation. Aircraft of the allied and associated powers shall have full liberty of passage and landing over and in German territory, equal treatment with German planes as to use of German airdromes, and with most favored nation planes as to internal commercial traffic in Germany. Germany agrees to accept allied certificates of nationality, airworthiness, competency or licenses and to apply the convention relative to aerial navigation concluded between the allied and associated powers to her own aircraft over her own territory. These rules apply until 1923, unless Germany has since been admitted to the League of Nations or to the above convention.

SECTION XII—FREEDOM OF TRANSIT. Germany must grant freedom of transit through her territories by mail or water to persons, goods, ships, carriages, and mails from or to any of the allied or associated powers, without customs or transit duties, undue delays, restrictions, or discriminations based on nationality, means of transport, or place of entry or departure. Goods in transit shall be assured all possible speed of journey, especially perishable goods. Germany may not divert traffic from its normal course in favor of her own transport routes or maintain "control stations" in connection with transmigration traffic. She may not establish any tax discrimination against the ports of allied or associated powers; must grant the latter's seaports all factors and reduced tariffs granted her own or other nationals, and afford the allied and associated powers equal rights with those of her own nationals in her ports and waterways, save that she is free to open or close her maritime coasting trade.

Free Zones in Ports. Free zones existing in German ports on August 1, 1914, must be maintained with due facilities as to warehouses, packing, and shipping, without discrimination, and without charges except for expenses of administration and use. Goods leaving the free zones for consumption in Germany and goods brought into the free zones from Germany shall be subject to the ordinary import and export taxes.

International Rivers. The Elbe from the junction of the Ultava, the Ultava from Prague, the Oder from Oppa, the Niemen from Grodno, and the Danube from Ulm are declared international, together with their connections. The riparian states must ensure good conditions of navigation within their territories unless a special organization exists therefor. Otherwise appeal may be had to a special tribunal of the League of Nations, which also may arrange for a general international waterways convention.

The Elbe and the Oder are to be placed under international commissions to meet within three months, that for the Elbe composed of four representatives of Germany, two from Czecho-Slovakia, and one each from Great Britain, France, Italy, and Belgium; and that for the Oder composed of one each from Poland, Russia, Czecho-Slovakia, Great Britain, France, Denmark, and Sweden. If any riparian state on the Niemen should so request of the League of Nations, a similar commission shall be established there. These commissions shall upon request of any riparian state meet within three months to revise existing international agreement.

The Danube. The European Danube Commission reassumes its pre-war powers, but for the time being with representatives of only Great Britain, France, Italy and Roumania. The upper Danube is to be administered by a new international commission until a definitive statute be drawn up at a conference of the Powers nominated by the allied and associated governments within one year after the peace. The enemy governments shall make full reparation for all war damages caused to the European Commission; shall cede their river facilities in surrendered territory, and give Czecho-Slovakia, Servia and Roumania any rights necessary on their shores for carrying on improvements in navigation.

The Rhine and the Moselle. The Rhine is placed under the Central Commission to meet at Strassbourg within six months after the peace, and to be composed of four representatives of France, which shall in addition select the President, four of Germany, and two each of Great Britain, Italy, Belgium, Switzerland, and the Netherlands. Germany must give France on the course of the Rhine included between the two extreme points of her frontiers all rights to take water to feed canals, while herself agreeing not to make canals on the right bank opposite France. She must also hand over to France all her drafts and designs for this part of the river.

Belgium is to be permitted to build a deep draught Rhine-Meuse canal if she so desires within twenty-five years, in which case Germany must construct the part within her territory on plans drawn by Belgium, similarly the interested Allied governments may construct a Rhine-Meuse canal—both, if constructed, to come under the competent international commission. Germany may not object if the Central Rhine Commission desires to extend its jurisdiction over the lower Moselle, the upper Rhine, or lateral canals.

Germany must cede to the allied and associated governments certain tugs, vessels, and facilities for navigation on all these rivers, the specific details to be established by an arbiter named by the United States. Decision will be based on the legitimate needs of the parties concerned and on the shipping traffic during the five years before the war. The value will be included in the regular reparation account. In the case of the Rhine, shares in the German navigation companies and property such as wharves and warehouses held by Germany in Rotterdam at the outbreak of the war must be handed over.

Railways. Germany, in addition to most favored nation treatment on her railways, agrees to co-operate in the establishment of through ticket services for passengers and baggage; to ensure communication by rail between the allied, associated, and other States; to allow the construction or improvement within twenty-five years of such lines as necessary; and to conform her rolling stock to enable its incorporation in trains of the allied or associated powers. She also agrees to accept the denunciation of the St. Gothard convention if Switzerland and Italy so request, and temporarily to execute instructions as to the transport of troops and supplies and the establishment of postal and telegraphic service, as provided.

Czecho-Slovakia. To assure Czecho-Slovakia access to the sea, special rights are given her both north and south. Toward the Adriatic she is permitted to run her own through trains to Fiume and Trieste. To the north, Germany is to lease her for ninety-nine years spaces in Hamburg and Stettin, the details to be worked out by a commission of three representing Czecho-Slovakia, Germany, and Great Britain.

The Kiel Canal. The Kiel Canal is to remain free and open to war and merchant ships of all nations at peace with Germany, subjects, goods and ships of all States are to be treated on terms of absolute equality, and no taxes to be imposed beyond those necessary for upkeep and improvement for which Germany is to be responsible. In case of violation of or disagreement as to those provisions, any State may appeal to the League of Nations, and may demand the appointment of an international commission. For preliminary hearing of complaints Germany shall establish a local authority at Kiel.

SECTION XIII—INTERNATIONAL LABOR ORGANIZATION. Members of the League of Nations agree to establish a permanent organization to promote international adjustment of labor conditions, to consist of an annual international labor conference and an international labor office.

The former is composed of four representatives of each State, two from the Government, and one each from the employers and the employed. Each of them may vote individually. It will be a deliberative legislative body, its measures taking the form of draft conventions or recommendations for legislation, which, if passed by two-thirds vote, must be submitted to the lawmaking authority in every State participating. Each Government may either enact the terms into law; approve the principle, but modify them to local needs; leave the actual legislation in case of a Federal State to local legislatures; or reject the convention altogether without further obligation.

The international labor office is established at the seat of the League of Nations as part of its organization. It is to collect and distribute information on labor throughout the world and prepare agenda for the conference. It will publish a periodical in French and English, and possibly other languages. Each State agrees to make to it for presentation to the conference an annual report of measures taken to execute accepted conventions. The governing body, in its Executive, consists of twenty-four members, twelve representing the Governments, six the employers, and six the employes, to serve for three years.

On complaint that any Government has failed to carry out a convention to which it is a party, the governing body may make inquiries directly to that Government, and in case the reply is unsatisfactory, may publish the complaint with comment. A complaint by one Government against another may be referred by the governing body to a committee with a possibility of economic action in the background.

The first meeting of the conference will take place in October, 1919, at Washington, to discuss the eight-hour day or forty-eight-hour week, prevention of unemployment, extension and application of the international conventions adopted at Berne in 1906, prohibiting night work for women, and the use of white phosphorus in the manufacture of matches; and employment of women and children at night or in unhealthy work, of women before and after childbirth, including maternity benefit, and of children as regards minimum age.

Nine principles of labor conditions were recognized on the ground that "the well-being, physical and moral, of the industrial wage earners is of supreme international importance." With exceptions necessitated by differences of climate, habits and economic development, they include: the guiding principle that labor should not be regarded merely as a commodity or article of commerce; the right of association of employers and employes; a wage adequate to maintain a reasonable standard of life; the eight-hour day or forty-eight hour week; a weekly rest of at least twenty-four hours, which should include Sunday wherever practicable; abolition of child labor and assurance of the continuation of the education and proper physical development of children; equal pay for equal work as between men and women; equitable treatment of all workers lawfully resident therein, including foreigners; and a system of inspection in which women should take part.

Section XIV—Guarantees. As a guarantee for the execution of the treaty, German territory to the west of the Rhine, together with the bridgeheads, will be occupied by allied and associated troops for a fifteen years' period. If the conditions are faithfully carried out by Germany, certain districts, including the bridgehead of Cologne, will be evacuated at the expiration of five years; certain other districts, including the bridgehead of Coblenz, and the territories nearest the Belgian frontier will be evacuated after ten years, and the remainder, including the bridgehead of Mainz, will be evacuated after fifteen years. In case the Interallied Reparation Commission finds that Germany has failed to observe the whole or part of her obligations either during the occupation or after the fifteen years have expired, the whole or part of the area specified will be reoccupied immediately. If before the expiration of the fifteen years Germany complies with all the treaty undertakings, the occupying forces will be withdrawn immediately.

All German troops at present in territories to the east of the new frontier shall return as soon as the allied and associated governments deem wise. They are to abstain from all requisitions and are in no way to interfere with measures for national defense taken by the Government concerned.

All questions regarding occupation not provided for by the treaty will be regulated by a subsequent convention or conventions which will have similar force and effect.

SECTION XV—MISCELLANEOUS. Germany agrees to recognize the full validity of the treaties of peace and additional conventions to be concluded by the allied and associated powers with the powers allied with Germany, to agree to the decisions to be taken as to the territories of Austria-Hungary, Bulgaria, and Turkey, and to recognize the new States in the frontiers to be fixed for them.

Germany agrees not to put forward any pecuniary claims against any allied or associated powers signing the present treaty based on events previous to the coming into force of the treaty.

Germany accepts all decrees as to German ships and goods made by any allied or associated prize court. The Allies reserve the right to examine all decisions of German prize courts. The present treaty, of which the French and British texts are both authentic, shall be ratified and the depositions of ratifications made in Paris as soon as possible. The treaty is to become effective in all respects for each Power on the date of deposition of its ratification.

BY THE PRESIDENT OF THE UNITED STATES OF AMERICA

A PROCLAMATION

[Exportation of Arms or Munitions of War to Mexico Unlawful.]

Whereas, a Joint Resolution of Congress, approved March 14th, 1912, reads and provides as follows:

"That whenever the President shall find that in any American country conditions of domestic violence exist which are promoted by the use of arms or munitions of war procured from the United States, and shall make proclamation thereof, it shall be unlawful to export except under such limitations and exceptions as the President shall prescribe any arms or munitions of war from any place in the United States to such country until otherwise ordered by the President or by Congress;"

And whereas, it is provided by Section II of the said Joint Resolution,

"That any shipment of material hereby declared unlawful after such a proclamation shall be punishable by a fine not exceeding ten thousand dollars, or imprisonment not exceeding two years, or both;"

And whereas, by an Act of Congress, approved June 15th, 1917, it is provided as follows:

"Whenever an attempt is made to export or ship from or take out of the United States, any arms or munitions of war, or other articles, in violation of law, or whenever there shall be known or probable cause to believe that any such arms or munitions of war, or other articles, are being or are intended to be exported, or shipped from, or taken out of the United States, in violation of law, the several collectors, naval officers, surveyors, inspectors of customs, and marshals and deputy marshals of the United States, and every other person duly authorized for the purpose by the President, may seize and detain any articles or munitions of war about to be exported or shipped from, or taken out of the United States, in violation of law, and the vessels or vehicles containing the same, and retain possession thereof until released or disposed of as hereinafter directed. If upon due inquiry as hereinafter provided, the property seized shall appear to have been about to be so unlawfully exported, shipped from, or taken out of the United States, the same shall be forfeited to the United States."

And whereas, by the same Act of Congress, it is provided in Section 8 thereof as follows:

"The President may employ such part of the land or naval forces of the United States as he may deem necessary to carry out the purposes of this title."

Now, therefore, I, Woodrow Wilson, President of the United States of America, acting under and by virtue of the authority conferred in me by the said Joint Resolution and Act of Congress, do hereby declare and proclaim that I have found that there exist in Mexico such conditions of domestic violence promoted by the use of arms or munitions of war procured from the United States as contemplated by the said Joint Resolution and Act of Congress; and I do hereby admonish all citizens of the United States and every person to abstain from every violation of the provisions of the Joint Resolution and Act of Congress above set forth, hereby made applicable to Mexico, and I do hereby warn them that all violations of such provisions will be rigorously prosecuted.

VETO MESSAGES

[Repeal of Daylight Saving Law and Vocational Rehabilitation.]

THE WHITE HOUSE, *July 12, 1919.*

To the House of Representatives:

I take the liberty of returning H. R. 3157, "An act making appropriations for the Department of Agriculture for the fiscal year ending June 30, 1920," without my signature.

I realize, of course, the grave inconvenience which may arise from the postponement of the legislation at this time, but feel obliged to withhold my signature because of the clause which provides that "at and after two o'clock A. M. on Sunday, October 26, 1919, next, the act entitled 'An Act to save daylight and to provide standard time for the United States,' approved March 19, 1918, be, and the same hereby is, repealed."

I believe that the repeal of the act referred to would be of very great inconvenience to the country, and I think that I am justified in saying that it would constitute something more than an inconvenience. It would involve a serious economic loss. The act of March 19, 1918, "to save daylight," resulted not only from a careful study of industrial conditions by competent men familiar with the business operations of the country, but also from observation of the happy and beneficial consequences of similar legislation in other countries where legislation of this character has been for some time in operation and where it has resulted, as the act of March 19, 1918 has resulted in the United States, in substantial economies. That act was intended to place the chief business activities of the country as nearly as might be within the limits of daylight throughout the year. It resulted in very great economies of fuel and a substantial economy of energy because of the very different effects of work done in the daylight and work done by artificial light.

It, moreover, served the daily convenience of the many communities of the country in a way which gave all but universal satisfaction, and the overwhelming testimony of its value which has come to me convinces me that I should not be justified in acquiescing in its repeal.

WOODROW WILSON.

THE WHITE HOUSE, *July 12, 1919.*

To the House of Representatives:

Under the Vocational Rehabilitation bill, which became law June 27, 1918, the Congress has sought to fulfill the expectations of the country that the soldier, sailor, or marine disabled in the recent war should be given an opportunity to secure at the expense and under the fostering care of the General Government such training as he needs to overcome the handicap of his disability and to resume his place as a civilian able to earn a living upon something like an equal footing with those with whom he was associated before he made his great sacrifice for the honor and defense of the country.

The work of rehabilitation under this admirable law is now at its height and was to have been given greater speed and certainty by the amendment to Section 2 of the Vocational Rehabilitation bill, which

I have today signed, and which places the whole responsibility for vocational training in a single agency, virtually transferring from the War Risk Insurance Bureau to the Federal Board for Vocational Education $6,000,000 with which to support disabled men in training at the generous figures of $80 a month for a single man and $100 a month for a man and his wife.

It is a matter of very grave concern, therefore, that, at the very moment when these disabled men are coming in constantly increasing numbers to the Government to avail themselves of this general plan, there should appear in the sundry civil appropriation bill, which I now return, limiting clauses which will do much more than seriously cripple and retard the beneficial work of restoring these men to useful and contented lives. Those clauses would probably, in fact, if put into effect, nullify the whole purpose of the Act and render its administration practically impossible.

The section of the bill which I now return, which governs the appropriation for this work, provides the sum of $6,000,000 for all the expenses of rehabilitation, including the support of the disabled men in training, and this sum is stated to be "in lieu of the appropriation contained in the Act approved July —, 1919, amending Section 2 of the Act approved June 27, 1918." Inasmuch as there are already over 4,000 disabled soldiers, sailors, and marines in training and inasmuch as another 4,000 would be put into training now that the amendment to Section 2 has become law, it is clear that, even at the rate of only $80 a month, a sum approximating $8,000,000 will be required for the mere support of these men, and that under the present appropriation nothing will be available for their tuition and travel or for placing them where they can earn a living, and it will be impossible to meet the needs of the new thousands who are every week seeking the benefits of the Rehabilitation Act. In the offices of the board in the District of Columbia and in fourteen great centres of the United States immediate help is being given to men in need of these services, and these offices are used for the essential purpose of keeping accurate records, of providing proper medical survey to the men, of caring for them in their illness, and for the various administrative costs inseparable from different work of this kind, which must, in the present circumstances, reach to every corner of the United States.

Furthermore, the same section of the sundry civil bill places such limitations upon the salaries which the Federal Board for Vocational Education is permitted to pay that it will inevitably result in the loss by the Vocational Board of a very large number of men who have made themselves especially valuable, and indeed indispensable, in this new work by reason of their native ability, their proven general experience, and their special training, and to whose advice the disabled men must look, as well as for superintendence in the matter of training and employment. Among these are the vocational advisers, whose special duty it is to study the men in the hospitals, confer with them, and lay out their vocational plans. These hospital cases must, if these men are to be dismissed or allowed to resign, get along entirely without such advice and supervision until they have been able, after their discharge, to make their way on their own initiative to the distant offices of the Federal Board.

These serious limitations upon the amount of money available and the uses to which it is to be put involved therefore an actual disruption of a carefully built up service at the very moment when the disabled soldiers, sailors, and marines now in the country or returning to it are most immediately in need of help. This is a matter of the gravest consequence. It cannot but have far-reaching and disastrous effects upon the plan so carefully thought out for the immediate and thorough rehabilitation of men in the service of the country.

I therefore return the bill, with the hope that the Congress will reconsider this section of the law, restore the $6,000,000 appropriated under the Act amending Section 2, and most liberally revise the salary limitations, so that this beneficent work may go on, and go on at once. I am convinced that in this matter I speak the sentiments and the hopes of those who have most carefully studied the needs of the returning soldiers and who are best qualified to carry out a purpose which I am sure the country has very much at heart.

WOODROW WILSON.

The White House, *August 16, 1919.*

To the House of Representatives:

I return this bill, H. R. 3854, "An Act for the repeal of the Daylight Saving law," without my signature, but do so with the utmost reluctance. I realize the very considerable and in some respects very serious inconveniences to which the Daylight Saving law subjects the farmers of the country, to whom we owe the greatest consideration and who have distinguished themselves during these recent years of war and want by patriotic endeavors worthy of all praise. But I have been obliged to balance one set of disadvantages against another, and to venture a judgment as to which were the most serious for the country. The immediate and pressing need of the country is production, increased and increasing production in all lines of industry. Disorganization and dislocation caused by the war have told nowhere so heavily as at the industrial centres—in manufacture and in the many industries to which the country and the whole world must look to supply needs which cannot be ignored or postponed.

It is to these that the Daylight Saving law is of most service. It ministers to economy and to efficiency. And the interest of the farmer is not in all respects separated from these interests. He needs what the factories produce along with the rest of the world. He is profited by the prosperity which the success brings about. His own life and methods are more easily adjusted, I venture to think, than those of the manufacturer and the merchant.

These are the considerations which have led me to withhold my signature from this repeal. I hope that they are considerations which will appeal to the thoughtful judgment of the House and in the long run to the thoughtful judgment of the farmers of the country, who have always shown an admirable public spirit.

WOODROW WILSON.

MESSAGE TO CONGRESS

[Asking the grant of permanent rank of General for John J. Pershing, commander-in-chief of the American Expeditionary Forces during the Great War, and for Peyton C. March, chief of staff of the United States army during the most decisive days of the participation of the United States in the war; and the permanent rank of Admiral for William S. Sims, commander of the United States fleet in European waters during the war, and for William S. Benson, director of naval operations of the United States Navy during the war. The permanent rank of General had previously been granted to George Washington, Ulysses S. Grant, William T. Sherman and Philip H. Sheridan. The permanent rank of Admiral had previously been granted to David G. Farragut, David D. Porter and George Dewey.]

THE WHITE HOUSE, *July 18, 1919.*

To the Senate and House of Representatives:

I take the liberty of calling your attention to a matter which I am sure is at the heart of the whole country, and which I have had very much in mind throughout all these months when we were trying to arrange a peace that would be worthy of the spirit and achievements of the men who won the victory in the field and on the sea. After mature reflection I earnestly recommend that you give the permanent rank of General to John J. Pershing and Peyton C. March, expressing the law in such a way as to give precedence to General Pershing; and that you give the permanent rank of Admiral to William S. Benson and William S. Sims.

I take it for granted that I am only anticipating your own thoughts in proposing these orders for the men upon whom the principal responsibilities devolved for achieving the great results which our incomparable navy and army accomplished.

WOODROW WILSON.

NOTE TO MEXICO

[Threatening a Change in Policy toward that Country in case no Greater Protection Were Afforded American Citizens There.]

MEXICO CITY, *July 22, 1919.*

Sir—With reference to the Embassy's note, dated July 16, 1919, relative to the murder of Peter Catron, near Calles, San Luis Potosi, on or about July 7 last, I have the honor to inform you that I am now under telegraphic instructions from my Government to urge upon the Mexican Government the punishment of those responsible for this murder and the adoption of adequate measures to prevent a recurrence of the murder of American citizens.

I am also instructed to state that, should the lives of American citizens continue to remain unsafe and these murders continue by means of the unwillingness or inability of the Mexican Government to afford adequate protection, my Government may be forced to adopt a radical change in its policy with regard to Mexico.

Accept, Sir, the renewed assurances of my highest consideration.

GEORGE T. SUMMERLIN,
Chargé d'Affaires.

MESSAGE TO THE SENATE

[Laying Before It the Text of a Proposed Special Treaty with France, Promising Protection in Case of Unprovoked Aggression by Germany.]

THE WHITE HOUSE, *July 29, 1919.*

Gentlemen of the Senate:

I take pleasure in laying before you a treaty with the Republic of France, the object of which is to secure to that republic the immediate aid of the United States of America in case of any unprovoked movement of aggression against her on the part of Germany, I earnestly hope that the treaty will meet with your cordial approval and will receive an early ratification at your hands, along with the treaty of peace with Germany. Now that you have had an opportunity to examine the great document I presented to you two weeks ago, it seems opportune to lay before you this treaty, which is meant to be in effect a part of it.

It was signed on the same day with the treaty of peace and is intended as a temporary supplement to it. It is believed that the treaty of peace with Germany itself provides adequate protection to France against aggression from her recent enemy on the east, but the years immediately ahead of us contain many incalculable possibilities. The Covenant of the League of Nations provides for military action for the protection of its members only upon advice of the council of the

League—advice given, it is to be presumed, only upon deliberation and acted upon by each of the Governments of the member states only if its own judgment justifies such action. The object of the special treaty with France which I now submit to you is to provide for immediate military assistance to France by the United States in case of any unprovoked movement of aggression against her by Germany without waiting for the advice of the council of the League of Nations that such action will be taken. It is to be an arrangement not independent of the League of Nations but under it.

It is therefore expressly provided that this treaty shall be made the subject of consideration at the same time with the treaty of peace with Germany; that this special arrangement shall receive the approval of the council of the League, and that this special provision for the safety of France shall remain in force only until, upon the application of one of the parties to it, the council of the League, acting, if necessary, by a majority vote, shall agree that the provisions of the Covenant of the League afford her sufficient protection.

I was moved to sign this treaty by considerations which will, I hope, seem as persuasive and as irresistible to you as they seem to me. We are bound to France by ties of friendship which we have always regarded, and shall always regard, as peculiarly sacred. She assisted us to win our freedom as a nation. It is seriously to be doubted whether we could have won it without her gallant and timely aid.

We have recently had the privilege of assisting in driving enemies, who were also enemies of the world, from her soil; but that does not pay our debt to her. Nothing can pay such a debt. She now desires that we should promise to lend our great force to keep her safe against the power she has had most reason to fear. Another great nation volunteers the same promise. It is one of the fine reversals of history that that other nation should be the very power from whom France fought to set us free.

A new day has dawned. Old antagonisms are forgotten. The common cause of freedom and enlightenment has created new comradeships and a new perception of what it is wise and necessary for great nations to do to free the world of intolerable fear. Two Governments who wish to be members of the League of Nations ask leave of the council of the League to be permitted to go to the assistance of a friend whose situation has been found to be one of peculiar peril, without awaiting the advice of the League to act.

It is by taking such pledges as this that we prove ourselves faithful to the utmost to the high obligations of gratitude and tested friendship. Such an act as this seems to me one of the proofs that we are a people that sees the true heart of duty and prefers honor to its own separate course of peace.

WOODROW WILSON.

The text of the treaty was as follows:—

ARTICLE I

In case the following stipulations relating to the left bank of the Rhine contained in the treaty of peace with Germany signed at Versailles the 28th day of June, 1919, by the United States of America, the French Republic, and the British Empire, among other Powers—

"Article 42. Germany is forbidden to maintain or construct any fortifications either on the left bank of the Rhine or on the right bank to the west of a line drawn 50 kilometers to the west of the Rhine.

"Article 43. In the area defined above the maintenance and assembly of armed forces, either permanently or temporarily, and military maneuvers of any kind, as well as the upkeep of all permanent works for mobilization, are in the same way forbidden.

"Article 44. In case Germany violates in any manner whatsoever the provisions of Articles 42 and 43 she shall be regarded as committing a hostile act against the Powers signatory of the present treaty and as calculated to disturb the peace of the world."

may not at first provide adequate security and protection to France, the United States of America shall be bound to come immediately to her assistance in the event of any unprovoked movement of aggression against her being made by Germany.

ARTICLE II

The present treaty, in similar terms with the treaty of even date for the same purpose concluded between Great Britain and the French Republic, a copy of which treaty is annexed hereto, will only come into force when the latter is ratified.

ARTICLE III

The present treaty must be submitted to the council of the League of Nations and must be recognized by the council, acting if need be by a majority, as an engagement which is consistent with the Covenant of the League. It will continue in force until on the application of one of the parties to it the council, acting if need be by a majority, agrees that the League itself affords sufficient protection.

ARTICLE IV

The present treaty will be submitted to the Senate of the United States at the same time as the Treaty of Versailles is submitted to the Senate for its advice and consent to ratification. It will be submitted before ratification to the French Chamber of Deputies for approval. The ratification thereof will be exchanged on the deposit of ratifications of the Treaty of Versailles at Paris or as soon thereafter as shall be possible.

ADDRESS TO CONGRESS

[On the High Cost of Living, August 8, 1919.]

Gentlemen of the Congress:

I have sought this opportunity to address you because it is clearly my duty to call your attention to the present cost of living and to

by the allied and associated powers, and one each b
.rn
erms of which shall be fixed by the principal ance
shall be concluded between Poland and Danzig iaries,
hin the Polish customs frontiers, through a fre paration
and the free use of all the city's waterways, s will be
control and administration of the Vistula ar legislation,
within the city, and postal, telegraphic s to indemnify.
Poland and Danzig; provide ag al for local needs
city, and place its foreign rela asin extends from the
abroad in to rians north as far as Stwendel includ-
ier betwe Sarre as far as Sarre Holzbach and on the
popu
acuat hts and welfare of the population and guarantee
ith working the mines the territory will be governed
sou by the League of Nations and consisting of five
a native inhabitant of the Sarre, and three repre-
untries other than France and Germany. The League
of the Commission as Chairman to act as executive
commission will have all powers of government form-
rman Empire, Prussia and Bavaria, will administer the
ic services and have full power to interpret the treaty
s will continue, but subject to the Commission. Exist-
ill remain the basis of the law, but the Commission may
consulting a local representative assembly which it
ve the taxing power but for local purposes only. New
by this assembly. Labor legislation will consider the
r organizations and the labor program of the League.
may be freely utilized, the former being free to belong
rights acquired as to pensions and social insurance will
ny and the Sarre Commission.
litary service but only a local gendarmerie to preserve
ll preserve their local assemblies, religious liberties,
ut may vote only for local assemblies. They will keep
except so far as individuals may change it. Those
ave every facility with respect to their property. The
t of the French customs system, with no export tax
al products going to Germany nor on German products
or five years no import duties on products of the basin
erman products coming into the basin. For local con-
y may circulate without restriction.
a plebiscite will be held by communes to ascertain the
n as to continuance of the existing regime under the
on with France or union with Germany. The right to
nhabitants over twenty resident therein at the signature.
e opinions thus expressed the League will decide the
any portion restored to Germany the German Govern-
French mines at an appraised valuation. If the price is

urge upon
the legislati
it and bring
paying for e
live are not j
pective, and
by vicious pr
They constitute
cause we know
power and that
and made to squ
Some of the me
illegal, some of
energetically proc
under the law, an

I need not rec
demanded and pa
food markets, at t
city and in the v
talk of every dome
ances even. It is a
has set in which is li
rents and the whole
cycle to which there is

With the increase
mands for increase i
be no other means
wages there follows
whose producers have
increase, for the ma
—but an increase
and for which the a
an excuse. The lab
they demand it are li
worse. It checks pr
tribution and strips
to buy, and there is a
the scarcity.

These are facts a
familiar; but we ar
them, or because of
"natural" and inevita
their fatal results if
or reverse them. I

ontrol, and
d may be

e immediate
1. The free
mselves, and
full and na-
neither peace
ing fears and
o know when
shift for itself
will and concert
r to do and to

n the operating
y anaesthetic. It
1 upon which it
cannot think its
rovident direction

no energy in en-
no calculable basis
selling, no certain
business, no hopeful
mbling of the dis-
een established and.

ically disturbed and
ples whom the war
ging and destructive
y affected and dis-
ductive capacity, our
with those of other
ith the nations and
sion of the war fell
erative action of the

our ports to foreign
dstuffs merely, but
index of what our
the volume of our
is impossible yet to
will be able to find
h purchases on such

agree in advance to any convention with which the allied
may determine to replace them. She is to recognize
Belgium over the contested territory of Moresnet and
Moresnet, and to renounce in favor of Belgium all rig
Eupen and Malmedy, the inhabitants of which are to
months to protest against this change of sovereignty
part, the final decision to be reserved to the League of I
is to settle the details of the frontier, and various reg
nationality are laid down.

Luxemburg. Germany renounces her various treatie
the Grand Duchy of Luxemburg, recognizes that it ceas
German Zollverein from January first, last, renounces a
of the railroads, adheres to the abrogation of its neutra
vance any international agreement as to it reached by th
powers.

Left Bank of the Rhine. As provided in the military
not maintain any fortifications or armed forces less than
east of the Rhine, hold any manoeuvres, nor maintain
mobilization. In case of violation, "she shall be rega
hostile act against the Powers who sign the present trea
disturb the peace of the world." "By virtue of the pi
shall be bound to respond to any request for an explana
of the League of Nations may think it necessary to addre

Alsace-Lorraine. After recognition of the moral ol
wrong done in 1871 by Germany to France and the peop
the territories ceded to Germany by the Treaty of Fra
France with their frontiers as before 1871, to date fro
armistice, and to be free of all public debts.

Citizenship is regulated by detailed provisions disting
immediately restored to full French citizenship, those whe
applications therefor, and those for whom naturalizatic
years. The last named class includes German residents
distinguished from those who acquire the position of AI
fined in the treaty. All public property and all private
ex-sovereigns passes to France without payment or cr
stituted for Germany as regards ownership of the rail
concessions of tramway. The Rhine bridges pass to Fra
for their upkeep.

For five years manufactured products of Alsace-Lor
to Germany free of duty to a total amount not exceeding
age of the three years preceding the war and textile mate
from Germany to Alsace-Lorraine and re-exported free c
electric power from the right bank must be continued for
years, with possible extension to ten, the ports of Kehl
be administered as a single unit by a French admini
supervised by the Central Rhine Commission. Propert
guarded in both ports and equality of treatment as respe
nationals, vessels, and goods of every country.

Contracts between Alsace-Lorraine and Germans are
France's right to annul on grounds of public interest.
hold in certain classes of cases while in others a judi

urge upon you with all the persuasive force of which I am capable the legislative measures which would be most effective in controlling it and bringing it down. The prices the people of this country are paying for everything that it is necessary for them to use in order to live are not justified by a shortage in supply, either present or prospective, and are in many cases artificially and deliberately created by vicious practises which ought immediately be checked by law. They constitute a burden upon us which is the more unbearable because we know that it is wilfully imposed by those who have the power and that it can by vigorous public action be greatly lightened and made to square with the actual conditions of supply and demand. Some of the methods by which these prices are produced are already illegal, some of them criminal, and those who employ them will be energetically proceeded against; but others have not yet been brought under the law, and should be dealt with at once by legislation.

I need not recite the particulars of this critical matter, the prices demanded and paid at the sources of supply, at the factory, in the food markets, at the shops, in the restaurants and hotels, alike in the city and in the village. They are familiar to you. They are the talk of every domestic circle and of every group of casual acquaintances even. It is a matter of familiar knowledge, also, that a process has set in which is likely, unless something is done, to push prices and rents and the whole cost of living higher and yet higher, in a vicious cycle to which there is no logical or natural end.

With the increase in the prices of the necessaries of life come demands for increase in wages—demands which are justified if there be no other means of enabling men to live. Upon the increase of wages there follows close an increase in the price of the products whose producers have been accorded the increase—not a proportionate increase, for the manufacturer does not content himself with that —but an increase considerably greater that the added wage cost and for which the added wage cost is oftentimes hardly more than an excuse. The laborers who do not get an increase in pay when they demand it are likely to strike, and the strike only makes matters worse. It checks production, it affects the railways, it prevents distribution and strips the markets, so that there is presently nothing to buy, and there is another excessive addition to prices resulting from the scarcity.

These are facts and forces with which we have become only too familiar; but we are not justified because of our familiarity with them, or because of any hasty and shallow conclusion that they are "natural" and inevitable, in sitting inactively by and letting them work their fatal results if there is anything that we can do to check, correct, or reverse them. I have sought this opportunity to inform the Congress what the Executive is doing by way of remedy and control, and to suggest where effective legal remedies are lacking and may be supplied.

We must, I think, frankly admit that there is no complete immediate remedy to be had from legislation and executive action. The free processes of supply and demand will not operate of themselves, and no legislative or Executive action can force them into full and natural operation until there is peace. There is now neither peace nor war. All the world is waiting—with what unnerving fears and haunting doubts who can adequately say?—waiting to know when it comes—a peace in which each nation shall make shift for itself as it can, or a peace buttressed and supported by the will and concert of the nations that have the purpose and the power to do and to enforce what is right.

Politically, economically, socially, the world is on the operating table, and it has not been possible to administer any anaesthetic. It is conscious. It even watches the capital operation upon which it knows that its hope of healthful life depends. It cannot think its business out or make plans or give intelligent and provident direction to its affairs while in such a case.

Where there is no peace of mind there can be no energy in endeavor. There can be no confidence in industry, no calculable basis for credits, no confident buying or systematic selling, no certain prospect of employment, no normal restoration of business, no hopeful attempt at reconstruction or the proper reassembling of the dislocated elements of enterprise until peace has been established and, so far as may be, guaranteed.

Our national life has no doubt been less radically disturbed and dismembered than the national life of other peoples whom the war more directly affected, with all its terrible ravaging and destructive force, but it has been, nevertheless, profoundly affected and disarranged, and our industries, our credits, our productive capacity, our economic processes are inextricably interwoven with those of other nations and peoples—most intimately of all with the nations and peoples upon whom the chief burden and confusion of the war fell and who are now most dependent upon the co-operative action of the world.

We are just now shipping more goods out of our ports to foreign markets than we ever shipped before—not foodstuffs merely, but stuffs and materials of every sort; but this is no index of what our foreign sales will continue to be or of the effect the volume of our exports will have on supplies and prices. It is impossible yet to predict how far or how long foreign purchasers will be able to find the money or the credit to pay for or sustain such purchases on such a scale; how soon or to what extent foreign manufacturers can resume their former production, foreign farmers get their accustomed crops from their own fields, foreign mines resume their former output, foreign merchants set up again their old machinery of trade with the ends of the earth.

All these things must remain uncertain until peace is established and the nations of the world have concerted the methods by which normal life and industry are to be restored. All that we shall do, in the meantime, to restrain profiteering and put the life of our people upon a tolerable footing will be makeshift and provisional. There can be no settled conditions here or elsewhere until the treaty of peace is out of the way and the work of liquidating the war has become the chief concern of our Government and of other Governments of the world. Until then business will inevitably remain speculative, and sway now this way and again that, with heavy losses or heavy gains, as it may chance, and the consumer must take care of both the gains and the losses. There can be no peace prices so long as our whole financial and economic system is on a war basis.

Europe will not, can not, recoup her capital or put her restless, distracted peoples to work until she knows exactly where she stands in respect of peace; and what we will do is for her the chief question upon which her quietude of mind and confidence of purpose depend. While there is any possibility that the peace terms may be changed or may be held long in abeyance or may not be enforced because of divisions of opinion among the powers associated against Germany, it is idle to look for permanent relief.

But what we can do we should do, and should do at once. And there is a great deal that we can do, provisional though it be. Wheat shipments and credits to facilitate the purchase of our wheat can and will be limited and controlled in such a way as not to raise, but rather to lower, the price of flour here. The Government has the power, within certain limits, to regulate that. We cannot deny wheat to foreign peoples who are in dire need of it, and we do not wish to do so; but, fortunately, though the wheat crop is not what we hoped it would be, it is abundant, if handled with provident care. The price of wheat is lower in the United States than in Europe, and can with proper management be kept so.

By way of immediate relief, surplus stocks of both food and clothing in the hands of the Government will be sold, and, of course, sold at prices at which there is no profit. And by way of a more permanent correction of prices, surplus stocks in private hands will be drawn out of storage and put upon the market.

Fortunately, under the terms of the Food Control act the hoarding of foodstuffs can be checked and prevented; and they will be, with the greatest energy. Foodstuffs can be drawn out of storage and sold by legal action, which the Department of Justice will institute wherever necessary; but so soon as the situation is systematically dealt with, it is not likely that the courts will often have to be resorted to.

Much of the accumulating of stocks has no doubt been due to the sort of speculation which always results from an uncertainty. Great surpluses were accumulated because it was impossible to foresee what the market would disclose and dealers were determined to be ready for whatever might happen, as well as eager to reap the full advantage of rising prices. They will now see the disadvantage, as well as the danger, of holding off from the new process of distribution.

Some very interesting and significant facts with regard to stocks on hand and the rise of prices in the face of abundance have been disclosed by the inquiries of the Department of Agriculture, the Department of Labor, and the Federal Trade Commission. They seem to justify the statement that in the case of many necessary commodities effective means have been found to prevent the normal operation of the law of supply and demand.

Disregarding the surplus stocks in the hands of the Government, there was a greater supply of foodstuffs in this country on June 1 of this year than at the same date last year. In the combined total of a number of the most important foods in dry and cold storage the excess is quite 19 per cent. And yet prices have risen. The supply of fresh eggs on hand in June of this year, for example, was greater by nearly 10 per cent than the supply on hand at the same time last year, and yet the wholesale price was 40 cents a dozen as against 30 cents a year ago.

The stock of frozen fowls had increased more than 298 per cent., and yet the price had risen also from 34½ cents per pound to 37½ cents. The supply of creamery butter had increased 129 per cent., and the price from 41 to 53 cents per pound. The supply of salt beef had been augumented 3 per cent., and the price had gone up from $34 a barrel to $36 a barrel. Canned corn had increased in stock nearly 92 per cent., and had remained substantially the same in price.

In a few foodstuffs the prices had declined, but in nothing like the proportion in which the supply had increased. For example, the stock of canned tomatoes had increased 102 per cent., and yet the price had declined only 25 cents per dozen cans. In some cases there had been the usual result of an increase of price following a decrease of supply, but in almost every instance the increase of price had been disproportionate to the decrease in stock.

The Attorney General has been making a careful study of the situation as a whole and of the laws that can be applied to better it, and is convinced that, under the stimulation and temptation of

A GERMAN AIRPLANE COMES INTO RANGE

A GERMAN AIRPLANE COMES INTO RANGE.

The illustration shows the crews of two British anti-aircraft guns rushing to take a shot at a German plane which has ventured within range behind the battlefront.

exceptional circumstances, combinations of producers and combinations of traders have been formed for the control of supplies and of prices which are clearly in restraint of trade, and against these, prosecutions will be promptly instituted and actively pushed which will in all likelihood have a prompt corrective effect.

There is reason to believe that the prices of leather, of coal, of lumber, and of textiles have been materially affected by forms of concert and co-operation among the producers and marketers of these and other universally necessary commodities which it will be possible to redress. No watchful or energetic effort will be spared to accomplish this necessary result. I trust that there will not be many cases in which prosecution will be necessary. Public action will no doubt cause many who have perhaps unwittingly adopted illegal methods to abandon them promptly and of their own motion.

And publicity can accomplish a great deal. The purchaser can often take care of himself if he knows the facts and influences he is dealing with; and purchasers are not disinclined to do anything, either singly or collectively, that may be necessary for their self-protection. The Department of Commerce, the Department of Agriculture, the Department of Labor, and the Federal Trade Commission can do a great deal toward supplying the public, systematically and at short intervals, with information regarding the actual supply of particular commodities that is in existence and available, and with regard to supplies which are in existence but not available because of hoarding, and with regard to the methods of price fixing which are being used by dealers in certain foodstuffs and other necessaries.

There can be little doubt that retailers are in part—sometimes in large part—responsible for exorbitant prices; and it is quite practicable for the Government through the agencies I have mentioned to supply the public with full information as to the prices at which retailers buy and as to the cost of transportation they pay, in order that it may be known just what margin of profit they are demanding. Opinion and concerted action on the part of purchasers can probably do the rest.

That is, these agencies may perform this indispensable service provided the Congress will supply them with the necessary funds to prosecute their inquiries and keep their price lists up to date. Hitherto the appropriation committee of the Houses have not always, I fear, seen the full value of these inquiries, and the departments and commissions have been very much straitened for means to render this service.

That adequate funds be provided by appropriation for this purpose, and provided as promptly as possible, is one of the means of greatly ameliorating the present distressing conditions of livelihood that I have come to urge, in this attempt to concert with you the best ways to serve the country in this emergency. It is one of the absolutely necessary means, underlying many others, and can be supplied at once.

There are many other ways. Existing law is inadequate. There are many perfectly legitimate methods by which the Government can exercise restraint and guidance.

Let me urge, in the first place, that the present Food Control Act should be extended, both as to the period of time during which it shall remain in operation and as to the commodities to which it shall apply. Its provisions against hoarding should be made to apply not only to food, but also to feedstuffs, to fuel, to clothing, and to many other commodities which are indispensably necessaries of life. As it stands now, it is limited in operation to the period of the war and becomes inoperative upon the formal proclamation of peace.

But I should judge that it was clearly within the constitutional power of the Congress to make similar permanent provisions and regulations with regard to all goods destined for interstate commerce, and to exclude them from interstate shipment if the requirements of law are not complied with. Some such regulation is imperatively necessary. The abuses that have grown up in the manipulation of prices by the withholding of foodstuffs and other necessaries of life cannot otherwise be effectively prevented. There can be no doubt of either the necessity or the legitimacy of such measures. May I not call attention to the fact, also, that, although the present act prohibits profiteering, the prohibition is accompanied by no penalty? It is clearly in the public interest that a penalty should be provided which will be persuasive.

To the same end I earnestly recommend, in the second place, that the Congress pass a law regulating cold storage as it is regulated, for example, by the laws of the state of New Jersey, which limit the time during which goods may be kept in storage, prescribe the methods of disposing of them if kept beyond the permitted period, and require that goods released from storage shall in all cases bear the date of their receipt.

It would materially add to the serviceability of the law, for the purpose we now have in view, if it were also prescribed that all goods released from storage for interstate shipment should have plainly marked upon each package the selling or market price at which they went in storage. By this means the purchaser would always be able to learn what profits stood between him and the producer or the wholesale dealer.

It would serve as a useful example to the other communities of the country, as well as greatly relieve local distress, if the Congress were to regulate all such matters very fully for the District of Columbia, where its legislative authority is without limit.

I would also recommend that it be required that all goods destined for interstate commerce should in every case, where their form or package makes it possible, be plainly marked with the price at which they left the hands of the producer. Such a requirement would bear a close analogy to certain provisions of the Pure Food Act, by which it is required that certain detailed information be given on the labels of packages of food and drugs.

And it does not seem to me that we can confine ourselves to detailed measures of this kind, if it is indeed our purpose to assume national control of the processes of distribution. I take it for granted that that is our purpose and our duty. Nothing less will suffice. We need not hesitate to handle a national question in a national way. We should go beyond the measures I have suggested.

We should formulate a law requiring a Federal license of all corporations engaged in interstate commerce and embodying in the license, or in the conditions under which it is to be issued, specific regulations designed to secure competitive selling and prevent unconscionable profits in the method of marketing. Such a law would afford a welcome opportunity to effect other much needed reforms in the business of interstate shipment and in the methods of corporations which are engaged in it; but for the moment I confine my recommendations to the object immediately in hand, which is to lower the cost of living.

May I not add that there is a bill now pending before Congress which, if passed, would do much to stop speculation and to prevent the fraudulent methods of promotion by which our people are annually fleeced of many millions of hard earned money? I refer to the measure proposed by the Capital Issues Committee for the control of security issues. It is a measure formulated by men who know the actual conditions of business, and its adoption would serve a great and beneficent purpose.

We are dealing, gentlemen of the Congress, I need hardly say, with very critical and very difficult matters. We should go forward with confidence along the road we see, but we shall also seek to comprehend the whole of the scene amidst which we act. There is no ground for some of the fearful forecasts I hear uttered about me, but the condition of the world is unquestionably very grave and we should face it comprehendingly.

The situation of our own country is exceptionally fortunate. We of all peoples can afford to keep our heads and to determine upon moderate sensible courses of action which will insure us against the passions and distempers which are working such deep unhappiness for some of the distressed nations on the other side of the sea. But we may be involved in their distresses unless we help, and help with energy and intelligence.

The world must pay for the appalling destruction wrought by the Great War, and we are part of the world. We must pay our share. For five years now the industry of all Europe has been slack and disordered. The normal crops have not been produced; the normal quantity of manufactured goods has not been turned out. Not until there are the usual crops and the usual production of manufactured goods on the other side of the Atlantic can Europe return to the former conditions; and it was upon the former conditions, not the present, that our economic relations with Europe were built up.

We must face the fact that unless we help Europe to get back to her normal life and production a chaos will ensue there which will inevitably be communicated to this country. For the present, it is manifest, we must quicken, not slacken, our own production. We, and we alone, now hold the world steady. Upon our steadfastness and self-possession depend the affairs of nations everywhere.

It is in this supreme crisis—the crisis for all mankind—that America must prove her mettle. In the presence of a world confused, distracted, she must show herself self-possessed, self-contained, capable of sober and effective action. She saved Europe by her action in arms; she must now save it by her action in peace. In saving Europe she will save herself, as she did upon the battlefields of the war. The calmness and capacity with which she deals with and masters the problems of peace will be the final test and proof of her place among the peoples of the world.

And, if only in our own interest, we must help the people overseas. Europe is our biggest customer. We must keep her going or thousands of our shops and scores of our mines must close. There is no such thing as letting her go to ruin without ourselves sharing in the disaster.

In such circumstances, face to face with such tests, passion must be discarded. Passion and a disregard for the rights of others have no place in the counsels of a free people. We need light, not heat, in these solemn times of self-examination and saving action. There must be no threats. Let there be only intelligent counsel, and let the best reasons win, not the strongest brute force. The world has just destroyed the arbitrary force of a military junta. It will live under no other. All that is arbitrary and coercive is in the discard. Those who seek to employ it only prepare their own destruction.

We cannot hastily and overnight revolutionize all the processes of our economic life. We shall not attempt to do so. These are days of deep excitement and of extravagant speech; but with us these are things of the surface. Every one who is in real touch with the silent masses of our great people knows that the old strong fibre and steady self-control are still there, firm against violence or any distempered action that would throw their affairs into confusion. I am serenely confident that they will readily find themselves, no matter what the circumstances, and that they will address themselves to the tasks of peace with the same devotion and the same stalwart preference for what is right that they displayed to the admiration of the whole world in the midst of war.

And I entertain another confident hope. I have spoken today chiefly of measures of imperative regulation and legal compulsion, of prosecutions and the sharp correction of selfish processes; and these no doubt are necessary. But there are other forces that we may count on besides those resident in the Department of Justice. We have just fully awakened to what has been going on and to the influences, many of them very selfish and sinister, that have been producing high prices and imposing an intolerable burden on the mass of our people. To have brought it all into the open will accomplish the greater part of the result we seek.

I appeal with entire confidence to our producers, our middlemen, and our merchants to deal fairly with the people. It is their opportunity to show that they comprehend, that they intend to act justly, and that they have the public interest sincerely at heart. And I have no doubt that housekeepers all over the country and every one who buys the things he daily stands in need of will presently exercise a greater vigilance, a more thoughtful economy, a more discriminating care as to the market in which he buys or the merchant with whom he trades than he has hitherto exercised.

I believe, too, that the more extreme leaders of organized labor will presently yield to a sober second thought and, like the great mass of their associates, think and act like true Americans. They will see that strikes undertaken at this critical time are certain to make matters worse, not better—worse for them and for everybody else.

The worst thing, the most fatal thing, that can be done now is to stop or interrupt production or to interfere with the distribution of goods by the railways and the shipping of the country. We are all involved in the distressing results of the high cost of living, and we must unite, not divide, to correct it.

There are many things that ought to be corrected in the relations between capital and labor, in respect of wages and conditions of labor, and other things even more far-reaching, and I, for one, am ready to go into conference about these matters with any group of my fellow-countrymen who know what they are talking about and are willing to remedy existing conditions by frank counsel rather than by violent contest.

No remedy is possible while men are in a temper, and there can be no settlement which does not have as its motive and standard the general interest. Threats and undue insistence upon the interest of a single class make settlement impossible.

I believe, as I have hitherto had occasion to say to the Congress, that the industry and life of our people and of the world will suffer irreparable damage if employers and workmen are to go on in a perpetual contest as antagonists. They must, on one plan or another, be effectively associated. Have we not steadiness and self-possession and business sense enough to work out that result? Undoubtedly we have, and we shall work it out.

In the meantime—now and in the days of readjustment and recuperation that are ahead of us—let us resort more and more to frank and intimate counsel and make ourselves a great and triumphant nation by making ourselves a united force in the life of the world. It will not then have looked to us for leadership in vain.

STATEMENTS

[Power of Ending War-Time Prohibition. Made Public July 28, 1919.]

I am convinced that the Attorney General is right in advising me that I have no legal power at this time in the matter of the ban on liquor. Under the Act of November, 1918, my power to take action is restricted. The Act provides that after June 30, 1919, "until the conclusion of the present war and thereafter until the termination of demobilization, the date of which shall be determined and proclaimed by the President, it shall be unlawful, etc." This law does not specify that the ban shall be lifted with the signing of peace, but with the termination of the demobilization of the troops, and I cannot say that this has been accomplished. My information from the War Department is that there are still a million men in the army under the emergency call. It is clear, therefore, that the failure of Congress to act upon the suggestion contained in my message of the twentieth of May, 1919, asking for a repeal of the Act of November 21, 1918, so far as it applies to wines and beers, makes it impossible for me to act in this matter at this time. When demobilization is terminated, my power to act without Congressional action will be exercised.

WOODROW WILSON.

[The Grant of Temporary Possession of the Shantung Peninsula of China to Japan, by the Peace Conference of Paris.]

THE WHITE HOUSE, *August 6, 1919.*

The Government of the United States has noted with the greatest interest the frank statement made by Viscount Uchida with regard to

Japan's future policy respecting Shantung. The statement ought to serve to remove many misunderstandings which had begun to accumulate about this question.

But there are references in the statement to an agreement entered into between Japan and China in 1915 which might be misleading if not commented upon in the light of what occurred in Paris when the clauses of the treaty affecting Shantung were under discussion. I therefore take the liberty of supplementing Viscount Uchida's statement with the following:

In the conference of the 30th of April last, where this matter was brought to a conclusion among the heads of the principal allied and associated powers, the Japanese delegates, Baron Makino and Viscount Chinda, in reply to a question put by myself, declared that:

"The policy of Japan is to hand back the Shantung peninsula in full sovereignty to China, retaining only the economic privileges granted to Germany, and the right to establish a settlement under the usual conditions at Tsing-tao.

"The owners of the railway will use special police only to insure security for traffic. They will be used for no other purpose.

"The police forces will be composed of Chinese, and such Japanese instructors as the Directors of the railway may select will be appointed by the Chinese Government."

No reference was made to this policy being in any way dependent upon the execution of the agreement of 1915 to which Viscount Uchida appears to have referred. Indeed, I felt it my duty to say that nothing that I agreed to must be construed as an acquiescence on the part of the Government of the United States in the policy of the notes exchanged between China and Japan in 1915 and 1918, and reference was made in the discussion to the enforcement of the agreements of 1915 and 1918 only in case China failed to co-operate fully in carrying out the policy outlined in the statement of Baron Makino and Viscount Chinda.

I have, of course, no doubt that Viscount Uchida had been apprised of all the particulars of the discussion in Paris, and I am not making this statement with the idea of correcting his, but only to throw a fuller light of clarification upon a situation which ought to be relieved of every shadow of obscurity or misapprehension.

WOODROW WILSON.

[On Attitude Toward Demand by Railroad Shopmen for Wage Increases.]

THE WHITE HOUSE, *August 25, 1919.*

My Fellow Citizens—A situation has arisen in connection with the administration of the railways which is of such general significance that I think it my duty to make a public statement concerning it, in order that the whole country may know what is involved.

The railroad shopmen have demanded a large increase in wages. They are now receiving 58, 63, and 68 cents per hour. They demand 85 cents per hour. This demand has been given careful and serious consideration by the board which was constituted by the Railroad Administration to adjust questions of wages, a board consisting of an equal number of representatives of employes and of the operating managers of the railroad companies. This board has been unable to come to an agreement, and it has therefore devolved upon the Director General of Railroads and myself to act upon the merits of the case.

The shopmen urge that they are entitled to higher wages because of the higher wages for the present received by men doing a similar work in shipyards, navy yards, and arsenals, as well as in a number of private industries, but I concur with the Director General in thinking that there is no real basis of comparison between the settled employment afforded mechanics by the railroads under living conditions as various as the location and surroundings of the railway shops themselves and the fluctuating employment afforded in industries exceptionally and temporarily stimulated by the war and located almost without exception in industrial centres where the cost of living is highest.

The substantial argument which the shopmen urge is the very serious increase in the cost of living. This is a very potent argument indeed. But the fact is that the cost of living has certainly reached its peak, and will probably be lowered by the efforts which are now everywhere being concerted and carried out. It will certainly be lowered so soon as there are settled conditions of production and of commerce; that is, so soon as the Treaty of Peace is ratified and in operation, and merchants, manufacturers, farmers, miners, all have a certain basis of calculation as to what their business will be and what the conditions will be under which it must be conducted.

The demands of the shopmen, therefore, and all similar demands, are in effect this: That we make increases in wages, which are likely to be permanent, in order to meet a temporary situation which will last nobody can certainly tell how long, but in all probability only for a limited time. Increases in wages will, moreover, certainly result in still further increasing the costs of production and, therefore, the cost of living, and we should only have to go through the same process again. Any substantial increase of wages in leading lines of industry at this time would utterly crush the general campaign which the Government is waging, with energy, vigor, and substantial hope of success, to reduce the high cost of living. And the increases in the cost of transportation which would necessarily result from increases in the wages of railway employes would more certainly and more immediately have that effect than any other enhanced wage costs. Only by keeping the cost of production on its present level, by increasing production and by rigid economy and saving on the part of the people can we hope for large decreases in the burdensome cost of living which now weighs us down.

The Director General of Railroads and I have felt that a peculiar responsibility rests upon us, because in determining this question we are not studying the balance sheets of corporations merely, we are in effect determining the burden of taxation which must fall upon the people of the country in general. We are acting, not for private corporations, but in the name of the Government and the public and must assess our responsibility accordingly. For it is neither wise nor feasible to take care of increases in the wages of railroad employes at this time by increases in freight rates. It is impossible at this time, until peace has come and normal conditions are restored, to estimate what the earning capacity of the railroads will be when ordinary conditions return. There is no certain basis, therefore, for calculating what the increases of freight rates should be, and it is necessary, for the time being at any rate, to take care of all increases in the wages of railroad employes through appropriations from the public treasury.

In such circumstances, it seems clear to me, and I believe will seem clear to every thoughtful American, including the shopmen themselves when they have taken second thought, and to all wage earners of every kind, that we ought to postpone questions of this sort till normal conditions come again and we have the opportunity for certain calculation as to the relation between wages and the cost of living. It is the duty of every citizen of the country to insist upon a truce in such contests until intelligent settlements can be made, and made by peaceful and effective common council. I appeal to my fellow-citizens of every employment to co-operate in insisting upon and maintaining such a truce, and to co-operate also in sustaining the Government in what I conceive to be the only course which conscientious public servants can pursue. Demands unwisely made and passionately insisted upon at this time menace the peace and prosperity of the country as nothing else could, and thus contribute to bring about the very results which such demands are intended to remedy.

There is, however, one claim made by the railway shopmen which ought to be met. They claim that they are not enjoying the same advantages that other railway employes are enjoying because their wages are calculated upon a different basis. The wages of other railroad employes are based upon the rule that they are to receive for eight hours' work the same pay they received from the longer workday that was the usual standard of the pre-war period. This claim is, I am told, well founded; and I concur in the conclusion of the Director General that the shopmen ought to be given the additional 4 cents an hour which the readjustment asked for will justify. There are certain other adjustments, also pointed out in the report of the Director General, which ought in fairness to be made, and which will be made.

Let me add also that the position which the Government must in conscience take against general increases in wage levels while the present exceptional and temporary circumstances exist will of course not preclude the Railroad Administration from giving prompt and careful consideration to any claims that may be made by other classes of employes for readjustments believed to be proper to secure impartial treatment for all who work in the railway service.

WOODROW WILSON.

MESSAGE TO CONGRESS

[Recommending Continuance of War-Time Passport Control.]

THE WHITE HOUSE, *August 25, 1919.*

To the Senate and House of Representatives:

I transmit herewith a communication from the Secretary of State, suggesting that the Passport-Control Act of May 22, 1918, be extended for one year after peace shall have been concluded between the United States and the Central Powers of Europe, and that ample appropriation be made for an efficient execution of that act and the regulations made under it during the remainder of the fiscal year.

This recommendation brings up for your consideration a very important question of policy which has an intimate relation to the welfare of the country. Information from the agents of the Government in foreign countries indicates that as soon as the existing restrictions upon travel are removed many persons will seek admission to this country, and that among the number are not only persons undesirable from the point of view of becoming future citizens, but persons whose origin and affiliations make it inadvisable that they should be permitted to enter the United States. The Act of May 22, 1918, which makes possible the prevention of undesirable individuals from departing for the United States, will automatically cease to be operative upon the establishment of a condition of peace. Individuals will then be free to come here for whatever purpose they choose, and many will come for purposes which we cannot approve and which may indeed be dangerous to the country and to its institutions. The immigration officials enforcing the immigration laws at the ports of the United States will not be able successfully to prevent the entry of all improper and dangerous persons because of the impracticability of developing a system of intelligence and investigation abroad to work in sufficiently close relationship to the immigration organization in the United States to be thoroughly effective in distinguishing between those individuals whose right to admission would be injurious to the country. The experience gained during the war shows that an efficient system of passport control administered by the Department of State through the diplomatic and consular officers in foreign countries can be depended upon to exclude practically all persons whose admission to the United States would be dangerous or contrary to the public interests. If the Congress concur in the view that the national welfare requires that the class of persons to which I have alluded should not enter this country, it is my belief that the simplest and most effective method that can be adopted would be to continue the system of control now being carried on by the Department of State, working in close co-operation with the Commissioner General of Immigration.

It is obvious that effectiveness of control can only be obtained through supplementing the regular diplomatic and consular personnel with a sufficient number of reliable and capable men, and such men as would be useful can be had only through the payment of adequate compensation. The Secretary of State estimates the expenditure required for the remainder of the current fiscal year at $750,000, including a number of additional employes in the Department of State who would be charged to supplement the administrative organization now maintained there. I quite agree with the view that it is entirely useless to make any outlay upon this work unless sufficient money is provided with which to make control effective. It would be most unwise to permit the public to rest under the impression that an effective control was being exerted over persons seeking admission to this country, when in fact, owing to inadequate personnel and an inefficient administration of the law, dangerous persons were freely crossing our boundaries.

It is important that I should add that the increase in the number of persons desiring to come to the United States has already almost overwhelmed the existing organization abroad, and that it is very doubtful whether the system of control can be kept in operation for more than a few weeks longer without additional appropriation.

With the relaxation of restrictions upon transportation which are gradually taking place, the burden of examining applicants' passport visas will become so great as to be entirely beyond the capacity of the number of officers whose employment existing appropriations make possible. Therefore, it is of the utmost importance that if the Congress should decide, as I hope it may, that the public interest requires that the existing system of control should be maintained and extended it will enact the necessary legislation, preferably by joint resolution, and make ample appropriation at the earliest possible moment.

WOODROW WILSON.

[Asking Appropriation for Expenses of American Peace Commission in Paris.]

THE WHITE HOUSE, *August 28, 1919.*

To the Senate and House of Representatives:

At the close of the last session of Congress, after it had become certain that the Peace Conference at Paris would not be able to conclude its work until after the expiration of the fiscal year on June 30, 1919, when the existing appropriation from which the expenses of the American Commission were being paid would cease to be available, the acting Secretary of State submitted at my direction a request for an additional appropriation of $5,000,000.

That amount was requested, first, in order to defray the expenses of the American participation in the conference at Paris until the close of its deliberations, and, second, to meet the initial expenses of the American participation in the various commissions and agencies which the treaty with Germany provides shall be set up immediately after the ratification of the treaty.

No action having been taken on that request by Congress, the Secretary of the Treasury, at my direction, in a letter to the Chairman of the Committee on Appropriations of the House of Representatives, in June last, pointed out the urgency of providing for the expenses of the American Commission, and this was followed by a communication from the Acting Secretary of State further explaining the necessity of the appropriation.

No steps have yet been taken to provide for the expenses of the American delegation in Paris, or of the agencies necessary to the discharge of its duties since July 1, 1919, when the appropriation for the national security and defense ceased to be available. It is therefore incumbent upon me again to bring the matter to your attention and point out the urgency of making suitable appropriations for the expenses of the commission. Meanwhile I have been compelled to make use of part of the emergency fund of the Department of State for the expenses of the commission, which is unfortunate in view of the large demand which it is foreseen will be made upon that fund during the current fiscal year.

Inasmuch as there might be objection to providing money at this time for the execution of any of the provisions of the treaty, when ratified, it is not desired now to ask your attention to that part of the estimate submitted.

I assume that no explanation is necessary of the continued presence of the commission in Paris since everyone knows that, although the treaty with Germany is now before the Senate, treaties with Austria, Turkey and Bulgaria are yet to be completed, and many other matters of actual and potential concern to this country require careful attention of the American representatives.

The purposes for which an additional appropriation is needed will be indicated by the enclosed statement of the expenditures already made and the liabilities growing out of the Peace Conference. In considering these expenses and estimates it should be borne in mind that for a time the personnel of the American delegation numbered more than 1,300 persons, and on July 31, last, had been reduced to about 400, about eighty-eight of whom were civilians, the remainder being from the army and navy.

The conference has been held at a time when conditions in France are abnormal, prices of food being more than 120 per cent. greater than a year ago, railroad transportation having increased more than 150 per cent.; fuel not only difficult to obtain, but only obtainable at prices over 200 per cent. higher than before the war. Although an army commissary had been utilized for the most part, the prices paid have notwithstanding been vastly greater than in pre-war times.

Then, too, means of communication and the usual channels of information have been so greatly impaired as a result of the war that not only has it been necessary to maintain an expensive courier system, but in many instances commissions have had to be dispatched for the purposes of investigation in order that the American Commission might be in a position to act intelligently and upon information the accuracy of which had been positively established.

These unusual conditions have made the work of the commission expensive, although I have no hesitation in saying that, considering the magnitude of the task, and the extent to which the commission was obliged to rely upon its own agencies, instead of upon those available in normal times, the expenses have been and are very modest.

It is obviously not possible at present to estimate how much longer the conference may be in session, but assuming that its work shall extend to the end of the calendar year, December 31, 1919, which I think may be regarded as the maximum, the sum of $825,000 will be required for the expenses. I hope that this amount may be appropriated at an early date.

WOODROW WILSON.

The statement of expenditures mentioned in the letter, to June 30, 1919, is as follows:

Travel and subsistence, $15,843.48.
Subsistence, $144,914.03.
Salaries, $103,815.95.
Wages to employes of Hotel Crillon, $53,345.33.
Stationery, office supplies, printing, furniture and fixtures, repairs, newspapers and miscellaneous expenditures, $40,432.71.

Rents, $5,720.06.

Food and hotel supplies, $128,828.10.

Hire and laundry of hotel linens, $31,583.48.

Fuel, heat, light, and compressed air, $20,038.78.

Telephone, $166.17.

Inventories and legal services, $3,329.75.

Special allotments to investigating commissions dispatched to the Baltic provinces, Poland, Turkey, the Balkans, Russia and the Caucasus, $105,610.26.

Confidential expenses, $13,587.19.

Purchase of automobiles, $14,602.96.

Total $666,859.29.

Traveling expenses, stationery and supplies, (disbursements by the Department of State in Washington), $38,009.02. Total, $704,868.31.

Reimbursement of the Government by members of the American Commission to negotiate peace on account of subsistence furnished their wives; official entertainment by the Secretary of State and Edward House; unexpended allotments, and miscellaneous items, $18,721.42.

Total net expenses December 1, 1918, to June 30, 1919, exclusive of the rent of the Hotel Crillon and telegraph charges, $686,146.89.

LIABILITIES

Rental of Hotel Crillon from December 1, 1918, to September 30, 1919, including damages, the amount of which are not yet known, approximately $35,000 monthly, $350,000.

Telegraph and cable service through the War Department, bills not yet received and amount not yet known, though the expense will be large.

Expenses of the commission from July 1, 1919, to July 30, 1919, exclusive of rent and telegraph service, $150,629.74.

Expenses of the commission from August 1, 1919, to August 31, 1919, exclusive of rent and telegraph service, estimated, $125,000.

Expenses of the commission from September 1, 1919, to December 31, 1919, estimated for four months, $440,000.

Total estimated and actual liabilities, so far as known, to date, $1,250,629.74.

Less rental of the Hotel Crillon to June 30, 1919, which is payable out of the appropriation for the national security and defense, $245,000.

Total appropriation required on the assumption that the conference may be prolonged to December 31, 1919, $820,629.74.

Total expense of commission, actual and estimated, $1,566,776.63.

EXECUTIVE ORDERS

[Re-Transferring Coast Guard to Treasury Department.]

THE WHITE HOUSE, *August 28, 1919.*

By virtue of the authority conferred by "An Act authorizing the President to coordinate or consolidate executive bureaus, agencies, and offices, and for other purposes, in the interest of economy and the more efficient concentration of the Government," approved May 20, 1918, I do hereby make and publish the following order:

The important purposes for which operation of the Coast Guard was temporarily transferred to the navy under the Act approved January 28, 1915, entitled "An Act to Create the Coast Guard by combining therein the existing Life Saving Service and Revenue Cutter Service" having been accomplished, and, it being for the best interests of the Government and for the efficient service of the Coast Guard in connection with the collection of the Revenue that the Coast Guard be under the supervision of the Treasury Department, it is hereby directed that the Coast Guard shall on and after this date operate under the Treasury Department.

WOODROW WILSON.

[Lifting War-Time Check Upon Government Expenditures.]

THE WHITE HOUSE, *August 28, 1919.*

Whereas by the Act of Congress approved July 8, 1918, Public No. 189, 65th Congress, it is provided

"That except as expressly otherwise authorized herein no part of the sums appropriated by this Act shall be expended in the purchase from private manufacturers of any material at a price in excess of twenty-five per centum more than the cost of manufacturing such material by the Government, or, where such material is not or has not been manufactured by the Government, at a price in excess of twenty-five per centum more than the estimated cost of manufacture by the Government: Provided, That whenever in the opinion of the President the situation is such as to justify such action he may waive the limitations contained in this section,"

And whereas, in view of the practical impossibility under existing conditions of making the estimates necessary to comply fully and adequately with said provisions, it appears that the situation is such as to justify a waiver of said provisions,

It is hereby ordered that during the present national emergency the limitations contained in the above section be and the same are hereby waived.

WOODROW WILSON.

LABOR DAY MESSAGE

THE WHITE HOUSE, *August 31, 1919.*

I am encouraged and gratified by the progress which is being made in controlling the cost of living. The support of the movement is widespread and I confidently look for substantial results, although I must counsel patience as well as vigilance, because such results will not come instantly or without team work.

Let me again emphasize my appeal to every citizen of the country to continue to give his personal support in this matter, and to make it as active as possible. Let him not only refrain from doing anything which at the moment will tend to increase the cost of living, but let him do all in his power to increase production; and, further than that, let him at the same time himself carefully economize in the matter of consumption. By common action in this direction we shall overcome a danger greater than the danger of war. We will hold steady a situation which is fraught with possibilities of hardship and suffering to a large part of our population; we will enable the processes of production to overtake the processes of consumption; and we will speed the restoration of an adequate purchasing power for wages.

I am particularly gratified at the support which the Government's policy has received from the representatives of organized labor, and I earnestly hope that the workers generally will emphatically indorse the position of their leaders and thereby move with the Government instead of against it in the solution of this greater domestic problem.

I am calling for as early a date as practicable a conference in which authoritative representatives of labor and of those who direct labor will discuss fundamental means of bettering the whole relationship of capital and labor and putting the whole question of wages upon another footing.

WOODROW WILSON.

ADDRESS

[When the United States Senate opened the discussion of the peace treaty with Germany, in which the Covenant of the League of Nations was included as an integral part, there was strong opposition on the part of many Senators to the ratification of the treaty. Most of the opposition centered around the Covenant of the League of Nations, although there was strong opposition also to the grant of the Shantung peninsula of China to Japan for an indefinite period of time. Some Senators were altogether opposed to the treaty in the form submitted; others were in favor of amending it; others were in favor of qualifying clauses. Naturally, the President was able to swing most of the Democratic Senators behind the treaty, but by the elections in the fall of 1918, the Republicans had achieved a majority in the Senate. After some eight weeks' consultation and discussion of the treaty with Senators in Washington, President Wilson undertook a "swing around the circle" to present the case for the treaty directly to the American people. The President's tour began on September 3, 1919, and in the course of it he reached the Pacific Coast. The tour was suddenly abandoned at Wichita, Kansas, on September 26, when the President was headed back toward Washington, five days before its scheduled termination, because of the complete prostration of the President as a result of nervous exhaustion due to overwork, both during and after the Peace Conference in Europe.

The following address was delivered in Columbus, Ohio, on September 4, 1918, as the first extensive address of the President's tour.]

Mr. Chairman, Governor Campbell and My Fellow-Citizens:

It is with very profound pleasure that I find myself face to face with you. I have for a long time chafed at the confinement of Washington. I have for a long time wished to fulfill the purpose with which my heart was full when I returned to our beloved country, namely, to go out and report to my fellow-countrymen concerning those affairs of the world which now need to be settled.

The only people I owe any report to are you and the other citizens of the United States, and it has become increasingly necessary, apparently, that I should report to you. After all the various angles at which you have heard the treaty held up perhaps you would like to know what is in the treaty. I find it very difficult in reading some of the speeches that I have read to form any conception of that great document. It is a document unique in the history of the world for many reasons, and I think I cannot do you a better service or the peace of the world a better service than by pointing out to you just what this treaty contains and what it seeks to do.

In the first place, my fellow-countrymen, it seeks to punish one of the greatest wrongs ever done in history, the wrong which Germany sought to do to the world and to civilization, and there ought to be no weak purpose with regard to the application of the punishment. She attempted an intolerable thing, and she must be made to pay for the attempt. The terms of the treaty are severe, but they are not unjust. I can testify that the men associated with me at the Peace Conference in Paris had it in their hearts to do justice and not wrong, but they knew, perhaps with a more vivid sense of what had happened than we could possibly know on this side of the water, the many solemn covenants which Germany had disregarded, the long preparation she had made to overwhelm her neighbors, the utter disregard which she had shown for human rights, for the rights of women and children and those who were helpless. They had seen their lands devastated by an enemy that devoted itself not only to the effort of victory, but to the effort of terror, seeking to terrify the people whom he fought, and I wish to testify that they exercised restraint in the terms of this treaty. They did not wish to overwhelm any great nation, and they had no purpose of overwhelming the German people, but they did think that it ought to be burned into the consciousness of men forever that no people ought to permit its government to do what the German Government did.

In the last analysis, my fellow-countrymen, as we in America would be the first to claim, a people are responsible for the acts of their Government; if their Government purposes things that are wrong, they ought to take measures and see to it that that purpose is not executed. Germany was self-governed. Her rulers had not concealed the purposes that they had in mind, but they had deceived their people as to the character of the methods they were going to use, and I believe from what I can learn that there is an awakened consciousness in Germany itself of the deep iniquity of the thing that was attempted.

When the Austrian delegates came before the Peace Conference they, in so many words, spoke of the origination of the war as a crime, and admitted in our presence that it was a thing intolerable to contemplate. They knew in their hearts that it had done them the deepest conceivable wrong; that it had put their people and the people of Germany at the judgment seat of mankind; and throughout this treaty every term that was applied to Germany was meant not to humiliate Germany, but to rectify the wrong that she had done. And you will see that if you will look into the severe terms of reparation, for there was no indemnity—no indemnity of any sort was claimed—merely reparation, merely paying for the destruction done, merely making good the losses, so far as the losses could be made good which she had unjustly inflicted, not upon the Governments (for the reparation is not to go to the Governments), but upon the people whose rights she had trodden upon, with absolute absence of everything that even resembled pity.

There is no indemnity in this treaty, but there is reparation, and even in the terms of reparation a method is devised by which the reparation shall be adjusted to Germany's ability to pay it.

I am astonished at some of the statements I see made about this treaty, and the truth is that they are made by persons who have not read the treaty or who, if they have read it, have not comprehended its meaning. There is a method of adjustment in the treaty by which the reparation shall not be pressed beyond the point which Germany can pay, but will be pressed to the utmost point that she can pay, which is just, which is righteous. It would be intolerable if there had been anything else, for, my fellow-citizens, this treaty is not meant merely to end this single war; it is meant as a notice to every Government which in the future will attempt this thing that mankind will unite to inflict the same punishment.

There is no national triumph sought to be recorded in this treaty. There is no glory sought for any particular nation. The thought of the statesmen collected around that table was of their people, of the sufferings that they had gone through, of the losses they had incurred, that great throbbing heart which was so depressed, so forlorn, so sad in every memory that it had had of the five tragical years that have gone. Let us never forget those years, my fellow countrymen. Let us never forget the purpose, the high purpose, the disinterested purpose, with which America lent its strength, not for its own glory, but for the defense of mankind.

And, as I said, this treaty was not intended merely to end this war; it was intended to prevent any similar war.

I wonder if some of the opponents of the League of Nations have forgotten the promises we made our people before we went to that peace table. We had taken by processes of law the flower of our youth from every countryside, from every household, and we told those mothers and fathers and sisters and wives and sweethearts that we were taking those men to fight a war which would end business of that sort, and if we do not end it, if we do not do the best that human concert of action can do to end it, we are of all men the most unfaithful—the most unfaithful to the loving hearts who suffered in this war, the most unfaithful to those households bowed in grief, yet lifted with the feeling that the lad laid down his life for a great thing—among other things in order that other lads might not have to do the same thing.

That is what the League of Nations is for, to end this war justly, and it is not merely to serve notice on Governments which would contemplate the same thing which Germany contemplated, that they will do so at their peril, but also concerning the combination of power which will prove to them that they will do it at their peril. It is idle to say the world will combine against you because it may not, but it is persuasive to say the world is combined against you and will remain combined against any who attempt the same things that you attempted.

The League of Nations is the only thing that can prevent the recurrence of this dreadful catastrophe and redeem our promises. And the character of the League is based upon the experience of this very war.

I did not meet a single public man who did not admit these things—that Germany would not have gone into this war if she had thought Great Britain was going into it, and that she most certainly would never have gone into this war if she had dreamed America was going into it, and they have all admitted that a notice beforehand that the greatest powers of the world would combine to prevent this sort of thing would have prevented it absolutely.

When gentlemen tell you, therefore, that the League of Nations is intended for some other purpose than this, merely reply this to them, "If we do not do this thing, we have neglected the Central Covenant that we made to our people," and there will be no statesman of any country who can thereafter promise his people any alleviation from the perils of war.

The passions of this world are not dead; the rivalries of this world have not cooled; they have been rendered hotter than ever. The harness that is to unite nations is more necessary now than it ever was before, and unless there is this sureness of combined action before wrong is attempted, wrong will be attempted just as soon as the most ambitious nations can recover from the financial stress of this war.

Now look what else is in the treaty. This treaty is unique in the history of mankind because the centre of it is the redemption of weak nations. There never was a congress of nations before that considered the rights of those who could not enforce their rights. There never was a congress of nations before that did not seek to effect some balance of power brought about by means of serving the strength and interest of the strongest powers concerned, whereas this treaty builds up nations that never could have won their freedom in any other way. It builds them up by gift, by largess, not by obligation; builds them up because of the conviction of the men who wrote the treaty that the rights of people transcended the rights of Governments, because of the conviction of the men who wrote that treaty that the fertile source of war is wrong; that the Austro-Hungarian Empire, for example, was held together by military force and consisted of peoples who did not want to live together; who did not have the spirit of nationality as toward each other; who were constantly chafing at the bonds that held them.

Hungary, though a willing partner of Austria, was willing to be her partner because she could share Austria's strength for accomplishing her own ambitions, and her own ambitions were to hold under her the Jugo-Slavic peoples that lay to the south of her; Bohemia, an unhappy partner—a partner by duress, beating in all her veins the strongest national impulse that was to be found anywhere in Europe; and north of that, pitiful Poland, a great nation divided up among the great powers of Europe, torn asunder—kinship disregarded, natural ties treated with contempt and an obligatory division among sovereigns imposed upon her, a part of her given to Russia, a part of her given to Austria, and a part of her given to Germany, and great bodies of Polish people never permitted to have the normal intercourse with their kinsmen for fear that that fine instinct of the heart should assert itself which binds families together.

Poland could never have won her independence. Bohemia never could have broken away from the Austro-Hungarian combination. The Slavic peoples to the south, running down into the great Balkan peninsula, had again and again tried to assert their nationality and their independence, and had as often been crushed, not by the immediate power they were fighting, but by the combined power of Europe.

The old alliances, the old balances of power, were meant to see to it that no little nation asserted its rights to the disturbance of the peace of Europe, and every time an assertion of rights was attempted it were suppressed by combined influence and force. And this treaty tears away all that and says these people have a right to live their own lives under the governments which they themselves choose to set up. That is the American principle and I was glad to fight for it, and when strategic consideration were urged I said (not I alone, but it was a matter of common counsel) that strategic conditions were not in our thoughts; that we were not now arranging for future wars, but were giving people what belonged to them.

My fellow-citizens, I do not think there is any man alive who has a more tender sympathy for the great people of Italy than I have, and a very stern duty was presented to us when we had to consider some of the claims of Italy on the Adriatic, because strategically, from the point of view of future wars, Italy needed a military foothold on the other side of the Adriatic, but her people did not live there except in little spots. It was a Slavic people, and I had to say to my Italian friends: "Everywhere else in this treaty we have given territory to the people who lived on it, and I do not think that it is for the advantage of Italy, and I am sure it is not for the advantage of the world, to give Italy territory where other people live."

I felt the force of the argument for what they wanted, and it was the old argument that had always prevailed, namely, that they needed it from a military point of view, and I have no doubt that if there is no League of Nations they will need it from a military point of view. But if there is a League of Nations they will not need it from a military point of view. If there is no League of Nations the military point of view will prevail in every instance and peace will be brought into contempt, but if there is a League of Nations Italy need not fear the fact that the shores on the other side of the Adriatic tower above her sandy shores on her side of the sea, because there will be no threatening guns there, and the nations of the world will have concerted not merely to see that the Slavic peoples have their rights but that the Italian people have their rights as well. I would rather have everybody on my side than be armed to the teeth; and every settlement that is right, every settlement that is based upon the principles I have alluded to, is a safe settlement because the sympathy of mankind will be behind it.

Some gentlemen have feared with regard to the League of Nations that we will be obliged to do things we don't want to do. If the treaty were wrong, that might be so; but if the treaty is right, we will wish to preserve right. I think I know the heart of this great people, whom I for the time being have the high honor to represent, better than some other men that I hear talk.

I have been bred and am proud to have been bred in the old Revolutionary stock which set this Government up when America was set up as a friend of mankind, and I know, if they do not, that America has never lost that vision or that purpose.

But I haven't the slightest fear that arms will be necessary if the purpose is there. If I know that my adversary is armed and I am not, I do not press the controversy; and if any nation entertains selfish purposes set against the principles established in this treaty, and is told by the rest of the world that it must withdraw its claims, it will not press them.

The heart of this treaty, then, my fellow-citizens, is not even that it punishes Germany—that is a temporary thing—it is that it rectifies the age-long wrongs which characterized the history of Europe.

There were some of us who wished that the scope of the treaty would reach some other age-long wrongs. It was a big job, and I don't say that we wished that it were bigger; but there were other wrongs elsewhere than in Europe, and of the same kind, which no doubt ought to be righted, and some day will be righted, but which we could not draw into the treaty because we could deal only with the countries whom the war had engulfed and affected. But, so far as the scope of our authority went, we rectified the wrongs which have been the fertile source of war in Europe.

Have you ever reflected, my fellow-countrymen, on the real source of revolutions? Men don't start revolutions in a sudden passion. Do you remember what Thomas Carlyle said about the French revolution? He was speaking of the so-called Hundred Days Terror which reigned, not only in Paris, but throughout France, in the days of the French revolution; and he reminded his readers that back of that Hundred Days of Terror lay several hundred years of agony and of wrong. The French people had been deeply and consistently wronged by their Government; robbed; their human rights disregarded; and the slow agony of those hundreds of years had after a while gathered into a hot anger that could not be suppressed.

Revolutions don't spring up over night; revolutions gather through the ages; revolutions come from the long suppression of the human spirit; revolutions come because men know that they have rights and that they are disregarded.

And when we think of the future of the world in connection with this treaty, we must remember that one of the chief efforts of those who made this treaty was to remove that anger from the heart of great peoples—great peoples who had always been suppressed and always been used, who had always been the tools in the hands of governments —generally of alien governments—not their own. And the makers of the treaty knew that if these wrongs were not removed, there could be no peace in the world, because, after all, my fellow-citizens, war comes from the seed of wrong, and not from the seed of right. This treaty is an attempt to right the history of Europe, and in my humble judgment it is a measurable success.

I say "measurable," my fellow-citizens, because you will realize the difficulty of this: Here are two neighboring peoples. The one people have not stopped at a sharp line, and the settlements of the other people, or their migrations, begun at that sharp line; they have intermingled. There are regions where you can't draw a national line and say there are Slavs on this side and Italians on that; there is this people here and that people there. It can't be done. You have to approximate the line. You have to come as near to it as you can, and then trust to the process of history to redistribute, it may be, the people who are on the wrong side of the line. And there are many such lines drawn in this treaty and to be drawn in the Austrian treaty, and where, perhaps, there are more lines of that sort than in the German treaty.

When we came to draw the line between the Polish people and the German people (not the line between Germany and Poland—there wasn't any Poland, strictly speaking) there were districts like the upper part of Silesia, or rather the eastern part of Silesia, which is called "Upper Silesia" because it is mountainous and the other part is not. Upper Silesia is chiefly Polish, and when we came to draw a line to represent Poland it was necessary to include Upper Silesia if we were really going to play fair and make Poland up of the Polish people wherever we found them in sufficiently close neighborhood to one another. But it wasn't perfectly clear that Upper or High Silesia wanted to be part of Poland. At any rate, there were Germans in Upper Silesia who said that it did not, and therefore we did there what we did in many other places—we said, "Very well, then, we will let the people that live there decide. We will have a referendum within a certain length of time after the war under the supervision of an international commission which will have a sufficient armed force behind it to preserve order and see that nobody interferes with the elections. We will have an absolutely free vote, and Upper Silesia shall go either to Germany or to Poland, as the people in Upper Silesia prefer."

And that illustrates many other cases where we provided for a referendum, or a plebiscite, as they choose to call it; and are going to leave it to the people themselves, as we should have done, what Government they shall live under.

It is none of my prerogatives to allot peoples to this Government and the other. It is nobody's right to do that allotting except the people themselves, and I want to testify that this treaty is shot through with the American principle of the choice of the governed.

Of course, at times it went further than we could make a practical policy of, because various peoples were keen upon getting back portions of their populations which were separated from them by many miles of territory, and we could not spot Europe with little pieces of separated States. I even had to remind my Italian colleagues that if they were going to claim every place where there was a large Italian population we would have to cede New York to them, because there are more Italians in New York than in any Italian city.

But I believe—I hope—that the Italians in New York City are as glad to stay there as we are to have them. I would not have you suppose that I am intimating that my Italian colleagues entered any claim for New York City.

We, of all peoples in the world, my fellow-citizens, ought to be able to understand the questions of this treaty without anybody explaining them to us; for we are made up out of all the peoples of the world. I dare say that in this audience there are representatives of practically all the peoples dealt with in this treaty. You don't have to have me explain national ambitions to you. You have been brought up on them; you have learned of them since you were children, and it is those national aspirations which we sought to realize, to give an outlet to, in this great treaty.

But we did much more than that. This treaty contains, among other things, a Magna Charta of labor—a thing unheard of until this interesting year of grace. There is a whole section of the treaty devoted to arrangements by which the interests of those who labor with their hands all over the world, whether they be men or women or children, are all of them to be safeguarded. And next month there is to meet the first assembly under this section of the League—and let me tell you it will meet, whether the treaty is ratified by that time or not—there is to meet an assembly which represents the interests of laboring men throughout the world. Not their political interests, there is nothing political about it. It is the interests of men concerning the conditions of their labor, concerning the character of labor which women shall engage in, the character of labor which children shall be permitted to engage in; the hours of labor, and, incidentally, of course, the remuneration of labor, that labor shall be remunerated in proportion, of course, to the maintenance of the standard of living which is proper for the man who is expected to give his whole brain and intelligence and energy to a particular task.

I hear very little said about the Magna Charta of labor which is embodied in this treaty. It forecasts the day, which ought to have come long ago, when statesmen will realize that no nation is fortunate which is not happy, and that no nation can be happy whose people are not contented—contented in their industry, contented in their lives, and fortunate in the circumstances of their lives.

If I were to state what seems to me to be the central idea of this treaty it would be this (it is almost a discovery in international conventions):—"Nations do not consist of their Government, but consist of their people."

That is a rudimentary idea; it seems to go without saying to us in America; but, my fellow-citizens, it was never the leading idea in any other international congress that I ever heard of, that is to say international congress made up of the representatives of Government. They were always thinking of national policy, of national advantages, of the rivalries of trade, of the advantages of territorial conquest.

There is nothing of that in this treaty. You will notice that even the territories which are taken away from Germany, like her colonies, are not given to anybody. There isn't a single act of annexation in this treaty. But territories inhabited by people not yet able to govern themselves, either because of economic or other circumstances or the stage of their development, are put under the care of powers who are to act as trustees—trustees responsible in the forum of the world, at the bar of the League of Nations, and the terms upon which they are to exercise their trusteeship are outlined. They are not to use those people by way of profit and to fight their wars for them; they are not to permit any form of slavery among them or of enforced labor. They are to see to it that there are humane conditions of labor with regard not only to the women and children, but to the men, also. They are to establish no fortifications; they are to regulate the liquor and opium traffic; they are to see to it, in other words, that the lives of the people whose care they assume—not sovereignty over whom they assume, but whose care they assume—are kept clean and safe and wholesome. There again the principle of the treaty comes out, that the object of the arrangement is the welfare of the people who live there and not the advantages of the Government which is the trustee.

It goes beyond that, and it seeks to gather under the common supervision of the League of Nations the various instrumentalities by which the world has been trying to check the evils that were in some places debasing men, like the opium traffic, like the traffic—for it was a traffic —in men, women, and children; like the traffic in other dangerous drugs; like the traffic in arms among uncivilized peoples, who could use arms only for their detriment; for sanitation; for the work of the Red Cross.

Why, those clauses, my fellow-citizens, draw the hearts of the world into league; draw the noble impulses of the world together and make a poem of them.

I used to be told that this was an age in which mind was monarch, and my comment was that if that were true then mind was one of those modern monarchs that reign and do not govern; but as a matter of fact we were governed by a great representative assembly made up of the human passions, and that the best we could manage was that the high and fine passions should be in a majority, so that they could control the baser passions, so that they could check the things that were wrong. This treaty seeks something like that. In drawing the humane endeavors of the world together, it makes a league of the fine passions of the world, of its philanthrophic passions, of its passion of pity, of the passion of human sympathy, of the passion of human friendliness and helpfulness, for there is such a passion. It is the passion that has lifted us along the slow road of civilization; it is the passion that has made ordered government possible; it is the passion that has made justice and established it in some happy parts of the world.

That is the treaty. Did you ever hear of it before? Did you ever know before what was in this treaty? Did anybody before ever tell you what the treaty was intended to do?

I beg, my fellow-citizens, that you and the rest of these Americans with whom we are happy to be associated all over this broad land will read the treaty for yourselves, or (if you won't take time to do that, for it is a technical document that is hard to read) that you will accept the interpretation of those who made it and know what the intentions were in the making of it.

I hear a great deal, my fellow-citizens, about the selfishness and the selfish ambitions of other Governments, but I would not be doing justice to the gifted men with whom I was associated on the other side of the water if I didn't testify that the purposes that I have outlined were their purposes. We differed as to the method, very often; we had discussions as to the details, but we never had any serious discussion as to the principle. And while we all acknowledge that the principles might, perhaps, in detail have been better realized, really we are all back of those principles. There is a concert of mind and of purpose and of policy in the world that was never in existence before. I am not saying that by way of credit to myself or to those colleagues to whom I have alluded, because what happened to us was that we got messages from our people; we were there under instructions, whether they were written down or not, and we didn't dare come home without fulfilling those instructions. If I could not have brought back the kind of treaty I brought back I never would have come back, because I would have been an unfaithful servant and you would have had the right to condemn me in any way that you chose to use. So that I testify that this is an American treaty not only, but it is a treaty that expresses the heart of the peoples—of the great peoples who were associated together in the war against Germany.

I said at the opening of this informal address, my fellow-citizens, that I had come to make a report to you. I want to add to that a little bit. I have not come to debate the treaty. It speaks for itself, if you will let it. The arguments directed against it are directed against it with a radical misunderstanding of the instrument itself. Therefore, I am not going anywhere to debate the treaty. I am going to expound it and I am going, right here now today, to urge you, in every vocal method that you can use, to assert the spirit of the American people in support of it. Don't let men pull it down. Don't let men misrepresent it. Don't let men lead this nation away from the high purposes with which this war was inaugurated and fought.

As I came through that line of youngsters in khaki a few minutes ago I felt that I could salute it because I had done the job in the way I promised them I would do it, and when the treaty is accepted men in khaki will not have to cross the seas again. That is the reason I believe in it. I say "when it is accepted," for it will be accepted. I have never entertained a moment's doubt of that, and the only thing I have been impatient of has been the delay. It is not a dangerous delay, except for the temper of the peoples scattered throughout the world who are waiting. Do you realize, my fellow-citizens, that the whole world is waiting on America? The only country in the world that is trusted at this moment is the United States, and they are waiting to see whether their trust is justified or not.

That has been the ground of my impatience. I knew their trust was justified, but I begrudge the time that certain gentlemen oblige us to take in telling them so. We shall tell them so in a voice as authentic as any voice in history, and in the years to come men will be glad to remember that they had some part in the great struggle which brought this incomparable consummation of the hopes of mankind.

MESSAGES

[Greeting General John J. Pershing, Commander-in-Chief of the American Expeditionary Forces in Europe During the Great War. Delivered by Secretary of War Newton D. Baker, on General Pershing's Return from Europe on September 8, 1919.]

My dear General Pershing, I am distressed that I cannot greet you in person. It would give me the greatest pleasure to grasp your hand and say to you what is in my heart and in the hearts of all true Americans as we hail your return to the home land you have served so gallantly. Notwithstanding my physical absence, may I not, as your Commander in Chief and as spokesman of our fellow-countrymen, bid you an affectionate and enthusiastic welcome—a welcome warmed with the ardor of genuine affection and deep admiration? You have served the country with fine devotion and admirable efficiency, in a war forever memorable as the world's triumphant protest against injustice and as its vindication of liberty, the liberty of peoples and of nations.

We are proud of you and of the men you command. No finer armies ever set their indomitable strength and unconquerable spirit against the forces of wrong. Their glory is the glory of the nation, and it is with a thrill of profound pride that we greet you as their leader and commander. You have just come from the sea and from the care of the men of the navy, who made the achievements of our arms on land possible, and who so gallantly assisted to clear the seas of their lurking peril. Our hearts go out to them, too. It is delightful to see you home again, well and fit for the fatigues you must endure before we are done with our welcome. I will not speak now of our associates on the other side of the sea. It will be delightful on many occasions to speak their praise. I speak now only of our personal joy that you are home again and that we have the opportunity to make you feel the warmth of our affectionate welcome.

[Opposing Organization of District of Columbia Policemen Into Associations to Exert Pressure Upon the Public. The Message Was Dispatched to the President of the Board of Commissioners of the District of Columbia, Following a Strike of the Police Force in Boston, and Was Made Public on September 18, 1919.]

I hope that you understood my brief telegram of the other day. I am quite willing that you should tell the Senate committee that my position in my conversations with you was exactly the same as I have expressed recently in speeches here in the West, and, of course, I am desirous, as you are, of dealing with the police force in the most just and generous way, but I think that any association of the police force of the Capital City, or of any great city, whose object is to bring pressure upon the public or the community such as will endanger the public peace or embarrass the maintenance of order, should in no case be countenanced or permitted.

WOODROW WILSON.

President Wilson's remarks on the strike of the Boston policemen, referred to above, are well exemplified in these words, from his address at Helena, Montana, on September 11, 1919:

I want to say this, that a strike of the policemen of a great city, leaving that city at the mercy of an army of thugs, is a crime against civilization.

In my judgment the obligation of a policeman is as sacred and direct as the obligation of a soldier. He is a public servant, not a private employe, and the whole honor of the community is in his hands. He has no right to prefer any private advantage to the public safety.

I hope that that lesson will be burned in so that it will never again be forgotten, because the pride of America is that it can exercise self-control.

QUESTIONS.

1. What was the attitude of the Wilson administration toward American business men? Pages 7871, 8015, 8038, 8151, 8714.

2. Why did President Wilson veto the bill containing a literacy test for immigrants and how did conditions after the war compel him to urge certain checks upon immigration? Pages 8043, 8778.

3. In what way did the Wilson administration assist the American farmer? Pages 7908, 8018, 8116.

4. What was President Wilson's attitude toward disorders in Mexico? Pages 7982, 8032, 8131, 8155, 8762.

5. How did President Wilson try to open peace mediations in the Great War before America was drawn into it, and with what success? Pages 8190, 8199.

6. What were the various steps by which Germany's submarine warfare brought the United States into the Great War? Pages 8057, 8062, 8121, 8125, 8204, 8206, 8209, 8221.

7. How did the conception of a League of Nations grow in President Wilson's mind as the Great War continued? Pages 8191, 8200, 8288, 8402, 8425, 8593.

8. Why did President Wilson urge the passage of the Woman Suffrage amendment to the United States Constitution? Pages 8163, 8375, 8599, 8639, 8719.

9. What reform in our currency system do we owe to the Wilson administration? Pages 7879, 7908, 8026, 8151.

10. What were the "Fourteen Points?" Page 8423.

11. Did the terms of peace given Germany square with the terms of peace promised her? Pages 8421, 8447, 8481, 8534, 8596 and 8737-8756.

12. How were alien enemies and their property treated during America's participation in the Great War? Pages 8243, 8392, 8372, 8380.

13. What was President Wilson's attitude toward demands by Labor which he thought unreasonable? Pages 8581, 8773, 8775.

14. What were President Wilson's remedies for the high cost of living? Page 8764.

15. What was President Wilson's conception of the service rendered the world by the formation of the League of Nations and by the peace imposed upon Germany? Pages 8670, 8696, 8727, 8785.

SUGGESTIONS.

The changes in the tariff policy of the United States due to the Wilson Administration will be found on pages 7869, 7872, 8030, 8151, 8158.

The message in which President Wilson urged that the United States enter the lists against the Imperial German Government will be found on page 8226.

The text of the League of Nations Covenant is on pages 8673-8681.

The attitude of the Wilson administration toward the problem of the ownership and management of the railroads of the United States is discussed on pages 8018, 8117, 8159, 8409, 8412, 8418, 8644, 8719.

The official summary of the peace treaty with Germany will be found on pages 8737-8756.

The various details of the selective draft system used to recruit the American Expeditionary Forces for the war against the Central Powers will be found on pages 8256, 8306, 8385, 8574.

The policy of the United States toward revolutionary Russia is discussed on pages 8230, 8270, 8403, 8422, 8424, 8469, 8483, 8501, 8589.

The armistice negotiations of the Great War are given on pages 8603-8617.

President Wilson's actions with respect to Prohibition may be found outlined on pages 8583, 8720, 8774.

NOTE.

For further suggestions on Wilson's administration see Wilson, Woodrow, Encyclopedic Index.

By reading the Foreign Policy of each President, and by scanning the messages as to the state of the nation, a thorough knowledge of the history of the United States will be acquired from the most authentic sources; because, as has been said, "Each President reviews the past, depicts the present and forecasts the future of the nation."

authority of an Executive Order issued by me dated August 23, 1917, appointing the said United States Fuel Administrator, and all subsequent Executive Orders, and in furtherance of the purpose of said orders and of the Act of Congress therein referred to, and approved August 10, 1917, did on January 31, 1919, and on February 20, 1919, execute and issue orders suspending until further order by the President certain rules, regulations, orders and proclamations theretofore promulgated, relating to the fixing of prices, the production, sale, shipment, distribution, apportionment, storage and use of coal and coke; and whereas, by an Executive Order dated October 30, 1919, the said orders of January 31, 1919, and of February 20, 1919, were revoked and annulled to the extent set forth in the said Executive Order of October 30, 1919; and whereas it appears that it may become necessary to restore and maintain during the war certain other of the said rules, regulations, orders and proclamations.

Now, Therefore, I, Woodrow Wilson, President of the United States of America, acting under authority of the aforesaid Act of Congress, approved August 10, 1917, do hereby order and direct that the United States Fuel Administrator shall, as occasion may require, restore, change or make such rules, regulations, orders and proclamations fixing the prices or regulating the production, sale, shipment, distribution, apportionment, storage or use, of all coal or coke as in his judgment may be necessary.

WOODROW WILSON.

By the President of the United States of America.

PROCLAMATIONS

[Thanksgiving—1919.]

The season of the year has again arrived when the people of the United States are accustomed to unite in giving thanks to Almighty God for the blessings which He has conferred upon our country during the twelve months that have passed. A year ago our people poured out their hearts in praise and thanksgiving that through divine aid the right was victorious and peace had come to the nations which had so courageously struggled in defense of human liberty and justice. Now that the stern task is ended and the fruits of achievement are ours, we look forward with confidence to the dawn of an era where the sacrifices of the nations will find recompense in a world at peace.

But to attain the consummation of the great work to which the American people devoted their manhood and the vast resources of their country they should, as they give thanks to God, reconsecrate themselves to those principles of right which triumphed through His merciful goodness. Our gratitude can find no more perfect expres-

279

sion than to bulwark with loyalty and patriotism those principles for which the free peoples of the earth fought and died.

During the past year we have had much to make us grateful. In spite of the confusion in our economic life resulting from the war, we have prospered. Our harvests have been plentiful, and of our abundance we have been able to render succor to less favored nations. Our democracy remains unshaken in a world torn with political and social unrest. Our traditional ideals are still our guides in the path of progress and civilization.

These great blessings, vouchsafed to us, for which we devoutly give thanks, should arouse us to a fuller sense of our duty to ourselves and to mankind to see to it that nothing that we may do shall mar the completeness of the victory which we helped to win. No selfish purpose animated us in becoming participants in the World War, and with a like spirit of unselfishness we should strive to aid by our example and by our cooperation in realizing the enduring welfare of all peoples and in bringing into being a world ruled by friendship and good will.

Wherefore, I, Woodrow Wilson, President of the United States of America, hereby designate Thursday, the twenty-seventh day of November next, for observance as a day of thanksgiving and prayer by my fellow-countrymen, inviting them to cease on that day from their ordinary tasks and to unite in their homes and in their several places of worship in ascribing praise and thanksgiving to God, the Author of all blessings and the Master of our destinies.

In witness whereof, I have hereunto set my hand and caused the seal of the United States to be affixed.

Done in the District of Columbia this fifth day of November, in the year of our Lord, one thousand nine hundred and nine-
[SEAL.]   teen, and of the independence of the United States the one hundred and forty-fourth.

WOODROW WILSON.

By the President:

ROBERT LANSING, *Secretary of State.*

[Fourteenth Decennial Census of the United States.]

Whereas, by the Act of Congress approved March 3, 1919, the Fourteenth Decennial Census of the United States is to be taken beginning on the second day of January, 1920; and

Whereas, a correct enumeration of the population every ten years is required by the Constitution of the United States for the purpose of determining the representation of the several States in the House of Representatives; and

Whereas, it is of the utmost importance to the interests of all the people of the United States that this Census should be a complete and accurate report of the population and resources of the Nation;

Now, therefore, I, Woodrow Wilson, President of the United States of America, do hereby declare and make known that, under the law aforesaid, it is the duty of every person to answer all questions on the census schedules applying to him and the family to which he belongs, and to the farm occupied by him or his family, and that any person refusing to do so is subject to penalty.

The sole purpose of the census is to secure general statistical information regarding the population and resources of the country and replies are required from individuals only to permit the compilation of such general statistics. No person can be harmed in any way by furnishing the information required. The Census has nothing to do with taxation, with military or jury service, with the compulsion of school attendance, with the regulation of immigration or with the enforcement of any national, state or local law or ordinance. There need be no fear that any disclosure will be made regarding any individual person or his affairs. For the due protection of the rights and interests of the persons furnishing information every employee of the Census Bureau is prohibited, under heavy penalty, from disclosing any information which may thus come to his knowledge.

I therefore earnestly urge upon all persons to answer promptly, completely and accurately all inquiries addressed to them by the enumerators or other employees of the Census Bureau and thereby to contribute their share toward making this great and necessary public undertaking a success.

In witness whereof I have hereunto set my hand and caused the seal of the United States to be affixed.

Done in the District of Columbia this tenth day of November, in the year of our Lord one thousand nine hundred and nine-

[SEAL.] teen, and of the independence of the United States the one hundred and forty-fourth.

WOODROW WILSON.

By the President:

WILLIAM PHILLIPS, *Acting Secretary of State.*

ADDRESS TO FELLOW-COUNTRYMEN

[The first anniversary of the signing of the armistice with Germany in the World War.]

THE WHITE HOUSE, *November 11, 1919.*

A year ago today our enemies laid down their arms in accordance with an armistice which rendered them impotent to renew hostilities, and gave to the world an assured opportunity to reconstruct its shattered order and to work out in peace a new and juster set of international relations.

The soldiers and people of the European Allies had fought and endured for more than four years to uphold the barrier of civilization against the aggressions of armed force. We ourselves had been in the conflict something more than a year and a half.

With splendid forgetfulness of mere personal concerns, we remodeled our industries, concentrated our financial resources, increased our agricultural output, and assembled a great army, so that at the last our power was a decisive factor in the victory. We were able to bring the vast resources, material and moral, of a great and free people to the assistance of our associates in Europe who had suffered and sacrificed without limit in the cause for which we fought.

Out of this victory there arose new possibilities of political freedom and economic concert. The war showed us the strength of great nations acting together for high purposes, and the victory of arms foretells the enduring conquests which can be made in peace when nations act justly and in furtherance of the common interests of men.

To us in America the reflections of Armistice Day will be filled with solemn pride in the heroism of those who died in the country's service, and with gratitude for the victory, both because of the thing from which it has freed us and because of the opportunity it has given America to show her sympathy with peace and justice in the councils of nations.   WOODROW WILSON.

By the President of the United States of America.

A PROCLAMATION

[Relinquishment of Federal control of railroads and systems of transportation.]

Whereas, in the exercise of authority committed to me by law, I have heretofore, through the Secretary of War, taken possession of and have, through the Director General of Railroads, exercised control over certain railroads, systems of transportation and property appurtenant thereto or connected therewith; including systems of coastwise and inland transportation, engaged in general transportation and owned or controlled by said railroads or systems of transportation; including also terminals, terminal companies and terminal associations, sleeping and parlor cars, private cars and private car lines, elevators, warehouses, telegraph and telephone lines, and all other equipment and appurtenances commonly used upon or operated as a part of such railroads and systems of transportation; and

Whereas, I now deem it needful and desirable that all railroads, systems of transportation and property now under such Federal control, be relinquished therefrom;

Now, therefore, under authority of Section 14 of the Federal Control Act approved March 21, 1918, and of all other powers and provisions of law thereto me enabling, I, Woodrow Wilson, President of the United States, do hereby relinquish from Federal control, effective the first day of March, 1920, at 12:01 o'clock A. M. all railroads, systems of transportation and property, of whatever kind, taken or held under such Federal control and not heretofore relinquished, and restore the same to the possession and control of their respective owners.

Walker D. Hines, Director General of Railroads, or his successor in office, is hereby authorized and directed, through such agents and agencies as he may determine, in any manner not inconsistent with the provisions of said Act of March 21, 1918, to adjust, settle and close all matters, including the making of agreements for compensation, and all questions and disputes of whatsoever nature arising out of or incident to Federal control, until otherwise provided by proclamation of the President or by Act of Congress; and generally to do and perform, as fully in all respects as the President is authorized to do, all and singular the acts and things necessary or proper in order to carry into effect this proclamation and the relinquishment of said railroads, systems of transportation and property.

For the purposes of accounting and for all other purposes, this proclamation shall become effective on the first day of March, 1920, at 12:01 o'clock A. M.

In witness whereof, I have hereunto set my hand and caused the seal of the United States to be affixed.

Done by the President, through Newton D. Baker, Secretary of War, in the District of Columbia, this twenty-fourth day [SEAL.] of December, in the year of our Lord one thousand nineteen hundred and nineteen and of the Independence of the United States the one hundred and forty-fourth.

WOODROW WILSON.

By the President:

ROBERT LANSING, *Secretary of State.*

NEWTON D. BAKER, *Secretary of War.*

[On the same day, a similar proclamation was issued regarding the American Railway Express Company (see page 8632).]

EXECUTIVE ORDERS

[Taking possession and title in German vessels.]

THE WHITE HOUSE, *November 24, 1919.*

Whereas the following Joint Resolution adopted by Congress was approved by the President May 12, 1917:

Joint Resolution Authorizing the President to take over for the United States the possession and title of any vessel within its jurisdiction, which at the time of coming therein was owned in whole or in part by any corporation, citizen, or subject of any nation with which the United States may be at war, or was under register of any such nation, and for other purposes.

Resolved by the Senate and House of Representatives of the United States of America in Congress Assembled, That the President be, and he is hereby, authorized to take over to the United States the immediate possession and title of any vessel within the jurisdiction thereof, including the Canal Zone and all territories and insular possessions of the United States except the American Virgin Islands, which at the time of the coming into such jurisdiction was owned in whole or in part by any corporation, citizen, or subject of any nation with which the United States may be at war when such vessel shall be taken, or was flying the flag of or was under register of any such nation or any political subdivision or municipality thereof; and, through the United States Shipping Board, or any department or agency of the Government, to operate, lease, charter, and equip such vessel in any service of the United States, or in any commerce, foreign or coastwise.

Sec. 2. That the Secretary of the Navy be, and he is hereby, authorized and directed to appoint, subject to the approval of the President, a board of survey, whose duty it shall be to ascertain the actual value of the vessel, its equipment, appurtenances and all property contained therein, at the time of its taking, and to make a written report of their findings to the Secretary of the Navy, who shall preserve such report with the records of his department. These findings shall be considered as competent evidence in all proceedings on any claim for compensation.

And whereas from time to time during the period of the war, vessels which were at the time of coming into the jurisdiction of the United States owned in whole or in part by a corporation, citizen or subject of the Empire of Germany, a nation with which the United States is now at war, or vessels which were flying the flag or under the register of the Empire of Germany or of a political subdivision or municipality thereof, or of any nation with which the United States is at war, have been taken over and operated by the United States or in the service of the United States.

Now therefore, the possession and title of the United States in all such vessels is taken over in accordance with Joint Resolution adopted by Congress and approved by the President May 12, 1917.

WOODROW WILSON.

[Conditions of employment for the permanent force for the Panama Canal.]

The White House, *November 25, 1919.*

By virtue of the authority vested in me by law, Section 3 of an Executive Order providing conditions of employment for the permanent force of the Panama Canal, issued February 2, 1914, is hereby amended so as to read as follows:

3. The compensation and conditions of employment of persons employed in the United States will be specified in the appointments. The compensation of such persons will begin upon date of embarkation at port of departure from the United States, and they will be granted free transportation from port of departure, including meals on the steamer, but no compensation or expenses for the journey to the port; but former employees from the United States whose services were terminated other than on account of reduction of force, and whose next preceding service with The Panama Canal was less than one year, shall be paid only from date of entry into the service on the Isthmus, and will be allowed only such reduced rates of transportation to the Isthmus as may be available for Government employees.

Employees appointed at an hourly rate will be paid for the period of transit to the Isthmus on the basis of an eight-hour day exclusive of Sundays. Except in case of discharge or other separation from the service beyond the employees control, payment of salary from date of embarkation to date of arrival on the Isthmus will not be made unless service on the Isthmus continues for thirty days.

This order shall take effect on and after this date.

WOODROW WILSON.

NOTE TO MEXICO

[December 1, 1919, demanding the release of William O. Jenkins. Jenkins was the United States Consul to Mexico at Puebla, arrested by the Mexican Government on charges of being in collusion with bandits by whom he had been captured and to whom a ransom had been paid for his release. Jenkins refused to give bail himself, but the strained relations between the two nations involved were greatly relieved when he was released on bail furnished by a private American citizen.]

I have not failed to transmit to my Government the note of the Mexican Government, dated November 26, 1919, with reference to the case of William O. Jenkins, American Consular Agent at Puebla, and I am now in receipt of a reply from the Government of the United States which I am instructed immediately to transmit to you.

The Government of the United States declines to be drawn into a juridical discussion of irrelevant matters or unimportant incidents brought forward in connection with this case. The Mexican Government cannot be misled, as it intimates, by the citation by the United States of "no principle or precedent of international law and not even a reason" for Jenkins' release; for obviously no such citation is necessary for the enlightenment of a Government of the present day.

The Mexican Government believes, and rightly so, that the American request for Jenkins' release is not based on "solely the strength of the country which makes it;" for it knows the request is founded on the justice of the right of an American citizen and United States consular officer to fair treatment while residing and discharging his duties within Mexican jurisdiction, with the knowledge and approval of the Mexican Government. The Mexican Government may contend that the imprisonment of the victim is necessary for the investigation by a judge under the "constant vigilance of public opinion" of the truth regarding his abduction, and that a right of release on bail is palliative for such wrongful imprisonment, but the United States is constrained to the opinion that such arguments are mere excuses.

The Government of the United States invites and desires the fullest possible examination and investigation of this case, but it cannot admit that it is necessary in order to ascertain the facts that Mr. Jenkins should be retained in prison even with the privilege of applying for bail. My Government will not and is satisfied that

Mr. Jenkins will not place any obstacle in the way of a complete and full examination of himself or of his witnesses or of the events leading up to and connected with his abduction.

The Mexican Government prefers to attribute the American note to an imperfect knowledge of the Mexican penal laws and proceeds to explain with refinement the intricacies of Mexican penal proceedings. But the Government of the United States fails to discern in their application to this case at the hands of Mexican authorities any approximation to impartial treatment of Jenkins, and the Mexican Government knows the absence of such treatment is the reason for the American request.

The Mexican Government maintains that it cannot grant the request of the United States for Jenkins' release for the reason that under international law no diplomatic intervention is appropriate unless a denial of justice has occurred and because the Mexican Government is not in a position to demand Jenkins' release in view of the separation of the executive and judicial powers under the Mexican form of government and the independence of the state courts, by one of which Jenkins is held. The succinct answer to this contention is, as every one knows, that a denial of justice has already taken place, and also because the Mexican Constitution specifically gives the Federal tribunal's jurisdiction of "all cases concerning diplomatic agents and consular officers."

The United States is not to be driven by such subtle argument into a defense of its request for the release of Mr. Jenkins. It is for Mexico to show cause for his detention, not for the United States to plead for his liberation. Stripped of extraneous matter, with which the Mexican note of November 26 endeavors to clothe it, the naked case of Jenkins stands forth: Jenkins, a United States consular agent accredited to the Government of Mexico, is imprisoned for "rendering false judicial testimony" in connection with the abduction of which he was the victim. This is the substance of the Mexican note.

My Government is pleased to learn that the imprisonment of Jenkins stands on this single and well-defined ground, and that the reported statements that Mexican authorities had caused the imprisonment of Jenkins because of collusion with his abductors and rebellion against the State are not seriously regarded by your Government.

In whose interest, then, is the charge of false swearing brought against Jenkins? His abductors? He is in equity the complainant in the case of his abduction, not the defendant, as the Mexican Government now makes him out to be. The Mexican Government is prosecuting the victim instead of the perpetrators of the crime. While the outlaws who endangered his life and took away a large part of his fortune enjoy their freedom, the Mexican authorities now deprive Jenkins of his liberty. Moreover, the ground expressed for the imprisonment of Jenkins, namely, that he is supposed "to be responsible for the crime of rendering false judicial testimony," must be taken—and my Government directs special attention to this point —as merely an expression of opinion on the part of the Mexican Government, as it is entirely unsupported by evidence. There is not produced any of the testimony rendered by him, or any extracts from such testimony tending to show the correctness of this opinion.

The Mexican Government cannot expect the United States to accept in the grave circumstances of this case such a bare, unsupported statement as a valid excuse for the imprisonment of an American consular officer, particularly in view of the fact that the investigation of the case by the representatives of the United States in Mexico, so far as it has proceeded, fails utterly to support this opinion of your Government. On the contrary, the investigation gives the Government of the United States every reason to believe that Mr. Jenkins has not knowingly given any false testimony in respect of vital points in his case, although he has been harassed by Mexican authorities to give such testimony, even while lying in the hospital too weak and exhausted to make them as a result of his treatment by the abductors, and while he knew evidence was being obtained against him through intimidation of witnesses. So stands the single, unsupported and, my Government believes, utterly unfounded, ground alleged for Jenkins' imprisonment.

What conclusion is to be drawn from such a reply of the Mexican Government other than there has been a studied effort on the part of Mexican authorities to ensnare Jenkins in the intricacies of legal proceedings by alleging the commission of a technical offense and by bringing unsupported charges against him, for a purpose: In the first place, to divert the attention of the American public and the American Government, and indeed of Mexicans themselves, from the actual situation, namely, that Puebla, the capital of the State of Puebla, and perhaps the second largest city in Mexico, is without adequate protection from outlaws who infest the immediate neighborhood and who are accustomed openly and freely to visit the city without hindrance, that by the failure to furnish adequate protection in this district the Mexican authorities have, through their negligence, made possible the abduction of Jenkins, and that in harmony with such an attitude on the part of the Mexican authorities they have failed to carry out the duty and obligation incumbent upon them to apprehend and punish the bandits concerned in the crime of which Jenkins was the victim. And in the second place, it appears to have been the purpose of the Mexican Government to assume a wilful indifference to the feelings of the American people that have been aroused to the point of indignation by the exposure, hardships, and physical suffering endured by Jenkins during his abduction and his subsequent treatment at the hands of Mexican authorities.

In view of the considerations which have been set forth, and in view particularly of the belief of my Government that the charge against Jenkins of deliberate false swearing is unfounded, the Government of the United States must renew its request for the immediate release of Consular Agent Jenkins from further imprisonment.

LANSING.

SEVENTH ANNUAL MESSAGE TO CONGRESS

[This was the first of President Wilson's annual messages to Congress to be read instead of delivered in person, the President being confined to the White House by illness.]

THE WHITE HOUSE, *December 2, 1919.*

TO THE SENATE AND HOUSE OF REPRESENTATIVES:

I sincerely regret that I cannot be present at the opening of this session of the Congress. I am thus prevented from presenting in as direct a way as I could wish the many questions that are pressing for solution at this time. Happily, I have had the advantage of the advice of the heads of the several executive departments who have kept in close touch with affairs in their detail and whose thoughtful recommendations I earnestly second.

In the matter of the railroads and the readjustment of their affairs growing out of Federal control, I shall take the liberty at a later date of addressing you.

I hope that Congress will bring to a conclusion at this session legislation looking to the establishment of a budget system. That there should be one single authority responsible for the making of all appropriations and that appropriations should be made not independently of each other, but with reference to one single comprehensive plan of expenditure properly related to the nation's income, there can be no doubt. I believe the burden of preparing the budget must, in the nature of the case, if the work is to be properly done and responsibility concentrated instead of divided, rest upon the executive. The budget so prepared should be submitted to and approved or amended by a single committee of each House of Congress and no single appropriation should be made by the Congress, except such as may have been included in the budget prepared by the executive or added by the particular committee of Congress charged with the budget legislation.

Another and not less important aspect of the problem is the ascertainment of the economy and efficiency with which the moneys appropriated are expended. Under existing law the only audit is for the purpose of ascertaining whether expenditures have been lawfully made within the appropriations. No one is authorized or equipped to ascertain whether the money has been spent wisely, economically and effectively. The auditors should be highly trained officials with permanent tenure in the Treasury Department, free of obligations to or motives of consideration for this or any subsequent administration, and authorized and empowered to examine into and make report upon the methods employed and the results obtained by the executive departments of the Government. Their reports should be made to the Congress and to the Secretary of the Treasury.

I trust that the Congress will give its immediate consideration to the problem of future taxation. Simplification of the income and profits taxes has become an immediate necessity. These taxes performed indispensable service during the war. They must, however, be simplified, not only to save the taxpayer inconvenience and expense, but in order that his liability may be made certain and definite.

With reference to the details of the Revenue Law, the Secretary of the Treasury and the Commissioner of Internal Revenue will lay before you for your consideration certain amendments necessary or desirable in connection with the administration of the law—recommendations which have my approval and support. It is of the utmost importance that in dealing with this matter the present law should not be disturbed so far as regards taxes for the calendar year 1920, payable in the calendar year 1921. The Congress might well consider whether the higher rates of income and profits taxes can in peace times be effectively productive of revenue, and whether they may not, on the contrary, be destructive of business activity and productive of waste and inefficiency. There is a point at which in peace times high rates of income and profits taxes discourage energy, remove the incentive to new enterprises, encourage extravagant expenditures and produce industrial stagnation with consequent unemployment and other attendant evils.

The problem is not an easy one. A fundamental change has taken place with reference to the position of America in the world's affairs. The prejudice and passions engendered by decades of controversy between two schools of political and economic thought,—the one believers in protection of American industries, the other believers in tariff for revenue only,—must be subordinated to the single consideration of the public interest in the light of utterly changed conditions. Before the war America was heavily the debtor of the rest of the world and the interest payments she had to make to foreign countries on American securities held abroad, the expenditures of American travelers abroad and the ocean freight charges she had to pay to others, about balanced the value of her pre-war favorable balance of trade. During the war America's exports have been greatly stimulated, and increased prices have increased their value. On the other hand, she has purchased a large proportion of the American securities previously held abroad, has loaned some $9,000,000,000 to foreign governments, and has built her own ships. Our favorable balance of trade has thus been greatly increased and Europe has been deprived of the means of meeting it heretofore existing. Europe can have only three ways of meeting the favorable balance of trade in peace times: by imports into this country of gold or of goods, or by establishing new credits. Europe is in no position at the present time to ship gold to us nor could we contemplate large further imports of gold into this country without concern. The time has nearly passed for international governmental loans and it will take time to develop in this country a market for foreign securities. Anything, therefore, which would tend to prevent foreign countries from settling for our exports by shipments of goods into this country could only have the effect of preventing them from paying for our exports and therefore of preventing the exports from being made. The productivity of the country, greatly stimulated by the war, must find an outlet by exports to foreign countries, and any measures taken to prevent imports will inevitably curtail exports, force curtailment of production, load the banking machinery of the country with credits to carry unsold products and produce industrial stagnation and unemployment. If we want to sell, we must be prepared to buy. Whatever, therefore, may have been our views during the period of growth of American business concerning tariff legislation, we must now adjust our own economic life to a changed condition growing out of the fact that American business is full grown and that America is the greatest capitalist in the world.

No policy of isolation will satisfy the growing needs and opportunities of America. The provincial standards and policies of the past, which have held American business as if in a strait-jacket, must yield and give way to the needs and exigencies of the new day in which we live, a day full of hope and promise for American business, if we will but take advantage of the opportunities that are ours for the asking. The recent war has ended our isolation and thrown upon us a great duty and responsibility. The United States must share the expanding world market. The United States desires for itself only equal opportunity with the other nations of the world, and that through the process of friendly cooperation and fair competition the legitimate interests of the nations concerned may be successfully and equitably adjusted.

There are other matters of importance upon which I urged action at the last session of Congress which are still pressing for solution. I am sure it is not necessary for me again to remind you that there is one immediate and very practicable question resulting from the war which we should meet in the most liberal spirit. It is a matter of recognition and relief to our soldiers. I can do no better than to quote from my last message urging this very action:

"We must see to it that our returning soldiers are assisted in every practicable way to find the places for which they are fitted in the daily work of the country. This can be done by developing and maintaining upon an adequate scale the admirable organization created by the Department of Labor for placing men seeking work; and it can also be done, in at least one very great field, by creating new opportunities for individual enterprise. The Secretary of the Interior has pointed out the way by which returning soldiers may be helped to find and take up land in the hitherto undeveloped regions of the country which the Federal Government has already prepared, or can readily prepare, for cultivation and also on many of the cut-over or neglected areas which lie within the limits of the older states; and I once more take the liberty of recommending very urgently that his plans shall receive the immediate and substantial support of the Congress."

In the matter of tariff legislation, I beg to call your attention to the statements contained in my last message urging legislation with reference to the establishment of the chemical and dyestuffs industry in America:

"Among the industries to which special consideration should be given is that of the manufacture of dyestuffs and related chemicals. Our complete dependence upon German supplies before the war made the interruption of trade a cause of exceptional economic disturbance. The close relation between the manufacture of dyestuffs, on the one hand, and of explosive and poisonous gases, on the other, moreover, has given the industry an exceptional significance and value. Although the United States will gladly and unhesitatingly join in the programme of international disarmament, it will, nevertheless, be a policy of obvious prudence to make certain of the successful maintenance of many strong and well-equipped chemical plants. The German chemical industry, with which we will be brought into competition, was and may well be again, a thoroughly knit monopoly capable of exercising a competition of a peculiarly insidious and dangerous kind."

During the war the farmer performed a vital and willing service to the nation. By materially increasing the production of his land, he supplied America and the Allies with the increased amounts of food necessary to keep their immense armies in the field. He indispensably helped to win the war. But there is now scarcely less need of increasing the production in food and the necessaries of life. I ask the Congress to consider means of encouraging effort along these lines. The importance of doing everything possible to promote production along economical lines, to improve marketing, and to make rural life more attractive and healthful, is obvious. I would urge approval of the plans already proposed to the Congress by the Secretary of Agriculture, to secure the essential facts required for the proper study of this question, through the proposed enlarged programmes for farm management studies and crop estimates. I would urge, also, the continuance of Federal participation in the building of good roads, under the terms of existing law and under the direction of present agencies; the need of further action on the part of the States and the Federal Government to preserve and develop our forest resources, especially through the practice of better forestry methods on private holdings and the extension of the publicly owned forests; better support for country schools and the more definite direction of their courses of study along lines related to rural problems; and fuller provision for sanitation in rural districts and the building up of needed hospital and medical facilities in these localities. Perhaps the way might be cleared for many of these desirable reforms by a fresh, comprehensive survey made of rural conditions by a conference composed of representatives of the farmers and of the agricultural agencies responsible for leadership.

I would call your attention to the widespread condition of political restlessness in our body politic. The causes of this unrest, while various and complicated, are superficial rather than deep-seated. Broadly, they arise from or are connected with the failure on the part of our Government to arrive speedily at a just and permanent peace permitting return to normal conditions, from the transfusion of radical theories from seething European centers pending such delay, from heartless profiteering resulting in the increase of the cost of living, and lastly from the machinations of passionate and malevolent agitators. With the return to normal conditions, this unrest will rapidly disappear. In the meantime, it does much evil. It seems to me that in dealing with this situation Congress should not be impatient or drastic but should seek rather to remove the causes. It should endeavor to bring our country back speedily to a peace basis, with ameliorated living conditions under the minimum of restrictions upon personal liberty that is consistent with our reconstruction problems. And it should arm the Federal Government with power to deal in its criminal courts with those persons who by violent methods would abrogate our time-tested institutions. With the free expression of opinion and with the advocacy of orderly political change, however fundamental, there must be no interference, but towards passion and malevolence tending to incite crime and insurrection under guise of political evolution there should be no leniency. Legislation to this end has been recommended by the Attorney General and should be enacted. In this direct connection, I would call your attention to my recommendations on August 8th, pointing out legislative measures which would be effective in controlling and bringing down the present cost of living, which contributes so largely to this unrest. On only one of these recommendations has the Congress acted. If the Government's campaign is to be effective, it is necessary that the other steps suggested should be acted on at once.

I renew and strongly urge the necessity of the extension of the present Food Control Act as to the period of time in which it shall remain in operation. The Attorney General has submitted a bill providing for an extension of this Act for a period of six months. As it now stands, it is limited in operation to the period of the war and becomes inoperative upon the formal proclamation of peace. It is imperative that it should be extended at once. The Department of Justice has built up extensive machinery for the purpose of enforcing its provisions; all of which must be abandoned upon the conclusion of peace unless the provisions of this Act are extended.

During this period the Congress will have an opportunity to make similar permanent provisions and regulations with regard to all goods destined for interstate commerce and to exclude them from interstate shipment, if the requirements of the law are not compiled with. Some such regulation is imperatively necessary. The abuses that have grown up in the manipulation of prices by the withholding of foodstuffs and other necessaries of life cannot otherwise be effectively prevented. There can be no doubt of either the necessity of the legitimacy of such measures.

As I pointed out in my last message, publicity can accomplish a great deal in this campaign. The aims of the Government must be clearly brought to the attention of the consuming public, civic organizations and state officials, who are in a position to lend their assistance to our efforts. You have made available funds with which to carry on this campaign, but there is no provision in the law authorizing their expenditure for the purpose of making the public fully informed about the efforts of the Government. Specific recommendation has been made by the Attorney General in this regard. I would strongly urge upon you its immediate adoption, as it constitutes one of the preliminary steps to this campaign.

I also renew my recommendation that the Congress pass a law regulating cold storage as it is regulated, for example, by the laws of the State of New Jersey, which limit the time during which goods may be kept in storage, prescribe the method of disposing of them if kept beyond the permitted period, and require that goods released from storage shall in all cases bear the date of their receipt. It would materially add to the serviceability of the law, for the purpose we now have in view, if it were also prescribed that all goods released from storage for interstate shipment should have plainly marked upon each package the selling or market price at which they went into storage. By this means the purchaser would always be able to learn what profits stood between him and the producer or the whole-sale dealer.

I would also renew my recommendation that all goods destined for interstate commerce should in every case, where their form or package makes it possible, be plainly marked with the price at which they left the hands of the producer.

We should formulate a law requiring a Federal license of all corporations engaged in interstate commerce and embodying in the license, or in the conditions under which it is to be issued, specific regulations designed to secure competitive selling and prevent unconscionable profits in the method of marketing. Such a law would afford a welcome opportunity to effect other much needed reforms in the business of interstate shipment and in the methods of corporations which are engaged in it; but for the moment I confine my recommendations to the object immediately in hand, which is to lower the cost of living.

No one who has observed the march of events in the last year can fail to note the absolute need of a definite programme to bring about an improvement in the conditions of labor. There can be no settled conditions leading to increased production and a reduction in the cost of living if labor and capital are to be antagonists instead of partners. Sound thinking and an honest desire to serve the interests of the whole nation, as distinguished from the interests of a class, must be applied to the solution of this great and pressing problem. The failure of other nations to consider this matter in a vigorous way has produced bitterness and jealousies and antagonisms, the food of radicalism. The only way to keep men from agitating against grievances is to remove the grievances. An unwillingness even to discuss these matters produces only dissatisfaction and gives comfort to the extreme elements in our country which endeavor to stir up disturbances in order to provoke governments to embark upon a course of retaliation and repression. The seed of revolution is repression. The remedy for these things must not be negative in character. It must be constructive. It must comprehend the general interest. The real antidote for the unrest which manifests itself is not suppression, but a deep consideration of the wrongs that beset our national life and the application of a remedy.

Congress has already shown its willingness to deal with these industrial wrongs by establishing the eight-hour day as the standard in every field of labor. It has sought to find a way to prevent child labor. It has served the whole country by leading the way in developing the means of preserving and safeguarding lives and health in dangerous industries. It must now help in the difficult task of finding a method that will bring about a genuine democratization of industry, based upon the full recognition of the right of those who work, in whatever rank, to participate in some organic way in every decision which directly affects their welfare. It is with this purpose in mind that I called a conference to meet in Washington on December 1st, to consider these problems in all their broad aspects, with the idea of bringing about a better understanding between these two interests.

The great unrest throughout the world, out of which has emerged a demand for an immediate consideration of the difficulties between capital and labor, bids us put our own house in order. Frankly, there can be no permanent and lasting settlements between capital and labor which do not recognize the fundamental concepts for which labor has been struggling through the years. The whole world gave its recognition and endorsement to these fundamental purposes in the League of Nations. The statesmen gathered at Versailles recognized the fact that world stability could not be had by reverting to industrial standards and conditions against which the average workman of the world had revolted. It is, therefore, the task of the statesmen of this new day of change and readjustment to recognize world conditions and to seek to bring about, through legislation, conditions that will mean the ending of age-long antagonisms between capital and labor and that will hopefully lead to the building up of a comradeship which will result not only in greater contentment among the mass of workmen but also bring about a greater production and a greater prosperity to business itself.

To analyze the particulars in the demands of labor is to admit the justice of their complaint in many matters that lie at their basis. The workman demands an adequate wage, sufficient to permit him to live in comfort, unhampered by the fear of poverty and want in his old age. He demands the right to live and the right to work amidst sanitary surroundings, both in home and in workshop, surroundings that develop and do not retard his own health and well-being; and the right to provide for his children's wants in the matter of health and education. In other words, it is his desire to make the conditions of his life and the lives of those dear to him tolerable and easy to bear.

The establishment of the principles regarding labor laid down in the covenant of the League of Nations offers us the way to industrial peace and conciliation. No other road lies open to us. Not to pursue this one is longer to invite enmities, bitterness, and antagonisms which in the end only lead to industrial and social disaster. The unwilling workman is not a profitable servant. An employee whose industrial life is hedged about by hard and unjust conditions, which he did not create and over which he has no control, lacks that fine spirit of enthusiasm and volunteer effort which are the necessary ingredients of a great producing entity. Let us be frank about this solemn matter. The evidences of world-wide unrest which manifest themselves in violence throughout the world bid us pause and consider the means to be found to stop the spread of this contagious thing before it saps the very vitality of the nation itself. Do we gain strength by withholding the remedy? Or is it not the business of statesmen to treat these manifestations of unrest which meet us on every hand as evidences of an economic disorder and to apply constructive remedies wherever necessary, being sure that in the application of the remedy we touch not the vital tissues of our industrial and economic life? There can be no recession of the tide of unrest until constructive instrumentalities are set up to stem that tide.

Governments must recognze the right of men collectively to bargain for humane objects that have at their base the mutual protection and welfare of those engaged in all industries. Labor must not be longer treated as a commodity. It must be regarded as the activity of human beings, possessed of deep yearnings and desires. The business man gives his best thought to the repair and replenishment of his machinery, so that its usefulness will not be impaired and its power to produce may always be at its height and kept in full vigor and motion. No less regard ought to be paid to the human machine, which after all propels the machinery of the world and is the great dynamic force that lies back of all industry and progress. Return to the old standards of wage and industry in employment are unthinkable. The terrible tragedy of war which has just ended and which has brought the world to the verge of chaos and disaster would be in vain if there should ensue a return to the conditions of the past. Europe itself, whence has come the unrest which now holds the world at bay, is an example of standpatism in these vital human matters which America might well accept as an example, not to be followed but studiously to be avoided. Europe made labor the differential, and the price of it all is enmity and antagonism and prostrated industry. The right of labor to live in peace and comfort must be recognized by governments and America should be the first to lay the foundation stones upon which industrial peace shall be built.

Labor not only is entitled to an adequate wage, but capital should receive a reasonable return upon its investment and is entitled to protection at the hands of the Government in every emergency. No Government worthy of the name can "play" these elements against each other, for there is a mutuality of interest between them which the Government must seek to express and to safeguard at all cost.

The right of individuals to strike is inviolate and ought not to be interfered with by any process of Government, but there is a predominant right and that is the right of the Government to protect all of its people and to assert its power and majesty against the challenge of any class. The Government, when it asserts that right, seeks not to antagonize a class but simply to defend the right of the whole people as against the irreparable harm and injury that might be done by the attempt by any class to usurp a power that only Government itself has a right to exercise as a protection to all.

In the matter of international disputes which have led to war, statesmen have sought to set up as a remedy arbitration for war. Does this not point the way for the settlement of industrial disputes, by the establishment of a tribunal, fair and just alike to all, which will settle industrial disputes which in the past have led to war and disaster? America, witnessing the evil consequences which have followed out of such disputes between these contending forces, must not admit itself impotent to deal with these matters by means of peaceful processes. Surely, there must be some method of bringing together in a council of peace and amity these two great interests, out of which will come a happier day of peace and cooperation, a day that will make men more hopeful and enthusiastic in their various tasks, that will make for more comfort and happiness in living and a more tolerable condition among all classes of men. Certainly human intelligence can devise some acceptable tribunal for adjusting the differences between capital and labor.

This is the hour of test and trial for America. By her prowess and strength, and the indomitable courage of her soldiers, she demonstrated her power to vindicate on foreign battlefields her conceptions of liberty and justice. Let not her influence as a mediator between capital and labor be weakened and her own failure to settle matters of purely domestic concern be proclaimed to the world. There are those in this country who threaten direct action to force their will upon a majority. Russia today, with its blood and terror, is a painful object lesson of the power of minorities. It makes little difference what minority it is; whether capital or labor, or any other class; no sort of privilege will ever be permitted to dominate this country. We are a partnership or nothing that is worth while. We are a democracy, where the majority are the masters, or all the hopes and purposes of the men who founded this government have been defeated and forgotten. In America there is but one way by which great reforms can be accomplished and the relief sought by classes obtained, and that is through the orderly processes of representative government. Those who would propose any other method of reform are enemies of this country. America will not be daunted by threats nor lose her composure or calmness in these distressing times. We can afford, in the midst of this day of passion and unrest, to be self-contained and sure. The instrument of all reform in America is the ballot. The road to economic and social reform in America is the straight road of justice to all classes and conditions of men. Men have but to follow this road to realize the full fruition of their objects and purposes. Let those beware who would take the shorter road of disorder and revolution. The right road is the road of justice and orderly process.   VOODROW WILSON.

EXECUTIVE ORDER

[Constituting Board of Surveys and Maps.]

THE WHITE HOUSE, *December 30, 1919.*

In order to coordinate the activities of the various map-making agencies of the executive departments of the Government, to standardize results, and to avoid unnecessary duplication of work, I hereby constitute a Board of Surveys and Maps, to be composed of one representative of each of the following organizations:

1. Corps of Engineers, U. S. Army. 2. U. S. Coast & Geodetic Survey, Department of Commerce. 3. U. S. Geological Survey, Department of Interior. 4. General Land Office, Department of Interior. 5. Topography Branch, Post Office Department. 6. Bureau of Soils, Department of Agriculture. 7. U. S. Reclamation Service, Department of Interior. 8. Bureau of Public Roads, Department of Agriculture. 9. Bureau of Indian Affairs, Department of Interior. 10. Mississippi River Commission, War Department. 11. U. S. Lake Survey, War Department. 12. International (Canadian) Boundary Commission, Department of State. 13. Forest Service, Department of Agriculture. 14. U. S. Hydrographic Office, Navy Department.

The individual members of this Board shall be appointed by the Chiefs of the various organizations named and shall serve without additional compensation.

The Board is directed to make recommendations to the several Departments or to the President for the purpose of coordinating all map-making and surveying activities of the Government and to settle all questions at issue between executive departments relating to surveys and maps in so far as their decisions do not conflict with existing laws.

This Board shall perfect a permanent organization and shall hold meetings at stated intervals, to which representatives of the map-using public shall be invited for the purpose of conference and advice.

This Board shall establish a central information office in the U. S. Geological Survey for the purpose of collecting, classifying and furnishing to the public information concerning all map and survey data available in the several Government departments and from other sources.

All Government departments will make full use of the above board as an advisory body and will furnish all available information and data called for by the Board.

So much of the Executive Order of August 10, 1906, as grants additional advisory powers to the United States Geographic Board is hereby rescinded and these additional powers are transferred to the Board of Surveys and Maps.   WOODROW WILSON.

LETTER

[Read at the Jackson Day dinner, January 8, 1920, defining Treaty stand.]

THE WHITE HOUSE, *January 8, 1920.*

My Dear Mr. Chairman:

It is with keenest regret that I find that I am to be deprived of the pleasure and privilege of joining you and the other loyal Democrats who are to assemble tonight to celebrate Jackson Day and renew their vows of fidelity to the great principles of our party, the principles which must now fulfil the hopes not only of our own people but of the world.

The United States enjoyed the spiritual leadership of the world until the Senate of the United States failed to ratify the treaty by which the belligerent nations sought to effect the settlements for which they had fought throughout the war. It is inconceivable that at this supreme crisis and final turning point in the international relations of the whole world, when the results of the great war are by no means determined and are still questionable and dependent upon events which no man can foresee or count upon, the United States should withdraw from the concert of progressive and enlightened nations by which Germany was defeated, and all similar Governments (if the world be so unhappy as to contain any) warned of the consequences of any attempt at a like iniquity, and yet that is the effect of the course which the United States has taken with regard to the Treaty of Versailles.

Germany is beaten, but we are still at war with her, and the old stage is reset for a repetition of the old plot. It is now ready for a resumption of the old offensive and defensive alliances which made settled peace impossible. It is now open again to every sort of intrigue.

The old spies are free to resume their former abominable activities. They are again at liberty to make it impossible for governments to be sure what mischief is being worked among their own people, what internal disorders are being fomented.

Without the covenant of the League of Nations there may be as many secret treaties as ever, to destroy the confidence of governments in each other, and their validity cannot be questioned.

None of the objects we professed to be fighting for has been secured, or can be made certain of, without this nation's ratification of the treaty and its entry into the covenant. This nation entered the great war to vindicate its own rights and to protect and preserve free government. It went into the war to see it through to the end, and the end has not yet come. It went into the war to make an end of militarism, to furnish guarantees to weak nations, and to make a just and lasting peace. It entered it with noble enthusiasm.

Five of the leading belligerents have accepted the treaty and formal ratifications will soon be exchanged. The question is whether this country will enter and enter whole-heartedly. If it does not do so, the United States and Germany will play a lone hand in the world.

The maintenance of the peace of the world and the effective execution of the treaty depend upon the whole-hearted participation of the United States. I am not stating it as a matter of power. The point is that the United States is the only nation which has sufficient moral force with the rest of the world to guarantee the substitution of discussion for war. If we keep out of this agreement, if we do not give our guarantees, then another attempt will be made to crush the new nations of Europe.

I do not believe that this is what the people of this country wish or will be satisfied with. Personally, I do not accept the action of the Senate of the United States as the decision of the nation.

I have asserted from the first that the overwhelming majority of the people of this country desire the ratification of the treaty, and my impression to that effect has recently been confirmed by the unmistakable evidences of public opinion given during my visit to seventeen of the States.

I have endeavored to make it plain that if the Senate wishes to say what the undoubted meaning of the League is I shall have no objection. There can be no reasonable objection to interpretations accompanying the act of ratification itself. But when the treaty is acted upon, I must know whether it means that we have ratified or rejected it.

We cannot rewrite this treaty. We must take it without changes which alter its meaning, or leave it, and then after the rest of the world has signed it, we must face the unthinkable task of making another and separate treaty with Germany.

But no mere assertions with regard to the wish and opinion of the country are credited. If there is any doubt as to what the people of the country think on this vital matter, the clear and single way out is to submit it for determination at the next election to the voters of the nation, to give the next election the form of a great and solemn referendum, a referendum as to the part the United States is to play in completing the settlements of the war and in the prevention in the future of such outrages as Germany attempted to perpetrate.

We have no more moral right to refuse now to take part in the execution and administration of these settlements than we had to refuse to take part in the fighting of the last few weeks of the war which brought victory and made it possible to dictate to Germany what the settlements should be. Our fidelity to our associates in the war is in question and the whole future of mankind. It will be heartening to the whole world to know the attitude and purpose of the people of the United States.

I spoke just now of the spiritual leadership of the United States, thinking of international affairs. But there is another spiritual leadership which is open to us and which we can assume.

The world has been made safe for democracy, but democracy has not been finally vindicated. All sorts of crimes are being committed in its name, all sorts of preposterous perversions of its doctrines and practices are being attempted.

This, in my judgment, is to be the great privilege of the democracy of the United States, to show that it can lead the way in the solution of the great social and industrial problems of our time, and lead the way to a happy, settled order of life as well as to political liberty. The program for this achievement we must attempt to formulate, and in carrying it out we shall do more than can be done in any other way to sweep out of existence the tyrannous and arbitrary forms of power which are now masquerading under the name of popular government.

Whenever we look back to Andrew Jackson we should draw fresh inspiration from his character and example. His mind grasped with such a splendid definiteness and firmness the principles of national authority and national action. He was so indomitable in his purpose to give reality to the principles of the Government, that this is a very fortunate time to recall his career and to renew our vows of faithfulness to the principles and the pure practices of Democracy.

I rejoice to join you in this renewal of faith and purpose. I hope that the whole evening may be of the happiest results as regards the fortunes of our party and the nation.

With cordial regards,

Sincerely yours,

WOODROW WILSON.

STATEMENT

[Further participation by the United States in armed intervention in Russia. Made public January 16, 1920.]

The Government of the United States has given the most careful consideration to the subject matter of the communication from the Japanese Government, which was read to the Secretary of State by the Japanese Ambassador on December 8, and which concerns the recent unfavorable development of the military situation with which Admiral Kolchak's forces have been confronted, and which proposes three alternative courses for the Allied and associated powers to take.

The Government of the United States agrees that for it to send a reinforcement of sufficient strength to act on the offensive in cooperation with anti-Bolshevik forces is impracticable.

The Government of the United States believes that for it to continue to participate in guarding the districts now under Allied military protection is also, under present conditions, impracticable, for the reason that an agreement to send reinforcements to such extent as may be required, with a view to maintain the status quo, might involve the Government of the United States in an undertaking of such indefinite character as to be inadvisable. The amount of reinforcement which might become necessary for the execution of such an agreement might be so great that the Government of the United States would not feel justified in carrying it out.

Consideration has been given, therefore, to the alternative presented by the Government of Japan of entire or partial withdrawal. It will be recalled that the purposes of the expedition, as originally conceived by the United States and expressed in an aide memoire handed to the Japanese Ambassador at Washington July 17, 1918, were, first, to help the Czecho-Slovak troops, which had during their retirement along the Siberian Railway been attacked by the Bolsheviki and enemy prisoners of war in Siberia, to consolidate their forces and effect their repatriation by way of Vladivostok, and, second, to steady any efforts at self-government or self-defense in which the Russians themselves might be willing to accept assistance.

Not only are the Czecho-Slovak troops now successfully advancing into Eastern Siberia, but an agreement has been effected between the Governments of Great Britain and the United States providing for their repatriation from Vladivostok. American vessels will begin to arrive at that port by February 1, and a contingent of more than 10,000 Czecho-Slovak troops can be immediately embarked. It is expected that evacuation will proceed rapidly thereafter, and from that date the first purpose for which American soldiers were sent to Siberia may be regarded as accomplished.

With respect to the second purpose, namely, the steadying of efforts at self-government or self-defense on the part of the Russians, the Government of the United States is impressed with the political instability and grave uncertainties of the present situation in Eastern Siberia, as described in the aide memoire presented by the Japanese Ambassador on December 8, and is disposed to the view that further military effort to assist the Russians in the struggle toward self-government may, in the present situation, lead to complications which would have exactly the opposite effect, prolonging the period of readjustment and involving Japan and the United States in ineffective and needless sacrifices. It is felt accordingly to be unlikely that the second purpose for which American troops were sent to Siberia will be longer served by their presence there.

In view, then, of the fact that the main purposes for which American troops were sent to Siberia are now at an end, and of the considerations set forth in the communication of the Japanese Government of December 8, which subsequent events in Eastern Siberia have strengthened, the Government of the United States has decided to begin at once arrangements for the concentration of the American forces at Vladivostok, with a view to their embarkation and departure immediately after the leaving of the first important contingent of Czecho-Slovak troops—that is to say, about February 1.

Careful consideration has also been given to the possibility of continuing, after the departure of the American troops, the assistance of American railway experts in the operation of the Trans-Siberian and Chinese Eastern Railways. It will be recalled that it is expressly stipulated in the plan for the supervision of these railways which was submitted by the Japanese Ambassador at Washington on January 15, 1919, that the arrangement should cease upon the withdrawal of the foreign military forces from Siberia and that all foreign railway experts appointed under the arrangement should then be recalled forthwith. The experience of recent months in the operation of the railways under conditions of unstable civil authority and frequent local military interferences furnishes a strong reason for abiding by the terms of the original agreement. Arrangements will be made accordingly for the withdrawal of the American railway experts under the same conditions and simultaneously with the departure of the American military forces.

The Government of the United States desires the Japanese Government to know that it regrets the necessity for this decision, because it seems to mark the end, for the time being at least, of a cooperative effort by Japan and the United States to assist the Russian people, which had of late begun to bear important results and seemed to give promise for the future.

The Government of the United States is most appreciative of the friendly spirit which has animated the Government of Japan in this undertaking, and is convinced that the basis of understanding which has been established will serve in the future to facilitate the common efforts of the two countries to deal with the problems which confront them in Siberia.

The Government of the United States does not in the least relinquish the deep interest which it feels in the political and economic fate of the people of Siberia nor its purpose to cooperate with Japan in the most frank and friendly way in all practical plans which may be worked out for the political and economic rehabilitation of that region.

It is suggested that the Government of Japan may desire to communicate to the other principal Allied and associated Governments the substance of the aide memoire of December 8. This Government will likewise make known to them the substance of the present communication.

QUESTIONS.

1. What was the attitude of the Wilson administration toward American business men? Pages 7871, 8015, 8038, 8151, 8714.

2. Why did President Wilson veto the bill containing a literacy test for immigrants and how did conditions after the war compel him to urge certain checks upon immigration? Pages 8043, 8778.

3. In what way did the Wilson administration assist the American farmer? Pages 7908, 8018, 8116.

4. What was President Wilson's attitude toward disorders in Mexico? Pages 7892, 8032, 8131, 8155, 8762.

5. How did President Wilson try to open peace mediations in the Great War before America was drawn into it, and with what success? Pages 8190, 8199.

6. What were the various steps by which Germany's submarine warfare brought the United States into the Great War? Pages 8057, 8062, 8121, 8125, 8205, 8206, 8209, 8221.

7. How did the conception of a League of Nations grow in President Wilson's mind as the Great War continued? Pages 8191, 8200, 8288, 8402, 8425, 8593.

8. Why did President Wilson urge the passage of the Woman Suffrage amendment to the United States Constitution? Pages 8163, 8375, 8599, 8639, 8719.

9. What reform in our currency system do we owe to the Wilson administration? Pages 7879, 7908, 8026, 8151.

10. What were the "Fourteen Points?" Page 8423.

11. Did the terms of peace given Germany square with the terms of peace promised her? Pages 8421, 8447, 8482, 8534, 8596 and 8737-8756.

12. How were alien enemies and their property treated during America's participation in the Great War? Pages 8243, 8392, 8372, 8380.

13. What was President Wilson's attitude toward demands by Labor which he thought unreasonable? Pages 8581, 8773, 8775.

14. What were President Wilson's remedies for the high cost of living? Page 8764.

15. What was President Wilson's conception of the service rendered the world by the formation of the League of Nations and by the peace imposed upon Germany? Pages 8670, 8696, 8727, 8785.

SUGGESTIONS.

The changes in the tariff policy of the United States due to the Wilson Administration will be found on pages 7869, 7872, 8030, 8151, 8158.

The message in which President Wilson urged that the United States enter the lists against the Imperial German Government will be found on page 8226.

The text of the League of Nations Covenant is on pages 8673-8681.

The attitude of the Wilson administration toward the problem of the ownership and management of the railroads of the United States is discussed on pages 8018, 8117, 8159, 8409, 8412, 8418, 8644, 8719.

The official summary of the peace treaty with Germany will be found on pages 8737-8756.

The various details of the selective draft system used to recruit the American Expeditionary Forces for the war against the Central Powers will be found on pages 8256, 8306, 8385, 8574.

The policy of the United States toward revolutionary Russia is discussed on pages 8230, 8270, 8403, 8422, 8424, 8469, 8483, 8501, 8589.

The armistice negotiations of the Great War are given on pages 8603-8617.

President Wilson's actions with respect to Prohibition may be found outlined on pages 8583, 8720, 8774.

NOTE.

For further suggestions on Wilson's administration see Wilson, Woodrow, Encyclopedic Index.

By reading the Foreign Policy of each President, and by scanning the messages as to the state of the nation, a thorough knowledge of the history of the United States will be acquired from the most authentic sources; because, as has been said, "Each President reviews the past, depicts the present and forecasts the future of the nation."

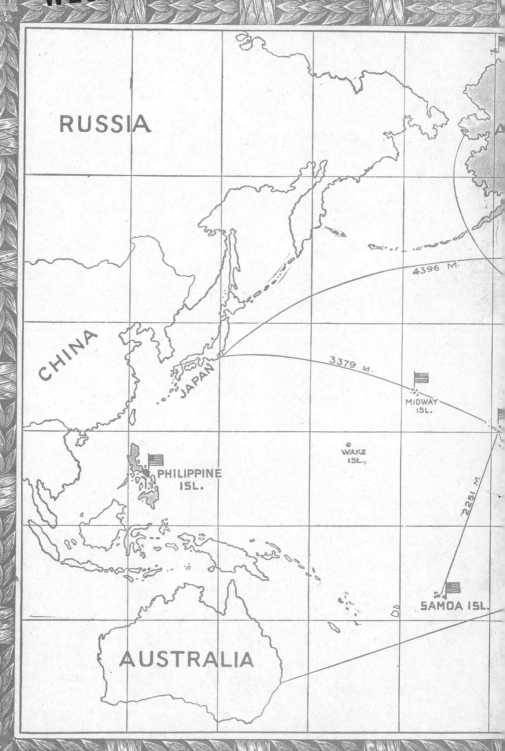

RUSSIA

CHINA

JAPAN

4396 M.

3379 M.

MIDWAY ISL.

WAKE ISL.

PHILIPPINE ISL.

2251 M.

SAMOA ISL.

AUSTRALIA